LISTEN to the MAX

실전모의고사 ❷

Michael A. Putlack   M.A. in History, Tufts University, Medford, MA, U.S.A.
Expert test developer of TOEFL, TOEIC, and TEPS

Stephen Poirier   Candidate for PhD in History, University of Western Ontario, Canada
Certificate of Professional Technical Writing, Carleton University, Canada

외고영어듣기대비 | Listen to the MAX

실전모의고사 ❷

지은이 Michael A. Putlack, Stephen Poirier
펴낸이 정규도
펴낸곳 (주)다락원

초판 1쇄 인쇄 2008년 7월 5일
초판 8쇄 발행 2021년 1월 4일

책임편집 홍혜정, 김명진, 김금발미
디자인 조화연
삽화 김인화

데 다락원 경기도 파주시 문발로 211
내용문의: (02)736-2031 내선 502
구입문의: (02)736-2031 내선 250~252
Fax: (02)732-2037
출판등록 1977년 9월 16일 제406-2008-000007호

Copyright © 2008, Darakwon, Inc.

값 17,000원 (MP3 CD1장 포함)

ISBN 978-89-5995-925-9 58740

http://www.darakwon.co.kr

• 다락원 홈페이지를 방문하시면 상세한 출판정보와 함께 동영상강좌, MP3자료
  등 다양한 어학 정보를 얻으실 수 있습니다.

외 고 영 어 듣 기 대 비

LISTEN to the MAX

실전모의고사 ❷

Michael A. Putlack | Stephen Poirier

다락원

LISTEN to the MAX 실전모의고사 시리즈에 대하여

해가 갈수록 외고에 대한 관심이 높아지면서 외고 입시를 준비하는 학생들 또한 늘어가는 추세이다. 이러한 관심 속에 외고의 입학 전형은 학교마다 그 특색을 더하며 다양화되고 있지만 가장 중요하고도 큰 비중을 차지하고 있는 영어듣기에서의 고득점은 외고 입학의 기본이자 필수 조건이라고 할 수 있다.

외고 입시 영어듣기 시험은 해마다 새로운 유형의 문제가 등장하고 있는 것은 물론, 스크립트 길이는 길어지고 보다 폭넓은 주제가 출제되고 있다. 또한 영어 교육의 중요성이 강화되고 있는 분위기 속에서 학생들의 실력도 나날이 늘고 있으므로 앞으로도 그 난이도가 더욱 심화될 가능성이 크다. **LISTEN to the MAX 실전모의고사** 시리즈는 그러한 영어듣기 시험에 대비해 효과적으로 리스닝 실력을 다지고 실전 감각을 키울 수 있도록 다양한 유형과 주제의 난이도 있는 문제들을 풍부하게 제공하고 있다.

먼저 실전모의고사 1권에서는 〈유형편〉 코너를 두어 실전 훈련에 돌입하기 전에 외고 영어듣기에 단골손님처럼 등장하는 주요 유형들에 대한 이해도를 높일 수 있도록 하였다. 이 〈유형편〉에서는 외고 영어듣기의 기본이 되는 주요 유형들은 물론, 외고 특유의 유형과 학생들이 어렵게 느끼는 유형까지, 총 14개의 유형에 대비할 수 있다.

실전모의고사 2권과 3권에서는 회당 40문제로 이루어진 실전모의고사를 각각 7회분씩 배치하여 본격적인 실전 감각을 키우게 하였다. 각 회의 모의고사는 다양한 외고에서 출제되고 있는 여러 가지 유형의 문제들을 두루 접해볼 수 있도록 구성하였으며 다양한 주제의 스크립트를 통하여 실전에서 어떤 주제의 듣기가 출제되어도 이해할 수 있는 생각의 토대를 마련해 주고자 하였다. 또한 실전모의고사에 대한 〈Dictation Test〉 코너에서는 단순히 문제를 풀어보고 끝나는 것이 아니라 보다 실질적인 리스닝 실력을 단련시킬 수 있다.

부디 이 **LISTEN to the MAX 실전모의고사** 시리즈가 보다 나은 내일을 위해 오늘도 열심히 노력하고 있는 상위권 학생들에게 최상의 대비서가 되기를 바라며, 이 책으로 공부하는 모든 학생들이 영어 리스닝 실력과 자신감, 성취감을 모두 얻을 수 있기를 바란다.

저자 일동

LISTEN to the MAX 실전모의고사 ❷의 구성과 특징

40문제의 모의고사 7회분

각 외고의 기출 문제들을 철저히 분석하여 최신 출제 경향을 완벽하게 반영한 7회의 실전모의고사를 통해 실전 감각을 키운다. 스크립트의 길이, 어휘 및 표현의 난이도, 대화 횟수 및 문장의 길이가 모두 가장 실전에 가깝게 했음은 물론, 모든 스크립트는 100% 원어민의 작업을 통해 실용적이고 수준 있는 표현들을 담았다.

━ 여러 외고의 갖가지 유형을 모두 풀어볼 수 있는 40문제

한 회의 실전모의고사 안에 각 외고 특유의 유형들이 모두 들어 있어 각종 유형들에 대한 기본 내공을 키울 수 있다.

━ 다양한 분야의 시사성 있는 토픽들

경제, 문화, 예술, 과학 등의 여러 분야에 대한 문제들을 통해 듣기 실력뿐만이 아닌 다양한 정보와 지식을 습득할 수 있게 하였다. 특히 최근 화제가 되는 여러 논점들을 다룸으로써, 폭넓은 분야의 시사성 있는 문제가 다양하게 등장하고 있는 외고영어듣기시험에 대한 완벽한 대비가 가능하다.

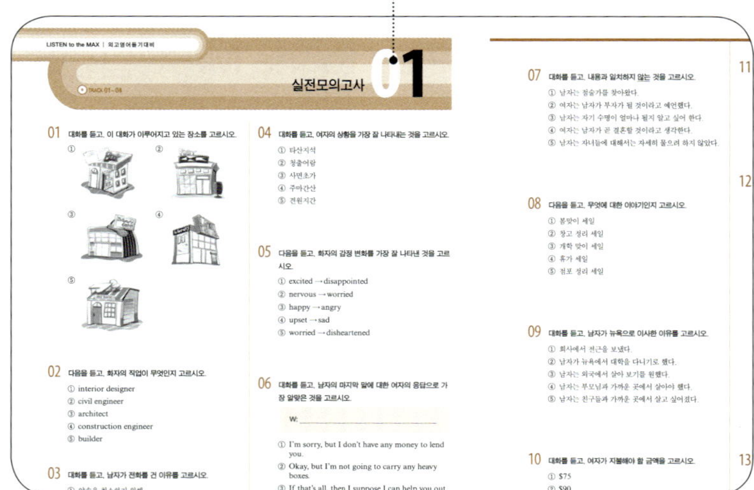

Dictation Test

7회의 실전모의고사에 대한 7회의 Dictation Test. 단순히 문제만 풀어보고 끝나는 것이 아니라 직접 받아 써봄으로써 궁극적인 리스닝 실력을 키울 수 있고 자신의 취약점이 무엇인지 알 수 있다.

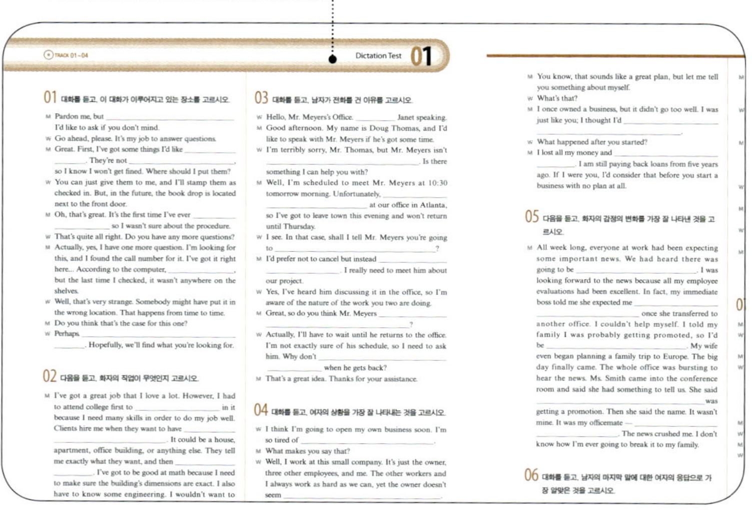

정답 및 해석

보기 편하도록 별책으로 제공되는 정답 및 해석에서는 **실전모의고사 7회분**에 실린 모든 문제의 스크립트와 해석을 제공한다. Dictation Test의 정답도 여기에서 찾아볼 수 있다.

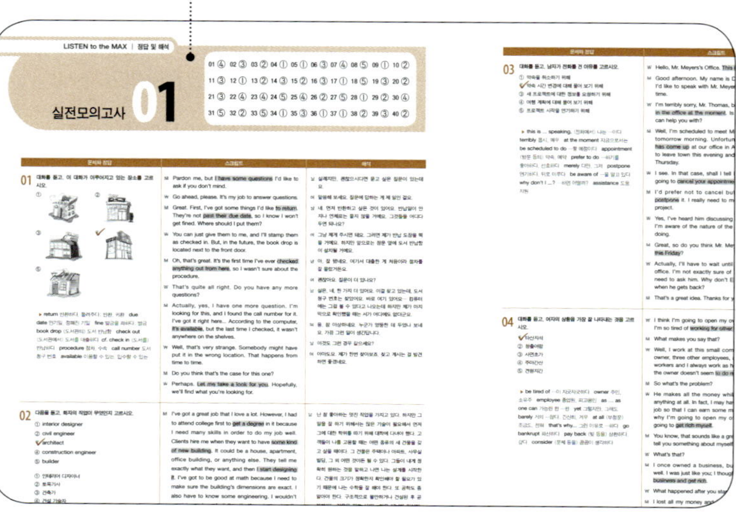

CONTENTS

실전모의고사

실전모의고사 01

- **No.01~No.10 :** ⊙ TRACK 01
- **No.11~No.20 :** ⊙ TRACK 02
- **No.21~No.30 :** ⊙ TRACK 03
- **No.31~No.40 :** ⊙ TRACK 04

실전모의고사 01

01 대화를 듣고, 이 대화가 이루어지고 있는 장소를 고르시오.

① 
② 
③ 
④ 
⑤ 

02 다음을 듣고, 화자의 직업이 무엇인지 고르시오.

① interior designer
② civil engineer
③ architect
④ construction engineer
⑤ builder

03 대화를 듣고, 남자가 전화를 건 이유를 고르시오.

① 약속을 취소하기 위해
② 약속 시간 변경에 대해 물어 보기 위해
③ 새 프로젝트에 대한 정보를 요청하기 위해
④ 여행 계획에 대해 물어 보기 위해
⑤ 프로젝트 시작을 연기하기 위해

04 대화를 듣고, 여자의 상황을 가장 잘 나타내는 것을 고르시오.

① 타산지석
② 청출어람
③ 사면초가
④ 주마간산
⑤ 견원지간

05 다음을 듣고, 화자의 감정 변화를 가장 잘 나타낸 것을 고르시오.

① excited → disappointed
② nervous → worried
③ happy → angry
④ upset → sad
⑤ worried → disheartened

06 대화를 듣고, 남자의 마지막 말에 대한 여자의 응답으로 가장 알맞은 것을 고르시오.

W: ___________________________________

① I'm sorry, but I don't have any money to lend you.
② Okay, but I'm not going to carry any heavy boxes.
③ If that's all, then I suppose I can help you out tonight.
④ Okay, but we're going to have to take your car.
⑤ But I have no idea where exactly you live.

07 대화를 듣고, 내용과 일치하지 <u>않는</u> 것을 고르시오.

① 남자는 점술가를 찾아왔다.
② 여자는 남자가 부자가 될 것이라고 예언했다.
③ 남자는 자기 수명이 얼마나 될지 알고 싶어 한다.
④ 여자는 남자가 곧 결혼할 것이라고 생각한다.
⑤ 남자는 자녀들에 대해서는 자세히 물으려 하지 않았다.

08 다음을 듣고, 무엇에 대한 이야기인지 고르시오.

① 봄맞이 세일
② 창고 정리 세일
③ 개학 맞이 세일
④ 휴가 세일
⑤ 점포 정리 세일

09 대화를 듣고, 남자가 뉴욕으로 이사한 이유를 고르시오.

① 회사에서 전근을 보냈다.
② 남자가 뉴욕에서 대학을 다니기로 했다.
③ 남자는 외국에서 살아 보기를 원했다.
④ 남자는 부모님과 가까운 곳에서 살아야 했다.
⑤ 남자는 친구들과 가까운 곳에서 살고 싶어졌다.

10 대화를 듣고, 여자가 지불해야 할 금액을 고르시오.

① $75
② $90
③ $105
④ $165
⑤ $200

11 다음을 듣고, 이 이야기가 어떤 질문에 대한 대답인지 고르시오.

① What are the costs involved in pet therapy?
② What is the success rate of pet therapy?
③ Who can benefit from pet therapy?
④ Why is pet therapy so effective?
⑤ Which doctors prescribe pet therapy?

12 다음을 듣고, 주어진 그래프에 대해 사실이 <u>아닌</u> 것을 고르시오.

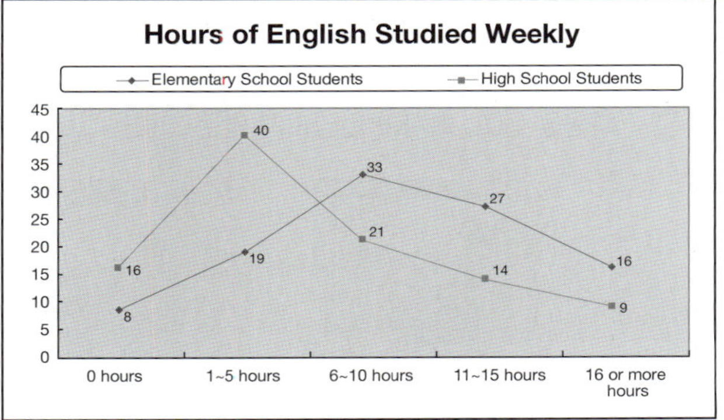

① 고등학교 학생들보다 더 많은 초등학교 학생들이 영어에 주당 1~5시간을 쓴다.
② 전반적으로 초등학교 학생들은 고등학교 학생들보다 영어 학습에 더 많은 시간을 쓴다.
③ 영어에 주당 16시간 이상을 쓰는 고등학교 학생들 수는 주당 1~5시간을 학습하는 초등학교 학생들 수보다 적다.
④ 초등학교 학생들의 2배에 이르는 고등학교 학생들은 전혀 영어를 공부하지 않는다.
⑤ 고등학교 학생들의 거의 2배에 이르는 초등학교 학생들이 영어에 주당 11~15시간을 쓴다.

13 대화를 듣고, 두 사람이 대화를 마치고 할 일을 고르시오.

① Apply for passports
② Purchase some books
③ Enroll in a language class
④ Pack their luggage
⑤ Buy some new clothes

14 대화를 듣고, 파스타를 만드는 순서가 알맞게 나열된 것을 고르시오.

> ⓐ Sprinkle the grated cheese over the pasta.
> ⓑ Boil the pasta until it is finished.
> ⓒ Mix the pine nuts and raisins with the pasta.
> ⓓ Fry some spinach and mix it with the pasta.

① ⓑ – ⓐ – ⓒ – ⓓ
② ⓑ – ⓒ – ⓐ – ⓓ
③ ⓑ – ⓓ – ⓒ – ⓐ
④ ⓓ – ⓑ – ⓐ – ⓒ
⑤ ⓓ – ⓒ – ⓑ – ⓐ

15 다음을 듣고, 화자가 언급하지 <u>않은</u> 그림을 고르시오.

① 
② 
③ 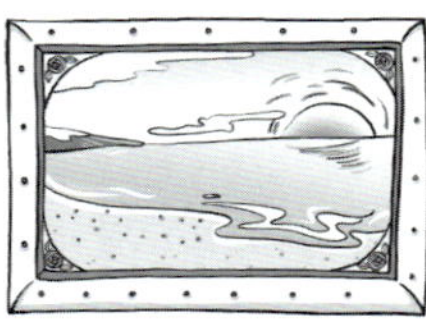
④ 
⑤ 

16 대화를 듣고, 두 사람이 이야기하고 있는 책의 장르와 그 책이 인기 있는 이유가 올바로 짝지어진 것을 고르시오.

① Science Fiction – It keeps people interested in the story.
② Nonfiction – It teaches people about politics.
③ Biography – It tells a very inspiring story.
④ Thriller – The plot is really amazing.
⑤ Mystery – It makes the reader very curious.

17 다음을 듣고, 남자의 미래에 대한 태도를 가장 잘 나타낸 것을 고르시오.

① Optimistic
② Frightened
③ Nervous
④ Apprehensive
⑤ Worried

18 대화를 듣고, 남자의 마지막 말로 유추할 수 있는 것을 고르시오.

① He will talk to his apartment supervisor.
② He will find out his neighbor's phone number.
③ He will ask the woman for some more advice.
④ He will file a complaint about his neighbor.
⑤ He is not going to talk to his neighbor.

19 대화를 듣고, 남자와 여자가 만날 시간을 고르시오.

① 6:30
② 7:00
③ 7:30
④ 8:00
⑤ 8:30

20 다음을 듣고, 불면증을 치료하기 위한 방법으로 제안되지 <u>않은</u> 것을 고르시오.

① Make the room as dark as possible.
② Do not read before going to sleep.
③ Avoid drinks that have caffeine in them.
④ Establish a moderate temperature in the room.
⑤ Do not exercise prior to going to bed.

21 대화를 듣고, 수잔에 대해 사실이 <u>아닌</u> 것을 고르시오.

① 수잔은 이름을 잘 기억한다.
② 수잔은 마음이 넓은 사람일 것이다.
③ 수잔은 가끔 회사에 지각한다.
④ 수잔은 컴퓨터 프로그램에 대해 잘 모른다.
⑤ 수잔은 성실하게 일하는 사람이다.

22 다음을 듣고, 화자의 요지가 무엇인지 고르시오.

① 컴퓨터 칩이 매년 더 작아지고 있다.
② 지구의 천연자원을 보존하는 것이 중요하다.
③ 20세기에는 위대한 많은 발명품이 있었다.
④ 소형화는 소중한 기술적 발전이다.
⑤ DVD플레이어는 작을 뿐만 아니라 휴대할 수도 있다.

23 대화를 듣고, 두 사람이 서울에서의 생활에 대해 불만스럽게 생각하는 것이 무엇인지 고르시오.

	남자의 불만	여자의 불만
①	지하철이 너무 느리다.	아파트가 너무 비싸다.
②	택시가 너무 느리다.	보도에 사람들이 너무 많다.
③	도시가 너무 크다.	택시를 타면 회사에 늦는다.
④	집값이 너무 비싸다.	교통이 너무 막힌다.
⑤	물가가 너무 비싸다.	지하철 시스템이 효율적이지 않다.

24 다음을 듣고, 이야기에서 말하는 내용의 예로 알맞은 것을 고르시오.

① mature – premature
② cycle – recycle
③ form – inform
④ view – preview
⑤ please – displease

25 대화를 듣고, 점원이 여자의 요구를 거절한 이유를 고르시오.

① The store does not give refunds to any customer.
② The customer forgot to bring her receipt with her.
③ The store only allows customers to exchange items.
④ The item the customer purchased is not damaged.
⑤ The customer bought the product too many days ago.

26 다음을 듣고, 화자의 의견에 동의하는 진술을 고르시오.

① Sumi: Parents shouldn't allow their children to play so many video games.
② Minho: I love video games since I've learned to work well with others from them.
③ Soohee: Video games are a waste of time, especially since students should be studying more.
④ Mina: I managed to set a new high score on the video game I was recently playing.
⑤ Taeho: Because of video games, I've made a lot of new friends at my school.

27 대화를 듣고, 두 사람이 기다리는 인물이 어디에서 왔는지 고르시오.

5:30	Tokyo
5:50	Athens
5:50	Rome
6:15	Sydney
6:20	Cairo

① Rome
② Cairo
③ Athens
④ Tokyo
⑤ Sydney

28 다음을 듣고, 화자가 설명하는 포즈로 알맞은 것을 고르시오.

① 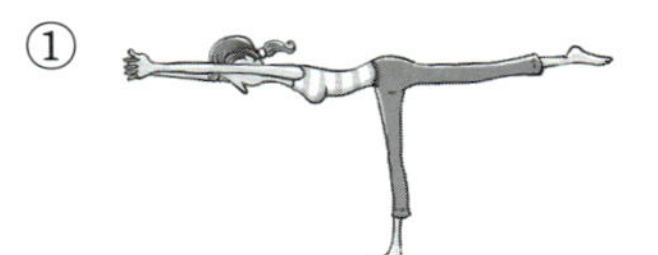　② 

③ 　④ 

⑤ 

29 대화를 듣고, 다음 중 두 사람이 먼저 해야 할 일들을 모두 고르시오.

ⓐ make some copies
ⓑ go to lunch
ⓒ attend a meeting with the department heads
ⓓ make some phone calls
ⓔ send a facsimile
ⓕ prepare for a meeting
ⓖ deliver some papers

① ⓐ, ⓒ, ⓕ, ⓖ
② ⓐ, ⓔ, ⓕ, ⓖ
③ ⓑ, ⓒ, ⓓ, ⓔ, ⓕ
④ ⓒ, ⓓ, ⓔ, ⓖ
⑤ ⓐ, ⓒ, ⓔ, ⓖ

30 다음을 듣고, 다음 문장의 빈 칸에 들어갈 알맞은 말을 고르시오.

> When you go to the United States, you should ________________________.

① always pay for your share of the meal at a restaurant
② stand close to people when speaking to them
③ give strong opinions on various topics
④ avoid talking about a number of specific subjects
⑤ be sure to ask about a person's religious beliefs

〔31-34〕 31번부터 34번까지는 문제와 보기를 모두 듣고 푸는 문제입니다. 대화나 이야기를 듣고, 영어로 들려주는 질문에 대한 알맞은 답을 고르시오.

31　①　②　③　④　⑤

32　①　②　③　④　⑤

33　①　②　③　④　⑤

34　①　②　③　④　⑤

35 다음을 듣고, 이어지는 영어 질문에 대한 알맞은 답을 고르시오.

① cold and snowy
② hot and rainy
③ warm and cloudy
④ hot and bright
⑤ cool and rainy

36 주어진 시간 동안 아래 지문을 주의 깊게 읽고, 들려주는 영어 질문에 답하시오. 〔1분〕

> After the heart, the brain is one of the most important organs in the body. Without an operational brain, a person would not be able to think for him or herself. Unsurprisingly, the human brain is an extremely complicated organ, and scientists have not yet determined everything it is capable of doing. However, what they have determined shows that the brain is simply incredible. For example, it is responsible for accepting all of the information that the five senses—sight, smell, touch, taste, and hearing—register, and then it must process that information. The brain also lets people think, speak, and imagine things. It controls people's emotions, of which they have a very large number. And the brain also controls the body's motor reflexes. These are what enable people to walk, talk, breathe, and move all of their various body parts. The brain even controls the rate at which a person's heart beats and a person's body temperature, among other things. There are simply a stunning amount of responsibilities that the brain, a relatively small organ, is responsible for.

Q: _______________________

① The Functions of the Brain
② How the Brain Works
③ The Brain and Motor Reflexes
④ The Complexity of the Brain
⑤ The Brain: The Most Important Organ

〔37-38〕 대화를 듣고, 이어지는 두 개의 질문에 답하시오.

37 Which of the following is NOT true about the woman's apartment?

① Her bedroom is not as big as she had thought.
② The wallpaper in the kitchen needs to be fixed.
③ She can see a nearby mountain from there.
④ There was no electricity when she moved in.
⑤ There is a problem with her bathroom sink.

38 Which of the following is the man's response to the woman?

① You'd better get that sink fixed immediately.
② So, not everything about your apartment is bad.
③ You must be paying a lot of money for that.
④ I'd be upset about the previous tenant if I were you.
⑤ What are you going to do about that wallpaper?

〔39-40〕 대화를 듣고, 이어지는 두 개의 질문에 답하시오.

39 Who are the speakers talking about?

① Frank D. Roosevelt
② Tony Blair
③ Winston Churchill
④ Douglas MacArthur
⑤ George Bush

40 Which of the following is NOT true about the person?

① He was once the prime minister of England.
② He often spoke to the British people on television.
③ He was the author of some books.
④ He once had a job as a journalist in a foreign country.
⑤ He had several different jobs in the government.

실전모의고사

실전모의고사 02

- **No.01~No.10** : ⊙ TRACK 05
- **No.11~No.20** : ⊙ TRACK 06
- **No.21~No.30** : ⊙ TRACK 07
- **No.31~No.40** : ⊙ TRACK 08

TRACK 05~08

01 대화를 듣고, 여자가 가려고 하는 곳을 고르시오.

Maple street

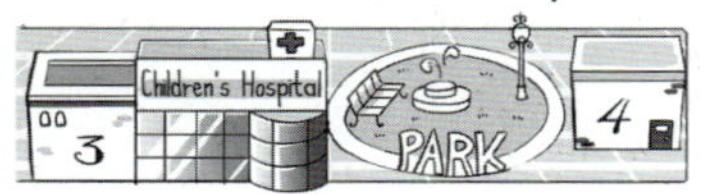

02 대화를 듣고, 이 대화가 이루어지고 있는 장소를 고르시오.

① at a car rental agency
② at a garage
③ at an auto showroom
④ at a used car sales lot
⑤ at a gas station

03 다음을 듣고, 이야기 속의 This가 무엇인지 고르시오.

① 자동차 ② 컴퓨터 ③ 라디오
④ 텔레비전 ⑤ 전화기

04 다음을 듣고, 화자가 무엇에 대해 이야기하고 있는지 고르시오.

① 울릉도 ② 제주도 ③ 완도
④ 여의도 ⑤ 진도

05 대화를 듣고, 남자가 MP3플레이어를 사기 위해 지불한 금액을 고르시오.

① one hundred fifty dollars
② one hundred dollars
③ fifty dollars
④ almost two hundred dollars
⑤ more than two hundred dollars

06 대화를 듣고, 남자가 어떤 스포츠를 하는 선수인지 고르시오.

① 축구
② 미식 축구
③ 아이스 하키
④ 농구
⑤ 야구

07 대화를 듣고, 남자의 마지막 말에 대한 여자의 응답으로 알맞은 것을 고르시오.

W: ____________________________________

① I'll be there by nine o'clock.
② I don't know where you live.
③ Sorry, but I have too much work to do.
④ Okay, I'll see if he wants to go.
⑤ No, I'm sorry, but I don't enjoy parties.

08

다음을 듣고, 이 이야기를 하는 목적을 고르시오.

① 레스토랑의 가격에 대해 불평하기 위해
② 레스토랑의 인테리어에 대해 이야기하기 위해
③ 그 음식이 어떻게 요리한 것인지 설명하기 위해
④ 그 레스토랑에서 식사하는 것을 추천하기 위해
⑤ 레스토랑의 서비스에 대해 불평하기 위해

09

대화를 듣고, 다음 중 헌혈에 대해 사실이 <u>아닌</u> 것을 고르시오.

① 헌혈을 매일 하면 건강에 좋지 않다.
② 헌혈하는 사람들에게 병원 측은 돈을 지불하지 않는다.
③ 헌혈을 하면 질병을 얻을 수 있다.
④ 병원에서는 많은 새로운 헌혈자들을 필요로 한다.
⑤ 인체는 빠져나간 혈액을 다시 채우기 위해 시간을 필요로 한다.

10

다음을 듣고, 은하수에 대해 사실이 <u>아닌</u> 것을 고르시오.

① 대부분의 사람들은 은하수가 나선형이라고 생각한다.
② 은하수는 우주에 있는 많은 은하들 중 하나이다.
③ 지구는 은하수 가장자리 근처에 있다.
④ 우주에 있는 은하는 약 130억 개로 추정된다.
⑤ 은하의 지름은 약 십만 광년이다.

11

대화를 듣고, 두 사람이 대화 후에 할 일을 고르시오.

① Go to a restaurant with healthier food
② Order some hamburgers and French fries
③ Complain to the restaurant owner
④ Go to the health club to work out
⑤ Return to their office and eat there

12

다음을 듣고, 1960년대 이후 10대 비만율의 변화를 가장 잘 보여 주는 그래프를 고르시오.

① 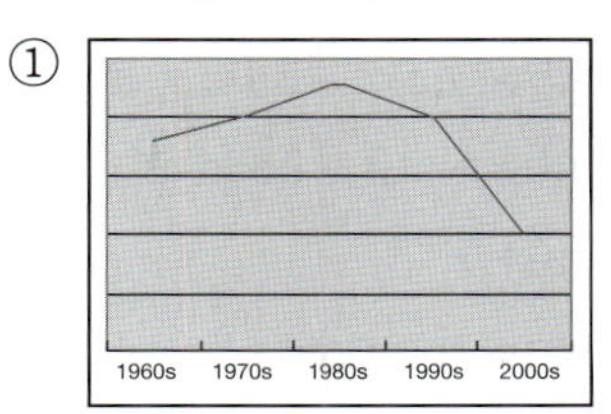
② 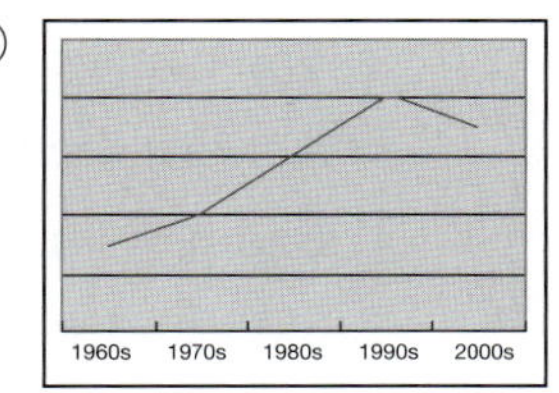
③ 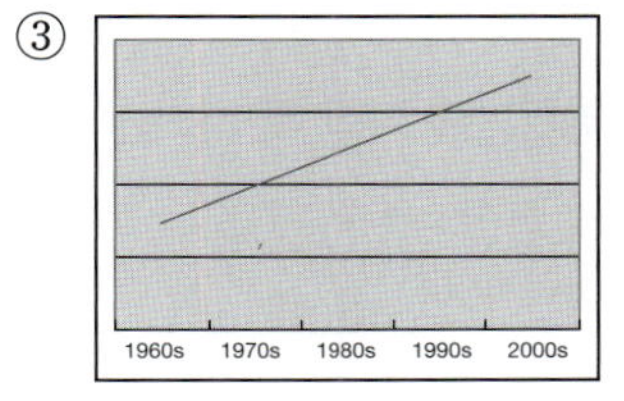
④ 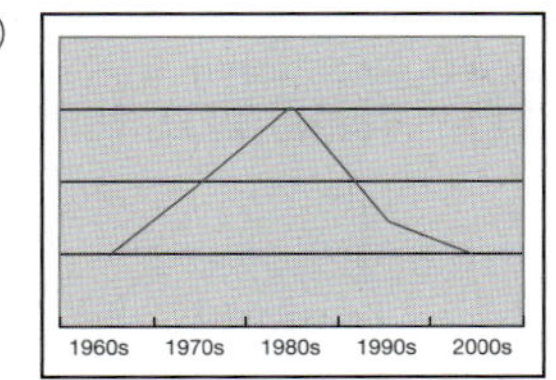
⑤ 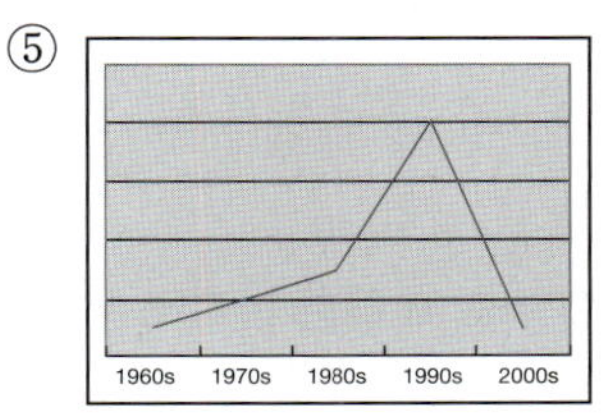

13

대화를 듣고, 두 사람이 방문할 장소를 순서대로 나열한 것을 고르시오.

ⓐ The Empire State Building
ⓑ Madison Square Garden
ⓒ Central Park
ⓓ The Metropolitan Museum of Modern Art

① ⓐ – ⓑ – ⓒ – ⓓ
② ⓑ – ⓒ – ⓓ – ⓐ
③ ⓒ – ⓐ – ⓓ – ⓑ
④ ⓒ – ⓓ – ⓑ – ⓐ
⑤ ⓓ – ⓒ – ⓐ – ⓑ

14

다음을 듣고, 화자가 이야기하고 있는 그림의 장르를 고르시오.

① a landscape
② a still-life
③ a portrait
④ a historical painting
⑤ a cartoon image

15 대화를 듣고, 상황을 가장 잘 나타내는 속담을 고르시오.

① Look before you leap.
② You cannot have your cake and eat it, too.
③ Actions speak louder than words.
④ Bad news travels fast.
⑤ Slow and steady wins the race.

16 다음을 듣고, 이야기의 분위기를 가장 잘 나타낸 것을 고르시오.

① happy   ② confident
③ nervous   ④ disappointed
⑤ relaxed

17 대화를 듣고, 여자의 마지막 말에 대한 남자의 응답으로 가장 알맞은 것을 고르시오.

M: _______________________________

① That's not a problem. In fact, it will last forever.
② It would be cheaper, but a new one would be better.
③ Yes, we can provide you with a faster Internet connection.
④ Yes, we just upgraded your computer to make it better.
⑤ No, your son should really be here instead of you.

18 다음을 듣고, 화요일의 날씨를 고르시오.

① cloudy and cold
② sunny and warm
③ rainy and cool
④ snowy and cold
⑤ windy and warm

19 대화를 듣고, 남자가 알람시계를 설정해 달라고 부탁한 시각을 고르시오.

① 새벽 3시
② 오후 3시
③ 새벽 2시 45분
④ 오후 2시 45분
⑤ 새벽 2시 50분

20 대화를 듣고, 두 사람이 가장 싫어하는 음식을 고르시오.

	Man	Woman
①	oatmeal	corn
②	oatmeal	beans
③	lobster	fish
④	corn	oatmeal
⑤	lobster	corn

21 다음을 듣고, 화자의 요지가 무엇인지 고르시오.

① Smoking can kill people of any age.
② Adults enjoy smoking as much as teens.
③ More teens are smoking these days.
④ Many famous people are smokers.
⑤ Smoking starts from peer pressure.

22 대화를 듣고, 여자가 남자의 요청을 듣지 못한 이유를 고르시오.

① There was a lot of construction noise.
② He was speaking very softly into the phone.
③ Someone else was trying to talk to her.
④ His cell phone connection was bad.
⑤ A large bus was passing his car.

23 다음을 듣고, 이 이야기의 장르를 고르시오.

① a short story
② an essay
③ a fairy tale
④ a fable
⑤ a sonnet

24 대화를 듣고, 두 사람이 무엇에 대해 이야기하고 있는지 고르시오.

① a snowstorm
② an earthquake
③ a volcano
④ a tornado
⑤ a typhoon

25 다음을 듣고, 제품에 대해 사실이 <u>아닌</u> 것을 고르시오.

① 이 제품은 토요일까지 세일을 한다.
② 다양한 색상으로 나오고 있다.
③ 작고 휴대성이 있다.
④ 열 가지 다른 부속품들이 있다.
⑤ 1년의 보증 기간이 있다.

26 다음을 듣고, 화자의 의견에 동의하는 진술을 고르시오.

① Minsu: The death penalty is barbaric and unjust.
② Jaehee: All murderers deserve to be executed.
③ Sungmin: Keeping killers in prison cells is a waste of money.
④ Changhoon: Everyone convicted of a crime should be in prison.
⑤ Jeonga: DNA testing shouldn't be used in criminal cases.

27 다음을 듣고, 화자의 집을 가장 잘 나타낸 것을 고르시오.

① 
② 
③ 
④ 
⑤ 

28 대화를 듣고, 두 사람이 현재까지 주문한 음식값으로 지불하게 될 금액을 고르시오.

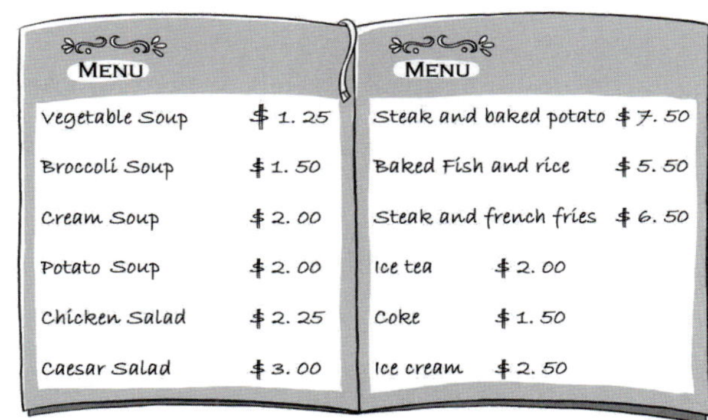

① $18.50
② $19.50
③ $20.00
④ $20.50
⑤ $21.50

29 대화를 듣고, 두 사람이 이상적인 친구에게서 원하는 공통 요소들을 모두 고르시오.

ⓐ intelligence   ⓑ good looks
ⓒ wealth   ⓓ honesty
ⓔ a sense of humor

① ⓐ, ⓑ, ⓒ
② ⓑ, ⓒ, ⓓ, ⓔ
③ ⓐ, ⓒ, ⓓ, ⓔ
④ ⓐ, ⓓ, ⓔ
⑤ ⓐ, ⓑ, ⓒ, ⓔ

30 다음을 듣고, 화자의 마지막 말에 이어질 내용으로 가장 알맞은 것을 고르시오.

So before the test, you'd better sleep __________ __________.

① as little as possible
② around seven hours or so
③ about three or four hours
④ a couple of hours and study the rest
⑤ as much as you can

〔31-34〕 31번부터 34번까지는 문제와 보기를 모두 듣고 푸는 문제입니다. 대화나 이야기를 듣고, 영어로 들려주는 질문에 대한 알맞은 답을 고르시오.

31 ①   ②   ③   ④   ⑤

32 ①   ②   ③   ④   ⑤

33 ①   ②   ③   ④   ⑤

34 ①   ②   ③   ④   ⑤

35 다음을 듣고, 이어지는 영어 질문에 답하시오.

① $6
② $7
③ $9
④ $10
⑤ $11

36 주어진 시간 동안 아래 지문을 주의 깊게 읽고, 들려주는 영어 질문에 답하시오. 〔1분〕

Welcome to History 103, European History in the Twentieth Century. The following is the syllabus for our course for the next month. During the first week, we will examine the events leading to World War I and the war itself. During the second week, our discussion turns to the post-war years, the Great Depression, and the rise of dictators like Adolf Hitler. After that, in the third week, our attention will be focused on the causes of World War II and the war in both Europe and the Pacific Ocean. In the final week, we will look at the end of the war and the start of the Cold War between the Soviet Union and the United States. All students are responsible for reading the chapters for these sections. There will be a quiz at the end of each week and a test at the end of every month. Each student will also prepare a topic for a major essay, which will be turned in at the end of the month. Come to my office in room 409 on Tuesdays from 3~5 p.m. if there are any problems.

Q: __________

① The causes of World War II
② The causes of World War I
③ The end of World War I
④ The Great Depression
⑤ The start of the Cold War

[37-38] 다음을 듣고, 이어지는 두 개의 질문에 답하시오.

37 What is the purpose of this talk?

① To warn people about purchasing pets
② To explain how some pets might get sick
③ To complain about the high costs of pets
④ To describe the reasons why people buy pets
⑤ To inform people on how to raise a pet

38 Which is NOT true about a good pet owner?

① A good owner will give the pet anything to eat.
② A good owner will make sure the pet sees a veterinarian.
③ A good owner will give the pet a place to sleep.
④ A good owner will love the pet like a child.
⑤ A good owner will never abandon the pet.

[39-40] 대화를 듣고, 이어지는 두 개의 질문에 답하시오.

39 What are the speakers talking about?

① the city's corrupt government
② the number of people who voted
③ a person's responsibility to vote
④ the reasons why they should not vote
⑤ the person they think will win the election

40 What is the woman's response to the man?

W: ___________________________

① I guess you are right after all.
② Maybe I won't vote the next time either.
③ No, but you've made some good points.
④ I still believe everyone's vote is important.
⑤ Please be sure to vote the next time.

LISTEN to the MAX | 외고영어듣기대비

실전모의고사

실전모의고사 03

- **No.01~No.10 :** TRACK 09
- **No.11~No.20 :** TRACK 10
- **No.21~No.30 :** TRACK 11
- **No.31~No.40 :** TRACK 12

TRACK 09~12

실전모의고사 03

01 대화를 듣고, 남자가 여자친구를 위해 살 선물을 고르시오.

① 

② 

③ 

④ 

⑤ 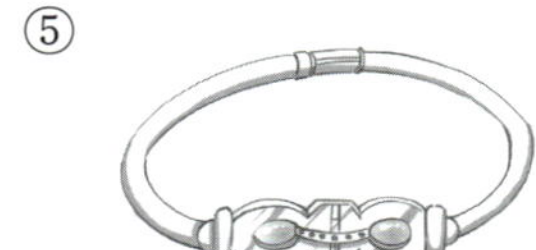

02 다음을 듣고, 화자의 장래희망이 무엇인지 고르시오.

① doctor
② animal trainer
③ nurse
④ animal groomer
⑤ veterinarian

03 대화를 듣고, 두 사람의 관계를 가장 잘 나타낸 것을 고르시오.

① bank teller – customer
② loan officer – customer
③ bank president – bank teller
④ customer – security guard
⑤ bank teller – loan officer

04 대화를 듣고, 두 사람이 만나기로 한 식당을 고르시오.

① Mitchell's
② Thai Delights
③ The Hot Tamale
④ Pomodoros
⑤ The Hungry Fisherman

05 다음을 듣고, 이야기의 제목으로 가장 알맞은 것을 고르시오.

① Why Soccer Has Become Popular
② A Brief History of Soccer
③ Some of the Rules of Soccer
④ The World Cup and Soccer
⑤ Soccer in Ancient Greece and Rome

06 대화를 듣고, 여자에 대해 사실이 <u>아닌</u> 것을 고르시오.

① 급여에 대한 것은 여자에게 중요한 문제이다.
② 직업의 안정성이 그녀가 원하는 것이다.
③ 여자는 더 이상 학업을 계속하기를 원하지 않는다.
④ 정부에 관련된 일자리가 여자의 흥미를 끈다.
⑤ 여자의 전공은 그녀의 직업 선택에 영향을 주지 않을 것이다.

07 다음을 듣고, 이야기의 분위기를 가장 잘 나타낸 것을 고르시오.

① displeased　② relaxed　③ bored
④ confused　⑤ agitated

08 대화를 듣고, 남자의 마지막 말에 대한 여자의 응답으로 가장 알맞은 것을 고르시오.

W: ______________________________

① She's at her parents' house right now.
② I think she's still working at the office.
③ She should be at the museum by three.
④ Sorry, but nothing has arrived for you yet.
⑤ I'd say probably in a couple of hours.

09 대화를 듣고, 여자의 마지막 말에 대한 남자의 응답으로 가장 알맞은 것을 고르시오.

M: ______________________________

① I think I need some more time to decide when I want to go.
② Are you sure there are no tickets available on Saturday?
③ I'd love two tickets for the Sunday afternoon performance.
④ I'll take two front-row tickets for the Thursday night show.
⑤ Do you mind if I trade these tickets for two on Saturday night?

10 다음을 듣고, 대피라미드에 대해 사실이 <u>아닌</u> 것을 고르시오.

① They are the most popular tourist sites ever.
② They are located all throughout Egypt.
③ There are three pyramids located at Giza.
④ They were used to bury people in.
⑤ No one is sure how they were built.

11 대화를 듣고, 여자가 신발을 사기 위해 지불할 금액을 고르시오.

① $85　　② $115　　③ $120
④ $150　　⑤ $200

12 대화를 듣고, 이 상황에 가장 어울리는 영어 속담을 고르시오.

① A stitch in time saves nine.
② The grass is always greener on the other side.
③ Never look a gift horse in the mouth.
④ Too many cooks spoil the broth.
⑤ The early bird always gets the worm.

13 다음을 듣고, 화자가 여행할 나라들을 차례대로 나열한 것을 고르시오.

ⓐ Greece
ⓑ Switzerland
ⓒ Italy
ⓓ Germany

① ⓐ – ⓑ – ⓒ – ⓓ
② ⓑ – ⓒ – ⓐ – ⓓ
③ ⓒ – ⓐ – ⓓ – ⓑ
④ ⓒ – ⓑ – ⓐ – ⓓ
⑤ ⓒ – ⓑ – ⓓ – ⓐ

14 대화를 듣고, 두 사람이 이야기하고 있는 사진을 고르시오.

① 　② 

③ 　④ 

⑤ 

15 대화를 듣고, 여자가 아들이 깨어난 직후 무엇을 할지 고르시오.

① Take him inside the house
② Give him some water to drink
③ Put a cold towel on his forehead
④ Let him walk around
⑤ Take him to the hospital

16 다음을 듣고, 서울의 현재 날씨를 고르시오.

① It is raining just a little.
② There is a moderate amount of rain.
③ There are some thunderstorms.
④ It is experiencing heavy rain.
⑤ The typhoon is dropping heavy rain.

17 대화를 듣고, 남자가 먹은 음식에 들어 있는 칼로리가 총 얼마인지 고르시오.

① 1,000
② 1,400
③ 1,500
④ 1,620
⑤ 1,720

18 다음을 듣고, 이야기의 내용과 일치하지 <u>않는</u> 것을 고르시오.

① 총 비행시간은 9시간이 걸릴 것이다.
② 항공기는 더 빨리 도착할 예정이다.
③ 파리의 날씨는 화창할 것으로 예상된다.
④ 비행기는 지중해를 통과했다.
⑤ 기온은 72도까지 오를 것이다.

19 대화를 듣고, 남자가 새 컴퓨터를 사지 <u>못하는</u> 이유를 고르시오.

① 남자는 신용카드를 가지고 오는 것을 잊었다.
② 남자는 할부로 결제하기를 원하지 않는다.
③ 남자는 충분한 현금을 가지고 있지 않다.
④ 남자의 신용카드가 최근에 기한이 만료되었다.
⑤ 남자는 최근에 신용카드를 너무 많이 사용했다.

20 대화를 듣고, 여자가 남자에게 해 준 충고가 <u>아닌</u> 것을 고르시오.

① Have some hot food to eat.
② Take some vitamin tablets.
③ Drink a lot of liquids.
④ Take some cough drops.
⑤ Get as much rest as possible.

21 다음을 듣고, 화자의 감정 변화를 가장 잘 나타낸 것을 고르시오.

① nervous → disappointed
② hopeful → angry
③ eager → sad
④ concerned → distrustful
⑤ pleased → confused

22 다음을 듣고, 지도에서 남자의 집을 고르시오.

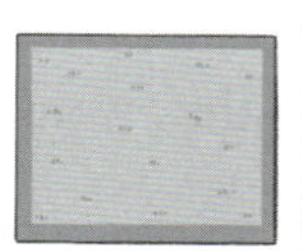

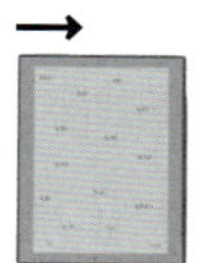
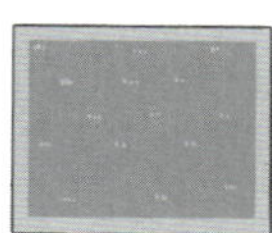
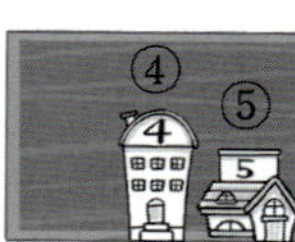

23 다섯 개의 대화문을 듣고, 자연스럽지 <u>않은</u> 것을 고르시오.

①   ②   ③   ④   ⑤

24 대화를 듣고, 두 사람에 대해 유추할 수 있는 것을 고르시오.

① 그들은 신혼부부이다.
② 그들은 정장을 주로 입는다.
③ 그들은 원하는 물건을 모두 구입할 예정이다.
④ 그들은 매일 밤 손님을 맞는다.
⑤ 그들에게는 충분한 예산이 있다.

25 다음을 듣고, 쇼트 프로그램과 롱 프로그램 점수를 합산한 점수가 가장 높아 스케이트 대회에서 우승한 사람이 누구일지 고르시오.

① Lisa Thompson
② Nancy Logan
③ Emily Bender
④ Mayu Fujikawa
⑤ Katrina Schmidt

26 대화를 듣고, 아들의 마지막 질문에 대한 여자의 응답으로 알맞은 것을 고르시오.

W: _______________________________________

① The laboratory where he did most of his work was in New Jersey.
② People still remember Edison for the important research he did.
③ He invented the phonograph, which could play sounds like music.
④ He never finished school since his teacher thought he was stupid.
⑤ He filed a patent for his electric light bulb in 1879.

27 대화를 듣고, 두 사람이 딸에게 취할 태도로 올바르지 <u>않은</u> 것을 고르시오.

① 딸이 더 일찍 잠자리에 들게 한다.
② 주말에 딸이 집에 있으면서 공부를 하게 한다.
③ 딸이 숙제를 끝내면 그것을 검사한다.
④ 가끔씩 딸이 외출하는 것을 못하게 한다.
⑤ 딸이 친구들을 만나는 것을 허락하지 않는다.

28 다음을 듣고, 화자의 의견에 동의하는 진술을 고르시오.

① 래리: 우리는 사람들이 환경을 파괴하지 못하도록 하는 새로운 법이 필요하다.
② 스티브: 나는 개발을 저지하려는 환경론자들 때문에 아주 짜증이 난다.
③ 제레미: 우리가 계속 땅을 개발하지 않으면 경제는 악화될 것이다.
④ 카렌: 우리는 많은 기존 건물을 파괴하고 자연이 그 지역을 대체하도록 해야 한다.
⑤ 제니: 우리는 개발업자들의 사업을 금지시켜 그들이 자연을 더 이상 손상시키지 않도록 해야 한다.

29 대화를 듣고, 두 사람이 먹을 음식을 모두 고르시오.

ⓐ baked potato	ⓑ corn
ⓒ chicken wings	ⓓ broiled scallops
ⓔ mushroom soup	ⓕ potato skins
ⓖ roast fish	ⓗ vegetable soup

① ⓐ, ⓑ, ⓒ, ⓓ, ⓖ
② ⓐ, ⓑ, ⓓ, ⓕ, ⓗ
③ ⓐ, ⓑ, ⓒ, ⓓ, ⓕ
④ ⓒ, ⓓ, ⓔ, ⓕ, ⓖ
⑤ ⓐ, ⓒ, ⓓ, ⓕ, ⓖ

다음을 듣고, 화자의 마지막 말에 이어질 내용으로 가장 알맞은 것을 고르시오.

> So, when meeting American businessmen for the first time, you'd better ______________________________________.

① be as outgoing as possible
② remember to speak with everyone
③ try not to offend anyone
④ offer to shake hands with everyone
⑤ pass out your business cards to them

〔31-34〕 31번부터 34번까지는 문제와 보기를 모두 듣고 푸는 문제입니다. 대화나 이야기를 듣고, 영어로 들려주는 질문에 대한 알맞은 답을 고르시오.

31 ① ② ③ ④ ⑤

32 ① ② ③ ④ ⑤

33 ① ② ③ ④ ⑤

34 ① ② ③ ④ ⑤

35 다음을 듣고, 이어지는 영어 질문에 답하시오.

① 4:00
② 6:00
③ 7:00
④ 8:00
⑤ 10:00

36 주어진 시간 동안 아래 지문을 주의 깊게 읽고, 대화를 들은 후 질문에 답하시오. 〔1분〕

> In recent years, there has been something of a revolution in the way that people take care of their banking needs. In the past, people had to go into physical banks to do all sorts of transactions. Once ATMs were invented, then many transactions could be done through these machines. However, thanks to the newest innovation in banking services, many people no longer even need to leave their homes to do their banking. The reason is that Internet banking is becoming popular. Thanks to Internet banking, customers can enter their login and password onto the computer and can then do almost every transaction they want. They can check their account balance, transfer money, and even pay their bills. This keeps them from having to go to the bank for many transactions. However, they still cannot deposit or withdraw money online, but they can apply for loans, including personal loans and mortgages. Best of all is that Internet banking is completely safe. The banks use the most advanced software, which is protected with many safeguards. So long as the customer does not let anyone know his or her login and password, the customer's account information is entirely safe.

Q: _____________________________________

① Well, you can apply for personal loans online.
② I've just got to transfer some money really quickly.
③ Actually, you still can't deposit money online yet.
④ It keeps me from having to visit an ATM all of the time.
⑤ The software is completely protected from hackers.

37 Which of the following questions does the talk answer?

① Why did Bram Stoker write the novel *Dracula*?
② What are the characteristics of a vampire?
③ What is the best way to destroy a vampire?
④ Where do most vampires prefer to live?
⑤ How can a regular person become a vampire?

38 Which of the following is NOT true about vampires?

① They are much stronger than most people.
② They can turn other people into vampires.
③ They must drink any kind of blood to survive.
④ They can be destroyed by a stake in the heart.
⑤ They can turn themselves into other animals.

〔39-40〕 대화를 듣고, 이어지는 두 개의 질문에 답하시오.

39 Which of the following is NOT true about the man?

① He makes a lot of money.
② He is currently employed.
③ He thinks his job is boring.
④ He lacks confidence in his abilities.
⑤ He is considering getting another job.

40 What is the woman trying to say?

① Making money is the most important aspect of working.
② Experience is the best way to get a new job.
③ Even in a bad economy, people can still get hired.
④ Enjoying one's job is better than being bored.
⑤ It is more important to be employed than to be happy.

실전모의고사

실전모의고사 04

- No.01~No.10 : ⊙ TRACK 13
- No.11~No.20 : ⊙ TRACK 14
- No.21~No.30 : ⊙ TRACK 15
- No.31~No.40 : ⊙ TRACK 16

실전모의고사 04

1 다음을 듣고, 이야기와 그림 속의 상황이 일치하지 <u>않는</u> 것을 고르시오.

2 대화를 듣고, 여자는 다음 중 누구와 친한 친구가 될 수 있을 것인지 고르시오.

① 수미: 난 친구들과 외출하는 걸 좋아하지만 같이 있을 때 말은 별로 안 해. 대신 친구들이 말하는 걸 뭐든 그냥 듣는 걸 더 좋아해.

② 진희: 나는 친구들을 위해 선물을 사는 걸 좋아해. 또 친구들과 집에서 영화를 보며 수다 떠는 것을 좋아하지.

③ 사라: 내가 잘 들어주기 때문에 친구들은 항상 내게 전화해서 문제를 얘기해. 다행히 친구들은 내게 점심이나 저녁 사주기를 좋아하는데, 때로 내가 돈이 부족하기 때문이야.

④ 미미: 난 함께 외출해서 친구들에게 돈을 쓰는 걸 좋아해. 항상 수다를 떨지만 친구들의 말에도 뭐든지 주의를 기울이려고 노력해.

⑤ 정아: 영화를 보러 가는 게 가장 좋아. 또 친구들이 별로 말을 하지 않아도 친구들과 얘기하는 걸 좋아해. 주로 내가 얘기를 가장 많이 하지.

3 다음을 듣고, 이 이야기가 무엇을 위한 것인지 고르시오.

① 상대방의 친절에 감사를 표하기 위해
② 최근의 여행을 되돌아 보기 위해
③ 자기를 도와준 두 남자를 칭찬하도록 추천하기 위해
④ 사업 관계를 더욱 돈독히 하고자 하는 마음을 드러내기 위해
⑤ 미래의 여행 계획을 세우기 위해

4 대화를 듣고, 여자에게 주어진 임무가 <u>아닌</u> 것을 고르시오.

① 항공편을 예약하는 것
② 회의의 일정을 잡는 것
③ 중요한 파일을 다시 입력하는 것
④ 컴퓨터 문제를 처리하는 것
⑤ 남자를 위해 호텔을 예약하는 것

5 다음을 듣고, 화자의 심정을 가장 잘 나타낸 것을 고르시오.

① concerned   ② depressed
③ nervous   ④ amused
⑤ optimistic

6 대화를 듣고, 영화에 대한 화자들의 의견이 바르게 반영된 것을 고르시오.

	좋았던 점	좋지 않았던 점
① 남자:	음악	특수효과
② 여자:	폭력성	배우들의 연기
③ 남자:	배우들의 연기	음악
④ 여자:	재미있는 대사	폭력성
⑤ 남자:	재미있는 대사	특수효과

7 다섯 개의 대화문을 듣고, 자연스럽지 <u>않은</u> 것을 고르시오.

①   ②   ③   ④   ⑤

8 다음을 듣고, 이야기 속의 This가 무엇인지 고르시오.

① history   ② philosophy
③ economics   ④ sociology
⑤ physics

9 대화를 듣고, 남자의 마지막 말에 대한 여자의 응답으로 알맞은 것을 고르시오.

W: ________________________________

① Okay, then let's meet at two o'clock.
② Oh, I'm sorry, but I won't be here.
③ That's fine with me. I'll see you then.
④ Sorry, but that's too late in the day.
⑤ I look forward to seeing you on Monday.

10 다음을 듣고, 이 이야기가 어떤 질문에 대한 대답인지 고르시오.

① How did Asians introduce tea to the West?
② What is the process by which people make tea?
③ Why do people in the East enjoy tea so much?
④ How do people in various countries consume tea?
⑤ Why do the British and Russians enjoy different kinds of teas?

11 대화를 듣고, 여자가 돌려 받게 될 금액이 얼마인지 고르시오.

① $4.50   ② $5.00
③ $5.50   ④ $6.00
⑤ $6.50

12 대화를 듣고, 이 상황에 가장 잘 어울리는 영어 속담을 고르시오.

① A stitch in time saves nine.
② Nothing ventured, nothing gained.
③ Every cloud has a silver lining.
④ The early bird catches the worm.
⑤ Don't count your chickens before they are hatched.

13 다음을 듣고, 이것이 누가 누구에게 하는 이야기인지 고르시오.

① coach → team
② mayor → city residents
③ manager → employees
④ president → citizens
⑤ professor → students

14 대화를 듣고, 두 사람이 이야기하고 있는 동작을 고르시오.

①    ② 

③    ④ 

⑤ 

15 대화를 듣고, 대화 후에 남자가 할 행동을 고르시오.

① Call his friend and apologize
② Call his parents to ask for money
③ Pay his friend twenty dollars
④ Borrow some money from his friend
⑤ Get his paycheck from his company

16 다음을 듣고, 이 내용에 대한 예로 알맞은 것을 고르시오.

① 중국의 많은 사람들이 바다 근처에서 산다.
② 유럽 전역에는 많은 농장들이 있다.
③ 힌두교도들은 종교적 신념을 이유로 쇠고기를 먹지 않는다.
④ 전 세계의 많은 나라들에는 저마다의 독특한 문화가 있다.
⑤ 어떤 나라에는 엄청난 폭우가 내린다.

17 대화를 듣고, 다음 중 대화 속에서 언급되지 <u>않은</u> 것을 고르시오.

① 남자가 원하는 방의 개수
② 이용 가능한 대중교통
③ 학교와 관련된 집의 위치
④ 마당의 유무
⑤ 남자가 지불할 수 있는 임대료 액수

18 대화를 듣고, 두 사람의 직업이 무엇인지 고르시오.

	Man	Woman
①	lawyer	florist
②	fireman	teacher
③	businessman	wedding planner
④	security guard	photographer
⑤	policeman	artist

19 다음을 듣고, 이 이야기의 내용이 어떤 장르에 속하는지 고르시오.

① a magazine article
② a newspaper report
③ a crime novel
④ a movie review
⑤ a textbook excerpt

20 대화를 듣고, 앞으로 소년이 잠자리에 들 시각을 고르시오.

① 11 p.m.
② 11:30 p.m.
③ Midnight
④ 12:30 a.m.
⑤ 1 a.m.

21 다음을 듣고, 그래프에 대해 사실이 <u>아닌</u> 것을 고르시오.

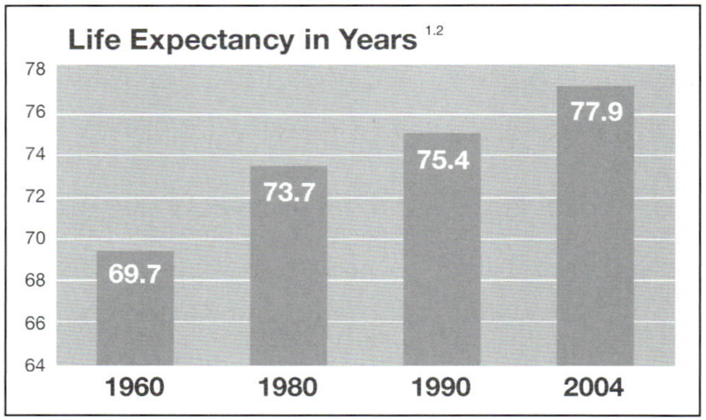

① Koreans lived longer on average in 1990 than in 1980.
② The life expectancy of the average Korean is steadily increasing.
③ The increase in life expectancy from 1960 to 1980 was greater than the increase from 1980 to 1990.
④ There was an increase in life expectancy of three and a half years from 1990 to 2004.
⑤ The increase in life expectancy of the average Korean from 1960 to 2004 was less than ten years.

대화를 듣고, 남자의 마지막 말을 완성하는 것을 고르시오.

> M: If I had done my best, ______________________________
> ______________________________.

① I'd be successful like you
② I never managed to go to college
③ I have to go back to work soon
④ I haven't gotten married yet
⑤ I'm not really interested in law

23

다음을 듣고, 여자가 휴가에 대해 가장 만족했던 것을 고르시오.

① chatting with her family
② watching the fireworks
③ staying in the cabin
④ having a picnic on the mountain
⑤ going to the barbecue

24

대화를 듣고, 여자의 좌석 위치를 고르시오.

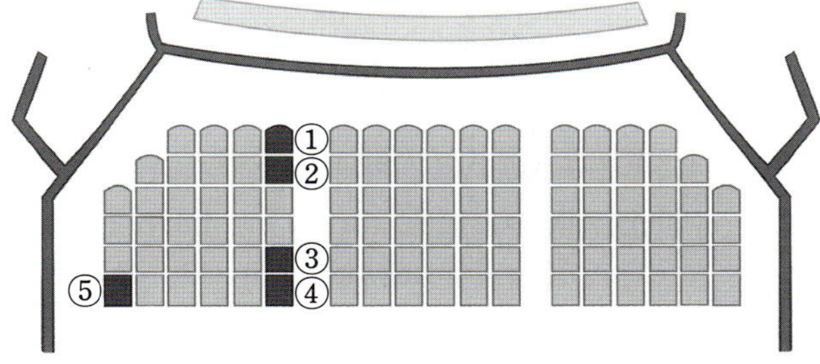

25

다음을 듣고, 원어민이 절대로 하지 않을 말이 무엇인지 고르시오.

① That's a nice jacket you're wearing.
② You are the same age as me.
③ I will see you in church.
④ You ought to go on a diet.
⑤ That movie had so many bad words.

26

대화를 듣고, 남자가 제출해야 하는 것을 모두 고르시오.

> ⓐ a copy of his driver's license
> ⓑ a copy of his passport
> ⓒ a financial statement
> ⓓ a copy of his ID card
> ⓔ a criminal background report

① ⓐ, ⓑ, ⓒ, ⓓ
② ⓑ, ⓓ, ⓔ, ⓐ
③ ⓐ, ⓑ, ⓓ, ⓔ
④ ⓑ, ⓒ, ⓓ, ⓔ
⑤ ⓐ, ⓒ, ⓓ, ⓔ

27

Why did the woman miss her flight?

① There were too many passengers on the flight.
② She forgot to confirm her reservation.
③ The flight was cancelled because of a problem.
④ She did not get to the airport on time.
⑤ She forgot to pay for her ticket.

28

Which of the following people agrees with the speaker?

① Jaegyu: I can't wait to retire at 65. It's my dream.
② Hyemi: I'm 65 years old but still healthy. I'm not interested in retiring.
③ Dongsook: Older people can't work as well as younger people.
④ Myungho: The government should make the retirement age lower.
⑤ Chulsoo: I'm happy I retired at 65. I have a lot of free time now.

29 **Which of the following is NOT true about the conversation?**

① They will go to her mother's house on Sunday.
② They will see the baseball game on Saturday.
③ They will see both games this weekend.
④ The man bought tickets for both games.
⑤ The woman likes baseball more than basketball.

30 **Which is the best title for this talk?**

① How Our Body Works
② Why People Can Taste Things
③ The Eye and the Brain
④ The Five Senses
⑤ Understanding the Environment

〔31-34〕 31번부터 34번까지는 질문과 보기를 모두 듣고 푸는 문제입니다. 대화나 이야기를 듣고, 영어로 들려주는 질문에 대한 알맞은 답을 고르시오.

31 ① ② ③ ④ ⑤

32 ① ② ③ ④ ⑤

33 ① ② ③ ④ ⑤

34 ① ② ③ ④ ⑤

35 다음을 듣고, 이어지는 영어 질문에 답하시오.

① Monday   ② Wednesday
③ Thursday   ④ Friday
⑤ Saturday

36 주어진 시간 동안 아래 지문을 주의 깊게 읽고, 들려주는 질문에 답하시오. 〔1분〕

In eastern Asia, many people visit both Western-trained doctors and Oriental medicine doctors. Oriental medicine differs greatly from Western medicine. To begin with, there is less reliance on surgery and synthetic medicines in Oriental medicine. Instead, it uses methods like acupuncture and herbal remedies to treat patients' aliments. The sick person's body is treated as a whole; the doctor does not just focus upon the particular part that is not functioning properly. For example, if a person had a foot problem, a Western doctor would examine them, take X-rays, and perhaps perform surgery or prescribe medicine for the foot problem. The Oriental doctor, however, would treat the body as one entity by using acupuncture on the feet, by massaging the joints in the back and legs to relieve pressure on the feet, and by giving herbal medicine for high blood pressure, which could be the cause of the foot problem. Western doctors are typically skeptical about Oriental medicine and often believe it has no merits. But this is more a case of professional jealousy than something grounded in fact. Oriental medicine is reliable, it is less expensive than Western methods, and the patient often recovers faster.

Q: ___________________________________

① 환자들에게 수술을 시행한다.
② 환자들에게 마사지를 시행한다.
③ 환자들에게 약을 처방한다.
④ 환자들에게 침을 놓는다.
⑤ 환자들의 엑스레이를 찍는다.

[37-38] 다음을 듣고, 이어지는 두 개의 질문에 답하시오.

37 Which of the following is NOT true about the speaker?

① She is married.
② She lives in Busan.
③ She is a school teacher.
④ She has children.
⑤ She studied in Australia.

38 Choose the title of a book which the speaker most likely wants to read.

① *Journey to the Stars*
② *Korea in the Nineteenth Century*
③ *Child Care and You*
④ *New Methods in Education*
⑤ *Adventures in the Jungle*

[39-40] 대화를 듣고, 이어지는 두 개의 질문에 답하시오.

39 Which TV program do the speakers like in common?

① sports programs
② science fiction shows
③ soap operas
④ reality shows
⑤ comedy shows

40 What is the reason the woman dislikes reality programs?

① She is easily bored by them.
② She finds them too realistic.
③ She thinks they are staged.
④ They are too violent for her.
⑤ They do not have realistic situations.

LISTEN to the MAX │ 외고영어듣기대비

실전모의고사

실전모의고사 **05**

- **No.01~No.10** : ⊙ TRACK 17
- **No.11~No.20** : ⊙ TRACK 18
- **No.21~No.30** : ⊙ TRACK 19
- **No.31~No.40** : ⊙ TRACK 20

실전모의고사 05

01 다음을 듣고, 여자가 찾아갈 가게들이 순서대로 나열된 것을 고르시오.

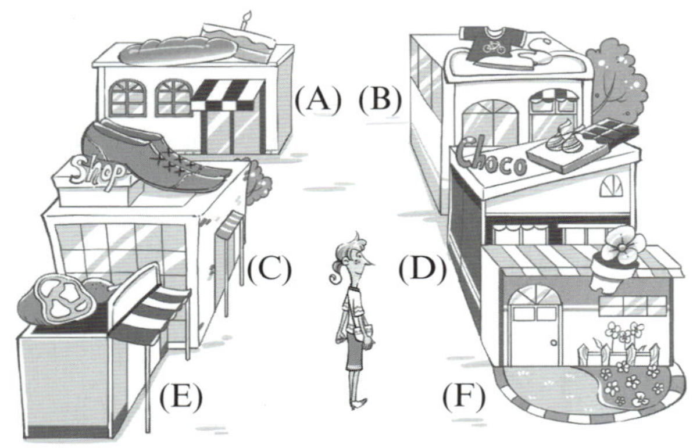

① (A) – (C) – (D) – (F)
② (B) – (D) – (F) – (E)
③ (F) – (C) – (D) – (A)
④ (E) – (F) – (C) – (B)
⑤ (F) – (D) – (C) – (A)

02 대화를 듣고, 남자의 직업이 무엇인지 고르시오.

① doctor ② businessman
③ librarian ④ lawyer
⑤ teacher

03 대화를 듣고, 두 사람의 관계를 가장 잘 나타낸 것을 고르시오.

Man	Woman
① interviewer	interviewee
② employer	employee
③ professor	student
④ manager	employee
⑤ company president	manager

04 다음을 듣고, 화자의 심정을 가장 잘 나타낸 것을 고르시오.

① regretful
② angry
③ jealous
④ ecstatic
⑤ uncaring

05 대화를 듣고, 남자가 목적지까지 가는 데 가장 좋은 교통수단이 무엇인지 고르시오.

① by taxi
② by bus
③ by car
④ by commuter train
⑤ by subway

06 대화를 듣고, 이 대화가 이루어지고 있는 장소를 고르시오.

① 공항 출국장
② 백화점
③ 슈퍼마켓
④ 면세점
⑤ 기념품 가게

07 다섯개의 대화문을 듣고, 자연스럽지 않은 것을 고르시오.

① ② ③ ④ ⑤

08 다음을 듣고, 이야기 속의 This가 무엇인지 고르시오.

① a text message
② an e-mail
③ a blog
④ a homepage
⑤ a chat room

09 대화를 듣고, 여자가 원래 받았어야 할 거스름돈이 얼마인지 고르시오.

① $3.50
② $5.60
③ $5.70
④ $6.30
⑤ $8.00

10 대화를 듣고, 여자의 마지막 말을 완성하는 가장 알맞은 것을 고르시오.

> W: Just hope you don't get fired. After all, _______________________________.

① as you sow, so shall you reap
② it's better to be safe than sorry
③ look before you leap
④ a bird in the hand is worth two in the bush
⑤ a penny saved is a penny earned

11 다음을 듣고, 우주여행에 대해 사실이 <u>아닌</u> 것을 고르시오.

① 한국 우주인이 우주정거장에서 실험을 했다.
② 우주선에 탄 세 명의 우주인 중 한 명은 전에 우주를 방문했다.
③ 이 우주선은 한국이 아닌 다른 국가에서 발사되었다.
④ 우주선에는 2개국의 우주인이 있었다.
⑤ 그 우주선은 이틀 뒤 우주정거장과 도킹했다.

12 대화를 듣고, 여자에게 주어진 조언이 <u>아닌</u> 것을 고르시오.

① Ask her parents for help with her work
② Ask the teacher more questions in class
③ Get a tutor to help with her studies
④ Go over her lessons much more carefully
⑤ Talk to the teacher after class finishes

13 다음을 듣고, 이 이야기가 어떤 질문에 대한 대답인지 고르시오.

① Where did you go to university?
② Can you tell me about your family?
③ When did you get married?
④ How did you meet your spouse?
⑤ Have you ever been on a blind date?

14 대화를 듣고, 두 사람에 의해 언급된 교통 표지판이 <u>아닌</u> 것을 고르시오.

① 
② 
③ 
④ 
⑤ 

15 대화를 듣고, 남자가 대화 후에 할 행동을 고르시오.

① 파티에 사람들을 초대한다.
② 제과점에 케이크를 주문한다.
③ 슈퍼마켓에서 음식을 구입한다.
④ 집이 깨끗한지 확인한다.
⑤ 파티를 위해 음식을 준비하기 시작한다.

16 다음을 듣고, 화자의 스케줄 표 중 빠진 부분에 들어갈 알맞은 것을 고르시오.

Schedule	
9 a.m.	Arrive at Work
10 a.m.	Sales Meeting
12 p.m.	Lunch with Friend
3 p.m.	Sales Meeting
5:30 p.m.	Meet the President
6:45 p.m.	Go to Airport

	Time	Activity
①	1 p.m.	Lunch with President
②	2 p.m.	Managers' Meeting
③	1:30 p.m.	Sales Meeting
④	2:30 p.m.	Managers Meeting
⑤	12:30 p.m.	Go Back to Office

17 다음을 듣고, 다음 중 이야기의 내용과 관련이 <u>없는</u> 것을 고르시오.

① J.R.R. 톨킨의 〈반지의 제왕〉
② 에밀리 브론테의 〈폭풍의 언덕〉
③ J.K. 롤링의 〈해리 포터와 불사조 기사단〉
④ 박경리의 〈토지〉
⑤ 윈스턴 처칠의 〈제2차 세계대전〉

18 대화를 듣고, 현재 시각을 고르시오.

Movie Timetable	
Spider-Man 3	4:30
Shrek 3	5:50
Titanic	7:00
The Lord of the Rings	7:30

① 5:30　　② 6:00　　③ 6:20
④ 6:40　　⑤ 7:10

19 다음을 듣고, 무엇에 대해 이야기하고 있는지 고르시오.

① 모델 선발　　② 패션쇼
③ 연기자 오디션　　④ 미인대회
⑤ 탤런트 쇼

20 대화를 듣고, 남자의 요지를 고르시오.

① 정부는 숭례문의 연소에 대해 사과해야 한다.
② 아무도 숭례문의 연소를 상상할 수 없었을 것이다.
③ 일부 국보가 파괴되는 것은 불가피하다.
④ 국보를 보호하는 데 많은 비용을 들일 필요는 없다.
⑤ 국보를 보호하는 것은 정부의 책임이다.

21 대화를 듣고, 남자가 말하고자 하는 것이 무엇인지 고르시오.

① Extreme diets help people quickly lose a lot of weight.
② The woman needs to go on a diet as soon as possible.
③ It is ideal to eat a little amount of food for several days.
④ The woman should be careful about the diet she goes on.
⑤ Eating only one kind of food is an example of an extreme diet.

22 다음을 듣고, 이야기의 내용이 그래프에 <u>잘못</u> 반영된 것을 고르시오.

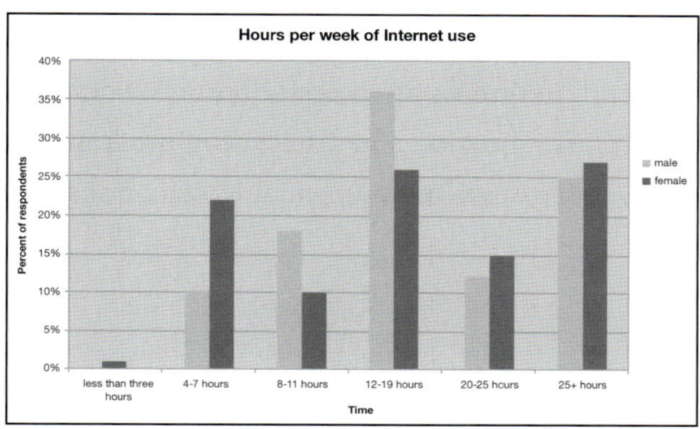

① 최고치를 보인 남성 사용자의 주당 시간
② 주당 25시간이 넘게 인터넷을 사용하는 여성의 퍼센트
③ 주당 3시간 미만을 인터넷을 사용하는 남성의 퍼센트
④ 주당 4시간에서 7시간을 사용하는 남성과 여성 사용자의 비교
⑤ 주당 20시간에서 25시간을 사용하는 남성과 여성 사용자의 비교

23 대화를 듣고, 화자들이 할 행동을 순서대로 나열한 것을 고르시오.

> ⓐ Go shopping at the department store
> ⓑ Have dinner with the man's parents
> ⓒ Take their children to the amusement park
> ⓓ Watch a movie with the woman's sister

① ⓐ – ⓓ – ⓑ – ⓒ
② ⓑ – ⓐ – ⓓ – ⓒ
③ ⓑ – ⓐ – ⓒ – ⓑ
④ ⓓ – ⓐ – ⓒ – ⓑ
⑤ ⓒ – ⓐ – ⓓ – ⓑ

24 다음을 듣고, 화자의 현재 취미가 무엇인지 고르시오.

① jazz dancing
② astronomy
③ painting
④ photography
⑤ sculpting

25 다음을 듣고, 남자의 마지막 말에 들어갈 가장 알맞은 것을 고르시오.

In conclusion, _________________________.

① Koreans will likely never accept foreigners in their country
② there will be many changes in Korea in the future
③ the government is likely to restrict the number of foreigners it allows in
④ all foreigners should be given equal treatment in Korea
⑤ there will be more foreigners than Koreans in a few years

26 대화를 듣고, 민수의 성격을 가장 잘 나타낸 것을 고르시오.

① Polite
② Tense
③ Selfish
④ Flashy
⑤ Considerate

27 대화를 듣고, 여자의 반지가 있던 위치를 고르시오.

28 다음을 듣고, 화자의 의견에 동의하는 진술을 고르시오.

① 수진: 부자만이 성형수술을 할 여유가 있으므로 그에 대한 제약이 있어야 한다.
② 은주: 얼굴에 손을 좀 대지 않았다면 나는 결코 이 일을 얻을 수 없었을 것이다.
③ 미희: 사무실에 있는 모든 여성들이 성형수술을 받았기 때문에 모두 똑같아 보인다.
④ 현정: 내 친구는 지난 해에 성형수술을 받은 뒤에 몇몇 심각한 문제로 고통을 받았다.
⑤ 정화: 채용은 그 사람의 외모가 아니라 실력에 근거해야 한다.

29 What can be inferred by the woman's last words?

① She thinks the man's grades are not very good.
② She does not consider the man a good friend.
③ She has very few close friends at her school.
④ She does not enjoy socializing with her friends.
⑤ She has not been out with her friends in a while.

30 What is the purpose of this talk?

① To announce a program time change
② To promote a new doll business
③ To discuss a successful businesswoman
④ To mention a new television program
⑤ To describe an unusual Korean household

〔31-34〕 31번부터 34번까지는 질문과 보기를 모두 듣고 푸는 문제입니다. 대화나 이야기를 듣고, 영어로 들려주는 질문에 대한 알맞은 답을 고르시오.

31 ① ② ③ ④ ⑤

32 ① ② ③ ④ ⑤

33 ① ② ③ ④ ⑤

34 ① ② ③ ④ ⑤

35 다음을 듣고, 이어지는 영어 질문에 답하시오.

① swimming
② baseball
③ golf
④ table tennis
⑤ volleyball

 주어진 시간 동안 아래 지문을 주의 깊게 읽고, 들려주는 질문에 답하시오. 〔1분〕

At the start of the twentieth century, Earth's population was estimated at around 1.6 billion people. In slightly more than one hundred years, however, that number has increased to somewhere around 6.6 billion individuals. This is an astonishing rate of increase in population as the number of people living on Earth has more than tripled in approximately a century. Interestingly enough, some countries around the world are either experiencing negative population growth or are witnessing birthrates lower than necessary for a country to sustain its population. For example, Russia is seeing its population decline while countries like Japan, Italy, and several other European nations all have incredibly low birthrates. For these countries, it is just a matter of time before their populations also begin to decrease. As a general rule, developed countries have lower birthrates while developing countries have much higher ones. The result is that much of the world's population increase is being driven by countries in Asia, the Middle East, and Africa. Unfortunately, many people in these countries cannot economically support such large families, which thereby causes numerous social and health problems because of these countries' quickly increasing populations.

Q: ______________________

① The world's population will triple in the next hundred years.
② Several Asian countries are seeing their populations decrease.
③ Many countries with increasing populations have social problems.
④ There is room for about 1.6 billion more people to live on Earth.
⑤ The populations in some developing countries are growing rapidly.

〔37-38〕 대화를 듣고, 이어지는 두 개의 질문에 답하시오.

37 **Which of the following is NOT an English loanword from another language?**

① sushi
② steak
③ pizza
④ cafe
⑤ aloha

38 **Why is the woman reading the book?**

① She has a class assignment on it.
② Someone gave it to her as a present.
③ Her major at school is linguistics.
④ She is interested in the topic.
⑤ She is taking a class on the topic.

〔39-40〕 다음을 듣고, 이어지는 두 개의 질문에 답하시오.

39 **What is the best title of this article?**

① Coming Summer Fashion Trends
② The New Spring Look
③ The Return of Sunglasses
④ The Styles of Earrings
⑤ Fashion from Around the World

40 **What is NOT mentioned as a hot item for the spring?**

① miniskirts
② colored stockings
③ sunglasses
④ plaid skirts
⑤ gold earrings

실전모의고사

실전모의고사 06

- **No.01~No.10** : TRACK 21
- **No.11~No.20** : TRACK 22
- **No.21~No.30** : TRACK 23
- **No.31~No.40** : TRACK 24

TRACK 21~24

01 대화를 듣고, 여자가 구입한 치마를 고르시오.

①  ② 

③  ④ 

⑤ 

02 대화를 듣고, 두 사람이 만나는 요일과 시간을 고르시오.

① 화요일 오후 2시
② 수요일 오전 10시
③ 목요일 오후 3시
④ 목요일 오후 4시
⑤ 금요일 오후 1시

03 다음을 듣고, 이야기 속의 This가 무엇인지 고르시오.

① a telescope
② a microscope
③ eyeglasses
④ a camera
⑤ binoculars

04 대화를 듣고, 여자의 감정 변화를 가장 잘 나타낸 것을 고르시오.

① concerned → encouraged
② depressed → worried
③ annoyed → amused
④ sad → pessimistic
⑤ angry → pleased

05 다음을 듣고, 화자가 고등학생일 때 어디에서 살았는지 고르시오.

① Kenya
② The United States
③ India
④ Saudi Arabia
⑤ Malaysia

06 다섯 개의 대화문을 듣고, 자연스럽지 않은 것을 고르시오.

①   ②   ③   ④   ⑤

07 다음을 듣고, 입장료의 총액이 얼마인지 고르시오.

① $10
② $15
③ $20
④ $24
⑤ $26

08 대화를 듣고, 남자의 마지막 말에 대한 여자의 응답으로 알맞은 것을 고르시오.

> W: ______________________________

① No, I haven't gotten a job yet.
② Yes, I will talk to him later.
③ No, I didn't have time to go.
④ Yes, I suppose I should try your method.
⑤ Yes, it's getting really frustrating.

09 다음을 듣고, 이 이야기의 목적이 무엇인지 고르시오.

① To instruct
② To complain
③ To warn
④ To criticize
⑤ To praise

10 대화를 듣고, 남자가 조깅 대신 수영을 시작한 이유를 고르시오.

① 남자는 건강을 증진시키고 싶어 한다.
② 조깅을 하기에는 거리가 너무 혼잡하다.
③ 의사가 수영을 하라고 지시했다.
④ 남자의 아내가 함께 운동을 하기를 원했다.
⑤ 남자는 아침 일찍 일어나는 것이 싫었다.

11 대화를 듣고, 약에 대해 사실이 <u>아닌</u> 것을 고르시오.

① 아무런 부작용이 없다.
② 하루에 네 번 복용한다.
③ 액체 상태의 약이다.
④ 일어난 직후 복용해야 한다.
⑤ 이 약은 복용해도 졸리지 않을 것이다.

12 다음을 듣고, 이 이야기가 어떤 질문에 대한 대답인지 고르시오.

① What are two happy stories about lottery winners?
② Why do lottery winners lose their money so quickly?
③ What happened to two different lottery winners?
④ Can winning the lottery change my life?
⑤ Do men and women handle success differently?

13 다섯 개의 대화문을 듣고, 아래 그림의 상황에 가장 잘 어울리는 것을 고르시오.

①　　②　　③　　④　　⑤

14 대화를 듣고, 두 사람의 관계를 가장 잘 나타낸 것을 고르시오.

	Woman	Man
①	eyewitness	police officer
②	driver	insurance agent
③	pedestrian	tow truck driver
④	shopkeeper	traffic control officer
⑤	passenger	mechanic

15 다음을 듣고, 슬로푸드 운동에 대해 사실이 <u>아닌</u> 것을 고르시오.

① 슬로푸드 운동을 하는 사람들은 어떤 종류의 패스트푸드도 먹지 않는다.
② 슬로푸드 운동은 모든 음식이 유기농으로 재배되어야 한다고 말한다.
③ 슬로푸드 운동을 하는 사람들은 요리가 음식을 먹는 것만큼이나 중요하다고 생각한다.
④ 슬로푸드 운동의 초창기 회원 들은 북미 지역에 살았다.
⑤ 슬로푸드 운동은 전자레인지의 사용을 지양한다.

16 대화를 듣고, 카페인 복용의 장단점을 고르시오.

	장점	단점
①	경계심 증진	위암 유발
②	지능 증진	손떨림 유발
③	기억력 증진	신경쇠약 유발
④	각성 효과	인체에 해로움
⑤	집중력 증진	체중 증가

17 다음을 듣고, 일기예보와 일치하지 <u>않는</u> 것을 고르시오.

① 토요일의 기온은 30도 가까이 될 것이다.
② 일요일은 덥고 맑은 날이 될 것이다.
③ 토요일은 남부지방이 몹시 흐릴 것이다.
④ 토요일에 비가 올 가능성이 몹시 높다.
⑤ 월요일에 더 많은 비가 예상된다.

18 다음을 듣고, 이야기의 분위기를 가장 잘 나타낸 것을 고르시오.

① comedic　　② thrilling
③ silly　　④ boring
⑤ nervous

19 다음을 듣고, 화자의 직업이 무엇인지 고르시오.

① photographer
② artist
③ choreographer
④ film director
⑤ wedding planner

20 대화를 듣고, 남자에 대해 사실이 <u>아닌</u> 것을 고르시오.

① He wants to stay close to his parents.
② He is not very concerned about money.
③ He does not want to drive his own car.
④ He is not eager to go to the countryside.
⑤ He would prefer to fly to his destination.

21 대화를 듣고, 다음 그래프에 대해 사실이 <u>아닌</u> 것을 고르시오.

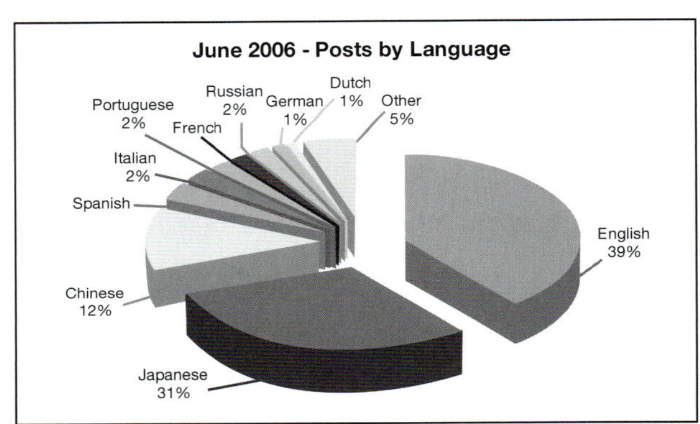

① Japanese people often use cell phones to update their blogs.
② More blogs use English than any other language.
③ Chinese is about to pass Japanese for the number-two position.
④ Lots of Chinese are getting connected to the Internet.
⑤ Many European languages will not get higher rankings in the future.

22 대화를 듣고, 남자의 마지막 말에 들어갈 말로 가장 알맞은 것을 고르시오.

① a little leak will sink a great ship
② all that glitters is not gold
③ empty vessels make the most noise
④ great haste makes great waste
⑤ look before you leap

23 대화를 듣고, 현금지급기의 사용 방법을 순서대로 나열한 것을 고르시오.

ⓐ Select the amount of money
ⓑ Choose the transaction to be made
ⓒ Select the PIN
ⓓ Swipe the bank card

① ⓓ – ⓑ – ⓐ – ⓒ
② ⓑ – ⓓ – ⓐ – ⓒ
③ ⓓ – ⓑ – ⓒ – ⓐ
④ ⓑ – ⓓ – ⓒ – ⓐ
⑤ ⓓ – ⓒ – ⓑ – ⓐ

24 대화를 듣고, 여자의 마지막 말에 담긴 의도가 무엇인지 고르시오.

① To be sarcastic
② To be considerate
③ To express her anger
④ To be generous
⑤ To express her sadness

25 대화를 듣고, 두 사람이 이야기하고 있는 도자기를 고르시오.

① 　② 

③ 　④ 

⑤ 

26 What best completes the speaker's last sentence?

① understand the method of greeting before visiting a different country
② always use the method of greeting people from your own culture
③ know that French women only kiss people whom they like
④ initiate a handshake with another person when in Eastern Asia
⑤ be sure to greet people with "hello" whenever you meet them

27 Which of the following is NOT true about Hangeul?

① It was created in the fourteenth century.
② It has ten different vowel sounds.
③ A Korean king is credited with inventing it.
④ It can be learned very quickly by some people.
⑤ Several people probably created it together.

28 Which of the following people agrees with the speaker?

① Jason: My business overseas tripled after the free-trade agreement was ratified.
② Bruce: I need to learn English so that I can have more opportunities at home and abroad.
③ Samantha: My company must expand overseas if it wants to compete at an international level.
④ Iris: All of my country's citizens should only buy products made in our country.
⑤ Richard: I'll buy a foreign product if it's cheaper and better than what is made here.

29 What is this food?

① hamburgers
② apple pie
③ pizza
④ cake
⑤ sandwiches

30 What are they mostly talking about?

① The housewarming parties they disliked
② Various aspects of past housewarming parties
③ When to have their own housewarming party
④ The housewarming party they liked the most
⑤ What to serve at their upcoming housewarming party

〔31-34〕 31번부터 34번까지는 질문과 보기를 모두 듣고 푸는 문제입니다. 대화나 이야기를 듣고, 영어로 들려주는 질문에 대한 알맞은 답을 고르시오.

31 ① ② ③ ④ ⑤

32 ① ② ③ ④ ⑤

33 ① ② ③ ④ ⑤

34 ① ② ③ ④ ⑤

35 주어진 시간 동안 아래 지문을 주의 깊게 읽고, 대화를 들은 후 질문에 답하시오. 〔1분〕

One of the greatest advocates for civil rights the United States has ever produced was Martin Luther King, Jr. The son of a preacher, King would go on to become a reverend himself. But that was not what he would become most famous for. It was King's dedication to civil rights that made him a world-renowned figure and, in fact, won him the Nobel Peace Prize in 1964. In the 1950s, many black Americans were upset with the segregation that was going on in the country, particularly in the South. Blacks and whites would often use different facilities, and blacks were not afforded the same treatment that whites were. Many people were ready to resort to violence, but King advocated a nonviolent approach. He led many sit-ins, boycotts, and other events in an attempt to gain equal rights for all Americans, particularly minorities. This culminated in 1963 when he gave his "I Have a Dream" speech in Washington, D.C. Just one year later, the Civil Rights Act became law, thereby giving all Americans equal treatment under the law. Unfortunately, King was assassinated in 1968, but his dream of equal rights still lives today.

Q: ______________________________

① He won the Nobel Peace Prize in 1964.
② He believed in using nonviolent methods.
③ He got the Civil Rights Act passed.
④ He became a preacher like his father.
⑤ He wanted blacks to be treated equally.

36 다음을 듣고, 이어지는 영어 질문에 답하시오.

① Sunday
② Monday
③ Tuesday
④ Wednesday
⑤ Thursday

〔37-38〕 대화를 듣고, 이어지는 두 개의 질문에 답하시오.

37 What is the woman's occupation?

① TV reporter
② newspaper reporter
③ hospital patient
④ magazine journalist
⑤ TV show host

38 Which of the following are proven false by the doctor? Check all that apply.

ⓐ An all-meat diet can be healthy.
ⓑ It is safe to lose several pounds very quickly.
ⓒ A person needs to eat a balanced diet.
ⓓ It is good to eat a lot of meat.
ⓔ No-vegetable diets are effective.

① ⓐ, ⓑ
② ⓐ, ⓑ, ⓒ
③ ⓐ, ⓑ, ⓓ
④ ⓑ, ⓓ
⑤ ⓑ. ⓓ. ⓔ

〔39-40〕 다음을 듣고, 이어지는 두 개의 질문에 답하시오.

39 What is the best title of this talk?

① Historic London Places
② The Best Sights in London
③ A Tour Package to London
④ How to Get to London
⑤ The History of London

40 Which of the following is NOT true about this tour?

① The cost of the hotel is not included.
② There are lower prices for groups.
③ The tours will be done by bus and boat.
④ A palace visit is part of the tour.
⑤ The package is available for three months.

실전모의고사

실전모의고사 07

- No.01~No.10 : ◉ TRACK 25
- No.11~No.20 : ◉ TRACK 26
- No.21~No.30 : ◉ TRACK 27
- No.31~No.40 : ◉ TRACK 28

TRACK 25~28

실전모의고사 07

01 대화를 듣고, 두 사람이 이야기하고 있는 장소를 고르시오.

①    ② 

③    ④ 

⑤ 

02 대화를 듣고, 여자가 책장을 파는 이유를 고르시오.

① 책장이 너무 낡아서
② 책장이 부서져서
③ 그녀의 새 아파트에 놓기에는 너무 커서
④ 남자가 책장을 정말로 필요로 하기 때문에
⑤ 그녀의 새 아파트에 놓기에는 너무 작아서

03 대화를 듣고, 인터뷰를 위해 준비된 것으로 언급되지 <u>않은</u> 것을 고르시오.

① 단정한 복장   ② 추천장   ③ 자격 요건
④ 경험   ⑤ 자기 소개서

04 대화를 듣고, 여자가 외출할 수 <u>없는</u> 이유를 고르시오.

① 그녀는 수업을 위해 해야 할 숙제가 있다.
② 그녀는 내일 회사 프레젠테이션이 있다.
③ 그녀는 실직해서 돈이 없다.
④ 그녀는 전날 늦게까지 밖에 있었다.
⑤ 그녀는 대학 시험을 준비중이다.

05 대화를 듣고, 남자가 쇼핑몰에 다녀오는 방법을 가장 잘 나타낸 것을 고르시오.

	쇼핑몰까지	집까지
①	5번 버스	어머니의 차
②	어머니의 차	친구 어머니의 차
③	5번 버스	친구 어머니의 차
④	어머니의 차	5번 버스
⑤	5번 버스	어머니의 차

06 다음을 듣고, 알프레드 노벨이 다섯 가지 상을 제정한 이유를 고르시오.

① 그는 매우 유명한 과학자였다.
② 그는 새로운 발명품들을 선전하고 싶었다.
③ 그는 부정한 방법으로 벌어들인 돈에 대해 양심의 가책을 느꼈다.
④ 그는 군에 의해 사용되는 자신의 발명품에 대해 괴로워했다.
⑤ 그는 돈이 너무 많았다.

07 대화를 듣고, 남자가 바커 인터내셔널 회사에서 일하는 것에 대해 걱정하는 점이 무엇인지 고르시오.

① 일이 힘들지 않은지
② 회사의 급여조건과 혜택이 좋은지
③ 연장 근무를 할 필요가 없는지
④ 상사가 좋은 사람인지
⑤ 점심식사가 무료인지

08 대화를 듣고, 여자의 마지막 말에 대한 남자의 응답으로 알맞은 것을 고르시오.

M: _______________________________

① Stop complaining.
② It will be easy. Don't worry.
③ I look forward to seeing you then.
④ Don't forget to wear shoes.
⑤ If you don't feel like going, call me after lunch.

09 대화를 듣고, 화자들이 이야기하고 있는 사람을 고르시오.

10 다음을 듣고, 대기에 대한 설명으로 옳지 <u>않은</u> 것을 고르시오.

① 대기는 지구를 둘러싼 가스층이다.
② 대기는 태양으로부터의 자외선을 흡수한다.
③ 대기는 기온을 낮춰 준다.
④ 카르만 선은 대기와 우주의 경계를 나타낸다.
⑤ 대기는 수소와 산소, 아황산가스과 기타 가스들로 구성되어 있다.

11 대화를 듣고, 남자가 여자만큼 배가 고프지 <u>않은</u> 이유를 고르시오.

① The man ate an apple and drank some water.
② The man ate breakfast, but the woman did not.
③ The man ate some doughnuts earlier.
④ The man ate some cookies earlier.
⑤ The man is trying not to think about food.

12 대화를 듣고, 남자가 구입하려고 하는 것을 모두 고르시오.

ⓐ computer	ⓑ washing machine
ⓒ television	ⓓ iron
ⓔ toaster	ⓕ microwave oven
ⓖ refrigerator	ⓗ bed
ⓘ stove	

① ⓐ, ⓒ, ⓓ, ⓔ, ⓕ, ⓗ
② ⓒ, ⓔ, ⓕ, ⓖ, ⓗ, ⓘ
③ ⓐ, ⓑ, ⓓ, ⓕ, ⓘ
④ ⓑ, ⓒ, ⓓ, ⓔ, ⓖ, ⓗ, ⓘ
⑤ ⓐ, ⓒ, ⓔ, ⓕ, ⓖ, ⓗ

13 다음을 듣고, 임주영 박사가 대학에서 가르치기 시작한 해를 고르시오.

① 1970
② 1977
③ 1986
④ 1987
⑤ 2008

14 대화를 듣고, 상황에 가장 잘 어울리는 속담을 고르시오.

① It's like talking to a wall.
② Too many cooks spoil the broth.
③ Spare the rod and spoil the child.
④ The grass is always greener on the other side.
⑤ There is no use crying over spilt milk.

15 다음을 듣고, 집을 짓는 과정을 순서대로 나열한 것을 고르시오.

> ⓐ Negotiate the contract
> ⓑ Select the plan for the home
> ⓒ Determine a budget
> ⓓ Choose the designer and builders
> ⓔ Find a plot of land

① ⓔ – ⓒ – ⓑ – ⓓ – ⓐ
② ⓒ – ⓓ – ⓔ – ⓐ – ⓑ
③ ⓔ – ⓓ – ⓑ – ⓒ – ⓐ
④ ⓒ – ⓒ – ⓓ – ⓐ – ⓑ
⑤ ⓒ – ⓔ – ⓓ – ⓑ – ⓐ

16 대화를 듣고, 내용과 일치하는 것을 고르시오.

① The man wants salt on his popcorn.
② The woman forgot to buy the tickets online.
③ The couple wants to see the new action movie.
④ The line moved faster when a new counter opened.
⑤ The couple gave up on seeing the movie they wanted

17 다음을 듣고, 다음 문장의 빈칸에 어울리지 <u>않는</u> 것을 고르시오.

> When people are outside in the summer, they need to ________________________.

① drink water every couple of hours
② keep their bodies dehydrated
③ try to keep from sweating too much
④ wear long-sleeved clothes and hats
⑤ protect themselves from the sun

18 대화를 듣고, 여자의 마지막 말에 대한 남자의 응답으로 알맞은 것을 고르시오.

> M: ________________________

① No, I already have a copy of the book.
② I think that I'll pass on the offer.
③ Yes, I'd love to talk to that person.
④ Yes, it is a really interesting book.
⑤ I'm pretty sure he wants too much for it.

19 다음을 듣고, 화자의 의견에 동의하는 진술을 고르시오.

① Sungmin: I haven't had much time to prepare for my interview.
② Yujin: I had someone look over my application for errors.
③ Hyowon: I told my interviewer about the problems his company has.
④ Jaegyu: I didn't bother dressing up for my interview.
⑤ Soohee: I brought an old copy of my resume to give to the interviewer.

20 대화를 듣고, 내용과 일치하는 것을 고르시오.

① It is very difficult to be a vegetarian.
② The man has found healthy alternatives to meat.
③ The man avoided meat to improve his health.
④ The people are going to an Italian vegetarian restaurant.
⑤ The woman will become a vegetarian.

21 대화를 듣고, 두 사람이 주로 무엇에 대해 이야기하고 있는지 고르시오.

① How hard it is to make business contacts
② How difficult learning to play golf is
③ How important golf is in business
④ How they should meet to play golf
⑤ How to find a nice club to play golf at

22 대화를 듣고, 총 몇 명이 식사를 할 것인지 고르시오.

① 6　　② 5　　③ 4
④ 3　　⑤ 2

23 대화를 듣고, 남자가 무엇을 팩스로 받을지 고르시오.

① An invitation to a party
② An invitation to the party for his partner
③ A recipe for garlic bread
④ Directions to the woman's house
⑤ A list of things to bring to the party

24 대화를 듣고, 남자의 직업을 고르시오.

① He is a salesperson.
② He works at an advertising company.
③ He works at a marketing company.
④ He is an office worker.
⑤ He is the manager of a clothing store.

25 다음을 듣고, 화자의 요지를 가장 잘 나타낸 것을 고르시오.

① Homeschooling should not be allowed according to the law.
② Homeschooled students perform better than public school students.
③ While homeschooling is effective, not every student should try it.
④ Virtually every homeschooled student gets accepted to prestigious universities.
⑤ Public schools are too restrictive, so homeschooling is a better option.

26 대화를 듣고, 다음 공지사항 중 <u>잘못된</u> 부분을 고르시오.

Restaurant

Qualifications: ⓐenergetic and outgoing person
ⓑPrevious experience is essential.
When: ⓒon Wednesday, 7 August from 8:00 a.m. to 6:00 p.m.
Where: ⓓat Seoul City Restaurant, Gangnam
Open positions: ⓔ16

① ⓐ　　② ⓑ　　③ ⓒ　　④ ⓓ　　⑤ ⓔ

27 대화를 듣고, 대화의 내용과 물건의 위치가 일치하지 <u>않는</u> 것을 고르시오.

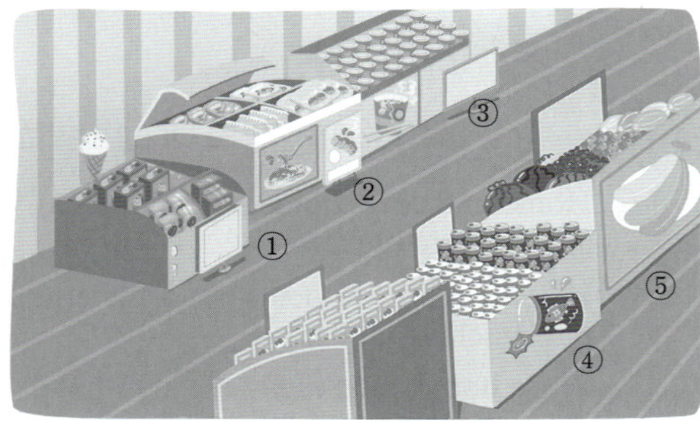

28 Why must the woman remind the man about the meeting after work?

① He does not have an assistant.
② He does not know that the flight has been delayed.
③ He forgot about the last meeting.
④ He has too few staff members.
⑤ He did not receive an email about it.

29 Why is blushing similar to stuttering in a social situation?

① They are both due to shyness.
② They are both due to a lack of confidence.
③ It is possible to hide these two things.
④ People need to control them.
⑤ It will not stop once it starts.

30 What will probably happen next?

① The man will receive a new order of fried rice.
② The man will start shouting at the waiter.
③ The man will speak to the manager and then leave.
④ The man will sit down at a different table.
⑤ The man will rush back to work.

〔31-34〕 31번부터 34번까지는 질문과 보기를 모두 듣고 푸는 문제입니다. 대화나 이야기를 듣고, 영어로 들려주는 질문에 대한 알맞은 답을 고르시오.

31 ①　②　③　④　⑤

32 ①　②　③　④　⑤

33 ①　②　③　④　⑤

34 ①　②　③　④　⑤

35 다음을 듣고, 이어지는 영어 질문에 답하시오.

① Monday　　② Wednesday
③ Thursday　　④ Saturday
⑤ Sunday

36 주어진 시간 동안 아래 지문을 주의 깊게 읽고, 대화를 들은 후 질문에 답하시오. 〔1분〕

> Anyone who has seen the movie *Armageddon* knows that asteroids present a constant threat to our planet. An asteroid impact wiped out the dinosaurs, and a disaster of equal or greater proportion could happen again. Unlike the characters in the movie though, we probably will not see the big rock coming; it would be invisible to the naked eye until it hit Earth's atmosphere. If a telescope happened to spot the deadly asteroid in time to give a warning, which is highly unlikely, we could still do nothing but wait. At the moment, there are no missiles in existence powerful enough to escape Earth's gravity, and there are no rockets capable of going even as far as the moon.

① And it could be worse than the one that killed the dinosaurs.
② But there are better ways to stop an asteroid.
③ But there is nothing we can do about it.
④ And it is possible a telescope would find it first.
⑤ But I just do not like the ending of the movie.

〔37-38〕 대화를 듣고, 이어지는 두 개의 질문에 답하시오.

37 Which of the following is true of the conversation?

① The boy is eager to attend the summer camp.
② The boy is going to visit his grandparents this summer.
③ The girl still wants to receive an allowance every week.
④ Both their parents don't usually change their minds easily.
⑤ The girl thinks going to the camp is a good idea.

38 What does the girl imply she is going to do during summer vacation?

① She will stay at her grandparents' home.
② She is going to find a part-time job.
③ She will work as a waitress at a restaurant.
④ She is going to hang out with the boy.
⑤ She will go to the same summer camp as the boy.

〔39-40〕 대화를 듣고, 이어지는 두 개의 질문에 답하시오.

39 남자의 취직에 대한 생각을 가장 잘 요약한 것은 무엇인가?

① 면접이 취직하는 데 가장 중요한 것이다.
② 월급이 근무 환경보다 더 중요하다.
③ 일의 종류와 근무 시간은 중요하지 않다.
④ 취직이 힘들기 때문에 면접관들에게 좋은 인상을 주는 것이 중요하다.
⑤ 일요일에 일하는 건 문제가 된다.

40 여자가 "It's only a job."이라고 말한 이유는 무엇인가?

① 남자가 인터뷰에 너무 많은 시간을 투자해서
② 남자가 일자리 찾느라 공부를 소홀히 해서
③ 남자가 인터뷰 복장에 너무 신경을 써서
④ 남자가 구직에 실패한 것을 위로하려고
⑤ 여자가 구직에 실패한 것을 변명하려고

실전모의고사
Dictation Test 01~07

01 대화를 듣고, 이 대화가 이루어지고 있는 장소를 고르시오.

M Pardon me, but _________________________________
I'd like to ask if you don't mind.

W Go ahead, please. It's my job to answer questions.

M Great. First, I've got some things I'd like ___________
_________. They're not ___________________,
so I know I won't get fined. Where should I put them?

W You can just give them to me, and I'll stamp them as
checked in. But, in the future, the book drop is located
next to the front door.

M Oh, that's great. It's the first time I've ever ___________
_______________ so I wasn't sure about the procedure.

W That's quite all right. Do you have any more questions?

M Actually, yes, I have one more question. I'm looking for
this, and I found the call number for it. I've got it right
here... According to the computer, ________________,
but the last time I checked, it wasn't anywhere on the
shelves.

W Well, that's very strange. Somebody might have put it in
the wrong location. That happens from time to time.

M Do you think that's the case for this one?

W Perhaps. _________________________________
_________. Hopefully, we'll find what you're looking for.

02 다음을 듣고, 화자의 직업이 무엇인지 고르시오.

M I've got a great job that I love a lot. However, I had
to attend college first to ___________________ in it
because I need many skills in order to do my job well.
Clients hire me when they want to have ___________
_________________________. It could be a house,
apartment, office building, or anything else. They tell
me exactly what they want, and then ______________
_________. I've got to be good at math because I need
to make sure the building's dimensions are exact. I also
have to know some engineering. I wouldn't want to
make a building that's not structurally sound or which
collapses soon after it gets erected. Finally, ___________
_____________________ for the structure, I
work closely with the builder to ensure that the building
is completed ___________________________.

03 대화를 듣고, 남자가 전화를 건 이유를 고르시오.

W Hello, Mr. Meyers's Office. __________ Janet speaking.

M Good afternoon. My name is Doug Thomas, and I'd
like to speak with Mr. Meyers if he's got some time.

W I'm terribly sorry, Mr. Thomas, but Mr. Meyers isn't
_________________________. Is there
something I can help you with?

M Well, I'm scheduled to meet Mr. Meyers at 10:30
tomorrow morning. Unfortunately, _______________
___________________ at our office in Atlanta,
so I've got to leave town this evening and won't return
until Thursday.

W I see. In that case, shall I tell Mr. Meyers you're going
to _______________________________?

M I'd prefer not to cancel but instead _______________
_________________. I really need to meet him about
our project.

W Yes, I've heard him discussing it in the office, so I'm
aware of the nature of the work you two are doing.

M Great, so do you think Mr. Meyers ________________
_______________________________?

W Actually, I'll have to wait until he returns to the office.
I'm not exactly sure of his schedule, so I need to ask
him. Why don't _________________________
_______________ when he gets back?

M That's a great idea. Thanks for your assistance.

04 대화를 듣고, 여자의 상황을 가장 잘 나타내는 것을 고르시오.

W I think I'm going to open my own business soon. I'm
so tired of _________________________.

M What makes you say that?

W Well, I work at this small company. It's just the owner,
three other employees, and me. The other workers and
I always work as hard as we can, yet the owner doesn't
seem _________________________________.

M So what's the problem?

W He makes all the money while we barely earn anything
at all. In fact, I may have to get a second job so that I
can earn some more money. That's why I'm going to
open my own business. I'm going to ______________
_________________.

M You know, that sounds like a great plan, but let me tell you something about myself.

W What's that?

M I once owned a business, but it didn't go too well. I was just like you; I thought I'd ________________________ ________________________.

W What happened after you started?

M I lost all my money and ________________________ ____________. I am still paying back loans from five years ago. If I were you, I'd consider that before you start a business with no plan at all.

05 다음을 듣고, 화자의 감정의 변화를 가장 잘 나타낸 것을 고르시오.

M All week long, everyone at work had been expecting some important news. We had heard there was going to be ________________________. I was looking forward to the news because all my employee evaluations had been excellent. In fact, my immediate boss told me she expected me ________________________ ________________________ once she transferred to another office. I couldn't help myself. I told my family I was probably getting promoted, so I'd be ________________________. My wife even began planning a family trip to Europe. The big day finally came. The whole office was bursting to hear the news. Ms. Smith came into the conference room and said she had something to tell us. She said ________________________ was getting a promotion. Then she said the name. It wasn't mine. It was my officemate — ________________________ ________________________. The news crushed me. I don't know how I'm ever going to break it to my family.

06 대화를 듣고, 남자의 마지막 말에 대한 여자의 응답으로 가장 알맞은 것을 고르시오.

M Lisa, ________________________ ________________________. I really need your help.

W No way, Jason. I remember the last time you asked me for assistance. I was stuck at your house all day long helping you take everything out of those boxes. I'll never do that again.

M Oh, right. Well, I did tell you it was going to be an all-day job, and you accepted, so you should have known ________________________.

W I suppose you're right. But ________________________ you're going to convince me to do anything for you this time.

M But, really, ________________________ ________________________. I don'tneed help moving, and I don't need to borrow any money from you either.

W That's a relief because I've barely got enough to make it to payday.

M So, um, don't you want to hear what favor I need from you?

W I guess so. But chances are that ________________________ ________________________. I'm going to say no.

M Well, the favor I need is ________________________ ________________________ tonight. It shouldn't be too hard since we're neighbors.

07 대화를 듣고, 내용과 일치하지 <u>않는</u> 것을 고르시오.

M ________________________ about my future?

W I see many things, both good and bad, in your future. What is it you'd like to know?

M Am I going to be rich?

W ________________________, you will find success. However, the road to becoming rich will not be easy. There will be times when you will ____________ ________________________. But do not despair. For, in the end, you will be a rich man.

M Okay, that sounds pretty good to me.

W What else would you like me to tell you?

M How about my personal life? Will I ever get married?

W Let me see your hand… Aha… I see ________________________ ________________________. And you will have three children. Alas, I cannot tell how many will be boys or girls. My inner sight does not give me those details.

M That's quite all right. I'd prefer to be surprised myself. So, um, can you tell me ________________________ ________________________?

W Yes, do you see your lifeline right here? According to it, you will live to be an old man.

08 다음을 듣고, 무엇에 대한 이야기인지 고르시오.

W Be sure that you come down to Martin's Department Store this weekend ___________________________

___________________________ for the very last time. We are having a sale where everything literally must go. For starters, everything in our store is going to be on sale ___________________________

___________________________. That's much more than any of the local stores are offering even during their spring sales. And be sure to visit ___________

___________________________ as well since some of them will be offering sales at up to eighty percent off. This includes the electronics department and the children's clothing department. Finally, ___________

___________________________, everything has got to go. Make us a reasonable offer, and we won't ___________________________. So come down to Martin's Department Store this weekend for the sale of a lifetime. ___________________________

___________________________.

09 대화를 듣고, 남자가 뉴욕으로 이사한 이유를 고르시오.

W Johnny, is that really you? What are you doing here?
M Hey, Carmen. I'm just back here for the weekend ___________

___________________________.
W I heard someone say that you had moved to New York City. Are you going to college there or something?
M No, it's not that. You know, I never really thought I'd move there, but, sure enough, it's the place I call home now.
W But you always talked about how you loved living near all your friends and how you ___________________________

___________________________. What made you suddenly go away?
M To be honest, I didn't have much of a choice in the matter. My boss told me ___________________________

___________________________. He gave me a choice between New York and Paris, and I had no desire to live abroad.
W Oh, I see. ___________________________

___________________________ like that.
M Yeah, I had to sell my house really quickly before I left. I don't even have one in New York. I'm just renting now.

W It sounds like your life is really different. Well, ___________

___________________________. I hope to see you around.

10 대화를 듣고, 여자가 지불해야 할 금액을 고르시오.

M Good afternoon, ma'am. Is there anything particular you're looking for?
W I'm looking for something nice to wear to work. It needs to ___________________________

___________________________.
M Why don't I show you some of our new blouses? They arrived just a couple of days ago, and, from what I've heard, they're the most fashionable clothes this winter.
W That sounds great. Let's take a look.
M Here's the first one you might like. Notice it's one of the top brands on the market. It ___________________________

___________________________, but it's on sale right now for only $165.
W That's ___________________________

___________________________. I'm on a limited budget, so I can only spend about half that amount.
M That's no problem at all. We've got a number of excellent looking blouses at lower prices. How about this white one, ___________________________

___________________________?
W Maybe, but could you show me some others first?
M I've got two more you may like. There's this black one that sells for ___________________________, and I've got a yellow blouse for only ___________________________. So, what will it be?
W I like them all, but I think ___________________________

___________________________. It looks the best.

11 다음을 듣고, 이 이야기가 어떤 질문에 대한 대답인지 고르시오.

W One unique way that some doctors have begun treating people is ___________________________
This involves pairing a patient with a pet in order to achieve certain benefits. The pets are usually dogs, but they may also be cats, birds, or even fish. As a general rule, pets help to ___________________________ and also enable their patients to take their minds off of their

own problems since they must in turn take care of their pets. Pet therapy has helped ______________________ ______________________ achieve longer lives, and it has also tremendously helped ______________________ ______________________. Sometimes pet therapy has even been used on ________ ______________________, where it has seen a certain level of success as well. Of course, not all attempts at using pet therapy are successful, but the numbers do not lie: More and more patients are living happier, healthier, and longer lives ______________________ ______________________.

12 다음을 듣고, 주어진 그래프에 대해 사실이 <u>아닌</u> 것을 고르시오.

M ______________________ on the number of hours of English studied by students in both elementary and high school. The study revealed a number of shocking results. For instance, despite the importance that society places on learning English, ____ ______________________ high school students, compared with ______________________ ______________________ elementary school students, never study English. Additionally, the overall numbers point toward elementary school students spending more class time studying English than high school students. Upon further investigation, __________ ______________________.

First, society places a heavy emphasis on learning English from a young age. This accounts for the huge number of hours — over sixteen a week for many elementary school students — that some students focus on English. Additionally, ______________________ ______________________ that high school students have many more subjects to study, they are ______________ ______________________.

This accounts for the relatively low number of hours many high schoolers spend studying English.

13 대화를 듣고, 두 사람이 대화를 마치고 할 일을 고르시오.

M I'm so excited we've decided to travel to Europe. It should really be a lot of fun.

W You're right, but now we've got lots of things we need to prepare before leaving. For example, do you even own a passport?

M Now that you mention it, I don't. I guess ______________ ______________________ since we're leaving in two months.

W It usually takes six weeks to process, so you have enough time. But you still should apply for it sometime this week. We've also got to ______________________ ______________________ so we can figure out what to see.

M Good thinking. And I'm enrolling in a foreign language course. Since we're visiting Italy, I want to speak at least basic Italian. ______________________ ______________________.

W That's a good plan.

M ______________________?

W Well, we ought to figure out what the weather is going to be like when we go. Since we can't take too much luggage, ______________________ ______________________.

M Oh, yeah, I hadn't thought of that. In the meantime, ______________________ I want to grab a travel guide or two.

W That's a plan. Let's get going.

14 대화를 듣고, 파스타를 만드는 순서가 알맞게 나열된 것을 고르시오.

W I'm starving. Why don't we order something for dinner?

M Actually, I was thinking of cooking this evening. ______ ______________________ for dinner?

W Wow, I had no idea you even knew how to cook. So, what are you making tonight?

M I'm going to cook a pasta dish my mother taught me. ______________________, but it tastes really delicious. All you need is some pasta, spinach, raisins, pine nuts, and grated cheese.

W It sounds great. What do you do first? I'm guessing you cook the spinach, right?

M Sorry, but that's wrong. You need to _______________ _______________. After that, you fry the spinach in some oil for a few minutes and then _______________.

W Yum, that already sounds delicious to me. Okay, so what do you do with the pine nuts and raisins?

M It's simple. You put them in the pasta and sprinkle the grated cheese _______________ _______________. Then you mix it all up, and it's ready to serve.

W You sound like you're a chef. Anyway, all that talk is making me hungry. Hurry up and start cooking.

15 다음을 듣고, 화자가 언급하지 <u>않은</u> 그림을 고르시오.

M My family and I just returned from the local museum. At first, I was _______________ _______________, but now I'm glad I went there. The museum was having an art exhibition featuring some paintings from the nineteenth century, and they were so nice to look at. For example, there was one painting that just showed _______________ _______________. I know it sounds pretty simple, but the way the artist used colors was simply amazing. Another painting portrayed _______________. I still can't forget how nice it looked. There was another painting which was just _______________ _______________. As you can tell, I prefer simple paintings so long as they are done well. Finally, the last picture that stood out was one with _______________ _______________ while walking down a rainy street. There were many others, but those were my favorites.

16 대화를 듣고, 두 사람이 이야기하고 있는 책의 장르와 그 책이 인기 있는 이유가 올바로 짝지어진 것을 고르시오.

W I'd really love to buy a book here, but they all look so boring. I'm sorry, but _______________ _______________.

M That's too bad because this is a really good book about politics.

W Well, I'd rather read a science fiction book or a mystery. Those genres really get me involved in the story, so I love reading them.

M Hey, I've got a great book for you. How about this one here? It's a bestseller, _______________ _______________. It's a really great work of literature.

W Hmm… Tell me some more about it, and then I might consider buying it.

M Okay, it's a story about _______________ _______________.

W You've got to be kidding me! There's no way that kind of book could possibly become a bestseller.

M Well, you'd be surprised. I read it and found the story to be amazing. This guy visited every continent on the world and had lots of adventures while he was searching for precious relics. _______________ _______________ about how he lived his life.

W You make it sound like it's a really great book. Maybe I will get it.

M Trust me. _______________ _______________.

17 다음을 듣고, 남자의 미래에 대한 태도를 가장 잘 나타낸 것을 고르시오.

W _______________ _______________ because I'm not pleased with what I'm doing now. In fact, I must say that _______________ _______________. I've got a job and make decent money, but there are few opportunities for me to get promoted. Basically, I've got _______________ job and don't want to be stuck with it forever. So I've decided to go back to school and get another degree. That way, with a better education, I'll be able to find a job that _______________ and which gives me _______________ _______________. Also, this time, I'm going to study a subject I'm interested in, not one which my parents demand that I learn. This change in my life is going to require a lot of hard work, but I really want to do it. I hope I can turn my life around and give myself _______________ _______________,

18 대화를 듣고, 남자의 마지막 말로 유추할 수 있는 것을 고르시오.

W You look really beat down this morning. Didn't you get enough sleep last night?

M Unfortunately, ____ . He got a dog two weeks ago, and it won't stop barking at night. It's big, too, so it makes a whole lot of noise. It's driving me crazy.

W ____ about it?

M I've visited his house a couple of times, but he wasn't home. And I can't give him a call since I don't know his number.

W That isn't good. Your neighbor sounds impolite. You live in an apartment, don't you?

M Yeah, so that makes it worse. He lives right above me, so it sounds like his dog is ____ .

W I've got an idea for you. Why don't you have a chat with the apartment supervisor? Your apartment complex must have ____ .

M I've considered that, but my neighbor could get in trouble and might even get kicked out of the building.

W So what? He's being rude and doesn't seem to care about you. Why should you care about him?

M I'll just give it some time and ____ .

19 대화를 듣고, 남자와 여자가 만날 시간을 고르시오.

M Jenny, are we still watching that movie together tonight?

W Yeah, I'm totally looking forward to seeing it. But I forgot... ____ ? It's a nine-thirty showing, right?

M Uh, no, it actually begins at nine. But we ought to meet before it starts.

W Okay, so ____ ? I've never been to that theater before, so I'd rather not meet there. I'd hate to get lost.

M That makes sense. ____

I've got to leave for a meeting soon, but I can be at the station at, say, seven o'clock. How does that sound?

W ____ . I don't know if I'll be finished working by then.

M Hmm… Well, it's going to take at least thirty minutes to get to the theater, and I was hoping to grab a bite to eat beforehand, so we shouldn't leave too much later.

W Well, ____ , that should get us there in plenty of time to have dinner.

M That sounds perfect to me.

W Great. Go to your meeting, and I'll see you in a few hours.

20 다음을 듣고, 불면증을 치료하기 위한 방법으로 제안되지 않은 것을 고르시오.

W ____ , which means they either cannot get to sleep at night or have a difficult time getting to sleep. These sufferers might spend hours tossing and turning in their beds. ____ , reflexes, and moods. Fortunately, there are several ways to cure insomnia. Something important to remember is to avoid drinks with caffeine in them. A lack of caffeine in the body will help your body relax and get to sleep easier. Also, ____ going to bed since this will stimulate your body and keep you from sleeping. Some people say you shouldn't read before bed, but I disagree with them. Another thing is to make your room as dark as possible by ____ . This will create a relaxing atmosphere. Finally, make sure ____ . Follow these instructions, and you should have no problems beating insomnia.

21 대화를 듣고, 수잔에 대해 사실이 <u>아닌</u> 것을 고르시오.

M What do you think of that new employee?

W Are you talking about Susan? ______________________ ______________________. I'm impressed with her work ethic and the way she keeps working on a project until it's finished. You know, she stayed here until ten thirty last night.

M ______________________. She's only been here for three weeks, and ______________________ ______________________.

W She's pretty generous, too. She gave me half of her lunch the other day when I mentioned I'd forgotten to bring something from home.

M What a nice young lady.

W What's your impression of her? You must have dealt with Mary once or twice since she's started.

M I'd say that ______________________ ______________________. I met her with some other employees on her first day of work, and she remembered my name two days ago, which was the next time she met me. That was impressive. She must be smart to have a memory like that.

W Yes, she is quite intelligent. ______________________ ______________________ that she doesn't know how to use the computer software very well.

M ______________________ ______________________. I'm sure she'll get the hang of it.

22 다음을 듣고, 화자의 요지가 무엇인지 고르시오.

M The twentieth century saw ______________________ ______________________, and the same thing is happening in the twenty-first century. Of all of the great discoveries and inventions people have made recently, I believe that there is one which stands out above all the others. I'm talking about miniaturization. This is the process that ______________________ ______________________. Take computer chips for example. Not only are they getting incredibly small these days, but they are also becoming more powerful. So this enables scientists to put more chips in a computer, thereby making it more powerful. Miniaturization is not just for computers though. It's in

all kinds of technology. Think about DVD players, for example. They were once large, but ______________________ ______________________.

Thanks to miniaturization, people can use fewer valuable natural resources yet not lose any of the benefits of a larger machine. ______________________ ______________________.

23 대화를 듣고, 두 사람이 서울에서의 생활에 대해 불만스럽게 생각하는 것이 무엇인지 고르시오.

W You've been living in Seoul for almost a year now. How do you like it?

M ______________________ ______________________, but that's not really a problem even though I'm originally from the country. Overall, I'd say I'm having a great time here.

W Really? You mean ______________________ ______________________?

M I guess that real estate prices are a little too high, so the rent I pay on my apartment is too much. But that's my only real complaint. How about you?

W I managed to get a really cheap yet nice place, so ______________________. And I just love the way the sidewalks are crowded with people. It seems like everyone has something important to do.

M Oh, right. You walk all the time, don't you?

W Yeah, I do. I tried taking taxis, but ______________________ ______________________, especially after I was late for a few meetings. I'll never take them again. So now ______________________ ______________________.

M What do you think of the subway system?

W It's awesome. It gets me almost anywhere in the city I want to be.

24 다음을 듣고, 이야기에서 말하는 내용의 예로 알맞은 것을 고르시오.

W Something interesting about the English language is that it's possible ______________________ ______________________. The way to accomplish that is to use prefixes. Prefixes are syllables that may be attached to the front of a word. They have their own meanings and may, of course, ____. Think, of the root "cycle." Adding "bi," which means "two," gets the word bicycle. Therefore ____. And something what's really interesting is how some new words, once a prefix is added, can have meanings opposite their roots. The word possible means that something can be done. However, by adding "im," which means "not," to it, you get impossible. This, of course, is the opposite of possible. Likewise, the word moral, when an "a" is added to it, becomes amoral. ____, all due to the ____.

25 대화를 듣고, 점원이 여자의 요구를 거절한 이유를 고르시오.

M Good evening, miss. Is there anything I can do for you?

W Yes, there is. I purchased this product from your store last Saturday, ____.

M Okay, did you remember to bring the receipt with you? We aren't allowed to refund any items ____.

W Sure, I have my receipt right here. You can see how I used my credit card to purchase it.

M Okay, and ____. Why didn't it work properly?

W I'm sorry? What are you talking about? I just bought this product but didn't like it once I tried it, so that's why I'm returning it.

M In that case, I'm terribly sorry, but ____.

W Why not? I've got my receipt here just like you requested.

M As you can see from this sign here, ____. Your reason for wanting to return this item is simply that you don't like it. We could, however, let you exchange it for something else.

W That's okay. I'll just hold on to it then.

26 다음을 듣고, 화자의 의견에 동의하는 진술을 고르시오.

M Although parents and teachers love complaining about video games and ____, there are actually some benefits people can get from playing these games. While it's true that many youths waste time playing games, depending upon the game they play, ____. Here's an example. Many video games require players ____. These two-player or multi-player games simply won't permit one player, no matter how good he is, to win the game by himself. This forces players to cooperate with one another. They must therefore learn ____. This is excellent preparation for the future after they graduate from school. It's highly likely these graduates will find jobs requiring them to work with their coworkers on various projects. ____, they'll already be able to work well with others.

27 대화를 듣고, 두 사람이 기다리는 인물이 어디에서 왔는지 고르시오.

W I wonder when Sara's flight is going to arrive. I sure hope ____.

M Let's take a look at the information board and see what time it's supposed to arrive.

W Good thinking. Hey, there's a flight arriving at 5:30. That's in just a few minutes.

M That's great, but it's too bad she's not on that flight.

W I know. I just like looking at all of the different cities people are coming from. See, ____. That's only a few minutes after the other one. And there's another flight getting here at 5:50.

M Yeah, that's great. But I'm still looking for Sara's flight. It would be nice if you could help me out.

W All right... Oh no! One of the flights has been

delayed, so it won't arrive until 6:15 this evening. It's barely going to beat a different flight that's getting in on time at 6:20.

M Okay, we've found her flight. _________________________
_________________________________. We've got some time, so let's get something to eat while we wait.

W That sounds all right to me.

28 다음을 듣고, 화자가 설명하는 포즈로 알맞은 것을 고르시오.

W Now that you've all been learning yoga for a few weeks, I want to teach you a new pose. We've already covered the splits, and _________________________________
____.
And many of you have even mastered the lotus position by sitting with your legs crossed. Well, tonight's pose is going to be a little different. What I want you to do is ____
_________________________. Choose whichever foot is the strongest. Then, I want you to lean forward. At the same time, _________________________________
____
— the one that's not on the ground — behind you. You should eventually get to where your legs form a ninety-degree angle with the leg on the ground straight up and ____
_________________________. I know that it sounds a little complicated, but it's a great stretch, so let's see if we can do it. Is everyone ready to begin?

29 대화를 듣고, 다음 중 두 사람이 먼저 해야 할 일들을 모두 고르시오.

M How's your day going? It seems like you're really busy.

W Yeah, ____
_________________________. For example, the boss just told me to get all this photocopying done within the next ten minutes, but I've also got to send ____
____.

M Wow, and I thought I was busy since I have to deliver some papers to Mr. Shim now.

W Well, at least my afternoon gets a little easier. I just have to make a few phone calls then, but ________________

____.

M That's good to know. After lunch, I'll attend a meeting with the department heads. It's pretty important, so I need to prepare for it immediately.

W I'd give you some help, but I don't have any time.

M Don't worry about that. I know you're busy. Say, _________
____
____?
We can talk about how much of our work we've gotten done and what we haven't finished.

W I'd love to, but I can't. _________________________________
_________________________.

M That sounds fine. Well, good luck with everything.

30 다음을 듣고, 다음 문장의 빈 칸에 들어갈 알맞은 말을 고르시오.

M These days, people are beginning to travel to many of the world's countries and are _________________________
____
_________________________. Unfortunately, the majority of people are often unaware of foreign cultures, so they wind up making cultural mistakes. It's crucial that people learn about other cultures _________________________
____.
For example, most Americans don't like people invading their personal space. They don't want anyone, no matter who the person is, _________________________
____.
It makes them feel extremely uncomfortable. Something else Americans dislike is when people they don't know well talk to them about personal topics like religion or politics. Furthermore, if an American host invites you out to dinner at a restaurant, _________________
Your host will take care of it. Finally, _________________
____.
That could offend some Americans, especially if you don't know them very well.

〔31-34〕 31번부터 34번까지는 문제와 보기를 모두 듣고 푸는 문제입니다. 대화나 이야기를 듣고, 영어로 들려주는 질문에 대한 알맞은 답을 고르시오.

31

M ____ ________________________ for the last few days, and I was hoping you could let me know what you think I should do about it.

W Sure, go ahead and tell me what's up.

M It's about Dave. He's the guy I share an office with. He's been driving me crazy lately, and I just don't know what to say to him.

W What's he been doing that's bothering you? He seems like a pretty nice guy.

M He is, but he has ________________________________ ____. It's not really loud, but, since our desks are next to each other, I have to hear every word he sings. I've already asked my boss about changing desks, but he won't let me.

W ____ ____________________________________?

M Oh, he knows he's doing it. I've mentioned to him before about how much it bothers me, but he won't stop singing. It's starting to get on my nerves really badly.

W I can imagine. ____________________________________ ________________________. You've got to do something about that as soon as possible.

M Okay, ____ ________________________________?

Q : *What is the best response to the man?*

M ① Just ignore him, and maybe he'll stop.
   ② Sing along with him whenever he starts.
   ③ Ask if you can get a new office somewhere else.
   ④ Pretend that his singing does not bother you at all.
   ⑤ Have a talk with him, and ask him to quit singing.

32

W I'm looking forward to this weekend since I'm planning ____.

M What are you doing with them?

W We're going to the mountain near my home to have a picnic. The whole family will be there, so it'll be a fantastic time.

M What are you planning to do after you eat? Will you play games or go hiking?

W We'll probably do some of both. I love nature, so I imagine ____ but some of my family members enjoy playing sports, so I'm sure they'll do that.

M That sounds much more exciting than my weekend. ____.

W Why are you going alone? I thought you had a girlfriend. The two of you should go together.

M I'd love that, but she's going out of town on a business trip this weekend, so I don't have much of a choice.

W If that's the case, ____ ____________________________________? Everyone knows you, so you won't be intruding on us.

M Hey, that's a great idea, ________________________________ ____________________________.

Q : *What was the man's original plan for the weekend?*

M ① To go on a picnic
   ② To see a movie
   ③ To go on a business trip
   ④ To go hiking
   ⑤ To stay at home alone

33

M Good evening, ma'am. My name is Trevor, and I'll be your waiter tonight. Would you care to order your dinner now?

W Yes, I think I'm all ready to order. For starters, ____________ ____?

M All right. That's a good choice. What kind of dressing would you like to have with it?

W I'll take ranch dressing. Also, I'd like to have the sirloin steak, please. I'd like it cooked medium rare.

M No problem. ______________________________________
________________________. That comes with a choice of
baked potato, rice pilaf, and soup. And it also includes
a small plate of vegetables.

W Oh my goodness. I had no idea I was ordering so much
food. ____.
Is it all right if I make a change to my order?

M That's no problem at all.

W Great. Thanks. Instead of the steak and garden salad,
just get me the chicken salad with ranch dressing.
____.

M That should take about ten minutes or so. __________
____
____?

W I'll just have an unsweetened ice tea, please.

Q : *Why does the woman change her order?*

M ① She is not particularly hungry.
② She has just finished her diet.
③ Her original meal is too expensive.
④ She does not want any vegetables.
⑤ She wants to order less food.

34

W One of the things you need to remember is that you're
going to have a lot of free time while you're here.
However, ____
____. Just three
years ago, ____.
I got here and wasted all my free time. Instead of going
to the library and studying after class, I hung out in the
dormitory and played computer games with my friends.
It was really fun, ____
____. You wouldn't
believe how angry my parents were. So, be sure that you
don't spend all of your time sleeping, playing games, or
even just goofing off. ____
________________________________, and I've been trying
____
____. If you do things
right, however, you'll get off to a good start and never
have any academic problems.

Q : *Which of the following best shows the relationship
between the speaker and the listener?*

M ① A senior and a freshman
② A professor and a senior
③ A guidance counselor and a junior
④ An advisor and a sophomore
⑤ An interviewer and a senior

35 다음을 듣고, 이어지는 영어 질문에 대한 알맞은 답을 고르
시오.

M Mr. Bryant is thinking of taking a vacation soon, but
he's not sure exactly where he wants to go __________
____
________________________. He can't stand ______
____ and he
doesn'treally enjoy extremes in either heat or cold.
He also doesn't like it when the weather is completely
sunny ____
________________________.

Q : *Which kind of weather conditions does Mr. Bryant like?*

36 주어진 시간 동안 아래 지문을 주의 깊게 읽고, 들려주는 영
어 질문에 답하시오.

Q : *What is the best title of this passage?*

[37-38] 대화를 듣고, 이어지는 두 개의 질문에 답하시오.

W You wouldn't believe ____
____.
It seems that so many things have gone wrong.

M Like what? I haven't moved in so long that I've
forgotten what it was like.

W For one thing, ____
____
when I moved in. The previous tenant hadn't
paid his bills, so I had to call both utility companies
to get someone to come out and turn them on. I was
trying to move everything in while it was dark.

M Ouch. That couldn't have been fun.

W No kidding. And get a load of this ... ____________

When I checked it out two weeks ago, it was fine. But now it's got lots of stains on it, and it's even peeling in a few places. ______________________________________ ______________________________________. Oh, and the sink in the bathroom leaks, too.

M It sounds like you've got some home repairs in your future. Aren't there at least one or two good things about your apartment? ______________________________ ______________________________________.

W Hmm… Well, the bedroom was bigger than I expected, so I've got more than enough room for my bed, wardrobe, and dresser. I was pleasantly surprised by that.

M Is there anything else?

W Hmm… ______________________________________ ______________________ since my window looks out on the mountain behind me.

37 Which of the following is NOT true about the woman's apartment?

38 Which of the following is the man's response to the woman?

M Are you still reading that biography? I never imagined you'd be the kind of person who'd enjoy that.

W ______________________________________. But, I must say this is one of the most amazing stories I've ever read.

M ______________________________________?

W It's definitely the way he encouraged the British people not to give up during World War II even when it looked like the Germans were going to win.

M Yeah, that was really inspiring. ______________________ ______________________________________ that were about how they were going to fight their hardest and not lose the war.

W It's a good thing he was the prime minister of England during the war and that the country wasn't being led by someone else. If that had been the case, ______________ ______________________________________.

M You're right about that. I think he was such a good leader because he had tons of experience. He had been a reporter in another country, he had written several books, and he had served in several government positions. ______________________________________ ______________________________________.

W Yeah, but why did the British people elect someone else right after the war ended? That seemed kind of strange.

M Well, ______________________________________ the book to find that one out.

W All right. In that case, let me get back to my reading.

Q : *Who are the speakers talking about?*

39 Who are the speakers talking about?

40 Which of the following is NOT true about the person?

01 대화를 듣고, 여자가 가려고 하는 곳을 고르시오.

W Excuse me, sir, but _______________________________________ Saint Paul's? I'm from out of town, and my friend is getting married today at two o'clock.

M Sure. Okay, let me see. We are on Main Street right next to the bank. So _______________________________________.

W Okay, so I need to head toward Second Avenue. Then what do I do?

M Turn right at Second Avenue. _______________________________________.

W Okay, that sounds pretty easy so far.

M Then, when you get to Maple Street, take a left.

W No problem. Where do I go after that?

M After that, walk along Maple Street _______________________________________. It's called Children's Hospital. It's located right next to Stanley Park. _______________________________________.

W Okay. Let me make sure I have this correct. Go straight west to Second Avenue, and then turn right. After that, go two blocks to Maple Street, and then turn left. Then walk until I see Stanley Park and Children's Hospital. Saint Paul's is opposite the hospital. Okay, thanks a lot.

M _______________________________________.

02 대화를 듣고, 이 대화가 이루어지고 있는 장소를 고르시오.

M Good day, madam. Welcome to the Swift Car Company. How can I help you?

W _______________________________________.

M Oh, that's not good. What seems to be the trouble?

W Well, it was fine until last night. But, this morning when I started it, the engine was making a lot of noise. I drove for about two blocks and started looking for a garage _______________________________________, so I stopped.

M That's terrible. I apologize for the inconvenience _______________________________________. We will get you a new car right away.

W Thank you very much.

M Don't mention it. First, can you tell me where you left the other car?

W It's on the corner of Duke Street and Queen Avenue right next to an Italian restaurant. It should be easy to spot. Here are the keys.

M Thank you. I'll send one of our men to take care of it immediately. Now, _______________________________________.

W Thanks. You've been so helpful.

03 다음을 듣고, 이야기 속의 This가 무엇인지 고르시오.

M This was created in the early twentieth century by three different men in three different countries _______________________________________. Inventors in the United States, Russia, and England all created a similar device that could _______________________________________. But American Philo Farnsworth is often given credit for being the inventor of this device. Unfortunately, he didn't get rich off of his invention. Poor judgment on his part caused him _______________________________________.

After a long legal battle, he was paid a fraction of what his invention is worth today. Although it was invented in the early twentieth century, it didn't become popular until the 1950s. Now, there is _______________________________________.

It is one of people's major sources of entertainment, and many people are even addicted to watching it. In fact, this invention is partially _______________________________________.

04 다음을 듣고, 화자가 무엇에 대해 이야기하고 있는지 고르시오.

W On today's tour, we are going to explore one of Korea's greatest treasures, _______________________________________.

It's far out to sea and takes many hours to get there, but it's a trip you won't regret taking. We will arrive there tonight and go on our tour tomorrow. The island is about seventy-three square kilometers in area and has about 10,000 people living there. Most people

_______________________________________ .
The island is volcanic in origin, and its highest point is a mountain almost 1,000 meters high called Sunginbong Peak. We can also see a waterfall, go hiking and fishing, and eat some delicious raw fish, which the island is famous for, while we're there. There are many cruise boats _______________________________________ and to others nearby. These cruises take about three hours, and we'll be taking one _______________________________________ .

05 대화를 듣고, 남자가 MP3플레이어를 사기 위해 지불한 금액을 고르시오.

W Did you find what you were looking for today?
M Yes, I got the latest and best MP3 player they had. Take a look at it.
W Wow, it looks pretty fancy. So, _______________________________________ ?
M Most were selling for about a hundred dollars, but _______________________________________ .
W What? That's way too expensive. You can get them for much less you know. Why on earth didn't you look around for a better deal?
M Actually, I did shop around. I checked out _______________________________________ before I decided on this one. I got it since it has the most song capacity.
W But you don't have a big music collection at all.
M True, but now _______________________________________ and store all my songs on this small device.
W That sounds good, but I still think you paid an arm and a leg for it.
M There were many cheaper ones, In fact, the cheapest was around fifty dollars, but those inexpensive ones weren't very good. Some others were _______________________________________ , but they didn't have very much song capacity.

06 대화를 듣고, 남자가 어떤 스포츠를 하는 선수인지 고르시오.

W Here we are with Chris Thomas, one of the best players in the league today. His team has just made the playoffs thanks to a three to two win tonight. How do you feel, Chris?
M I'm tired but very satisfied. We had a good season, and _______________________________________ .
W You must be happy with the way you played tonight. You scored the winning goal.
M Yeah, _______________________________________ , and that helped us win, so I'm very happy with my performance.
W What are your expectations for the playoffs?
M We want to win it all, but you have to win sixteen games, so it's difficult.
W What do you think about Boston, _______________________________________ ?
M They have a great team. They skate well, have a great goalie and defensemen, and are very good at penalty killing. And _______________________________________ .
W How's the injury you had earlier in the year?
M I still have some pain in my foot, so that makes skating difficult, but _______________________________________ , so it's safe to play.

07 대화를 듣고, 남자의 마지막 말에 대한 여자의 응답으로 알맞은 것을 고르시오.

W It's a busy day, isn't it?
M It sure is. Oh, do you have a moment to talk?
W Okay, _______________________________________ , or I'll never get out of here.
M It sounds like you already have plans for tonight.
W Yeah, I have a date with one of the guys in the Accounting Department. I'm so excited because he's such a nice person.
M That's great. Anyway, what I wanted to ask you is _______________________________________ , but I guess you won't be. It's my wife's birthday, and she'd love to see you again.
W Oh, is that tonight? I heard someone mention it. I

enjoyed the last party you had, especially since your house is so beautiful. Well, sorry, _______________

____.

It ends around nine thirty.

M Then why don't you come to the party after the movie? We'll still be there, and lots of people are coming.

W Maybe, but I'll have to see what my date wants to do first.

M ____,

too. Why don't you ask him?

08 다음을 듣고, 이 이야기의 목적을 고르시오.

W There's a new restaurant on Wilson Street that I went to last night. My husband took me, of course, and

____.

It was a Russian restaurant, and they had _______________

____.

The waitresses all wore traditional Russian costumes, and they even had a small band playing Russian folk music. We had a lovely bottle of Russian wine, some caviar, and thick brown bread for an appetizer. Then came the traditional Russian soup called borsch, which is made from red beets. It was fantastic. After that, _____

____.

We dined on roasted salmon, a plate of boiled potatoes with herbs, carrots in a special sauce, and then a lovely roast beef dish. ____

_______________________. You should definitely try the food there. ____, and everyone was so friendly. The only problem was the price. It was somewhat expensive, but _______________

____.

09 대화를 듣고, 다음 중 헌혈에 대해 사실이 <u>아닌</u> 것을 고르시오.

W Hey, Joe, I'm sorry, but I can't have dinner with you tonight. I'm going to the hospital to donate some blood after school. Do you want to come?

M I'm not sure... ____

_______________________. Is it safe? I heard that some people have gotten diseases after giving blood and

____.

W You must have heard wrong. They use a new needle for each person, so ____

____.

M Okay, I believe you. Hey, can I get paid if I give blood?

W No, Joe, they don't pay blood donors. Sorry, but you can't get rich by sellling your blood.

M That's too bad. If they paid for it, _______________

____.

W That's dangerous. If you gave blood every day, then you would probably get sick. Your body needs time to replace the blood they take out of you. _______________

____.

M I guess that makes sense. Do they have enough donors?

W No, that's why I'm going and why you should come, too. Hospitals never have enough blood in storage for what they need.

M Okay, I'll come with you. Then let's have dinner after donating blood.

10 다음을 듣고, 은하수에 대해 사실이 <u>아닌</u> 것을 고르시오.

M A galaxy ____

_______________________ by gravity. Astronomers estimate that there are forty to fifty billion galaxies in the universe. The most distant object ever seen from Earth is a galaxy almost thirteen billion light years away. Earth's galaxy is called the Milky Way, and _______________

____

_______________________. The few exceptions are other galaxies so far away from the planet that they appear as mere points of light in the sky. The Milky Way is about

____

and ____.
No one has ever seen the Milky Way in its entirety, but astronomers can make educated guesses about its shape and size from their observations of other galaxies. Most believe the Milky Way is shaped like a spiral nebula.

____

_______________________ and is very small in the grand vastness of the universe.

11 대화를 듣고, 두 사람이 대화 후에 할 일을 고르시오.

W What would you like to have for lunch?

M I'm not sure. There are so many good things on this menu that I want to try them all.

W Well, _________________________________ _________________________ on this menu, too. I wouldn't recommend the hamburgers here. They are so bad for you.

M What are you talking about? This place has the most delicious hamburgers in the city.

W They are the most delicious but _________________ _________________. They're full of fat, red meat, and cheese, all of which are bad for your heart. And this restaurant always serves them with greasy French fries which are deep fried in oil and covered in salt. Salt is very bad for your blood pressure.

M ____?

W I'm worried about your health. You've gained some weight recently.

M What? Oh, I've only put on a few kilos. And _________ _________________________. But maybe you're right. The food here is very unhealthy, so perhaps we shouldn't eat here.

W So, what do you want to do? I'm still hungry.

M So am I. It's a good thing we still have fifty minutes _________________________________.

12 다음을 듣고, 1960년대 이후 십대 비만율의 변화를 가장 잘 보여 주는 그래프를 고르시오.

W One of ____ ____. Becoming overweight at such an early age leads to long-term health problems for many teens when they become adults. Diabetes, kidney problems, and heart disease are ____ _________________. One of the main causes has been the rise in junk food consumption and the lack of exercise. The explosion of the fast-food and snack-food industries began in the 1960s. _________________________ _________________________ instead of going outdoors, this led to a trend of increasing teenage obesity. This trend increased rapidly through the 1970s, 1980s, and 1990s as more delicious junk food

was created and cable television, VCRs, video games, and then the Internet allowed teens to be entertained indoors. ____ ____, with teen obesity decreasing slightly. Experts attribute this to more parents and teens _________________ _________________________.

13 대화를 듣고, 두 사람이 방문할 장소를 순서대로 나열한 것을 고르시오.

M Wow, I can't believe we're in New York City. This is one of the most amazing cities in the world.

W Where do you want to go first? There's so much to see here.

M ____. I've always wanted to go to the top and look at everything down below.

W ____. Central Park is right across the street, so we should make that our first stop.

M Okay, then why don't we visit the Empire State Building after doing that?

W That sounds good. After lunch, _________________ _________________________.

M The weather forecast said it's supposed to rain this afternoon.

W Really? That's terrible. _________________________ _________________________?

M There's a basketball game at Madison Square Garden. We already have tickets for it.

W But that's at six o'clock. What can we do in the meantime?

M I know. ____ _________________________. I know just the place. The Metropolitan Museum of Modern Art isn't far away.

W That's a great idea. I've heard it's got an awesome art collection. ____ _________________________.

14 다음을 듣고, 화자가 이야기하고 있는 그림의 장르를 고르시오.

M I went to the local art gallery with my class the other day. Art usually bores me, but ________________________________. There was this one painting being exhibited there which showed a bowl of fruit on a table. That's a pretty common painting, right? But this painting was so good that I wanted to eat the fruit in it. There were apples, oranges, bananas, and grapes. The apples were on the bottom and were bright red. The bananas were so yellow that _________________________________. The grapes were the green kind, not the purple kind they serve in our school cafeteria. The bright mix of colors — orange, yellow, red, and green — ________________ ____________________________________.

Even though the painting didn't depict any people nor did it have an action scene in it, I was totally impressed by it. __________________________________ ___________________________________.

15 대화를 듣고, 상황을 가장 잘 나타내는 속담을 고르시오.

M I feel terrible. ___________________________ _______________________________.

W I thought you were good friends with the owner's son, so that was going to help you.

M We are good friends. I talk with him on the phone all the time, we have lunch once a week, and I even play golf with him two or three times a month. __________ ____________________________________. This other guy, Bill Williams, got the promotion. I don't know what I did wrong.

W Well, why don't you tell me about Bill Williams and what kind of worker he is?

M He always comes in before everyone else. He works late and ______________________________________ _______________ and ______________________ ___________________. He volunteers for some charity, and he helped promote the addition of the daycare center in the building.

W He sounds like a wonderful guy.

M Sure, but that's no reason for him to get the promotion instead of me.

W Well, ___________________________? Bill

sounds like the ideal worker, yet you haven't told me about anything that you do ___________________ ________________________________ all the time.

16 다음을 듣고, 이야기의 분위기를 가장 잘 나타낸 것을 고르시오.

W I started a new job ___________________________ ________________ about six months ago. At first, I was very scared I would get fired. I made a lot of mistakes. On my second day on the job, I spilled coffee all over a legal document, so I had to retype it right away. I could never remember the lawyers' names, and _____________ ____.

Also, I accidentally deleted a file from the computer. Thankfully, it was backed up in another place. I was so nervous during those first few weeks. I cried almost every night, and I bit my fingernails to almost nothing. However, ______________________________________ ____________________, so I feel much more comfortable. I know what to do, and ___________________________ __________________. I think that by making mistakes, we learn how to do things the right way. If I ever have my own company, __________________________________ ________________.

17 대화를 듣고, 여자의 마지막 말에 대한 남자의 응답으로 가장 알맞은 것을 고르시오.

M Welcome to Startek Electronics. How can I help you today?

W I'm not sure actually. My son recommended that I get a new computer, but I still like my old one. I guess I need some advice on computers.

M That's not a problem. We can give you a new one or upgrade the old one. First, can you tell me about your current computer?

W My son wrote it all down. Let's see... Here it is.

M Yes, ___________________________________. You still have a dial-up modem and a three-point-five-inch floppy disk drive. Those are not very useful these days. Most people use a broadband modem or Ethernet connection.

W Yes, _____________________________________

_________________. That's one reason why I'm here.

M Also, you have a very slow CD-ROM drive. And your processor and memory capacity are quite low. Pretty soon, ____.

W So, what do you think I should do?

M I can set you up with new computer for less than a thousand dollars.

W Oh, ____. What about upgrading this one?

18 다음을 듣고, 화요일의 날씨를 고르시오.

W Now, let me provide you with ____. The storm system that we're experiencing now will be over by Saturday night, so Sunday will be clear and sunny. On Monday, ____ and cooler temperatures. This will continue on Tuesday, so ____ at the beginning of the week. By Wednesday, the rainy period will end, but the cloudy skies and colder temperatures will continue. On Thursday, ____, so it will be much warmer than it was earlier in the week. However, that will soon end. Starting on Friday, ____, so it's possible we'll see the first snowstorm of the season. Depending on the temperature, the weekend will either be very snowy, or we will have more rainy weather. And that's it for the weather that you can be expecting over the next few days.

19 대화를 듣고, 남자가 알람시계를 설정해 달라고 부탁한 시각을 고르시오.

M Oh, no. The soccer game that I want to watch is on at three in the morning.

W That's really late for a sports event. ____?

M It's a World Cup game from South Africa, so it's seven hours behind our time. I'll be asleep when the game is on.

W If it's so important, why don't you just record it on your VCR and watch it after work tomorrow?

M That's not the same as watching it live. All my friends will be watching it, so someone will tell me the score, or ____.

W Okay, how about this idea? You should just go to bed early — maybe around nine o'clock — ____.

M Yeah, that would work, but I'll be so tired at work tomorrow. I don't think that will impress my boss very much.

W ____, including your boss. I'll set the alarm clock. What time do you want to get up?

M ____.

W No problem. Hey, now it's time for bed if you want to get up on time.

20 대화를 듣고, 두 사람이 가장 <u>싫어하는</u> 음식을 고르시오.

M Someone sent us a survey in the mail. It's all about things we like and don't like. Do you want to answer it?

W Sure, why not? ____. I think I know everything you like and don't like.

M Oh, really? What about food? What kind of food do I dislike the most?

W Oh, that's easy. ____.

M No, that's not exactly true. I like some kinds of fish, like cod and salmon. And lobster is okay, too. You don't know what kind of food I really hate, do you?

W Okay, so I don't know. What's the answer?

M ____. I guess I ate too much of it as a child.

W Really? I don't think I've ever seen you eat it, and now I know why. Okay, so now it's your turn. ____?

M Let's see. You never eat any kind of beans, so I'd say that's the answer.

W You're close. I like the taste of beans but just never eat them. ____. I guess we don't know each other as well as we thought.

21 다음을 듣고, 화자의 요지가 무엇인지 고르시오.

M ____
______________________________________ shows that,
while the number of adult smokers is decreasing,
____
______________________________. In the 13-19
year old age group, there has been a fifteen-percent
increase in the number of smokers today compared to
ten years ago. At the same time, there has been ________
____.
The growing number of teen smokers is the result of
two factors: They are peer pressure and the influence
of advertising and the media. Teens try smoking
because ______________________________________,
so they feel pressured to conform and act like their
peers. Many teens see their favorite singers and
television and movie stars smoking — both on and off
the screen — so ______________________________
____.
The sad truth is that the most addictive smokers are
those who start smoking when they are teenagers.
Unfortunately for them, by smoking, they are risking b
oth ____
______________________________________.

22 대화를 듣고, 여자가 남자의 요청을 듣지 <u>못한</u> 이유를 고르시오.

W Hello, Johnson Architects. This is Janice speaking.
How may I help you?

M Hi, Janice. It's Peter Donaldson. ________________
__________________________________, but I've been
delayed because of ____________________________
______________________________.

W Where are you now, Peter?

M I'm near the Tenth Street overpass on Ventura
Boulevard. ____________________________________,
so it may be thirty minutes to an hour before I can get
there. I'm really sorry about that.

W Okay, thanks for calling. I'll tell the others, and we'll
delay the meeting until you arrive.

M I'd appreciate that. By the way, can you...

W What was that? ______________________________
Peter. Could you repeat that?

M Sorry, but it's really noisy here. I asked if you could
prepare my PowerPoint presentation. I'm sending it to
your e-mail from my laptop right now. That will save us
some time when I arrive.

W Okay, send it. Oh, it's here already. I got your e-mail. I'll
set it up in the conference room.

M Thanks a lot, Janice. ________________________
__________________________________. Bye.

23 다음을 듣고, 이 이야기의 장르를 고르시오.

W Soon, however, ______________________________
__________________________, so the king banished her
from the kingdom. A few months later, right in the
middle of the night, the king's daughter, the princess,
suddenly disappeared. The king's men searched for her
for years and years, but they couldn't find her anywhere.
____
____,
but there was no trace of her anywhere. One day, a
stranger came to the castle and told the king he knew
where the princess was. He said she was being held
prisoner by the witch deep in the darkest part of the
forest. ____
__________________________, but the king
told them that he alone must go there to battle the
witch. The soldiers weren't pleased, __________________
__________________________. But the king
himself was a great warrior, so he knew what he had to
do.

24 대화를 듣고, 두 사람이 무엇에 대해 이야기하고 있는지 고르시오.

M That was quite a storm we had. I've never seen anything
like that before.

W ____?
My house has three broken windows, and we still don't
have any electricity.

M What? It's been three days since it finished. We got our
power back last night.

W I guess ______________________________________
__________________________. They had to restore power to the
hospitals and police and fire stations first.

M Those are essential services, so it makes sense. We still have a lot of trees down in my neighborhood.

W It's the same here. The wind was really powerful. Someone said it was over one hundred and fifty kilometers per hour.

M I know. The wind was really howling for hours. ________ __________________________, and maybe twenty people were lost.

W That's terrible. Some people in the town ten kilometers away got hurt when they went outside as the eye of the storm passed over them.

M I guess they thought the storm was over, but __________ _______________________.

W The weather service said this one was almost 100 kilometers wide. That's a class two storm.

25 다음을 듣고, 제품에 대해 사실이 <u>아닌</u> 것을 고르시오.

M Right now, on sale until Saturday at Stan's Electronics on Fulton Avenue is the Bronco Super Duper Dust Devil Vacuum Cleaner. That's right, folks, from now until Saturday, ________________________________ ______________________________________, our lowest price in years. It's powerful enough to clean any carpet or floor and small enough to fit in your closet. It's portable and can be easily carried from room to room and up and down the stairs. ______________ ____________________________, the Super Duper Dust Devil __________________________ ____________________, which allow you to clean those hard-to-reach places. Under beds, in corners, behind bookcases, and on top of cupboards, __________ ____________________. Our product has a full parts and service warranty for one year after purchase. If you're not satisfied, return it within one week of purchase for a refund. So, come down to Stan's Electronics, and ____ __________________.

26 다음을 듣고, 화자의 의견에 동의하는 진술을 고르시오.

W Currently, __________________________________ ________________________________ is causing a great deal of controversy. While the death penalty still exists, no one in my country has been executed for several years. I, for one, __________________________ _______________________. It is inhumane for our government to take the life of another person no matter what that individual did. If we execute people, we're no better than the criminals themselves. A much better punishment would be to keep them locked in prison for the rest of their lives. This way, ____, and they must pay the penalty for those they did. I'm sure many people don't agree with me, yet there have been many recent cases where DNA testing has proved that ____ ____ _______________. If they had been executed, then we would have killed innocent people. It's far better to respect the human rights of all people _______________ __________________.

27 다음을 듣고, 화자의 집을 가장 잘 나타낸 것을 고르시오.

W My family just moved into a new house we bought. I'm so pleased with it because it looks like the house I've always dreamed of owning. For one thing, ________ ____________________________, so it's great to have both an upstairs and a downstairs. And there are ____, so the house is going to get a lot of light. That's a good thing because I love having a bright house. Oh, and we've also got __________________________________ ____________________, so there's _______________ __________________________. I'm planning to have lots of fires in wintertime, so that should help keep the house warm. We've even got a front yard with ________ __________________________. It looks so nice. I'm sure that the kids are going to love climbing the tree and playing in the yard. It's going to be so great living here.

28 대화를 듣고, 두 사람이 현재까지 주문한 음식값으로 지불하게 될 금액을 고르시오.

W What do you want to order, Derek?

M I'm not sure yet. I'm afraid that ____. Everything looks so good.

W I think I'm going to start with a salad, but I don't know which one.

M Try the chicken salad. One of my friends had it here, and she said it was great.

W That sounds good. Are you going to have a salad, too?

M No, I believe ____ and then have the steak and French fries.

W French fries are so unhealthy. Instead of them, you should have ____.

M Maybe you're right. Okay, I'll have the baked potato. And, for a drink, I think ____.

W Yeah, I'll have an ice tea, too. And for the main dish, I'll have the baked fish and rice. What about dessert? Do you want some ice cream or pie?

M ____ and then decide about dessert? I'm not sure if I'll have any room after all this food.

29 대화를 듣고, 두 사람이 이상적인 친구에게서 원하는 공통 요소들을 모두 고르시오.

M What do you think would make ____? If you had to pick some qualities, what would they be?

W I'm not sure. I think it's impossible to find an ideal mate. ____. I can't stand people who lie. If I had a boyfriend who lied to me, I'd break up with him immediately.

M I'd have to agree with you there. Also, I think I could only be with someone who has the same education as me. Intelligence is a must.

W You're right. I don't want a boyfriend ____.

W What about looks? I think looks are important.

W Well, I can do without them so long as he's a nice person.

M She'd have to ____, too. I can't stand being around serious people.

W Yeah, that's a must. How about money? Do you want a rich girlfriend?

M Not really. Then she'd always be expecting me to buy her expensive presents.

W I can understand that, but I'd love to have a rich boyfriend ____.

30 다음을 듣고, 화자의 마지막 말에 이어질 내용으로 가장 알맞은 것을 고르시오.

W Students must always take tests. ____, but tests are used to grade a student's progress, so they're necessary. Getting a good grade on a test can be easy if you know what to do. First, make sure you study with a partner. ____, it's easier to understand the information and to remember it. Second, turn off all radios, TVs, computers, and other distractions. You must concentrate on what you are studying. Third, ____. Study a little bit each day for several days, and you'll do much better. Finally, ____. Most people have trouble sleeping before an exam, but it's the most important thing to do. ____, but ____, or you'll be too relaxed during the test. So before the test, you'd better sleep...

[31-34] 31번부터 34번까지는 문제와 보기를 모두 듣고 푸는 문제입니다. 대화나 이야기를 듣고, 영어로 들려주는 질문에 대한 알맞은 답을 고르시오.

31

M We're going to be late for the exam.

W ____.
I need it for the test I'm taking today. It was right here in my bag last night, but now I can't find it.

M Okay, I'll help you look for it. Where is it? Aha, ________ ________________________________. Now let's get out of here.

W Just a minute. Let me put my shoes on. What's the rush anyway? ____ ________________________________.

M It's nine thirty now, and the traffic on the way to the university is going to be bad.

W Let's take the subway then. It's much faster than your car, and ____ ________________________________.

M I need my car for after school to pick up Fred from the airport.

W Well, I'm taking the subway. I don't want to be late for this exam. If I miss it, ________________________ ________________.

M All right, we'll take the subway. I'll just come back and get my car after school. Can we go now? ____________ ________________.

W Yeah, let's go.

Q : *Which best shows the mood of this conversation?*

M ① urgent
② desperate
③ calm
④ comedic
⑤ serious

32

M Now, let's turn to our local news report. A fire broke out in an apartment building on Seventh Avenue at three in the morning, resulting in several injuries and severe property damage. ____________________________ ________________________________ and were still on the scene this morning. Residents were awakened by a smoke detector and rushed to evacuate. ____________ ____ and is in stable condition in a local hospital. He's expected to survive. Two men attempted to extinguish the flames but were overcome by smoke inhalation and had to be treated by medics before being released. ____________ ____, but it's suspected that electrical wiring caused it. The owner of the building has been brought in for questioning. Meanwhile, as a result of the fire, ________ ____. Donations to the victims can be made at St. Joseph's Church on Seventh Avenue.

Q : *What is this news story about?*

M ① a heart attack victim
② some homeless people
③ two men hurt in an accident
④ a fire in a building
⑤ the cause of an accident

33

M Come in, Mrs. Delaney, and have a seat, please. How can I help you today?

W Thank you, Mr. Fraser. The reason I'm here is that ____.

M Oh, that's not good to hear. What exactly is the problem?

W I ordered the bone china from Dresden, Germany, for my shop, but ________________________________, many pieces were chipped, and some were cracked. ____.

M I apologize on behalf of the company. Of course, we will compensate you for any product that was damaged.

W I would expect nothing less. Also, ____________________ ____.

M But that order has already been shipped from Germany and will arrive two days from now. It's too late to cancel it.

W It seems you don't understand, Mr. Fraser. ____________ ____. I will not accept and will not pay for this recent order.

M I understand, Mrs. Delaney. Again, I apologize for not providing you with satisfactory service.

W I'm sure ________________________.
   Good day, Mr. Fraser.

Q : *Why is the woman unhappy with the products she ordered?*

M ① They were damaged in shipping.
   ② They are overly expensive.
   ③ They were late in arriving.
   ④ Her customers were unhappy with them.
   ⑤ She did not order the items she received.

34

W Mr. Smith, I need to speak to you about my apartment.
M What seems to be the problem this time?
W ________________________.
   The bathroom sink is still leaking. Water is spilling all over the floor, so we have to use the kitchen sink to brush our teeth and wash our hands.
M I fixed that two weeks ago, yet ________________________ ________________________?
W It was fine for a week, but then the leak started again in the same place. I think you need to replace the entire sink.
M ________________________ ________________________, then I'm going to have to raise the rent.
W That's not fair. We have a lease that's good for another six months. And it says that ________________________ ________________________ to the apartment.
M All right, don't get so excited. Are you going to be home on Tuesday afternoon?
W No, I'm working all day Tuesday. Wednesday is better.
M Okay, so on Wednesday, ________________________ ________________________. Hopefully, that will be the end of this problem.

Q : *Which best shows the relationship between the two speakers?*

M ① a customer and a hotel manager
   ② an employee and a director
   ③ a tenant and a landlord
   ④ a renter and a real estate agent
   ⑤ a buyer and a seller

35 다음을 듣고, 이어지는 영어 질문에 답하시오.

M Tom, Joe, and David ate together at a restaurant during their lunch break. ________________________ ________________________. Tom's share of the bill was nine dollars. ________________________ ________________________, and David paid the rest of the bill.

Q : *How much money did David pay?*

36 주어진 시간 동안 아래 지문을 주의 깊게 읽고, 들려주는 영어 질문에 답하시오. 〔1분〕

Q : *Today is the first day of class. What will they study?*

〔37-38〕 다음을 듣고, 이어지는 두 개의 질문에 답하시오.

W ________________________.
   You are taking care of a living thing and should show it all the love and care you would give to your own child. First, you must be sure to get all the proper injections that the pet needs to protect it from diseases. ________________________ ________________________.
   Second, your pet needs the best nutrition available and must have a balanced diet. There are many pet food products on the market today, so choose wisely. Third, all pets need a place to sleep that is warm and comfortable. ________________________.
   Next, pets need exercise and attention. Take you pet for a walk, play with it, and show it that you care about it. ________________________ ________________________. Of course, this is not possible with all pets, such as birds, fish, or turtles, but even they need all of your love and attention. ________________________ ________________________. If you plan to move away or you can no longer take care of your pet, please take it to an animal shelter.

37 What is the purpose of this talk?

38 Which is NOT true about a good pet owner?

〔39-40〕 대화를 듣고, 이어지는 두 개의 질문에 답하시오.

W Hi, Bill. I just heard that ____. Did you vote in the election yesterday?

M No, I was too busy to make it to the voting station. I had a lot of work to do. Besides it was raining a lot yesterday.

W What? That's terrible. ____. It's your civic responsibility. I can't believe you didn't vote.

M ____.

Not everyone votes. In fact, none of my coworkers voted yesterday. No one thinks his or her vote will ___________________________________.

To tell the truth, I've never voted in any election.

W That's a cynical attitude. Everyone's vote is important. You know that in some countries, ____, or they are forced to vote for someone. Here, at least we have the freedom to vote for the people we want to lead us.

M I've heard all of that before. It doesn't matter what I do. I just have one vote, and, besides, it's already decided who will win.

W _______________________________________.

It's because of people like you that our country has so many problems.

M No, it's because of the corrupt political system. No one cares if I vote or not. ____?

39 What are the speakers talking about?

40 What is the woman's response to the man?

01 대화를 듣고, 남자가 여자친구를 위해 살 선물을 고르시오.

M Hello. I was wondering if you could help me with a problem.

W Sure, what are you looking for?

M Tomorrow is my girlfriend's birthday, so I want to get her something nice. _______________________________________
_______________________________________.

W Well, you've come to the right place for birthday presents. Have you considered getting her _______________
_______________________________?

M I bought her one for her last birthday, so I'd like to get something different. _______________________________
_______________________________.

W Those are nice, but let me tell you something… You shouldn't get her one for her birthday. Instead, _________
_______________________________?
She'll probably appreciate those more. Take this pair, for example.

M Yes, those look quite spectacular, but don't you think
_______________________________________?

W They're fine, but not as presents. In fact, lots of men usually wind up purchasing something similar to what I just showed you.

M Is that true? In that case, _______________________
_______________________. How much do I owe you?

W Your total comes to seventy-five dollars, sir.

02 다음을 듣고, 화자의 장래희망이 무엇인지 고르시오.

W Even though I haven't finished high school, I still constantly think about my future. Nowadays, there are so many things a person can do. I feel as if _______________________________________. For example, I could become an astronaut, doctor, lawyer, or even an engineer. They're all great jobs, but they aren't the ones for me. The job I'd really love to do involves taking care of animals. I love animals and even own a couple of pets. _______________________
_______________________. That makes me feel so sad, so I want to take care of them until they get better. _______________________

_______________________. I'd be a doctor, but one who takes care of animals. People tell me I'm really good around animals, so I'm sure _______________
_______________________.

03 대화를 듣고, 두 사람의 관계를 가장 잘 나타낸 것을 고르시오.

W Good morning. Is there something I can help you with?

M Yes, _______________________________________,
_______________________.

W Are you interested in a savings or checking account? Or perhaps you'd like something different?

M As of now, _______________________________
_______________________, but I'm sure I'll open up some other accounts when I get more settled. So, what exactly do I have to do?

W You can start _______________________________
_______________________. It should only take you a couple of minutes. Oh, I'll also need to see some photo identification.

M Sure. Is a driver's license acceptable?

W Yes, but I'll need to see two forms of ID. _______________
_______________________, would you?

M Actually, I brought my passport with me just in case, so I guess it's my lucky day. Is there anything else you'd like me to do?

W No, there isn't. Just complete those papers while I go to make copies of your IDs. _______________________
_______________________.

M Take your time.

04 대화를 듣고, 두 사람이 만나기로 한 식당을 고르시오.

M Why don't we have dinner together this weekend?

W That sounds like a good plan. Where shall we go?

M Well, I love the Hot Tamale. It's _______________
_______________________. Why don't we have dinner there?

W I'm sorry, but I can't stomach Mexican food. I was thinking that the Hungry Fisherman _______________
_______________________________________.

M I'm allergic to shellfish, so that's not an option. Sorry.

Hmm... We could visit Pomodoros, which is an outstanding Italian restaurant, or Thai Delights, a Thai restaurant ______________________________ ______________________. How about one of those?

W Okay, that doesn't sound too bad. Or we could even visit Mitchell's, ______________________________ ______________________. I was just there a few days ago and loved the food.

M That sounds delicious, but ______________________________ ____?

W Yeah, you're probably right. I don't get out very often, so it's probably best to eat at another restaurant. Why don't we go to the Italian place? ______________________ ______________________.

M Really? You'll love it. I'll make reservations for seven o'clock this Saturday.

05 다음을 듣고, 이야기의 제목으로 가장 알맞은 것을 고르시오.

M Countless cultures have a tradition of playing a game where players on opposing teams ______________________ ____. The ancient Romans, Greeks, and Chinese all played some form of soccer. However, soccer as people know it today wasn't played until the early nineteenth century, when various British schools attempted to codify the game's rules. During the nineteenth century, soccer and rugby, ______ ______________________________________, ______________ ____. Indeed, for almost a hundred years, the rules of soccer were altered. It wasn't until 1869 that players were banned from touching the ball with their hands. ______________ ____ ____. Soccer quickly increased in popularity, with many amateur and professional leagues developing everywhere. Today, soccer is the most popular sport in the world, and the World Cup, soccer's championship tournament, ______ ____.

06 대화를 듣고, 여자에 대해 사실이 <u>아닌</u> 것을 고르시오.

M We're graduating next year. Have you thought about ____ ______________________?

W Yeah, I've put lots of thought into it.

M Really? What do you think you're going to do?

W Well, ____, but I don't think I have to find a job connected to my major. Instead, ____ ____.

M That sounds interesting. What kind of work are you thinking of?

W I'd love to become a teacher. It would be ______________ ____. However, if I want to teach for a long time, I'll have to return to school to get a teaching degree, and I have no desire to do that.

M I'm pretty tired of school myself.

W That's why I'll most likely find some kind of government job. I'd absolutely love to work for the city in a position where ____ ______________________.

M That sounds nice.

W Not only does the government provide good jobs, but the pay and benefits are excellent, and ______________ ____, too.

07 다음을 듣고, 이야기의 분위기를 가장 잘 나타낸 것을 고르시오.

W I recently left my home in the city ______________________ ____. I must confess that it's not nearly what I'd expected to experience. I'm used to the hustle and bustle of the city. There, something is always going on twenty-four hours a day. However, life here is considerably slower-paced than in the city. For example, ____ ____ anywhere. I can drive for several miles without even seeing another car. And people live really far away from each other, too. You can't even see another house from the one I'm living at. ____ ____. I've actually come to enjoy sitting out in my yard and doing nothing. There's a

small pond on my property, so, if I'm really quiet,
____

visiting the pond all day long. It's a different life down
here, but I really enjoy it.

08 대화를 듣고, 남자의 마지막 말에 대한 여자의 응답으로 가장 알맞은 것을 고르시오.

M Hello, may I please speak with Stephanie?
W I'm sorry, but she's not in at the moment. ___________
____?
M Sure, this is her friend Mark.
W Oh, hi, Mark. It's Rachel. We met a couple of weeks
ago when you dropped by the house. Is there anything
that I can do for you?
M Well, I was calling to speak with Stephanie. I wanted to
know _______________________________________
_________________________________ with me this
weekend. She hasn't mentioned anything to you about
it, has she?
W No, I'm afraid she hasn't. I'm sorry about that.
However, I did hear her say something about having to
drop by her parents' house this weekend. I hope _______
_________________________________.
M Hmm… It might since I haven't heard anything about
that. I hope it won't. There's an exhibition at the
museum we've both been dying to see.
W Well, why don't ________________________________
_________________________________?
M That would be great. About when do you expect her to
arrive?

09 대화를 듣고, 여자의 마지막 말에 대한 남자의 응답으로 가장 알맞은 것을 고르시오.

M Good afternoon. I was hoping to make reservations for
the musical that's being performed here. ___________
____?
W I apologize, sir, but Saturday night's show has been sold
out for two weeks.
M Oh, no. I was really looking forward to attending it.
W There are _____________________________________
___________________ if you're interested.
M Yes, I'd like to learn more about them. What nights are

they?
W Well, there are performances on Thursday night and
Sunday evening. The Thursday night show ___________
____________________________ while the
Sunday performance _____________________________
_________________________________.
M That's wonderful. Both of the days and times fit my
schedule. Tell me something though… What kinds of
seats are available for each performance?
W The Sunday show has almost sold out, so ___________
___________________________, and
most aren't very good. However, the Thursday night
performance still has seats everywhere, ___________
_________________.
M Ah, that's where I always like to sit.
W So, what would you like me to do?

10 다음을 듣고, 대피라미드에 대해 사실이 <u>아닌</u> 것을 고르시오.

M Egypt has a large number of pyramids ________________
____.
However, when most people talk about its pyramids,
they're referring to the ones located at Giza. People
know them as the Great Pyramids. Found near Cairo,
____
_________________. These pyramids were constructed
over 4,500 years ago in a process that took a long
amount of time to complete. However, _______________
____
_________________________________ even in
the present. People do, though, know their use: The
pyramids were burial chambers for Egyptian pharaohs.
For hundreds of years, the Great Pyramid of Giza was
____
_________________________. From its completion until
around 1300 AD, nothing else manmade was higher
than it. The pyramids are among the most famous
structures in the world, and it is believed that more
tourists have visited them _________________________
_________________________.

11 대화를 듣고, 여자가 신발을 사기 위해 지불할 금액을 고르시오.

W Good evening. I saw your advertisement for shoes in the local paper, and I was hoping that you'd be able to point out to me which ones are on sale.

M Sure, that won't be a problem. As you probably know, ________________________________, not our entire collection.

W Yes, I read that in the ad. So I'm guessing that this pair of loafers is not on sale.

M That's correct. They cost $150 though in case you're interested.

W Well, ________________________________, but not at that price. How about these black high heels? How much are they?

M They retail for $120, but, since they're on sale, ________________________________.

W That's quite a bargain. You must really want to move a lot of your products.

M We're trying ________________________________. How about this pair of brown shoes? They usually cost $200 but are only $115 now. You can't beat that bargain.

W I'd have to agree with you, but I'm not that impressed by the way they look. ________________________________, please.

M All right. Let me go and wrap them up for you.

12 대화를 듣고, 이 상황에 가장 어울리는 영어 속담을 고르시오.

M You're not going to believe all the problems we're having on this project I'm working on.

W Is that the one where you're teaming up with five or six other employees?

M ________________________________. We were supposed to start last week, but, unfortunately, we've ________________________________.

W What exactly is the problem? From what I've heard, you've got some really good employees working on your team. You all should be able to handle this work easily.

M You'd like to think that, wouldn't you? However, ________________________________. Every member of the team is convinced that he should be the leader. I'm the team leader, but no one is respecting my position.

W That's not good.

M You're telling me. Everybody keeps trying to give me suggestions and is telling me how they think the project should be run.

W You've got to do something about that, ________________________________.

M I know. It's a total mess since no one wants to be a follower, and everyone wants to be the leader. I just hope we can get this project finished on time.

W Good luck with that. ________________________________.

13 다음을 듣고, 화자가 여행할 나라들을 차례대로 나열한 것을 고르시오.

W I'm taking a trip to Europe in three weeks, so I had to complete ________________________________. I haven't been to Europe before, so I need to make sure I can visit as many places as possible. The first place ________________________________. I love the art and architecture there, so it'll be wonderful to see places like Rome, Venice, and Florence in person. I'd originally planned to visit Switzerland next, but ________________________________. That works for me. I'll have a great time cruising the islands there. Next, I'm going to fly to Germany because ________________________________. I haven't seen them in a while, so that should be nice. Hopefully, they'll show me some of the local sights. Finally, before I go home, I'm going to make it to ________________________________. I can't wait to take in some of the mountain scenery in that country.

14 대화를 듣고, 두 사람이 이야기하고 있는 사진을 고르시오.

M Hey, who's this a picture of? I didn't know you had a sister.

W I don't. That's actually a picture of my grandmother from a few decades ago. She looks much different now than she did in the past, doesn't she?

M Yeah, I never would've guessed it's her in this photograph. To begin with, ____.

W You're right. My grandmother got tired of taking care of her hair, so she cut it off. Now it's fairly short and curly.

M Here's something strange. The woman in the photograph ________________________________, but I don't remember seeing your grandmother in them.

W ________________________________. She used to wear glasses, but now she doesn't since she wears contact lenses instead.

M Oh, well, that makes sense. You know, now that I think about it, your grandmother in this picture looks kind of like you.

W Do you think so? Many people have said ____________, but I don't see it.

M Yeah, there is. You both have similar eyes and noses.

W I'll be sure to tell my grandmother you said that the next time I see her.

15 대화를 듣고, 여자가 아들이 깨어난 직후 무엇을 할지 고르시오.

M 911, please state the nature of your emergency.

W ________________________________, and I'm not sure what to do.

M Okay, first, check to see if he's still breathing.

W Yes, he's breathing, but he hasn't woken up yet. He passed out a minute ago, and I'm starting to get worried.

M Can you tell me ____?

W He was outside running around with his friends. They'd been playing a game for about thirty minutes or so when he suddenly just passed out.

M All right, ____. It's a hot day today, so he's probably ____. You need to cool him off a lot. I recommend putting a cold towel on his forehead ________________________________. Then, you need to give him ________________________________. And keep him on the ground for at least ten minutes.

W But what if he tries to stand up?

M He probably won't have the energy to. However, once he can walk, take him inside the house to a cool place. He'll be all right, but you should take him to the hospital ________________________________.

16 다음을 듣고, 서울의 현재 날씨를 고르시오.

W Most of the country is ____ that has been steadily approaching the country from Taiwan. It finally made landfall last night near Busan, and it's causing heavy rains all across the country's southern provinces. There have been reports of ________________________________, and citizens are urged to take caution when driving. The government is even recommending that people stay indoors until the typhoon passes. Meanwhile, the storm is expected to ____, where it should cause even more damage. Seoul should face the brunt of the storm tomorrow although it's currently experiencing only light rain. ____, and tomorrow, the capital should receive several inches of rain. The Han River is expected to rise by several feet, which will cause flooding all throughout various parts of Gyeonggi Province. Meteorologists predict ____, but it will still remain here long enough to cause extensive damage.

17 대화를 듣고, 남자가 먹은 음식에 들어 있는 칼로리가 총 얼마인지 고르시오.

W What's the matter? You don't look particularly happy today.

M I started a diet last week, but ____________________ ____________________. It's getting really frustrating.

W I didn't know you were dieting. Actually, I'm on a diet too, so I always carry this book with me. It tells me how many calories are in various foods, so I can be careful about what I eat at all times.

M Hey, do you think you could check out some of the foods I had today?

W Sure. Just tell me what you ate.

M Okay. ____________________. And then I had some spaghetti for lunch.

W According to this book, the apple had ____________________ ____________________, so you're doing well there. And I saw you had sauce with your spaghetti, ____________________ ____________________. Did you have anything else?

M Um, well, I had two cheeseburgers for a snack. I was a little hungry in the afternoon.

W That's why you aren't losing any weight. ____________________ ____________________. You had over 1,000 calories just for a snack. If you keep eating like that, you're never going to lose any weight.

M Yeah, but they taste really good.

18 다음을 듣고, 이야기의 내용과 일치하지 않는 것을 고르시오.

M Good morning, everyone. This is Captain Reynolds speaking. We're about to begin our final descent into Paris, where we'll be on the ground ____________________ ____________________. The temperature in Paris is a balmy seventy-two degrees Fahrenheit, so it's a beautiful spring day in the city. The weather forecast ____________________ ____________________, so be sure to get out and enjoy the city as soon as we land. By the time we arrive, ____________________. We're going to be landing at Gate 19 at approximately nine thirty-five, which makes us about ten minutes early thanks to those tailwinds we caught ____________________

____________________. We'd like to thank all of you for flying with us today. If Paris is your final destination, ____________________ ____________________. If you are transferring to another city, there are agents waiting at the gate who can provide you ____________________ ____________________. Have a great day, everybody.

19 대화를 듣고, 남자가 새 컴퓨터를 사지 못하는 이유를 고르시오.

M Check out that computer over there. It's the latest model and is so much better than the one I'm using now.

W In that case, ____________________? I know you use a computer for your work all the time, so this upgraded version might help you become more productive.

M I'd love to buy it, but it's got a steep price tag.

W ____________________ ____________________?

M I never make big purchases with cash. I use my credit card for items like this since it's easier to get my money refunded if it gets lost, broken, or stolen.

W What are you waiting for then? Take out your credit card, and buy that computer. Oh, wait. You forgot to bring your card, didn't you?

M No, it's not that. It's just that ____________________ ____________________ because I've been using my card for several purchases lately.

W Couldn't you purchase it ____________________ ____________________? I know most stores allow that.

M I don't think ____________________ ____________________. Remember that I just moved last month, so I had to buy a lot of things for my house.

W Oh, well. I hope you can get this computer sooner rather than later.

20 대화를 듣고, 여자가 남자에게 해 준 충고가 아닌 것을 고르시오.

W Why are you still at work? I could hear you coughing from the elevator. ____________________ ____________________.

M I'd love to, but I've got too much work to finish here.

W That's ridiculous. So, are you at least doing anything to try to get better?

M Not really. I haven't seen a doctor because I know he's going to tell me to take some medicine and stay in bed. ____.

W I'd say you have more than a cold. You'd better go home and get some rest. And drink a lot of liquids. They'll help you get over your sickness more quickly.

M ____?

W Yes. My father's a doctor, so he taught me a lot. You need to eat some hot foods, like soup or something similar. And also take some vitamin C tablets, which ____.

M Okay, I'll stop at one on my way home.

W That's good to hear. But, most important of all, ______ ____. Your body needs to get stronger, and sleep will help you do that.

M I'll be sure to take your advice. Thanks for everything.

21 다음을 듣고, 화자의 감정 변화를 가장 잘 나타낸 것을 고르시오.

W Six days ago, I was surfing my favorite clothing store's website. While browsing their selections, I saw the most wonderful coat. It was made of cashmere and could be worn either casually or formally. And it was even being offered at a bargain price. Naturally, ______________ ____. I simply couldn't wait to receive it, especially since I was planning to wear it to an upcoming work event. Finally, I saw the deliveryman pull up to my house with a big package. It felt like my birthday as ______________________ ____.

____ than the one I had expected. The color was right, but the style wasn't the same. ______________________________ ______________________________________, too. I checked to see if there had been a mistake, but that was really the coat I had ordered. I was so steamed ______________________________ ______________________________________. I'm never going to purchase anything from them again.

22 다음을 듣고, 지도에서 남자의 집을 고르시오.

M Hello, Gina. This is Chuck. I was expecting ______________ ____, but I got your answering machine instead. Okay, I'm going to leave some directions on how to get to my house for tonight's party. I hope they make sense because I might not be able to answer the phone if you call. Now, you'll be coming from your house on Oak Street. So ____ ______________________________________ Oak Street and Second Avenue. You'll need to go past Third Avenue. However, once you get to Fourth Avenue, I want you to take a right and go one block. That's going to lead to Franklin Road, where you should hang ______________ ____.

My house is located ______________________________________ ______________________________. ______________________________ ______________________________________.

There will probably be several cars in front of the house, so you can't miss it. I hope to see you soon.

23 다섯 개의 대화문을 듣고, 자연스럽지 <u>않은</u> 것을 고르시오.

① **M** Do you have any plans for this ______________________ ____?

W I haven't really given it too much thought. Did you have something in mind?

② **W** Have you decided ______________________________________ ______________________________?

M No, I haven't. Everything on the menu looks so delicious that I can't make up my mind.

③ **M** You look really happy about something. ______________ ______________________________________?

W Mr. Park just gave me my new work assignment, and he's going to let me be the team leader.

④ **W** We're running a little late, so we ought ______________ ____.

M Are you sure about that? At this time of night, traffic in that area might not be so good.

⑤ **M** I haven't been feeling very well these days. I think that I'm coming down with something.

W Yeah, he told me that I have the flu, so ______________ ____.

24 대화를 듣고, 두 사람에 대해 유추할 수 있는 것을 고르시오.

W Let's go to the furniture department. We need to purchase some furniture for our house since there's practically nothing in it now.

M It'd be nice to furnish our house, but ____?

W I know ____, but we really need some things. I mean, we've got a bed and a dresser, but we don't even own a couch.

M Yeah, I suppose it doesn't look good when we have company and don't have a sofa for them to sit on.

W It was so embarrassing when Jack and Lisa were at our place the other night.

M All right, so let's get a sofa. ____?

W I was thinking of getting a dining table with four chairs. That should be perfect for whenever we're eating alone or when we've got another couple over. And you'll be able to work at it when we aren't having dinner.

M I like the sound of that. Hey, how about that wardrobe over there? ____.

W I don't know if we can afford it. Let's just keep them in the closet for now.

25 다음을 듣고, 쇼트 프로그램과 롱 프로그램 점수를 합산한 점수가 가장 높아 스케이트 대회에서 우승한 사람이 누구일 지 고르시오.

W Now, let's move to the recent news from women's figure skating, where the gold medal was awarded tonight. The top three performers in the short program were Katrina Schmidt, ____, Mayu Fujikawa ____, and Emily Bender ____. The short program was one of the most exciting in recent memory as a number of skaters performed exceptionally well. However, those three came out best out of all of the performers. Now, let's take a look at ____. We have the top five performers from the long program for you. Nancy Logan won ____

____ 97 points. Unfortunately, her short program routine, where ____, kept her from achieving overall victory. In second place was Mayu Fujikawa ____, and in third was Lisa Thompson with 94 points. Emily Bender and Katrina Schmidt both got scores of 92 in their long programs.

26 대화를 듣고, 아들의 마지막 질문에 대한 여자의 응답으로 알맞은 것을 고르시오.

M Mom, we learned about Thomas Edison in history class today, but I don't think ____. Do you know anything about him?

W Well, I know a few things. For example, he was one of the greatest inventors in all history. I believe that ____.

M Wow, he must have been really busy inventing things.

W That's true, but he also had a huge number of technicians and scientists working for him. He was a brilliant man, but ____.

M What exactly did he invent? I know he was the first person ____.

W Actually, he wasn't the first person to make a light bulb. Several other people managed to make light bulbs before Edison did. However, he was the first to make one that was practical and could be sold to the public. ____.

M Oh, I didn't realize that.

W Most people don't. But that still doesn't mean he didn't accomplish great things. There were also several other important inventions ____.

M Like what? Can you tell me?

27 대화를 듣고, 두 사람이 딸에게 취할 태도로 올바르지 <u>않은</u> 것을 고르시오.

M I'm concerned about Sue since it seems ____.

W I agree. I think she might be hanging out with some

students who are bad influences. Her grades have been dropping lately, and, if they keep getting worse, ______________________________.

M We've got to do something. What do you suggest?
W Hmm… We could stop granting her permission to go out on the weekends so that she'd have to stay home and study.
M I like that idea. And why don't we make sure ______________________________. She's always exhausted and could really use a good night's sleep.
W All right. But do you think we should forbid her from seeing her friends?
M I don't think that's right. ______________________________.
W I'm not so sure, but we'll go with your idea for now. But I definitely feel we should go over her homework with her every night. That way we'll confirm that she's doing it and doing it well.
M I agree. You can look at the humanities while I'll cover math and science.
W ______________________________.

28 다음을 듣고, 화자의 의견에 동의하는 진술을 고르시오.

M ______________________________.

It's important to protect and preserve the environment, but people also need to develop places in order to erect homes and buildings, construct roads, and complete other construction projects. It's a fine line people are walking: ______________________________, but they simply can't leave it alone, or else humans won't be able to prosper. That's why I believe the government ______________________________. These could be areas that are abundant in wildlife. For example, there's a huge forest near my home which is teeming with animals. Some local developers ______________________________, but I don't think they should be allowed to do so. If they cut down the forest, what'll happen to all of the animals? Instead, the developers should use land that has already been developed. This way, they can construct their new buildings ______________________________.

29 대화를 듣고, 두 사람이 먹을 음식을 모두 고르시오.

W I'm so glad we decided to come here for dinner. I haven't eaten anything all day long, and this is my favorite restaurant.
M I know what you mean. The chicken wings here are really delicious.
W Are you going to be ordering those? I was thinking about it, but I'm going to go with ______________________________.
M That's a nice, healthy choice. As for me, I'm going to get the potato skins for starters. I love the way they cook them here. What about your entrée?
W I'm definitely getting ______________________________. And I think I'll get the baked potato for my side dish.
M Yum, that sounds absolutely delicious. I'm not nearly as hungry as you though, so I think I'm just going to order the roast fish.
W What? ______________________________? You tried my fish but couldn't stand it.
M Oh, right. That completely slipped my mind. On second thought, instead of that, I'm going to have the broiled scallops. And I'm going to get some corn with it.
W Those are much better choices.
M Okay, so ______________________________.

30 다음을 듣고, 화자의 마지막 말에 이어질 내용으로 가장 알맞은 것을 고르시오.

W You're all visiting the United States on a business trip next week. You need to remember that American business culture is much different than ours, so ______________________________.

First, when you meet American businessmen, they're all going to shake hands with you. If there are any women, they also might offer to shake hands with you. Should they do that, ______________________________.
Then they're going to chat with you for a few minutes.

They'll ask you about your flight and how you like the country. ____
_________________________. You want to seem positive in all of your comments. And don't make any comments about what the Americans look like. Even if the person is handsome or beautiful, _________________________
_____________________. And definitely don't say anything about a person who might be overweight or not be very good-looking. If you do that, _________________________
_________________________. So, when meeting American businessmen for the first time, you'd better...

〔31-34〕 31번부터 34번까지는 문제와 보기를 모두 듣고 푸는 문제입니다. 대화나 이야기를 듣고, 영어로 들려주는 질문에 대한 알맞은 답을 고르시오.

31

W I'm absolutely stunned to be standing up here in front of everyone this evening. After all, there are so many others ____
_____________________________. And I'd like for everyone to know that there's no way that _____________
____.
I owe my success to a lot of different people. These people have made tonight possible, and, without them, I'm sure I never would have been able to become an actor in the first place. First, I'd like to thank my parents Allen and Wendy for encouraging me when most people doubted I'd ever make it in acting. _________
_________________________, and they made sure I never gave up my dream. And my director, John Davidson, was tremendous, as were the rest of _________
_________________________. They're the ones who should be up here tonight instead of me.

Q: *What is this speech for?*

M ① To promote a movie
② To accept an award
③ To congratulate her parents
④ To announce a new film
⑤ To give some advice

32

M One of the most important holidays in the United States falls on July 4. _________________________
_________________________________, for it is the day back in 1776 when the American colonies declared their independence from England, their colonial master. For more than 200 years, Americans have ____
_________________________________. As it's a national holiday in the U.S., the majority of people get the day off from work. While not so many people take the time to reflect upon their freedoms anymore, countless Americans attempt to make the most out of their day off. Since Independence Day falls in the summer, many Americans ____.
They may have picnics with their families, go camping, watch parades, or even attend baseball games. Additionally, they often have cookouts or barbecues, where hamburgers, hotdogs, and steaks are the main foods. ____
_________________________.

Q: *What is this talk about?*

M ① Why the Americans declared their independence from England
② The history of July 4 from 1776 to the present
③ The foods that most Americans eat on July 4
④ How many Americans celebrate Independence Day
⑤ Where Americans socialize on Independence Day

33

W Are you still watching that football game? I thought you said it was about to end thirty minutes ago.
M There are still two minutes left. Sometimes _____________
____.
W I don't know how you can stand watching those games. You should try another sport like soccer.
M You've got to be kidding. That's the most boring sport imaginable. ____
____.
W That's yet another sport which takes forever to end.
M I guess you're right about that. _________________________
____.

W I think the reason is that my brothers both played it when they were young. But, come to think of it, they also played volleyball, and I don't enjoy that sport either.

M I sometimes just think you don't appreciate sports at all. You ought to give them a chance. They're great exercise and really fun to play and watch.

W I don't know. ___________________________

____________________________.

M Anyway, the game's about to finish. Let me get back to watching it.

Q : *Which of the following sports do the speakers like in common?*

M ① Baseball
　② Volleyball
　③ Football
　④ Basketball
　⑤ Soccer

34

M Good afternoon, Mrs. Lee. What brings you here today?

W I think Choco's got something wrong with her skin. She keeps scratching herself all the time and won't stop.

M ___________________________________?
For example, has she been suffering from a loss of appetite? Or perhaps she may seem lethargic at times?

W Oh, goodness no. I don't think I've ever seen a more active dog. Choco loves to run around the house and play with her toys. ___________________________

____________________________.

M That's good to hear. I was worried it might be something serious.

W No, it seems the constant scratching is all that's bothering her. ___________________________

____

____________________________.

M Okay, I think I know what her problem is then. Let me take some skin samples first, but that's really just a formality.

W Why is that? What's wrong?

M She probably picked up some fleas while she was outside. But don't worry. I'll give her some special

shampoo and medicine, and ___________________________

____________________________.

W That's great to hear.

Q : *Which is the relationship between the speakers?*

M ① A dog owner and a pet shop owner
　② A veterinarian and a nurse
　③ A nurse and a dog groomer
　④ A veterinarian and a dog owner
　⑤ A pet shop owner and a veterinarian

35 다음을 듣고, 이어지는 영어 질문에 답하시오.

M At twelve o'clock in the afternoon, Sally and Lisa go to the beach and ___________________________

____________________________. Sally already had eight seashells while Lisa had none. Sally finds a pretty seashell ____________________________, but Lisa looks harder, so she finds a pretty seashell ___________________________

____________________________.

Q : *What time will Lisa have the same number of seashells as Sally?*

36 주어진 시간 동안 아래 지문을 주의 깊게 읽고, 대화를 들은 후 질문에 답하시오. 〔1분〕

W Are you ready to go? We're going to be late.

M Hold on a second while I do some banking.

W How are you going to do any banking from your office? Isn't it a little late to be calling your banker?

M No, I'm doing Internet banking. I haven't paid a couple of my most recent bills, ___________________________

____________________________.

W Is that something new? ___________________________

____________________________.

M It's been around for a while, but not everyone uses it.

W Well, I can understand that. After all, with all of those computer hackers out there, what happens if someone unauthorized gets access to your account? ___________________________

____________________________.

M I suppose that could happen, but it's actually pretty safe.

W I'm not so confident about that. ___________________________

____________________________?

M In 1897, Bram Stoker ___________________

____.

In it, he chronicled the story of Count Dracula, a vicious, bloodsucking vampire from Transylvania. While many people believe Stoker created the Dracula legend himself, stories of vampires have actually been around for hundreds, if not thousands, of years. _________________________________, vampires are undead creatures. That is, they are neither living nor dead but something in between. Vampires survive

____

____.

However, when a vampire bites a person, usually in the neck, that person will soon become a vampire. Legends attribute many special powers to vampires. _________________________, _________________ _________________, and can sometimes turn themselves into a bat, a wolf, or even a cloud of gas. In addition, vampires show no reflections in mirrors. ___________ _________________________, vampires can be defeated. A person can kill a vampire by driving a wooden stake into its heart. Also, vampires, being evil creatures, react badly to crosses and holy water. And vampires cannot be exposed to the sun. If any sunlight touches them,

____.

37 **Which of the following questions does the talk answer?**

38 **Which of the following is NOT true about vampires?**

M I've been doing a lot of thinking about my job lately. I'm not sure if I should stay at my current position or not. In fact, ___________________________ ____.

W Really? What's wrong with the job you're doing now?

M Well, it's just really boring. ___________________ _________________________________. It's just that I had been hoping to do something a little more exciting with my life.

W In that case, _____________________________ _________________ and look for a position in another field?

M You know... I'd love to do that, but what happens if things don't go too well? My job is completely boring, but it's still a job. What if I don't succeed in something new?

W Who cares? _______________________________ _______________. Even if you fail, it'll still be a learning experience for you.

M I don't know. At first, I thought getting a new job would be all right, but _______________________ _________________. What happens if I don't get hired by someone else?

W You've got a lot of talent and abilities. I'm sure someone will give you a job.

M Do you think so? I'm not so sure about that.

W Of course I do. Anyway, you only live once. Take a risk, and try to find a job you'll actually enjoy. ___________ ____.

39 **Which of the following is NOT true about the man?**

40 **What is the woman trying to say?**

01 다음을 듣고, 이야기와 그림 속의 상황이 일치하지 <u>않는</u> 것을 고르시오.

W My friend is a painter ____. Last week, she visited a local farm and subsequently created a wonderful painting of a rural farming scene. I saw it and realized that she had completely captured the way a farm looks. The focus of the piece was ________________________ of the painting. To the right of the barn ________________________ and other birds swimming in it. ________________________ which are grazing in the field located on the left-hand side of the painting. And, ________________________, so it's ________________________ and also giving off a red light. I was so impressed by this painting. I grew up on a farm, and she accurately managed to depict the essence of a farm. Her painting really reminded me of my earlier life.

02 대화를 듣고, 여자는 다음 중 누구와 친한 친구가 될 수 있을 것인지 고르시오.

M I just had a huge argument with my best friend. I don't think we're ever going to talk to each other again.

W That's too bad. Perhaps you need to choose your friends better in the future.

M I suppose you're right. Well, ____?

W That's a good question. I'm a pretty outgoing person, so ____. I don't think that would be a good match.

M Yeah, you're probably correct about that. What else?

W I like to go out a lot, so I need to be friends with a person ________________________. Oh, and my best friend should be a good listener, too.

M Yeah, that's a really important characteristic. That's key for me as well.

W There's one more... ________________________. I can't stand hanging out with people who never pay for their fair share or who are always begging to borrow money from you.

M It looks like you've thought about this a lot.

W I have, and that's why I have a really good best friend. ____ and almost never have any problems.

03 다음을 듣고, 이 이야기가 무엇을 위한 것인지 고르시오.

M ____ during my recent trip to your city. In particular, I wish to note that the hotel you set me up in was excellent; the room was lovely, and the food was fantastic. I would also like you to say thanks to Bob Davies and Fred Thompson ____ concluded. In addition, everyone in your office was polite and showed the efficiency and professionalism I had expected from your company. ____. Finally, I want to extend a personal invitation to anyone in your company to visit my company and city anytime. I'm not sure if I can provide the same level of hospitality as you and your people did, but I will do my best. Once again, I am really ____.

04 대화를 듣고, 여자에게 주어진 임무가 <u>아닌</u> 것을 고르시오.

M Can I see you for a moment?

W Of course. What can I do for you?

M First, I need the Williams account file ________________________ I've made. ________________________ tomorrow. Also, can you make a reservation for me on a flight to Incheon on March 24? I'll be returning on March 27. ________________________, too.

W No problem, sir. I'll get on it right away. ____?

M Yes. The computer specialist is coming to my office this afternoon to check my computer for viruses, but I'm going to be in meetings all afternoon. Please make sure he gets in, but stay in the office while he works. I don't want him copying anything or ___________________________ ___________________________.

W I'm positive there won't be any problems with that since he's very reliable.
M I know, but we have a lot of sensitive material and need to be careful.
W I understand. ___________________________ ___________________________. Is that everything you need me to do?
M That's it for now. I'm going to lunch and then those meetings. See you tomorrow.

05 다음을 듣고, 화자의 심정을 가장 잘 나타낸 것을 고르시오.

W I've had ___________________________, and sometimes it seems like it's never going to change. For example, I'd been dating the same guy for two years, but his company just transferred him to another office, so he moved all the way across the country. We had to break up because of that. Additionally, I feel like ___________________________. It isn't stimulating at all, so I don't get any satisfaction out of it. I'd love to find another one, but ___________________________, so I doubt I'd be able to get hired anywhere else. Finally, I'm probably going to have to move to a smaller apartment because my neighborhood is getting more expensive. Rent rates are rising, and ___________________________. It seems like nothing is going right for me nowadays. I sure wish things would turn around and ___________________________.

06 대화를 듣고, 영화에 대한 화자들의 의견이 바르게 반영된 것을 고르시오.

W How was your past weekend?
M It was boring except for the movie I watched on Saturday night.
W I saw one on Saturday, too. What did you see?
M I went to that science fiction movie that was based on the television show. ___________________________ ___________________________.

W I don't particularly care for science fiction. My husband and I went to a drama about some people in Los Angeles. How was your movie?
M Well, to begin with, ___________________________ ___________________________. Additionally, ___________________________ ___________________________, and the story itself was pretty good with lots of funny dialog. The only problem was the music. It just didn't seem to match the mood of the movie. ___________________________?
W Well, I had mixed feelings about it. For one thing, the acting and story were quite good. Those really impressed me a lot.
M But what did you dislike about the movie? There was obviously something.
W You're right. I thought it had too much bad language and violence in it. ___________________________ ___________________________.
M That's too bad. I guess I won't bother watching it in the future.

07 다섯 개의 대화문을 듣고, 자연스럽지 않은 것을 고르시오.

① M Excuse me, ___________________________ ___________________________? I'm trying to catch the seven-thirty train.
    W It's twenty-five after seven. You'd better hurry if you don't want to be late.
    M Thanks a lot. ___________________________.

② W And then I told him I didn't have time to meet until next weekend.
    M Oh, so ___________________________?
    W He wasn't happy, but he understood my situation.

③ M I'm sorry, but Joey isn't home right now. ___________________________ ___________________________?
    W Thanks. It's Sue from school. Can you ask him to call me later?
    M Sure, I can do that for you. I'll have him contact you as soon as he gets home.

④ W So, ___________________________ ___________________________?
    M He told me I need to get some rest because I've been working too hard.
    W In that case, why don't we go hiking this weekend?

It should be a lot of fun.

⑤ M I'm really sorry, but I'm going to be late for dinner tonight.

W Oh? ____
________________?

M Traffic is bad since there was an accident on the road.

08 다음을 듣고, 이야기 속의 This가 무엇인지 고르시오.

W ____
that deals with the thoughts of men on various subjects. In particular, ideas on where we come from, our existence in the universe, ethics, logic, and the meaning of life are all central to this discipline. Some of the most famous practitioners have ________________
________________, ________________.
Plato, Socrates, and Aristotle are among the most famous of the Greek thinkers associated with this field. Plato, who was Socrates's student, ________________
________________, and his works are often used as primary sources of instruction and study. His student Aristotle didn't agree with many of these methods, so he developed his own methods of inquiry, ________________
________________. In the recent past, the most important practitioners have come from Germany and include such famous thinkers as Immanuel Kant and Friedrich Hegel.

09 대화를 듣고, 남자의 마지막 말에 대한 여자의 응답으로 알맞은 것을 고르시오.

W Good morning, this is the First Bank of New York. This is Betty White speaking. How can I help you?

M Good day, Mrs. White. This is Scott Andrews. We had an appointment for two o'clock this afternoon, ________
________________.

W May I ask why you can't make the appointment, Mr. Andrews?

M Of course. My company is sending me out of town today on a business trip. ________________
________________, and I can't get out of it.

W I understand. So we'd better reschedule our appointment, hadn't we? Let's see. Today is Tuesday. ____?

M I'm sorry, but that's not good for me. I won't be back in town until Friday evening.

W Then we can meet sometime next week. ________________
________________.

M Actually, I was hoping to meet sooner than that. I need to take care of this matter before next Monday.

W We're open on Saturday morning until noon. I wasn't planning to come in, but I suppose that I could make an exception.

M ____.
How does ten Saturday morning sound to you?

10 다음을 듣고, 이 이야기가 어떤 질문에 대한 대답인지 고르시오.

M Tea has been drunk in various parts of the world, the Far East in particular, since ancient times. Only after Western explorers reached these lands during the Middle Ages was tea brought to the countries of Europe. ________________
________________, all of which depend upon the culture. In the West, black tea is the preferred drink. Many people take it with sugar and either milk or cream. ____,
where four in the afternoon is considered "tea time." Additionally, ________________
________________. However, Russians enjoy black tea with lemon or honey and drink it after every meal. In the East, green tea is the preferred choice, and many people believe it contains healthy properties.
____
________________, an elaborate ritual in which the setting of dishes, the making of the tea, and the pouring and drinking are ________________
________________.

11 대화를 듣고, 여자가 돌려 받게 될 금액이 얼마인지 고르시오.

M Good evening. ____
________________?

W Yes, I think so. I've got this sweater I'd like to purchase, and I've also got a pair of blue jeans.

M Okay, the sweater costs fifty dollars while the jeans are on sale, so ____. That's quite a bargain you're getting.

W I agree. That's why I'm purchasing them. By the way, when is the sale ending?

M Actually, today is the last day of the sale, ____ now unless you like paying higher prices.

W Hmm... That's a good point. I tell you what. I think ____. That's probably the smart thing to do. Oh, I've also got this card I'd like to use with my purchase. I'm not exactly sure what it does though.

M Ah, this is a family card which gives you five percent back on everything you purchase here.

W Well, that sounds great. So, do you just give me the discount right here?

M No. You pay the full price here, and then you take your receipt to the counter downstairs ____.

12 대화를 듣고, 이 상황에 가장 잘 어울리는 영어 속담을 고르시오.

W I heard your new Internet business is doing really well. Congratulations.

M Thanks. It's really growing faster than I'd ever expected. I think I'll have to hire three new people ____.

W I wish I could have my own business. I don't particularly like my job.

M What's stopping you then? ____.

W I know. It's just that it's a huge step. I'm nervous about investing my money and time into something I'm not sure will work.

M ____. Find something you really like because if you're not enjoying yourself, you won't be happy. Then do some research on it. Finally, ___________________________________ for the first six months since most new businesses don't make a profit at first.

W Now you're making me even more nervous. I don't think I'll ever have that much money.

M ____, you can do it.

W I don't know if I'm ready to do so much work and take such a big gamble.

M There is some risk involved, ____.

13 다음을 듣고, 이것이 누가 누구에게 하는 이야기인지 고르시오.

M It's a pleasure to be with everyone today. It's an election year, and ____. Thanks to my leadership, the economy is stronger than ever, and experts predict even more future growth thanks to the tax cuts I had enacted. ____. We're in the middle of an unprecedented economic boom, so, if you want it to continue, you'll reelect me next month. In addition to keeping the economy running, I'm going to make sure the federal government intrudes on your lives as little as possible. As I've always said, ____. My opponent wants to pass legislation that will control too many aspects of your lives. I say that people tend to know what's best for themselves and don't need the government to tell them what to do. And you'll get more of this hands-off approach ____.

14 대화를 듣고, 두 사람이 이야기하고 있는 동작을 고르시오.

W I was wondering if you could give me some advice on making ____. I'm particularly concerned about my thighs.

M Then jogging, riding a bike, and doing aerobics are the best things to do. Here's one for you... ____ is great for toning and firming the legs.

W What kind of exercise is that? Could you show me how to do it?

M Just lie on your back like I'm doing now. Lift your legs,

and then ______________________________
__________________________. But make sure
your elbows are on the floor and aren't raised.

W Okay, ____________________________________?
It feels somewhat strange.

M But that's exactly what you should be doing. Now, lift
your legs higher in the air, and move them in a circular
motion __________________________________
______________.

W Am I doing it properly?

M Just raise your legs a little more, and then you'll have it.
Yes, that's perfect.

W I can already feel my legs burning. This isn't going to
hurt later, is it?

M ______________________________, but, after a
while, your legs will look and feel great.

15 대화를 듣고, 대화 후에 남자가 할 행동을 고르시오.

W ____?
You look like you lost your best friend.

M As a matter of fact, I have. We had a big fight yesterday,
and he said he never wants to talk to me again.

W I'm so sorry about that. What happened to cause the
fight?

M It was about money. He lent me a hundred dollars
two months ago, but I still haven't paid him back.
____
______________________________.

W Have you tried borrowing money from your parents or
someone else?

M I thought of that, but then ____________________
______________________.

W That's a good point. Maybe you could pay him a small
amount of money each week. You just need to call him,
say you made a mistake, and ______________________
______________________.

M That's a good idea. Thanks for your help. The only
problem is that my next payday isn't for another week,
so I can't pay him anything now.

W If he's a true friend, he'll understand. Apologize to
him, and say that ______________________________
______________________.

M I appreciate your help. Thanks for your advice.

16 다음을 듣고, 이 내용에 대한 예로 알맞은 것을 고르시오.

W Every country has its own unique food and customs for
food consumption. Much of this is influenced by the
country's climate, culture, and terrain. In Asia, many
nations eat large amounts of rice ____________________
____.
In contrast, Europeans and
North Americans eat lots of bread, which comes from
wheat. The climates in these lands are suitable for
growing wheat. Additionally, ________________________
______________________________________ because
of their beliefs. For example, some religions do not
condone the eating of beef because __________________
______________________________. Other people
don't consume pork because pigs are unclean animals
in their belief system. Finally, ____________________
______________________________. Countries
near the sea have diets heavy in seafood because fishing
grounds are so close by. Meanwhile, mountainous
countries have little arable land, so their fields are used
to grow grains and vegetables, not for grazing cows. In
contrast, flat prairie lands are ideal for raising cattle.

17 대화를 듣고, 다음 중 대화 속에서 언급되지 <u>않은</u> 것을 고르시오.

W Why don't you tell me exactly __________________
______________________?

M I have three children in my family, so we'll require at
least four bedrooms and two bathrooms. The bigger the
house, the better it is.

W That's not a problem. We have several of those kinds of
homes ____________________________________.

M Great. Also, since my kids are all attending school, I
need a house in a good school district and ____________
______________________________________.

W Of course. I should be able to find you a place close
to the local schools. What about your budget? Do you
have ____
______________________?

M I'd love to be able to spend less than $1,500 a month
______________________________________.

W Well, that's going to make it somewhat more difficult
since you need such a large home, but I'll see what's

available.

M Oh, and there's one more thing. I'd really appreciate it if the places you show me _______________ _______________________________. They're pretty active, so they need a place to run around.

W Sure, most of the homes in this area have yards.

18 대화를 듣고, 두 사람의 직업이 무엇인지 고르시오.

M Do you think everyone has a job that _______________ _______________________________?

W I'm not sure. My brother is a teacher, and he's one of the shyest people I know. I guess he's a different person when he's in front of his class.

M You're certainly different than him. _______________ _______________________________.

W What do you mean?

M You're so creative even when you aren't working with flowers in your shop. I've seen your drawings and paintings, and they're excellent.

W Having creativity is necessary in my profession. I have to prepare for so many events, like weddings, funerals, and parades, and _______________________________ _______________________________.

M I'm certainly glad you took care of all the flowers for my wedding.

W Well, what about your personality? It certainly doesn't match your job. _______________________________ _______________________________.

M That's what my wife says. I actually wanted to be a fireman because I like helping people. But you know, when I'm in a courtroom standing in front of the jury and looking a criminal in the eye, _______________ _______________________________.

W Maybe your personality goes with your job after all.

19 다음을 듣고, 이 이야기의 내용이 어떤 장르에 속하는지 고르시오.

M The large number of crimes over the weekend has shocked local residents. _______________________________ _______________________________, and a convenience store on Palm Street was robbed at 2 a.m. on Saturday morning. A large amount of cash was stolen, but no one was hurt. Police say that all four crimes may be connected, and they are searching for members of a local gang that may be responsible. Residents are advised to _______________________________ _______________________________ when opening the door to strangers. During one of the robberies, the criminals pretended to be gas inspectors checking for leaks. They tied up the elderly couple and then ransacked the house, taking all of the valuables. Although shaken up, the couple was, fortunately, _______________________________ _______________________________. If anyone has any information regarding these crimes, call Crime Stoppers at 555-6789, or stop by a local police station. _______________________________ _______________________________, and _______________________________ _______________________________.

20 대화를 듣고, 앞으로 소년이 잠자리에 들 시각을 고르시오.

M Mom, I'd like to talk about my daily schedule. I think _______________________________.

W What's the matter with it?

M I'd really like to have some more free time, especially so that I can watch television. It would be great to be able to watch some TV before I go to bed every night.

W I don't think that's such a good idea. You're in high school now, and _______________________________ _______________________________.

M But I'm so busy all day that I never have any fun. I'm in school until six o'clock, and after that, I study at the art academy until eight p.m.

W Yes, and then you come home at eight thirty, do your homework for three hours, and then go to bed.

M It's not fair. All my friends' parents _______________ _______________________________.

W _______________________________

____________________________________.

M What if I went to bed half an hour later? Then I could watch something,

W Maybe. ____________________________________

____________________________. But if you're too tired and your grades go down, then we're going to end this experiment.

21 다음을 듣고, 그래프에 대해 사실이 <u>아닌</u> 것을 고르시오.

W The life expectancy for Koreans nowadays is greater than it has been at any point in the nation's history. There are many reasons for this dramatic improvement in how long people live. For example, ____________________

____________________, and the medical treatment Koreans receive is tremendously better than what it was merely thirty or forty years ago. The result is that ____________

____

____________________________________ but instead can focus on long-term goals and desires. A simple look at a graph will show how, in the past forty-four years, the life expectancy of the average Korean went ____________________________________

____________________________________. This is a number similar to those of the world's developed countries, showing that Korea has reached standards near what people in these countries have. ____________

____ is expected to stay around eighty years of age, this is welcome increase from past years.

22 대화를 듣고, 마지막 남자의 말을 완성하는 것을 고르시오.

M ____

____________________________________.

W It's been at least ten years. In fact, I don't believe we've seen each other since our high school graduation ceremony.

M Yeah, I've been out of touch with lots of people from school. ____________________________________,
but I didn't.

W I thought you'd wanted to become an engineer.

M I did, but I didn't study very hard at school. So, none of the good universities would accept me. I guess I should

have paid more attention in class and tried to plan for my future. What are you doing these days?

W ____

in Seoul, and I just got married a while ago.

M That's fantastic. You always studied hard, so __________

____. I was too busy having fun and playing games in school.

W Well, are you working somewhere around here?

M Yes, I'm employed at my father's store and help him out. It's an okay job I guess, ____________________

____________________________________.

W What do you think would have happened had you studied harder at school?

M If I had done my best...

23 다음을 듣고, 여자가 휴가에 대해 가장 만족했던 것을 고르시오.

W I just returned from my summer holiday, which was absolutely fantastic. My family went to a cabin by a lake in the mountains. ____________________________________

____________________________________.

Unfortunately, there was a downpour the first day, but we still entertained ourselves indoors by playing games and just chatting. On the second day, we went fishing, and my son caught a big trout. He was so proud of it. The day after that, we went hiking up a mountain and had a picnic at the top, ____________________________________

____________________________________. But the last day was even better. The local town sponsored this huge barbecue. There was a concert and a fireworks show.

____________________________________.

The fireworks simply ____________________________________

____________________________________. My children laughed and had a great time watching everything. I'm already planning our vacation for next summer, and

____________________________________.

24 대화를 듣고, 여자의 좌석 위치를 고르시오.

M Welcome to Cineplex Theater. How may I help you?

W Hi, I'd like to get a seat for the 8 p.m. showing of that action movie.

M We have tickets, but most of them have already been

sold. ________________________________, and
they're all on the ________________________________
________________________. Take a look at this seating chart,
and tell me what you like. The ones available are
marked in blue.

W I ________________________________,
so I'd prefer something as far away as possible.

M How about seat number twenty-four? It's pretty far
away from the screen.

W It is, but it's also on the far left-hand side near the wall,
so ________________________________.
Is there anything better?

M How about a seat in the aisle? What about this one
here? It's still empty.

W That's in the aisle, ________________________________
________________________. Isn't there anything in the last row?

M Yes, there is. This seat is free, and it's exactly what you
want. Here's your ticket. That will be eight dollars and
fifty cents, please.

W Here you are. Thanks for your help.

25 다음을 듣고, 원어민이 절대로 하지 <u>않을</u> 말이 무엇인지 고르시오.

M There are many expressions in English that English
speakers find offensive. Foreigners who meet English
speakers or visit their countries should be aware of
____
and then take care not to use them lest there be a bad
result. For example, one should ________________________
________________________________. Calling
someone "fat" is very insulting. In addition, just
about any negative remark on a person's appearance
may cause offense. Never ask people their height or
why they have a handicap or other physical problem.
________________________________,
so refrain from saying that someone is "too old."
In fact, you shouldn't even ask how old a person is.
The clothes people wear let them express themselves,
so ________________________________.
In addition, there are many swear words that are
regularly used in English-language movies, but ________
________________________________. Finally, be
careful about saying something negative about a
person's politics or religion.

26 대화를 듣고, 남자가 제출해야 하는 것을 모두 고르시오.

W Good afternoon, sir. Welcome to the Elite Golf Club.
How can I be of service?

M I'm interested in joining your club and would like to
know ________________________________.

W That's not a problem at all. Here's our application
form. Please fill this out at your leisure, and then mail it
to the club or submit it in person.

M I'm sorry, but according to this, ________________________
________________________________. Why is that?

W Our club has a very expensive annual membership fee,
and we must ensure that you can afford it should you
join.

M Of course. There's one more thing I'd like to ask about.
I'm also required to provide ________________________
________________. Is this necessary?

W Absolutely, sir. We pride ourselves on having a top
safety record and ________________________________
________________________________. We don't
want those kinds of people in our club.

M That's good to know. Is there anything else I need to
bring?

W Yes, we require copies of ________________________________
________________________________.

M I'll take this home and mail it as soon as possible with
all the proper documents.

27 Why did the woman miss her flight?

W I recently had a terrible experience at the airport. I was
going to Tokyo from Beijing for an important meeting.
Unfortunately, ________________________________
________________________, so ________________________________.
By the time I got to the check-in counter, they had
stopped taking any more passengers. I was so upset that
the airline agent promised to get me on the first flight in
the morning, which was at 5 a.m. I had to be in Seoul
for an 11 a.m. meeting the next day, so I told her to
book the flight. Then, I tried to check into the airport
hotel, ________________________________,
so I had to spend the night in the passenger lounge.
________________________________, and I was
worried someone would steal my bags, so I hardly slept
at all. It was weird since no one else was in the airport

at night. It felt so strange being alone in such a big
building. __________________________________ .

28 Which of the following people agrees with the speaker?

M Some people __________________________________
__________________ . This is known as ________________
______________________ . Many countries or companies
have laws regarding this situation. In Korea, according
to law, the retirement age is sixty-five. However, some
companies force their employees to retire when they
are even younger. I have a problem with mandatory
retirement, especially because many people are being
forced to retire __________________________________
__________________________________ . Additionally,
many people in their sixties have accumulated a
wealth of experience and wisdom at their jobs and
are extremely valuable employees for their firms.

__________________________________ ,
then companies should find another way to enable them
to contribute. Also, many elderly people are unable
to survive just with their company or government
pensions. They need their salaries to live decent lives,
especially because __________________________________
__________________________ . The government
needs to change the current policy and let people work
until they want to retire.

29 Which of the following is NOT true about the conversation?

W What are we going to do this weekend?

M There's a baseball game on Saturday afternoon and a
basketball game on Sunday night. __________________
__________________________________ , and I already
have the tickets.

W You're going to both of them? I know you love sports,
but I think two games in one weekend are too much for
me.

M Come on. It'll be fun. You like baseball, and the home
team is trying to win enough games to make the
playoffs. You'll have a great time if you go.

W I'll go to the baseball game, but I certainly don't want

to see the basketball game. You know __________________
__________________________________ .

M The champs are coming to town. It's going to be a great
game.

W Sorry, but Sunday is our day to do something together
with our family. My mother wants us to come for
dinner.

M But I bought __________________________________
__________________________ .

W I'm sure one of your friends will buy them from you, or
you can just give them away instead.

M I guess __________________________________
__________________ . Call your mother, and tell her
that we'll be there.

30 Which is the best title for this talk?

W Our bodies get information from the environment
through the various senses. There are five of them, and
they are, in no particular order, __________________
__________________________________ . People are able
to hear thanks to their ears and the other auditory
organs found inside the head. What we hear as noise
are __________________________________
__________________________________ . The eyes are
connected to the brain by the optical nerves, and the
brain records the images the eyes see. The nose picks
up smells through a series of olfactory sensors in the
nasal passages. The tongue, mouth, and lips have
sensors __________________________________
__________________________ , both pleasant and not so
pleasant, that people experience. These allow people to
distinguish between a large number of different tastes.
The skin covers the entire body. Every skin cell contains
sensors that feel sensations __________________________

__________________________________ .

Without our senses, we would have a very difficult time
living in our world's environment.

〔31-34〕 31번부터 34번까지는 문제와 보기를 모두 듣고 푸는 문제입니다. 대화나 이야기를 듣고, 영어로 들려주는 질문에 대한 알맞은 답을 고르시오.

31

M My department supervisor got promoted to head manager last week, so we have a new supervisor in our department. So far, the new supervisor is excellent. In fact, she's much better than the person she replaced. ____ if they make a mistake. She knows a lot about her position, which makes our jobs much easier. She also always arrives at work on time and only takes an hour for lunch. The last boss would always come late and would often ____. Every day this week, she stayed late to help us finish a project in order to complete it by the deadline. Our previous supervisor was out the door at five o'clock sharp every day. Sometimes I wonder ____.

Anyway, I'm totally satisfied with my new boss. I just hope she doesn't get promoted, too.

Q : *Which is NOT a reason this speaker likes the new boss?*

M ① She always has lunch with the staff.
② She is never late for work.
③ She often stays late to help others.
④ She is very nice to the employees.
⑤ She does her job very well.

32

M May I see your ____ please, ma'am?

W Yes, officer. Here they are. Could you tell me what I did wrong?

M Actually, ____. First, you were driving ten kilometers ____. The posted limit is only sixty kilometers per hour, yet you were doing seventy.

W Sorry. I'm late for work, so I was in a hurry.

M That's no excuse, ma'am. Second, ____.

W I guess I forgot, but no one else was signaling, so why did you stop me?

M I stopped you because you also have a broken taillight cover ____ ____. Today would be a good time to do it.

W I'll go to the repair shop at lunchtime. Is that everything, officer?

M No, there's one more thing. You were ________________ ____, so try to keep a safe distance in the future. Here's your ticket. Please drive carefully from now on, ma'am.

W I will. Thanks for being so nice.

Q : *Which of the following offenses did the woman NOT commit?*

M ① She was too close to another car.
② She did not signal a lane change.
③ She was driving too fast.
④ She did not have her seatbelt on.
⑤ She had a broken car part.

33

W The English language has many expressions which can convey subtle meanings for events or people's personalities. Many expressions come from ________________ ____. An example is "____." This saying comes from the tale of a man with a basket of eggs. He was walking with a basket full of eggs in his arms while thinking about the dozens of chickens he would have ____. Some chickens he would sell for money, some he would cook for his family, and others he would keep to lay more eggs. Soon, he would have hundreds of chickens. ________________ ____ when he tripped, fell, and broke every egg in the basket. The moral of this fable is you shouldn't depend on something until it happens. The man was already thinking of chickens while he only had eggs and thus lost everything ________________ ____.

Q : *What is an example of "Don't count your chickens before they're hatched"?*

M ① A boy gets the birthday present he was hoping for from his parents.

② A student studies hard and receives a very good grade on an exam.

③ A woman buys a lottery ticket and then goes to look at new cars.

④ A man starts a business and becomes very successful after some time.

⑤ A little girl dreams of becoming a ballerina when she grows up.

34

M Yes, ma'am. How can I help you?

W I was just robbed. A man just stole my purse from my hands right on the street.

M Just relax, ma'am. I know ________________ ____________, but I need to ask you some questions. Please have a seat at my desk here. Okay, first, what's your name and address?

W I'm sorry, officer, but it was so shocking. My name is Jessica Smith, and I live at 120 Eastern Avenue.

M Now ________________ ____________?

W I was leaving the library near the university just down the street from here. I work there. This man drove by on a motorcycle and ________________ ____________ before I knew what was happening.

M What kind of motorcycle was he riding?

W Oh, I don't know much about them. It wasn't a big one. It was more like a scooter. I think it was white with red strips.

M All right. ________________________________?

W I didn't get a look at his face because he was wearing a helmet with a dark visor.

Q : *Where is this conversation taking place?*

M ① In a library
② In a police station
③ At 120 Eastern Avenue
④ At the motorcycle repair shop
⑤ At a university

35 다음을 듣고, 이어지는 영어 질문에 답하시오.

M Terry, Jimmy, and Fred share an apartment together. All three of them like watching television at their home at night. Terry usually watches television ________________ ____________ but ________________ because he goes out with his friends then. Jimmy doesn't watch TV as much as the others because he's a student and needs to study. He enjoys his favorite shows __________ ________________. Fred can be found in front of the television ________________ ____________ because he really loves it.

Q : *Which day of the week do all three roommates watch television together at home?*

36 주어진 시간 동안 아래 주어진 지문을 주의 깊게 읽고, 들려주는 질문에 답하시오. 〔1분〕

Q : *Which is NOT a difference between Western and Oriental medicine?*

〔37-38〕 다음을 듣고, 이어지는 두 개의 질문에 답하시오.

W Please allow me to introduce myself. My name is Park Heejin, and I'm thirty-nine years old. I was born in Busan and have two older sisters and one younger brother. ________________ ____________ but have since retired. I finished high school in 1987 and entered Seoul National University to study education. I graduated with my degree in 1992. I was employed as an elementary school teacher for three years ________________ ____________ for a year. Following that, I returned to Korea, where I found my current job, which is teaching English at a Seoul middle school. I got married in 1999 and now have two daughters. I like watching baseball and television dramas and __________ ________________. I love hiking, and my husband and I also enjoy socializing with our friends by going out to eat a lot. Reading is my other passion. ________________ ____________. There's nothing better than staying at home and reading a good book.

37 Which of the following is NOT true about the speaker?

38 Choose the title of a book which the speaker most likely wants to read.

39 Which TV program do the speakers like in common?

40 What is the reason the woman dislikes reality programs?

〔39-40〕 대화를 듣고, 이어지는 두 개의 질문에 답하시오.

M _________________________________ to go to the park.

W I guess we can spend the entire day here. My _________ _________________. Turn on the television, please.

M I don't know how you can watch soap operas. They are so unrealistic. My mother watches one show that has a character who has been married and divorced so many times I've lost track.

W Well, _________________________________ you like. They must be scripted. I don't believe those programs are spontaneous, and I bet those people are all paid actors.

M There's no script for those shows, and they aren't actors. Everything you see really happens. Hey, the TV guide says that new science fiction show is starting tonight at nine o'clock after the comedy hour.

W I forgot about that. I really want to see that show because _____________________________.

M Yeah, I can't wait to see it. Oh, the soccer game is on another channel right now. It's the Premier league. Can I change the channel?

W Wait until my show is over. You know I'm not a big fan of sports. People are always hitting each other and getting hurt. It's just too much. Why don't you record it?

M But it's my favorite team. _____________________.

W Okay, just wait until I set up the VCR to record my show.

01 다음을 듣고, 여자가 찾아갈 가게들이 순서대로 나열된 것을 고르시오.

W I've got some shopping to do today. There are a lot of things to buy, yet I'm pretty short of time. Fortunately, there's _________________________ _________________________. Now, let me think about the best way to do this. First, I need some flowers for my sister's birthday, so I think _________________________

_________________________.

Oh, I should _________________________ _________________________. She loves chocolate, and I heard that the shop is having a sale today. Then, I can cross the street and pick up the shoes I left to get fixed at the store last week after I broke a heel while working. Finally, I need _________________________

_________________________.

I don't want to carry it around everywhere and risk dropping it or anything.

02 대화를 듣고, 남자의 직업이 무엇인지 고르시오.

W How's your new job been going? _________________________ _________________________ because I haven't seen you around much lately.

M Well, the job's going quite well to tell the truth. I absolutely love it, especially because I don't have to wear a suit like I did at my previous job.

W Yeah, you were always at the office and going on business trips a lot. I remember how busy you used to be.

M But it's much different nowadays. _________________________ _________________________, and there's really not that much stress in my life.

W That's a relief. I never enjoyed hearing stories about all your trips to the doctor's office since you were so stressed.

M You won't hear about those any more. _________________________

_________________________.

W That's good to hear. What about your hours?

M I work a standard nine-to-six day even though we're open until nine. But I get to go home early.

W It sounds like you've found the ideal job for you.

Congratulations.

M Yeah, _________________________ _________________________ _________________________.

03 대화를 듣고, 두 사람의 관계를 가장 잘 나타낸 것을 고르시오.

M What is your take on the current job market?

W _________________________ _________________________. The economy was great for a couple of years, but it looks like it's about to take a nosedive.

M That's our assessment as well. We're positive a number of companies are going to begin laying off workers relatively soon.

W _________________________.

M Not at all. If it were, you and I wouldn't be talking today. However, that means we can be picky about whom we choose to employ.

W I suppose _________________________

_________________________.

M Yes, that's true, but we're impressed with your qualifications. Depending upon how well you do today, we may call you in for a second round.

W That's exactly what I'm hoping for. Like I said earlier, I'm not confident in the economy, so I need to secure some employment really soon.

M _________________________

_________________________, I'd say you'll be sure to do that. Now, why don't I introduce you to some of the other people with whom you'll be speaking today?

W That sounds great to me.

04 다음을 듣고, 화자의 심정을 가장 잘 나타낸 것을 고르시오.

M I just found out that _________________________ _________________________ in Seoul, and, in hindsight, missing out on this opportunity was my own fault. _________________________

_________________________, but I successfully passed the first two rounds. However, the night before the last interview, _________________________

_________________________.

It was fun, but now I wish I'd never gone. I returned home late and forgot to set my alarm clock. I woke up

thirty minutes before the interview and was already
____.
I hurried there but was out of breath and sweaty when I
arrived. I didn't shave, and my tie was even on crooked.
Today, I received an e-mail saying they weren't going to
hire me. ____
____________________________________.

05 대화를 듣고, 남자가 목적지까지 가는 데 가장 좋은 교통수단이 무엇인지 고르시오.

M ____?

W I'm going to stay home with my family. How about
you?

M My family and I are going downtown to the new
shopping mall this Saturday. We're going to drive there
in the afternoon.

W Oh, it's quite nice, but _______________________
____________________________.

M Why do you say that?

W The parking lots there are simply jam-packed with cars.
I drove there last weekend and spent thirty minutes
looking around for a parking spot. You'd be better off
going there by subway.

M Oh, I didn't know that. I'm not sure about the subway
though. There's not a station anywhere near our house.

W Hmm… ____________________________________
______________________. You're nowhere
near the commuter train, are you?

M We live in the suburbs, so we could take it, but my
youngest is kind of scared of them. It sounds silly, but
it's the truth. __________________________________
___________________.

W I agree. That sounds like the best way to get to the mall
and back.

06 대화를 듣고, 이 대화가 이루어지고 있는 장소를 고르시오.

W Come here and take a look at this. Do you think I
ought to buy it?

M Can't you purchase it somewhere else back at home?

W Well, I might have to look around, but I'm sure I could
find it at a store somewhere.

M ____

_________________________ on it here?

W The reason is that it's much cheaper here. __________
____,
it costs less than if I were to get it at the complex near
our house.

M I never thought about it like that. In that case, ________
_____________________________________?
We're on vacation after all.

W That's so nice of you to say that. Now, after I get this,
let's go to that section over there. We absolutely must
buy some presents for everyone back home.

M Okay, _______________________________ hurry
____.

W Right. I hadn't noticed how little time we have left.

M Then let's buy what we need to and get out of here.

07 다섯 개의 대화문을 듣고, 자연스럽지 <u>않은</u> 것을 고르시오

① M I talked to Jeremy's teacher for a while after school.

   W Really? ______________________________
_________________________________?

   M She told me he was doing well in school but that he
doesn't always do his homework.

   W We'll have to make sure he finishes it every night
from now on.

② W Did you remember to bring the shopping list with
you? I've got to get a lot of stuff today.

   M Actually, I don't have it. ____________________
_________________________________.

   W Great. Why don't you let me have it so that we can
get our shopping done?

③ M Do you have a copy of that memo which Mr. Park
sent to everyone?

   W Yeah, I think I've got one right here. ____________
________________________________?

   M I inadvertently threw it away with some other files.

   W You've got to be more careful about that. You might
wind up getting rid of something really important
one of these days.

④ W _____________________________________
Sara and Greg?

   M Did they finally decide to get married or something?
It's about time that they tie the knot.

   W Actually, ___________________________________.
They broke up with each other last night.

⑤ M ____
to see your parents?

W It was nice to spend time with them, but the trip was
not particularly relaxing.

M Oh? I thought your parents lived out in the country
where there's nothing to do.

W That's true, but I had to visit ___________________
____ that
I never got a chance to rest.

08 다음을 듣고, 이야기 속의 This가 무엇인지 고르시오.

W This is something _________________________________
___________________________, and it can only be found there.
It often consists of mundane stories about a person's
life, giving details of that individual's daily routine and
various ups and downs. In many ways, _______________
____.
It's sometimes very opinionated, giving a person's
thoughts on particular issues. Others may cover a
specific topic, such as movie reviews, a sports team,
or even someone's favorite type of pet. Some become
quite popular _____________________________________
____ and then
leave comments. Others are set up so that only friends
and family members can view them, so permission
must be granted before new people can obtain access.
Some people who write them just for fun get noticed
and become famous all _____________________________
____.

09 대화를 듣고, 여자가 원래 받았어야 할 거스름돈이 얼마인지 고르시오.

W Excuse me, but I think you just made a mistake. _______
____.

M I don't think so. The cash register says you should get
back seven dollars and thirty cents, so that's what I
returned to you.

W ____
___________________________, but I don't think your manager
would appreciate it if you did that. Would it be okay to
go over my purchases in order to check?

M I guess not. There's no one in line behind you.

W All right, I bought this cold medicine ________________
__________________________. And this box of candy cost
three dollars and fifty cents.

M Right. And the aspirin costs ________________________
____.

W Okay, and there's one more item I purchased. Let me
see what the price is here.

M It's this DVD, ___________________________________
___________________________.

W So, I gave you thirty dollars for my purchase. Did you
give me the right amount of change?

M Oops. It looks like ________________________________
___________________________. Thanks for being so honest.

10 대화를 듣고, 여자의 마지막 말을 완성하는 가장 알맞은 것을 고르시오.

M I just got chewed out by the boss for ten minutes
____.

W You haven't finished that project? Didn't you start it a
month ago?

M Yeah, ____
___________________________. I never expected the project to
take this long.

W You should've known to get your work done on time.
Why didn't you work weekends to finish it? I've been
here every weekend for the past two months to ensure
that ____.

M You don't really think I should give up my weekends,
do you? I'd much rather hang out with my friends and
do stuff with them.

W Yeah, that would be nice. But you still need to get your
work done.

M I'm sorry, but ___________________________________
___________________________. My free time is important to
me.

W That's a pretty bad attitude. You need to focus on your
work.

M Sorry, but I disagree with you. And I really don't
appreciate the boss yelling at me. ___________________
____.

W Just hope you don't get fired. After all,...

11 다음을 듣고, 우주여행에 대해 사실이 <u>아닌</u> 것을 고르시오.

M Humans have gone into space since 1961 when the first Russian astronaut, Yuri Gagarin, orbited the Earth. ____ since, and now Korea has joined this exclusive club. In April 2008, Korea's first astronaut blasted off from a launch pad in Kazakhstan, and, two days later, ________________________________ ____________________________. With the Korean astronaut were two Russians. It was the first time in space for all three of them. The Korean astronaut ____ ________________ before returning to Earth. During this time, she conducted experiments on the effects of space travel on fruit flies and the effects of zero gravity on her facial features. Other experiments included monitoring dust storms that originate in China and blow into Korea. She returned to Earth ____ ____ on the space station.

12 대화를 듣고, 여자에게 주어진 조언이 <u>아닌</u> 것을 고르시오.

M Your mother told me that your last mathematics test wasn't very good. What's been going on with your studies lately? You used to be such a good student, ____ ____.

W I have no idea. It's just that some of the material we cover in class seems too hard. I simply don't understand it much of the time.

M In that case, ____ ____?

W Are you serious? Then I'd look stupid in front of all my friends. I can't do that.

M I bet that your friends are all confused too ____________ ____.

W Well, you may be right about that. Their test scores aren't good either.

M Okay, then you should see about getting a tutor to help you.

W Yeah, the school provides them. I can do that. Is there anything else that I should do?

M Sure. ____

____ and ask your mother or me for help. Remember that we went to school too, so we can assist you with your schoolwork.

W Oh, right. ____.
Thanks a lot, Dad.

13 다음을 듣고, 이 이야기가 어떤 질문에 대한 대답인지 고르시오.

M ____ ________________________________ that my friend and her friend set up for us. At the time, we were both university students although we attended different colleges. Our first date was in a coffee shop near her university. ____________ ________________________________, and I think she was, too. But we got settled down, had some coffee, and then talked for a long time. It was on our very first date that ____ ________________________________. At the end of the evening, I asked for her phone number, and she gladly provided it for me. We had many more dates after that, and I think we knew we were in love soon after. About one year later, I graduated from university and started working. Then she took me to meet her parents, ____________ ____. That was ten years ago. Now we have two children, a boy and a girl, and we're very happy.

14 대화를 듣고, 두 사람에 의해 언급된 교통 표지판이 <u>아닌</u> 것을 고르시오.

M How am I ever going to pass my driver's license exam? I've got so many things to learn that I'll never remember them all.

W Why don't you let me help you? Here, ____________ ____

____.

M I know most of them, but some are pretty hard.

W In that case, let's practice. What's this one with ____ with a line through it?

M Hmm... I think it means you cannot turn right. And I know what the picture of the arrow going straight ahead and then curving backwards with a line through

it means, too. ______________________________
______________________________.

W Wow, it looks like you know your signs. How about this sign ______________________________
______________________________? That's a little confusing.

M I think it means there's ______________________________
______________________________.

W Bingo. You're exactly right about that. Here's one I don't recognize. It's got an arrow that curves back and forth then goes straight ahead.

M Oh, it's indicating that ______________________________
______________________________.

W You know, I don't think you have anything to worry about on your test.

15 대화를 듣고, 남자가 대화 후에 할 행동을 고르시오.

M Mom's big birthday party is tomorrow. Why don't we go over everything we're going to do one last time?

W Yeah, we ought to do that since we wouldn't want to forget anything.

M Now, we're going to cook dinner for her at six o'clock.
____
______________________________?

W I haven't gotten all of them, but here's a list of what we have. We'll have to visit the supermarket tomorrow to get the rest.

M Okay, ______________________________.
What about the cake? Are you going to make that?

W Uh, ______________________________
______________________________.

M That's not good. We'd better call the bakery and order a cake for Mom since I doubt either of us will have time to make it.

W Then you ought ______________________________
 since we'll want it specially ordered. What about inviting everyone to the party?

M ______________________________
______________________________, but we should call them again tomorrow to confirm that they're going to show up. And we need to clean the house as well. This place is a mess.

W All right. I'll take care of that right now, and ______
______________________________.

16 다음을 듣고, 화자의 스케줄 표 중 빠진 부분에 들어갈 알맞은 것을 고르시오.

W I have many things to do every day, so I always make sure that ______________________________
______________________________. This Tuesday, I'll arrive at work at nine a.m. as usual. After I check my e-mail and have some coffee to help me wake up, ______________________________
______________________________. I anticipate it'll take about two hours. I plan to meet my friend for lunch at twelve o'clock and return to my office by one. At two, ______________________________
______________________________, which will hopefully conclude by three o'clock since I have another sales meeting at that time. That one should finish by half past four. Then, I'm scheduled to meet with the president of our company at half past five, during which time he wants to go over the current sales figures. Finally, ______________________________
______________________________ that evening, so I promised to meet him at the airport by a quarter to seven.

17 다음을 듣고, 다음 중 이야기의 내용과 관련이 <u>없는</u> 것을 고르시오.

W Writing a readable story takes great skill and a lot of time. ______________________________
______________________________, creating an intriguing plot, developing believable characters, and then putting them all together in an enjoyable manner. All good stories start with imagination. It doesn't matter if the genre is science fiction, crime, fantasy, or romance. Without imagination, there would be no story. ______________________________
______________________________, such as the setting, the time, the basic situation, and the progress of the story. ______________________________
______________________________ by not giving away vital information until absolutely necessary. The best novels are those which ______________________________
______________________________. Lastly, a brilliant plot made with a fantastic imagination is wasted if no

one believes in or likes the characters. Once authors create the characters that people can see themselves in, they will be on their way to making a great story ______
____ .

18 대화를 듣고, 현재 시각을 고르시오.

M I'm so excited to be going to the movies. ________________
____
_______________________ .

W It's the same for me. Well, let's take a look at what films are playing.

M I haven't seen a good action movie in a while. I hope that *Spider-Man 3* is playing here.

W Well, ____
________________________ . The good news is that the movie's playing here, but the bad news is that it's already over. I'm sorry about that.

M That's all right. ________________________________
______________________ . Say, what do you think about watching *The Lord of the Rings*? I've heard great things about that movie.

W But do you really want to wait around for almost an hour? What are we going to do in the meantime?

M I suppose we could get some dinner. What do you think about that?

W Actually, I had dinner already, so ________________
______________________ . Hey, I've got a better idea. *Titanic* is going to be starting in about twenty minutes. Let's just see that.

M Okay, ____ .

W I'll get the tickets, and you go to buy the popcorn and cokes.

19 다음을 듣고, 무엇에 대해 이야기하고 있는지 고르시오.

M This competition ________________________________
____ . The women are judged ________________________________
____ and skills at a particular activity. One of the first things in the competition is the evening gown competition. Each lady wears a lovely dress, and the judges rate her on her poise and elegance. The next step in the contest is the

bathing suit judging. In this segment, each lady wears a similar bathing suit and walks before the judges and the audience. ____
____ . Here, each contestant must do a performance of some kind. Singing, dancing, and playing music are among the most common of these talents although some will do activities of a different nature. At last, the judges select several finalists, usually five, and ask difficult questions about ____
____ .

Finally, after much discussion, the judges make their selection on who ________________________________ .

20 대화를 듣고, 남자의 요지를 고르시오.

W I can't believe what happened to Sungnyemun. It bothers me that ________________________________
____ .

M You're right. The government needs to do a better job of protecting them.

W But what can it do? I mean, who'd ever suspect somebody would want to burn something like Sungnyemun down? It never would occur to most people to do that.

M That's true. However, ________________________________
____ , and Sungnyemun belonged to all Korean citizens.

W What do you suggest they do?

M Well, it's too late for Sungnyemun, but ________________
____ for our national treasures. And, of course, it should put smoke alarms and more fire extinguishers near them.

W But who's going to pay for these security guards?

M I've got an idea. All of those riot police ________________
____ . The government is paying them to stand around and do nothing most of the time. They should be employed as guards for all national treasures.

W That idea just might work.

M I hope so. After all, we can rebuild Sungnyemun, ____ . We don't want to lose any more of our country's treasures.

21 대화를 듣고, 남자가 말하고자 하는 것이 무엇인지 고르시오.

W I'm really concerned about my weight. I've been looking at myself in the mirror, and I seem like I've put on some weight lately. I think I'm going to go on a diet.

M Well, ____ ____.

W Huh? Why do you say that?

M There are a large number of different diets that people are following these days. In fact, it's something of a fad to go on an extreme diet.

W ____. What exactly is it?

M There are many different kinds, but they typically involve eating very little for several days or eating only one type of food. Those diets often help people lose a lot of weight fast, but there are some problems.

W ____ __________________? That's exactly what I need.

M It's actually quite unhealthy. You can cause serious harm to your body by going on a crash diet.

W Hmm… I never thought of it that way.

M Yeah, so ____ __________________________________. You don't want to do any harm to your body, or you might have a hard time recovering from an extreme diet.

22 다음을 듣고, 이야기의 내용이 그래프에 잘못 반영된 것을 고르시오.

M A recent survey of Internet users resulted in some interesting numbers. The survey asked both women and men ____ ____. According to the survey, about thirty-six percent of the male respondents claimed to use the Internet for twelve to nineteen hours each week. This was the largest category for men. Meanwhile, __________________________ ____ — about twenty-seven percent — said they use the Internet over twenty-five hours per week. On the lower end of the scale, about two percent of males and females who responded ____ __________________________________. More females than males spend four to seven hours a week on the Internet, yet more males than females spend eight to eleven hours a week online. Finally, slightly more females than males use the Internet for twenty to twenty-five hours per week. ____ __________________________________ may be reflected in ____ __________________________________.

23 대화를 듣고, 화자들이 할 행동을 순서대로 나열한 것을 고르시오.

M I'm so relieved we've got a holiday coming up. I could use a break from work, so __________________________ __________________________________.

W But don't you remember we promised to take the kids to the amusement park this weekend?

M Oh, that's right. Well, __________________________, __________________________, so let's go there on Sunday. I guess that'll be the day with the fewest visitors since most people are likely to go on Friday or Saturday.

W That sounds fine, but what do you want to do on the other two days?

M ____, but it sounds like you've got some other plans in mind. Am I right?

W Your parents want us to visit them for dinner, so I thought we'd do that on Friday night. And we've got to go shopping at the department store and see a movie with my sister.

M ____ __________________________________.

W Yeah, I'm sorry about that.

M That's fine. Okay, __________________________________ __________________________, let's get the shopping out of the way. We can watch the movie __________________ __________________________________.

W Great. I'll give her a call and let her know our plans.

24 다음을 듣고, 화자의 현재 취미가 무엇인지 고르시오.

W I love doing so many things, but __________________ __________________________________. I guess it's because of my moody personality. I get really excited about something, but, the next day, I want to

try something else. For example, ___________
___________________, and I immediately signed up for
photography classes. Previously, ___________
___________________ but dropped that when
I decided to learn how to make sculptures. But I soon
got frustrated with that because it takes too much time
to finish anything. Besides, I'd just begun studying
astronomy with my son's telescope. ___________
___________________, so, after
a week, I started taking jazz dance lessons. At first
it was fun, but the instructor was especially strict, so
I had too many problems. But I think I'll continue
with ___________
___________. ___________
___________________. However, there's always the
possibility I'll get interested in something else soon.

25 다음을 듣고, 남자의 마지막 말에 들어갈 가장 알맞은 것을 고르시오.

M It's never been clearer than before that ___________
___________________.
For the majority of its existence, Korea has been a
closed society with Koreans considering foreigners
to be outsiders. Now, there are many signs indicating
this will change. There are currently over one million
foreigners from all over the world living and working in
Korea. In addition, ___________
___________________. It is estimated that,
by 2030, ten percent of Koreans will be married to
foreigners while their children will represent five percent
of the population. Despite this, Korean society is
having a difficult time accepting non-Koreans. In many
nations, ___________
___________________. Koreans
need to adjust their definition of what a Korean is and
should learn to accept non-Koreans as full citizens and
neighbors. Only then will Korea be able to accept all of
its citizens, ___________
___________________, as
Koreans and not as strangers. In conclusion,...

26 대화를 듣고, 민수의 성격을 가장 잘 나타낸 것을 고르시오.

M I didn't expect to see you here tonight. I thought you
said that you didn't have any money to spend.

W Well, that's true, but one of my friend's gave me some
cash because he knew how much I wanted to see this
movie with everyone.

M So ___________
___________________?

W Oh, I don't have to reimburse him at all. Minsu gave me
the money. ___________
___________________.

M You're right about that. I ___________
___________________. I had lost my notebook,
and we were taking a test the next day. Minsu
photocopied all of his notes for me and then let me
have them. I couldn't believe it.

W That's a good one. I have another story about him as
well.

M Go ahead, and tell me what he did.

W He didn't do this for me, so I heard about it from
someone else. Do you remember that thunderstorm we
had last week?

M Yeah, how can I forget it? It was awful.

W Well, Minsu gave Eunmi ___________
___________________. He got
soaked in the process, but he didn't seem to mind.

27 대화를 듣고, 여자의 반지가 있던 위치를 고르시오.

W Can you come and help me for a minute? I think I've
lost my ring. It's somewhere in the living room, but I
can't remember where I put it.

M Did you lose your ring again? Okay, let me help you
find it. ___________
___________________ like it was the last time you lost
it.

W I already checked, but it's not there. Why don't you
____
___________________?

M Okay, but I don't know how it could have gotten there.

W In the meantime, I'll look on the bookshelves. I
sometimes put things there and then forget about them.
Are you having any luck?

M Not yet. It's kind of dark here. Let me get a flashlight,

and ____.
Why don't you look on the TV stand? It might be there.

w No, I already searched there twice. I'll never find it.

M Okay, I've got the flashlight. ________________________
________________________________.

w This is horrible. It's not even next to the lamp like it usually is.

M ________________________. Hold on a second, and I'll be able to grab it for you.

28 다음을 듣고, 화자의 의견에 동의하는 진술을 고르시오.

w ____
in Korea nowadays. Many people spend a lot of money so that they can look their best. Most people who get work done say that they need the surgery ____________
____.
Getting a good job and finding the perfect husband or wife is not easy, so looking like a model or movie star is a must. ____
________________________. Modern society is all about competition, and, if getting plastic surgery is necessary to be successful, then a person should do it. Unfortunately, attending a good university or having the best skills no longer guarantees employment.
________________________________. After all, in Korea, a personal photograph must be attached to all job applications. Discrimination based on appearance is illegal yet impossible to prove. Therefore, many young people ________________________
________________________________. Getting married is also on most young people's minds, and being beautiful or handsome is ________________________________
________________________.

29 What can be inferred by the woman's last words?

M Some of us are going out to eat tonight. Would you care to join us?

w I'd love to, but I've got to finish this paper, so __________
________________________________.

M Are you talking about that paper for your literature class? I thought it wasn't due until next week.

w You're right, but I like turning in my work as quickly as possible. Besides, I've got several other assignments to work on, so it'll be good to finish this paper tonight.

M Oh, come on. Forget about that report, and have dinner with us. ____
________________________________.

w Yeah, but I'm here to get good grades and learn as much as I can. I don't want to disappoint my parents.

M But it's just one time. You don't have to stay the entire evening.

w I'm sorry, but I can't. You all go out and have fun together. Perhaps I can meet everyone in a few weeks when my workload gets lighter.

M I think you care too much about your grades and not enough about your friends.

w Well, ____
________________________________. It would help you a lot.

30 What is the purpose of this talk?

M Kim Minhee was ________________________________
who loved making dolls at home. One day, a friend suggested that she start selling dolls over the Internet. Minhee decided to try it, and, overnight, ____________
________________________________.
Unfortunately, this has created a number of problems for her. Her husband is jealous that she makes more money than he does, and her children want her
____
________________________. Additionally, a large corporation has recently offered to buy her doll business provided that she gives up the rights to her creation. What should Minhee do? ________________________
________________________ from Monday to Friday at eleven a.m. to find out. *Life in the Dollhouse* ________________
________________________________. Be sure to remember the new time since you won't want to miss Korea's most popular morning TV program, and then you can find out how Minhee will solve her problems in her *Life in the Dollhouse*.

31

W I've called this meeting once again to stress the importance of doing this. Too many people have not followewd _______________________ _______________________. You must be sure to sort every item into the different bags and containers at the collection point. First, _______________________ _______________________. Plastic bottles and any other kinds of plastic container go into container number one. Into container number two go newspapers, paper bags, _______________________ _______________________. Put glass bottles of any type and tin cans into container number three. Finally, too many people are dumping animal, fruit, and vegetable waste matter into the regular garbage bags.

_______________________ _______________________. This includes meat and fish bones, eggshells, apple cores, orange and banana peels, and any leftover or spoiled food. Please cooperate in this matter, and then there shouldn't be any more problems in the future.

Q : *What is this talk about?*

M ① A new government law for apartments
② Garbage separation at an apartment complex
③ Recycling glass, plastic, and paper
④ Thanking people for following some rules
⑤ The punishment for failing to follow the rules

32

W Mr. Johnson, do you mind if I ask you a few questions? I'm curious about _______________________ _______________________.

M Weren't you listening in class yesterday? I went over everything then.

W Actually, I wasn't there since I was at the doctor's office. _______________________.

M In that case, go ahead and ask whatever you want.

W First, are we going to be tested on the section about the Impressionists?

M Yes, you should know about them, so _______________________ _______________________ since they'll help you understand that time period.

W Okay, thanks. But what about the information on Art Deco? Do we need to know that?

M No, _______________________, so you can set that aside to study another day.

W Great, and are there any books I should study that would help me _______________________?

M In addition to your textbook, there's a list of books _______________________ _______________________. Read that list, do some extra reading, and you should do well on the exam.

Q : *Which of the following will the student NOT do?*

M ① Learn about Art Deco
② Read a list on her syllabus
③ Study chapters 4 and 5
④ Learn about the Impressionists
⑤ Get some extra books to study

33

M I'm still in high school, but, in the future, I hope to have a successful career, so right now _______________________ _______________________. I need to get accepted to a good university first, so I must study hard in school. Mathematics is important for my job because it requires a lot of navigational skills, so I'm taking extra math classes now. Also, _______________________ _______________________ and its main language is English, I need to ensure that my English is as good as possible. Next, I need _______________________ _______________________ since perfect vision is required for this position. After I finish university, I'll apply to all the big airlines for training. _______________________ _______________________, then I'll go to a private flying club and get my private license first. After that, I am sure one of them will hire me.

Q : *According to the talk, what does the speaker want to be in the future?*

M ① a flight attendant
② a surgeon
③ a math teacher

④ a tour guide
⑤ an airline piloty

34

M Is there something I can help you with today?
W Yes, ____
________________________, please.
M All right. There are a few seats left on the bus. Do you have any preference as to where you'd like to sit?
W I didn't know we could choose our seats on the bus. If that's the case, how about giving me an aisle seat near the front?
M Sure, I can do that for you. Now, _______________
_______________________________, so that's about fifteen minutes from now. You should have plenty of time to get there before it leaves.
W That's good to hear. I'm in a hurry and _____________
________________________________.
M Well, you've got a ticket on the express bus, so, once it starts going, ___________________________________
________________________________.
W That sounds wonderful. Oh, how much do I owe you for the ticket?
M Your total comes to sixty dollars.
W Here's the cash. Thanks so much for your assistance.

Q : *How long will the bus take to get to New York?*

M ① 4 hours
② 4 hours and thirty minutes
③ 5 hours
④ 5 hours and thirty minutes
⑤ 6 hours

35 다음을 듣고, 이어지는 영어 질문에 답하시오.

M Eric thinks _______________________________________,
so he wants to start playing a new sport. However, he's not particularly good at sports _____________________
_______________________. In addition, he prefers to play sports where he doesn't have any teammates. Finally, he doesn't particularly enjoy being outdoors, and

____

________________.

Q : *Which of the following sports is Eric likely to try?*

36 주어진 시간 동안 아래 지문을 주의 깊게 읽고, 들려주는 질문에 답하시오. 〔1분〕

Q : *According to the passage, which of the following statements is true?*

[37-38] 대화를 듣고, 이어지는 두 개의 질문에 답하시오.

M What book are you looking at there?
W It's a book about the English language I'm reading for fun. ____.
Did you know that large numbers of English words come from other languages?
M Sure, but don't most languages borrow from each other? I'm not sure there's anything special about that.
W Well, of course _________________________________
_____________________; however, large numbers of English words have been taken straight from other languages and put into English _________________
_______________________. For example, the word "sushi" comes from Japanese. In English, it has the same meaning as the Japanese word. Linguists call these loanwords.
M Ah, I see what you're talking about. That's pretty fascinating. What are some other words that come from different languages?
W Hmm… Let me see. The word "café" comes from a French word. And the word "aloha," which we use to mean "hello," _______________________________
____________________________.
M I never realized there were _____________________
____________________________.
W Yeah, I'm totally amazed as well. Here, check this out. The word "gulag," which is a prison, comes from the same Russian word. And, your favorite food, pizza, comes from the Italian word with the same meaning.
M Yum, I'm getting hungry just thinking about that. Let's go get a steak or something to eat.
W Okay, ____________________________________,
and then I'll join you for dinner.

37 Which of the following is NOT an English loanword from another language?

38 Why is the woman reading the book?

〔39-40〕 다음을 듣고, 이어지는 두 개의 질문에 답하시오.

M Women's spring fashions are about to hit the catwalk from Milan to New York, and we have the latest news on _______________________________________ _______________. As temperatures start warming, blue jeans will go out of style and more _______________ _____________________________________. While plaid skirts are definitely in, make sure they're below the knee because miniskirts are no longer fashionable. The best plaid skirts should be gray, red, or brown and have a slight slit at the side. Along with the skirt, ____, with dark tones in black, brown, blue, and green being the most popular choices. As for accessories, ____: sunglasses and gold earrings. Sunglasses — the bigger the better — are back in style after disappearing for a few years. Now they're being worn by everyone, so grab a pair for yourself. _______________________________ _______________, and gold earrings are the hottest items out there. It doesn't matter what kind of earrings you wear. They could be hoops or simple studs. But make sure they're gold, and _______________________ _______________.

39 What is the best title of this article?

40 What is NOT mentioned as a hot item for the spring?

01 대화를 듣고, 여자가 구입한 치마를 고르시오.

W Excuse me, but do you think you could help me out for a few minutes?

M Sure, _________________________________?

W Well, I'm interested in getting a new skirt, but I'm not exactly sure what is in and out of style these days.

M I think I can help you out with that problem. How about this miniskirt? _________________________ _______________.

W It's nice, but I am not interested in that or in anything that is too long. So I don't want a skirt _____________ _________________________________.

M Okay, then I won't show you any of those in stock. Here's a nice skirt that has stripes. What do you think of it?

W Ugh. That doesn't do anything for me at all. _________ _________________________________.

M Hmm… I've got two of those. Here's one which has some flower designs on it, and here's one that's a nice solid color.

W _________________________________.

That's exactly what I'm looking for.

M That's an excellent decision. Just let me wrap it up for you.

02 대화를 듣고, 두 사람이 만나는 요일과 시간을 고르시오.

M Anne, I've been meaning to contact you about sitting down for a meeting sometime soon. Do you have any time to get together this week?

W Well, let me think about that for a minute… _________ _________________________________, but I think Wednesday or Thursday is a definite possibility.

M Hmm… I'm going to be out of the office on a business trip both of those days, so do you think we could meet on Friday instead?

W _________________________________. What time were you hoping to see me?

M I think anytime in the morning works for me. How does ten a.m. sound to you?

W Sorry, but _________________________________ _________________. I've got a meeting in Mr. Drummond's office at that time. How about the afternoon? Do you have any time then?

M Well, I could meet you at either one or four o'clock, but only for an hour.

W How much time do you think you'll need?

M This should _________________________________.

W In that case, let's get together right after lunch on that day.

03 다음을 듣고, 이야기 속의 This가 무엇인지 고르시오.

W This is a device which is used _________________ _________________________________. It is typically found in hospitals, research laboratories, and educational institutes. It can be small enough to sit on a person's desk _________________________________ _________________________. To use it, the specimen to be observed is placed on a rectangular piece of glass called a slide. _________________________________ must then be covered by a second smaller square piece of glass. The slide is subsequently set underneath a powerful lens. The user looks through the lens at the specimen and can even adjust the intensity in order to see the item at various magnifications. The most basic ones can _________________________________ while huge electronic ones can observe even the tiniest organisms living on Earth. Without this device, much scientific research into diseases and the structure of the atom _________________________________.

04 대화를 듣고, 여자의 감정 변화를 가장 잘 나타낸 것을 고르시오.

M You've been looking a little down lately. I hope you don't have any family problems.

W No, it's just that _________________________________ _________________. I'm simply not pleased with anything right now. I can't stand my major and feel like I don't have any goals in my life.

M Hey, calm down a bit. _________________________________ _________________, nothing's that bad.

w   Of course it is. With my major, there's no way I'll ever get a decent job.

M   If you're really not happy with your major, then ____?

w   That would be impossible to do. After all, I've been here for two years, so it's too late to change.

M   That's not exactly true. My best friend was in the same situation as you last year. ____________________________, and now he's much happier.

w   Really? Are you sure about that?

M   Totally. He might have to stay here for an extra semester, but ____.

w   I agree. Thanks. I'm going to check into this right away.

05 다음을 듣고, 화자가 고등학생일 때 어디에서 살았는지 고르시오.

M   When I was growing up, my family moved many times because of my father's job. He was a civil engineer for a construction company, so they sent him to several countries on building projects. Since they were long-term contracts, ______________________________. I spent three years in India during elementary school while he helped build a dam there. Soon after that, we moved to Kenya, where his company constructed a highway and an airport. ______________________________ Saudi Arabia when he was working on an oil refinery. From ______________________________, we lived in Malaysia, where my father was the supervisor of a massive seaport project. Finally, I attended university in the United States when my father was assigned to the head office there in New York. ______________________________, but I've seen some fascinating places.

06 다섯 개의 대화문을 듣고, 자연스럽지 <u>않은</u> 것을 고르시오.

① M   Where are you going with that big pile of clothes?

  w   I'm ______________________________. My washer broke down the other day, and the repairman hasn't made it to my house yet.

  M   In that case, ______________________________ to do your laundry. That's better than heading to the laundromat.

② w   I know you're really busy with your work today, but would you mind ______________________________?

  M   Okay, what exactly do you need assistance with?

  w   It's the project you're working on now. You're doing it all wrong.

③ M   I've decided to take up a new hobby.

  w   That sounds nice. Do you know what you're going to do yet?

  M   I haven't made up my mind, but I was thinking about learning how to play chess.

  w   Good luck. ______________________________, so it might take you a while to learn how to play it really well.

④ w   You look exhausted. ______________________________?

  M   Yeah, you wouldn't believe how busy things have gotten. Ever since Mr. Martin got transferred here, ______________________________.

  w   You should have a chat with him and tell him what he's doing.

  M   No way. I don't want to say anything that could jeopardize my job.

⑤ M   Have you purchased everything we need to make dinner tonight?

  w   I'm pretty sure I have. ______________________________, and I picked up some chicken at the supermarket as well.

  M   What about the dessert? Did you remember to make that?

  w   ______________________________, so I bought something from the bakery instead.

07 다음을 듣고, 입장료의 총액이 얼마인지 고르시오.

w   Last Tuesday, my family went to the natural history museum to see the dinosaur exhibition. There were myself, my husband, ______________________________, and ______________________________. The museum opened at ten a.m. and closed at seven p.m., and we spent most of the day there. We wanted to go on Monday, but _______________________ _______________________. The entrance fees are _______________________ _______________________, five dollars for senior citizens, _______________________, and _______________________ _______________________. They were offering a ten-percent discount for groups of five or more. It was a bit expensive, _______________________ _______________________. The exhibition was fantastic, and we saw their wonderful collection of dinosaur bones. My son enjoyed it most of all, but I think my teenage daughter was a little bored. She kept calling her friends on her cell phone.

08 대화를 듣고, 남자의 마지막 말에 대한 여자의 응답으로 알맞은 것을 고르시오.

M Have you managed to apply for any good jobs lately?

W Well, I've submitted my resume to a lot of different companies, but I'm not sure _______________________ _______________________.

M Yeah, I know what you mean. The job market doesn't seem like it's particularly good this year.

W True, but you're an engineer, so you shouldn't have too much of a hard time finding a job. My major is in liberal arts, _______________________ _______________________.

M I suppose you're right. _______________________ _______________________?

W I'm mostly searching for an office job, but I'm not going to be too picky about what I get. I've applied to some consulting firms, big businesses, _______________________ _______________________.

M Are you serious? It sounds like you need to focus a little better.

W Maybe, _______________________ _______________________.

M I agree, but focusing on one sector should help you get a job faster. That's what the job counselor told us. Didn't you attend that meeting on getting a job last week?

09 다음을 듣고, 이 이야기의 목적이 무엇인지 고르시오.

M After finishing university, many people enter the job market. One of the most important skills you need is how to do a job interview. _______________________ _______________________, so pay close attention. First, learn everything you can about the company you're interviewing with. For example, _______________________ _______________________, where its headquarters is, and who its president is. Second, make sure you dress your best and look presentable. _______________________ _______________________ any flashy jewelry or any kind of perfume or cologne. Next, make sure you arrive early for the interview. If you're late, you have already lost the job. During the interview, _______________________, and answer every question in a clear, strong manner. Finally, and most importantly, _______________________ _______________________. If you do, this shows you're there to help yourself, not to help the company.

10 대화를 듣고, 남자가 조깅 대신 수영을 시작한 이유를 고르시오.

W Are you still going on those two-mile jogs every morning?

M Actually, I quit doing those about a month or so ago.

W What? Aren't you the one who was always telling me how I needed to exercise? _______________________ _______________________?

M I'm not jogging anymore, but I'm still exercising regularly. Instead of jogging, _______________________ _______________________.

W Oh, that's interesting. I never imagined you were the kind of person who'd enjoy that.

M Me neither, but it's actually kind of fun.

W So, what made you take it up? Did you just get sick of jogging and having to run on those crowded city streets?

M Not exactly. My wife's doctor told her _______________________ _______________________. She didn't want to do it alone, so _______________________ _______________________. I wasn't that good at first, but now I can't wait to get to the pool.

W That sounds great. I swim a lot myself. _______________________

____.

M I hope so. We'll have to be sure to swim some laps together.

11 대화를 듣고, 약에 대해 사실이 <u>아닌</u> 것을 고르시오.

W I'm trying to find some medicine, but I'm not sure exactly what to buy.

M In that case, _______________________ _______________________, and I'll try to match the proper medicine for you?

W I've been coughing a lot lately, and I've got a sore throat as well. My nose is running, and I'm experiencing various aches and pains ________________________ ________________.

M All right, I think I know the perfect medicine for you. You want to get this medicine, which should help you feel better quickly.

W That sounds good. _______________________ ________________?

M You should take one spoonful ________________ ____________. Drink some _______________________ ________________.

W Is it going to make me drowsy or have any other side effects? I've got to take my kids to school, so I hope it won't do anything bad to me.

M Don't worry about that at all. People who have taken this medicine have reported that ________________ ________________________.

W That's good to hear. Is there anything else I should know?

M Yes, if you don't feel better after a couple of days, ________________________________.

12 다음을 듣고, 이 이야기가 어떤 질문에 대한 대답인지 고르시오.

M ________________________________ for many people, but it can also be a nightmare for others. Sudden wealth can bring riches as well as numerous problems when people get all that money. A California woman who recently won the lottery went from the rich house to the poorhouse ________________________________. After winning the lottery, she started buying everything she could. She soon met some disreputable people, who wound up conning her out of her fortune. Very quickly, all of her five million dollars in prize money was gone, and ________________________________. However, there are many people who manage to handle their sudden wealth much more appropriately than that unfortunate woman. A New York man who won the lottery started by quitting his job and then ____________ ________________________________. Afterwards, he invested the rest of the money in a business and the stock market. Today, he's successful, wealthy, and ________________________________ ________________________.

13 다섯 개의 대화문을 듣고, 아래 그림의 상황에 가장 잘 어울리는 것을 고르시오.

① **W** Why don't we stop working and ________________ ________________________________?

   M That sounds like a great idea. What do you want to get to eat?

   W I'm not exactly sure. Let's walk outside and see which restaurants aren't too busy.

② **M** What would you like to order for lunch today?

   W I think I'll have the chicken salad, please. I'd like that with ranch dressing.

   M All right, and ________________________________ ________________?

   W Yes, I'll have a glass of unsweetened ice tea, please.

③ **M** I'm so glad I've started ________________________ ________________________ these days.

   W Yeah, it's a lot healthier than eating at the employee cafeteria.

   M You can say that again. It's also cheaper, and ________ ________________________.

④ **W** Well, that was a really good lunch.

   M I have to agree with you, but it's about time that we head back to the office.

   W Yeah, I don't really want to go back, but ____________ ________________________________.

   M Exactly. My wife won't be happy if I come home from work late again tonight.

⑤ **W** What are you thinking of doing for lunch today?

   M Why don't we ________________________________ ________________?

W That sounds like a plan. I don't feel like going out in all this rain.

14 대화를 듣고, 두 사람의 관계를 가장 잘 나타낸 것을 고르시오.

W I can't believe what just happened. I saw the entire thing if you want to hear about it.

M Yes, I'd appreciate your giving me a statement. _________ _______________________________?

W I was waiting to cross the street here. Traffic going north-south was stopped while _______________ _______________.

M Please go on.

W I noticed the light was changing because most of the cars started slowing down. But that red car suddenly started speeding up like the driver wanted to make it through the light. ____________________________ _______________________, which was just beginning to move through the intersection.

M Okay, it sounds like you saw exactly what a couple of other people did as well.

W ___________________________. I just hope they can get a tow truck here quickly so that traffic won't be stopped for too long.

M We've already called one, so it's on its way. Oh, if you don't mind, I need your name and a telephone number where we can reach you.

W Sure, let me write them down for you.

M You'll probably get contacted by someone in my office as well as both drivers' insurance companies. _________ _______________.

15 다음을 듣고, 슬로푸드 운동에 대해 사실이 아닌 것을 고르시오.

W The slow-food movement is a relatively recent attempt to return people to the basics of good eating. Today's lifestyles _______________________________ ___________________, which leaves little time for eating. The emphasis in the slow-food movement is on taking one's time while dining, whether at home or in a restaurant. According to the members of this group, _______________________________, not a race to eat as quickly as one can. Members believe that the dining table is a place to relax, enjoy food, and talk to family and friends. Cooking as a group and teaching cooking to the next generation are also very important. Fresh, organically grown food is the choice of slow-food movement members, and _______________ _______________________________ ____________________. Naturally, they're also against any type of fast-food restaurant or instant food. _______________ _______________________________ and has since spread both to North America and Asia.

16 대화를 듣고, 카페인 복용의 장단점을 고르시오.

W Are you already drinking another cup of coffee? Isn't that the third cup you've had since lunch?

M I really need the caffeine to help me stay awake. I haven't gotten a good night's sleep ever since I started working on this project, so I need something to help me ____________________________.

W Well, that's true, but all that caffeine can't be good for your body. I read in a magazine that if you ingest too much caffeine, _____________________________ _______________.

M That's all right. I don't normally drink caffeine, so, once this project ends, I'll stop. Anyway, I feel so much more alert nowadays. It's a pretty good feeling.

W But look at _______________________________ _______________. They never did that before you drank all that coffee.

M Hmm… I hadn't noticed that before.

W And you're also speaking really quickly and moving around like you're nervous. Seriously, all that caffeine is bad for you. Do me a favor and stop drinking so much of it.

M Okay, I'll do that _______________________ _______________.

W Great. Your body will thank you for doing that. And you'll be protecting your health in the future.

17 다음을 듣고, 일기예보와 일치하지 <u>않는</u> 것을 고르시오.

M Now, let's take a look at the long-range forecast for the coming weekend on the Korean peninsula. In the south, there will be continued high winds and heavy seas from the typhoon _______________. People should remain indoors and refrain from driving since, while the typhoon will avoid us, we can still expect some heavy rain. Between fifty and one hundred millimeters are expected. However, _______________. On Saturday, the skies will still be cloudy in the south, and there will still be a a ten-percent chance of light rain. In the north, there will be fewer clouds, and, by Saturday afternoon, _______________. Temperatures on Saturday should be in the high twenties. Sunday is expected to be sunny and hot, with the temperature climbing to _______________ and twenty-nine degrees in Seoul and the west coast. This heat will bring increased humidity, and, thus, there will be more rainfall on Monday.

18 다음을 듣고, 이야기의 분위기를 가장 잘 나타낸 것을 고르시오.

M Detective Max Gordon leaped from his burning car and dashed into the nearby alley. As he ran, the rain continued to pour and completely drenched him. Not far behind were the two thugs on his tail, and Max _______________. He turned the corner but saw he was in a dead end. Max stopped to catch his breath and then noticed the lid of a garbage can. He listened closely, and then he _______________. A light overhead cast shadows on the ground, and Max could see two men approaching with guns drawn. When the first one came around the corner Max smashed the garbage lid across the thug's gun hand, and the gun skidded across the ground as the man shouted. _______________. There was an all-out brawl as

Max smashed, punched, and clawed at the two men _______________.

19 다음을 듣고, 화자의 직업이 무엇인지 고르시오.

M Is everyone ready to begin? This is going to be a family portrait with five people, so _______________. Mr. Kim, can you stand in the back, please? Yes, that's perfect. I want your son to stand next to you on the right. Okay, that's great where he's standing now. I'm going to place the three ladies in front of the men and have them sitting down. Mr. Kim's mother _______________, his daughter should sit right in front of her father, and his wife should be in front of her son. Is everyone fine? Good, everyone please hold that pose. Okay, I need to adjust the lights a bit. Mr. Kim, _______________? That yes, that looks better. Now I need the men to move apart just a bit. Both of you turn your shoulders a bit so that you're facing each other more. Thank you. _______________.

20 대화를 듣고, 남자에 대해 사실이 <u>아닌</u> 것을 고르시오.

W We need to talk about our trip to visit your parents in the countryside.
M I was hoping to fly there and then rent a car to drive around.
W _______________. Why don't we drive there instead?
M I hate driving all those hours to get there. And the roads there are going to be packed since it's a holiday weekend. Besides, money isn't important _______________.
W Well, I'd still rather drive there. Anyway, where are we staying? Your parents won't have any room at their place since your brother's family is already there.
M Yeah, _______________. I suppose we could stay at that hotel near their place.
W No way. That place is a dive. You know, I found a nice little bed and breakfast on the Internet that's about thirty minutes from their place. _______________.

M Sure, but we're going to be with my family most of the time. We won't have the chance to do any activities. And I'd rather be five minutes away than thirty.

W Well, let me see what I can find. ___________________
___________________ .

21 대화를 듣고, 다음 그래프에 대해 사실이 <u>아닌</u> 것을 고르시오.

M I have to get home soon. I've got this great idea _______
___________________ .

W You really love your blog a lot, don't you?

M That's the truth. Nowadays, more and more people all around the world are getting into them. However, ___________________
Check out this graph that I found.

W Wow, it seems that English and Japanese are by far the main languages people blog in. It's easy to understand why English is the leader since it's an international language. ___________________ ?

M I think many Japanese update their blogs through their cell phones. And you know how important the cell phone culture is in Japan, right?

W Totally. It looks like ___________________
___________________ .

M That's correct. The reason is that millions of Chinese are getting hooked up to the Internet.

W I'd be willing to bet that Chinese overtakes Japanese in a few years.

M That'll probably happen. But it looks like European languages like Russian, German, and Spanish _______
___________________ .

W I'm sure of that. Not enough people around the world speak those languages for them ___________________
___________________ .

22 대화를 듣고, 남자의 마지막 말에 들어갈 말로 가장 알맞은 것을 고르시오.

W I'm so excited ___________________
___________________ . I'm going to love spending time with my friends.

M You're driving to the beach this weekend, right?

W Yeah, I haven't been there in a while, so I'm going to

have fun. We're taking my car, but ___________________
___________________ .
After all, it's a four-hour drive.

M You're taking your car, huh? Are you sure that's a good idea?

W Why not? It has enough room for all six people going on the trip. If we tried to cram into someone else's car, there wouldn't be enough legroom.

M That's not what I'm talking about. Take a look at that little pool of liquid forming underneath your car. _______
___________________ .

W Oh, it's probably harmless. I'm not worried about ___________________
___________________ .

M You ought to care. That's brake fluid. It might seem like it's small, but losing some could be the difference between life and death. You might find yourself hitting the brakes ___________________ .

W Oh, I think I see what you mean. ___________________
___________________ , right?

M Exactly, or you'll have a huge problem. Just remember,...

23 대화를 듣고, 현금지급기의 사용 방법을 순서대로 나열한 것을 고르시오.

W ___________________ ?
I can't get it to work right.

M You're trying one of those new ATMs, aren't you? They work a little differently than the old kind.

W Don't I just put in my card and punch all of the buttons?

M No, not exactly. Actually, the first thing that you need to do is ___________________
___________________ .

W What? You mean I don't swipe my card first?

M No, you don't. You're going to make a withdrawal, right? In that case, go ahead and push the button for that. ___________________
___________________ .

W Okay, I can do that. But I really prefer the old style where the card stays in the machine. They're a lot easier to use.

M Yeah, I suppose that you're right about that.

W Okay, now the machine is asking me how much I want to take out. So I just hit the button, and then the money is going to come out. Is that correct?

M You forgot about one thing. You need to ___________ ___________, you know, your ___________ ___________, before you can get any money. Only then will you be all set.

24 대화를 듣고, 여자의 마지막 말에 담긴 의도가 무엇인지 고르시오.

M Take a look at your office. ___________.

W Well, I've been busy working on several projects simultaneously, so I haven't been able to clean it up.

M But how can you find anything in all this clutter? I mean, take a look at all of the papers and folders lying around here.

W Strangely enough, I actually seem to know ___________ ___________. It might look messy to you, but I can still find whatever I'm looking for.

M Are you sure about that? It sure doesn't look like ___________ ___________.

W Yeah, don't worry about me. At least my office is just messy and not dirty. I don't have any empty pizza boxes or fast-food wrappers lying around here like someone that I know.

M What? Are you talking about me?

W I sure am. You're the one ___________ ___________. While mine might have tons of papers lying around, yours is lucky ___________ ___________.

M Hmm… I suppose you may be partially right about that.

W I'm totally right. So, the next time I need some tips on how to straighten up my office, ___________ ___________. Okay, Mr. Clean?

25 대화를 듣고, 두 사람이 이야기하고 있는 도자기를 고르시오.

W Ah, we're in my favorite part of the museum. I absolutely love the oriental ceramics exhibition.

M ___________. Fine porcelain is really like artwork if you ask me. So, what's your favorite type of ceramics? I love ones that have wide bodies but thin bottlenecks.

W I can't say I agree with you. ___________ ___________. Here, let me point out my favorite one in the museum's collection. There it is.

M What, you mean the one with the flower designs painted all over it?

W No, not that one. I'm talking about the one with ___________ ___________.

M Ah, yes, that one is pretty nice. I love that ___________ ___________.

W Yes, it's practically the same size from the bottom to the top. I think that's why I like it so much. ___________ ___________.

M Yes, and it's somewhat unusual in that it has only one handle as opposed to two of them.

W You're absolutely right about that. ___________ ___________ can sometimes upset the balance of the work, which is why I feel it's so finely crafted.

M Wow, I had never considered that before.

26 What best completes the speaker's last sentence?

M There are many ways to greet people in different cultures. In the West, ___________ ___________, but there are some differences. In Russia, for instance, men shake hands virtually every time they meet while American men usually don't shake hands with people they see everyday. Both traditional Jewish and Muslim cultures ___________ ___________, so shaking hands is forbidden. In France, when a woman greets a man or woman, she gives a small kiss on the cheek whereas North Americans tend not to kiss unless they haven't met in a long time. In Eastern countries, particularly Japan, China, and Korea, people meet ___________ ___________. It's considered a sign of respect. Additionally, ___________ ___________, ___________ ___________. These cultures also use handshakes, but the older of the two people must initiate it. ___________ ___________, such as saying "hello" or "hi." This, of course, varies from culture to culture. So, you should…

27 Which of the following is NOT true about Hangeul?

M Learning Korean is hard, especially __________________

____.

W You're referring to Hangeul, right? Did you know Hangeul has a pretty interesting history?

M I heard some king invented it a long time ago, but that's about all I know.

W Yes, Hangeul ______________________________________

__________________, who lived from 1397 to 1450. He probably didn't create it by himself, but he's still given credit for it. Hangeul was made because there was no Korean script at the time. Literate Koreans used Chinese characters.

M That makes sense. ________________________________

____.

W You can say that again. After all, there are only fourteen consonants and ten vowels. But, since the symbols can be placed into different syllabic blocks,

____

______________________.

M Yeah, it seems like you can make so many words. I'm really impressed by that. It makes studying hard though.

W True, but the ease with which people can learn Hangeul has helped Korea decrease its illiteracy rate. After all, many people can learn Hangeul ______________________

__________________________.

M True, but they can't master it that quickly.

W No, but they can still start sounding out words that fast.

28 Which of the following people agrees with the speaker?

W ____

which is primarily concerned with two things: curbing the growing power of multinational corporations and limiting free-trade agreements. Many people fear that some companies are growing too powerful and may one day replace nations ____________________________

__________________________. Coupled with this is a sense that national pride and growth are being sacrificed by creating free-trade zones. Anti-globalization believers think that ______________________________________

________________________________. I couldn't agree more with these people. National industries must be protected from cheap products from other nations. When more foreign products enter a country, that country tends to lose jobs in its domestic industries, which increases unemployment. In addition, __________

____.

A nation is run by its duly-elected officials, not by the seemingly unlimited money some of these corporations have. Another aspect of anti-globalization is __________

____.

This can especially been seen in the growing use of English as an international language.

29 What is this food?

M This food originated long ago with the Greeks and Romans. They would put onions, olives, and other vegetables on flat pieces of bread and then eat them as meals or snacks. ______________________________________

______________________________________, even after the decline of Rome and Greece. In the late nineteenth century in Naples, Italy, ______________________________

____ for Queen Margarita's visit. It had green peppers, white mozzarella cheese, and red tomatoes on flat bread and was arranged in the shape of the Italian flag. The queen tried it and loved it, and it soon spread all over Italy. When ______________________________________,
they brought this dish with them and even established restaurants in many American cities. During World War II, American soldiers carried this food all over the world, ____.
It has even been eaten aboard the space station. Today, almost every country has some version of it, and it's estimated that ______________________________________

__________________.

30 What are they mostly talking about?

W Now that we've finally gotten settled down in our house, we need to start thinking about hosting a housewarming party.

M Yeah, that would let all of our friends see where we live.
____
_______________________________, too.

W You're right. So I was thinking that we could have the party catered like Dave and Lisa did for theirs.

M No, I don't like that idea. _______________________
_____________________________________, much like John and Nancy did. It'll be a lot of work, but I think we can do it if we team up.

W Okay, the food at John and Nancy's place was really good, so we'll do that. _________________________
__________________ Dave and Lisa's party?

M It was great. It wasn't too loud, nor was it too soft, so it didn't interfere with anyone's conversation.

W Yeah, that was the best thing about it. And I really liked that John and Nancy had us _______________
_____________________________________.

M You're right. They were excellent icebreakers since all their friends didn't know each other.

W We should do the same thing at ours.

M ____.

〔31-34〕 31번부터 34번까지는 질문과 보기를 모두 듣고 푸는 문제입니다. 대화나 이야기를 듣고, 영어로 들려주는 질문에 대한 알맞은 답을 고르시오.

31

W You won't believe the new roommate I just got. _______
_____________________________________.

M Really? I thought you told me she seemed nice when you met her the first time.

W Looks can be deceiving. _________________________
_______________________________.

M What exactly has she done?

W Well, as soon as she got settled in the apartment, she walked into my room and _____________________
___________________________. Can you believe that?

M That wasn't very considerate of her.

W Oh, that's not all. She even started rearranging all of the furniture in the living room. She told me I have no sense of style and that she wanted to redo the house. And when she saw a picture of my boyfriend, she started
____

_____________________________. She wasn't complimentary at all.

M That's awful. Is there any way for you to get rid of her?

W I need to have a chat with her.

M _____________________________________. You ought to tell her _______________________________
_______________________________.

Q: *Which sentence is the woman likely to say to her roommate?*

M ① Don't poke your nose where it doesn't belong.
② There's more than one way to skin a cat.
③ You are such a yellow-bellied person.
④ You have really come out of your shell.
⑤ That's just the icing on the cake.

32

W Hello, I just wanted to say how satisfied I am with the Brew Master 600 that I ordered from your company. It has a faster brewing time than my previous coffee machine, and ___________________________________
_____________________________. And the twelve-cup-capacity pot is great since everyone in my family enjoys drinking a good cup of coffee. _______________________________
_____________________________, and I always set it so that the coffee is ready exactly when we wake up. All my friends asked about it, and I gave them your number. Three of them have received it already, and they say it's the best coffee machine they've ever bought. By the way, the reason I'm calling is that _____________________________
_____________________________.
It's my sister's birthday in a week, and I think the Brew Master 600 would make _______________________.

Q: *What is the purpose of the phone call?*

M ① to complain about a product
② to make an order
③ to advertise something
④ to inform someone about an item
⑤ to return a purchase

33

M Winter is just around the corner as the balmy fall days are ending. Expect temperatures to drop this week ________________________ ________________________. While no snow is expected at the beginning of the week, temperatures will drop to almost freezing on Monday. ________________________ ________________________, and there is an eighty-percent chance of rain and freezing rain on Tuesday and Wednesday. On Thursday, ________________________ ________________________.

Please use caution when driving as there will be serious whiteout conditions on all highways, especially near the ocean. The snow will continue on Saturday ________________________ ________________________.

The east coast mountains are going to get at least ten centimeters of snow by Saturday. A new cold front is expected to move through the area by Sunday, ________________________ ________________________ ________________________.

Q : *Which of the following is NOT true according to the weather forecast?*

M ① Monday will not experience any snowfall.
　② The roads near the ocean will be dangerous on Friday.
　③ The coldest day of the week will be Sunday.
　④ Hardly any snow will fall on the east coast.
　⑤ There is a good chance of rain on Tuesday.

34

W Jim, I'm sorry I couldn't make it to your office today. Why don't we reschedule our meeting as soon as possible?

M That sounds good. I'm in favor of getting together as soon as possible because we've got a lot to talk about and ________________________.

W All right, well, today is Monday, and I'm all tied up, so ________________________?

M It's good, but only in the afternoon. I'm out of the office in the morning.

W Then that's no good for me since I'll be on the factory floor all afternoon.

M In that case, how about the day after tomorrow? ________________________ ________________________?

W I've got a lot of free time. What time are you thinking of meeting?

M I was hoping for either nine in the morning or four in the afternoon. I've got a luncheon from twelve to three, so ________________________ ________________________.

W Let's go for the morning time. We can chat, and then ________________________.

M Great. I'll see you then.

Q : *When are the speakers going to meet?*

M ① Monday at 10 a.m.
　② Monday at 4 p.m.
　③ Tuesday at noon
　④ Wednesday at 10 a.m.
　⑤ Wednesday at 3 p.m.

35 주어진 시간 동안 아래 지문을 주의 깊게 읽고, 대화를 들은 후 질문에 답하시오. 〔1분〕

M I've got to write a report on Martin Luther King, Jr., but I don't know that much about him.

W Are you serious? He was ________________________ ________________________. He helped change the entire country.

M I know he was big on civil rights, but I'm not exactly sure how.

W Well, he managed to get some legislation passed ________ ________________________. Remember that several decades ago, not everyone was treated the same in the U.S.

M Right, but I'm a little confused about his tactics. ________ ________________________?

W No, he didn't. Some other groups did, but the people who followed King ________________________ ________________________.

M Like what? What did they do?

W Well, King led the Montgomery Bus Boycott from 1955 to 1956. ________________________, but he got the city of Montgomery to change its laws.

M Why didn't he ever resort to physically fighting?

Q : *Which is the best answer to the man's last words?*

36 다음을 듣고, 이어지는 영어 질문에 답하시오.

M Today is Sunday, so Sumi is taking her dog for a walk in the local park like she did yesterday. She always takes her dog __________________________________. Then she takes her dog for a walk next to the river __________________. Next, she takes her dog to a local school's playground __________________________________. Finally, she goes to the lake for one day and then returns to the park the next day.

Q : *On which day will Sumi take her dog to the lake?*

[37-38] 대화를 듣고, 이어지는 두 개의 질문에 답하시오.

W Dr. Weston, because there are so many fad diets out there these days, our readers are very interested in learning __________________________________ __________________________________.

M It's true that many people are following some strange diets, which can wind up hurting them more than helping them.

W Now, I've heard it's possible for a person __________________ __________________________________. What do you think about that?

M I'm sorry, but that's just wrong. A person can lose several pounds very quickly, but __________________ __________________________________. Plus, most of the weight loss tends to be water, which the person can quickly regain.

W What about the notion of an all-meat diet being very healthy.

M You must be kidding. A person needs to eat a balanced diet, one which includes fruits, grains, and vegetables. __________________________________ __________________________________.

W But isn't a lot of meat supposed to be good for you since it is high in protein? I believe our own magazine had an article about that not too long ago.

M Well, meat, of course, does have a lot of protein, but a person should be careful about eating too much of it, __________________________________. It can clog up arteries and lead to heart problems if you overeat it and enjoy it too much.

W Well, that's very interesting to know.

37 What is the woman's occupation?

38 Which of the following are proven false by the doctor? Check all that apply.

[39-40] 다음을 듣고, 이어지는 두 개의 질문에 답하시오.

M Are you looking for an exciting place to visit? Why not come to London? It's a fantastic city with a mix of both the old and the new. __________________________________ __________________________________. Our package tour includes the cost of the flight, four days and three nights at a lovely hotel, and a bus tour of London on a real double-decker bus. On the first day, you will check out Buckingham Palace, Trafalgar Square, the Tower of London, and Westminster Abby __________________________________ __________________________________. On the second day, you will go on a Thames River boat cruise to be followed by a visit to the Millennium Dome and the London Eye, one of the world's biggest Ferris wheels. The last full tour day will be yours for shopping or to take in any of the other sights you may wish to enjoy. __________________________________ __________________________________ and is affordable for all. Call one of our operators at our office at 555-2309. And remember to ask about ________ __________________________________.

39 What is the best title of this talk?

40 Which of the following is NOT true about this tour?

01 대화를 듣고, 두 사람이 이야기하고 있는 장소를 고르시오.

W May I have your name and address please?

M I live at 12 Baker Street.

W And ____
____, please?

M It's 555-6691.

W Okay, I think that should just about do it. Here is your reservation.

M Thanks. I'm glad that we got that taken care of.

W You reserved a small car, right? _________________________
_________________________________?

M Yes, I will be the only one who will be driving.

W Let me make a copy of your license for our records. I'll be right back in a couple of seconds.

M Okay.

W Oh, I see that your license is damaged. Do you have ___
_________________________________ with you?

M I'm afraid that I don't. You know, I've never had anyone else tell me that there's a problem with my license before.

W My manager is very strict, so _______________________
_________________________ I have copies of two forms of identification that belong to you.

M Here's my passport. _________________________________
_________________________?

W Yes, thank you very much. Have a seat over there. I'll have everything ready for you in a minute.

02 대화를 듣고, 여자가 책장을 파는 이유를 고르시오.

M Hello. May I speak to Mrs. Robinson, please?

W This is Mrs. Robinson speaking.

M Hello, my name is Jack Smith. I'm calling _____________
_________________________________. I only saw the advertisement this morning. You haven't sold it yet, have you?

W Actually, you're the first person to call about the ad. So, no, ____.

M The ad mentioned that you're selling it for $50. Is that the correct price?

W Yes, and ____.
I've only had it for two years, but I'm moving to a

smaller apartment, so I'm afraid that _________________
_________________________________.

M I think $50 is a good price. I really want the bookcase, but the problem is that I don't have a car. Do you think that you could hold on to it for a few more days until I can arrange to have one of my friends drive me over to pick it up?

W Let's see… Today's Sunday, and _____________________
_________________________________. So I've got to get rid of it by then. Is that going to be possible for you?

M I don't think so. Let me call you back so that I can figure out some way to get that bookshelf out of your place.

03 대화를 듣고, 인터뷰를 위해 준비된 것으로 언급되지 <u>않은</u> 것을 고르시오.

M So, how was your interview?

W I haven't gone to the interview yet. It's tomorrow morning. I'm already nervous.

M Don't worry. You'll be fine. You have _________________
_________________________________. You'll be the best person for the job.

W I hope so. Say, would you write ______________________
_________________________ for the job?

M No problem. I'm sure they'll ask you for one anyway. I'll say that you work well with people and that you're hard working and responsible.

W I sound really boring!

M Nonsense, ____
_________________________.

W Thanks for the help.

M Good luck with the interview tomorrow. ______________
_________________________________. You'll be fine.

04 대화를 듣고, 여자가 외출할 수 <u>없는</u> 이유를 고르시오.

M Jane, how are you doing?

W Oh, hi, Mark. Life is crazy these days, and when I'm not at work, I'm at college.

M I know what you mean. _____________________________
_________________________________. I'm

calling because I'm getting together with Lisa and Mike tonight. We're probably going out to eat and then maybe we'll have coffee together. ____________________ ____________________?

W I'd really love to, but I have an important work presentation tomorrow.

M That's too bad. But you know ____________________ ____________________. We should be home by 11 p.m. at the latest. Maybe you need a break. ____________________ ____________________? It's time to get a life.

W You don't understand. There's nothing I'd like more. But I haven't finished the presentation yet and the meeting is first thing in the morning.

M All right then. But next time no excuses. You need to relax more. Everyone has been complaining that ______ ____________________.

W You're right. There's more to life than working and studying.

M I'll give you a call soon, and hopefully you'll be less busy next time.

W I promise I'll be available.

05 대화를 듣고, 남자가 쇼핑몰에 다녀오는 방법을 가장 잘 나타낸 것을 고르시오.

M Mom, how do I get to the Woods Shopping Mall? I'm planning to go there for a while.

W You can take bus number 5, but if you want to go now, ____________________.

M Thanks, Mom. Can you wait while I take a shower?

W Sure, I can wait for you, but don't be too long. I've got to meet some friends of my own after I finish shopping. ____________________ ____________________.

M I won't, Mom. I'm supposed to meet Jim outside the shoe store in thirty minutes. His mother is buying him some new shoes, and he wants me to help him choose a cool pair.

W That's a good idea. ____________________ ____________________ with him?

M We might see a movie after we find the shoes, or maybe we will get some dinner while we're there.

W I won't wait for you at the mall then since I've got other things to do. You had better take the bus back home.

M Okay, but Jim said that ____________________ ____________________, so that's how I plan to get home.

06 다음을 듣고, 알프레드 노벨이 다섯 가지 상을 제정한 이유를 고르시오.

W Nobel Prizes have been awarded in ____________________ ____________________ and ____________________ since 1901. Alfred Nobel, a Swedish scientist, used his will to institute the first five prizes in 1895. The prize for economics was instituted by Sweden's central bank in 1968. ____________________ ____________________. Except for the peace prize, which is handed out in Oslo, Norway, they are all awarded in Stockholm, Sweden, at an annual ceremony on December 10, the anniversary of Nobel's death. Nobel was himself ____________________ ____________________. Before his death Nobel became ____________________ ____________________ and therefore decided to leave 94% of his total assets for the establishment of the five prizes to promote study and research.

07 대화를 듣고, 남자가 바커 인터내셔널 회사에서 일하는 것에 대해 걱정하는 점이 무엇인지 고르시오.

M Pardon me, but is anyone sitting here?

W No.

M Then do you mind if I join you?

W Please go ahead.

M It's just that… How can I put this? I know that you work for Barker International, and I'm dying to get a job there. ____________________ ____________________?

W I don't mind at all although I had assumed that you wanted the pleasure of my company for lunch.

M You must think I'm so rude.

W ____________________.

M Are you happy working at that company?

W What a difficult question. Yes, I think I am happy although I have a pretty stressful job and a very tough boss.

M ____________________, isn't it?

W It's a good salary, yes, and ________________________
________________________.
M Such as?
W That's a very personal question.
M But it's important. My present company offers no perks at all.
W I think that you might want to work at Barker International ________________________.
Yes, the company pays us very well. But, in return, ____
________________________.

08 대화를 듣고, 여자의 마지막 말에 대한 남자의 응답으로 알맞은 것을 고르시오.

M I'm starting to run before work in the morning since I absolutely have to get into shape.
W Where do you run when you go out?
M I always jog at Center Park. It takes about 35 minutes to go around the park once. I'd love to do more, _______
________________________.
W That sounds very tiring, especially if you're going before work.
M Not really. I feel so much better after jogging. I even have more energy, and ________________________.
W I used to run in the evenings a long time ago. ________________________.
M Why don't you come with me one morning, and we'll run around the park once? If you don't like it, you don't have to come with me again. But if you do, we can run together every morning. It would be __________
________________________.
W I don't know if I could do it every day, but I suppose ________________________.
M Let's meet at the entrance to the park at about 6 a.m.
W That's so early that I'm sure I'll still be yawning, but okay.

09 대화를 듣고, 화자들이 이야기하고 있는 사람을 고르시오.

W How are you enjoying the party? Have you met a lot of people tonight?
M I'm surprised to say this, but I'm having a good time. I don't usually get out, but ________________________

________________________.
W You know, there's someone whom you absolutely have to meet. His name is Kevin. Have you talked to him yet?
M No, I'm afraid I haven't had the pleasure of being introduced to him. Is he one of those guys standing over there in the corner?
W Yes, he is. ________________________
________________________, so you'll be sure to like him. He's
________________________.
M The one on the right who is kind of short?
W Oh, no. That's Lewis. Kevin is fairly tall and pretty skinny. He's also got medium-length hair.
M We'll there are two guys like that. Is he the one wearing
________________________,
or is he the person with the T-shirt and shorts?
W He's got the button-down shirt on. He actually usually wears suits, so he's going casual tonight.
M Okay, I'll be sure to talk to him if you think that
________________________.

10 다음을 듣고, 대기에 대한 설명으로 옳지 않은 것을 고르시오.

M The atmosphere is ________________________
________________________ and which is held in place by gravity. It is made up of nitrogen, oxygen, argon, carbon dioxide, water vapor, and other gases. This mixture of gases is commonly known as air.
________________________.
This helps to lower the temperature of the planet, which makes life possible. ________________________
________________________.
________________________. There is no clear boundary between the atmosphere and outer space. The higher it goes, the thinner the atmosphere becomes until it finally fades away into space. The Karman line, which is 100 kilometers above the Earth, is commonly used
____
________________________. However, it's different in other countries. In the United States, for example, people who travel above a height of 80.5 kilometers above the planet are considered astronauts.

11

대화를 듣고, 남자가 여자만큼 배가 고프지 <u>않은</u> 이유를 고르시오.

W I'm starving right now. _______________________
_______________________?

M It's 11:30 a.m., so we've got another half an hour until lunch.

W I won't survive unless I get something to eat right now.

M Here, why don't you have some water?

W Water? I'd like some food _______________________
_______________________. I was running late and barely got here on time.

M Stop thinking about food, and you should be fine.

W Don't you have a snack that I can eat to help hold me over until lunch?

M Like what? All I have is water and apples.

W You've always got healthy food. However, _______________________ like cookies or perhaps a doughnut.

M That sounds terrible. You know that you won't feel like eating lunch if you start eating cookies now, don't you?

W _______________________ since I don't have any cookies with me right now. I'm usually fine if I eat breakfast in the morning, but I'm simply starving today.

M It's never a good idea to miss breakfast. _______________________. That's why I'm feeling fine and you're not.

12

대화를 듣고, 남자가 구입하려고 하는 것을 모두 고르시오.

M I'm so excited. I just signed a contract to rent an apartment, so I'll be moving there in a couple of weeks.

W Congratulations. You must be so excited finally to be getting out of your parents' home _______________________.

M I am, but now I've got to spend a lot of money on furniture and stuff. _______________________.

W Wow, that's going to be expensive.

M You're telling me. I won't have enough money for everything I need, so I'll have to figure out what the most important things are.

W That's smart. Well, you'll definitely need _______________________
_______________________.

M I agree on everything except the washing machine. I'll just have to go to a laundromat for the first couple of months.

W Well, that's not too bad. _______________________
_______________________? Surely you'll need one of those.

M I'm going to get both since they're fairly inexpensive. And _______________________ but not a computer. I'll just use the one I have at work.

W Great. And I can give you an iron if you want it. I've got an extra one lying around my home.

13

다음을 듣고, 임주영 박사가 대학에서 가르치기 시작한 해를 고르시오.

W The Seoul Chamber of Commerce would like to congratulate Dr. Yim Ju Young _______________________ the Seoul Chamber of the Arts and Literature. He will take up his appointment on May 30, 2008. Dr. Yim graduated from the Department of English Literature of Seoul National University in 1970. He immigrated to the United States in 1977, _______________________ in English Literature at the State University of New York. He taught at the University of Wisconsin _______________________
_______________________. He also serves as president of the Korea Foundation for the Arts.

14

대화를 듣고, 상황에 가장 잘 어울리는 속담을 고르시오.

W How did your presentation go this morning?

M _______________________. So many things went wrong that it was really embarrassing.

W But you worked so hard. How could that have happened? What went wrong?

M I prepared the presentation, but, during the meeting, the entire team _______________________
_______________________.

W But I thought you'd decided that one person would do the presentation and everyone else would answer the questions afterwards.

M Yes, that's what we had decided. But in the meeting, everyone seemed to have forgotten __________________ __________________________.

W You must have been really angry. I know that I would have been.

M I was. We looked as if we hadn't prepared properly. My manager said that he wants to see me in his office tomorrow morning. __________________ __________________________.

W You should explain exactly what happened. The situation could easily have been avoided, especially since you worked so hard and for so many hours. __________________________.

15 다음을 듣고, 집을 짓는 과정을 순서대로 나열한 것을 고르시오.

M These days, many people are choosing not to purchase homes that have already been built. Instead, they're having their own homes __________________ __________________________. Unfortunately, this process is often complicated, especially for first-time homeowners. But there are a few things they can do to ensure their home gets built as smoothly and as easily as possible. The first thing a future homeowner should do __________________ __________________________. After that, he or she should choose the lot where the house is going to be built. This, of course, should be accounted for in the budget. __________________ __________________________, the individual needs to pick both the architect and the builders. Next, since the architect will undoubtedly present at least two or three different designs for the house, the plan to be followed needs to be selected. Finally, __________________ __________________________. Once this is done, construction on the new house can begin.

16 대화를 듣고, 내용과 일치하는 것을 고르시오.

W What a disaster. __________________________.
It looks like we're going to have to wait for a long time before we get to the front.

M I'm sorry that I didn't book the tickets online like you asked me to. We could have been sitting down already.

W I don't think we'll even get in. The tickets will be sold out __________________ __________________________.

M Don't worry. I don't think anyone wants to see the movie we're going to watch. Most people are here to see __________________________.

W You may be right about that. Look over there. They've opened a new counter, __________________ __________________________.

M I've got an idea. I'll stand in line while you go get our drinks. After all, we don't want to walk in after the movie starts.

W Okay. Would you like me to get you some popcorn?

M I'd really appreciate it, but make sure __________________ __________________________, please. Oh, and I want a diet soda, too.

W No problem. I'll meet you in a couple of minutes.

17 다음을 듣고, 다음 문장의 빈칸에 어울리지 <u>않는</u> 것을 고르시오.

W Now that summer is beginning, __________________ __________________________. Unfortunately, most people don't take all the precautions they should so wind up suffering from heatstroke or developing other heat-related problems. __________________________, people should remember to do a few important things. First, and most importantly, people need to __________________ __________________________. So long as they are outside in the sun, they should drink lots of water. Even when they're not thirsty, they still need water, especially if they're sweating a lot. Without water, __________________ __________________________. Additionally, people shouldn't stay in the sun for too long. Remaining under the blazing sun can cause people __________________ __________________________. Finally, if people have to be in the sun for any length of time, they should wear sunscreen and protect themselves with the proper clothes. They should wear light clothes, not dark ones, and protect their heads from __________________ __________________________.

18 대화를 듣고, 여자의 마지막 말에 대한 남자의 응답으로 알
맞은 것을 고르시오.

W Eric, you'll never guess what I found today.

M I give up. Go ahead and tell me.

W Well, I know you've been looking all over for that book
on early American history. You know what I'm talking
about, right? It's the one ________________________
____.

M Sure, that's the book by Roger Jackson. I know what
you're talking about… Wait a second. ________________
________________________________. You
didn't, did you?

W Well… I didn't exactly find a copy, but I got the next
best thing.

M Okay, hurry up and tell me about it. You know I've
been dying to get my hands on a copy of that book.

W All right, let me see. I was at the local used bookstore
____
________________. Well, for some reason, I decided to ask
the clerk if they had the Jackson book.

M Did they?

W No, they didn't. But ________________________________
________________________, and he mentioned that he had
two copies of that book in his collection and would be
willing to part with one if the price was right. So, ______
____?

19 다음을 듣고, 화자의 의견에 동의하는 진술을 고르시오.

M When going to a job interview, you must be careful to
____ with
the people who may eventually become your employers.
Too many people, ________________________________
________________________, fail to prepare sufficiently for
their interviews and therefore don't get hired. All it
takes is a little bit of common sense to avoid making
these foolish mistakes. Interviewees should make sure
____
________________________. Wearing blue jeans and a
T-shirt to an interview is a sure way not to get hired.
Additionally, resumes and cover letters ________________
____.
Many potential employers will throw out any job
applications that are poorly written or which have

mistakes in them. Interviewees should also be kind,
courteous, and well-spoken. They should take every
opportunity ____
________________________________, yet they should also be
careful not to come across as arrogant. By acting in
this manner, the chances of a person getting hired will
____.

20 대화를 듣고, 내용과 일치하는 것을 고르시오.

W Thanks for your help on that project. I couldn't have
done it without you.

M ____ so don't
worry about it.

W I'd like to buy you lunch at that new Italian place that
just opened as a way of thanking you.

M That sounds nice, but ________________________________
________________________________?

W I didn't know that. What made you decide to give up
meat?

M I just stopped enjoying it and then decided that I
should stop eating it altogether.

W So what do you eat instead?

M I eat eggs and drink milk, or I have nuts and soy foods.
____
________________________. As a matter of fact, we
actually have many choices.

W It sounds as if your diet is very healthy as well.

M It is. And my doctor says that I'm in much better shape
____.

W Well, I'll find a restaurant that serves the kind of food
you'd like to eat, and then we'll go there.

21 대화를 듣고, 두 사람이 주로 무엇에 대해 이야기하고 있는
지 고르시오.

W Do you still play golf these days?

M Of course I do. I love to play that game. Why do you
ask?

W My husband is learning to play and ________________
____.

M Tell him to give me a call. I'd love to play a game or two
with him. How good is he?

W I don't think he's very good yet since he's only been

playing for about two months.

M If he's just a beginner, then it's possible that I could teach him a few things.

W He'd love that and really appreciate it. It's so important to him to play well because _______________________. He thinks it's a good way _______________________.

M He's absolutely right. _______________________. I got tired of having to buy people dinner all the time. Now I just invite my contacts to play golf instead. Most businesspeople enjoy playing the game after all.

W My husband will probably give you a call this evening. I hope _______________________.

22 대화를 듣고, 총 몇 명이 식사를 할 것인지 고르시오.

W Good evening, sir. _______________________?

M Yes, I do.

W What is your name?

M My name is Brad Pitt.

W Let's see. Oh yes, _______________________. Is that correct?

M Yes, that's correct. _______________________?

W It shouldn't be too much of a problem. I'll tell your waiter to set an extra place at the table.

M Thank you.

W Your reservation is _______________________, isn't it?

M Yes, non-smoking please.

W Come this way, please. We have a table for you _______________________.

M That's great. We can look out over the river while we eat.

W I hope you enjoy your evening.

23 대화를 듣고, 남자가 무엇을 팩스로 받을지 고르시오.

M Hi, how are you doing today?

W I'm doing well today. Thank you for asking.

M I just received an invitation to your party next weekend. _______________________.

W I really hope that you can come. I haven't thrown a

birthday party in about three years.

M So it's next Saturday at your house, right?

W That's right. _______________________.

M Oh, yes. Do you think I can call you to learn the way to your house on the day before the party? I always end up driving around in places I don't know and then get hopelessly lost.

W _______________________, so you shouldn't have any problems.

M That's even better.

W So you're definitely going to come, right? Shall I add you to my list?

M Please do that. _______________________?

W You could bring some of that delicious garlic bread that you make.

M Great.

24 대화를 듣고, 남자의 직업을 고르시오.

M We're having a big sale tomorrow. All dresses and shoes will be on sale for 25% off.

W Wow! _______________________.

M Our doors open at 7:30 a.m., and I imagine that we'll be very busy all day long.

W I hate the crowds that show up at these sales.

M We hate them, too. Most of us will come to work at about 7 a.m. and wind up leaving at about 10 p.m. tomorrow.

W That's too bad. _______________________?

M It's only going to last one day.

W What a pity. I don't know if I'll have a chance to come and look at everything. I'm going to be busy at the office.

M All the best garments _______________________. Why don't you stop by the store before going to work?

W I don't know if I'll have enough time. I'll see.

M _______________________ will be next year. _______________________.

W Now I see why you do such good work at your job. You've convinced me to show up.

M Excellent.

25 다음을 듣고, 화자의 요지를 가장 잘 나타낸 것을 고르시오.

W A popular trend among American parents is for them ____.

This is referred to as homeschooling. While it may appear unusual, homeschoolers often do very well in comparison to students at regular schools. For example, on average, ____, win more contests like spelling bees, and get into higher ranking schools more often than students attending public schools. Parents homeschool their children for several reasons. Some feel that ____, so they prefer to do it themselves. Others like teaching their children subjects, like religion, for example, that aren't covered in public schools. And others feel that public schools are bad influences on their children ____.

Whatever the case, many homeschooled students are highly motivated and, as it turns out, extremely well-educated upon finishing their high school curriculum. Undoubtedly, more students will be choosing __________ ____.

26 대화를 듣고, 다음 공지사항 중 잘못된 부분을 고르시오.

M The biggest and busiest restaurant in Seoul is seeking rising stars to join its team of dedicated professionals. ____ and are looking for a challenge, we would like to meet you. We are looking for mature, neatly groomed, and energetic people. An outgoing personality is a must, and ____. ____.

If these characteristics describe you, then submit an application as soon as you can. If you do not meet these qualifications, then your enquiry or application will not be considered. ____, August 7, from 8:00 a.m. to 6:00 p.m. at Seoul City Restaurant. The location of our restaurant is Gangnam. Please call

us for an appointment. We only have ________________ ____.

27 대화를 듣고, 대화의 내용과 물건과 위치가 일치하지 않는 것을 고르시오.

M Excuse me, but could you let me know where your pasta section is?

W It's right over there ____.

M Okay, and where are the sauces? I need to purchase some tomato sauce, too.

W You can find that in the canned goods section, ________ ____.

M Well, thanks. Oh, by the way, do you sell spices?

W Sure, they're all over here.

M I need to get some oregano and basil.

W Here they are. Will you be needing anything else?

M Well, I guess I could use some vegetables. Let's see… I need ____.
And that should be everything I need.

W Sir, you can find the vegetables in our produce section. ____.

M Oh, there is one last thing. Do you happen to sell fedelini?

W I've never heard of it. It sounds like it's a type of pasta.

M Yes, it is. It's a lot like vermicelli only thicker.

W You could check in the pasta section, sir, but I can't guarantee you'll find it.

M Thanks so much.

28 Why must the woman remind the man about the meeting after work?

W I'm sorry to interrupt you right now, but I have a message for you.

M What's wrong? Is there something I need to fix right now?

W It's not bad news. I'm just supposed to give you this reminder ____ ____.

M Oh, yes. I'd completely forgotten about tonight's meeting.

W I knew you were going to do that ________________________ ____.

M With all the extra work I have right now, it's not surprising that I can't remember to do everything.

W You've still got too few staff members in your office, don't you?

M Yes, but I have just hired two new employees who will start working for me next week.

W That's a relief. Maybe ____.

M Yes, and then you won't have to remind me about all of the important things any more.

W ____.

M Why are we having it so late after work?

W We are meeting the Japanese clients, but their flight has been delayed by a couple of hours.

29 Why is blushing similar to stuttering in a social situation?

M Hello, it's so good to see you today.

W Hi, I'm so glad that you made it here tonight.

M ____.

W Why don't you come in to the dining room? A few other people have already arrived.

M It looks as if I know almost everyone here. What a relief. You know I'm really shy, so when I meet new people, I often start stuttering. It's a habit I had as a child, and ____.

W I had no idea that you stuttered. You're always so confident when we're in the office.

M ____. ____. I worry that I'll start stuttering and that people will think I'm strange.

W When I was a teenager, _______________________________. I used to blush whenever a stranger said something to me. It's like stuttering in a way. It's something you can't hide. But I've since learned to control my blushing, so now I'm fine.

M That's lucky for you. Unfortunately, ____.

30 What will probably happen next?

M I'd like to see the manager, please.

W Could you hold on for a moment, please? ____.

M Tell him that there's an angry customer waiting to speak to him.

W Is there ____, sir?

M I'm so angry. I just found some seafood in my fried rice. And I don't eat seafood.

W I'm sorry. ____ _______________________.

M I usually don't mind getting the wrong order, and I don't get angry very easily. But I told the waiter that I'm allergic to seafood. I get really sick if I eat it, but he still managed to get my order wrong. I don't think he was listening to a word that I said.

W I can understand why you're angry. _______________________ ____? I'll make sure that the chef prepares a new order for you. And your meal will be on the house.

M ____. I want to see the manager, and then I'm leaving.

[31-34] 31번부터 34번까지는 질문과 보기를 모두 듣고 푸는 문제입니다. 대화나 이야기를 듣고, 영어로 들려주는 질문에 대한 알맞은 답을 고르시오.

31

W Why don't we take a break for lunch right now? _______ ____ since we arrived here this morning.

M I agree. What do you feel like eating?

W I feel like having a toasted sandwich and a cup of strong coffee.

M ____. It's just a snack. Let's go to the restaurant around the corner and get some proper food.

W I'd like that, but we don't have enough time to go out for a long lunch.

M ____, so we'll be back in an hour.

W Maybe I'll try their spaghetti and tomato sauce with basil. Didn't you have that last time we went there together?

M I did. It was so delicious. In fact, I think that __________ ____.

W Why don't we call and ask them ____________________ ___________________________________?

M I'd like that, but I don't think they deliver food.

W Let's try at least. We really need to finish these statistics before the end of the day.

Q : *How does the man probably respond to the woman?*

M ① Don't worry. I'll go to the restaurant alone.
   ② I'll bring you a sandwich from the restaurant.
   ③ Okay, I'll call them and ask if they deliver.
   ④ I'm not hungry anymore.
   ⑤ I think their food is terrible anyway.

32

W The Great Mall is _________________________________ ____. A series of special events are being organized __________ ___________________________. Most of the stores in the mall will run special promotions during July. Designer stores will be offering up to 70% off selected goods on July 12 starting at nine in the morning. ______________ ____, the Face Store will pamper you with a free makeover. Sorry, guys, but this is an offer for ladies only. The best hairdressers, stylists, and beauty therapists will be on hand ____ _____________________. The first fifty customers that day receive a 50% discount on a treatment and beauty package.

Q : *What is the reason the Great Mall is offering special promotions?*

M ① to promote the mall
   ② to celebrate the tenth annual fundraiser for shopaholics
   ③ to celebrate its tenth anniversary
   ④ to hold its year-end clearance sale
   ⑤ to offer free makeovers for mall patrons

33

M I saw you at the coffee shop last night, but you didn't even greet me. Why didn't you say hi to me?

W I wasn't at the coffee shop last night. I was here at home studying all night long.

M No, you weren't. __________________________________.

W ____ ________________________________. We're twins, so people often get confused.

M I didn't know you had a twin. ___________________ ___________________________, aren't you?

W Yes, we are.

M And ____.

W But we don't dress the same, so that's one way to tell us apart.

M Do your parents ever confuse the two of you?

W They haven't done that in a long time. They can always tell the difference between us.

M What about your friends? It must be easy to fool some of them.

W Well, sometimes we play tricks on them. Last week, I went to the movies with her friends, and they didn't realize I had tricked them. ___________________________.

Q : *Why is it so easy for the women to trick people?*

M ① They dress the same.
   ② They have the same friends.
   ③ They have the same hairstyles.
   ④ They are identical twins.
   ⑤ They like to have fun.

34

M My boss says that he's so happy with my work that he might promote me very soon. I've been waiting for this day for a really long time.

W That's good news. Did he say ____________________ ____?

M No, he didn't, but it will probably happen soon. _______ __________________________________.

W Just make sure you don't get lazy and give him a reason not to promote you.

M I won't. I'm going to focus on the vacation we'll go on when I get the promotion. I think we should go to

Hawaii. The weather there is great, and we can swim in the ocean every day. You can read your books there, and _______________________________.

W I'd love to go to Hawaii. I've wanted to go there for years.

M And when we come back, _______________________ _______________________ you love so much. Perhaps we can even find one that's red. You can drive it wherever you want when I'm not using it.

W ____.

Q: *What advice do you think the woman offers the man?*

M ① Don't put all your eggs in one basket.
   ② Don't believe everything you're told.
   ③ Don't count your chicken before they're hatched.
   ④ Don't daydream too much.
   ⑤ Don't dream too big.

35 다음을 듣고, 이어지는 질문에 답하시오.

M Minsu met his friend and saw a movie together with him _______________________. _______________________ _______________________, they had agreed to have dinner together _______________________________, but, when they met, they changed their minds so that they could watch a film instead.

Q: *What day is it today?*

36 주어진 시간 동안 아래 지문을 주의 깊게 읽고, 대화를 들은 후 질문에 답하시오. 〔1분〕

M I picked up some DVDs. Want to watch *Armageddon* with me?

W Okay. I've already seen it, but I promise I won't give away the ending.

M Oh, ___________________________________.
   A big, scary asteroid is about to smash into the Earth, so a group of heroes flies off into space and destroys it, ___________________________________.

W Right. It's a great story, but I wish movies would treat scientific topics more realistically. The plot of that movie is ___________________________________.

M It's not completely different. Asteroids are real, and there are huge numbers of them that cross Earth's orbit

_______________________________________. One of them could head for us at any time.

W That's true....

Q: *Which best completes the woman's last words?*

[37-38] 대화를 듣고, 이어지는 두 개의 질문에 답하시오.

M Do you mind if I talk to you? ___________________ ____.

W I'm all ears. Go ahead and let me know what's going on.

M I'm trying to decide what to do during summer vacation. My parents really want me to go to summer camp, ___________________________________.
   Instead, I'd rather get a part-time job at a restaurant and spend the rest of the time hanging out with my friends.

W What kind of summer camp is it?

M It's actually more of a study camp. It's a five-week program where they teach you extra classes to help you prepare for college. _______________________________ _______________________. Plus, I don't need to go since my grades are already really good.

W Have you tried explaining this to your parents ________ _________________________? If you did that, you might convince them _______________________ _______________________.

M I tried earlier, but both my parents are set on sending me to camp.

W That's too bad. But you ought to try talking to them again. After all, my parents wanted to send me to my grandparents' for the summer, _______________________ ____.

M How'd you manage that? _______________________ ____.

W Actually, it was pretty easy. I told them that if I got a part-time job, they wouldn't have to pay me an allowance anymore. They jumped at that opportunity.

37 Which of the following is true of the conversation?

38 What does the girl imply she is going to do during summer vacation?

〔39-40〕 대화를 듣고, 이어지는 두 개의 질문에 답하시오.

W _______________________________. Where are you going?

M I'm going to a job interview. I sent an application letter to a bank, and they wrote an email saying that they wanted to interview me. Do you think I look all right for an interview?

W You look good. They might think you're trying to impress them. _______________________________.

M But I do want to impress them. Don't you understand _______________________________

_______________________________? Most of the students in my class have jobs with the best companies. I've been trying to find a job for two months now.

W You're right. All I think about are my studies.

M You should think about finding a job when you graduate next year. It's more difficult than you think. You have to write _______________________________

_______________________________. And if they decide to interview you, _______________________________

_______________________________.

W You sound as if you know what you're talking about. How much money do you think they'll offer you?

M I don't know. It depends on the kind of work and the working hours. I can only work in the afternoon and perhaps on weekends.

W But banks aren't open on weekends.

M _______________________________.

Sometimes the office staff works on Saturdays.

W But do you want to work on weekends, too?

M _______________________________.

I don't even mind working Sundays, too.

39 남자의 취직에 대한 생각을 가장 잘 요약한 것은 무엇인가?

40 여자가 "It's only a job."이라고 말한 이유는 무엇인가?

MEMO
Listen to the max

MEMO
Listen to the max

LISTEN to the MAX

실전모의고사 ❷

Michael A. Putlack | Stephen Poirier

정답 및 해석

다락원

외고영어듣기대비

LISTEN to the MAX

실전모의고사 ❷

정답 및 해석

Michael A. Putlack | Stephen Poirier

다락원

실전모의고사 01

01 ④	02 ③	03 ②	04 ①	05 ①	06 ③	07 ④	08 ⑤	09 ①	10 ②
11 ③	12 ①	13 ②	14 ③	15 ②	16 ③	17 ①	18 ⑤	19 ③	20 ②
21 ③	22 ④	23 ④	24 ⑤	25 ④	26 ②	27 ⑤	28 ①	29 ②	30 ④
31 ⑤	32 ②	33 ⑤	34 ①	35 ③	36 ①	37 ①	38 ②	39 ③	40 ②

문제와 정답	스크립트	해석

01

대화를 듣고, 이 대화가 이루어지고 있는 장소를 고르시오.

① 　② 

③ 　④ 

⑤ 

▶ **return** 반환하다, 돌려주다; 반환, 귀환　**due date** 만기일, 정해진 기일　**fine** 벌금을 과하다; 벌금　**book drop** (도서관의) 도서 반납함　**check out** (도서관에서) 도서를 대출하다　*cf.* **check in** (도서를) 반납하다　**procedure** 절차, 수속　**call number** 도서 청구 번호　**available** 이용할 수 있는, 입수할 수 있는

M Pardon me, but I have some questions I'd like to ask if you don't mind.

W Go ahead, please. It's my job to answer questions.

M Great. First, I've got some things I'd like to return. They're not past their due date, so I know I won't get fined. Where should I put them?

W You can just give them to me, and I'll stamp them as checked in. But, in the future, the book drop is located next to the front door.

M Oh, that's great. It's the first time I've ever checked anything out from here, so I wasn't sure about the procedure.

W That's quite all right. Do you have any more questions?

M Actually, yes, I have one more question. I'm looking for this, and I found the call number for it. I've got it right here... According to the computer, it's available, but the last time I checked, it wasn't anywhere on the shelves.

W Well, that's very strange. Somebody might have put it in the wrong location. That happens from time to time.

M Do you think that's the case for this one?

W Perhaps. Let me take a look for you. Hopefully, we'll find what you're looking for.

남 실례지만, 괜찮으시다면 묻고 싶은 질문이 있는데요.

여 말씀해 보세요. 질문에 답하는 게 제 일인 걸요.

남 네. 먼저 반환하고 싶은 것이 있어요. 반납일이 안 지나 연체료는 물지 않을 거예요. 그것들을 어디다 두면 되나요?

여 그냥 제게 주시면 돼요. 그러면 제가 반납 도장을 찍을 거예요. 하지만 앞으로는 정문 옆에 도서 반납함이 설치될 거예요.

남 아, 잘 됐네요. 여기서 대출한 게 처음이라 절차를 잘 몰랐거든요.

여 괜찮아요. 질문이 더 있나요?

남 실은, 네, 한 가지 더 있어요. 이걸 찾고 있는데, 도서 청구 번호는 찾았어요. 바로 여기 있어요… 컴퓨터에는 그걸 볼 수 있다고 나오는데 하지만 제가 마지막으로 확인했을 때는 서가 어디에도 없었더군요.

여 음, 참 이상하네요. 누군가 엉뚱한 데 두었나 봐요. 가끔 그런 일이 생긴답니다.

남 이것도 그런 경우 같으세요?

여 아마도요. 제가 한번 찾아보죠. 찾고 계시는 걸 발견하면 좋겠네요.

02

다음을 듣고, 화자의 직업이 무엇인지 고르시오.

① interior designer
② civil engineer
③ architect ✓
④ construction engineer
⑤ builder

① 인테리어 디자이너
② 토목기사
③ 건축가
④ 건설 기술자
⑤ 건축업자

▶ **degree** 학위　**dimension** 치수, 크기　**engineering** 공학, 엔지니어링　**collapse** 무너지다, 붕괴하다　**erect** (건물을) 세우다, 짓다　**once** 일단 …하면; (과거의) 한때, 이전에

M I've got a great job that I love a lot. However, I had to attend college first to get a degree in it because I need many skills in order to do my job well. Clients hire me when they want to have some kind of new building. It could be a house, apartment, office building, or anything else. They tell me exactly what they want, and then I start designing it. I've got to be good at math because I need to make sure the building's dimensions are exact. I also have to know some engineering. I wouldn't want to make a building that's not structurally sound or which collapses soon after it gets erected. Finally, once I create the plans for the structure, I work closely with the builder to ensure that the building is completed exactly the way I drew it.

남 난 참 좋아하는 멋진 직업을 가지고 있다. 하지만 그 일을 잘 하기 위해서는 많은 기술이 필요해서 먼저 그에 대한 학위를 따기 위해 대학에 다녀야 했다. 고객들이 나를 고용할 때는 어떤 종류의 새 건물을 갖고 싶을 때이다. 그 건물은 주택이나 아파트, 사무실 빌딩, 그 외 어떤 것이든 될 수 있다. 그들이 내게 정확히 원하는 것을 말하고 나면 나는 설계를 시작한다. 건물의 크기가 정확한지 확인해야 할 필요가 있기 때문에 나는 수학을 잘 해야 한다. 또 공학도 좀 알아야 한다. 구조적으로 불안하거나 건설된 후 곧 붕괴하는 건물을 짓고 싶지는 않을 테니까 말이다. 마지막으로 일단 건축물에 대한 계획을 짜고 나면, 건축업자와 긴밀히 작업하여 그 건물이 정확히 내가 그린 대로 완공되는지 확인한다.

<table>
<tr><th>문제와 정답</th><th>스크립트</th><th>해석</th></tr>
</table>

03 대화를 듣고, 남자가 전화를 건 이유를 고르시오.

① 약속을 취소하기 위해
✓ 약속 시간 변경에 대해 물어 보기 위해
③ 새 프로젝트에 대한 정보를 요청하기 위해
④ 여행 계획에 대해 물어 보기 위해
⑤ 프로젝트 시작을 연기하기 위해

▶ this is … speaking. (전화에서) 나는 …이다 terribly 몹시, 매우 at the moment 지금으로서는 be scheduled to do …할 예정이다 appointment (방문 등의) 약속, 예약 prefer to do …하기를 좋아하다, 선호하다 merely 다만, 그저 postpone 연기하다, 뒤로 미루다 be aware of …을 알고 있다 why don't I …? …하면 어떨까? assistance 도움, 지원

W　Hello, Mr. Meyers's Office. This is Janet speaking.

M　Good afternoon. My name is Doug Thomas, and I'd like to speak with Mr. Meyers if he's got some time.

W　I'm terribly sorry, Mr. Thomas, but Mr. Meyers isn't in the office at the moment. Is there something I can help you with?

M　Well, I'm scheduled to meet Mr. Meyers at 10:30 tomorrow morning. Unfortunately, something has come up at our office in Atlanta, so I've got to leave town this evening and won't return until Thursday.

W　I see. In that case, shall I tell Mr. Meyers you're going to cancel your appointment?

M　I'd prefer not to cancel but instead merely postpone it. I really need to meet him about our project.

W　Yes, I've heard him discussing it in the office, so I'm aware of the nature of the work you two are doing.

M　Great, so do you think Mr. Meyers can meet me this Friday?

W　Actually, I'll have to wait until he returns to the office. I'm not exactly sure of his schedule, so I need to ask him. Why don't I have him call you when he gets back?

M　That's a great idea. Thanks for your assistance.

여　네, 마이어스 씨 사무실의 재닛입니다.

남　안녕하세요, 제 이름은 더그 토머스인데, 마이어스 씨가 시간이 된다면 얘기를 좀 하고 싶습니다.

여　토머스 씨, 정말 죄송합니다만 마이어스 씨는 지금 사무실에 안 계십니다. 제가 도와드릴 일이 없을까요?

남　음, 내일 오전 10시 30분에 마이어스 씨를 만나기로 되어 있어요. 안타깝게도 애틀랜타 사무실에 일이 생겨 오늘 저녁에 출장을 가야 해서 목요일까지 돌아오지 않을 겁니다.

여　알겠습니다. 그럼 마이어스 씨께 약속을 취소하실 거라고 말씀 드릴까요?

남　제가 바라는 건 취소가 아니라 그냥 연기를 하는 겁니다. 저희 프로젝트에 관해 마이어스 씨를 정말 만나야 하거든요.

여　네, 사무실에서 마이어스 씨가 그 논의를 하시는 걸 들어서 두 분이 하시는 작업의 성격을 알고 있습니다.

남　잘 됐군요, 그럼 마이어스 씨가 이번 주 금요일에 저를 만날 수 있을 것 같으세요?

여　사실은 마이어스 씨가 사무실에 돌아오실 때까지 기다려야 합니다. 그 분의 일정을 정확히 알 수 없어서 여쭤봐야 하거든요. 돌아오시면 전화 드리라고 하면 어떨까요?

남　좋습니다. 도와줘서 고마워요.

---

04 대화를 듣고, 여자의 상황을 가장 잘 나타내는 것을 고르시오.

✓ 타산지석
② 청출어람
③ 사면초가
④ 주마간산
⑤ 견원지간

▶ be tired of …이 지긋지긋하다 owner 주인, 소유주 employee 종업원, 피고용인 as … as one can 가능한 한 …한 yet 그렇지만, 그래도 barely 거의 …않다; 간신히, 겨우 at all (부정문) 조금도, 전혀 that's why… 그런 이유로 …하다 go bankrupt 파산하다 pay back (빚 등을) 상환하다, 갚다 consider (문제 등을) 곰곰이 생각하다

W　I think I'm going to open my own business soon. I'm so tired of working for other people.

M　What makes you say that?

W　Well, I work at this small company. It's just the owner, three other employees, and me. The other workers and I always work as hard as we can, yet the owner doesn't seem to do much of anything.

M　So what's the problem?

W　He makes all the money while we barely earn anything at all. In fact, I may have to get a second job so that I can earn some more money. That's why I'm going to open my own business. I'm going to get rich myself.

M　You know, that sounds like a great plan, but let me tell you something about myself.

W　What's that?

M　I once owned a business, but it didn't go too well. I was just like you; I thought I'd start my own business and get rich.

W　What happened after you started?

M　I lost all my money and went bankrupt. I am still paying back loans from five years ago. If I were you, I'd consider that before you start a business with no plan at all.

여　곧 내 사업을 시작할 것 같아. 다른 사람들을 위해 일하는 게 아주 지긋지긋해.

남　왜 그런 말을 해?

여　음, 내가 일하는 데는 아주 작은 회사야. 사장과 다른 직원 세 명과 나뿐이지. 다른 직원들과 난 항상 가능한 한 열심히 일하는데도 사장은 별로 일 하는 게 없는 것 같아.

남　그래서 뭐가 문제인데?

여　사장은 모든 돈을 버는 반면에 우린 거의 얻는 게 없어. 사실 나는 돈을 좀 더 벌 수 있게 부업을 얻어야 할지도 몰라. 그래서 내 사업을 시작하려고 하는 거야. 난 정말 부자가 될 거야.

남　있잖아, 훌륭한 계획 같기는 한데 내 얘기를 좀 해줄게.

여　뭔데?

남　난 한때 사업체를 소유했지만 일이 너무 안 됐어. 나도 꼭 너 같았어. 내 사업을 시작해서 부자가 되려고 생각했지.

여　시작한 뒤 어떻게 됐어?

남　돈을 몽땅 잃고 파산했어. 5년 전부터 아직까지 대출금을 갚고 있어. 내가 너라면 아무 계획 없이 사업을 시작하기 전에 신중히 생각해 볼 거야.

05

다음을 듣고, 화자의 감정 변화를 가장 잘 나타낸 것을 고르시오.

- ☑ ① excited → disappointed
- ② nervous → worried
- ③ happy → angry
- ④ upset → sad
- ⑤ worried → disheartened

① 흥분한 → 실망한
② 긴장한 → 걱정되는
③ 행복한 → 화난
④ 화난 → 슬픈
⑤ 걱정되는 → 낙심한

▶ promotion 승진 look forward to …을 고대하다 employee evaluation (직원들에 대한) 인사고과, 업무평가 immediate 직접적인, 바로 이웃의 position 직(職), 책무 transfer 전근시키다, 이동시키다 can't help …을 어쩔 수가 없다 burst to do …하고 싶어 못 견디다 deserved 그만한 가치가 있는 crush (희망 등을) 꺾다, 맥을 못 추게 하다 break (뉴스 등을) 알리다

M All week long, everyone at work had been expecting some important news. We had heard there was going to be a big promotion. I was looking forward to the news because all my employee evaluations had been excellent. In fact, my immediate boss told me she expected me to get promoted to her position once she transferred to another office. I couldn't help myself. I told my family I was probably getting promoted, so I'd be making more money. My wife even began planning a family trip to Europe. The big day finally came. The whole office was bursting to hear the news. Ms. Smith came into the conference room and said she had something to tell us. She said someone in our office was getting a promotion. Then she said the name. It wasn't mine. It was my officemate—a guy I didn't feel deserved the job. The news crushed me. I don't know how I'm ever going to break it to my family.

남 한 주 내내 직장의 모든 사람이 어떤 중요한 소식을 기다리고 있었다. 우리는 대대적인 승진이 있을 것이라고 들었다. 나는 인사고과가 모두 훌륭했기 때문에 이 소식을 고대하고 있었다. 사실 바로 위 상사는 내게 일단 자신이 다른 사무실로 이동하면 내가 그 직책으로 승진될 것이 예상된다고 말했다. 난 참을 수가 없었다. 식구들에게 어쩌면 승진이 되어서 돈을 더 벌게 될지도 모른다고 말했다. 아내는 심지어 유럽 가족여행을 계획하기 시작했다. 드디어 그 중요한 날이 왔다. 온 사무실이 그 소식을 듣고 싶어 못 견뎌 했다. 스미스 씨가 회의실로 와서 우리에게 할 말이 있다고 했다. 그녀는 우리 사무실의 누군가가 승진할 것이라고 말했다. 그런 다음 그 이름을 발표했다. 내가 아니었다. 사무실 동료였는데, 내 생각에 그 일을 맡을 자격이 없는 사람이었다. 그 소식으로 나는 절망감이 들었다. 가족에게 그 소식을 어떻게 알려야 할지 모르겠다.

06

대화를 듣고, 남자의 마지막 말에 대한 여자의 응답으로 가장 알맞은 것을 고르시오.

W: _______________________________

- ① I'm sorry, but I don't have any money to lend you.
- ② Okay, but I'm not going to carry any heavy boxes.
- ☑ ③ If that's all, then I suppose I can help you out tonight.
- ④ Okay, but we're going to have to take your car.
- ⑤ But I have no idea where exactly you live.

① 미안하지만, 네게 빌려 줄 돈이 없어.
② 좋아, 하지만 무거운 상자는 안 나를 거야.
③ 그 정도라면 오늘밤 너를 도울 수 있을 것 같아.
④ 좋아, 하지만 네 차를 가져야 해.
⑤ 하지만 난 네가 정확히 어디에 사는지 전혀 몰라.

▶ favor 부탁, 호의 stick 같히게 하다, 꼼짝 못하게 하다 get into (어떤 상태에) 들어가다, 빠지다 suppose 생각하다, 추정하다 convince 설득하다 relief 안도, 안심 make it 잘해내다, (…에) 용케 도달하다 payday 봉급일 (the) chances are… 아마 …일 것이다 unless …하지 않는다면

M Lisa, I've got a favor to ask of you. I really need your help.

W No way, Jason. I remember the last time you asked me for assistance. I was stuck at your house all day long helping you take everything out of those boxes. I'll never do that again.

M Oh, right. Well, I did tell you it was going to be an all-day job, and you accepted, so you should have known what you were getting into.

W I suppose you're right. But there's no chance you're going to convince me to do anything for you this time.

M But, really, I'm not going to ask for anything big. I don't need help moving, and I don't need to borrow any money from you either.

W That's a relief because I've barely got enough to make it to payday.

M So, um, don't you want to hear what favor I need from you?

W I guess so. But chances are that unless it's something really small, I'm going to say no.

M Well, the favor I need is a ride home after work tonight. It shouldn't be too hard since we're neighbors.

W _______________________________

남 리사, 부탁이 하나 있는데. 당신 도움이 정말 필요해.

여 절대 안 돼, 제이슨. 지난번에 도와달라고 했을 때 기억하고 있거든. 네가 그 상자들에서 온갖 걸 꺼내는 걸 돕느라고 온종일 네 집에 틀어박혀 있었잖아. 다시는 절대로 안 그럴 거야.

남 아, 알았어. 근데 난 일이 온종일 걸리는 거라고 말해 줬어. 그리고 당신은 허락했고, 그러니까 네가 하게 될 일이 뭔지는 알았어야지.

여 네 말이 맞는 것 같네. 하지만 이번에는 당신을 위해 뭔가를 하도록 나를 설득할 수 없을 거야.

남 하지만 정말로 대단한 걸 부탁하진 않을 거야. 물건 옮기는 것도 아니고 네게 돈을 꿔야 하는 것도 아니야.

여 그 말에 안심이 되네. 봉급날까지 겨우 지낼 정도밖에 없으니까 말이야.

남 그러니까, 음, 내 부탁이 뭔지 들어 볼래?

여 그래. 하지만 정말 작은 일이 아니라면 안 된다고 할 거야.

남 음, 내 부탁은 오늘밤 퇴근 후에 집까지 태워 달라는 거야. 우린 이웃이니까 너무 어렵지 않잖아.

07

대화를 듣고, 내용과 일치하지 **않는** 것을 고르시오.

① 남자는 점술가를 찾아왔다.
② 여자는 남자가 부자가 될 것이라고 예언했다.
③ 남자는 자기 수명이 얼마나 될지 알고 싶어 한다.
✓④ 여자는 남자가 곧 결혼할 것이라고 생각한다.
⑤ 남자는 자녀들에 대해서는 자세히 물으려 하지 않았다.

▶ **matter** 문제, 일 **despair** 절망하다, 체념하다 **in the end** 결국, 마지막에 **how about ...?** …은 어떤가? **personal** 개인적인 **alas** (슬픔, 연민 등을 나타내어) 아아, 슬프다 **inner** 영적인, 내적인 **sight** 판단, 시력 **detail** 세부적인 것 **lifeline** (손금의) 생명선

M What can you tell me about my future?

W I see many things, both good and bad, in your future. What is it you'd like to know?

M Am I going to be rich?

W In money matters, you will find success. However, the road to becoming rich will not be easy. There will be times when you will lose all your money and feel hopeless. But do not despair. For, in the end, you will be a rich man.

M Okay, that sounds pretty good to me.

W What else would you like me to tell you?

M How about my personal life? Will I ever get married?

W Let me see your hand… Aha… I see you will be married twice in your life. And you will have three children. Alas, I cannot tell how many will be boys or girls. My inner sight does not give me those details.

M That's quite all right. I'd prefer to be surprised myself. So, um, can you tell me how long I'm going to live?

W Yes, do you see your lifeline right here? According to it, you will live to be an old man.

남 내 미래에 대해 뭘 말할 수 있죠?

여 당신의 미래에 많은 것이 보이네요. 좋은 것과 나쁜 것 모두요. 뭘 알고 싶죠?

남 내가 부자가 될까요?

여 돈 문제라면 성공할 거예요. 하지만 부자가 되는 길은 쉽지 않을 거예요. 돈을 모두 잃고 희망이 없을 때가 있을 겁니다. 하지만 절망하지는 마세요. 결국에는 부자가 될 거니까요.

남 알았어요. 아주 좋은 소리네요.

여 또 뭘 말해 줄까요?

남 개인적인 삶은 어때요? 결혼하게 될까요?

여 손을 한번 볼게요… 아하… 살면서 두 번 결혼하게 될 걸로 보이네요. 또 자녀가 세 명 있고요. 안타깝지만 아들이나 딸이 몇명인지는 말해 줄 수 없어요. 영적인 능력은 그런 세세한 것은 알려 주지 않는답니다.

남 그건 괜찮아요. 나도 놀라움을 맛보는 게 더 좋으니까요. 그리고, 얼마나 오래 살지 말해 줄 수 있나요?

여 그럼요, 바로 여기 생명선이 보이죠? 생명선에 따르면 노인이 될 때까지 살 거라고 하네요.

08

다음을 듣고, 무엇에 대한 이야기인지 고르시오.

① 봄맞이 세일
② 창고 정리 세일
③ 개학 맞이 세일
④ 휴가 세일
✓⑤ 점포 정리 세일

▶ **sale** 할인 판매 **literally** 글자 뜻대로; 완전히, 정말로 **for starters** 우선, 첫째로 **off** 할인하여, 공제하여 **offer** 제공하다; 부르는 값, 매물 **individual** 개별적인 **as well** …도, 마찬가지로 **up to** (수에 대해) …까지 **department** (상품별) 매장, 코너 **reasonable** (가격이) 합당한, 비싸지 않은 **turn ... down** …을 물리치다, 거절하다

W Be sure that you come down to Martin's Department Store this weekend from Friday to Sunday before we close our doors for the very last time. We are having a sale where everything literally must go. For starters, everything in our store is going to be on sale for a minimum of fifty percent off. That's much more than any of the local stores are offering even during their spring sales. And be sure to visit each of our individual departments as well since some of them will be offering sales at up to eighty percent off. This includes the electronics department and the children's clothing department. Finally, before we close on Sunday, everything has got to go. Make us a reasonable offer, and we won't turn you down. So come down to Martin's Department Store this weekend for the sale of a lifetime. You won't want to miss it.

여 마지막으로 폐점을 하기 전인 금요일에서 일요일까지의 이번 주말에 마틴스 백화점에 오시는 걸 잊지 마세요. 말 그대로 모든 물건을 처리해야 하는 할인 판매를 합니다. 우선, 당점포의 모든 제품이 최소 50퍼센트 할인 판매에 들어갈 것입니다. 이것은 심지어 지역 상점들이 봄맞이 할인 판매에서 제공하는 것보다 훨씬 더 많습니다. 또한 개별 매장도 꼭 방문해 보세요. 일부 매장은 최고 80퍼센트까지 할인이 됩니다. 여기에는 전자제품 매장과 아동복 매장이 포함됩니다. 마지막으로, 일요일에 폐점하기 전에 모든 제품이 처리되어야 합니다. 합리적인 가격을 제시해 주시면 여러분을 실망시켜 드리지 않을 겁니다. 그러니 이번 주말에 평생에 기억될 할인 판매를 하는 마틴스 백화점을 방문해 주십시오. 놓치면 후회하실 겁니다.

09 대화를 듣고, 남자가 뉴욕으로 이사한 이유를 고르시오.

✓① 회사에서 전근을 보냈다.
② 남자가 뉴욕에서 대학을 다니기로 했다.
③ 남자는 외국에서 살아 보기를 원했다.
④ 남자는 부모님과 가까운 곳에서 살아야 했다.
⑤ 남자는 친구들과 가까운 곳에서 살고 싶어졌다.

▶ **sure enough** (예상대로) 확실히, 정말로 **to be honest** 솔직히 말해 **transfer** 전근시키다 **choice** 선택권 **desire** 욕망, 소망 **abroad** 해외에서 **rent** (남에게서) 임차하다, 빌리다 **run into** …을 우연히 만나다 **see you around** (헤어지면서) 안녕, 또 만나

W Johnny, is that really you? What are you doing here?

M Hey, Carmen. I'm just back here for the weekend seeing a few of my old friends.

W I heard someone say that you had moved to New York City. Are you going to college there or something?

M No, it's not that. You know, I never really thought I'd move there, but, sure enough, it's the place I call home now.

W But you always talked about how you loved living near all your friends and how you couldn't stand to leave your family. What made you suddenly go away?

M To be honest, I didn't have much of a choice in the matter. My boss told me I was getting transferred. He gave me a choice between New York and Paris, and I had no desire to live abroad.

W Oh, I see. It's too bad that he made you choose like that.

M Yeah, I had to sell my house really quickly before I left. I don't even have one in New York. I'm just renting now.

W It sounds like your life is really different. Well, it was great running into you. I hope to see you around.

여 조니, 정말 너니? 여기서 뭐하는 거야?

남 안녕, 카르멘. 주말 동안 옛날 친구 몇 명 보려고 막 여기 왔어.

여 누가 네가 뉴욕시로 이사했다고 말하는 걸 들었는데. 거기서 대학 같은 데 다니는 거니?

남 아니, 그건 아니고. 너도 알겠지만, 나는 거기로 이사 갈 거라곤 정말 전혀 생각 못했는데 이젠 정말로 고향집이라고 부르는 곳이 되었어.

여 하지만 넌 항상 친구들 가까이 사는 게 얼마나 좋은지, 또 가족을 떠나 사는 것이 얼마나 참을 수 없는 일인지 말했잖아. 갑자기 떠나간 이유가 뭐야?

남 솔직히 그 문제에서는 선택의 여지가 별로 없었어. 상사가 내게 전출될 거라고 말했거든. 뉴욕과 파리 사이에서 선택할 수 있었는데, 난 해외에서 살 마음은 전혀 없었어.

여 아, 그렇구나. 그런 선택을 해야 했다니 참 유감이다.

남 그래, 떠나기 전에 정말 급하게 집을 팔아야 했지. 뉴욕에는 집조차 없어. 지금은 그냥 세 들어 살고 있거든.

여 네 생활이 정말 달라진 것 같다. 널 만나게 돼 반가웠어. 또 만나면 좋겠다.

---

10 대화를 듣고, 여자가 지불해야 할 금액을 고르시오.

① $75
✓② $90
③ $105
④ $165
⑤ $200

▶ **particular** 특별한, 각별한 **formal** 정장용의, 격식 차린 **a couple of** 둘의, 두셋의 **fashionable** 유행의, 최신식인 **notice** 주목하다, 알아차리다 **normally** 보통은, 일반적으로 **go for** (가격)에 팔리다 **a bit** 다소, 약간 **range** 폭, 범위 **limited** 한정된, 부족한 **budget** 경비, 예산

M Good afternoon, ma'am. Is there anything particular you're looking for?

W I'm looking for something nice to wear to work. It needs to look good but not be too formal.

M Why don't I show you some of our new blouses? They arrived just a couple of days ago, and, from what I've heard, they're the most fashionable clothes this winter.

W That sounds great. Let's take a look.

M Here's the first one you might like. Notice it's one of the top brands on the market. It normally goes for $200, but it's on sale right now for only $165.

W That's a bit out of my price range. I'm on a limited budget, so I can only spend about half that amount.

M That's no problem at all. We've got a number of excellent looking blouses at lower prices. How about this white one, which goes for just $90?

W Maybe, but could you show me some others first?

M I've got two more you may like. There's this black one that sells for $105, and I've got a yellow blouse for only $75. So, what will it be?

W I like them all, but I think I'll take the white one. It looks the best.

남 안녕하십니까, 손님. 특별히 찾는 게 있으세요?

여 일할 때 입기 좋은 것을 찾고 있어요. 보기에 괜찮으면서 너무 정장답지 않아야 하죠.

남 신상품 블라우스를 좀 보여 드릴까요? 바로 며칠 전에 도착한 것인데, 제가 듣기에 이번 겨울에 가장 유행할 만한 의상이라더군요.

여 좋아요. 한 번 보죠.

남 여기 좋아하실 만한 첫 번째 옷입니다. 시장에서 최고급 브랜드 중 하나이죠. 정상가는 200달러이지만 지금은 단돈 165달러에 할인중입니다.

여 제가 생각한 가격대에서 좀 벗어나네요. 예산이 좀 빠듯해서 그 금액의 절반 정도만 쓸 수 있거든요.

남 괜찮습니다. 더 저렴한 가격에 멋진 블라우스가 많이 있답니다. 이 흰색은 딱 90달러인데, 어떠세요?

여 괜찮을 것도 같네요. 하지만 다른 것들을 먼저 좀 보여 주시겠어요?

남 좋아하실 만한 제품이 두 벌 더 있습니다. 105달러에 판매되는 이 검정 블라우스와 75달러밖에 안 하는 노란색 블라우스가 있습니다. 자, 어떠세요?

여 모두 마음에 들지만 흰색으로 해야 겠어요. 그게 제일 좋아 보이네요.

11

다음을 듣고, 이 이야기가 어떤 질문에 대한 대답인지 고르시오.

① What are the costs involved in pet therapy?
② What is the success rate of pet therapy?
✔ Who can benefit from pet therapy?
④ Why is pet therapy so effective?
⑤ Which doctors prescribe pet therapy?

① 애완동물 치료에 드는 비용은 얼마인가?
② 애완동물 치료의 성공률은 얼마인가?
③ 애완동물 치료에서 혜택을 얻을 수 있는 사람은 누구인가?
④ 애완동물 치료가 그렇게 효과적인 이유는?
⑤ 어떤 의사들이 애완동물 치료를 처방하는가?

▶ unique 독특한, 고유의 treat 치료하다 involve 의미하다, 수반하다 pair 짝을 짓다 benefit 혜택 as a general rule 일반적으로, 대체로 take one's mind off …의 일을 잊게 하다 in turn 이번에는, 차례가 되어 tremendously 엄청나게 elderly 연세가 지긋한, 초로인 lie 거짓말하다 thanks to …덕분에

W One unique way that some doctors have begun treating people is to use pet therapy. This involves pairing a patient with a pet in order to achieve certain benefits. The pets are usually dogs, but they may also be cats, birds, or even fish. As a general rule, pets help to lower people's stress levels and also enable their patients to take their minds off of their own problems since they must in turn take care of their pets. Pet therapy has helped heart attack victims achieve longer lives, and it has also tremendously helped the elderly and AIDS patients. Sometimes pet therapy has even been used on mentally ill patients, where it has seen a certain level of success as well. Of course, not all attempts at using pet therapy are successful, but the numbers do not lie: More and more patients are living happier, healthier, and longer lives thanks to their pets.

여 일부 의사들이 사람들을 치료하기 시작한 독특한 방법 중 한 가지는 애완동물을 치료에 이용하는 것이다. 이것은 특정한 혜택을 얻기 위해 환자를 애완동물과 짝을 지어 주는 것을 의미한다. 그 애완동물들은 보통은 개이지만 고양이나 새, 심지어 물고기가 될 수도 있다. 일반적으로 애완동물들은 사람들의 스트레스 수준을 낮추는 데 도움을 주며 또한 환자들이 이번에는 애완동물들을 보살펴 줘야 하기 때문에 자신의 문제에 대해 잊어버릴 수 있게 해 준다. 애완동물 치료는 심근경색 환자들이 더 오래 살도록 도움을 주었으며, 노인 및 에이즈 환자들에게도 상당한 도움을 주었다. 때때로 애완동물 치료는 정신 질환이 있는 환자들에게까지 사용되기도 했는데, 이 부문에서도 일정 수준의 성공을 보여주었다. 물론 애완동물을 이용한 모든 시도가 성공적이지는 않지만 통계는 거짓말을 하지 않는다. 더욱 더 많은 환자들이 애완동물 덕분에 더 행복하고, 더 건강하며 더 오래 살고 있다.

12

다음을 듣고, 주어진 그래프에 대해 사실이 <u>아닌</u> 것을 고르시오.

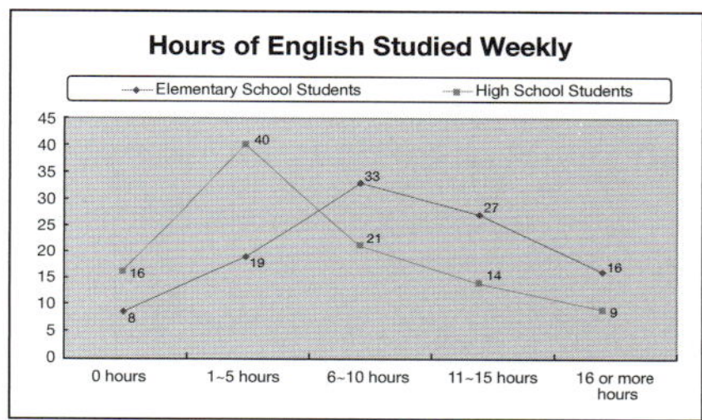

✔ 고등학교 학생들보다 더 많은 초등학교 학생들이 영어에 주당 1~5시간을 소비한다.
② 전반적으로 초등학교 학생들은 고등학교 학생들보다 영어 학습에 더 많은 시간을 쓴다.
③ 영어에 주당 16시간 이상을 쓰는 고등학교 학생들 수는 주당 1~5시간을 학습하는 초등학교 학생들 수보다 적다.
④ 초등학교 학생들의 2배에 이르는 고등학교 학생들은 전혀 영어를 공부하지 않는다.
⑤ 고등학교 학생들의 거의 2배에 이르는 초등학교 학생들이 영어에 주당 11~15시간을 쓴다.

▶ study 조사, 연구 carry out (조사 등을) 수행하다 reveal 드러내다 for instance 예를 들면, 가령 place on (신뢰, 희망 등을) …에 두다, 걸다 additionally 더구나, 게다가 point toward (증거, 조사 등이) … 경향을 보이다 emphasis 중요시, 강조 account for …의 이유를 설명하다, 원인이 되다 due to … 때문에 relatively 상대적으로, 비교적

M A recent study was carried out on the number of hours of English studied by students in both elementary and high school. The study revealed a number of shocking results. For instance, despite the importance that society places on learning English, a full sixteen percent of high school students, compared with eight percent of elementary school students, never study English. Additionally, the overall numbers point toward elementary school students spending more class time studying English than high school students. Upon further investigation, two reasons for this were discovered. First, society places a heavy emphasis on learning English from a young age. This accounts for the huge number of hours—over sixteen a week for many elementary school students—that some students focus on English. Additionally, due to the fact that high school students have many more subjects to study, they are less able to focus upon English. This accounts for the relatively low number of hours many high schoolers spend studying English.

남 최근 초등학교와 고등학교 모두에서 학생들의 영어 학습 시간에 대해 조사가 실시되었다. 이 조사에서 많은 놀라운 결과가 드러났다. 예를 들어 사회가 영어 학습에 부여하는 중요성에도 불구하고 고등학교 학생들의 16퍼센트가 전혀 영어를 공부하지 않는데, 이것은 초등학교 학생들의 8퍼센트와 비교되는 수치이다. 게다가 전반적인 통계는 초등학교 학생들이 고등학교 학생들보다 더 많은 수업시간을 영어 공부에 쓰는 경향이 나타났다. 추가 조사에서 이에 대한 두 가지 이유가 밝혀졌다. 첫째로 사회가 어린 나이에서부터의 영어 학습을 과도하게 강조하는 것이다. 이것은 어떤 학생들이 영어에 집중하는 엄청난 양의 시간, 많은 초등학교 학생들의 경우 주당 16시간이 넘는 시간을 설명해 준다. 더욱이 고등학교 학생들은 공부해야 할 과목이 더 많다는 사실 때문에 영어에 덜 집중할 수 있다. 이것은 많은 고등학생들이 영어 학습에 상대적으로 적은 시간을 쓰는 것을 설명해 준다.

13 대화를 듣고, 두 사람이 대화를 마치고 할 일을 고르시오.

① Apply for passports
✓ Purchase some books
③ Enroll in a language class
④ Pack their luggage
⑤ Buy some new clothes

① 여권을 신청한다
② 책을 몇 권 구입한다
③ 어학 수업에 등록한다
④ 짐을 싼다
⑤ 새 옷을 산다

▶ passport 여권　now that you mention it 네가 그렇게 말하니까　had better …해야 한다, 하는 것이 낫다　apply for …을 신청하다　process (서류 등을) 처리하다　pick up …을 얻다, 사다　figure out …을 해결하다, 생각해내다　enroll 등록하다　in the meantime 그 사이에, 그럭저럭하는 동안에　hit (어떤 장소에) 닿다, 도착하다　grab 재빨리 손에 넣다

M　I'm so excited we've decided to travel to Europe. It should really be a lot of fun.

W　You're right, but now we've got lots of things we need to prepare before leaving. For example, do you even own a passport?

M　Now that you mention it, I don't. I guess I'd better hurry and apply for one since we're leaving in two months.

W　It usually takes six weeks to process, so you have enough time. But you still should apply for it sometime this week. We've also got to pick up some travel books so we can figure out what to see.

M　Good thinking. And I'm enrolling in a foreign language course. Since we're visiting Italy, I want to speak at least basic Italian. That should help us out a lot.

W　That's a good plan.

M　What else do you think we should do?

W　Well, we ought to figure out what the weather is going to be like when we go. Since we can't take too much luggage, we'll need to pack properly.

M　Oh, yeah, I hadn't thought of that. In the meantime, let's hit the bookstore. I want to grab a travel guide or two.

W　That's a plan. Let's get going.

남　유럽으로 여행하기로 결정해서 아주 신나. 분명 엄청 재미있을 거야.

여　그래, 하지만 이제 떠나기 전에 준비해야 할 게 많아. 예를 들면 넌 여권이라도 있니?

남　네가 말하니까 말인데, 없어. 두 달 후에 떠나야 하니까 서둘러서 신청해야겠어.

여　보통 처리하는 데 6주가 걸리니까 시간은 충분해. 하지만 그래도 이번 주중에 신청을 해야 할 거야. 또 뭘 구경할지 생각할 수 있게 여행 책자도 좀 사야지.

남　좋은 생각이야. 또 난 외국어 강좌를 등록할 거야. 이탈리아를 방문할 거니까 최소한 기본적인 이탈리아어는 하고 싶거든. 그럼 우리한테 많은 도움이 될 거야.

여　좋은 계획이구나.

남　그밖에 또 뭘 해야 할 것 같니?

여　음, 우리가 갈 때 날씨가 어떨지 생각해 봐야 해. 큰 짐을 갖고 갈 수 없으니까, 적절하게 짐을 쌀 필요가 있을 거야.

남　아, 그래, 그 생각은 못했다. 그 사이에 우리 서점에 들러 보자. 여행 안내서 한두 권 정도는 빨리 사고 싶어.

여　괜찮은 계획이야. 나가자.

---

14 대화를 듣고, 파스타를 만드는 순서가 알맞게 나열된 것을 고르시오.

ⓐ Sprinkle the grated cheese over the pasta.
ⓑ Boil the pasta until it is finished.
ⓒ Mix the pine nuts and raisins with the pasta.
ⓓ Fry some spinach and mix it with the pasta.

ⓐ 파스타 위에 치즈 간 것을 뿌린다.
ⓑ 파스타를 익을 때까지 삶는다.
ⓒ 잣과 건포도를 파스타에 섞는다.
ⓓ 시금치 약간을 볶고 파스타와 섞는다.

① ⓑ – ⓐ – ⓒ – ⓓ
② ⓑ – ⓒ – ⓐ – ⓓ
✓ ⓑ – ⓓ – ⓒ – ⓐ
④ ⓓ – ⓑ – ⓐ – ⓒ
⑤ ⓓ – ⓒ – ⓑ – ⓐ

▶ care to …을 좋아하다, 바라다　ingredient (음식의) 재료　raisin 건포도　pine nut 잣　grated 갈아 놓은　sprinkle 흩뿌리다　be ready to …할 준비가 되다　serve 대접하다　chef 요리사

W　I'm starving. Why don't we order something for dinner?

M　Actually, I was thinking of cooking this evening. Would you care to join me for dinner?

W　Wow, I had no idea you even knew how to cook. So, what are you making tonight?

M　I'm going to cook a pasta dish my mother taught me. It only has a few ingredients, but it tastes really delicious. All you need is some pasta, spinach, raisins, pine nuts, and grated cheese.

W　It sounds great. What do you do first? I'm guessing you cook the spinach, right?

M　Sorry, but that's wrong. You need to boil the pasta in water until it's done first. After that, you fry the spinach in some oil for a few minutes and then mix that with the pasta.

W　Yum, that already sounds delicious to me. Okay, so what do you do with the pine nuts and raisins?

M　It's simple. You put them in the pasta and sprinkle the grated cheese on top of everything. Then you mix it all up, and it's ready to serve.

W　You sound like you're a chef. Anyway, all that talk is making me hungry. Hurry up and start cooking.

여　배고파 죽을 것 같아. 저녁 시켜먹지 않을래요?

남　실은 오늘 저녁에는 요리할 생각이었어요. 나랑 같이 저녁하지 않을래요?

여　우와, 당신이 요리까지 할 줄 아는지는 전혀 몰랐어요. 그래서, 오늘밤에 뭘 만들 건데요?

남　어머니가 가르쳐 주신 파스타 요리를 할 거예요. 재료는 몇 가지뿐이지만 정말 맛있거든요. 필요한 거라고는 파스타 약간과 시금치, 건포도, 잣, 치즈 간 게 다예요.

여　근사한데요. 먼저 뭘 할 거죠? 내 생각엔 시금치를 요리할 것 같은데, 그렇죠?

남　미안하지만 틀렸어요. 먼저 파스타를 물에 넣어서다 익을 때까지 삶아야 해요. 그 후에 시금치를 몇 분간 기름에다 볶은 다음 파스타와 섞는 거예요.

여　얌얌, 벌써 맛있게 느껴지네요. 좋아요. 그럼 잣과 건포도로는 뭘 해요?

남　간단해요. 파스타에 넣고 모든 것 위에 치즈 간 것을 뿌리면 되죠. 그 다음에 그 모든 걸 섞으면 대접할 준비가 된 거예요.

여　그렇게 말하니 당신이 요리사 같군요. 아무튼 그 얘기를 다 하다보니 배고파지네요. 얼른 요리를 시작해요.

15 다음을 듣고, 화자가 언급하지 않은 그림을 고르시오.

①  ② 

③ 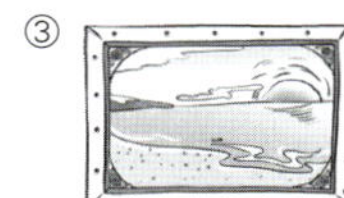 ④ 

⑤ 

▶ **somewhat** 다소 **reluctant** 마음이 내키지 않는, 꺼리는 **feature** 특집으로 다루다 **portray** (그림, 조각 등으로) 표현하다, 그리다 **sit** (물건이 고정해) 위치하다, 놓여 있다 **tell** 분간하다, 식별하다 **so long as**…하는 한은, …하기만 하면 **stand out** (사물이) 두드러지다, 눈에 띄다

M My family and I just returned from the local museum. At first, I was somewhat reluctant to go there, but now I'm glad I went there. The museum was having an art exhibition featuring some paintings from the nineteenth century, and they were so nice to look at. For example, there was one painting that just showed the sun setting on the beach. I know it sounds pretty simple, but the way the artist used colors was simply amazing. Another painting portrayed a man and a woman sitting at a table in a garden. I still can't forget how nice it looked. There was another painting which was just a bowl of fruit sitting on a table. As you can tell, I prefer simple paintings so long as they are done well. Finally, the last picture that stood out was one with a woman holding an umbrella while walking down a rainy street. There were many others, but those were my favorites.

여 나는 가족과 함께 지역 박물관에서 막 돌아왔다. 처음에는 그곳에 가는 것이 다소 싫었지만 이제는 거기 갔던 것이 기쁘다. 박물관은 19세기의 회화 일부를 특징적으로 보여 주는 미술 전시회를 열고 있었는데, 아주 볼 만했다. 예를 들어 해변의 석양을 보여주는 그림이 하나 있었다. 아주 단순하게 들릴 거라는 걸 알지만 화가가 색상을 사용한 방식이 정말 놀라웠다. 또 다른 그림은 정원의 탁자에 앉아 있는 남자와 여자를 묘사했다. 그것이 얼마나 근사하게 보였는지 아직도 잊을 수가 없다. 또 다른 그림에는 탁자 위에 놓인 과일 그릇 하나만 있었다. 알 수 있겠지만 나는 훌륭하기만 하다면 단순한 그림을 선호한다. 눈에 띄었던 마지막 그림은 우산을 든 여자가 비오는 거리를 걸어가고 있는 그림이었다. 다른 것들이 많이 있었는데, 그것들은 내가 좋아하는 것이었다.

---

16 대화를 듣고, 두 사람이 이야기하고 있는 책의 장르와 그 책이 인기 있는 이유가 올바로 짝지어진 것을 고르시오.

① Science Fiction – It keeps people interested in the story.
② Nonfiction – It teaches people about politics.
③ Biography – It tells a very inspiring story.
④ Thriller – The plot is really amazing.
⑤ Mystery – It makes the reader very curious.

① 공상과학소설 – 사람들로 하여금 이야기에 흥미를 갖게 한다.
② 비소설 – 사람들에게 정치학에 대한 것을 알려 준다.
③ 전기 – 매우 감동적인 이야기이다.
④ 스릴러 – 플롯이 멋지다.
⑤ 미스터리 – 독자의 호기심을 자극한다.

▶ **be into** …에 열중하다, 몹시 흥미를 갖다 **would rather** 오히려 …하고 싶다 **involve in** …에 몰두하다 **archaeologist** 고고학자 **You've got to be kidding me!** 농담이겠지! **continent** 대륙 **precious** 귀중한, 가치 있는 **relics** (역사적) 유물, 유적 **inspiring** (사람을) 고무하는, 감동시키는

W I'd really love to buy a book here, but they all look so boring. I'm sorry, but I'm just not into nonfiction.

M That's too bad because this is a really good book about politics.

W Well, I'd rather read a science fiction book or a mystery. Those genres really get me involved in the story, so I love reading them.

M Hey, I've got a great book for you. How about this one here? It's a bestseller, but don't let that fool you. It's a really great work of literature.

W Hmm… Tell me some more about it, and then I might consider buying it.

M Okay, it's a story about the life of a famous archaeologist.

W You've got to be kidding me! There's no way that kind of book could possibly become a bestseller.

M Well, you'd be surprised. I read it and found the story to be amazing. This guy visited every continent on the world and had lots of adventures while he was searching for precious relics. It's a really inspiring story about how he lived his life.

W You make it sound like it's a really great book. Maybe I will get it.

M Trust me. You won't regret buying it at all.

여 정말로 여기서 책을 사고 싶지만 모든 게 아주 따분해 보여. 미안하지만 난 비소설엔 흥미가 없어.

남 안 됐다. 이건 정치에 관한 정말 괜찮은 책인데.

여 음, 난 오히려 공상과학이나 추리소설을 읽고 싶어. 그 장르들은 정말이지 이야기에 몰두하게 되니까 그것들을 읽는 게 참 좋아.

남 이봐, 네게 좋은 책이 있어. 여기 이건 어때? 베스트셀러지만 거기에 속지는 마. 정말 훌륭한 작품이니까.

여 흠… 좀 더 얘기해 봐, 그럼 사는 걸 고려해 볼 수도 있어.

남 알았어, 이건 유명한 고고학자의 삶에 대한 이야기야.

여 농담이겠지! 그런 책이 베스트셀러가 될 리가 없어.

남 음, 너도 놀랄 거야. 난 그걸 읽었는데 굉장한 이야기였어. 이 사람은 세계의 모든 대륙을 방문해서 귀중한 유물을 찾아 많은 모험을 했어. 이 책은 그 사람이 어떤 삶을 살았는지에 관한 정말 감동적인 이야기야.

여 네 말을 들으니 정말 대단한 책 같구나. 아마도 그걸 사야 겠다.

남 날 믿어. 산 걸 절대로 후회하지 않을 거야.

17 다음을 듣고, 남자의 미래에 대한 태도를 가장 잘 나타낸 것을 고르시오.

✓① Optimistic
② Frightened
③ Nervous
④ Apprehensive
⑤ Worried

① 긍정적인
② 겁먹은
③ 긴장한
④ 염려하는
⑤ 걱정하는

▶ **lately** 최근에 **I must say** 진짜로, 정말로 **currently** 현재는, 지금은 **disappointed with** …에 낙담한, 실망한 **decent** 상당한, 쏠쏠한 **dead-end** 막다른, 앞이 막힌 **turn around** …을 나쁜 상태에서 좋은 상태로 바꾸다, 호전시키다

M I've been thinking about my life a lot lately because I'm not pleased with what I'm doing now. In fact, I must say that I'm currently disappointed with my life. I've got a job and make decent money, but there are few opportunities for me to get promoted. Basically, I've got a dead-end job and don't want to be stuck with it forever. So I've decided to go back to school and get another degree. That way, with a better education, I'll be able to find a job that pays me more money and which gives me a chance for promotions. Also, this time, I'm going to study a subject I'm interested in, not one which my parents demand that I learn. This change in my life is going to require a lot of hard work, but I really want to do it. I hope I can turn my life around and give myself a future I can look forward to, not one I'm afraid of.

남 지금 하고 있는 것에 만족하지 않기 때문에 최근 내 삶에 대해 많은 생각을 해오고 있다. 사실 나는 현재 내 삶에 정말 실망이다. 직업이 있고 돈을 상당히 벌지만 승진할 기회가 거의 없다. 기본적으로 나는 미래가 없는 일을 갖고 있는데 그 일에 영원히 매달려 있고 싶지는 않다. 그래서 학교로 돌아가서 다른 학위를 따야겠다고 결정했다. 그렇게 해서 더 나은 교육을 받아서 더 많은 보수와 승진 기회를 주는 일자리를 찾을 수 있을 것이다. 또 이번에는 부모님이 내게 배우라고 요구하는 것이 아니라 내가 흥미 있는 과목을 공부할 것이다. 내 인생에서 이 변화에는 많은 노력이 필요하겠지만 난 정말 그걸 하고 싶다. 내가 삶을 전환해서 내가 두려워하는 것이 아니라 고대할 수 있는 미래를 나 자신에게 선사할 수 있기를 바란다.

---

18 대화를 듣고, 남자의 마지막 말로 유추할 수 있는 것을 고르시오.

① He will talk to his apartment supervisor.
② He will find out his neighbor's phone number.
③ He will ask the woman for some more advice.
④ He will file a complaint about his neighbor.
✓⑤ He is not going to talk to his neighbor.

① 그는 아파트 관리인과 얘기할 것이다.
② 그는 이웃의 전화번호를 알아낼 것이다.
③ 그는 여자에게 조언을 더 구할 것이다.
④ 그는 이웃에게 소송을 제기할 것이다.
⑤ 그는 이웃과 얘기하지 않을 것이다.

▶ **beat down** …을 때려눕히다 **a whole lot of** 많은 **impolite** 무례한, 버릇없는(= rude) **chat** 마음 놓고 이야기하다, 잡담하다 **supervisor** 관리인 **apartment complex** 아파트 단지 **care about** …을 염려하다, …에 관심이 있다

W You look really beat down this morning. Didn't you get enough sleep last night?

M Unfortunately, my neighbor's dog kept me up all night. He got a dog two weeks ago, and it won't stop barking at night. It's big, too, so it makes a whole lot of noise. It's driving me crazy.

W Have you tried talking to your neighbor about it?

M I've visited his house a couple of times, but he wasn't home. And I can't give him a call since I don't know his number.

W That isn't good. Your neighbor sounds impolite. You live in an apartment, don't you?

M Yeah, so that makes it worse. He lives right above me, so it sounds like his dog is barking right above my head.

W I've got an idea for you. Why don't you have a chat with the apartment supervisor? Your apartment complex must have rules about making noise at night.

M I've considered that, but my neighbor could get in trouble and might even get kicked out of the building.

W So what? He's being rude and doesn't seem to care about you. Why should you care about him?

M I'll just give it some time and see if the barking stops.

여 오늘 아침에는 정말 초췌해 보여. 간밤에 잠을 충분히 못 잤어?

남 불행히도 이웃집 개 때문에 밤새 깨어 있었어. 2주 전에 개가 생겼는데, 그 개가 밤에 짖는 걸 멈추지를 않아. 소리도 커서 소음이 엄청 나요. 미치겠어.

여 이웃한테 그 얘기 하려고 해봤어?

남 두어 번 그 집을 방문했는데, 집에 없었어. 번호를 몰라서 전화도 못해.

여 안 됐다. 이웃이 무례한 것 같네. 아파트에 살고 있지, 그렇지?

남 그래, 그래서 상황이 더 악화되는 거야. 그가 바로 윗집에 살아서 개가 내 머리 바로 위에서 짖는 것 같거든.

여 좋은 수가 있어. 아파트 관리인에게 얘기해 보면 어때? 아파트 단지에 야간 소음에 대한 규정이 분명히 있을 거야.

남 그 생각을 해 봤지만 이웃이 곤란해질 수 있고 아파트에서 쫓겨날지도 몰라.

여 그럼 어때? 그 사람은 무례하고 널 염려하지도 않는 것 같은데. 넌 왜 그 사람 걱정을 하니?

남 그냥 좀 더 시간을 두고 개가 짖는 것을 멈추는지 봐야겠어.

<table>
<tr><th>문제와 정답</th><th>스크립트</th><th>해석</th></tr>
</table>

19

대화를 듣고, 남자와 여자가 만날 시간을 고르시오.

① 6:30
② 7:00
✔ 7:30
④ 8:00
⑤ 8:30

▶ **totally** 완전히, 전적으로 **showing** 상연, 상영 **make sense** 말이 되다, 이해할 수 있다 **grab a bite** 간단히 먹다, 요기하다 **beforehand** 미리, 사전에 **plenty of** 많은, 다수의

M Jenny, are we still watching that movie together tonight?

W Yeah, I'm totally looking forward to seeing it. But I forgot… What time does it begin? It's a nine-thirty showing, right?

M Uh, no, it actually begins at nine. But we ought to meet before it starts.

W Okay, so where do you think we should get together? I've never been to that theater before, so I'd rather not meet there. I'd hate to get lost.

M That makes sense. Let's meet at the subway station nearby work. I've got to leave for a meeting soon, but I can be at the station at, say, seven o'clock. How does that sound?

W That's too early for me. I don't know if I'll be finished working by then.

M Hmm… Well, it's going to take at least thirty minutes to get to the theater, and I was hoping to grab a bite to eat beforehand, so we shouldn't leave too much later.

W Well, if we leave an hour and a half before the movie begins, that should get us there in plenty of time to have dinner.

M That sounds perfect to me.

W Great. Go to your meeting, and I'll see you in a few hours.

남 제니, 오늘밤 영화 같이 보는 거야?

여 응, 정말 기대하고 있어. 하지만 깜빡했는데… 몇 시에 시작하는 거지? 9시 반 상영이지, 맞아?

남 아니, 사실은 9시에 시작해. 하지만 우린 영화 시작하기 전에 만나야 해.

여 알았어, 그럼 어디서 같이 만나는 게 좋을까? 난 그 극장에 전에 가 본 적이 없어서 거기서는 안 만나고 싶은데. 길 잃는 건 싫어.

남 그래. 회사 근처 지하철역에서 만나자. 곧 회의하러 가야 하지만 7시에 역에 갈 수 있어. 어때?

여 그건 나한테는 너무 빨라. 그때까지 일을 마칠지 모르겠어.

남 흠… 극장에 도착하는 데 최소한 30분이 걸릴 거고 그 전에 뭘 좀 먹었으면 좋겠으니까 너무 늦게 출발하면 안 돼.

여 음, 영화가 시작되기 1시간 반 전에 떠나면 거기 도착해서 저녁 먹을 시간이 충분히 있을 거야.

남 딱 좋은 것 같다.

여 좋아. 회의에 가 봐. 몇 시간 뒤에 봐.

20

다음을 듣고, 불면증을 치료하기 위한 방법으로 제안되지 않은 것을 고르시오.

① Make the room as dark as possible.
✔ Do not read before going to sleep.
③ Avoid drinks that have caffeine in them.
④ Establish a moderate temperature in the room.
⑤ Do not exercise prior to going to bed.

① 방을 가능한 한 어둡게 만들어라.
② 잠들기 전에 책을 읽지 말아라.
③ 카페인이 함유된 음료수를 피하라.
④ 방의 온도를 알맞게 유지하라.
⑤ 잠자리에 들기 전에 운동을 하지 말아라.

▶ **insomnia** 불면증 **sufferer** 고통받는 사람, 환자 **toss and turn** 몸을 엎치락뒤치락하다 **reflex** 반사 행동, 반사 능력 **relax** 편히 쉬다, 긴장을 풀다 **stimulate** 자극하다, 흥분시키다 **make sure** 확인하다, 꼭 …하다 **instruction** 지시, 명령

W Sometimes people get insomnia, which means they either cannot get to sleep at night or have a difficult time getting to sleep. These sufferers might spend hours tossing and turning in their beds. A lack of sleep can affect people's mental abilities, reflexes, and moods. Fortunately, there are several ways to cure insomnia. Something important to remember is to avoid drinks with caffeine in them. A lack of caffeine in the body will help your body relax and get to sleep easier. Also, try not to exercise two hours before going to bed since this will stimulate your body and keep you from sleeping. Some people say you shouldn't read before bed, but I disagree with them. Another thing is to make your room as dark as possible by removing all the lights. This will create a relaxing atmosphere. Finally, make sure the temperature in your room is neither too hot nor too cold. Follow these instructions, and you should have no problems beating insomnia.

여 때때로 사람들은 불면증에 걸리는데, 그것은 밤에 잠을 수 없거나 잠드는 데 어려움을 겪는 것을 의미한다. 이러한 환자들은 몇 시간을 잠자리에서 뒤척이며 보내기도 한다. 수면 부족은 사람들의 정신적 능력과 반사 능력, 기분에 영향을 미칠 수 있다. 다행히 불면증을 치료하는 몇 가지 방법이 있다. 기억해야 할 중요한 것은 카페인이 든 음료를 피하라는 것이다. 체내에 카페인이 부족하면 몸의 긴장이 풀리며 잠드는 것이 더 쉬워질 수 있다. 또한 몸을 흥분시키고 잠드는 것을 방해하기 때문에 잠자리에 들기 2시간 전에는 운동을 하지 않도록 하라. 어떤 사람들은 잠자기 전에 독서를 해서는 안 된다고 말하지만, 나는 그것에 동의하지 않는다. 또 다른 것은 모든 불빛을 없애서 방을 최대한 어둡게 하라는 것이다. 이것은 편안한 분위기를 만들어 줄 것이다. 마지막으로 방 온도가 너무 덥거나 너무 춥지 않도록 하라. 이러한 지시를 따르면 불면증을 없애는 데 전혀 문제가 없을 것이다.

<table>
<tr><th>문제와 정답</th><th>스크립트</th><th>해석</th></tr>
</table>

21 대화를 듣고, 수잔에 대해 사실이 <u>아닌</u> 것을 고르시오.

① 수잔은 이름을 잘 기억한다.
② 수잔은 마음이 넓은 사람일 것이다.
③ 수잔은 가끔 회사에 지각한다. ✓
④ 수잔은 컴퓨터 프로그램에 대해 잘 모른다.
⑤ 수잔은 성실하게 일하는 사람이다.

▶ incredible 엄청난, 놀랄 만한 impress 감명을 주다, 인상을 갖게 하다 ethic 가치 체계, 윤리 make a name for oneself 유명해지다 generous 관대한 deal with …을 상대하다, 관계하다 intelligent 머리가 좋은, 명석한 negative 단점, 결점 get the hang of …의 사용법을 알다, 터득하다

M What do you think of that new employee?

W Are you talking about Susan? She's incredible. I'm impressed with her work ethic and the way she keeps working on a project until it's finished. You know, she stayed here until ten thirty last night.

M That's impressive. She's only been here for three weeks, and she's already making a name for herself.

W She's pretty generous, too. She gave me half of her lunch the other day when I mentioned I'd forgotten to bring something from home.

M What a nice young lady.

W What's your impression of her? You must have dealt with Susan once or twice since she's started.

M I'd say that what stood out the most was her memory. I met her with some other employees on her first day of work, and she remembered my name two days ago, which was the next time she met me. That was impressive. She must be smart to have a memory like that.

W Yes, she is quite intelligent. The only negative I can think of is that she doesn't know how to use the computer software very well.

M That's something which takes time to learn. I'm sure she'll get the hang of it.

남 그 신입 직원 어떻게 생각해요?

여 수잔 말하는 거예요? 놀라워요. 그녀의 업무 윤리와 일을 마무리할 때까지 꾸준히 프로젝트에 임하는 방식에 감명받았어요. 있잖아요, 그녀는 지난밤에는 10시 30분까지 여기 남아 있었어요.

남 대단하군요. 이곳에 온 지 3주밖에 안 됐는데, 벌써 유명해졌네요.

여 또 아주 너그럽기도 해요. 요전날 내가 깜빡하고 집에서 아무 것도 못 갖고 왔다고 했더니 나한테 점심의 반을 주더라고요.

남 정말 마음씨 착한 아가씨네요.

여 그녀에 대한 당신 인상은 어때요? 그녀가 시작한 후 분명히 한두 번은 수잔을 겪어 봤을 텐데요.

남 아마도 가장 두드러진 건 그녀의 기억력일 거예요. 업무 첫날 다른 직원들 몇 명과 함께 그녀를 만났는데, 이틀 전에 두 번째로 만났을 때 내 이름을 기억했어요. 아주 인상적이었어죠. 그런 기억력을 지닌 걸로 봐서 총명한 게 분명해요.

여 그래요, 꽤 머리가 좋아요. 내가 생각할 수 있는 유일한 단점은 단지 그녀가 컴퓨터 소프트웨어를 잘 사용할 줄 모른다는 거예요.

남 그것은 배우는 데 시간이 걸리잖아요. 틀림없이 해낼 거라고 봐요.

---

22 다음을 듣고, 화자의 요지가 무엇인지 고르시오.

① 컴퓨터 칩이 매년 더 작아지고 있다.
② 지구의 천연자원을 보존하는 것이 중요하다.
③ 20세기에는 위대한 많은 발명품이 있었다.
④ 소형화는 소중한 기술적 발전이다. ✓
⑤ DVD플레이어는 작을 뿐만 아니라 휴대할 수도 있다.

▶ miniaturization 소형화 device (기계적) 장치 computer chip 컴퓨터 칩 incredibly 대단히 enable …을 가능하게 하다 portable 휴대가 가능한 valuable 값진, 귀중한 natural resources 천연자원 feat 위업, 공적

M The twentieth century saw a large number of technological advances, and the same thing is happening in the twenty-first century. Of all of the great discoveries and inventions people have made recently, I believe that there is one which stands out above all the others. I'm talking about miniaturization. This is the process that lets people make machines and devices smaller and smaller. Take computer chips for example. Not only are they getting incredibly small these days, but they are also becoming more powerful. So this enables scientists to put more chips in a computer, thereby making it more powerful. Miniaturization is not just for computers though. It's in all kinds of technology. Think about DVD players, for example. They were once large, but they're getting really smaller and are even portable now. Thanks to miniaturization, people can use fewer valuable natural resources yet not lose any of the benefits of a larger machine. What an impressive feat of technology.

남 20세기는 상당한 기술적 발전을 이뤘고, 동일한 일이 21세기에 일어나고 있다. 인간이 최근에 이룬 모든 위대한 발견과 발명 가운데, 나는 다른 모든 것들보다 뛰어난 것이 하나 있다고 생각한다. 내가 말하는 것은 소형화이다. 이것은 사람들이 기기와 장비를 점점 더 작게 만들게 되는 과정이다. 컴퓨터 칩을 예로 들어 보자. 이것들은 요즈음 믿을 수 없을 정도로 작을 뿐만 아니라 더욱 강력해지고 있다. 그래서 이것으로 과학자들은 컴퓨터 하나에 더 많은 칩을 넣을 수 있고 그리하여 컴퓨터는 더욱 강력해진다. 하지만 소형화는 비단 컴퓨터에만 해당되는 것은 아니다. 그것은 모든 종류의 기술에 들어 있다. 예를 들어 DVD플레이어에 대해 생각해 보자. 그것들은 한때는 컸지만 지금은 굉장히 작아지고 있으며, 심지어는 휴대할 수도 있다. 소형화 덕분에 사람들은 소중한 천연자원을 덜 사용하면서도 더 큰 기기의 혜택 중 어떤 것도 잃지 않을 수 있다. 얼마나 놀라운 기술의 업적인가.

23 대화를 듣고, 두 사람이 서울에서의 생활에 대해 불만스럽게 생각하는 것이 무엇인지 고르시오.

남자의 불만	여자의 불만
① 지하철이 너무 느리다.	아파트가 너무 비싸다.
② 택시가 너무 느리다.	보도에 사람들이 너무 많다.
③ 도시가 너무 크다.	택시를 타면 회사에 늦는다.
✔ 집값이 너무 비싸다.	교통이 너무 막힌다.
⑤ 물가가 너무 비싸다.	지하철 시스템이 효율적이지 않다.

▶ **even though** 비록 …일지라도, …인데도 **originally** 출신은, 원래는 **overall** 전반적으로 **complaint** 불만, 불평 **real estate** 부동산 **work out** (문제 따위가) 풀리다 **sidewalk** 인도, 보도 **traffic** 교통(량) **awesome** 아주 인상적인, 최고의

W You've been living in Seoul for almost a year now. How do you like it?

M It's a lot bigger than I had imagined it would be, but that's not really a problem even though I'm originally from the country. Overall, I'd say I'm having a great time here.

W Really? You mean you don't even have a single complaint?

M I guess that real estate prices are a little too high, so the rent I pay on my apartment is too much. But that's my only real complaint. How about you?

W I managed to get a really cheap yet nice place, so that worked out fine for me. And I just love the way the sidewalks are crowded with people. It seems like everyone has something important to do.

M Oh, right. You walk all the time, don't you?

W Yeah, I do. I tried taking taxis, but the traffic here is so slow that I just gave up, especially after I was late for a few meetings. I'll never take them again. So now I either walk or take the subway.

M What do you think of the subway system?

W It's awesome. It gets me almost anywhere in the city I want to be.

여 이제 서울에 사신 지 1년 가까이 됐죠. 어때요?

남 생각했던 것보다 훨씬 더 큰데, 제가 원래 시골 출신이긴 하지만 그건 정말 문제가 되지 않아요. 전반적으로는 여기서 좋은 시간을 보내고 있다고 해야겠네요.

여 정말요? 불만이 하나도 없다는 말이에요?

남 부동산 가격은 좀 너무 높아서 아파트에 내는 집세가 너무 많은 것 같아요. 하지만 그게 내가 가진 유일한 실질적인 불만이에요. 당신은 어때요?

여 난 정말로 값싸지만 괜찮은 곳을 겨우 구해서 그 문제는 괜찮게 해결됐어요. 그리고 난 인도가 사람들로 혼잡한 것이 좋아요. 모두가 뭔가 해야 할 중요한 일이 있는 것 같거든요.

남 아, 그래요. 당신은 항상 걸어다니죠, 안 그래요?

여 맞아요, 그렇죠. 택시를 타려고 해 봤지만 여기 교통이 너무 막혀요. 특히 몇몇 회의에 지각한 뒤로 그냥 포기했어요. 다시는 택시를 안 탈 거예요. 그래서 이제는 걷거나 지하철을 타죠.

남 지하철 시스템은 어떻게 생각해요?

여 훌륭해요. 시내에 원하는 곳이면 거의 어디든 갈 수 있어요.

---

24 다음을 듣고, 이야기에서 말하는 내용의 예로 알맞은 것을 고르시오.

① mature – premature
② cycle – recycle
③ form – inform
④ view – preview
✔ please – displease

① 성숙한 – 조숙한
② 순환하다 – 재생하다
③ 형성하다 – 알리다
④ 바라보다 – 미리 보다
⑤ 기쁘게 하다 – 불쾌하게 하다

▶ **construct** 구성하다 **root** (파생어 등의) 어근 **prefix** 접미사 **syllable** 음절 **attach** 붙이다 **opposite** 반대의 **likewise** 마찬가지로, 더욱이 **addition** 첨가, 추가된 물건

W Something interesting about the English language is that it's possible to construct many new words from one basic root word. The way to accomplish that is to use prefixes. Prefixes are syllables that may be attached to the front of a word. They have their own meanings and may, of course, change the meaning of a word when added to it. Think, of the root "cycle." Adding "bi," which means "two," gets the word bicycle. Therefore a new word with its own meaning is created. And something what's really interesting is how some new words, once a prefix is added, can have meanings opposite their roots. The word possible means that something can be done. However, by adding "im," which means "not," to it, you get impossible. This, of course, is the opposite of possible. Likewise, the word moral, when an "a" is added to it, becomes amoral. Moral and amoral are also two words with opposite meanings, all due to the mere addition of a prefix.

여 영어에 관한 흥미로운 것은 기본적인 하나의 어근 단어로 많은 새로운 단어를 구성할 수 있다는 것이다. 그것이 가능한 방법은 접미사를 이용하는 것이다. 접미사는 단어의 앞에 붙을 수 있는 음절이다. 이것들은 그 자체 의미가 있고 물론 한 단어에 붙을 때 그 단어의 의미를 변화시킬 수도 있다. 어근 'cycle'을 생각해 보라. '둘'을 의미하는 'bi'를 붙이면 '두발자전거'가 된다. 따라서 그 자체 의미를 띤 새 단어가 탄생한다. 그리고 정말 흥미로운 것은 어떤 새 단어들이 일단 접미사가 붙으면, 그들의 어근에 반대되는 의미를 띨 수 있는 방식이다. 'possible'이라는 단어는 할 수 있는 어떤 것을 의미한다. 하지만 '아닌'을 의미하는 'im'을 붙이면 '불가능한'이 된다. 물론 이것은 possible의 반대이다. 이처럼, moral(도덕적)이란 단어는 'a'가 붙으면 amoral(비도덕적)이 된다. 도덕적과 비도덕적은 또한 반대의 뜻을 지닌 두 단어로, 모든 것이 단순히 접미사 하나를 덧붙인 것에서 기인한다.

<table>
<tr><th>문제와 정답</th><th>스크립트</th><th>해석</th></tr>
</table>

25 대화를 듣고, 점원이 여자의 요구를 거절한 이유를 고르시오.

① The store does not give refunds to any customer.
② The customer forgot to bring her receipt with her.
③ The store only allows customers to exchange items.
✓ The item the customer purchased is not damaged.
⑤ The customer bought the product too many days ago.

① 이 가게는 어떠한 고객에게도 환불을 하지 않는다.
② 고객이 영수증을 가져오는 것을 잊었다.
③ 이 가게는 제품을 교환하는 것만 허용한다.
④ 고객이 구입한 물품에 하자가 없다.
⑤ 고객이 제품을 산 것이 너무 오래 전 일이다.

▶ purchase 구입하다 receipt 영수증 refund 환불하다 customer 고객 request 요청하다 permit 허용하다 damaged 손상된 hold on to …을 내놓지 않다, 매달리다

M Good evening, miss. Is there anything I can do for you?

W Yes, there is. I purchased this product from your store last Saturday, but I'd like to return it.

M Okay, did you remember to bring the receipt with you? We aren't allowed to refund any items unless the customer provides a receipt.

W Sure, I have my receipt right here. You can see how I used my credit card to purchase it.

M Okay, and what exactly was wrong with the product? Why didn't it work properly?

W I'm sorry? What are you talking about? I just bought this product but didn't like it once I tried it, so that's why I'm returning it.

M In that case, I'm terribly sorry, but I'm afraid we can't refund your money after all.

W Why not? I've got my receipt here just like you requested.

M As you can see from this sign here, refunds are only permitted in case of damaged items. Your reason for wanting to return this item is simply that you don't like it. We could, however, let you exchange it for something else.

W That's okay. I'll just hold on to it then.

남 안녕하세요, 손님. 뭘 도와드릴까요?

여 네. 지난 토요일에 이 가게에서 이 제품을 구입했는데, 반환하고 싶어요.

남 알겠습니다, 영수증을 갖고 오셨나요? 고객이 영수증을 제시하지 않으면 어떤 물품도 환불이 안 됩니다.

여 네, 여기 영수증 있어요. 구입하면서 신용카드를 사용한 걸 아시게 될 거예요.

남 네, 정확히 이 제품에 뭐가 잘못됐나요? 왜 제대로 작동하지 않았죠?

여 뭐라고요? 무슨 말씀하시는 거예요? 전 이 물건을 샀고 한번 사용해 보니까 마음에 들지 않아서 반납하려는 거예요.

남 그렇다면, 정말 죄송합니다만 유감스럽게도 돈을 환불해드릴 수 없습니다.

여 왜 안 돼죠? 요구하신 대로 여기 영수증이 있어요.

남 여기 이 표시에서 보시다시피, 환불은 손상 제품에 대해서만 허용됩니다. 손님이 이 품목을 반환하시려는 이유는 단지 마음에 들지 않기 때문이잖아요. 하지만 다른 것으로 교환해 드릴 수는 있습니다.

여 알겠습니다. 그렇다면 그냥 그걸로 할게요.

---

26 다음을 듣고, 화자의 의견에 동의하는 진술을 고르시오.

① Sumi: Parents shouldn't allow their children to play so many video games.
✓ Minho: I love video games since I've learned to work well with others from them.
③ Soohee: Video games are a waste of time, especially since students should be studying more.
④ Mina: I managed to set a new high score on the video game I was recently playing.
⑤ Taeho: Because of video games, I've made a lot of new friends at my school.

① 수미: 부모들은 자녀들이 너무 많은 비디오 게임을 하도록 허용해서는 안 된다.
② 민호: 나는 비디오 게임을 좋아하는데, 그로 인해 다른 사람들과 효과적으로 작업하도록 배웠기 때문이다.
③ 수희: 비디오 게임은 시간 낭비인데, 특히 학생들은 더 많이 공부해야 하기 때문에 그렇다.
④ 미나: 나는 최근 즐기는 비디오 게임에서 겨우 새로운 고득점을 세웠다.
⑤ 태호: 비디오 게임 때문에 나는 학교에서 새 친구들을 많이 사귀었다.

▶ depend upon …에 달려 있다 lesson 교훈 cooperate 협력하다 no matter how 어떻게 보아도, 아무리 …해도 burden 짐, 부담 in conjunction with …와 함께, …에 관련하여 likely …할 것 같은

M Although parents and teachers love complaining about video games and how they're ruining young people's lives, there are actually some benefits people can get from playing these games. While it's true that many youths waste time playing games, depending upon the game they play, they may gain some valuable life lessons. Here's an example. Many video games require players to cooperate with one another in order to win. These two-player or multi-player games simply won't permit one player, no matter how good he is, to win the game by himself. This forces players to cooperate with one another. They must therefore learn to share burdens and to use their own abilities in conjunction with those of others. This is excellent preparation for the future after they graduate from school. It's highly likely these graduates will find jobs requiring them to work with their coworkers on various projects. Thanks to the skills they learned about teamwork by playing video games, they'll already be able to work well with others.

남 학부모와 교사들이 비디오 게임과 그것이 젊은이들의 삶을 어떻게 파괴하는지에 관해 불만을 털어 놓는 것을 좋아하지만, 실제로 사람들이 이런 게임을 하는 것에서 얻을 수 있는 이점도 일부 있다. 많은 청년들이 게임을 하는 데 시간을 낭비하면서 그 게임에 의존하고 있다는 것은 사실이지만 그들은 몇몇 소중한 삶의 교훈을 얻을 수도 있다. 여기에 일례가 있다. 많은 비디오 게임은 게임을 하는 사람들이 승리를 위해 서로 협력하기를 요구한다. 이런 두 명 또는 여러 명의 사람들이 참여하는 게임은, 아무리 게이머가 숙련하더라도, 단순히 한 사람의 게이머가 혼자서 게임에 승리하도록 허용하지 않을 것이다. 이로 인해 게이머들은 서로 협력할 수밖에 없다. 따라서 그들은 부담을 공유하고 그들 자신의 능력을 다른 사람들의 능력과 연계하여 사용하는 것을 배워야만 한다. 이것은 이들이 학교를 졸업한 뒤 미래를 위한 훌륭한 준비가 된다. 이런 졸업생들은 다양한 프로젝트에서 동료들과 같이 작업해야 하는 일을 발견할 가능성이 크다. 비디오 게임을 함으로써 팀워크에 대해 습득한 기술 덕분에 그들은 이미 다른 사람들과 효과적으로 작업할 수 있을 것이다.

<table>
<tr><th>문제와 정답</th><th>스크립트</th><th>해석</th></tr>
</table>

27 대화를 듣고, 두 사람이 기다리는 인물이 어디에서 왔는지 고르시오.

5:30	Tokyo
5:50	Athens
5:50	Rome
6:15	Sydney
6:20	Cairo

① Rome
② Cairo
③ Athens
④ Tokyo
✓⑤ Sydney

① 로마
② 카이로
③ 아테네
④ 도쿄
⑤ 시드니

▶ flight 정기 항공편   delay 연기하다   be supposed to …하기로 되어 있다   beat 먼저 도착하다, 앞지르다   get in 도착하다, 오다   on time 정각에, 제시간에

스크립트

W I wonder when Sara's flight is going to arrive. I sure hope it hasn't been delayed.

M Let's take a look at the information board and see what time it's supposed to arrive.

W Good thinking. Hey, there's a flight arriving at 5:30. That's in just a few minutes.

M That's great, but it's too bad she's not on that flight.

W I know. I just like looking at all of the different cities people are coming from. See, there's another international flight arriving here at 5:42 at Gate 30. That's only a few minutes after the other one. And there's another flight getting here at 5:50.

M Yeah, that's great. But I'm still looking for Sara's flight. It would be nice if you could help me out.

W All right… Oh no! One of the flights has been delayed, so it won't arrive until 6:15 this evening. It's barely going to beat a different flight that's getting in on time at 6:20.

M Okay, we've found her flight. She's arriving at Gate 42 on the 6:15 flight. We've got some time, so let's get something to eat while we wait.

W That sounds all right to me.

해석

여 사라의 비행기가 언제 도착할지 모르겠어. 연착되지 않았으면 정말 좋겠는데.

남 안내판을 보고 몇 시에 도착 예정인지 보자.

여 좋은 생각이야. 이봐, 5시 30분에 도착하는 항공편이 있어. 겨우 몇 분 후인데.

남 좋아, 하지만 사라가 그 항공편에 타지 않았다는 게 안타까운걸.

여 나도 알아. 그냥 사람들이 오는 여러 도시를 보는 게 좋아. 봐, 30번 게이트에서 5시 42분에 여기 도착하는 다른 국제 항공편이 있어. 그건 다른 것의 단 몇 분 뒤야. 그리고 5시 50분에 이곳에 도착하는 또 다른 항공편이 있어.

남 그래, 괜찮네. 하지만 난 여전히 사라의 항공편을 찾고 있어. 네가 날 도와준다면 좋을 거야.

여 알았어… 이런! 항공편 하나가 연착돼서 오늘 저녁 6시 15분까지 도착하지 않을 거래. 6시 20분에 맞춰 정시에 도착할 다른 항공편보다 먼저 온다는데.

남 좋아, 그녀의 항공편을 찾았군. 6시 15분 항공편으로 42번 게이트에 도착할 거야. 시간이 좀 있으니까 기다리는 동안 뭘 좀 먹으러 가자.

여 좋아.

---

28 다음을 듣고, 화자가 설명하는 포즈로 알맞은 것을 고르시오.

✓① 
② 
③ 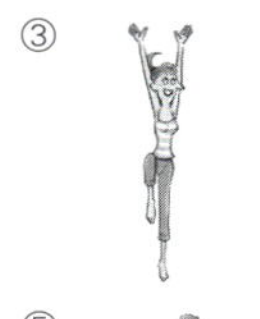
④ 
⑤ 

▶ pose 자세   cover 포함하다; …을 다루다   splits 스플리츠: (댄스 등의) 두 다리를 일직선으로 벌려 바닥에 앉는[뛰어오르는] 연기   lotus 연꽃   whichever 어느 쪽이든   lean forward 앞으로 기울이다, 구부리다   stretch 쭉 뻗다; 뻗기   angle 각도

스크립트

W Now that you've all been learning yoga for a few weeks, I want to teach you a new pose. We've already covered the splits, and I'm proud most of you are doing well with that. And many of you have even mastered the lotus position by sitting with your legs crossed. Well, tonight's pose is going to be a little different. What I want you to do is to stand on only one foot. Choose whichever foot is the strongest. Then, I want you to lean forward. At the same time, stretch your hands out in front of you while extending your other leg—the one that's not on the ground—behind you. You should eventually get to where your legs form a ninety-degree angle with the leg on the ground straight up and the leg in the air straight behind you. I know that it sounds a little complicated, but it's a great stretch, so let's see if we can do it. Is everyone ready to begin?

해석

여 이제 여러분 모두가 몇 주간 요가를 배우고 있기 때문에 새 자세를 가르쳐 드리고 싶습니다. 이미 스플리츠를 배웠고, 대부분이 그걸 잘 하고 있는 게 뿌듯해요. 심지어 여러분 중 많은 분이 다리를 꼬고 앉아서 하는 연꽃 자세도 습득했지요. 자, 오늘밤의 자세는 약간 다를 겁니다. 내가 바라는 건 여러분이 한 발로만 서 있는 거예요. 어느 쪽 발이 더 강한지 선택하세요. 그 다음에 앞으로 몸을 기울이세요. 동시에 두 손을 앞으로 쭉 뻗고 바닥에 있지 않는 다른 다리는 뒤로 펴세요. 결국 다리를 90도 각도로 해서 바닥에 있는 다리는 쭉 펴고 공중에 있는 다리는 뒤로 펴야 해요. 좀 복잡하게 들린다는 건 알지만 훌륭한 스트레칭이니 여러분이 할 수 있는지 한번 봅시다. 모두 시작할 준비가 됐나요?

29 대화를 듣고, 다음 중 두 사람이 먼저 해야 할 일들을 모두 고르시오.

ⓐ make some copies
ⓑ go to lunch
ⓒ attend a meeting with the department heads
ⓓ make some phone calls
ⓔ send a facsimile
ⓕ prepare for a meeting
ⓖ deliver some papers

ⓐ 복사를 한다
ⓑ 점심을 먹는다
ⓒ 부서장들과의 회의에 참석한다
ⓓ 전화를 건다
ⓔ 팩스를 보낸다
ⓕ 회의 준비를 한다
ⓖ 서류를 전달한다

① ⓐ, ⓒ, ⓕ, ⓖ
② ⓐ, ⓔ, ⓕ, ⓖ ✓
③ ⓑ, ⓒ, ⓓ, ⓔ, ⓕ
④ ⓒ, ⓓ, ⓔ, ⓖ
⑤ ⓐ, ⓒ, ⓔ, ⓖ

▶ photocopying 사진 복사   urgent 긴급한   client 고객   terribly 매우   attend 참석하다

M How's your day going? It seems like you're really busy.

W Yeah, I've got a million things to do but no time at all. For example, the boss just told me to get all this photocopying done within the next ten minutes, but I've also got to send an urgent fax to one of our clients right now.

M Wow, and I thought I was busy since I have to deliver some papers to Mr. Baker now.

W Well, at least my afternoon gets a little easier. I just have to make a few phone calls then, but none of them are too terribly important.

M That's good to know. After lunch, I'll attend a meeting with the department heads. It's pretty important, so I need to prepare for it immediately.

W I'd give you some help, but I don't have any time.

M Don't worry about that. I know you're busy. Say, why don't we have lunch together a couple of hours from now? We can talk about how much of our work we've gotten done and what we haven't finished.

W I'd love to, but I can't. How about tomorrow?

M That sounds fine. Well, good luck with everything.

남 오늘 어때요? 정말 바쁜 것 같네요.

여 그래요, 할 일이 엄청 많은데 시간이 전혀 없어요. 예를 들어 상사는 방금 내게 이 복사를 모두 앞으로 10분 내에 끝내라고 말했지만 난 지금 당장 고객 중 한 사람에게 긴급한 팩스를 보내야 해요.

남 우와, 난 지금 베이커 씨에게 서류를 좀 전달해야 해서 내가 바쁘다고 생각했는데.

여 음, 최소한 오후에는 좀 더 수월해요. 그때는 그냥 전화 몇 통화만 하면 되는데, 아주 상당히 중요한 건 하나도 없거든요.

남 알아 둘 필요가 없네요. 점심 후에 난 부서장들과 하는 회의에 참석할 거예요. 꽤 중요한 거라서 당장 그 준비를 해야 해요.

여 도와주고 싶지만 시간이 전혀 없네요.

남 그건 걱정 말아요. 당신이 바쁜 걸 아니까. 음, 지금부터 두어 시간 후에 같이 점심하는 거 어때요? 일이 얼마나 끝났고 어떤 것을 덜 끝냈는지 얘기할 수 있고.

여 그러고 싶지만 안 되겠어요. 내일은 어때요?

남 좋아요. 자, 모든 일에 행운을 빌어요.

---

30 다음을 듣고, 다음 문장의 빈 칸에 들어갈 알맞은 말을 고르시오.

When you go to the United States, you should _______________.

① always pay for your share of the meal at a restaurant
② stand close to people when speaking to them
③ give strong opinions on various topics
④ avoid talking about a number of specific subjects ✓
⑤ be sure to ask about a person's religious beliefs

당신이 미국에 가면, 당신은 _______________.

① 식당에서 자기몫의 돈을 늘 내야 한다
② 사람들과 얘기할 때 그들 가까이에 서야 한다
③ 다양한 주제에 대해 뚜렷한 의견을 내야 한다
④ 몇가지 특정 주제에 대해 얘기하는 것은 피해야 한다
⑤ 다른 사람의 종교적 신념에 대해 꼭 물어 봐야 한다

▶ invade 침해하다   host 주인, 주최자   opinionated 자기 의견을 고집하는, 독단적인   offend 기분을 상하게 하다, 불쾌감을 주다

M These days, people are beginning to travel to many of the world's countries and are meeting people from cultures other than their own. Unfortunately, the majority of people are often unaware of foreign cultures, so they wind up making cultural mistakes. It's crucial that people learn about other cultures to keep from embarrassing themselves. For example, most Americans don't like people invading their personal space. They don't want anyone, no matter who the person is, to come too close to them while they're talking. It makes them feel extremely uncomfortable. Something else Americans dislike is when people they don't know well talk to them about personal topics like religion or politics. Furthermore, if an American host invites you out to dinner at a restaurant, don't try to pay the bill. Your host will take care of it. Finally, feel free to give your opinion, but don't be too opinionated. That could offend some Americans, especially if you don't know them very well.

남 오늘날 사람들은 세계의 많은 국가들로 여행하기 시작하고 자신들의 문화가 아닌 다른 문화에 속한 사람들을 만나고 있다. 불행히도 상당수의 사람들이 종종 외국 문화에 대해 알지 못해 결국에는 문화적인 실수를 하고 만다. 사람들이 스스로 당황해하지 않도록 다른 문화에 대해 배우는 것은 중요하다. 예를 들어 대부분의 미국인들은 사람들이 자신의 사적 공간을 침해하는 것을 좋아하지 않는다. 그들은 그 사람이 누구이든 대화를 하는 동안 자신들에게 너무 가까이 오길 바라지 않는다. 그런 행동은 이들을 지극히 불편하게 만든다. 미국인들이 싫어하는 다른 것은 잘 모르는 사람들이 종교나 정치 같은 개인적인 주제에 관해 자신들에게 얘기할 때이다. 또한, 어떤 미국인이 여러분을 식당에서의 저녁식사에 초대한 경우라면 계산을 하려고 하지 말라. 당신을 초대한 사람이 알아서 할 것이다. 마지막으로 자유롭게 여러분의 의견을 제시하되 너무 고집하지는 말라. 그것은 어떤 미국인들, 특히 여러분이 잘 모르는 사람인 경우, 기분을 상하게 할 수 있다.

31

[모두 듣기] **What is the best response to the man?**

W: ______________________________.

① Just ignore him, and maybe he'll stop.
② Sing along with him whenever he starts.
③ Ask if you can get a new office somewhere else.
④ Pretend that his singing does not bother you at all.
✓ Have a talk with him, and ask him to quit singing.

남자의 말에 대한 가장 알맞은 대답은 무엇인가?
① 그냥 무시해, 그럼 아마 멈출 거야.
② 그가 노래를 시작하면 함께 부르도록 해.
③ 어딘가 다른 곳에 새 사무실을 얻을 수 있는지 물어 봐.
④ 그의 노래가 전혀 성가시지 않는 척을 해.
⑤ 그와 얘기를 하고 노래를 멈춰 달라고 요청해.

▶ bother 괴롭히다, 성가시게 하다 what's up 무슨 일인지 horrible 끔찍한, 몹시 불쾌한 get on one's nerves …의 신경을 거스르다, …를 화나게 하다 awful 몹시 나쁜, 싫은

M There's something that's been bothering me for the last few days, and I was hoping you could let me know what you think I should do about it.

W Sure, go ahead and tell me what's up.

M It's about Dave. He's the guy I share an office with. He's been driving me crazy lately, and I just don't know what to say to him.

W What's he been doing that's bothering you? He seems like a pretty nice guy.

M He is, but he has this horrible habit of singing at his desk all the time. It's not really loud, but, since our desks are next to each other, I have to hear every word he sings. I've already asked my boss about changing desks, but he won't let me.

W Do you think he realizes what he's doing?

M Oh, he knows he's doing it. I've mentioned to him before about how much it bothers me, but he won't stop singing. It's starting to get on my nerves really badly.

W I can imagine. That must be awful. You've got to do something about that as soon as possible.

M Okay, so what do you think I ought to do?

W ______________________________

남 지난 며칠간 날 괴롭히는 게 있는데 그것에 관해 내가 뭘 해야 할지 네 생각을 알고 싶어.

여 좋아, 계속해서 무슨 일인지 말해 봐.

남 데이브에 관한 거야. 그는 사무실을 같이 쓰는 사람이야. 최근 들어 날 미치게 만드는데, 그에게 무슨 말을 해야 할지 모르겠어.

여 그의 어떤 행동이 널 불편하게 하니? 꽤 착한 사람 같던데.

남 그래, 하지만 항상 책상에서 노래하는 지독한 버릇이 있어. 크게 시끄럽진 않지만 우린 책상이 서로 옆에 있어서 난 그가 부르는 모든 가사를 들어야 해. 이미 상사에게 자리 바꾸는 걸 요청해 놨지만 허락하지 않을 거야.

여 그가 자신이 하는 행동을 알고 있는 것 같니?

남 그럼, 그는 자기가 그러는 걸 알아. 전에 그게 얼마나 날 괴롭히는지 말했지만, 그는 노래하는 걸 멈추려 하지 않아. 정말 내 신경을 거슬리기 시작했어.

여 상상이 돼. 정말 끔찍하겠다. 가능한 한 빨리 뭔가 조치를 취해야겠구나.

남 그래, 그러니까 내가 어떻게 해야 할 것 같니?

여 ______________________________

32

[모두 듣기] **What was the man's original plan for the weekend?**

① To go on a picnic
✓ To see a movie
③ To go on a business trip
④ To go hiking
⑤ To stay at home alone

원래 남자의 주말 계획은 무엇이었는가?
① 소풍을 가는 것
② 영화 보러 가는 것
③ 출장 가는 것
④ 하이킹을 가는 것
⑤ 혼자 집에 있는 것

▶ go hiking 하이킹 가다 woods 숲, 삼림 intend 작정이다, 생각이다 catch a movie 영화를 보다 out of town 도시를 떠나 business trip 출장 intrude on 주제넘게 나서다, 방해하다

W I'm looking forward to this weekend since I'm planning to have a great time with my family.

M What are you doing with them?

W We're going to the mountain near my home to have a picnic. The whole family will be there, so it'll be a fantastic time.

M What are you planning to do after you eat? Will you play games or go hiking?

W We'll probably do some of both. I love nature, so I imagine I'll go for a hike in the woods, but some of my family members enjoy playing sports, so I'm sure they'll do that.

M That sounds much more exciting than my weekend. I was just intending to catch a movie by myself.

W Why are you going alone? I thought you had a girlfriend. The two of you should go together.

M I'd love that, but she's going out of town on a business trip this weekend, so I don't have much of a choice.

W If that's the case, then why don't you go on the picnic with us? Everyone knows you, so you won't be intruding on us.

M Hey, that's a great idea. Thanks a lot for inviting me.

여 이번 주말에 가족들과 즐거운 시간을 보낼 계획이어서 기대가 돼요.

남 뭘 할 건데요?

여 집 근처 산으로 소풍을 갈 거예요. 온 가족이 갈 거라서 아주 멋진 시간이 될 거예요.

남 식사 후에 뭘 할 계획이죠? 게임을 하거나 하이킹을 갈 건가요?

여 아마 둘 다 조금은 할 거예요. 난 자연을 좋아해서 숲속으로 하이킹하러 갈 생각이지만 식구들 중 일부는 운동하는 걸 즐기니까 분명히 그걸 하겠죠.

남 내 주말보다 훨씬 더 흥미진진한 것 같네요. 난 그냥 혼자 영화 볼 생각이었는데.

여 왜 혼자 가요? 여자친구가 있는 줄 알았는데. 둘이 같이 가야죠.

남 그러고 싶지만 그녀가 이번 주말에 출장을 가서 제가 별 선택의 여지가 없어요.

여 그런 상황이라면, 우리하고 소풍 안 갈래요? 모두 당신을 아니까 방해되지 않을 거예요.

남 와, 좋은 생각이네요. 초대해 줘서 정말 고마워요.

<table>
<tr><th>문제와 정답</th><th>스크립트</th><th>해석</th></tr>
</table>

33 〔모두 듣기〕 **Why does the woman change her order?**

① She is not particularly hungry.
② She has just finished her diet.
③ Her original meal is too expensive.
④ She does not want any vegetables.
✓ She wants to order less food.

여자는 왜 주문을 바꾸었는가?

① 그녀는 그다지 배가 고프지 않다.
② 그녀는 다이어트를 막 끝냈다.
③ 원래 시켰던 음식이 너무 비싸다.
④ 그녀는 채소를 원하지 않는다.
⑤ 그녀는 더 적은 음식을 주문하기를 원한다.

▶ dressing (요리에 얹는) 드레싱, 소스 sirloin 설로인: 소의 허리고기의 윗부분 medium rare 중간 정도의 설익히는 pilaf 필라프: 고기 수프로 조리한 쌀밥; 볶은 밥을 고기, 야채와 함께 수프로 찐 중동의 요리 plate 접시, (접시에 담은) 요리 ruin 망치다 care for …을 좋아하다, 바라다 unsweetened 달게 하지 않은

M Good evening, ma'am. My name is Trevor, and I'll be your waiter tonight. Would you care to order your dinner now?

W Yes, I think I'm all ready to order. For starters, how about getting me the garden salad?

M All right. That's a good choice. What kind of dressing would you like to have with it?

W I'll take ranch dressing. Also, I'd like to have the sirloin steak, please. I'd like it cooked medium rare.

M No problem. Our chef cooks an excellent steak. That comes with a choice of baked potato, rice pilaf, and soup. And it also includes a small plate of vegetables.

W Oh my goodness. I had no idea I was ordering so much food. My diet is going to be ruined. Is it all right if I make a change to my order?

M That's no problem at all.

W Great. Thanks. Instead of the steak and garden salad, just get me the chicken salad with ranch dressing. I think that ought to do it.

M That should take about ten minutes or so. Would you care for something to drink while you wait?

W I'll just have an unsweetened ice tea, please.

남 안녕하십니까, 고객님. 저는 트레버라고 하며 오늘 밤 손님을 접대할 겁니다. 지금 저녁식사를 주문하시겠습니까?

여 네, 주문해도 될 것 같네요. 우선 가든 샐러드 좀 주시겠어요?

남 알겠습니다. 훌륭한 선택이십니다. 곁들일 드레싱은 어떤 종류로 하시겠습니까?

여 랜치 드레싱으로 할게요. 또 설로인 스테이크도 부탁해요. 미디움 레어로 익혀 주시면 좋겠어요.

남 알겠습니다. 저희 요리사가 스테이크를 아주 잘 합니다. 스테이크에는 구운 감자와 쌀밥 필라프, 그리고 스프 중에서 선택할 수 있습니다. 또 작은 접시에 야채가 곁들여 나옵니다.

여 이런. 그렇게 많은 음식이 나오는지 몰랐어요. 다이어트가 엉망이 될 거예요. 주문을 바꿔도 될까요?

남 얼마든지 괜찮습니다.

여 잘 됐네요. 고마워요. 스테이크와 가든 샐러드 대신 그냥 랜치 드레싱을 한 치킨 샐러드를 주세요. 그거면 될 것 같네요.

남 한 10분 정도 걸릴 겁니다. 기다리시는 동안 음료를 드시겠습니까?

여 무설탕 아이스티 한 잔 주세요.

---

34 〔모두 듣기〕 **Which of the following best shows the relationship between the speaker and the listener?**

✓ A senior and a freshman
② A professor and a senior
③ A guidance counselor and a junior
④ An advisor and a sophomore
⑤ An interviewer and a senior

화자와 듣는 사람의 관계를 가장 잘 나타낸 것은 어느 것인가?

① 상급생과 신입생
② 교수와 상급생
③ 담당 카운셀러와 하급생
④ 조언자와 2학년생
⑤ 면접관과 상급생

▶ waste 낭비하다 hang out 서성거리다 dormitory 기숙사 goof off 빈둥거리다 disaster 재앙 grade 성적 ever 언제나 변함없이 do things right …을 제대로 하다 get off 출발하다

W One of the things you need to remember is that you're going to have a lot of free time while you're here. However, you've got to learn how to spend that time wisely. Just three years ago, when I was in your situation, I got here and wasted all my free time. Instead of going to the library and studying after class, I hung out in the dormitory and played computer games with my friends. It was really fun, but my grades suffered a lot. You wouldn't believe how angry my parents were. So, be sure that you don't spend all of your time sleeping, playing games, or even just goofing off. My first year was a disaster, and I've been trying to get my grades up ever since that time. If you do things right, however, you'll get off to a good start and never have any academic problems.

여 여러분이 기억해야 할 것들 중 한 가지는 여기 있는 동안 많은 자유 시간을 갖게 될 것이라는 것입니다. 하지만 그 시간을 현명하게 쓰는 방법을 배워야 합니다. 바로 3년 전에 내가 여러분의 처지에 있을 때 나는 여기 와서 모든 자유 시간을 낭비했습니다. 방과 후 도서관에 가서 공부하는 대신 기숙사에서 서성거리면서 친구들과 컴퓨터 게임을 하며 놀았지요. 그건 참 재미있었지만 성적은 상당히 타격을 받았어요. 부모님이 얼마나 화를 내셨는지 여러분은 믿지 못할 거예요. 그러니까 여러분이 가진 모든 시간을 잠을 자거나 게임을 하거나 그냥 빈둥거리는 데 쓰지 않도록 하세요. 내 1학년은 끔찍했고 나는 그 이후 성적을 올리려고 노력하고 있어요. 하지만, 여러분이 제대로 하면 좋은 출발을 하게 될 것이고, 학업에 대한 어떠한 문제도 없을 겁니다.

35 다음을 듣고, 이어지는 영어 질문에 대한 알맞은 답을 고르시오.

① cold and snowy
② hot and rainy
✓ warm and cloudy
④ hot and bright
⑤ cool and rainy

① 춥고 눈오는
② 덥고 비오는
③ 따뜻하고 구름 낀
④ 덥고 화창한
⑤ 시원하고 비오는

▶ be concerned about …을 염려하다
precipitation 강우(량) extremes 양극단, 곤경

M Mr. Bryant is thinking of taking a vacation soon, but he's not sure exactly where he wants to go because he is concerned about the weather in each place. He can't stand any kind of precipitation, and he doesn't really enjoy extremes in either heat or cold. He also doesn't like it when the weather is completely sunny since it's too bright for him.

Q: *Which kind of weather conditions does Mr. Bryant like?*

남 브라이언트 씨는 곧 휴가를 갈 생각이지만 정확히 어디로 가고 싶은지 확신이 없는데, 왜냐하면 곳곳의 날씨가 걱정스럽기 때문이다. 그는 어떠한 종류의 강우도 견디지 못하며 더위나 추위도 심한 것을 정말 좋아하지 않는다. 그는 또 날씨가 완전히 햇빛이 비칠 때도 좋아하지 않는데, 그건 그에게 너무 밝기 때문이다.

Q: *브라이언트 씨는 어떤 날씨를 좋아할까?*

---

36 주어진 시간 동안 아래 지문을 주의 깊게 읽고, 들려주는 영어 질문에 답하시오.〔1분〕

After the heart, the brain is one of the most important organs in the body. Without an operational brain, a person would not be able to think for him or herself. Unsurprisingly, the human brain is an extremely complicated organ, and scientists have not yet determined everything it is capable of doing. However, what they have determined shows that the brain is simply incredible. For example, it is responsible for accepting all of the information that the five senses—sight, smell, touch, taste, and hearing—register, and then it must process that information. The brain also lets people think, speak, and imagine things. It controls people's emotions, of which they have a very large number. And the brain also controls the body's motor reflexes. These are what enable people to walk, talk, breathe, and move all of their various body parts. The brain even controls the rate at which a person's heart beats and a person's body temperature, among other things. There are simply a stunning amount of responsibilities that the brain, a relatively small organ, is responsible for.

Q ______________

✓ The Functions of the Brain
② How the Brain Works
③ The Brain and Motor Reflexes
④ The Complexity of the Brain
⑤ The Brain: The Most Important Organ

① 뇌의 기능
② 뇌는 어떻게 작용하는가
③ 뇌와 운동신경의 반사능력
④ 뇌의 복잡성
⑤ 뇌: 가장 중요한 기관

Q: *What is the best title of this passage?*

심장 다음으로 뇌는 신체에서 가장 중요한 기관 중의 하나이다. 기능을 다하는 뇌가 없다면 사람은 스스로 생각할 수 없을 것이다. 인간의 뇌는 지극히 복잡한 기관이며 과학자들이 아직 뇌가 할 수 있는 모든 것을 판단하지 못한 것은 놀라운 일이 아니다. 하지만 그들이 판단한 것은 뇌가 그야말로 놀랍다는 것을 보여준다. 예를 들어 뇌는 시각과 후각, 촉각, 미각, 청각의 오감이 등록하는 모든 정보를 받아들인 다음 그 정보를 처리해야 할 책임이 있다. 뇌는 또한 사람들이 생각하고 말하고 상상할 수 있게 한다. 뇌는 사람들의 아주 많은 다양한 감정을 조절한다. 그리고 몸의 운동신경의 반사 능력도 조절한다. 이것들은 사람들이 걷고 말하고 숨쉬고 다양한 체내 부분을 모두 움직일 수 있게 하는 것이다. 뇌는 무엇보다도 사람의 심장 박동 수와 체온를 조절한다. 상대적으로 작은 기관인 뇌에는 그저 놀랍기만 한 담당해야 할 많은 책임이 있다.

Q: *이 이야기에 가장 알맞은 제목은 무엇인가?*

37 Which of the following is NOT true about the woman's apartment?

✔ ① Her bedroom is not as big as she had thought.

② The wallpaper in the kitchen needs to be fixed.

③ She can see a nearby mountain from there.

④ There was no electricity when she moved in.

⑤ There is a problem with her bathroom sink.

다음 중 여자의 아파트에 대해 사실이 <u>아닌</u> 것은 무엇인가?

① 그녀의 침실이 생각했던 것보다 크지 않다.

② 주방의 벽지는 다시 바를 필요가 있다.

③ 집에서 가까운 곳의 산을 바라볼 수 있다.

④ 그녀가 이사 왔을 땐 전기가 들어오지 않았다.

⑤ 화장실 배수구에 문제가 있다.

38 Which of the following is the man's response to the woman?

M: _______________________________

① You'd better get that sink fixed immediately.

✔ ② So, not everything about your apartment is bad.

③ You must be paying a lot of money for that.

④ I'd be upset about the previous tenant if I were you.

⑤ What are you going to do about that wallpaper?

여자의 마지막 말에 대한 남자의 대답으로 알맞은 것은?

① 즉시 배수구를 고치는 게 좋을 거야.

② 그렇다면, 아파트의 모든 것이 나쁜 건 아니구나.

③ 분명 그것에 돈을 많이 들일 거야.

④ 내가 너였다면 이전 세입자에게 화가 났을 거야.

⑤ 그 벽지를 어떻게 할 거니?

▶ **previous** 이전의 **tenant** (가옥 등의) 점유자 **utility** (전기, 전화 등의) 공익사업 **get a load of** …을 잘 보다, 주의를 기울이다 **stain** 얼룩 **peel** 벗겨지다 **replace** 교체하다 **sink** 세면대 **leak** (파이프 등이) 새다 **repair** 보수, 수리 **wardrobe** 옷장 **dresser** 화장대 **look out on** …으로 향하다, …을 바라보다

(37~38)

W You wouldn't believe how difficult moving in to a new apartment can be. It seems that so many things have gone wrong.

M Like what? I haven't moved in so long that I've forgotten what it was like.

W For one thing, there wasn't any electricity or gas in my apartment when I moved in. The previous tenant hadn't paid his bills, so I had to call both utility companies to get someone to come out and turn them on. I was trying to move everything in while it was dark.

M Ouch. That couldn't have been fun.

W No kidding. And get a load of this… The wallpaper in the kitchen was totally ruined. When I checked it out two weeks ago, it was fine. But now it's got lots of stains on it, and it's even peeling in a few places. I'm going to have to get it replaced. Oh, and the sink in the bathroom leaks, too.

M It sounds like you've got some home repairs in your future. Aren't there at least one or two good things about your apartment? There must be something positive to talk about.

W Hmm… Well, the bedroom was bigger than I had expected, so I've got more than enough room for my bed, wardrobe, and dresser. I was pleasantly surprised by that.

M Is there anything else?

W Hmm… The apartment has a great view since my window looks out on the mountain behind me.

M _______________________________

(37~38)

여 새 아파트로 이사하는 게 얼마나 힘든지 넌 이해하지 못할 거야. 아주 많은 것들이 잘못된 것 같아 보여.

남 이를테면? 난 아주 오랫동안 이사를 안 해서 그게 어떤 건지 잊어버렸어.

여 우선, 내가 이사해 왔을 때 이 아파트에 전기나 가스가 전혀 없었어. 예전 거주자가 청구서를 지불하지 않아서 누군가가 와서 그것들을 틀도록 내가 공익사업체에 전화해야 했어. 깜깜한 가운데 모든 걸 옮기려 하고 있었다고.

남 저런. 재미있을 수가 없겠는걸.

여 정말 그래. 그리고 이걸 잘 들어봐… 부엌 벽지가 완전히 엉망이었어. 2주 전에 확인했을 때는 괜찮았거든. 하지만 지금은 많은 얼룩이 있고 심지어 몇 군데는 벗겨져 있어. 교체를 해야 해. 아, 그리고 욕실 세면대도 물이 새고 있어.

남 앞으로 집 수리를 좀 해야 할 것 같다. 네 아파트에 최소한 한두 가지 좋은 점은 없어? 뭔가 얘기할 만한 긍정적인 게 분명히 있을 텐데.

여 흠… 침실은 예상했던 것보다 더 커서 침대랑 옷장, 화장대를 충분히 넣고도 남는 공간이 있어. 그건 기분 좋은 놀라움이었지.

남 다른 건 없어?

여 흠… 아파트 조망이 괜찮아. 뒤쪽 산으로 창문이 나 있거든.

남 _______________________________

39 Who are the speakers talking about?

① Frank D. Roosevelt
② Tony Blair
✓ Winston Churchill
④ Douglas MacArthur
⑤ George Bush

화자들은 누구에 대해 이야기하고 있는가?

① 프랭크 D. 루즈벨트
② 토니 블레어
③ 윈스턴 처칠
④ 더글라스 맥아더
⑤ 조지 부시

40 Which of the following is NOT true about the person?

① He was once the prime minister of England.
✓ He often spoke to the British people on television.
③ He was the author of some books.
④ He once had a job as a journalist in a foreign country.
⑤ He had several different jobs in the government.

이야기의 주인공에 대해 사실이 <u>아닌</u> 것은 무엇인가?

① 그는 한때 영국의 수상이었다.
② 그는 텔레비전에 나와 영국 국민에게 연설을 자주 했다.
③ 그는 책 몇권을 쓴 저자였다.
④ 그는 한때 외국에서 신문기자 일을 했다.
⑤ 그는 정부에서 몇 가지 일을 했다.

▶ biography 전기(물) definitely 확실히, 틀림없이 encourage 격려하다, 용기를 북돋우다 give up …을 포기하다 prime minister 수상 turn out 결국 …임이 드러나다, (결과가) …이 되다 tons of 상당한, 다수의

(39~40)

M　Are you still reading that biography? I never imagined you'd be the kind of person who'd enjoy that.

W　I'm rather surprised myself. But, I must say this is one of the most amazing stories I've ever read.

M　What's your favorite part about the book?

W　It's definitely the way he encouraged the British people not to give up during World War II even when it looked like the Germans were going to win.

M　Yeah, that was really inspiring. He gave lots of speeches to people on the radio that were about how they were going to fight their hardest and not lose the war.

W　It's a good thing he was the prime minister of England during the war and that the country wasn't being led by someone else. If that had been the case, things might have actually turned out differently.

M　You're right about that. I think he was such a good leader because he had tons of experience. He had been a reporter in another country, he had written several books, and he had served in several government positions. So he knew what to do during that time of trouble.

W　Yeah, but why did the British people elect someone else right after the war ended? That seemed kind of strange.

M　Well, you'll have to continue reading the book to find that one out.

W　All right. In that case, let me get back to my reading.

(39~40)

남　아직도 그 전기를 읽고 있어? 네가 그걸 좋아할 거라고는 전혀 생각 못 했는데.

여　나 스스로도 좀 놀라워. 하지만 이건 정말 지금껏 읽은 가장 놀라운 얘기들 중 하나야.

남　그 책에서 제일 좋아하는 부분이 뭔데?

여　물론 2차 세계대전 독일인이 승리할 것처럼 보였을 때도 영국인들에게 포기하지 말라고 격려한 부분이야.

남　그래, 그거 정말 감명 깊었어. 그는 사람들에게 직접, 혹은 라디오로 많은 연설을 했는데, 어떻게 열심히 싸우면서 전쟁에서 패배하지 않을 것인지에 대한 거였지.

여　그가 전쟁 동안 영국의 수상이었고 영국이 다른 사람의 지도를 받지 않았다는 것은 좋은 일이야. 상황이 실제로 다르게 나타났을지도 몰라.

남　그건 네 말이 맞아. 난 그가 엄청난 경험이 있었기 때문에 그처럼 훌륭한 지도자였다고 생각해. 그는 다른 나라에서 기자 생활을 했고 책을 몇 권 썼으며 정부에서도 몇 번 근무했어. 그래서 그 어려운 시기에 뭘 해야 할지 알았던 거야.

여　그래, 하지만 왜 영국 사람들은 전쟁이 끝난 직후에 다른 사람을 뽑았지? 좀 이상한 것 같아.

남　음, 그걸 알아내려면 그 책을 계속 읽어야 할 거야.

여　그래. 그렇다면 계속 책을 읽어야겠다.

실전모의고사 02

01 ①	02 ①	03 ④	04 ①	05 ④	06 ③	07 ④	08 ④	09 ③	10 ④
11 ①	12 ②	13 ③	14 ②	15 ③	16 ②	17 ②	18 ③	19 ③	20 ①
21 ③	22 ①	23 ③	24 ⑤	25 ②	26 ①	27 ⑤	28 ④	29 ④	30 ②
31 ①	32 ④	33 ①	34 ③	35 ②	36 ②	37 ⑤	38 ①	39 ③	40 ④

문제와 정답	스크립트	해석

01 대화를 듣고, 여자가 가려고 하는 곳을 고르시오.

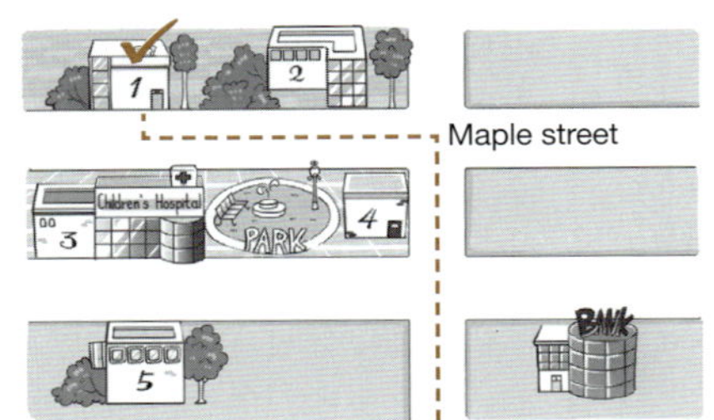

▶ out of town 도시를 떠나 avenue 큰 길, (거리명으로서) …가(街) go straight 곧장 가다 block (도시의) 한 구획, 블록 so far 여기까지, 이 정도까지 opposite 맞은편의, 반대쪽의

W Excuse me, sir, but can you tell me how to get to Saint Paul's? I'm from out of town, and my friend is getting married today at two o'clock.

M Sure. Okay, let me see. We are on Main Street right next to the bank. So you can go west to Second Avenue.

W Okay, so I need to head toward Second Avenue. Then what do I do?

M Turn right at Second Avenue. Then you go straight two blocks to Maple Street.

W Okay, that sounds pretty easy so far.

M Then, when you get to Maple Street, take a left.

W No problem. Where do I go after that?

M After that, walk along Maple Street until you see a hospital. It's called Children's Hospital. It's located right next to Stanley Park. The church that you're looking for is opposite the hospital.

W Okay. Let me make sure I have this correct. Go straight west to Second Avenue, and then turn right. After that, go two blocks to Maple Street, and then turn left. Then walk until I see Stanley Park and Children's Hospital. Saint Paul's is opposite the hospital. Okay, thanks a lot.

M Enjoy the wedding.

여 실례합니다만, 세인트 폴로 가는 방법을 알려 주시 겠어요? 다른 곳 출신인데 친구가 오늘 2시에 결혼 하거든요.

남 네. 자, 한번 볼까요. 우리가 있는 곳은 메인 스트리 트의 은행 바로 옆이에요. 그러니까 세컨드 애비뉴 쪽으로 서쪽으로 가면 되겠네요.

여 알겠어요, 그러니까 제가 세컨드 애비뉴 쪽으로 가 야 한다는 거죠. 그 다음에는 어떻게 해야 하죠?

남 세컨드 애비뉴에서 오른쪽으로 돌아요. 그런 다음 메이플 스트리트로 두 블록 곧장 가세요.

여 알겠어요, 아직까진 꽤 쉬운 것 같네요.

남 그런 다음 메이플 스트리트에 도착하면 왼쪽으로 돌 아요.

여 그러죠. 그 후에는 어디로 가면 되나요?

남 그 뒤에는 병원이 보일 때까지 메이플 스트리트를 따라 걸어가세요. 그 병원은 아동병원이에요. 스탠 리 공원 바로 옆에 있어요. 찾으시는 교회는 그 병원 맞은편에 있어요.

여 알겠어요. 제가 제대로 아는지 확인할게요. 세컨드 애비뉴로 서쪽으로 직진한 다음에 우회전하고요. 그 뒤에 메이플 스트리트로 두 블록을 간 다음에 좌회 전하고요. 그런 다음 스탠리 공원과 아동병원이 보 일 때까지 걷는 거죠. 세인트 폴은 병원 맞은편에 있 고요. 알겠네요, 정말 고맙습니다.

남 결혼식 즐겁게 보내요.

02 대화를 듣고, 이 대화가 이루어지고 있는 장소를 고르시 오.

✓① at a car rental agency
② at a garage
③ at an auto showroom
④ at a used car sales lot
⑤ at a gas station

① 렌터카 사무소에서
② 자동차 정비소에서
③ 자동차 전시장에서
④ 중고차 판매장에서
⑤ 주유소에서

M Good day, madam. Welcome to the Swift Car Company. How can I help you?

W I have a problem with the car that I rented yesterday.

M Oh, that's not good. What seems to be the trouble?

W Well, it was fine until last night. But, this morning when I started it, the engine was making a lot of noise. I drove for about two blocks and started looking for a garage when a lot of smoke started coming from the engine, so I stopped.

M That's terrible. I apologize for the inconvenience on behalf of the company. We will get you a new car right away.

W Thank you very much.

M Don't mention it. First, can you tell me where you left the other car?

남 안녕하세요, 사모님. 스위프트 자동차사에 잘 오셨 습니다. 뭘 도와드릴까요?

여 어제 렌트한 차에 문제가 있어요.

남 저런, 안됐군요. 뭐가 문제인 것 같습니까?

여 어젯밤까지는 괜찮았어요. 하지만 오늘 아침에 시동 을 걸었을 때 엔진에서 소음이 많이 났어요. 두 블록 정도 운전해 자동차 정비소를 찾기 시작했을 때 엔 진에서 연기가 많이 나기 시작해서 차를 세웠어요.

남 저런. 회사를 대신해 불편을 드린 점 사과드립니다. 당장 새 차를 가져다 드리겠습니다.

여 정말 고맙습니다.

남 천만에요. 우선 그 차를 어디다 두셨는지 말씀해 주 시겠습니까?

여 듀크 스트리트와 퀸 애비뉴 모퉁이에 있는 이탈리아 식당 바로 옆에 있어요. 찾기 쉬울 거예요. 여기 열 쇠가 있어요.

<table>
<tr><th>문제와 정답</th><th>스크립트</th><th>해석</th></tr>
</table>

문제와 정답	스크립트	해석
▶ rent (남에게서) 임차하다, 빌리다 garage 자동차 수리 공장, (자동차 수리도 하는) 주유소 apologize 사과하다 on behalf of …을 대신하여 Don't mention it. 천만에요, 별말씀을요. spot (소재를) 알아내다 immediately 즉시, 당장에 fill out (서류 등을) 작성하다 form 양식	W It's on the corner of Duke Street and Queen Avenue right next to an Italian restaurant. It should be easy to spot. Here are the keys. M Thank you. I'll send one of our men to take care of it immediately. Now, if you would just fill out this form, I can get you a new car right away. W Thanks. You've been so helpful.	남 고맙습니다. 직원 한 명을 보내 당장 처리하도록 하겠습니다. 이제, 이 양식을 작성하시기만 하면 바로 새 차를 드릴 수 있습니다. 여 고마워요. 큰 도움이 됐어요.

03

다음을 듣고, 이야기 속의 This가 무엇인지 고르시오.

① 자동차
② 컴퓨터
③ 라디오
✔ 텔레비전
⑤ 전화기

▶ practically 사실상, 실질적으로 device 장치 transmit 전송하다 airwaves (방송용 전파 같은) 공중파 give ... credit for …을 ~에 대해 인정하다 judgment 판단 on one's part …편에서는, …에 책임이 있는 give away 거저 주다, 수여하다 fraction 작은 부분 addict (나쁜 버릇 등에) 젖게 하다, 중독되게 하다 partially 부분적으로 be to blame for …의 책임을 져야 하다

M This was created in the early twentieth century by three different men in three different countries at practically the same time. Inventors in the United States, Russia, and England all created a similar device that could transmit images across airwaves. But American Philo Farnsworth is often given credit for being the inventor of this device. Unfortunately, he didn't get rich off of his invention. Poor judgment on his part caused him to give away most of his rights to some major corporations. After a long legal battle, he was paid a fraction of what his invention is worth today. Although it was invented in the early twentieth century, it didn't become popular until the 1950s. Now, there is one in almost every home in the developed world. It is one of people's major sources of entertainment, and many people are even addicted to watching it. In fact, this invention is partially to blame for the unhealthy lifestyles of many people.

남 이것은 20세기 초 사실상 같은 시기에 서로 다른 세 국가에서 세 명의 다른 남자에 의해 만들어졌다. 미국과 러시아, 영국의 발명가들은 모두 이미지를 공중파로 전송할 수 있는 유사한 장치를 만들었다. 하지만 미국인인 필로 판스워스가 종종 이 장치의 제작자로 인정받고 있다. 불행히도 그는 자신의 발명으로 부자가 되지는 못했다. 그의 잘못된 판단으로 그는 대부분의 권리를 몇몇 주요 기업에 양도해야 했다. 오랜 법적 투쟁 후에 그는 오늘날 자신의 발명 가치의 일부를 보상받았다. 비록 20세기 초에 발명되었지만 그것은 1950년대까지 대중화되지 않았다. 이제 그것은 선진국의 거의 모든 가정에 하나씩 있다. 그것은 사람들의 주요 오락처 가운데 하나이며 심지어 많은 사람들은 그것을 보는 데 중독되어 있다. 사실 이 발명품은 많은 사람들의 건강에 좋지 않은 생활양식에 대해서 부분적으로는 책임을 져야 한다.

04

다음을 듣고, 화자가 무엇에 대해 이야기하고 있는지 고르시오.

✔ 울릉도
② 제주도
③ 완도
④ 여의도
⑤ 진도

▶ explore 탐색하다 treasure 보물 regret 후회하다 make a living 생활비를 벌다 tourism industry 관광산업 volcanic 화산(성)의, 화산 작용으로 인한 peak 봉우리 raw fish 생선회 cruise 유람 항해, 순항 nearby 근처의

W On today's tour, we are going to explore one of Korea's greatest treasures, an island found in the East Sea off the coast of Korea. It's far out to sea and takes many hours to get there, but it's a trip you won't regret taking. We will arrive there tonight and go on our tour tomorrow. The island is about seventy-three square kilometers in area and has about 10,000 people living there. Most people make a living by fishing or by working in the tourism industry. The island is volcanic in origin, and its highest point is a mountain almost 1,000 meters high called Sunginbong Peak. We can also see a waterfall, go hiking and fishing, and eat some delicious raw fish, which the island is famous for, while we're there. There are many cruise boats which take tourists around the island and to others nearby. These cruises take about three hours, and we'll be taking one first thing tomorrow morning.

여 오늘 투어에서 우리는 한국의 가장 위대한 보물 중 하나인 한국의 연안인 동해에 있는 섬을 탐색해 볼 겁니다. 그 섬은 바다 멀리 떨어져 있고 그곳에 가려면 여러 시간이 걸리지만 후회하지 않을 여행입니다. 오늘밤에 그곳에 도착해서 내일 투어를 계속할 겁니다. 섬은 면적이 73제곱킬로미터 정도이며 그곳에는 1만 명 정도가 살고 있지요. 대부분의 사람들은 어업이나 관광산업에 종사해서 생활합니다. 그 섬은 원래 화산작용에 의한 것이며 최고봉은 성인봉이라고 부르는 거의 1천 미터 높이의 산입니다. 우리는 또 폭포를 구경하고 하이킹과 낚시를 즐기고 그곳에 있는 동안 섬의 명물인 맛있는 회를 먹을 수 있습니다. 많은 유람선이 있어서 관광객들을 그 섬과 근처에 있는 주변의 다른 곳으로 데려다 줄 겁니다. 이런 유람은 3시간 정도 걸리며 내일 아침 가장 먼저 하게 될 것입니다.

<table>
<tr><th>문제와 정답</th><th>스크립트</th><th>해석</th></tr>
</table>

05

대화를 듣고, 남자가 MP3플레이어를 사기 위해 지불한 금액을 고르시오.

① one hundred fifty dollars
② one hundred dollars
③ fifty dollars
④ ✓ almost two hundred dollars
⑤ more than two hundred dollars

① 150 달러
② 백 달러
③ 50달러
④ 거의 2백 달러
⑤ 2백 달러 이상

▶ latest 최신의 fancy 근사한, 멋진 cost (금액이) 들다 way 훨씬, 아주 on earth 도대체 deal 거래, 물건 capacity 용량 collection 수집(물) an arm and a leg 거액의 돈, 막대한 경비

스크립트

W Did you find what you were looking for today?

M Yes, I got the latest and best MP3 player they had. Take a look at it.

W Wow, it looks pretty fancy. So, how much did you pay for it?

M Most were selling for about a hundred dollars, but this one cost twice that amount.

W What? That's way too expensive. You can get them for much less you know. Why on earth didn't you look around for a better deal?

M Actually, I did shop around. I checked out about ten shops and compared a lot of players before I decided on this one. I got it since it has the most song capacity.

W But you don't have a big music collection at all.

M True, but now I can make my collection much bigger and store all my songs on this small device.

W That sounds good, but I still think you paid an arm and a leg for it.

M There were many cheaper ones, In fact, the cheapest was around fifty dollars, but those inexpensive ones weren't very good. Some others were around one hundred or one hundred fifty dollars, but they didn't have very much song capacity.

해석

여 오늘 찾고 있던 거 찾았어?

남 응, 최신 제품으로 가장 좋은 MP3플레이어를 샀어. 한 번 봐.

여 우와, 꽤 근사하다. 그래서 이거 얼마 줬는데?

남 대부분은 1백 달러 정도에 판매되는데 이건 그 2배야.

여 뭐라고? 너무 비싸잖아. 훨씬 더 싸게 살 수 있을 텐데, 알잖아. 대체 왜 더 좋은 거래를 위해 둘러보지 않았어?

남 사실은 쇼핑을 다녔어. 열 군데 상점을 확인해 보고 이걸로 결정하기 전에 많은 플레이어들을 비교해 봤어. 이게 노래를 담을 수 있는 용량이 제일 커서 이걸로 한 거야.

여 하지만 넌 모아놓은 음악도 별로 없잖아.

남 사실이야, 하지만 이젠 훨씬 더 많이 모을 수 있고 노래를 모두 이 작은 장치에 저장할 수 있어.

여 그건 좋은 것 같은데 그래도 난 네가 돈을 너무 많이 지불한 것 같아.

남 더 값싼 게 많이 있었어. 사실 가장 싼 건 50달러가량이었지만 그런 저렴한 것들은 별로 안 좋았어. 다른 것들은 어떤 건 1백 달러나 150달러 정도 했지만 노래 저장 용량이 크지 않았어.

06

대화를 듣고, 남자가 어떤 스포츠를 하는 선수인지 고르시오.

① 축구
② 미식 축구
③ ✓ 아이스하키
④ 농구
⑤ 야구

▶ league 경기 연맹, 리그 playoff 플레이오프, 챔피언 결정전 score 득점하다, 기록하다 period (시합의 전반, 후반 등의) 한 구분, 피리어드 performance 성과, 성취 expectation 기대, 예상 opponent 상대 goalie 골키퍼 penalty killing 페널티 킬링: 선수가 퇴장당한 팀이 퇴장 당한 시간동안 실점을 막으려는 플레이 injury 부상

스크립트

W Here we are with Chris Thomas, one of the best players in the league today. His team has just made the playoffs thanks to a three to two win tonight. How do you feel, Chris?

M I'm tired but very satisfied. We had a good season, and now we're in the playoffs for the first time in three years.

W You must be happy with the way you played tonight. You scored the winning goal.

M Yeah, I had two goals in the third period, and that helped us win, so I'm very happy with my performance.

W What are your expectations for the playoffs?

M We want to win it all, but you have to win sixteen games, so it's difficult.

W What do you think about Boston, your first opponent?

M They have a great team. They skate well, have a great goalie and defensemen, and are very good at penalty killing. And they also have home ice advantage.

W How's the injury you had earlier in the year?

M I still have some pain in my foot, so that makes skating difficult, but my skates have extra protection and support, so it's safe to play.

해석

여 오늘 이곳에는 저희와 함께 리그 최고의 선수 중 하나인 크리스 토머스가 나와 있습니다. 그의 팀은 오늘밤 3대 2로 승리한 덕분에 플레이오프에 진출했습니다. 기분이 어때요, 크리스?

남 피곤하지만 아주 만족합니다. 우린 시즌 성적이 좋았고 이제는 3년 만에 플레이오프에 진출했습니다.

여 오늘밤 경기 내용에 기분이 좋겠어요. 결승골을 기록했잖아요.

남 네, 3피리어드에 두 골을 넣었고 그게 우리 승리에 도움이 돼서 제 경기성적에 아주 기분이 좋습니다.

여 플레이오프는 어떨 것으로 예상하시죠?

남 모두 이기고 싶지만 16 경기를 이겨야 하니까 어려워요.

여 첫 번째 상대인 보스턴은 어떻게 생각해요?

남 훌륭한 팀이죠. 스케이트를 잘 타고 골키퍼와 수비진도 훌륭하고 페널티 킬링도 아주 잘 하죠. 또 홈 빙판이라는 이점도 있고요.

여 올해 초에 당한 부상은 어때요?

남 아직 발에 통증이 좀 있어서 스케이트 타는 게 힘들지만 제 스케이트에 추가 보호와 지지 장치가 있어서 안전하게 경기할 수 있어요.

07

대화를 듣고, 남자의 마지막 말에 대한 여자의 응답으로 알맞은 것을 고르시오.

W: ___________________________________

① I'll be there by nine o'clock.
② I don't know where you live.
③ Sorry, but I have too much work to do.
✓ Okay, I'll see if he wants to go.
⑤ No, I'm sorry, but I don't enjoy parties.

① 9시까지 갈게요.
② 난 당신이 어디에 사는지 몰라요.
③ 미안하지만, 할 일이 너무 많아요.
④ 알았어요, 그가 가길 원하는지 알아 볼게요.
⑤ 아니, 미안하지만 난 파티를 좋아하지 않아요.

▶ accounting 회계, 경리　date 데이트, 데이트 상대
Why don't you...? …하는 것이 어때?

W It's a busy day, isn't it?

M It sure is. Oh, do you have a moment to talk?

W Okay, but I've got a lot of work to do before five o'clock, so make it quick, or I'll never get out of here.

M It sounds like you already have plans for tonight.

W Yeah, I have a date with one of the guys in the Accounting Department. I'm so excited because he's such a nice person.

M That's great. Anyway, what I wanted to ask you is if you were coming to my party tonight, but I guess you won't be. It's my wife's birthday, and she'd love to see you again.

W Oh, is that tonight? I heard someone mention it. I enjoyed the last party you had, especially since your house is so beautiful. Well, sorry, but we're going to dinner and then will see that new action movie. It ends around nine thirty.

M Then why don't you come to the party after the movie? We'll still be there, and lots of people are coming.

W Maybe, but I'll have to see what my date wants to do first.

M He's welcome to join the party, too. Why don't you ask him?

W ___________________________________

여 바쁜 하루네요, 그렇죠?

남 정말 그래요. 아, 잠깐 얘기할 수 있어요?

여 좋아요, 하지만 다섯 시 전에 해야 할 일이 많으니 서둘러 줘요. 안 그러면 절대로 여기서 못 빠져나갈 거예요.

남 벌써 오늘밤의 계획이 있는 것 같네요.

여 그래요, 경리부에 있는 사람과 데이트가 있어요. 아주 좋은 사람이어서 참 흥분돼요.

남 잘됐네요. 어쨌거나 오늘밤 파티에 올 수 있는지 물어보고 싶었는데, 못 올 것 같군요. 아내 생일인데, 당신을 다시 보면 참 좋아할 거예요.

여 아, 그게 오늘밤이에요? 누가 말하는 것 들었어요. 지난번 파티는 특히나 집이 참 아름다워서 즐거웠어요. 음, 미안하지만 저녁을 먹은 다음 새 액션영화를 볼 거예요. 그게 9시 30분 쯤 끝나요.

남 그럼 영화 보고 파티에 오면 어때요? 우린 아직 거기 있을 거고 사람들이 많이 올 거예요.

여 어쩌면요, 하지만 먼저 데이트 상대가 원하는 걸 알아야 해요.

남 그도 파티에 오는 것 환영해요. 한 번 물어 보지 그래요?

여 ___________________________________

08

다음을 듣고, 이 이야기를 하는 목적을 고르시오.
① 레스토랑의 가격에 대해 불평하기 위해
② 레스토랑의 인테리어에 대해 이야기하기 위해
③ 그 음식이 어떻게 요리한 것인지 설명하기 위해
✓ 그 레스토랑에서 식사하는 것을 추천하기 위해
⑤ 레스토랑의 서비스에 대해 불평하기 위해

▶ decoration 장식, 장식물　costume 의상　folk music 민속 음악　caviar 캐비어　brown bread 흑빵　appetizer 애피타이저, 전채　red beet (채소) 근대　dish 요리, 음식　dine on …을 식사로 먹다

W There's a new restaurant on Wilson Street that I went to last night. My husband took me, of course, and we had a great time there. It was a Russian restaurant, and they had the most wonderful decorations. The waitresses all wore traditional Russian costumes, and they even had a small band playing Russian folk music. We had a lovely bottle of Russian wine, some caviar, and thick brown bread for an appetizer. Then came the traditional Russian soup called borsch, which is made from red beets. It was fantastic. After that, we had a number of dishes brought to our table. We dined on roasted salmon, a plate of boiled potatoes with herbs, carrots in a special sauce, and then a lovely roast beef dish. It was all wonderful and delicious. You should definitely try the food there. The service was great, and everyone was so friendly. The only problem was the price. It was somewhat expensive, but it was well worth it.

여 윌슨 스트리트에 지난 밤에 내가 간 새 식당이 있다. 남편이 데리고 갔는데 우리는 거기서 즐거운 시간을 보냈다. 그곳은 러시아 식당이었고 가장 훌륭한 장식이 있었다. 종업원들은 모두 전통 러시아 의상을 입었고 심지어는 러시아 민속음악을 연주하는 소규모 밴드도 있었다. 우리는 훌륭한 러시아 포도주 한 병과 캐비어 약간, 두꺼운 흑빵을 애피타이저로 먹었다. 그 다음에 보르시치라고 부르는 전통 러시아 수프가 나왔는데, 그것은 레드비트로 만든 것이다. 정말로 훌륭했다. 그 다음에 우리는 테이블로 서빙된 몇 가지 요리를 먹었다. 우리는 연어 구이와 허브와 함께 익힌 감자 한 접시, 특별 소스에 담긴 당근과 그 다음으로 훌륭한 쇠고기 구이 요리를 먹었다. 모두 훌륭하고 맛있었다. 꼭 거기서 음식을 맛보아야 한다. 서비스는 훌륭했고 모두가 아주 친절했다. 유일한 문제는 가격이었다. 다소 비쌌지만 그럴 만한 가치는 있었다.

<table>
<tr><th>문제와 정답</th><th>스크립트</th><th>해석</th></tr>
</table>

09 대화를 듣고, 다음 중 헌혈에 대해 사실이 <u>아닌</u> 것을 고르시오.

① 헌혈을 매일 하면 건강에 좋지 않다.
② 헌혈하는 사람들에게 병원 측은 돈을 지불하지 않는다.
✓ ③ 헌혈을 하면 질병을 얻을 수 있다.
④ 병원에서는 많은 새로운 헌혈자들을 필요로 한다.
⑤ 인체는 빠져나간 혈액을 다시 채우기 위해 시간을 필요로 한다.

▶ donate 기부하다 *cf.* donor 기부자, 헌혈자 disease 질병 needle 바늘 replace 대체하다, 보상하다 recommend 권유하다 make sense 말이 되다, 사리에 맞다 storage 저장, 보관

W Hey, Joe, I'm sorry, but I can't have dinner with you tonight. I'm going to the hospital to donate some blood after school. Do you want to come?

M I'm not sure… I've never donated blood before. Is it safe? I heard that some people have gotten diseases after giving blood and a few even died.

W You must have heard wrong. They use a new needle for each person, so you can't get sick from giving blood.

M Okay, I believe you. Hey, can I get paid if I give blood?

W No, Joe, they don't pay blood donors. Sorry, but you can't get rich by selling your blood.

M That's too bad. If they paid for it, I would be there every day.

W That's dangerous. If you gave blood every day, then you would probably get sick. Your body needs time to replace the blood they take out of you. Doctors recommend donating blood only once a month.

M I guess that makes sense. Do they have enough donors?

W No, that's why I'm going and why you should come, too. Hospitals never have enough blood in storage for what they need.

M Okay, I'll come with you. Then let's have dinner after donating blood.

여 안녕, 조, 미안하지만 오늘밤 저녁식사 같이 못하겠어. 수업 후에 헌혈을 하러 병원에 가야 해. 너도 갈래?

남 글쎄… 난 한 번도 헌혈해 본 적이 없는데. 안전하니? 어떤 사람들은 헌혈 후에 병에 걸리고 몇몇은 죽기까지 했다고 들었어.

여 분명히 잘못 들은 거야. 사람마다 새 바늘을 사용해서 헌혈로 병에 걸리지는 않아.

남 알았어, 널 믿는다. 이봐, 내가 헌혈하면 돈을 받을 수 있니?

여 아니야, 조, 헌혈하는 사람에게 돈을 지불하진 않아. 유감이지만 피를 팔아서 부자가 될 순 없어.

남 유감이군. 그걸로 돈을 준다면 매일 거기 갈 텐데.

여 위험한 생각이야. 매일 피를 준다면 넌 아마 몸이 아플 거야. 네 몸은 빠져 나가는 피를 대체할 시간이 필요해. 의사들은 한 달에 한 번만 헌혈하는 것을 권해.

남 일리가 있는 것 같다. 헌혈하는 사람은 충분하니?

여 아니, 그래서 내가 가려는 거고, 또 너도 가야 해. 병원은 결코 필요한 만큼의 혈액을 보유하지 못하거든.

남 알았어, 같이 갈게. 그럼 헌혈하고 나서 저녁 먹자.

10 다음을 듣고, 은하수에 대해 사실이 <u>아닌</u> 것을 고르시오.

① 대부분의 사람들은 은하수가 나선형이라고 생각한다.
② 은하수는 우주에 있는 많은 은하들 중 하나이다.
③ 지구는 은하수 가장자리 근처에 있다.
✓ ④ 우주에 있는 은하는 약 130억 개로 추정된다.
⑤ 은하의 지름은 약 십만 광년이다.

▶ galaxy 은하, 성운 gravity 중력 astronomer 천문학자 light year 광년 belong to …에 속하다, …의 소유이다 exception 예외 mere 단지 …에 불과한, 단순한 educated 지식(경험)에 의한, 근거가 있는 observation 관찰, 관측 spiral nebula 나선 은하(성운) vastness 광대함, 막대함

M A galaxy is a body of gas and stars held together by gravity. Astronomers estimate that there are forty to fifty billion galaxies in the universe. The most distant object ever seen from Earth is a galaxy almost thirteen billion light years away. Earth's galaxy is called the Milky Way, and most of what you see in the night sky belongs to it. The few exceptions are other galaxies so far away from the planet that they appear as mere points of light in the sky. The Milky Way is about one hundred thousand light years across and ten thousand light years thick. No one has ever seen the Milky Way in its entirety, but astronomers can make educated guesses about its shape and size from their observations of other galaxies. Most believe the Milky Way is shaped like a spiral nebula. The Earth lies along one edge of this spiral nebula and is very small in the grand vastness of the universe.

남 은하는 개스와 별들이 중력에 의해 밀착해 있는 것이다. 천문학자들은 우주에 400~500억 개의 은하가 있다고 추정한다. 현재까지 지구에서 본 가장 멀리 있는 것은 거의 130억 광년 떨어진 은하이다. 지구의 은하는 은하수라 불리는데 여러분이 밤하늘에서 보는 것의 대부분이 거기에 속한다. 몇 가지 예외는 지구에서 아주 멀리 떨어진 다른 은하로, 이것들은 하늘에서 단순히 빛나는 점으로 보인다. 은하수는 지름이 약 10만 광년에 두께는 1만 광년이다. 아무도 은하수 전체를 본 사람은 없지만 천문학자들은 다른 은하를 관측함으로써 그것의 모양과 크기에 관해 경험으로 추측할 수 있다. 대부분은 은하수가 나선 은하처럼 생겼다고 생각한다. 지구는 이 나선 은하의 한쪽 가장자리를 따라 놓여 있으며 엄청나게 거대한 우주에서 아주 작다.

11 대화를 듣고, 두 사람이 대화 후에 할 일을 고르시오.

☑ ① Go to a restaurant with healthier food
② Order some hamburgers and French fries
③ Complain to the restaurant owner
④ Go to the health club to work out
⑤ Return to their office and eat there

① 몸에 더 좋은 음식이 있는 레스토랑에 간다.
② 햄버거와 감자 튀김을 주문한다.
③ 레스토랑 주인에게 불만을 이야기 한다.
④ 운동을 하기 위해 헬스클럽에 간다.
⑤ 사무실로 돌아가 그곳에서 식사를 한다.

▶ **menu** 식단, 메뉴 **fat** 지방 **red meat** 붉은
고기, 살코기 **greasy** 지방이 많은, 기름진 **blood
pressure** 혈압 **gain weight** 체중이 늘다 **put on**
…을 늘리다

W What would you like to have for lunch?

M I'm not sure. There are so many good things on this menu that I want to try them all.

W Well, there's a lot of unhealthy food on this menu, too. I wouldn't recommend the hamburgers here. They are so bad for you.

M What are you talking about? This place has the most delicious hamburgers in the city.

W They are the most delicious but are certainly not the healthiest. They're full of fat, red meat, and cheese, all of which are bad for your heart. And this restaurant always serves them with greasy French fries which are deep fried in oil and covered in salt. Salt is very bad for your blood pressure.

M Are you a doctor now?

W I'm worried about your health. You've gained some weight recently.

M What? Oh, I've only put on a few kilos. And I'm going to join a health club. But maybe you're right. The food here is very unhealthy, so perhaps we shouldn't eat here.

W So, what do you want to do? I'm still hungry.

M So am I. It's a good thing we still have fifty minutes before our lunch break ends.

여 점심으로 뭐 먹고 싶어?

남 글쎄. 이 메뉴에 좋은 게 아주 많아서 다 맛보고 싶네.

여 음, 이 메뉴에는 건강에 안 좋은 음식도 많이 있어. 난 여기 햄버거는 권하지 않을 거야. 아주 나빠.

남 무슨 말을 하는 거야? 이곳은 시에서 가장 맛있는 햄버거가 있어.

여 가장 맛있지만 확실히 건강에는 가장 안 좋아. 지방과 살코기, 치즈로 가득한데, 그건 모두 심장에 나빠. 또 이 식당은 항상 기름에 푹 튀기고 소금 범벅인 기름진 감자튀김을 곁들여 내놓잖아. 소금은 혈압에 굉장히 나빠.

남 지금 네가 의사니?

여 네 건강을 걱정하는 거야. 최근에 체중이 좀 불었잖아.

남 뭐라고? 아, 겨우 몇 킬로만 찐 거야. 헬스클럽에 등록할 거야. 하지만 어쩌면 네 말이 맞아. 여기 음식은 몸에 좋지 않으니 여기서 먹지 말아야겠다.

여 그래서 뭘 먹고 싶어? 난 아직 배고픈데.

남 나도 그래. 점심시간이 끝나려면 아직 50분이 남아 있으니까 괜찮아.

---

12 다음을 듣고, 1960년대 이후 10대 비만율의 변화를 가장 잘 보여 주는 그래프를 고르시오.

① 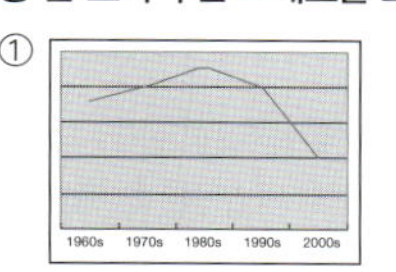 ② 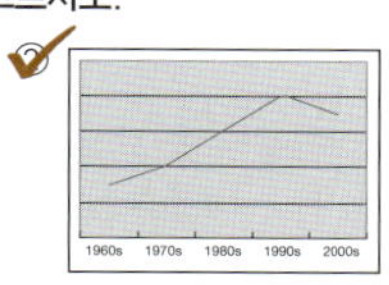

③ 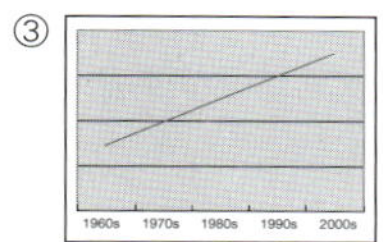 ④ 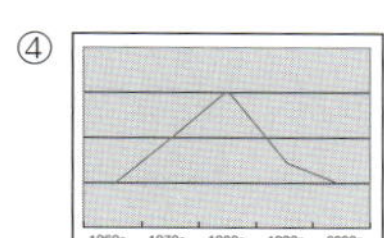

⑤ 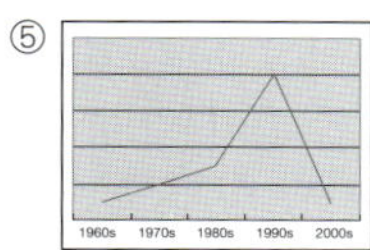

▶ **obesity** 비만 **diabetes** 당뇨병 **kidney**
신장, 콩팥 **face** 직면하다 **consumption** 소비
explosion 급증, 폭발 **couple** 결부시켜 생각하다
rapidly 급속히 **reverse** 완전히 바꾸다, 뒤집다
slightly 다소 **attribute A to B** A가 B에 기인한다고
생각하다

W One of the major health problems in our country is teenage obesity. Becoming overweight at such an early age leads to long-term health problems for many teens when they become adults. Diabetes, kidney problems, and heart disease are just some of the problems they face. One of the main causes has been the rise in junk food consumption and the lack of exercise. The explosion of the fast-food and snack-food industries began in the 1960s. Coupled with more and more teens watching television instead of going outdoors, this led to a trend of increasing teenage obesity. This trend increased rapidly through the 1970s, 1980s, and 1990s as more delicious junk food was created and cable television, VCRs, video games, and then the Internet allowed teens to be entertained indoors. Only in the current decade has this trend reversed itself, with teen obesity decreasing slightly. Experts attribute this to more parents and teens becoming aware of the health risks involved in teen obesity.

여 우리나라의 주요한 건강 문제 중 하나는 십대의 비만이다. 그처럼 이른 나이에 과체중이 되는 것은 많은 십대들이 성인이 될 때 장기적인 문제로 이어진다. 당뇨병과 신장 질환, 심장 질환은 그들이 부딪치는 문제들 중 일부일 뿐이다. 주요 원인의 하나는 정크푸드의 소비 증가와 운동 부족이 되어왔다. 패스트푸드와 가벼운 군것질 음식 산업의 급증은 1960년대에 시작됐다. 점점 더 많은 십대들이 야외로 나가는 대신 텔레비전을 보는 것과 관련되어 이것은 십대 비만이 증가하는 경향으로 이어졌다. 더 맛있는 정크푸드가 생기고 케이블 텔레비전과 비디오, 비디오 게임, 그 다음에는 인터넷으로 인해 십대들이 실내에서 즐거움을 찾을 수 있게 되면서. 이러한 경향은 1970년대와 80년대, 그리고 90년대를 거쳐 급속히 증가했다. 겨우 최근 10년 사이에 이런 경향은 십대 비만이 다소 감소하면서 바뀌었다. 전문가들은 이것을 더 많은 부모들과 십대들이 십대 비만에 관련된 건강의 위험에 대해 인식하고 있기 때문이라고 생각한다.

13 대화를 듣고, 두 사람이 방문할 장소를 순서대로 나열한 것을 고르시오.

ⓐ The Empire State Building
ⓑ Madison Square Garden
ⓒ Central Park
ⓓ The Metropolitan Museum of Modern Art

ⓐ 엠파이어 스테이트 빌딩
ⓑ 매디슨 스퀘어 가든
ⓒ 센트럴 파크
ⓓ 메트로폴리탄 현대 미술관

① ⓐ - ⓑ - ⓒ - ⓓ
② ⓑ - ⓒ - ⓓ - ⓐ
✓③ ⓒ - ⓐ - ⓓ - ⓑ
④ ⓒ - ⓓ - ⓑ - ⓐ
⑤ ⓓ - ⓒ - ⓐ - ⓑ

▶ **ferry** 페리, 연락선   **statue** 상, 입상   **weather forecast** 일기예보   **be supposed to do** …하기로 되어 있다   **in the meantime** 그 사이에, 그럭저럭하는 동안에   **metropolitan** 주요 도시의   **awesome** 아주 인상적인, 멋있는   **prior to** …이전에

M   Wow, I can't believe we're in New York City. This is one of the most amazing cities in the world.

W   Where do you want to go first? There's so much to see here.

M   Let's visit the Empire State Building first. I've always wanted to go to the top and look at everything down below.

W   It's too far from our hotel. Central Park is right across the street, so we should make that our first stop.

M   Okay, then why don't we visit the Empire State Building after doing that?

W   That sounds good. After lunch, we can take a ferry to the Statue of Liberty.

M   The weather forecast said it's supposed to rain this afternoon.

W   Really? That's terrible. What should we do if it rains?

M   There's a basketball game at Madison Square Garden. We already have tickets for it.

W   But that's at six o'clock. What can we do in the meantime?

M   I know. We can go to a museum or art gallery. I know just the place. The Metropolitan Museum of Modern Art isn't far away.

W   That's a great idea. I've heard it's got an awesome art collection. Let's do that prior to catching the game.

남   우와, 우리가 뉴욕시에 있다는 게 믿기지 않아. 여긴 세상에서 가장 놀라운 도시 중 하나야.

여   어딜 먼저 가고 싶어? 여기선 볼 게 아주 많아.

남   엠파이어 스테이트 빌딩 먼저 가보자. 항상 꼭대기에 가서 아래에 있는 모든 걸 보고 싶었어.

여   거긴 우리 호텔에서 너무 멀어. 센트럴 파크는 바로 길 건너에 있으니 거길 가장 먼저 들러야 할 것 같은데.

남   알았어, 그럼 그러고 난 후에 엠파이어 스테이트 빌딩에 가보는 게 어때?

여   좋아. 점심 식사 후에는 자유의 여신상까지 페리를 탈 수 있어.

여   일기예보에는 오늘 오후에 비가 올 거라고 했어.

여   정말? 안 되는데. 비가 오면 뭘 해야 하지?

남   매디슨 스퀘어 가든에서 농구 경기가 있어. 이미 표도 갖고 있잖아.

여   하지만 그건 여섯 시야. 그 사이에 뭘 할 수 있을까?

남   내가 알지. 박물관이나 미술관에 가면 돼. 좋은 데를 내가 알아. 메트로폴리탄 현대 미술관이 멀지 않은 곳에 있어.

여   좋은 생각이야. 놀라운 미술 소장품들이 있다고 들었어. 경기를 보기 전에 그렇게 하자.

---

14 다음을 듣고, 화자가 이야기하고 있는 그림의 장르를 고르시오.

① a landscape
✓② a still-life
③ a portrait
④ a historical painting
⑤ a cartoon image

① 풍경화
② 정물화
③ 초상화
④ 역사화
⑤ 만화

▶ **bore** 지루하게 하다   **bottom** 아래, 바닥   **peel** (과일의) 껍질을 벗기다   **even though** 비록 …하더라도   **depict** 묘사하다, 그리다   **impressed** 감명을 받은   **easily** 확실히, 단연   **ever** 언젠가, 이전에   **in person** (사진이 아닌) 실물로, (몸소) 직접

M   I went to the local art gallery with my class the other day. Art usually bores me, but this time I had a better experience. There was this one painting being exhibited there which showed a bowl of fruit on a table. That's a pretty common painting, right? But this painting was so good that I wanted to eat the fruit in it. There were apples, oranges, bananas, and grapes. The apples were on the bottom and were bright red. The bananas were so yellow that I wanted to reach out and take one and peel it. The grapes were the green kind, not the purple kind they serve in our school cafeteria. The bright mix of colors—orange, yellow, red, and green—made the painting come alive. Even though the painting didn't depict any people nor did it have an action scene in it, I was totally impressed by it. It was easily the best painting I've ever seen in person before.

남   나는 요전날 반친구들과 함께 지역 미술관에 갔다. 미술은 보통 따분한데, 이번에는 더 좋은 경험을 했다. 그림 하나가 거기에 전시돼 있었는데, 탁자 위에 과일 그릇이 그려진 것이다. 그건 꽤 흔한 그림이다, 안 그런가? 하지만 그 그림은 아주 훌륭해서 그 안에 있는 과일들을 먹고 싶었다. 사과와 오렌지, 바나나, 포도가 있었다. 사과는 아래쪽에 있었고 밝은 적색이었다. 바나나는 너무 노란 빛이어서 손을 뻗어 하나를 잡아 껍질을 벗기고 싶었다. 포도는 우리 학교 식당에서 나오는 자주색 종류가 아니라 청포도류였다. 오렌지빛과 노란색, 붉은색, 초록의 색들이 밝게 혼합되어 그림이 살아 있었다. 비록 그 그림에서 사람을 묘사하거나 어떤 행동을 하는 장면도 전혀 없었지만 난 완전히 그것에 매료되었다. 그건 단연코 내가 지금까지 직접 본 그림들 중 최고의 그림이었다.

문제와 정답	스크립트	해석

15 대화를 듣고, 상황을 가장 잘 나타내는 속담을 고르시오.

① Look before you leap.
② You cannot have your cake and eat it, too.
✓ Actions speak louder than words.
④ Bad news travels fast.
⑤ Slow and steady wins the race.

① 돌다리도 두드려 보고 건너라.
② 두 마리의 토끼를 다 잡을 수는 없다.
③ 행동이 말보다 낫다.
④ 나쁜 소식은 빨리 퍼진다.
⑤ 더디더라도 착실하게 하면 결국 이긴다.

▶ promotion 승진 owner 소유주, 주인 hand in …을 제출하다 on time 제시간에 charity 자선단체 daycare center 보육원, 탁아소 promote 진척시키다, 승진시키다 instead of …대신 ideal 이상적인 aside from …이외에 hang out with …와 어울리다, 사귀다

스크립트 (15)

M I feel terrible. I didn't get the promotion I was hoping for.

W I thought you were good friends with the owner's son, so that was going to help you.

M We are good friends. I talk with him on the phone all the time, we have lunch once a week, and I even play golf with him two or three times a month. I thought the promotion was mine. This other guy, Bill Williams, got the promotion. I don't know what I did wrong.

W Well, why don't you tell me about Bill Williams and what kind of worker he is?

M He always comes in before everyone else. He works late and hands in all of his reports on time and in perfect condition. He volunteers for some charity, and he helped promote the addition of the daycare center in the building.

W He sounds like a wonderful guy.

M Sure, but that's no reason for him to get the promotion instead of me.

W Well, what have you done? Bill sounds like the ideal worker, yet you haven't told me about anything that you do aside from hanging out with the owner's son all the time.

해석 (15)

남 기분이 엉망이야. 바라던 승진을 못했어.

여 난 네가 소유주 아들과 사이 좋은 친구여서 그게 도움이 될 거라고 생각했는데.

남 사이좋은 친구지. 항상 전화로 얘기하고, 일주일에 한 번 점심도 먹고, 심지어 한 달에 두세 번은 골프를 치기도 해. 난 승진이 내 거라고 생각했어. 빌 윌리엄스라는 다른 녀석이 승진했어. 내가 뭘 잘못했는지 모르겠어.

여 음, 빌 윌리엄스란 사람에 대해서 그리고 그가 어떤 직원인지 말해 줄래?

남 그는 항상 다른 모든 사람들보다 일찍 와. 늦게까지 일하고 모든 보고서를 제시간에 완벽한 상태로 제출해. 자선단체를 위해 봉사하고 건물 내에 보육실을 추가하는 걸 진척시키는 데 도움을 주기도 했어.

여 훌륭한 사람 같구나.

남 응, 하지만 그게 나 대신 그가 승진한 이유는 안 돼.

여 음, 넌 어떻게 했는데? 빌은 이상적인 직원 같지만 넌 항상 소유주 아들과 노는 것 외엔 어떤 것도 네가 한 일에 대해 말한 게 없잖아.

---

16 다음을 듣고, 이야기의 분위기를 가장 잘 나타낸 것을 고르시오.

① happy
✓ confident
③ nervous
④ disappointed
⑤ relaxed

① 행복한
② 자신감 있는
③ 긴장되는
④ 실망한
⑤ 편안한

▶ get fired 해고되다 spill 엎지르다 legal 법적인 accidentally 우연히 back up (컴퓨터 디스크 등)의 백업을 복사하다 lately 요사이, 최근에

스크립트 (16)

W I started a new job as a secretary in a law firm about six months ago. At first, I was very scared I would get fired. I made a lot of mistakes. On my second day on the job, I spilled coffee all over a legal document, so I had to retype it right away. I could never remember the lawyers' names, and I answered the phone like I would at home. Also, I accidentally deleted a file from the computer. Thankfully, it was backed up in another place. I was so nervous during those first few weeks. I cried almost every night, and I bit my fingernails to almost nothing. However, things have changed a lot lately, so I feel much more comfortable. I know what to do, and I've learned to relax and be calm. I think that by making mistakes, we learn how to do things the right way. If I ever have my own company, I will give new people a chance.

해석 (16)

여 난 6개월 전에 법률 회사에서 비서로 새 일을 시작했다. 처음에는 해고를 당할까봐 아주 겁이 났다. 나는 실수를 많이 했다. 일을 한 둘째 날에는 법률 문서 위에 온통 커피를 엎질러 당장 타이핑을 다시 해야 했다. 변호사들의 이름을 도무지 기억할 수 없었고 집에서처럼 전화를 받았다. 또한 우연히 컴퓨터에서 파일을 삭제했다. 기쁘게도 그건 다른 곳에 백업되어 있었다. 처음 몇 주 동안에는 정말 긴장이 되었다. 거의 매일 밤 울었고 손톱이 거의 남아 있지 않을 정도로 물어뜯었다. 하지만 상황은 최근 많이 변했고 나는 훨씬 더 편안하다. 뭘 해야 할지 알고 긴장을 풀고 진정하는 법을 배웠다. 실수를 함으로써 우리는 일을 제대로 하는 법을 배우는 것 같다. 언젠가 내 회사를 갖는다면 나는 새로운 사람들에게 기회를 줄 것이다.

17

대화를 듣고, 여자의 마지막 말에 대한 남자의 응답으로 가장 알맞은 것을 고르시오.

M: ________________________

① That's not a problem. In fact, it will last forever.
② ✔ It would be cheaper, but a new one would be better.
③ Yes, we can provide you with a faster Internet connection.
④ Yes, we just upgraded your computer to make it better.
⑤ No, your son should really be here instead of you.

① 문제 없습니다. 사실은 그건 영원히 지속될 겁니다.
② 그건 더 싸겠지만 새 것이 더 나을 겁니다.
③ 네, 더 빠른 인터넷 연결을 제공해 드릴 수 있습니다.
④ 네, 방금 고객님의 컴퓨터를 더 좋게 업그레이드했습니다.
⑤ 아니오, 고객님 대신 아드님이 정말로 여기에 오셔야 합니다.

▶ electronics 전자 기기, 전자 공학 current 현재의, 지금의 outdated 시대에 뒤진 dial-up modem 전화 접속 모뎀 broadband (무선) 광대역의 connection (전화의) 접속, 연결 application (컴퓨터) 응용 프로그램, 애플리케이션 set up with …을 공급하다, 설비하다.

M Welcome to Startek Electronics. How can I help you today?

W I'm not sure actually. My son recommended that I get a new computer, but I still like my old one. I guess I need some advice on computers.

M That's not a problem. We can give you a new one or upgrade the old one. First, can you tell me about your current computer?

W My son wrote it all down. Let's see... Here it is.

M Yes, it seems a bit outdated. You still have a dial-up modem and a three-point-five-inch floppy disk drive. Those are not very useful these days. Most people use a broadband modem or Ethernet connection.

W Yes, my Internet connection is very slow. That's one reason why I'm here.

M Also, you have a very slow CD-ROM drive. And your processor and memory capacity are quite low. Pretty soon, your computer won't be able to add any new applications.

W So, what do you think I should do?

M I can set you up with new computer for less than a thousand dollars.

W Oh, that sounds a little too expensive for me. What about upgrading this one?

M ________________________

남 스타텍 일렉트로닉스에 오신 걸 환영합니다. 오늘은 뭘 도와드릴까요?

여 실은 잘 모르겠어요. 아들이 새 컴퓨터를 사길 권했지만 난 아직 옛날 것이 좋거든요. 컴퓨터에 관해 조언이 좀 필요한 것 같아요.

남 문제없습니다. 저희는 새 것을 드리거나 오래된 걸 업그레이드해 드릴 수 있습니다. 먼저 현재 고객님의 컴퓨터에 대해 말씀을 해 주시겠습니까?

여 아들이 모두 적어 줬어요. 어디 보자… 여기 있어요.

남 네, 약간 오래된 것 같네요. 아직 전화 접속 모뎀과 3.5인치 플로피 디스켓을 사용하시는군요. 그것들은 요즘은 별로 유용하지 않답니다. 대부분의 사람들은 광대역 모뎀이나 이더넷 접속을 사용하죠.

여 네, 인터넷 연결이 아주 느려요. 그게 여기 온 한 가지 이유에요.

남 또 속도가 아주 느린 시디롬 드라이브를 갖고 계시네요. 프로세서와 메모리 용량이 아주 낮고요. 조만간 고객님의 컴퓨터에는 새 응용프로그램을 아무 것도 추가하지 못할 거에요.

여 그럼 어떻게 해야 하죠?

남 천 달러 미만으로 새 컴퓨터를 설치해 드릴 수 있습니다.

여 아, 그건 좀 너무 비싼 것 같아요. 이걸 업그레이드하면 어떨까요?

남 ________________________

18

다음을 듣고, 화요일의 날씨를 고르시오.

① cloudy and cold
② sunny and warm
③ ✔ rainy and cool
④ snowy and cold
⑤ windy and warm

① 구름끼고 추운
② 맑고 따뜻한
③ 비오고 서늘한
④ 눈오고 추운
⑤ 바람 불고 따뜻한

▶ extended 연장한, 장기간에 걸친 temperature 기온 storm system 폭풍 (전선) snowstorm 눈보라 depending on …에 따라 either … or … 이거나 …한

W Now, let me provide you with the extended forecast for the coming week. The storm system that we're experiencing now will be over by Saturday night, so Sunday will be clear and sunny. On Monday, expect some rain showers with light winds and cooler temperatures. This will continue on Tuesday, so don't forget your umbrellas at the beginning of the week. By Wednesday, the rainy period will end, but the cloudy skies and colder temperatures will continue. On Thursday, the sun will show up again, so it will be much warmer than it was earlier in the week. However, that will soon end. Starting on Friday, there will be another storm system moving through, so it's possible we'll see the first snowstorm of the season. Depending on the temperature, the weekend will either be very snowy, or we will have more rainy weather. And that's it for the weather that you can be expecting over the next few days.

여 이제, 다가오는 한 주에 대한 장기 일기예보를 말씀 드리겠습니다. 지금 겪고 있는 폭풍은 토요일 밤쯤 끝나서 일요일은 맑은 날씨에 해를 볼 수 있겠습니다. 월요일에는 약한 바람과 기온이 더 선선해지면서 비가 약간 내릴 것으로 예상됩니다. 이것은 화요일에도 계속되니 주초에는 우산을 잊지 마십시오. 수요일경에는 비는 끝나겠지만 흐린 하늘과 더 찬 기온이 지속될 겁니다. 목요일에는 다시 해가 비쳐서 주초보다 훨씬 더 따뜻해지겠습니다. 하지만 그건 곧 사라지겠습니다. 금요일을 시작으로 또 다른 폭풍이 이동해 와서 이번 계절 첫 눈보라가 있을 가능성이 있습니다. 기온에 따라 주말은 아주 눈이 많이 내리거나 비가 더 내리는 날씨가 되겠습니다. 이것으로 다음 며칠간의 날씨를 예보해 드렸습니다.

19

대화를 듣고, 남자가 알람시계를 설정해 달라고 부탁한 시각을 고르시오.

① 새벽 3시
② 오후 3시
✓ 새벽 2시 45분
④ 오후 2시 45분
⑤ 새벽 2시 50분

▶ How about...? …은 어때? work 유효하게 작용하다, 효과가 있다 it's time for …할 시간이다 on time 제시간에

M Oh, no. The soccer game that I want to watch is on at three in the morning.

W That's really late for a sports event. Are you sure you have the right time?

M It's a World Cup game from South Africa, so it's seven hours behind our time. I'll be asleep when the game is on.

W If it's so important, why don't you just record it on your VCR and watch it after work tomorrow?

M That's not the same as watching it live. All my friends will be watching it, so someone will tell me the score, or I'll see it in the newspaper.

W Okay, how about this idea? You should just go to bed early—maybe around nine o'clock—and then wake up for the game.

M Yeah, that would work, but I'll be so tired at work tomorrow. I don't think that will impress my boss very much.

W Everyone will be tired, including your boss. I'll set the alarm clock. What time do you want to get up?

M Make it about fifteen minutes before the game starts.

W No problem. Hey, now it's time for bed if you want to get up on time.

남 어, 이런. 보고 싶은 축구 경기가 오전 3시에 하네.

여 운동 경기치곤 정말 늦다. 시간이 맞는 게 확실해?

남 이건 남아프리카에서 하는 월드컵 경기라서 우리 시간보다 몇 시간 더 늦어. 경기가 방송될 때 난 잠들어 있을 거야.

여 그게 그렇게 중요하면 그냥 비디오로 녹화해서 내일 퇴근 후에 보면 어때?

남 그건 생방송으로 보는 것과 달라. 내 친구들은 모두 볼 테니 누가 점수를 얘기해 주거나, 아니면 신문에서 보게 되겠지.

여 알았어, 이건 어때? 그냥 일찍, 한 9시쯤 자러 간 다음 경기할 때 일어나는 거야.

남 그래, 그럼 되겠지만 내일 직장에서 아주 피곤할 거야. 그건 상사에게 좋은 인상을 못 줄 테고.

여 당신 상사를 포함해서 모두가 피곤할 거야. 내가 알람시계를 맞춰 놓을게. 몇 시에 일어나고 싶어?

남 경기 시작 15분쯤 전으로 해놔.

여 알았어. 자, 이제 제시간에 일어나고 싶으면 자야 할 시간이야.

20

대화를 듣고, 두 사람이 가장 싫어하는 음식을 고르시오.

Man	Woman
✓ oatmeal	corn
② oatmeal	beans
③ lobster	fish
④ corn	oatmeal
⑤ lobster	corn

남자	여자
① 오트밀	옥수수
② 오트밀	콩
③ 랍스터	생선
④ 옥수수	오트밀
⑤ 랍스터	옥수수

▶ survey 조사(서) cod 대구 salmon 연어 turn 차례 least 가장 적게, 아주 근소하게 I'd say 아마 …이겠지요 close (정도가) 가까운, 비슷한 as … as …만큼 ~한

M Someone sent us a survey in the mail. It's all about things we like and don't like. Do you want to answer it?

W Sure, why not? We've been married for ten years. I think I know everything you like and don't like.

M Oh, really? What about food? What kind of food do I dislike the most?

W Oh, that's easy. You really hate to eat fish.

M No, that's not exactly true. I like some kinds of fish, like cod and salmon. And lobster is okay, too. You don't know what kind of food I really hate, do you?

W Okay, so I don't know. What's the answer?

M It's any kind of oatmeal. I guess I ate too much of it as a child.

W Really? I don't think I've ever seen you eat it, and now I know why. Okay, so now it's your turn. What's my least favorite food?

M Let's see. You never eat any kind of beans, so I'd say that's the answer.

W You're close. I like the taste of beans but just never eat them. I really can't stand corn. I guess we don't know each other as well as we thought.

남 누가 우리한테 우편으로 설문지를 보냈어. 우리가 좋아하고 싫어하는 것들에 관한 거야. 대답할래?

여 그래, 안 될 것 없잖아? 우린 결혼한 지 10년이 됐어. 난 당신이 좋아하고 싫어하는 것을 모두 알 것 같은데.

남 그래, 정말? 음식은 어때? 내가 가장 싫어하는 음식 종류가 뭐야?

여 아, 그건 쉽지. 생선을 정말 싫어하잖아.

남 아니야, 그건 정확한 사실이 아니야. 난 대구나 연어 같은 생선은 좋아해. 또 바닷가재도 괜찮아. 당신은 내가 정말 싫어하는 종류의 음식이 뭔지 모르는구나, 그렇지?

여 알았어, 그래 나 몰라. 그게 뭔데?

남 모든 종류의 오트밀이야. 어릴 때 그걸 너무 많이 먹은 것 같아.

여 정말? 당신이 그걸 먹는 걸 여태 못 본 것 같은데, 이제 이유를 알겠다. 됐어, 그럼 이제는 당신 차례야. 내가 가장 싫어하는 음식은 뭐야?

남 잠깐만. 당신은 콩은 어떤 것이든 절대로 안 먹으니까, 그게 답일 것 같은데.

여 비슷해. 콩 맛은 좋아하지만 그냥 절대로 먹지는 않아. 옥수수는 정말 못 참겠어. 우린 생각만큼 서로에 대해 잘 모르는 것 같다.

21

다음을 듣고, 화자의 요지가 무엇인지 고르시오.

① Smoking can kill people of any age.
② Adults enjoy smoking as much as teens.
✓ More teens are smoking these days.
④ Many famous people are smokers.
⑤ Smoking starts from peer pressure.

① 흡연은 모든 연령의 사람들을 죽일 수 있다.
② 성인들은 10대만큼 흡연을 즐긴다.
③ 요즘 더 많은 10대들이 흡연하고 있다.
④ 많은 유명인들이 흡연자이다.
⑤ 흡연은 동료 집단과의 경쟁심에서 시작된다.

▶ compared to …와 비교해 볼 때 decrease 감소하다 factor 요인, 요소 peer pressure 동류 집단 압력, 동료와의 경쟁심 conform (형상, 성질이) 같아지다, 순응하다 imitate 흉내 내다, 모방하다 pick up (습관 등을) 몸에 익히다 addictive 습관성의, 중독되기 쉬운

M A recent national survey on cigarette smoking shows that, while the number of adult smokers is decreasing, the number of teenage smokers is increasing. In the 13-19 year old age group, there has been a fifteen-percent increase in the number of smokers today compared to ten years ago. At the same time, there has been a ten-percent decrease among adult smokers. The growing number of teen smokers is the result of two factors: They are peer pressure and the influence of advertising and the media. Teens try smoking because their friends are doing it, so they feel pressured to conform and act like their peers. Many teens see their favorite singers and television and movie stars smoking—both on and off the screen—so they try to imitate them and therefore pick up this bad habit. The sad truth is that the most addictive smokers are those who start smoking when they are teenagers. Unfortunately for them, by smoking, they are risking both their immediate and long-term health.

남 최근 흡연에 관한 전국적인 조사에 따르면 성인 흡연자의 수는 감소하는 반면 십대 흡연자의 수는 증가하고 있다. 13~19세 연령층에서 10년 전과 비교해 오늘날 흡연자 수가 15퍼센트 증가했다. 동시에 성인 흡연자들 가운데서는 10퍼센트가 감소했다. 십대 흡연자 수의 증가는 두 가지 요인에 따른 것인데, 그것들은 동료 집단에 대한 경쟁심과 광고와 미디어의 영향이다. 십대들은 친구들이 하기 때문에 흡연을 시도하는데 그래서 그들은 비슷해지고 동료들처럼 행동해야 할 압력을 느낀다. 많은 십대들은 좋아하는 가수와 TV와 영화 스타들이 화면 속에서나 밖에서 흡연하는 것을 보고 그들을 모방하려 하는데, 따라서 이런 나쁜 습관을 얻는다. 서글픈 사실은 가장 중독적인 흡연자들은 십대 때 흡연을 시작한 사람들이라는 것이다. 안타깝게도 흡연을 함으로써 그들은 눈앞의 건강과 장기적인 건강 둘 다를 위험에 빠뜨리고 있다.

22

대화를 듣고, 여자가 남자의 요청을 듣지 <u>못한</u> 이유를 고르시오.

✓ There was a lot of construction noise.
② He was speaking very softly into the phone.
③ Someone else was trying to talk to her.
④ His cell phone connection was bad.
⑤ A large bus was passing his car.

① 공사장의 소음이 심했다.
② 남자가 전화기에 대고 굉장히 작게 말했다.
③ 다른 사람이 여자에게 말을 걸고 있었다.
④ 남자의 휴대폰 연결 상태가 나빴다.
⑤ 큰 버스가 남자의 차 옆을 지나가고 있었다.

▶ architect 건축 기사, 설계자 This is ... speaking (전화에서) 저는 …입니다 delay 지연시키다 overpass 육교, 고가교차로 boulevard 대로, 넓은 가로수 길 appreciate 감사해 하다 by the way 그런데, 말이 난 김에 laptop 노트북 컴퓨터 save (시간, 노력을) 절약하다 as soon as …하자마자, …하자 곧

W Hello, Johnson Architects. This is Janice speaking. How may I help you?

M Hi, Janice. It's Peter Donaldson. I'm almost at your office, but I've been delayed because of some work they're doing on the road.

W Where are you now, Peter?

M I'm near the Tenth Street overpass on Ventura Boulevard. There's a lot of traffic, so it may be thirty minutes to an hour before I can get there. I'm really sorry about that.

W Okay, thanks for calling. I'll tell the others, and we'll delay the meeting until you arrive.

M I'd appreciate that. By the way, can you...

W What was that? I couldn't hear you, Peter. Could you repeat that?

M Sorry, but it's really noisy here. I asked if you could prepare my PowerPoint presentation. I'm sending it to your e-mail from my laptop right now. That will save us some time when I arrive.

W Okay, send it. Oh, it's here already. I got your e-mail. I'll set it up in the conference room.

M Thanks a lot, Janice. I'll see you as soon as I get through this traffic. Bye.

여 안녕하세요, 존슨 건축사 사무실의 제니스입니다. 뭘 도와드릴까요?

남 안녕 제니스. 피터 도널드슨이에요. 당신 사무실에 거의 다 왔는데 도로 공사 때문에 지체됐어요.

여 지금 어디예요, 피터?

남 텐스 스트리트 근처의 벤투라로 위 고가차로예요. 교통량이 많아 도착하기까진 30분 정도 될 것 같아요. 정말 미안해요.

여 괜찮아요, 전화 줘서 고마워요. 다른 사람들에게 말할게요, 도착할 때까지 회의를 연기하죠.

남 감사해요. 그런데 저…

여 뭐였죠? 못 알아들었어요, 피터. 다시 말씀해 주시겠어요?

남 미안하지만 여기가 정말 시끄럽네요. 제 파워포인트 프리젠테이션 준비를 해주실 수 있나 해서요. 지금 당장 노트북 컴퓨터로 이메일을 보낼게요. 그럼 내가 도착할 때 시간을 좀 벌 거예요.

여 알았어요, 보내세요. 아, 벌써 여기 왔네요. 이메일 받았어요. 회의실에 설치해 놓을게요.

남 정말 고마워요, 제니스. 이 교통상황에서 벗어나는 대로 곧 뵐게요. 잘 있어요.

23 다음을 듣고, 이 이야기의 장르를 고르시오.

① a short story
② an essay
✓ a fairy tale
④ a fable
⑤ a sonnet

① 단편소설
② 수필
③ 동화
④ 우화
⑤ 소네트

▶ banish 추방하다 disappear 사라지다 trace 흔적 prisoner 포로, 구속된 사람 witch 마녀 pleased 기분이 좋은 warrior 전사, 병사

W Soon, however, the witch began causing trouble, so the king banished her from the kingdom. A few months later, right in the middle of the night, the king's daughter, the princess, suddenly disappeared. The king's men searched for her for years and years, but they couldn't find her anywhere. The king himself often left his castle to search for the princess, but there was no trace of her anywhere. One day, a stranger came to the castle and told the king he knew where the princess was. He said she was being held prisoner by the witch deep in the darkest part of the forest. The king's soldiers started preparing for battle, but the king told them that he alone must go there to battle the witch. The soldiers weren't pleased, for the witch was strong in magic. But the king himself was a great warrior, so he knew what he had to do.

여 하지만 곧 마녀는 문제를 일으키기 시작했고 그래서 왕은 그녀를 왕국에서 추방했다. 몇 달 뒤의 한밤중에 왕의 딸인 공주가 갑자기 사라졌다. 왕의 부하들은 오랫동안 그녀를 찾았지만 어디에서도 그녀를 찾을 수 없었다. 왕은 종종 혼자서 성을 떠나 공주를 찾았지만 그녀의 흔적은 어디에도 없었다. 어느 날 이방인이 성에 와서 왕에게 공주가 어디에 있는지 안다고 말했다. 그는 공주가 숲의 가장 어두운 곳의 깊숙한 데에 마녀에게 붙잡혀 있다고 말했다. 왕의 군인들은 전투를 준비하기 시작했지만 왕은 그들에게 자기 혼자서 마녀와 싸우러 그곳에 가야만 한다고 말했다. 마녀가 강력한 마법을 지녔기 때문에 병사들은 좋아하지 않았다. 하지만 왕은 훌륭한 전사여서 자신이 뭘 해야 할지 알고 있었다.

---

24 대화를 듣고, 두 사람이 무엇에 대해 이야기하고 있는지 고르시오.

① a snowstorm
② an earthquake
③ a volcano
④ a tornado
✓ a typhoon

① 눈보라
② 지진
③ 화산
④ 토네이도
⑤ 태풍

▶ power 전력, 에너지 downtown 중심가, 도심(부) restore 회복시키다 essential 필수적인 service (전기, 가스 등의) 공급, 공급 시설 howling 윙윙거리는, 으르렁거리는 class 등급

M That was quite a storm we had. I've never seen anything like that before.

W Wasn't it just awful? My house has three broken windows, and we still don't have any electricity.

M What? It's been three days since it finished. We got our power back last night.

W I guess I live too far from downtown. They had to restore power to the hospitals and police and fire stations first.

M Those are essential services, so it makes sense. We still have a lot of trees down in my neighborhood.

W It's the same here. The wind was really powerful. Someone said it was over one hundred and fifty kilometers per hour.

M I know. The wind was really howling for hours. I also heard about ten ships were sunk at sea, and maybe twenty people were lost.

W That's terrible. Some people in the town ten kilometers away got hurt when they went outside as the eye of the storm passed over them.

M I guess they thought the storm was over, but the eye is just a calm area in the storm's center.

W The weather service said this one was almost 100 kilometers wide. That's a class two storm.

남 대단한 폭풍이었어. 그런 건 전에 한 번도 본 적이 없었어.

여 정말 끔찍하지 않았니? 우리 집은 창문이 세 개가 깨지고 아직도 전기가 안 들어와.

남 뭐라고? 폭풍이 끝난 지 3일이 됐잖아. 우린 어제 밤에 전기가 들어왔는데.

여 내가 도심에서 너무 멀리 살아서 그런가 봐. 병원과 경찰서, 소방서의 먼저 전기를 복구해야 했겠지.

남 그것들은 필수 시설이니까 그럴 만해. 우리 동네엔 아직 나무가 많이 넘어져 있어.

여 여기도 똑같아. 바람이 정말 강력했거든. 누가 그러는데 지속 150킬로미터가 넘었대.

남 알아. 바람이 정말 몇 시간 동안 윙윙거렸어. 배가 열 척 정도 바다에 침몰하고 스무 명 정도가 실종됐다는 얘기도 들었어.

여 저런. 10킬로미터 떨어진 마을에 사는 어떤 사람들은 폭풍의 눈이 지나갈 때 외출해서 다쳤어.

남 그 사람들은 폭풍이 끝났다고 생각한 것 같지만 태풍의 눈은 그냥 태풍 중앙의 고요한 부분일 뿐이야.

여 기상청에 따르면 이번 건 범위가 거의 100킬로미터였대. 그건 2등급 폭풍이야.

25 다음을 듣고, 제품에 대해 사실이 <u>아닌</u> 것을 고르시오.

① 이 제품은 토요일까지 세일을 한다.
② 다양한 색상으로 나오고 있다.
③ 작고 휴대성이 있다.
④ 열 가지 다른 부속품들이 있다.
⑤ 1년의 보증 기간이 있다.

▶ on sale 판매중인, 특가의 dust 먼지 vacuum cleaner 진공청소기 portable 이동할 수 있는, 휴대용의 metallic 금속성인, 금속 비슷한 attachment 부속품 cupboard 찬장, 붙박이장 warranty 보증(서) purchase 구입 refund 환불하다, 반환하다

M Right now, on sale until Saturday at Stan's Electronics on Fulton Avenue is the Bronco Super Duper Dust Devil Vacuum Cleaner. That's right, folks, from now until Saturday, our famous vacuum cleaner is now only fifty-nine ninety-nine, our lowest price in years. It's powerful enough to clean any carpet or floor and small enough to fit in your closet. It's portable and can be easily carried from room to room and up and down the stairs. Sold only in basic black and metallic colors, the Super Duper Dust Devil comes with ten attachments, which allow you to clean those hard-to-reach places. Under beds, in corners, behind bookcases, and on top of cupboards, there is no place this machine cannot reach. Our product has a full parts and service warranty for one year after purchase. If you're not satisfied, return it within one week of purchase for a refund. So, come down to Stan's Electronics, and you'll walk away a happy customer.

남 지금 풀턴 애비뉴에 있는 스탠의 전자용품점에서 토요일까지 브롱코 수퍼 두퍼 더스트 데블 진공청소기가 할인 판매되고 있습니다. 그렇습니다, 여러분, 지금부터 토요일까지 당사의 유명한 진공청소기가 단돈 59.99달러로, 수년간 최저 가격입니다. 이 제품은 어떤 카펫이나 바닥도 청소할 정도로 충분히 강력하며 여러분의 옷장에 딱 들어갈 정도로 충분히 작습니다. 이동할 수 있어서 방에서 방으로 또 계단 위 아래로 쉽게 옮길 수 있습니다. 기본인 검정색과 메탈릭한 색상으로만 판매되는 이 수퍼 두퍼 더스트 데블에는 열 가지 부속품이 같이 나오는데, 그것으로 그런 손닿기 어려운 곳들을 청소할 수 있습니다. 침대 밑과 구석, 책장 뒤와 찬장 위, 이 기기가 닿을 수 없는 곳은 없습니다. 당사의 제품은 구입 후 1년 동안 완벽한 부품과 서비스를 보장합니다. 만족하시지 않는다면 구입 1주일 내에 돌려 주시면 환불이 됩니다. 그러니 스탠의 전자용품점에 오십시오, 나가실 때 행복한 고객이 되실 겁니다.

---

26 다음을 듣고, 화자의 의견에 동의하는 진술을 고르시오.

① Minsu: The death penalty is barbaric and unjust.
② Jaehee: All murderers deserve to be executed.
③ Sungmin: Keeping killers in prison cells is a waste of money.
④ Changhoon: Everyone convicted of a crime should be in prison.
⑤ Jeonga: DNA testing shouldn't be used in criminal cases.

① 민수: 사형은 야만적이며 부당하다.
② 재희: 모든 살인자들은 처형되어 마땅하다.
③ 성민: 살인자들을 감옥에 가두는 것은 돈 낭비이다.
④ 창훈: 범죄로 유죄판결을 받은 모든 사람은 감옥에 있어야 한다.
⑤ 정아: DNA 검사는 형사 사건에 사용되어서는 안 된다.

▶ death penalty 사형 punishment 처벌 criminal 범죄자 controversy 논란, 논쟁 execute 사형에 처하다 for one 한 예로서는, 개인으로서는 inhumane 비인도적인, 몰인정한 no matter what 아무리 …해도 no better than …이나 다름없는 death row (한 줄로 늘어선) 사형수 감방 innocent 무죄인, 결백한 convicted 유죄 판결을 받은

W Currently, the death penalty as a punishment for criminals is causing a great deal of controversy. While the death penalty still exists, no one in my country has been executed for several years. I, for one, disagree with the death penalty. It is inhumane for our government to take the life of another person no matter what that individual did. If we execute people, we're no better than the criminals themselves. A much better punishment would be to keep them locked in prison for the rest of their lives. This way, they cannot commit new crimes, and they must pay the penalty for those they did. I'm sure many people don't agree with me, yet there have been many recent cases where DNA testing has proved that people on death row are innocent of the crimes they've been convicted of. If they had been executed, then we would have killed innocent people. It's far better to respect the human rights of all people even if they are criminals.

여 현재 범죄자들에 대한 처벌인 사형은 상당히 많은 논란을 일으키고 있다. 사형제도는 아직 존재하지만 우리나라에서는 수년간 아무도 사형되지 않았다. 나도 사형제에 동의하지 않는다. 그 개인이 어떤 짓을 했더라도 정부가 다른 사람의 목숨을 앗는 것은 비인간적이다. 우리가 사람들을 사형시킨다면 우리는 범죄자들보다 나을 것이 전혀 없다. 훨씬 더 나은 처벌은 그들을 여생 동안 감옥에 가두는 것이다. 이렇게 하면 그들은 범죄를 새로 저지를 수 없고 자신들이 저지른 것에 대한 처벌을 받아야만 한다. 분명히 많은 사람들이 내게 동의하지 않겠지만 최근의 많은 사례들에 따르면 DNA 검사에서 사형선고를 받은 사람들이 유죄 판결을 받은 범죄에 무죄라는 것이 입증되었다. 그들이 처형되었다면, 우리는 죄 없는 사람들을 죽인 것이 된다. 설령 그들이 범죄자라 하더라도 모든 사람들의 인권을 존중하는 것이 훨씬 더 낫다.

27 다음을 듣고, 화자의 집을 가장 잘 나타낸 것을 고르시오.

①  ② 

③  ④ 

⑤ 

▶ for one thing 우선, 첫째로 fireplace (벽)난로 chimney 굴뚝 stick 튀어 나오다 so that 그러므로, 그 때문에 yard 마당

W My family just moved into a new house we bought. I'm so pleased with it because it looks like the house I've always dreamed of owning. For one thing, it's got two floors, so it's great to have both an upstairs and a downstairs. And there are two big windows on each floor, so the house is going to get a lot of light. That's a good thing because I love having a bright house. Oh, and we've also got a fireplace in the living room, so there's a chimney sticking out of the roof. I'm planning to have lots of fires in wintertime, so that should help keep the house warm. We've even got a front yard with a tree growing in it. It looks so nice. I'm sure that the kids are going to love climbing the tree and playing in the yard. It's going to be so great living here.

여 우리 가족은 구입한 새 집으로 방금 이사했다. 나는 기분이 아주 좋은데, 그 집이 항상 내가 갖기를 꿈꾸었던 집 같기 때문이다. 우선 층이 두 개여서 위층과 아래층이 모두 있다는 것이 아주 좋았다. 그리고 각 층에 커다란 창문이 두 개 있어서 집에 많은 빛이 들어올 것이다. 난 밝은 집을 좋아하기 때문에 그건 좋은 일이다. 그리고 또 거실에는 벽난로가 있어서 지붕 밖으로 굴뚝이 나와 있다. 겨울철에 불을 많이 피울 계획이니까 집을 따뜻하게 유지하는 데 도움이 될 것이다. 나무가 한 그루 자라는 앞마당도 있다. 정말 근사해 보인다. 분명히 아이들은 그 나무에 올라가고 마당에서 노는 걸 좋아할 것이다. 여기 사는 것은 정말 근사할 것이다.

---

28 대화를 듣고, 두 사람이 현재까지 주문한 음식값으로 지불하게 될 금액을 고르시오.

MENU		MENU	
Vegetable Soup	₩ 1.25	Steak and baked potato	₩ 7.50
Broccoli Soup	₩ 1.50	Baked Fish and rice	₩ 5.50
Cream Soup	₩ 2.00	Steak and french fries	₩ 6.50
Potato Soup	₩ 2.00	Ice tea	₩ 2.00
Chicken Salad	₩ 2.25	Coke	₩ 1.50
Caesar Salad	₩ 3.00	Ice cream	₩ 2.50

① $18.50
② $19.50
③ $20.00
④ $20.50
⑤ $21.50

▶ I'm afraid that (유감이지만) …라고 생각하다 baked 구워진 main meal 주요 음식 dessert 디저트, 후식 room 공간, 여유

W What do you want to order, Derek?

M I'm not sure yet. I'm afraid that I need a few more minutes. Everything looks so good.

W I think I'm going to start with a salad, but I don't know which one.

M Try the chicken salad. One of my friends had it here, and she said it was great.

W That sounds good. Are you going to have a salad, too?

M No, I believe I'll start with the vegetable soup and then have the steak and French fries.

W French fries are so unhealthy. Instead of them, you should have the rice or baked potato with the steak.

M Maybe you're right. Okay, I'll have the baked potato. And, for a drink, I think I'll order a glass of ice tea.

W Yeah, I'll have an ice tea, too. And for the main dish, I'll have the baked fish and rice. What about dessert? Do you want some ice cream or pie?

M Why don't we wait until we have our main meal first and then decide about dessert? I'm not sure if I'll have any room after all this food.

여 뭘 주문할 거야, 데릭?

남 아직 모르겠어. 좀 더 시간이 필요할 것 같은데. 모두 아주 좋아 보여.

여 난 샐러드로 시작하려고 하는데 어떤 걸로 해야 할지 모르겠어.

남 치킨 샐러드를 먹어봐. 친구 한 명이 여기서 먹었는데 훌륭하다고 했어.

여 좋아. 너도 샐러드 먹을 거니?

남 아니, 난 야채 수프로 시작한 뒤에 스테이크와 감자튀김을 먹을까봐.

여 감자튀김은 너무 몸에 안 좋아. 그 대신 밥이나 구운 감자를 스테이크와 같이 먹어야지.

남 어쩜 네 말이 맞는 거 같네. 알았어, 구운 감자를 먹을게. 그리고 음료수는 아이스티 한 잔을 주문해야겠어.

여 그래, 나도 아이스티로 할래. 주 요리로는 난 생선구이와 밥을 먹을게. 디저트는 어때? 아이스크림이나 파이를 좀 먹을래?

남 우선 주 요리를 먹을 때까지 기다렸다가 디저트에 대해 결정하면 안 될까? 이 음식을 다 먹은 뒤에 여유가 있을지 잘 모르겠거든.

29 대화를 듣고, 두 사람이 이상적인 친구에게서 원하는 공통 요소들을 모두 고르시오.

ⓐ intelligence
ⓑ good looks
ⓒ wealth
ⓓ honesty
ⓔ a sense of humor

① ⓐ, ⓑ, ⓒ
② ⓑ, ⓒ, ⓓ, ⓔ
③ ⓐ, ⓒ, ⓓ, ⓔ
✓④ ⓐ, ⓓ, ⓔ
⑤ ⓐ, ⓑ, ⓒ, ⓔ

▶ quality 특징, 특질 mate 짝 break up with …와 헤어지다 intelligence 지성, 총명함 must 필요한 것 don't have a clue 전혀 알지 못하다, 능력이 없다 looks 생김새, 용모 do without …이 없이 지내다, 필요없다 so long as …하는 한, …하기만 하면

M What do you think would make the ideal girlfriend or boyfriend? If you had to pick some qualities, what would they be?

W I'm not sure. I think it's impossible to find an ideal mate. But honesty is the most important thing for me. I can't stand people who lie. If I had a boyfriend who lied to me, I'd break up with him immediately.

M I'd have to agree with you there. Also, I think I could only be with someone who has the same education as me. Intelligence is a must.

W You're right. I don't want a boyfriend who doesn't have a clue about what's going on in the world.

M What about looks? I think looks are important.

W Well, I can do without them so long as he's a nice person.

M She'd have to have a good sense of humor, too. I can't stand being around serious people.

W Yeah, that's a must. How about money? Do you want a rich girlfriend?

M Not really. Then she'd always be expecting me to buy her expensive presents.

W I can understand that, but I'd love to have a rich boyfriend to take me out to some nice places.

남 이상적인 여자친구나 남자친구를 만드는 건 뭐라고 생각하니? 몇 가지 특징을 뽑아야 한다면 뭐일 것 같아?

여 글쎄. 내 생각엔 이상적인 짝을 찾는 건 불가능해. 하지만 솔직함이 나한텐 가장 중요한 거야. 난 거짓말하는 사람은 못 참거든. 나한테 거짓말하는 남자친구가 있다면 당장 헤어질 거야.

남 그건 너와 동감이야. 또 난 나만큼 교육받은 사람과만 지낼 수 있을 것 같아. 똑똑한 건 필수거든.

여 맞아. 난 세상이 어떻게 돌아가는지 갈피를 못잡는 남자친구는 필요없어.

남 외모는 어때? 난 외모가 중요한 것 같아.

여 음, 난 괜찮은 사람이기만 하면 그건 괜찮아.

남 또 훌륭한 유머감각도 있어야 해. 난 심각한 사람들과 있는 건 못 견디거든.

여 그래, 그건 필수야. 돈은 어때? 부자인 여자친구를 원하니?

남 별로. 그럼 그녀는 항상 내가 비싼 물건을 사 주길 기대할 거야.

여 알 것 같아. 하지만 난 나를 근사한 곳에 데려다 줄 부자 남자친구가 있으면 좋겠어.

---

30 다음을 듣고, 화자의 마지막 말에 이어질 내용으로 가장 알맞은 것을 고르시오

So before the test, you'd better sleep ______ ______.

① as little as possible
✓② around seven hours or so
③ about three or four hours
④ a couple of hours and study the rest
⑤ as much as you can

그러므로 시험 전에는 ______ 자는 것이 좋다.

① 가능한 한 적게
② 약 7시간 정도
③ 서너 시간 가량
④ 한두 시간만 자고 나머지는 공부를 하는 것이
⑤ 가능한 한 많이

▶ grade …의 등급을 매기다, 분류하다: 성적 평점, 평가 make sure 확인하다, 반드시 …하다 turn off (전원 등을) 끄다 distraction 마음을 산만하게 하는 것, 기분풀이 concentrate on …에 집중하다 had better …해야 하다, …이 더 낫다

W Students must always take tests. It's something that most of them dislike, but tests are used to grade a student's progress, so they're necessary. Getting a good grade on a test can be easy if you know what to do. First, make sure you study with a partner. When two people study together, it's easier to understand the information and to remember it. Second, turn off all radios, TVs, computers, and other distractions. You must concentrate on what you are studying. Third, don't leave all of your studying until the last moment. Study a little bit each day for several days, and you'll do much better. Finally, get enough rest the night before the exam. Most people have trouble sleeping before an exam, but it's the most important thing to do. More than six hours is best, but try not to sleep more than eight, or you'll be too relaxed during the test. So before the test, you'd better sleep ______.

여 학생들은 반드시 항상 시험을 치뤄야 한다. 그것은 그들 대부분이 싫어하는 것이지만 시험은 학생의 발전 등급을 매기는 데 사용되므로 필요하다. 시험에서 좋은 성적을 얻는 것은 여러분이 뭘 해야 할지를 안다면 쉬울 수 있다. 우선, 파트너와 같이 공부하도록 하라. 두 사람이 같이 공부하면 정보를 이해하고 기억하기가 더 쉽다. 둘째로 라디오와 TV, 컴퓨터, 기타 신경을 분산시킬 만한 것들을 모두 꺼라. 반드시 공부하는 데 집중해야 한다. 셋째로 모든 공부를 마지막 순간까지 내버려두지 마라. 며칠 동안 매일 조금씩 공부하면 훨씬 더 나을 것이다. 마지막으로 시험 전날 밤에는 충분히 쉬어라. 대부분의 사람들이 시험 전에 수면을 취하는 데 어려움을 겪지만 그것이 해야 할 가장 중요한 일이다. 6시간을 넘는 것이 최상이지만 8시간 넘게는 자지 않도록 하라, 그렇지 않으면 시험 동안 긴장이 너무 풀릴 것이다. 그래서 시험 전에는 ______ 자는 것이 좋다.

31 〔모두 듣기〕 **Which best shows the mood of this conversation?**

✔ ① urgent
② desperate
③ calm
④ comedic
⑤ serious

이 대화의 분위기를 가장 잘 나타낸 것은 무엇인가?

① 다급한
② 절망적인
③ 고요한
④ 우스운
⑤ 진지한

▶ calculator 계산기 rush 서두르다 parking space 주차 공간 pick up (사람을) 자동차로 마중 나가다, 차에 태우다

M We're going to be late for the exam.

W I can't find my calculator. I need it for the test I'm taking today. It was right here in my bag last night, but now I can't find it.

M Okay, I'll help you look for it. Where is it? Aha, there it is under the coffee table. Now let's get out of here.

W Just a minute. Let me put my shoes on. What's the rush anyway? The exam doesn't start until ten o'clock.

M It's nine thirty now, and the traffic on the way to the university is going to be bad.

W Let's take the subway then. It's much faster than your car, and we won't have to look for a parking space.

M I need my car for after school to pick up Fred from the airport.

W Well, I'm taking the subway. I don't want to be late for this exam. If I miss it, I'll fail the course.

M All right, we'll take the subway. I'll just come back and get my car after school. Can we go now? It's getting late.

W Yeah, let's go.

남 우리 시험에 늦겠다.

여 계산기를 못 찾겠어. 오늘 볼 시험에 필요한데. 간밤엔 가방 안에 있었는데, 지금은 못 찾겠어.

남 알았어, 내가 찾는 거 도와줄게. 어디 있지? 아아, 저기 커피 테이블 아래에 있다. 이제 나가자.

여 잠깐만. 신발 좀 신고. 대체 왜 서두르는 거야? 시험은 10시에나 시작하잖아.

남 지금 아홉시 반이고 학교에 가는 길의 교통상황이 나쁘잖아.

여 그럼 지하철을 타자. 네 차보다 훨씬 더 빠르고 주차장을 찾을 필요도 없잖아.

남 수업 후에 공항에 프레드를 데리러 가야 해서 필요해.

여 음, 난 지하철을 탈래. 이번 시험에 늦고 싶지 않아. 시험을 못 치면, 그 강의에서 낙제할 거야.

남 알았어, 지하철을 타자. 그냥 수업 후에 내가 돌아와서 차를 갖고 갈게. 이제 갈까? 늦겠다.

여 그래, 가자.

32 〔모두 듣기〕 **What is this news story about?**

① a heart attack victim
② some homeless people
③ two men hurt in an accident
✔ ④ a fire in a building
⑤ the cause of an accident

이 뉴스는 무엇에 관한 것인가?

① 심장마비 환자
② 집 없는 사람들
③ 사고로 부상당한 두 남자
④ 빌딩의 화재
⑤ 사고의 원인

▶ break out (화재 등이) 발생하다 property 재산, 소유물 scene 장소, 현장 resident 주민 detector 탐지기 evacuate 피난시키다, 주민을 옮기다 elderly 연세가 지긋한, 초로인 extinguish (불 등을) 끄다 inhalation 흡입 medic 의사, 의학도 suspect 의심하다 wiring 배선 (공사) questioning 심문

M Now, let's turn to our local news report. A fire broke out in an apartment building on Seventh Avenue at three in the morning, resulting in several injuries and severe property damage. Three fire stations responded to the call and were still on the scene this morning. Residents were awakened by a smoke detector and rushed to evacuate. One elderly man suffered a heart attack and is in stable condition in a local hospital. He's expected to survive. Two men attempted to extinguish the flames but were overcome by smoke inhalation and had to be treated by medics before being released. The cause of the fire is still under investigation, but it's suspected that electrical wiring caused it. The owner of the building has been brought in for questioning. Meanwhile, as a result of the fire, more than fifty people are now homeless. Donations to the victims can be made at St. Joseph's Church on Seventh Avenue.

남 이제, 지역 뉴스 보도 시간입니다. 오전 3시에 7번가 아파트 건물에서 화재가 발생해 수 명의 부상자와 심각한 재산피해가 발생했다고 합니다. 세 곳의 소방서가 신고를 받아 오늘 아침에도 현장에 있었습니다. 주민들은 연기 탐지기 때문에 깨서 급히 몸을 피했습니다. 노인 한 명은 심근경색을 일으켰는데 지역 병원에서 안정을 취하고 있습니다. 그는 생명에는 지장이 없는 듯합니다. 남자 두 명이 불길을 끄려고 해봤지만 연기를 너무 많이 들이마셔서 의료진의 치료를 받은 뒤 풀려났습니다. 화재 원인은 아직 조사중이지만 전기 배선으로 인한 것으로 추정됩니다. 건물 주인은 심문을 받기 위해 불려와 있는 상태입니다. 한편 화재 결과 50여 명의 사람들이 이제 집을 잃게 되었습니다. 7번가의 세인트 조셉 교회에서 피해자들을 위한 기부를 할 수 있습니다.

33

[모두 듣기] **Why is the woman unhappy with the products she ordered?**

✓① They were damaged in shipping.
② They are overly expensive.
③ They were late in arriving.
④ Her customers were unhappy with them.
⑤ She did not order the items she received.

여자가 주문한 상품에 대해 만족하지 못한 이유는 무엇인가?

① 그것들은 배송 중에 손상되었다.
② 그것들은 지나치게 비쌌다.
③ 그것들은 늦게 도착했다.
④ 그녀의 고객들이 그것들을 좋아하지 않았다.
⑤ 그녀는 자신이 받은 품목을 주문하지 않았다.

▶ bone china 본차이나, 자기 shipment 탁송 화물, 발송 chip (도자기 등의 이를) 빼다 cracked 금이 간, 깨진 unsatisfactory 만족스럽지 못한 compensate 보상하다, 갚다 no longer 더 이상 …않는 not entirely 전적으로 …한 것은 아닌

M Come in, Mrs. Delaney, and have a seat, please. How can I help you today?

W Thank you, Mr. Fraser. The reason I'm here is that there's a problem with my recent order.

M Oh, that's not good to hear. What exactly is the problem?

W I ordered the bone china from Dresden, Germany, for my shop, but when the shipment arrived, many pieces were chipped, and some were cracked. That's totally unsatisfactory.

M I apologize on behalf of the company. Of course, we will compensate you for any product that was damaged.

W I would expect nothing less. Also, I would like to cancel the order I placed a few days ago.

M But that order has already been shipped from Germany and will arrive two days from now. It's too late to cancel it.

W It seems you don't understand, Mr. Fraser. I no longer wish to do business with your company. I will not accept and will not pay for this recent order.

M I understand, Mrs. Delaney. Again, I apologize for not providing you with satisfactory service.

W I'm sure it's not entirely your fault. Good day, Mr. Fraser.

남 들어오세요, 들레이니 씨. 앉으시죠. 오늘은 뭘 도와 드릴까요?

여 고맙습니다, 프레이저 씨. 최근 주문에 문제가 있어서예요.

남 유감스러운 소식이네요.. 정확히 어떤 문제인가요?

여 제 가게에 쓰려고 독일 드레스덴에서 자기를 주문했는데 물건이 도착했을 때 여러 개가 이가 빠졌고 어떤 건 금이 가 있었어요. 정말 불만스럽더군요.

남 회사를 대신해 사과드립니다. 당연히 손상된 제품에 대해 보상해 드리겠습니다.

여 그러셔야죠. 또한 며칠 전에 한 주문을 취소하고 싶어요.

남 하지만 그 주문은 벌써 독일에서 선적되어서 이틀 뒤면 도착할 거예요. 취소하시기엔 너무 늦었습니다.

여 이해를 못하시는 것 같군요, 프레이저 씨. 그쪽 회사와 더 이상 거래하고 싶지 않아요. 이번 최근 주문은 받지 않을 거고 지불도 안 할 겁니다.

남 알겠습니다, 들레이니 씨. 다시 한 번 만족스러운 서비스를 제공해 드리지 못해 사과드립니다.

여 전적으로 당신 잘못은 아니에요. 안녕히 계세요, 프레이저 씨.

34

[모두 듣기] **Which best shows the relationship between the two speakers?**

① a customer and a hotel manager
② an employee and a director
✓③ a tenant and a landlord
④ a renter and a real estate agent
⑤ a buyer and a seller

두 화자의 관계를 가장 잘 나타낸 것은 무엇인가?

① 고객과 호텔 매니저
② 종업원과 감독
③ 세입자와 집주인
④ 임차인과 부동산 중개인
⑤ 구매자와 판매자

▶ sink 세면대 leak (파이프 등이) 새다 fix 고치다 replace 교체하다 raise 인상하다 fair 정당한, 타당한 lease 임대차 계약, 임대[임차] 기간 good (계약 등이) 유효한 repair 수리

W Mr. Smith, I need to speak to you about my apartment.

M What seems to be the problem this time?

W It's the same as it was the last time. The bathroom sink is still leaking. Water is spilling all over the floor, so we have to use the kitchen sink to brush our teeth and wash our hands.

M I fixed that two weeks ago, yet it's still giving you trouble?

W It was fine for a week, but then the leak started again in the same place. I think you need to replace the entire sink.

M If I start replacing things in these apartments, then I'm going to have to raise the rent.

W That's not fair. We have a lease that's good for another six months. And it says that you're responsible for any repairs that need to be done to the apartment.

M All right, don't get so excited. Are you going to be home on Tuesday afternoon?

W No, I'm working all day Tuesday. Wednesday is better.

M Okay, so on Wednesday, I'll come by and replace the sink. Hopefully, that will be the end of this problem.

여 스미스 씨, 아파트에 관해 말씀 드릴 게 있는데요.

남 이번에는 무슨 문제죠?

여 지난번과 똑같은 거예요. 욕실 세면대가 계속 물이 새고 있어요. 물이 바닥으로 온통 흘러내려서 부엌 싱크대를 사용해서 양치질하고 손을 씻어야 해요.

남 두 주 전에 고쳤는데, 아직도 문제가 있나요?

여 한 주는 괜찮았지만 그 다음 다시 똑같은 곳에서 물이 새기 시작했어요. 제 생각엔 세면대 전체를 교체해야 할 것 같아요.

남 이 아파트에서 물건들을 교체하기 시작한다면 임대료를 올려야 해요.

여 그건 부당해요. 우리의 임대 기간은 앞으로 6개월간은 더 유효해요. 그리고 아파트에 필요한 수리는 어떤 것이든 책임을 지신다고 돼 있잖아요.

남 알았어요, 너무 흥분하지 말아요. 화요일 오후에 집에 있을 거예요?

여 아니오, 화요일은 하루 종일 일을 해요. 수요일이 낫겠어요.

남 알았어요, 그럼 수요일에 들러서 세면대를 교체할게요. 그걸로 이번 문제가 끝났으면 좋겠네요.

<table><tr><th>문제와 정답</th><th>스크립트</th><th>해석</th></tr></table>

35 다음을 듣고, 이어지는 영어 질문에 답하시오.

① $6
✓ $7
③ $9
④ $10
⑤ $11

▶ lunch break 점심시간 bill 계산서 share 몫, 공유

M Tom, Joe, and David ate together at a restaurant during their lunch break. The bill came to a total of twenty-two dollars. Tom's share of the bill was nine dollars. Joe's share was three dollars less than Tom's, and David paid the rest of the bill.

Q: *How much money did David pay?*

남 톰과 조, 데이비드가 점심시간 동안 식당에서 같이 식사를 했다. 계산서는 총액이 22달러였다. 톰이 계산할 몫은 9달러였다. 조의 몫은 톰보다 3달러 적었고 데이비드는 나머지 금액을 지불했다.

Q: *데이비드는 얼마를 지불했는가?*

---

36 주어진 시간 동안 아래 지문을 주의 깊게 읽고, 들려주는 영어 질문에 답하시오. [1분]

Welcome to History 103, European History in the Twentieth Century. The following is the syllabus for our course for the next month. During the first week, we will examine the events leading to World War I and the war itself. During the second week, our discussion turns to the post-war years, the Great Depression, and the rise of dictators like Adolf Hitler. After that, in the third week, our attention will be focused on the causes of World War II and the war in both Europe and the Pacific Ocean. In the final week, we will look at the end of the war and the start of the Cold War between the Soviet Union and the United States. All students are responsible for reading the chapters for these sections. There will be a quiz at the end of each week and a test at the end of every month. Each student will also prepare a topic for a major essay, which will be turned in at the end of the month. Come to my office in room 409 on Tuesdays from 3-5 p.m. if there are any problems.

① The causes of World War II
✓ The causes of World War I
③ The end of World War I
④ The Great Depression
⑤ The start of the Cold War

① 2차 세계대전의 원인
② 1차 세계대전의 원인
③ 1차 세계대전의 종결
④ 대공황
⑤ 냉전의 시작

Q: *Today is the first day of class. What will they study?*

역사 103, 20세기 유럽사 수업에 온 걸 환영해요. 다음은 다음 달에 들을 강좌 요강이에요. 첫 주에는 1차 세계대전을 이끈 사건들과 그 전쟁을 살펴볼 거예요. 두 번째 주에는 전후 시기와 대공황, 아돌프 히틀러 같은 독재자의 부상에 대해 토론할 겁니다. 그 뒤 세 번째 주에는 2차 세계대전의 원인과 유럽 및 태평양 두 곳의 전쟁에 관해 집중적으로 살펴볼 겁니다. 마지막 주에는 전쟁의 종결과 소련과 미국 간의 냉전의 시작을 검토할 거예요. 모든 학생은 이 섹션들에 해당하는 챕터들을 읽어야 합니다. 매주 끝에 간단한 구두질문이 있고 매달 말에는 시험이 있을 거예요. 학생들은 각자 주요 에세이에 관한 주제도 준비해야 하는데, 그건 월말에 제출되는 겁니다. 무슨 문제가 있으면 매주 화요일 오후 3~5시에 내 사무실인 409호로 오세요.

Q: *오늘은 수업의 첫날이다. 무엇을 공부할 것인가?*

37 What is the purpose of this talk?

① To warn people about purchasing pets
② To explain how some pets might get sick
③ To complain about the high costs of pets
④ To describe the reasons why people buy pets
✓ To inform people on how to raise a pet

이 이야기의 목적은 무엇인가?

① 애완동물 구입에 대해 사람들에게 경고하기 위해
② 애완동물들이 어떻게 병에 걸리는지 설명하기 위해
③ 애완동물에 들어가는 높은 비용을 불평하기 위해
④ 사람들이 애완동물을 사는 이유를 설명하기 위해
⑤ 사람들에게 애완동물 기르는 법을 알리기 위해

38 Which is NOT true about a good pet owner?

✓ A good owner will give the pet anything to eat.
② A good owner will make sure the pet sees a veterinarian.
③ A good owner will give the pet a place to sleep.
④ A good owner will love the pet like the child.
⑤ A good owner will never abandon the pet.

좋은 애완동물 주인에 대해 사실이 아닌 것은 무엇인가?

① 좋은 주인은 애완동물에게 무엇이든 먹게 할 것이다.
② 좋은 주인은 애완동물을 꼭 수의사에게 진찰받게 할 것이다.
③ 좋은 주인은 애완동물이 잠잘 곳을 제공할 것이다.
④ 좋은 주인은 아이처럼 애완동물을 사랑할 것이다.
⑤ 좋은 주인은 절대로 애완동물을 버리지 않을 것이다.

▶ **responsibility** 책임, 의무 **injection** 주입, 주사(액) **obtain** 획득하다, 손에 넣다 **veterinarian** 수의사 **nutrition** 영양 섭취, 영양분 **overnight** 밤사이에 **care about** …에 마음 쓰다, …에 관심을 갖다 **such as** 이를테면, 예컨대 **abandon** 버리다 **shelter** 보호시설, 피난처

(37~38)

W Being a pet owner is a big responsibility. You are taking care of a living thing and should show it all the love and care you would give to your own child. First, you must be sure to get all the proper injections that the pet needs to protect it from diseases. These can be obtained from any veterinarian hospital. Second, your pet needs the best nutrition available and must have a balanced diet. There are many pet food products on the market today, so choose wisely. Third, all pets need a place to sleep that is warm and comfortable. Never leave your pet outside overnight. Next, pets need exercise and attention. Take you pet for a walk, play with it, and show it that you care about it. Dogs especially need to get outside and run around. Of course, this is not possible with all pets, such as birds, fish, or turtles, but even they need all of your love and attention. Finally, never abandon your pet. If you plan to move away or you can no longer take care of your pet, please take it to an animal shelter.

(37~38)

여 애완동물 주인이 된다는 것은 큰 책임이 따른다. 여러분은 살아 있는 것을 보살피고 자신의 자녀에게 주는 것과 같은 모든 사랑과 관심을 애완동물에게 보여 주어야 한다. 첫째로 애완동물이 질병에 걸리지 않는 데 필요한 적절한 주사를 모두 반드시 맞도록 해야 한다. 이것들은 모든 동물병원에서 받을 수 있다. 둘째로 여러분의 애완동물은 가능한 최고의 영양 섭취가 필요하며 반드시 균형 잡힌 식사를 해야 한다. 요즘 시장에는 많은 애완동물 먹이 상품이 있으므로 현명하게 선택하라. 셋째로 모든 애완동물들은 따뜻하고 편안한 잠자리가 필요하다. 절대로 밤 동안 애완동물을 밖에 두지 마라. 다음으로 애완동물들은 운동과 관심이 필요하다. 산책을 하러 데리고 가거나 같이 놀아 주고 신경을 쓰고 있다는 것을 보여 주라. 개들은 특히 밖에 나가서 돌아다녀야 할 필요가 있다. 물론 이것은 새나 물고기, 거북 같은 모든 애완동물에 가능하지는 않지만 그런 동물들조차 여러분의 모든 사랑과 관심을 필요로 한다. 마지막으로 절대로 애완동물을 버리지 마라. 멀리 이사를 계획하거나 더 이상 애완동물을 보살필 수 없다면 반드시 동물보호소에 데리고 가라.

39

What are the speakers talking about?

① the city's corrupt government
② the number of people who voted
✔ a person's responsibility to vote
④ the reasons why they should not vote
⑤ the person they think will win the election

화자들은 무엇에 대해 이야기하고 있는가?

① 도시의 부패한 정부
② 투표한 사람들의 수
③ 투표를 해야 하는 의무
④ 그들이 투표해서는 안 되는 이유
⑤ 그들이 선거에서 이길 거라고 생각하는 사람

40

What is the woman's response to the man?

W: _______________________________

① I guess you are right after all.
② Maybe I won't vote the next time either.
③ No, but you've made some good points.
✔ I still believe everyone's vote is important.
⑤ Please be sure to vote the next time.

남자의 말에 대한 여자의 응답으로 알맞은 것은?

① 결국은 네 말이 맞는 것 같아.
② 나도 다음 번에는 투표를 하지 말까봐.
③ 아니, 하지만 좋은 지적이었어.
④ 난 그래도 모두가 투표하는 것이 중요하다고 믿어.
⑤ 다음 번에는 꼭 투표해.

▶ **mayor** 시장 **elect** 선출하다 **term** 임기 **vote** 투표하다 **big deal** 대단한 일, 중대한 사건 **cynical** 냉소적인 **be forced to do** …하지 않을 수 없다 **at least** 최소한, 적어도 **besides** 게다가, 그밖에는 **attitude** 태도 **corrupt** 부패한

(39~40)

W Hi, Bill. I just heard that the mayor has been elected to another term. Did you vote in the election yesterday?

M No, I was too busy to make it to the voting station. I had a lot of work to do. Besides it was raining a lot yesterday.

W What? That's terrible. You should have made time to vote. It's your civic responsibility. I can't believe you didn't vote.

M It's not such a big deal. Not everyone votes. In fact, none of my coworkers voted yesterday. No one thinks his or her vote will make a difference anyway. To tell the truth, I've never voted in any election.

W That's a cynical attitude. Everyone's vote is important. You know that in some countries, people aren't allowed to vote, or they are forced to vote for someone. Here, at least we have the freedom to vote for the people we want to lead us.

M I've heard all of that before. It doesn't matter what I do. I just have one vote, and, besides, it's already decided who will win.

W I can't believe your poor attitude. It's because of people like you that our country has so many problems.

M No, it's because of the corrupt political system. No one cares if I vote or not. Can't you see that I'm right?

W _______________________________

(39~40)

여 안녕, 빌. 방금 시장이 연임에 선출됐다는 말을 들었어. 넌 어제 선거에서 투표했니?

남 아니, 너무 바빠서 투표소에 못 갔어. 할 일이 많았거든. 게다가 어젠 비가 많이 왔잖아.

여 뭐? 이럴 수가. 투표할 시간은 만들었어야지. 그건 너의 시민으로서의 의무야. 네가 투표를 안 했다니 믿을 수가 없다.

남 그건 그렇게 큰 문제가 아니야. 모든 사람이 투표하는 건 아니잖아. 사실 내 직장동료들은 어제 아무도 투표 안 했어. 자기 투표로 달라지는 게 있을 거라고 생각하는 사람은 아무도 없어. 사실을 말하면 난 어떤 선거든 한 번도 투표한 적이 없는걸.

여 그건 냉소적인 태도야. 모든 사람들의 투표는 중요해. 어떤 국가에선 사람들이 투표를 못하거나 누군가에게 투표하도록 강요당한다는 것을 너도 알잖아. 여기선 최소한 우리를 지도해 주길 원하는 사람들에게 투표할 자유가 있어.

남 그런 말은 모두 전에 들었어. 내가 뭘 하든 상관없어. 난 그냥 한 표일 뿐이고 게다가 이미 누가 이길지 정해졌잖아.

여 네가 형편없는 태도를 갖고 있다니 믿을 수가 없어. 우리나라가 그렇게 문제가 많은 건 너 같은 사람들 때문이야.

남 아니, 그건 부패한 정치체제 때문이야. 아무도 내가 투표를 하든 안 하든 신경 쓰지 않아. 내가 옳다는 걸 모르겠니?

여 _______________________________

실전모의고사 03

01 ③	02 ⑤	03 ①	04 ④	05 ②	06 ②	07 ②	08 ⑤	09 ④	10 ②
11 ①	12 ④	13 ③	14 ⑤	15 ②	16 ①	17 ③	18 ①	19 ⑤	20 ④
21 ②	22 ②	23 ⑤	24 ①	25 ④	26 ③	27 ⑤	28 ①	29 ②	30 ③
31 ②	32 ④	33 ①	34 ④	35 ④	36 ⑤	37 ②	38 ③	39 ①	40 ④

문제와 정답	스크립트	해석

01

대화를 듣고, 남자가 여자친구를 위해 살 선물을 고르시오.

①  ② 

③  ✓ ④ 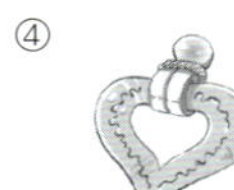

⑤ 

▶ I wonder if …인지 궁금해 하다 bracelet 팔찌 appreciate 고맙게 생각하다, 진가를 알다 spectacular 굉장한, 볼 만한 pendant (귀고리, 목걸이 따위의) 늘어뜨린 장식, 펜던트 purchase 구매하다 similar to …와 비슷한 in that case 그렇다면 owe (물건의) 대금을 빚지고 있다 total comes to 모두 해서 …이다

스크립트

M Hello. I was wondering if you could help me with a problem.

W Sure, what are you looking for?

M Tomorrow is my girlfriend's birthday, so I want to get her something nice. The only problem is I'm not sure what to buy.

W Well, you've come to the right place for birthday presents. Have you considered getting her a ring of some kind?

M I bought her one for her last birthday, so I'd like to get something different. I was actually thinking about a bracelet.

W Those are nice, but let me tell you something… You shouldn't get her one for her birthday. Instead, how about a nice pair of earrings? She'll probably appreciate those more. Take this pair, for example.

M Yes, those look quite spectacular, but don't you think a pendant or brooch would be better?

W They're fine, but not as presents. In fact, lots of men usually wind up purchasing something similar to what I just showed you.

M Is that true? In that case, let me have that pair then. How much do I owe you?

W Your total comes to seventy-five dollars, sir.

해석

남 안녕하세요. 좀 힘들어서 그런데 도와주실 수 있을까요.

여 그럼요, 찾으시는 게 뭔가요?

남 내일이 여자친구 생일이어서 뭔가 좋은 걸 주고 싶거든요. 유일한 문제는 뭘 사야 할지 모르겠다는 거예요.

여 음, 생일선물을 사기 좋은 곳에 오셨어요. 여자친구를 위한 반지 종류를 생각해 보셨어요?

남 지난번 생일 때 하나를 선물해서 다른 걸 하고 싶어요. 실은 팔찌를 생각하고 있었어요.

여 그것도 괜찮은데, 제 말 좀 들어 보세요… 팔찌는 생일선물로 하시면 안 돼요. 대신에 멋진 귀고리 한 쌍은 어떠세요? 아마 여자친구분은 그걸 더 좋아하실 거예요. 이를테면 이걸 보시죠.

남 네, 꽤 근사해 보이네요. 하지만 펜던트나 브로치가 더 낫지 않을까요?

여 그것도 괜찮지만 선물로는 아니죠. 사실 많은 남자분들이 보통 결국에는 제가 방금 보여 드렸던 것과 비슷한 것을 사세요.

남 정말요? 그렇다면 그걸로 할게요. 얼마를 드리면 되죠?

여 모두 해서 75달러입니다.

02

다음을 듣고, 화자의 장래희망이 무엇인지 고르시오.

① doctor
② animal trainer
③ nurse
④ animal groomer
⑤ veterinarian ✓

① 의사
② 동물 조련사
③ 간호사
④ 동물 미용사
⑤ 수의사

▶ constantly 끊임없이 nowadays 요즈음에는 unlimited 무제한의 take care of …을 돌보다 get better 호전되다, 좋아지다 heal (상처 등을) 고치다, 낫게 하다 cure (병을) 치료하다 whatever 어떤 …일지라도

스크립트

W Even though I haven't finished high school, I still constantly think about my future. Nowadays, there are so many things a person can do. I feel as if my options are unlimited. For example, I could become an astronaut, doctor, lawyer, or even an engineer. They're all great jobs, but they aren't the ones for me. The job I'd really love to do involves taking care of animals. I love animals and even own a couple of pets. But sometimes I see animals that get hurt. That makes me feel so sad, so I want to take care of them until they get better. That's the kind of job I'd love to do in the future. I'd be a doctor, but one who takes care of animals. People tell me I'm really good around animals, so I'm sure I'd be able to heal them and cure whatever problems they have.

해석

여 고등학교를 마치지 않았지만 난 여전히 미래에 대해 끊임없이 생각한다. 요즈음에는 사람이 할 수 있는 일이 아주 많다. 난 내가 선택할 수 있는 것이 무한한 것 같이 느껴진다. 예를 들면 우주비행사나 의사, 변호사, 기술자가 될 수도 있을 것이다. 그것들은 모두 훌륭한 직업이지만 나한테는 아니다. 내가 정말 하고 싶은 일은 동물들을 보살피는 것과 관련된 것이다. 난 동물을 좋아하고, 애완동물도 몇 마리 있다. 그런데 이따금은 상처받은 동물들을 본다. 그걸 보면 아주 슬퍼져서 나는 그 동물들이 나을 때까지 그것들을 보살펴 주고 싶다. 그것이 내가 미래에 하고 싶은 종류의 일이다. 나는 의사가 될 것인데, 동물을 보살피는 의사이다. 사람들은 내가 동물 관련 일에는 정말 솜씨가 좋다고 말하니까 난 내가 그것들을 낫게 하고 무슨 문제가 생기든 치료해 줄 수 있을 거라고 확신한다.

<table>
<tr><th>문제와 정답</th><th>스크립트</th><th>해석</th></tr>
</table>

03 대화를 듣고, 두 사람의 관계를 가장 잘 나타낸 것을 고르시오.

☑ ① bank teller – customer
② loan officer – customer
③ bank president – bank teller
④ customer – security guard
⑤ bank teller – loan officer

① 은행원 – 고객
② 대출 담당 직원 – 고객
③ 은행장 – 은행원
④ 고객 – 보안요원
⑤ 은행원 – 대출 담당 직원

▶ **open an account** (은행에) 계좌를 개설하다, …와 거래를 시작하다 **savings** 저축, 저금 **checking account** 당좌예금 계좌 **as of now** 현재로서는 **settled** 정착한 **fill out** (양식 등을) 작성하다 **paperwork** 문서 업무, 사무 절차 **identification** 신분증 **passport** 여권 **just in case** 만일을 위해 **take one's time** 천천히 하다

W Good morning. Is there something I can help you with?

M Yes, I just moved to this area, so I'd like to open an account with you.

W Are you interested in a savings or checking account? Or perhaps you'd like something different?

M As of now, I only want a checking account, but I'm sure I'll open up some other accounts when I get more settled. So, what exactly do I have to do?

W You can start by filling out this paperwork right here. It should only take you a couple of minutes. Oh, I'll also need to see some photo identification.

M Sure. Is a driver's license acceptable?

W Yes, but I'll need to see two forms of ID. You wouldn't happen to have a passport or some other form of identification, would you?

M Actually, I brought my passport with me just in case, so I guess it's my lucky day. Is there anything else you'd like me to do?

W No, there isn't. Just complete those papers while I go to make copies of your IDs. I'll be back in just a second.

M Take your time.

여 안녕하세요. 뭘 도와드릴까요?

남 네, 얼마 전 이 지역으로 이사 와서 이 은행의 계좌를 만들고 싶어요.

여 저축이나 당좌예금에 관심 있으세요? 아니면 뭔가 다른 걸 하고 싶으신가요?

남 지금으로선 당좌예금만 하고 싶지만 좀 더 정착되면 다른 계좌도 좀 개설할 거예요. 자, 제가 해야 할 게 정확히 뭐죠?

여 우선 바로 여기 이 서류를 작성하시죠. 단 몇 분이면 됩니다. 아, 또 사진이 있는 신분증도 좀 보여 주셔야겠네요.

남 그러죠. 운전면허증도 되나요?

여 네, 하지만 두 종류의 신분증이 필요해요. 혹시 여권이나 다른 종류의 신분증은 안 갖고 계시죠, 그렇죠?

남 실은 만일을 대비해 여권을 가져와서 운이 좋은 것 같네요. 제가 해야 할 다른 것이 있나요?

여 아니오, 없습니다. 제가 신분증을 복사하는 동안 그 서류를 완성하시기만 하면 됩니다. 잠시 후에 돌아올게요.

남 천천히 하세요.

---

04 대화를 듣고, 두 사람이 만나기로 한 식당을 고르시오.

① Mitchell's
② Thai Delights
③ The Hot Tamale
☑ ④ Pomodoros
⑤ The Hungry Fisherman

▶ **tamale** 타말리: 으깬 옥수수와 간 고기를 옥수수 껍질에 싸서 찐 멕시코 요리 **stomach** 맛있게 먹다, 소화하다 **allergic to** …에 대해 알레르기(성)의 **shellfish** (새우, 게 등의) 갑각류 동물, 조개 **option** 선택권, 선택할 수 있는 것 **outstanding** 저명한, 우수한 **make reservations** 예약을 하다

M Why don't we have dinner together this weekend?

W That sounds like a good plan. Where shall we go?

M Well, I love the Hot Tamale. It's that new Mexican restaurant down the street from the office. Why don't we have dinner there?

W I'm sorry, but I can't stomach Mexican food. I was thinking that the Hungry Fisherman would be a great place to eat instead.

M I'm allergic to shellfish, so that's not an option. Sorry. Hmm… We could visit Pomodoros, which is an outstanding Italian restaurant, or Thai Delights, a Thai restaurant right in our neighborhood. How about one of those?

W Okay, that doesn't sound too bad. Or we could even visit Mitchell's, which serves excellent steaks. I was just there a few days ago and loved the food.

M That sounds delicious, but do you really want to return there so soon?

W Yeah, you're probably right. I don't get out very often, so it's probably best to eat at another restaurant. Why don't we go to the Italian place? I've never been there.

M Really? You'll love it. I'll make reservations for seven o'clock this Saturday.

남 이번 주말에 같이 저녁식사 할까요?

여 좋은 생각인 것 같네요. 어디로 갈 거예요?

남 음, 난 핫 타말리가 좋아요. 사무실 길 아래에 있는 새로 생긴 멕시코 식당이에요. 거기서 저녁식사 하는 게 어때요?

여 미안하지만 난 멕시코 음식은 속이 불편해요. 내 생각엔 헝그리 피셔먼이 먹기 괜찮은 곳 같은데요.

남 난 조개류에 알레르기가 있어서 그건 안 되겠어요. 미안해요. 흠… 유명한 이탈리아 식당인 포모도르나 바로 근처에 있는 태국 식당인 타이 딜라이츠에 갈 수도 있을 것 같은데. 이들 중 하나 어때요?

여 좋아요, 그리 나쁘지 않은 것 같네요. 아니면 미첼스에 갈 수도 있을 것 같아요. 훌륭한 스테이크를 대접하는 곳이죠. 바로 며칠 전에 거기 갔는데, 음식이 훌륭했어요.

남 맛있을 것 같긴 한데, 정말 그렇게 빨리 거길 다시 가고 싶어요?

여 그래요, 당신 말이 맞겠네요. 그리 자주 외출하는 게 아니니 다른 식당에서 먹는 게 제일 좋겠네요. 이탈리아 식당에 가는 것 어때요? 거긴 못 가봤는데.

남 정말요? 마음에 들 거예요. 이번 주 토요일 7시로 예약해 놓을게요.

05 다음을 듣고, 이야기의 제목으로 가장 알맞은 것을 고르시오.

① Why Soccer Has Become Popular
✓ A Brief History of Soccer
③ Some of the Rules of Soccer
④ The World Cup and Soccer
⑤ Soccer in Ancient Greece and Rome

① 왜 축구는 인기를 얻었는가
② 간략한 축구의 역사
③ 축구의 몇 가지 규칙들
④ 월드컵과 축구
⑤ 고대 그리스와 로마에서의 축구

▶ tradition 전통 opponents 상대 ancient 고대의
codify 집대성하다, 체계화하다 entirely 완전히
ban 금지하다 adoption 채택 popularity 인기도
tournament 승자 진출전, 토너먼트; (각국 대표팀
등의) 종합 운동 경기 대회 planet 행성

M Countless cultures have a tradition of playing a game where players on opposing teams try kicking a ball into their opponents' net. The ancient Romans, Greeks, and Chinese all played some form of soccer. However, soccer as people know it today wasn't played until the early nineteenth century, when various British schools attempted to codify the game's rules. During the nineteenth century, soccer and rugby, which were similar at that time, became entirely different sports. Indeed, for almost a hundred years, the rules of soccer were altered. It wasn't until 1869 that players were banned from touching the ball with their hands. The adoption of that rule is when many say the modern game of soccer began. Soccer quickly increased in popularity, with many amateur and professional leagues developing everywhere. Today, soccer is the most popular sport in the world, and the World Cup, soccer's championship tournament, is the most watched sporting event on the planet.

남 수많은 문화에는 대항하는 선수들이 상대의 네트로 공을 차 넣으려고 하는 경기를 하는 전통이 있다. 고대 로마와 그리스, 중국인들은 모두 일종의 축구를 했다. 하지만 오늘날 사람들이 아는 것 같은 축구는 다양한 영국 학교들이 이 경기의 규칙을 체계화하려 시도한 19세기 초까지 이뤄지지 않았다. 당시에 비슷했던 축구와 럭비는 19세기 동안 완전히 다른 스포츠가 되었다. 실제로 축구 규칙은 거의 백년 동안에 바뀌었다. 1869년까지는 선수들이 손으로 공을 만지는 것이 금지되지 않았다. 그런 규칙을 채택한 것은 근대 축구 경기가 시작됐을 때라고 많은 사람들은 말한다. 축구는 급속히 인기를 얻게 되었고 곳곳에서 많은 아마추어와 프로리그가 발달했다. 오늘날 축구는 세상에서 가장 대중적인 스포츠이며 축구 챔피언십 토너먼트인 월드컵은 지구에서 가장 많은 사람들이 구경하는 스포츠 행사이다.

06 대화를 듣고, 여자에 대해 사실이 아닌 것을 고르시오.

① 급여에 대한 것은 여자에게 중요한 문제이다.
② 직업의 안정성이 그녀가 원하는 것이다.
③ 여자는 더 이상 학업을 계속하기를 원하지 않는다.
④ 정부에 관련된 일자리가 여자의 흥미를 끈다.
⑤ 여자의 전공은 그녀의 직업 선택에 영향을 주지 않을 것이다.

▶ major in …을 전공하다 connected to …에
연결된 public sector 공공 부문 pass on …을
전달하다 desire 욕구, 욕망 be tired of …이
싫증나다 likely 가능성 있는 absolutely 정말로,
완전히 not only A but (also) B A뿐만 아니라 B도
benefit 수당, 이득 factor 요인, 요소

M We're graduating next year. Have you thought about what job you're going to get after school's done?

W Yeah, I've put lots of thought into it.

M Really? What do you think you're going to do?

W Well, I'm majoring in economics, but I don't think I have to find a job connected to my major. Instead, I'll probably get a job in the public sector.

M That sounds interesting. What kind of work are you thinking of?

W I'd love to become a teacher. It would be fun to pass on knowledge to others. However, if I want to teach for a long time, I'll have to return to school to get a teaching degree, and I have no desire to do that.

M I'm pretty tired of school myself.

W That's why I'll most likely find some kind of government job. I'd absolutely love to work for the city in a position where I could help other citizens.

M That sounds nice.

W Not only does the government provide good jobs, but the pay and benefits are excellent, and those two factors are important to me, too.

남 우리 내년에 졸업하잖아. 학업을 마치면 무슨 일을 할지 생각해봤니?

여 응, 많이 해봤지.

남 정말? 뭘 하려고 하는데?

여 음, 난 경제학을 전공했지만 전공과 관련된 일을 찾아야 할 것 같진 않아. 대신 아마 공공 부문에서 일을 얻을 것 같아.

남 흥미로운걸. 어떤 종류의 일을 생각하는 거니?

여 난 교사가 되고 싶어. 다른 사람들에게 지식을 전수하는 건 재미있을 거야. 하지만 오랫동안 가르치려면 다시 학교로 돌아가서 교직을 이수해야 할 텐데 그러고 싶은 마음은 없어.

남 난 학교는 정말 지긋지긋해.

여 그래서 정부에 관련된 일자리 같은 걸 찾을 가능성이 제일 많아. 정말로 다른 시민들을 도울 수 있는 직책에서 시를 위해 일하고 싶어.

남 근사하다.

여 정부는 괜찮은 일자리를 제공할 뿐만 아니라 보수와 혜택도 뛰어난데, 그 두 가지는 나한테도 중요하거든.

07 다음을 듣고, 이야기의 분위기를 가장 잘 나타낸 것을 고르시오.

① displeased
✓ relaxed
③ bored
④ confused
⑤ agitated

① 화난
② 편안한
③ 지루한
④ 혼란스러운
⑤ 흥분한

▶ countryside 시골 confess 고백하다 not nearly 도저히 …아니다, …(에 가깝기는) 커녕 be used to …에 익숙하다 hustle and bustle 혼잡, 북새통 considerably 상당히 property 부동산, 땅

W I recently left my home in the city to live in the countryside. I must confess that it's not nearly what I'd expected to experience. I'm used to the hustle and bustle of the city. There, something is always going on twenty-four hours a day. However, life here is considerably slower-paced than in the city. For example, there's almost no traffic on the roads anywhere. I can drive for several miles without even seeing another car. And people live really far away from each other, too. You can't even see another house from the one I'm living at. That makes my neighborhood extremely quiet. I've actually come to enjoy sitting out in my yard and doing nothing. There's a small pond on my property, so, if I'm really quiet, I can watch lots of different animals visiting the pond all day long. It's a different life down here, but I really enjoy it.

여 나는 최근 시골에서 살기 위해 도시에 있는 집을 떠났다. 그것은 도저히 내가 경험하리라 예상한 것이 아니라고 고백해야겠다. 난 도시의 혼잡함에 익숙해 있다. 거기서는 항상 뭔가가 하루 스물네 시간 진행되고 있다. 하지만 이곳 생활은 도시보다 상당히 속도가 느리다. 예를 들어 어디든 도로에 통행이 거의 없다. 심지어 다른 차를 보지 않고 수마일을 운전할 수도 있다. 또 사람들이 서로 정말 멀리 떨어져 산다. 심지어 내가 살고 있는 곳에서는 다른 집이 안 보인다. 그래서 주변이 정말 조용하다. 사실 난 아무것도 하지 않고 마당에 나와 앉아 있는 걸 즐기게 되었다. 우리 땅에는 작은 연못이 있어서 내가 정말 조용히 있으면 하루 종일 연못에 찾아오는 많은 다양한 동물들을 지켜볼 수 있다. 여기는 다른 삶이지만 난 정말 그것을 즐기고 있다.

---

08 대화를 듣고, 남자의 마지막 말에 대한 여자의 응답으로 가장 알맞은 것을 고르시오.

W: ___________

① She's at her parents' house right now.
② I think she's still working at the office.
③ She should be at the museum by three.
④ Sorry, but nothing has arrived for you yet.
✓ I'd say probably in a couple of hours.

① 그녀는 지금 부모님 집에 있어.
② 그녀는 아직 사무실에서 일하고 있는 것 같아.
③ 그녀는 3시 쯤에는 박물관에 있을 거야.
④ 미안하지만 아직 네게 도착한 것이 아무것도 없어.
⑤ 아마 몇 시간 이내일 것 같아.

▶ at the moment 지금 drop by …에 들르다 mention 언급하다 affect 영향을 미치다 die to 몹시 …하고 싶다 as soon as …하는 대로 곧

M Hello, may I please speak with Stephanie?

W I'm sorry, but she's not in at the moment. May I ask who's calling, please?

M Sure, this is her friend Mark.

W Oh, hi, Mark. It's Rachel. We met a couple of weeks ago when you dropped by the house. Is there anything that I can do for you?

M Well, I was calling to speak with Stephanie. I wanted to know if she was still going to be able to visit the museum with me this weekend. She hasn't mentioned anything to you about it, has she?

W No, I'm afraid she hasn't. I'm sorry about that. However, I did hear her say something about having to drop by her parents' house this weekend. I hope that isn't going to affect your plans.

M Hmm… It might since I haven't heard anything about that. I hope it won't. There's an exhibition at the museum we've both been dying to see.

W Well, why don't I have her give you a call as soon as she comes home?

M That would be great. About when do you expect her to arrive?

W ___________

남 여보세요, 스테파니와 통화할 수 있을까요?

여 죄송하지만 지금 없는데요. 실례지만 누구시죠?

남 네, 저는 친구인 마크예요.

여 아, 안녕, 마크. 난 레이첼이야. 몇 주 전에 집에 들렀을 때 만났지. 내가 뭐 도와줄 거 있니?

남 음, 스테파니와 얘기하려고 전화했어. 이번 주말에 박물관에 같이 갈 수 있는지 알고 싶어서. 스테파니가 너에게 그 얘기 안 했지, 그렇지?

여 응, 안 했어. 어쩌니. 하지만 이번 주말에 부모님 집에 들러야 한다던가 하는 걸 들었어. 네 계획에 영향이 없었으면 좋겠다.

남 흠… 그런 얘긴 전혀 못 들어서 어쩜 그럴지도 모르겠어. 안 그랬으면 좋겠는데. 우리 둘다 정말 보고 싶어 하던 전시회가 박물관에서 하거든.

여 음, 스테파니에게 집에 오는 대로 네게 전화하라고 전할까?

남 그럼 좋겠어. 언제쯤 돌아올 것 같니?

여 ___________

09 대화를 듣고, 여자의 마지막 말에 대한 남자의 응답으로 가장 알맞은 것을 고르시오.

M: ____________________

① I think I need some more time to decide when I want to go.
② Are you sure there are no tickets available on Saturday?
③ I'd love two tickets for the Sunday afternoon performance.
✔④ I'll take two front-row tickets for the Thursday night show.
⑤ Do you mind if I trade these tickets for two on Saturday night?

① 언제 가고 싶은지 결정하는 데 시간이 좀 필요할 것 같군요.
② 토요일에 가능한 표가 없는 것이 확실한가요?
③ 일요일 오후 공연으로 표 두 장을 원해요.
④ 목요일 밤 쇼로 앞줄 좌석 두 장으로 하겠어요.
⑤ 이 표들을 토요일 밤 표 두 장과 교환해도 괜찮은가요?

▶ perform 상연하다 showing 상연, 상영 sold out 매진된, 품절된 look forward to …을 고대하다 attend 참석하다 performance 공연 last 지속하다 fit (의도, 시기 등에) 적합하다, 어울리다

M Good afternoon. I was hoping to make reservations for the musical that's being performed here. Could I get two tickets for the Saturday night showing?

W I apologize, sir, but Saturday night's show has been sold out for two weeks.

M Oh, no. I was really looking forward to attending it.

W There are two other performances this week if you're interested.

M Yes, I'd like to learn more about them. What nights are they?

W Well, there are performances on Thursday night and Sunday evening. The Thursday night show lasts from eight to ten while the Sunday performance starts at three and finishes at five.

M That's wonderful. Both of the days and times fit my schedule. Tell me something though… What kinds of seats are available for each performance?

W The Sunday show has almost sold out, so there are only a few seats remaining, and most aren't very good. However, the Thursday night performance still has seats everywhere, including a few located near the front.

M Ah, that's where I always like to sit.

W So, what would you like me to do?

M ____________________

남 안녕하세요. 여기서 공연중인 뮤지컬을 예약하고 싶습니다. 토요일 밤 상연하는 걸로 두 장 살 수 있을까요?

여 죄송합니다만 선생님, 토요일 밤 쇼는 2주간 매진되었습니다.

남 아, 저런. 그걸 정말 고대하고 있었는데.

여 관심이 있으시면 이번 주에 다른 공연 두 건이 있습니다.

남 그래요, 좀 더 알아보고 싶군요. 어느 요일밤에 하죠?

여 음, 목요일 밤과 일요일 저녁에 공연이 있습니다. 목요일 밤 쇼는 8시에서 10시까지 진행되고 일요일 공연은 세 시에 시작해서 다섯 시에 끝납니다.

남 잘됐네요. 날짜랑 시간이랑 제 일정에 맞네요. 하지만 좀 더 말씀해 주시겠어요… 각 공연에 가능한 좌석의 종류는 어떤가요?

여 일요일 쇼는 거의 매진이어서 남아 있는 좌석이 몇 석뿐인데, 대부분이 별로 좋지 않습니다. 하지만 목요일 밤 공연은 정면 가까운 몇 곳을 포함해서 아직 곳곳에 좌석이 있습니다.

남 아, 전 항상 거기 앉는 걸 좋아하죠.

여 그럼, 어떻게 하시겠어요?

남 ____________________

---

10 다음을 듣고, 대피라미드에 대해 사실이 <u>아닌</u> 것을 고르시오.

① They are the most popular tourist sites ever.
✔② They are located all throughout Egypt.
③ There are three pyramids located at Giza.
④ They were used to bury people in.
⑤ No one is sure how they were built.

① 대피라미드들은 가장 인기 있는 관광지이다.
② 대피라미드들은 이집트 곳곳에 위치해 있다.
③ 대피라미드들은 기자에 위치한 세 개의 피라미드이다.
④ 대피라미드들은 사람들을 매장하는 데 쓰였다.
⑤ 대피라미드들을 어떻게 건설했는지 아무도 확실히 알지 못한다.

▶ situated (어떤 장소에) 위치하고 있는, 있는 refer to …을 언급하다, 부르다 dominate 차지하다, 점유하다 process 방법, 공정 construction 건축, 공사 burial chamber 묘실 pharaoh 파라오

M Egypt has a large number of pyramids situated throughout the country. However, when most people talk about its pyramids, they're referring to the ones located at Giza. People know them as the Great Pyramids. Found near Cairo, there are three pyramids that dominate the area. These pyramids were constructed over 4,500 years ago in a process that took a long amount of time to complete. However, their method of construction is unknown and remains a mystery even in the present. People do, though, know their use: The pyramids were burial chambers for Egyptian pharaohs. For hundreds of years, the Great Pyramid of Giza was the tallest manmade structure in the world. From its completion until around 1300 AD, nothing else manmade was higher than it. The pyramids are among the most famous structures in the world, and it is believed that more tourists have visited them than any other place on Earth.

남 이집트에는 전국 곳곳에 많은 피라미드가 있다. 하지만 대부분의 사람들이 이집트의 피라미드에 대해 말할 때 기자에 있는 것을 언급하고 있다. 사람들은 그것들을 대피라미드로 알고 있다. 카이로 근처에서 발견된 세 개의 피라미드가 그 지역을 점하고 있다. 이 피라미드들은 4500여 년 전에 건축되었는데, 완공되는 데 오랜 시간이 걸렸다. 하지만 건축 방법은 알려져 있지 않으며 현재까지도 수수께끼로 남아 있다. 그래도 사람들은 그것들의 용도는 알고 있다. 그 피라미드들은 이집트 파라오들의 묘실이었다. 수백 년 동안 기자의 대피라미드는 인간이 만든 세계에서 가장 큰 건축물이었다. 완공된 후 서기 1300년경까지 인간이 만든 다른 어떤 것도 그것보다 더 크지 않았다. 그 피라미드들은 세상에서 가장 유명한 건축물에 포함되며, 지구상의 다른 어떤 곳보다 더 많은 관광객들이 그곳을 방문하고 있다고 믿어진다.

11 대화를 듣고, 여자가 신발을 사기 위해 지불할 금액을 고르시오.

☑ $85
② $115
③ $120
④ $150
⑤ $200

▶ advertisement 광고 on sale 팔려고 내놓은, 특가인 apply to …에 적용되다 entire 전체의 loafer 로퍼, 간편한 뒤축이 없는 일상화 in case …한 경우에는 retail for (상품이) … 값으로 소매되다 move (상품을) 팔다 beat a bargain 값을 깎다 wrap ... up …을 포장하다

W Good evening. I saw your advertisement for shoes in the local paper, and I was hoping that you'd be able to point out to me which ones are on sale.

M Sure, that won't be a problem. As you probably know, the sale only applies to a certain number of shoes, not our entire collection.

W Yes, I read that in the ad. So I'm guessing that this pair of loafers is not on sale.

M That's correct. They cost $150 though in case you're interested.

W Well, I do think that they're attractive, but not at that price. How about these black high heels? How much are they?

M They retail for $120, but, since they're on sale, you only have to pay $85.

W That's quite a bargain. You must really want to move a lot of your products.

M We're trying to make room for our spring collection. How about this pair of brown shoes? They usually cost $200 but are only $115 now. You can't beat that bargain.

W I'd have to agree with you, but I'm not that impressed by the way they look. I think I'll take the high heels, please.

M All right. Let me go and wrap them up for you.

여 안녕하세요. 지역 신문에서 구두 광고를 봤는데 세일중인 게 어떤 건지 좀 알려 주셨으면 좋겠어요.

남 네, 문제 없습니다. 아시겠지만 세일은 전체 품목이 아니라 특정 구두에만 해당됩니다.

여 네, 광고에서 읽었어요. 그러니까 이 로퍼는 특별가가 아니겠네요.

남 맞습니다. 하지만 관심이 있으시다면 가격은 150달러입니다.

여 음, 멋있긴 하지만 그 가격에는 안 되겠네요. 이 검정색 하이힐은 어때요? 얼마예요?

남 소매가로 120달러이지만 특별가 제품이니까 85달러만 내시면 됩니다.

여 꽤 싸네요. 제품을 많이 처분하고 싶은가 봐요.

남 봄 컬렉션을 위한 공간을 만들려고 해요. 이 갈색 구두는 어때요? 보통은 200달러이지만 지금은 115달러밖에 안 합니다. 그 가격 이하는 안 됩니다.

여 그렇겠네요. 하지만 모양이 그다지 마음에 들지 않네요. 그 하이힐을 살 게요.

남 알겠습니다. 가서 포장을 해드리겠습니다.

---

12 대화를 듣고, 이 상황에 가장 어울리는 영어 속담을 고르시오.

① A stitch in time saves nine.
② The grass is always greener on the other side.
③ Never look a gift horse in the mouth.
☑ Too many cooks spoil the broth.
⑤ The early bird always gets the worm.

① 시기 적적한 바늘 한 땀이 아홉 바늘의 수고를 던다.
② 건너편의 잔디가 늘 더 푸르러 보인다. (남의 떡이 커 보인다.)
③ 선물로 받은 말의 입 속을 보지 말아라. (선물 받은 것의 흠을 잡지 말아라)
④ 요리사가 많으면 죽을 망친다. (사공이 많으면 배가 산으로 간다.)
⑤ 일찍 일어나는 새가 벌레를 잡는다.

▶ work on …에 착수하다, 연구하다 be supposed to do …하기로 되어 있다 barely 거의 … 않다 handle (일을) 처리하다, (문제를) 다루다 convinced 확신에 찬, 신념 있는 respect 존중하다 mess 엉망 on time 제시간에 in a person's shoes 남과 같은 입장에, 남의 입장에 서서

M You're not going to believe all the problems we're having on this project I'm working on.

W Is that the one where you're teaming up with five or six other employees?

M That's exactly what I'm talking about. We were supposed to start last week, but, unfortunately, we've barely done any work yet.

W What exactly is the problem? From what I've heard, you've got some really good employees working on your team. You all should be able to handle this work easily.

M You'd like to think that, wouldn't you? However, here's what the problem is. Every member of the team is convinced that he should be the leader. I'm the team leader, but no one is respecting my position.

W That's not good.

M You're telling me. Everybody keeps trying to give me suggestions and is telling me how they think the project should be run.

W You've got to do something about that, or else you're never going to finish.

M I know. It's a total mess since no one wants to be a follower, and everyone wants to be the leader. I just hope we can get this project finished on time.

W Good luck with that. I'm glad I'm not in your shoes.

남 내가 작업중인 이 프로젝트에 있는 모든 문제를 넌 못 믿을 거야.

여 다른 직원 대여섯 명과 같이 팀으로 하고 있는 그것 말이니?

남 바로 그거야. 지난주에 시작하기로 돼 있었는데, 불행히도 아직 한 게 거의 없어.

여 정확히 뭐가 문제야? 내가 듣기로는 네 팀에는 정말 훌륭한 직원들이 있다던데. 모두가 이 작업을 쉽게 처리할 수 있을 텐데.

남 그렇게 생각하고 싶지, 그렇지? 하지만 문제는 이거야. 모든 팀원들이 자신이 리더가 돼야 한다고 확신하는 거야. 내가 팀장이지만 아무도 내 직책을 존중하지 않아.

여 안됐다.

남 정말 그래. 모두가 계속 나한테 제안하려 하고 프로젝트 운영방안에 대해 자기 생각을 말하고 있어.

여 뭔가 조치를 취해야겠다. 안 그러면 결코 끝내지 못할 거야.

남 알아. 아무도 따르려 하지 않아서 완전히 엉망이고 모두가 리더가 되고 싶어 해. 난 그냥 이번 프로젝트를 제때 끝낼 수 있길 바랄 뿐이야.

여 행운을 빈다. 내가 네 입장이 아니어서 다행이야.

13

다음을 듣고, 화자가 여행할 나라들을 차례대로 나열한 것을 고르시오.

ⓐ Greece
ⓑ Switzerland
ⓒ Italy
ⓓ Germany

① ⓐ - ⓑ - ⓒ - ⓓ
② ⓑ - ⓒ - ⓐ - ⓓ
③ ⓒ - ⓐ - ⓓ - ⓑ
④ ⓒ - ⓑ - ⓐ - ⓓ
⑤ ⓒ - ⓑ - ⓓ - ⓐ

▶ itinerary 여정, 여행 계획 as ... as possible 가능한 한 …한 architecture 건축 in person 본인이 직접 cruise 유람 항해하다 sights 명승지 scenery 경치, 풍경 can't wait to do 빨리 …하고 싶다 take in …을 구경하다, 방문하다

W I'm taking a trip to Europe in three weeks, so I had to complete my itinerary with my travel agent. I haven't been to Europe before, so I need to make sure I can visit as many places as possible. The first place I'm traveling to is Italy. I love the art and architecture there, so it'll be wonderful to see places like Rome, Venice, and Florence in person. I'd originally planned to visit Switzerland next, but my travel agent recommended I visit Greece instead. That works for me. I'll have a great time cruising the islands there. Next, I'm going to fly to Germany because I've got some relatives who live in the southern part of the country. I haven't seen them in a while, so that should be nice. Hopefully, they'll show me some of the local sights. Finally, before I go home, I'm going to make it to Switzerland for a couple of days. I can't wait to take in some of the mountain scenery in that country.

여 3주 후에 유럽으로 여행을 가게 되어 여행사 직원과 일정을 완성해야 했다. 이전에 유럽에 가 본 적이 없어서 가능한 한 많은 곳을 방문할 수 있도록 확인할 필요가 있다. 내가 여행할 첫 장소는 이탈리아이다. 그곳의 미술과 건축을 좋아하니까 로마와 베네치아, 피렌체 같은 장소들을 직접 보면 멋질 것이다. 다음으로는 원래 스위스를 방문할 계획이었지만 여행사에서 대신 그리스 방문을 권했다. 나는 그렇게 하기로 했다. 거기서 섬을 유람하며 멋진 시간을 보낼 것이다. 다음에는 독일로 비행기를 타고 갈 건데, 그곳 남부에 사는 친척들이 좀 있기 때문이다. 그 친척들을 한동안 못 봤기 때문에 그렇게 되면 좋을 것이다. 그들이 지역의 볼 만한 곳을 몇 군데 보여 주면 좋겠다. 마지막으로 귀국하기 전에 며칠간 스위스에 갈 것이다. 그 나라의 산악 경치를 빨리 보고 싶다.

14

대화를 듣고, 두 사람이 이야기하고 있는 사진을 고르시오.

①  ② 

③  ④ 

▶ decade 10년간 to begin with 우선, 첫째로 curly 곱슬곱슬한 observant 관찰력이 날카로운 make sense 말이 되다, 이해할 수 있다 kind of 어느 정도, 얼마간 resemblance 비슷함, 닮은 것

M Hey, who's this a picture of? I didn't know you had a sister.

W I don't. That's actually a picture of my grandmother from a few decades ago. She looks much different now than she did in the past, doesn't she?

M Yeah, I never would've guessed it's her in this photograph. To begin with, the woman in this picture has long, straight hair.

W You're right. My grandmother got tired of taking care of her hair, so she cut it off. Now it's fairly short and curly.

M Here's something strange. The woman in the photograph is wearing glasses, but I don't remember seeing your grandmother in them.

W That's pretty observant of you. She used to wear glasses, but now she doesn't since she wears contact lenses instead.

M Oh, well, that makes sense. You know, now that I think about it, your grandmother in this picture looks kind of like you.

W Do you think so? Many people have said there's a resemblance between the two of us, but I don't see it.

M Yeah, there is. You both have similar eyes and noses.

W I'll be sure to tell my grandmother you said that the next time I see her.

남 이봐, 이거 누구 사진이야? 난 네가 여자형제가 있는 줄 몰랐어.

여 없어. 그건 사실 몇 십 년 전에 찍은 할머니 사진이야. 할머닌 지금 과거랑 전혀 다르게 보여, 그렇지 않니?

남 그래, 이 사진에 있는 사람이 할머니라곤 전혀 생각 못했어. 우선 이 사진 속 여성은 머리가 길고 직모잖아.

여 맞아. 할머닌 머리를 손질하는 것에 질려서 자르셨지. 지금은 꽤 짧은 곱슬머리지.

남 여기 이상한 게 있어. 사진 속 여성은 안경을 끼고 있는데 네 할머니가 안경 낀 걸 본 기억이 없어.

여 눈썰미가 좋구나. 할머닌 예전엔 안경을 꼈지만 지금은 아니야, 대신 콘텍트렌즈를 끼셔.

남 아, 그럼, 말이 된다. 그 생각을 하니까 말인데, 이 사진 속의 할머니 약간 너 같아 보여.

여 그렇게 생각하니? 많은 사람들이 우리 두 사람이 닮았다고 하는데 난 모르겠어.

남 그래, 닮았어. 둘 다 눈과 코가 비슷해.

여 다음에 할머니를 뵙게 되면 네가 말한 걸 꼭 말씀드릴게.

<table>
<tr><th>문제와 정답</th><th>스크립트</th><th>해석</th></tr>
</table>

15 대화를 듣고, 여자가 아들이 깨어난 직후 무엇을 할지 고르시오.

① Take him inside the house
☑ Give him some water to drink
③ Put a cold towel on his forehead
④ Let him walk around
⑤ Take him to the hospital

① 아들을 집안으로 데리고 들어간다.
② 아들에게 마실 물을 준다.
③ 아들의 이마에 차가운 수건을 놓는다.
④ 아들을 걸어보게 한다.
⑤ 아들을 병원에 데리고 간다.

▶ **state** 정확히 말하다 **nature** 특징, 종류
emergency 응급 사태 **faint** 기절하다(=pass out)
see if …인지 보다 **suffer from** …을 앓다, 고생하다
heatstroke 열사병 **forehead** 이마 **dehydrated**
탈수상태인 **check out** …을 확인하다

M 911, please state the nature of your emergency.

W My son suddenly fainted, and I'm not sure what to do.

M Okay, first, check to see if he's still breathing.

W Yes, he's breathing, but he hasn't woken up yet. He passed out a minute ago, and I'm starting to get worried.

M Can you tell me what he was doing at the time he passed out?

W He was outside running around with his friends. They'd been playing a game for about thirty minutes or so when he suddenly just passed out.

M All right, I think I know what the problem is. It's a hot day today, so he's probably suffering from heatstroke. You need to cool him off a lot. I recommend putting a cold towel on his forehead until he wakes up. Then, you need to give him some water since he's probably dehydrated. And keep him on the ground for at least ten minutes.

W But what if he tries to stand up?

M He probably won't have the energy to. However, once he can walk, take him inside the house to a cool place. He'll be all right, but you should take him to the hospital to have a doctor check him out.

남 911입니다. 응급 상황을 말씀하세요.

여 아들이 갑자기 기절했는데 뭘 해야 할지 모르겠어요.

남 알겠습니다, 먼저 아직 숨을 쉬고 있는지 확인해 보세요.

여 네, 숨은 쉬고 있는데 아직 안 깨어났어요. 잠깐 전에 기절했는데, 걱정이 돼요.

남 기절했을 때 뭘 하고 있었는지 말씀해 주시겠어요?

여 밖에서 친구들과 뛰어다니고 있었어요. 30분 정도 운동을 하다 갑자기 그냥 기절했어요.

남 알겠습니다, 문제가 뭔지 알 것 같군요. 오늘 날이 더워서 아마 열사병을 일으킨 것 같네요. 아드님을 아주 시원하게 해 줘야 해요. 깨어날 때까지 찬 수건을 이마에 대어 주세요. 그 다음에 아마 탈수상태일 테니 물을 좀 주셔야 해요. 또 최소한 10분간 바닥에 누워있게 하세요.

여 하지만 일어나려고 하면 어떡하죠?

남 아마도 그럴 힘이 없을 거예요. 하지만 일단 걸을 수 있으면 집안의 시원한 곳으로 데리고 가세요. 괜찮겠지만 병원에 데리고 가서 의사의 진찰을 받아보세요.

---

16 다음을 듣고, 서울의 현재 날씨를 고르시오.

☑ It is raining just a little.
② There was a moderate amount of rain.
③ There are some thunderstorms.
④ It is experiencing heavy rain.
⑤ The typhoon is dropping heavy rain.

① 약간의 비만 오고 있다.
② 적당한 양의 비가 내렸다.
③ 천둥이 치고 있다.
④ 폭우가 내리고 있다.
⑤ 태풍이 심한 비를 뿌리고 있다.

▶ **batter** (바람 등이) 세게 부딪치다, 강타하다
landfall (비행기 등의) 착륙, 상륙 **province**
지방 **urge** 촉구하다, 재촉하다 **caution** 조심,
경계 **peninsula** 반도 **brunt** (공격, 타격의) 주력,
예봉 **capital** 수도 **throughout** …을 두루, 도처에
meteorologist 기상학자, 기상 전문가 **predict**
예보하다 **extensive** 막대한, 광범위한

W Most of the country is being battered by the typhoon that has been steadily approaching the country from Taiwan. It finally made landfall last night near Busan, and it's causing heavy rains all across the country's southern provinces. There have been reports of flooding in some coastal areas, and citizens are urged to take caution when driving. The government is even recommending that people stay indoors until the typhoon passes. Meanwhile, the storm is expected to continue north across the entire Korean peninsula, where it should cause even more damage. Seoul should face the brunt of the storm tomorrow although it's currently experiencing only light rain. This will steadily increase over the course of the day, and tomorrow, the capital should receive several inches of rain. The Han River is expected to rise by several feet, which will cause flooding all throughout various parts of Gyeonggi Province. Meteorologists predict the typhoon will leave the country in a couple of days, but it will still remain here long enough to cause extensive damage.

여 전국 대부분의 지역이 대만에서 서서히 접근중인 태풍의 타격을 받고 있습니다. 태풍은 드디어 지난밤에 부산 근처에 상륙해 남부 지방 전역에 많은 비를 뿌리고 있습니다. 몇몇 해안 지역에서는 범람이 보고되었고 시민들은 운전시 주의가 요구됩니다. 정부에서는 심지어 태풍이 지나갈 때까지 사람들이 실내에 머물러 있도록 권고하고 있습니다. 한편 폭풍이 북쪽을 향해 한반도 전역을 지나갈 것이 예상되면서 훨씬 더 많은 피해가 일어날 것으로 보입니다. 서울은 현재는 약한 비만 내리고 있지만 내일은 폭풍의 타격을 정면으로 받을 것 같습니다. 이로 인해 비가 하루 동안 서서히 증가하여 내일은 몇 인치의 강우가 있을 것으로 보입니다. 한강은 수피트 상승할 것으로 예상되는데, 이것은 경기도 여러 지역에 범람을 초래할 것입니다. 기상 전문가들은 이 태풍이 며칠 뒤면 사라지겠지만 여전히 막대한 피해를 일으키기에 충분히 오랜 시간 동안 지속될 것으로 예보하고 있습니다.

<table>
<tr><th>문제와 정답</th><th>스크립트</th><th>해석</th></tr>
</table>

17 대화를 듣고, 남자가 먹은 음식에 들어 있는 칼로리가 총 얼마인지 고르시오.

① 1,000
② 1,400
✓ 1,500
④ 1,620
⑤ 1,720

▶ matter 문제, 걱정 particularly 특히 lose weight 살을 빼다 frustrating 좌절감을 느낄 정도의, 초조한 snack 간식 that's why 그래서 …하다

W What's the matter? You don't look particularly happy today.

M I started a diet last week, but I don't seem to be losing any weight. It's getting really frustrating.

W I didn't know you were dieting. Actually, I'm on a diet too, so I always carry this book with me. It tells me how many calories are in various foods, so I can be careful about what I eat at all times.

M Hey, do you think you could check out some of the foods I had today?

W Sure. Just tell me what you ate.

M Okay. I had an apple early in the day. And then I had some spaghetti for lunch.

W According to this book, the apple had eighty calories, so you're doing well there. And I saw you had sauce with your spaghetti, so that was about 320 calories. Did you have anything else?

M Um, well, I had two cheeseburgers for a snack. I was a little hungry in the afternoon.

W That's why you aren't losing any weight. One cheeseburger has 550 calories. You had over 1,000 calories just for a snack. If you keep eating like that, you're never going to lose any weight.

M Yeah, but they taste really good.

여 무슨 일이야? 오늘 특별히 안 좋아 보이네.

남 지난주에 다이어트를 시작했는데 체중이 전혀 안 빠지는 것 같아. 정말 초조해져.

여 네가 다이어트중인 건 몰랐네. 사실 나도 다이어트 중이어서 항상 이 책을 갖고 다녀. 이 책으로 여러 음식에 얼마나 많은 칼로리가 있는지 알 수 있어서 항상 먹는 것에 주의할 수 있거든.

남 있잖아, 오늘 내가 먹은 음식 좀 확인해 줄 수 있니?

여 그럼. 뭘 먹었는지만 말해.

남 알았어. 오늘 일찍 사과 하나를 먹었어. 그리곤 점심으로 스파게티를 먹었고.

여 이 책에 따르면 사과에 80칼로리가 있다니까 넌 그 시점에서는 잘 하고 있어. 또 스파게티와 소스를 먹었으니까 그건 320칼로리쯤 되겠다. 다른 건 안 먹었어?

남 음, 어, 간식으로 치즈버거 두 개를 먹었어. 오후에 배가 좀 고팠거든.

여 그래서 네가 살이 전혀 안 빠지는 거야. 치즈버거 하나는 550칼로리가 들어 있어. 넌 간식으로만 1,000 칼로리 넘게 먹은 거야. 계속 그렇게 먹다가는 전혀 살을 못 뺄 거야.

남 그래, 하지만 정말 맛있어.

---

18 다음을 듣고, 이야기의 내용과 일치하지 <u>않는</u> 것을 고르시오.

✓ 총 비행시간은 9시간이 걸릴 것이다.
② 항공기는 더 빨리 도착할 예정이다.
③ 파리의 날씨는 화창할 것으로 예상된다.
④ 비행기는 지중해를 통과했다.
⑤ 기온은 72도까지 오를 것이다.

▶ be about to 막 …하려 하다 descent 내리기, 하강 balmy 온화한, 상쾌한 Fahrenheit 화씨 온도계[눈금] scattered 흩뿌려진, 산재한 get out (탈것에서) 내리다, 나가다 tailwind (항공기 등의) 뒷바람, 순풍 destination 목적지, 도착지 transfer 환승하다, 갈아타다 agent (공공 기관의) 직원

M Good morning, everyone. This is Captain Reynolds speaking. We're about to begin our final descent into Paris, where we'll be on the ground in approximately forty-five minutes. The temperature in Paris is a balmy seventy-two degrees Fahrenheit, so it's a beautiful spring day in the city. The weather forecast calls for sunny skies with just a few scattered clouds, so be sure to get out and enjoy the city as soon as we land. By the time we arrive, our flight will have taken eight hours to complete. We're going to be landing at Gate 19 at approximately nine thirty-five, which makes us about ten minutes early thanks to those tailwinds we caught while flying over the Mediterranean Sea. We'd like to thank all of you for flying with us today. If Paris is your final destination, please enjoy your stay there. If you are transferring to another city, there are agents waiting at the gate who can provide you with the transfer information you need. Have a great day, everybody.

남 안녕하세요, 승객 여러분. 저는 레이놀즈 기장입니다. 저희는 파리를 향해 마지막으로 하강할 예정이며 약 45분 뒤면 착륙할 것입니다. 파리의 기온은 화씨 72도로 온화해서 아름다운 봄날입니다. 일기 예보에 따르면 구름 몇 점만 끼는 햇빛 가득한 하늘이라니까, 착륙하는 대로 내리셔서 꼭 도시를 즐기시기 바랍니다. 도착할 때까지 우리 비행기는 총 8시간을 비행했을 것입니다. 지중해 위를 비행하는 동안 순풍이 분 덕분에 약 10분 정도 빠른 9시 35분경에 19번 게이트에 착륙할 예정입니다. 오늘 저희 항공기를 이용해 주셔서 여러분 모두에게 감사를 드립니다. 파리가 목적지인 분은 그곳에서 즐거운 체류가 되시길 바랍니다. 다른 도시로 이동하시려면 게이트에서 기다리고 있는 직원이 여러분에게 필요한 환승 정보를 제공해 드릴 겁니다. 여러분 모두 즐거운 하루 보내시기 바랍니다.

19 대화를 듣고, 남자가 새 컴퓨터를 사지 **못하는** 이유를 고르시오.

① 남자는 신용카드를 가지고 오는 것을 잊었다.
② 남자는 할부로 결제하기를 원하지 않는다.
③ 남자는 충분한 현금을 가지고 있지 않다.
④ 남자의 신용카드가 최근에 기한이 만료되었다.
✓⑤ 남자는 최근에 신용카드를 너무 많이 사용했다.

▶ upgrade (제품)의 품질을 높이다 productive 생산적인 steep (값, 금액 등이) 터무니없이 비싼, 엄청난 price tag 정가표, 가격표 credit card 신용카드 item 품목 refund 환불하다 credit limit 신용 한도(액) monthly installments (매달 내는) 할부, 월부 sooner rather than later 더 늦기 전에

M Check out that computer over there. It's the latest model and is so much better than the one I'm using now.

W In that case, why don't you purchase it? I know you use a computer for your work all the time, so this upgraded version might help you become more productive.

M I'd love to buy it, but it's got a steep price tag.

W Didn't you bring enough cash with you?

M I never make big purchases with cash. I use my credit card for items like this since it's easier to get my money refunded if it gets lost, broken, or stolen.

W What are you waiting for then? Take out your credit card, and buy that computer. Oh, wait. You forgot to bring your card, didn't you?

M No, it's not that. It's just that I'm nearing my credit limit because I've been using my card for several purchases lately.

W Couldn't you purchase it in monthly installments? I know most stores allow that.

M I don't think I even have that much credit left. Remember that I just moved last month, so I had to buy a lot of things for my house.

W Oh, well. I hope you can get this computer sooner rather than later.

남 저쪽에 있는 저 컴퓨터를 확인해 봐. 최신 모델인데 지금 내가 쓰는 것보다 훨씬 더 나아.

여 그럼 저걸 구입하지 그러니? 넌 일할 때 항상 컴퓨터를 사용하니까 업그레이드 버전인 이것이 네가 더 생산적이 되도록 도움을 줄 수 있잖아.

남 사고 싶지만 가격이 엄청 비싸.

여 현금을 충분히 안 가져 왔어?

남 난 큰 건은 절대로 현금으로 구입 하지 않아. 분실이나 고장, 도난 당할 경우에 환불 받기가 더 쉬워서 이런 물건은 신용카드를 사용해.

여 그럼 뭘 기다려? 신용카드를 꺼내서 그 컴퓨터를 사. 아, 잠깐. 카드 갖고 오는 것 잊어버렸구나, 그렇지 않니?

남 아니, 그게 아냐. 그냥 최근에 몇 건을 구매하느라 카드를 써버려서 카드 한도액이 다 돼 가서 그래.

여 할부로 구입할 수 없었어? 대부분의 가게에서는 그게 되는 걸로 아는데.

남 그 정도의 신용 한도도 안 남아 있을 거야. 내가 바로 지난 달에 이사 와서 집에 필요한 물건을 많이 사야 했던 걸 기억해봐.

여 아, 그래. 더 늦기 전에 네가 이 컴퓨터를 살 수 있으면 좋겠다.

---

20 대화를 듣고, 여자가 남자에게 해 준 충고가 **아닌** 것을 고르시오.

① Have some hot food to eat.
② Take some vitamin tablets.
③ Drink a lot of liquids.
✓④ Take some cough drops.
⑤ Get as much rest as possible.

① 뜨거운 음식을 먹어라.
② 비타민 정제를 먹어라.
③ 수분을 많이 마셔라.
④ 감기약을 먹어라.
⑤ 가능한 많은 휴식을 취하라.

▶ cough 기침하다 ridiculous 우스꽝스러운, 터무니없는 medicine (내복)약, 의약품 had better …해야 하다, …하는 것이 낫다 rest 휴식 liquid 액체, 유동체 get over …에서 회복하다, 극복하다 work (약 등이) 효과가 있다 tablet (약의) 정제 pharmacy 약국 stop at …에 들르다 on one's way …로 가는 길에[도중에]

W Why are you still at work? I could hear you coughing from the elevator. You need to go home and get better.

M I'd love to, but I've got too much work to finish here.

W That's ridiculous. So, are you at least doing anything to try to get better?

M Not really. I haven't seen a doctor because I know he's going to tell me to take some medicine and stay in bed. It's just a cold anyway.

W I'd say you have more than a cold. You'd better go home and get some rest. And drink a lot of liquids. They'll help you get over your sickness more quickly.

M Do you think that will work?

W Yes. My father's a doctor, so he taught me a lot. You need to eat some hot foods, like soup or something similar. And also take some vitamin C tablets, which you can get at any pharmacy nearby.

M Okay, I'll stop at one on my way home.

W That's good to hear. But, most important of all, you should sleep as much as you can. Your body needs to get stronger, and sleep will help you do that.

M I'll be sure to take your advice. Thanks for everything.

여 왜 아직 직장에 있어? 엘리베이터에서 네가 기침하는 게 들리던데. 집에 가서 좀 나아야지.

남 그러고 싶지만 여기서 끝내야 할 일이 너무 많아.

여 말도 안 돼. 그래서 낫기 위해 최소한 뭐라도 하고 있는 거야?

남 별로. 약 좀 먹고 누워 있으라고 말할 걸 아니까 진찰도 안 받았어. 그냥 감기야.

여 감기보다 더한 것 같은데. 집에 가서 좀 쉬는 게 낫겠다. 그리고 물 같은 걸 많이 마셔. 아픈 것이 더 빨리 낫는 데 도움이 될 거야.

남 그게 효과가 있을 것 같니?

여 그래. 우리 아버지가 의사라서 많이 가르쳐 주셨어. 수프나 뭐 비슷한 뜨거운 음식을 좀 먹어야 할 거야. 그리고 또 비타민 C 알약도 좀 먹어. 근처 아무 약국에서나 살 수 있어.

남 알았어, 집에 가는 길에 들러 볼게.

여 좋아. 하지만 가장 중요한 건 최대한 잠을 많이 자야 해. 몸이 더 튼튼해져야 하는데, 잠이 도움이 될 거야.

남 충고 꼭 들을게. 모든 게 고마워.

21 다음을 듣고, 화자의 감정 변화를 가장 잘 나타낸 것을 고르시오.

① nervous → disappointed
✓ hopeful → angry
③ eager → sad
④ concerned → distrustful
⑤ pleased → confused

① 긴장된 → 실망한
② 희망에 찬 → 화난
③ 갈망하는 → 슬픈
④ 걱정하는 → 의심하는
⑤ 즐거운 → 혼란스러운

▶ surf 인터넷 상의 정보를 찾아다니다 browse 대강 훑어보다 selection (구매 등을 위한) 전시품 offer 팔려고 내놓다 at a bargain price 싼값으로, 특가로 place an order 주문하다 upcoming 다가오는 deliveryman (상품) 배달인 pull up 차를 세우다. (차 등이) 서다 material 옷감, 직물 steam 노발대발하게 하다 trick 속이다

W Six days ago, I was surfing my favorite clothing store's website. While browsing their selections, I saw the most wonderful coat. It was made of cashmere and could be worn either casually or formally. And it was even being offered at a bargain price. Naturally, I placed an order for the coat. I simply couldn't wait to receive it, especially since I was planning to wear it to an upcoming work event. Finally, I saw the deliveryman pull up to my house with a big package. It felt like my birthday as I opened up the box and took a look at my new coat. But it was totally different than the one I had expected. The color was right, but the style wasn't the same. And the material felt strange, too. I checked to see if there had been a mistake, but that was really the coat I had ordered. I was so steamed since the company had tricked me. I'm never going to purchase anything from them again.

여 6일 전에 나는 좋아하는 옷가게의 웹사이트를 돌아다니고 있었다. 전시 품목을 훑어보다가 가장 멋진 코트를 봤다. 캐시미어 직물로 만들어졌고, 캐주얼로도 정장으로도 입을 수 있을 것 같았다. 그리고 그것은 심지어 특가로 판매되고 있었다. 당연히 난 그 코트를 주문했다. 특히 앞으로 있을 직장 행사에 그걸 입을 생각을 하니까 빨리 받고 싶었다. 드디어 배달원이 큰 소포를 가지고 우리 집에 차를 대는 걸 봤다. 상자를 열고 새 코트를 보는 것이 마치 생일 때 같았다. 하지만 그건 내가 예상했던 것과 완전히 달랐다. 색깔은 괜찮았지만 스타일이 똑같지 않았다. 소재도 이상한 것 같았다. 실수가 있었는지 확인해 보았지만 그건 정말 내가 주문한 코트였다. 그 회사가 날 속였기 때문에 난 아주 화가 났다. 다시는 거기서 아무것도 구입하지 않을 것이다.

22 다음을 듣고, 지도에서 남자의 집을 고르시오.

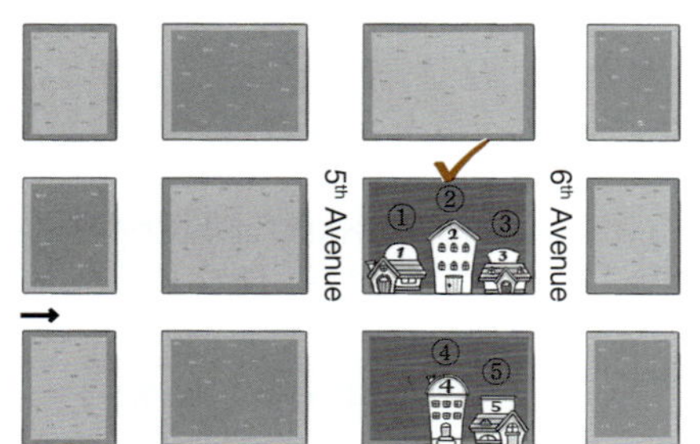

▶ answering machine 자동응답기 direction 지시, 방향 get to …에 이르다 intersection (주요 도로와의) 교차점 avenue 대로, (도로명으로서) …가 once 일단 …하면 lead to …에 이르다, …로 통하다 hang a left 왼쪽으로 돌다 be located (건물 등이) 위치하다 in front of … 앞에, 정면에

M Hello, Gina. This is Chuck. I was expecting to talk to you in person, but I got your answering machine instead. Okay, I'm going to leave some directions on how to get to my house for tonight's party. I hope they make sense because I might not be able to answer the phone if you call. Now, you'll be coming from your house on Oak Street. So go east for two blocks from the intersection of Oak Street and Second Avenue. You'll need to go past Third Avenue. However, once you get to Fourth Avenue, I want you to take a right and go one block. That's going to lead to Franklin Road, where you should hang an immediate left and go two more blocks. My house is located on the block between Fifth and Sixth avenues. It's the second house on the left-hand side of the road. There will probably be several cars in front of the house, so you can't miss it. I hope to see you soon.

남 안녕, 지나. 나 척이야. 직접 얘기하려고 했는데 대신 자동응답기가 받네. 좋아, 오늘밤 파티 때 우리 집에 오는 방법을 좀 남겨놓을게. 네가 전화해도 받을 수 없을지 모르니까 이해가 제대로 되면 좋겠다. 자, 넌 오크 스트리트에 있는 집에서 올 거잖아. 그러니까 오크 스트리트와 이번가 교차지점에서 두 블록 동쪽으로 가. 3번가를 지나야 해. 하지만 일단 사번가에 도착하면 우회전해서 한 블록을 가. 그럼 프랭클린 로드로 이어질 거야. 거기서 바로 왼쪽으로 돌아서 두 블록을 더 가. 우리 집은 5번가와 6번가 사이 블록에 있어. 그 도로 왼쪽 편에서 두 번째 집이야. 아마 집 앞에 차가 몇 대 있을 거니까 반드시 찾을 거야. 곧 만나길 바랄게.

23 다섯 개의 대화문을 듣고, 자연스럽지 <u>않은</u> 것을 고르시오.

①
②
③
④
✓

▶ make up one's mind 결정하다 assignment 임무, (임명된) 지위 trust 신뢰하다 ought to …해야 하다 cab 택시 have a point 일리가 있다 hurry 서두르다 come down with …병에 걸리다 flu 유행성 감기, 독감

① M Do you have any plans for this coming three-day weekend?

W I haven't really given it too much thought. Did you have something in mind?

② W Have you decided what you're going to order yet?

M No, I haven't. Everything on the menu looks so delicious that I can't make up my mind.

③ M You look really happy about something. What's going on?

W Mr. Smith just gave me my new work assignment, and he's going to let me be the team leader.

① 남 다가오는 3일 동안의 주말에 어떤 계획 있어?

여 그다지 생각 안 해 봤는데. 뭐 생각하는 거 있니?

② 여 뭘 주문할지 이미 결정했어?

남 아니, 못했어. 메뉴에 있는 게 모두 아주 맛있어 보여서 결정을 못하겠어.

③ 남 뭔가 정말 행복해 보이는데. 무슨 일이야?

여 스미스 씨가 방금 내게 새 업무를 부여했는데, 내가 팀장이 되게 해 줄 거야.

④ W We're running a little late, so we ought to take a cab to the opera house.

M Are you sure about that? At this time of night, traffic in that area might not be so good.

⑤ M I haven't been feeling very well these days. I think that I'm coming down with something.

W Yeah, he told me that I have the flu, so I need to stay in bed for a day or two.

④ 여 좀 늦었으니까 오페라하우스까지 택시를 타야겠어.

남 정말? 이런 밤 시간엔 그 지역 교통이 그다지 안 좋을 텐데.

⑤ 남 요즘 내 몸 상태가 별로 안 좋아. 무슨 병에 걸렸나봐.

여 그래, 그가 내가 독감이 걸려서 하루나 이틀 누워 있어야 한다고 했어.

---

24 대화를 듣고, 두 사람에 대해 유추할 수 있는 것을 고르시오.

✓① 그들은 신혼부부이다.
② 그들은 정장을 주로 입는다.
③ 그들은 원하는 물건을 모두 구입할 예정이다.
④ 그들은 매일 밤 손님을 맞는다.
⑤ 그들에게는 충분한 예산이 있다.

▶ department 매장 practically 사실상, 거의 …나 다름없이 furnish (집 등에 가구 등을) 갖추다, 비치하다 dresser 화장대, 찬장 couch (보통 등받이와 팔걸이가 있는) 긴 의자, 소파 company 동행, 친구(들) alone 단독으로 wardrobe 양복장, 옷장 suit (양복의) 한 벌, 슈트 afford …할 수 있다, 여유가 있다 closet 벽장 for now 당분간, 현재로선

W Let's go to the furniture department. We need to purchase some furniture for our house since there's practically nothing in it now.

M It'd be nice to furnish our house, but do you think we have enough money?

W I know the wedding and honeymoon last month cost a lot of money, but we really need some things. I mean, we've got a bed and a dresser, but we don't even own a couch.

M Yeah, I suppose it doesn't look good when we have company and don't have a sofa for them to sit on.

W It was so embarrassing when Jack and Lisa were at our place the other night.

M All right, so let's get a sofa. What else do you think we ought to buy?

W I was thinking of getting a dining table with four chairs. That should be perfect for whenever we're eating alone or when we've got another couple over. And you'll be able to work at it when we aren't having dinner.

M I like the sound of that. Hey, how about that wardrobe over there? I could use a place to hang my suits.

W I don't know if we can afford it. Let's just keep them in the closet for now.

여 가구 매장으로 가자. 지금 집에 사실상 아무것도 없으니까 필요한 가구를 좀 사야 해.

남 집에 가구를 들이는 건 좋겠지만 돈이 충분한 것 같니?

여 지난달에 결혼이랑 신혼여행 경비로 돈이 많이 든 건 알지만 정말 필요한 것들이 있어. 침대와 화장대는 있지만 소파도 없잖아.

남 그래, 손님들이 왔을 때 앉을 소파가 없으면 안 좋겠다.

여 요전날 밤에 잭과 리사가 집에 왔을 때 참 당황했어.

남 알았어, 그러니까 소파를 사자. 다른 건 뭘 사야 할 것 같니?

여 의자 네 개랑 식탁을 살 생각이었어. 그럼 우리끼리 먹을 때나 다른 커플들이 왔을 때나 언제든 완벽할 거야. 그리고 식사를 안 할 땐 거기서 일을 할 수도 있고.

남 좋은 생각이야. 이것 봐, 저기 있는 옷장은 어때? 내 양복을 걸어 둘 수 있을 것 같은데.

여 그걸 살 여력이 있을지 모르겠어. 당분간 양복은 그냥 벽장에 두기로 해.

---

25 다음을 듣고, 쇼트 프로그램과 롱 프로그램 점수를 합산한 점수가 가장 높아 스케이트 대회에서 우승한 사람이 누구일지 고르시오.

① Lisa Thompson
② Nancy Logan
③ Emily Bender
✓④ Mayu Fujikawa
⑤ Katrina Schmidt

▶ award (상 등을) 수여하다 performer 연기자, 선수 exceptionally 이례적으로, 유별나게 segment 부분, 구분 unheard 들어본 적 없는, 알려지지 않는 event 시합[경기], 종목 routine 정해진 순서, 판에 박힌 연기 keep from …을 삼가다 overall 전체에 걸친, 종합적인

W Now, let's move to the recent news from women's figure skating, where the gold medal was awarded tonight. The top three performers in the short program were Katrina Schmidt, who scored 95 points, Mayu Fujikawa with 94 points, and Emily Bender with 93 points. The short program was one of the most exciting in recent memory as a number of skaters performed exceptionally well. However, those three came out best out of all of the performers. Now, let's take a look at the scores from the long program. We have the top five performers from the long program for you. Nancy Logan won that segment of the event by scoring an unheard of 97 points. Unfortunately, her short program routine, where she fell down a couple of times, kept her from achieving overall victory. In second place was Mayu Fujikawa with a score of 95, and in third was Lisa Thompson with 94 points. Emily Bender and Katrina Schmidt both got scores of 92 in their long programs.

여 이제 오늘밤 금메달이 수여된 여자 피겨스케이팅의 최신 뉴스를 알아보죠. 쇼트 프로그램에서 세 명의 최고 선수는 95점을 기록한 카트리나 슈미트와 94점을 얻은 마유 후지카와, 그리고 93점을 얻은 에밀리 벤더입니다. 쇼트 프로그램은 많은 스케이트 선수들이 이례적으로 잘 연기했기 때문에 최근에 가장 흥미진진했던 것 중 하나로 기억됩니다. 하지만 모든 선수들 중에서 그 세 명이 최고로 드러났습니다. 이제, 롱 프로그램의 점수를 살펴보시죠. 롱 프로그램에는 다섯 명의 최고 선수들이 있습니다. 낸시 로건은 전례없는 97점을 기록해서 대회 해당 부문에서 승리를 거뒀습니다. 안타깝게도 쇼트 프로그램 연기에서 몇 번 넘어져서 전체적인 승리를 거두지는 못했습니다. 2위는 마유 후지카와로 95점을 받았으며 3위는 94점을 받은 리사 톰슨이었습니다. 에밀리 벤더와 카트리나 슈미트 두 선수는 롱 프로그램에서 92점을 얻었습니다.

<table>
<tr><th>문제와 정답</th><th>스크립트</th><th>해석</th></tr>
</table>

26 대화를 듣고, 아들의 마지막 질문에 대한 여자의 응답으로 알맞은 것을 고르시오.

W: ______________________________

① The laboratory where he did most of his work was in New Jersey.
② People still remember Edison for the important research he did.
✓③ He invented the phonograph, which could play sounds like music.
④ He never finished school since his teacher thought he was stupid.
⑤ He filed a patent for his electric light bulb in 1879.

① 그가 대부분의 작업을 한 실험실은 뉴저지에 있었단다.
② 사람들은 여전히 에디슨이 한 중요한 연구 때문에 그를 기억하지.
③ 그는 축음기를 발명했는데, 그건 음악 같은 소리를 낼 수 있었어.
④ 선생님이 그를 멍청하다고 생각했기 때문에 그는 결코 학교를 마치지 못했단다.
⑤ 그는 1879년에 자신의 전구에 대한 특허를 신청했어.

▶ **explanation** 설명 **inventor** 발명가 **hold** 보유하다, 확보하다 **patent** 특허 **brilliant** 명석한 **assist** 도와주다, 거들다 **electric light bulb** 전구 **manage to** 그럭저럭 해내다, 용케 …을 해내다 **the public** 일반 사람들, 대중 **accomplish** 이룩하다, 완성하다 **aside from** …이외에, …은 별도로 하고

M Mom, we learned about Thomas Edison in history class today, but I don't think our teacher's explanation was good enough. Do you know anything about him?

W Well, I know a few things. For example, he was one of the greatest inventors in all history. I believe that he even held over 1,000 patents.

M Wow, he must have been really busy inventing things.

W That's true, but he also had a huge number of technicians and scientists working for him. He was a brilliant man, but other people assisted him in making all of the inventions that he did.

M What exactly did he invent? I know he was the first person to make an electric light bulb.

W Actually, he wasn't the first person to make a light bulb. Several other people managed to make light bulbs before Edison did. However, he was the first to make one that was practical and could be sold to the public. That's an important difference.

M Oh, I didn't realize that.

W Most people don't. But that still doesn't mean he didn't accomplish great things. There were also several other important inventions that he made aside from the light bulb.

M Like what? Can you tell me?

W ______________________________

남 엄마, 오늘 역사 수업시간에 토머스 에디슨에 대해 배웠는데, 선생님 설명이 충분하지 않은 것 같아요. 그 사람에 대해 좀 아세요?

여 음, 약간 알아. 예를 들면 역사상 가장 위대한 발명가 중 한사람이었지. 특허를 1,000건이 넘게 보유하고 있을 거야.

남 우와, 물건을 발명하느라 정말로 바빴겠네요.

여 맞아, 하지만 그를 위해 일하는 기술자와 과학자들도 엄청나게 많이 있었어. 그는 명석한 사람이었지만 다른 사람들이 그가 모든 발명품을 만드는 걸 도왔지.

남 정확히 뭘 발명했어요? 최초로 전구를 만든 사람인 건 알아요.

여 사실은 그가 전구를 만든 최초의 사람은 아니었어. 다른 몇 사람이 에디슨 이전에 전구를 만들어냈단다. 하지만 에디슨이 실용적이고 대중들에게 판매할 수 있는 전구를 만든 최초의 사람이었지. 그게 중요한 차이야.

남 아, 그건 몰랐어요.

여 대부분의 사람들이 몰라. 하지만 그렇다고 해서 그가 훌륭한 일을 하지 않았다는 뜻은 아니야. 전구 외에도 다른 몇 가지 중요한 발명도 했어.

남 어떤 거요? 말해 주실래요?

여 ______________________________

---

27 대화를 듣고, 두 사람이 딸에게 취할 태도로 올바르지 <u>않</u>은 것을 고르시오.

① 딸이 더 일찍 잠자리에 들게 한다.
② 주말에 딸이 집에 있으면서 공부를 하게 한다.
③ 딸이 숙제를 끝내면 그것을 검사한다.
④ 가끔씩 딸이 외출하는 것을 못하게 한다.
✓⑤ 딸이 친구들을 만나는 것을 허락하지 않는다.

▶ **be concerned about** …에 대해 염려하다 **personality** 성격, 인격 **hang out with** …와 어울리다 **grant ... permission** …에게 허락하다 **forbid ... from** …이 ~하는 것을 금지하다 **socialize with** …와 격의없이 교제하다 **go with** …에게 동조하다, 동의하다 **go over** …을 잘 살펴보다, 검토하다 **confirm** 확인하다, 뒷받침하다 **humanities** 인문 과학 **turn ... around** …을 나쁜 상태에서 좋은 상태로 바꾸다, 호전시키다

M I'm concerned about Sue since it seems her personality has been changing lately.

W I agree. I think she might be hanging out with some students who are bad influences. Her grades have been dropping lately, and, if they keep getting worse, she'll never get accepted by a good college.

M We've got to do something. What do you suggest?

W Hmm… We could stop granting her permission to go out on the weekends so that she'd have to stay home and study.

M I like that idea. And why don't we make sure she goes to bed earlier every night. She's always exhausted and could really use a good night's sleep.

W All right. But do you think we should forbid her from seeing her friends?

M I don't think that's right. She should determine for herself which friends are okay to socialize with and which ones aren't.

W I'm not so sure, but we'll go with your idea for now. But I definitely feel we should go over her homework with her every night. That way we'll confirm that she's doing it and doing it well.

M I agree. You can look at the humanities while I'll cover math and science.

W I hope she can turn things around.

남 최근 수가 성격이 변하는 것 같아서 걱정이 돼.

여 동감이야. 일부 나쁜 영향을 주는 학생들과 어울리는 건 아닌가 몰라. 성적이 최근에 떨어지고 있는데, 계속 나빠지면 좋은 대학에 절대 들어갈 수 없을 거야.

남 뭔가 행동을 취해야겠는데. 뭐 없을까?

여 흠… 집에 남아서 공부하게 주말에 외출하는 걸 허락하지 않을 수도 있을 것 같은데.

남 그거 좋은 생각이야. 그리고 매일 밤 더 일찍 잠들게 하는 것 어때? 항상 지쳐 있으니까 잠을 잘 잘 수 있을 거야.

여 좋아. 그런데 친구 만나는 건 금지해야 할 것 같아?

남 그건 아닌 것 같아. 그 애 스스로 어떤 친구들이 어울리면 괜찮고 어떤 친구는 아닌지를 스스로 판단해야 해.

여 잘 모르겠지만 지금은 당신 생각을 따를게. 하지만 분명히 매일 밤 그 애 숙제를 봐줘야 할 것 같아. 그럼 그 애가 숙제를 하고 있고 잘 하는지 확인할 수 있잖아.

남 그래. 내가 수학과 과학을 맡을 테니 당신은 인문 분야를 보면 되겠다.

여 그 애 상황이 좋아지면 좋겠어.

<table>
<tr><th>문제와 정답</th><th>스크립트</th><th>해석</th></tr>
</table>

28 다음을 듣고, 화자의 의견에 동의하는 진술을 고르시오.

✔① 래리: 우리는 사람들이 환경을 파괴하지 못하도록 하는 새로운 법이 필요하다.
② 스티브: 나는 개발을 저지하려는 환경론자들 때문에 아주 짜증이 난다.
③ 제레미: 우리가 계속 땅을 개발하지 않으면 경제는 악화될 것이다.
④ 카렌: 우리는 많은 기존 건물을 파괴하고 자연이 그 지역을 대체하도록 해야 한다.
⑤ 제니: 우리는 개발업자들의 사업을 금지시켜 그들이 자연을 더 이상 손상시키지 않도록 해야 한다.

▶ be on a person's mind (사물이) 남의 마음에 걸려 있다 preserve 보존하다 cf. preservation 보존 erect (건조물을) 세우다, 설립하다 fine line 가느다란 줄, 좋은 것과 나쁜 것 두 가지 간에 차이를 구분하기 어려운 것 destroy 파괴하다 prosper 번영하다 set aside (물건 등을 미래를 위해) 떼어놓다, 제쳐놓다 abundant in …이 풍부한(＝teem with) wildlife 야생생물 obtain 획득하다

M Something that's on many people's minds now is the environment. It's important to protect and preserve the environment, but people also need to develop places in order to erect homes and buildings, construct roads, and complete other construction projects. It's a fine line people are walking: They don't want to destroy the environment, but they simply can't leave it alone, or else humans won't be able to prosper. That's why I believe the government should set aside certain lands for preservation. These could be areas that are abundant in wildlife. For example, there's a huge forest near my home which is teeming with animals. Some local developers are trying to obtain permission to construct houses on it, but I don't think they should be allowed to do so. If they cut down the forest, what'll happen to all of the animals? Instead, the developers should use land that has already been developed. This way, they can construct their new buildings without destroying any more of the environment than is necessary.

남 지금 많은 사람들이 염려하는 것이 환경이다. 환경을 보호하고 보존하는 것은 중요하지만 사람들은 또한 집과 건물을 세우고 도로를 건설하고 기타 건축 프로젝트를 완공하기 위해 곳곳을 개발할 필요가 있다. 그것은 사람들이 줄타기를 하는 것과 마찬가지로, 사람들은 환경을 파괴하고 싶지는 않지만 그냥 내버려 둘 수도 없다. 그렇지 않으면 인간들은 번영할 수 없을 것이다. 그래서 나는 정부가 보존을 위한 특정한 땅을 할당해 놓아야 한다고 생각한다. 이러한 땅은 야생생물이 풍부한 지역이 될 수 있을 것이다. 예를 들어 우리 집 근처에는 동물들이 많은 커다란 숲이 있다. 어떤 지역 개발업자들은 그 땅에 집을 건축하기 위해 허가를 얻으려 하고 있지만 난 그들이 그렇게 하도록 허용되어서는 안 된다고 생각한다. 만일 그들이 숲을 베어내면, 모든 동물들에게는 어떤 일이 일어날까? 대신에 개발업자들은 이미 개발된 땅을 사용해야 한다. 이런 방식으로 그들은 필요 이상으로 환경을 더 파괴하지 않고 새 건물을 건축할 수 있다.

---

29 대화를 듣고, 두 사람이 먹을 음식을 모두 고르시오.

ⓐ baked potato
ⓑ corn
ⓒ chicken wings
ⓓ broiled scallops
ⓔ mushroom soup
ⓕ potato skins
ⓖ roast fish
ⓗ vegetable soup

① ⓐ, ⓑ, ⓒ, ⓓ, ⓖ
✔② ⓐ, ⓑ, ⓓ, ⓕ, ⓗ
③ ⓐ, ⓑ, ⓒ, ⓓ, ⓕ
④ ⓒ, ⓓ, ⓔ, ⓕ, ⓖ
⑤ ⓐ, ⓒ, ⓓ, ⓕ, ⓖ

▶ appetizer 전채, (일반적으로) 식욕을 돋우는 것 as for …에 관한 한은, …은 어떠냐 하면 for starters 우선, 첫째로 entrée 앙트레: 생선 요리와 고기 요리 사이에 나오는 요리, 불고기 이외의 주요리 roast 구이 side dish 곁들임 요리, 반찬 not nearly 도저히[결코] …이 아니다 slip one's mind 잊어버리다, 생각나지 않다 on second thought 다시 생각해 보니 broil (고기 등을) (불에) 굽다, 석쇠 구이로 하다 scallop 가리비

W I'm so glad we decided to come here for dinner. I haven't eaten anything all day long, and this is my favorite restaurant.

M I know what you mean. The chicken wings here are really delicious.

W Are you going to be ordering those? I was thinking about it, but I'm going to go with the vegetable soup for an appetizer instead.

M That's a nice, healthy choice. As for me, I'm going to get the potato skins for starters. I love the way they cook them here. What about your entrée?

W I'm definitely getting the roast pork for dinner. And I think I'll get the baked potato for my side dish.

M Yum, that sounds absolutely delicious. I'm not nearly as hungry as you though, so I think I'm just going to order the roast fish.

W What? Don't you remember what happened the last time we were here? You tried my fish but couldn't stand it.

M Oh, right. That completely slipped my mind. On second thought, instead of that, I'm going to have the broiled scallops. And I'm going to get some corn with it.

W Those are much better choices.

M Okay, so if we're ready to order, let's find our waiter now.

여 여기로 저녁 먹으러 오게 돼서 정말 기뻐. 하루 종일 아무것도 못 먹었는데 여긴 내가 좋아하는 식당이거든.

남 무슨 말인지 알아. 여기 닭날개는 정말 맛있지.

여 너 그거 주문할 거야? 난 그걸 생각하고 있었지만 대신 애피타이저로 야채수프를 할게.

남 건강에 좋은 훌륭한 선택이야. 난 먼저 포테이토 스킨을 먹겠어. 여기 포테이토 스킨 요리 솜씨가 좋거든. 앙트레는 어떻게 할래?

여 당연히 저녁으론 돼지고기 구이를 먹을 거야. 그리고 구운 감자를 곁들여 먹을래.

남 와, 그거 정말 맛있겠다. 하지만 난 너만큼 배고프진 않으니까 그냥 생선 구이를 주문할게.

여 뭐라고? 지난번 여기 왔을 때 생긴 일 기억 안 나니? 내 생선을 먹어 보고서는 못 견뎌했잖아.

남 아, 맞다. 까마득히 잊어버렸어. 다시 생각해 보니까 그것 대신 조개 구이를 먹어야겠어. 또 옥수수도 같이 시켜야지.

여 그게 훨씬 나아.

남 됐어, 그럼 주문할 준비가 됐으면 이제 웨이터를 찾아보자.

30 다음을 듣고, 화자의 마지막 말에 이어질 내용으로 가장 알맞은 것을 고르시오.

> So, when meeting American businessmen for the first time, you'd better ___________ ___________.

① be as outgoing as possible
② remember to speak with everyone
✓③ try not to offend anyone
④ offer to shake hands with everyone
⑤ pass out your business cards to them

> 그러니까, 처음으로 미국인 사업가들을 만날 때는 ___________ ___________ 좋습니다.

① 가능한 사교적인 사람이 되는 것이
② 모든 사람과 이야기를 나눠야 한다는 것을 기억하는 것이
③ 누구의 감정도 상하지 않게 하는 것이
④ 모든 사람에게 악수를 청하는 것이
⑤ 그들에게 명함을 나눠 주는 것이

▶ **business trip** 출장 **shake hands** 악수하다 **offer** 청하다, …하려고 하다 **chat** 잡담하다 **flight** 비행기 여행 **negative** 부정적인 *cf.* positive 긍정적인 **comment** 의견, 비평 **overweight** 중량 초과의, 살이 찐 **ruin** 망쳐놓다

W You're all visiting the United States on a business trip next week. You need to remember that American business culture is much different than ours, so there are some things you must remember. First, when you meet American businessmen, they're all going to shake hands with you. If there are any women, they also might offer to shake hands with you. Should they do that, be sure to accept their offer. Then they're going to chat with you for a few minutes. They'll ask you about your flight and how you like the country. Be sure not to say anything negative. You want to seem positive in all of your comments. And don't make any comments about what the Americans look like. Even if the person is handsome or beautiful, you shouldn't mention that. And definitely don't say anything about a person who might be overweight or not be very good-looking. If you do that, you could ruin the entire meeting. So, when meeting American businessmen for the first time, you'd better ______ ________________.

여 여러분은 모두 다음주에 출장 차 미국을 방문하시게 됩니다. 미국의 사업 문화는 우리와 훨씬 달라서 반드시 기억하셔야 할 것들이 몇 가지 있다는 걸 알아 두실 필요가 있습니다. 먼저 미국인 사업가들을 만날 때 그들은 모두 여러분과 악수를 할 겁니다. 여성이 있으면 그들 또한 여러분에게 악수를 청할지도 모릅니다. 그럴 경우 그 청을 받아들이도록 하십시오. 그런 다음 그들은 잠시 여러분과 담소를 나눌 것입니다. 여러분의 비행과 그 나라를 어떻게 생각하는지에 관해 물어 볼 겁니다. 어떤 것이든 부정적인 말은 하지 마십시오. 여러분이 하는 말이 모두 긍정적이라는 인상을 주고 싶으시겠죠. 그리고 미국인들의 외모에 대해 어떤 언급도 하지 마십시오. 그 사람이 잘생겼거나 아름답더라도 그걸 언급해서는 안 됩니다. 그리고 절대로 뚱뚱해 보이거나 아주 잘 생겨 보이지 않는 사람에 관해 아무 것도 말하지 마십시오. 그렇게 하셨다가는 회의 전체를 망칠 수 있습니다. 그러니까, 처음으로 미국인 사업가들을 만날 때는 ___________ 좋습니다.

---

31 〔모두 듣기〕 **What is this speech for?**

① To promote a movie
✓② To accept an award
③ To congratulate her parents
④ To announce a new film
⑤ To give some advice

이 이야기는 무엇을 위한 것인가?

① 영화를 홍보하기 위해
② 수상을 받아들이기 위해
③ 부모님을 축하해 드리기 위해
④ 신작 영화를 발표하기 위해
⑤ 충고를 주기 위해

▶ **stun** 놀라게 하다, 아연하게 하다 **deserve of** …을 받을 만하다 **award** 상 **there's no way** 절대 …하지 않는다 **(all) by myself** 나 혼자 힘으로, 나 혼자서 **in the first place** 애당초, 처음부터 **encourage** 격려하다 **doubt** 의심하다, 믿지 않다 **make it** 잘해내다, 성공하다 **gave up** 포기하다 **tremendous** 굉장히 멋진〔좋은〕

W I'm absolutely stunned to be standing up here in front of everyone this evening. After all, there are so many others who are much more deserving of this award than I am. And I'd like for everyone to know that there's no way that I could have accomplished this all by myself. I owe my success to a lot of different people. These people have made tonight possible, and, without them, I'm sure I never would have been able to become an actor in the first place. First, I'd like to thank my parents Allen and Wendy for encouraging me when most people doubted I'd ever make it in acting. They had faith in me, and they made sure I never gave up my dream. And my director, John Davidson, was tremendous, as were the rest of my co-stars in the film. They're the ones who should be up here tonight instead of me.

여 저는 오늘 저녁 모든 분 앞에서 이곳에 서게 되어 정말로 놀랐습니다. 어쨌거나 저보다 훨씬 더 이 상을 받을 만한 분들이 아주 많이 계십니다. 그리고 저 혼자서는 이 모든 것을 절대로 이룰 수 없었을 것이라는 점을 모든 분께 말씀 드리고 싶습니다. 저의 성공은 많은 다른 분들의 덕분입니다. 이 분들 때문에 오늘밤이 가능했고 그들이 없었다면 저는 결코 처음부터 배우가 될 수 없었을 것입니다. 먼저, 많은 사람들이 제가 연기로 성공할 수 있을지 의아해 했을 때 저를 격려해 주신 것에 대해 부모님인 앨런과 웬디 두 분께 감사 드리고 싶습니다. 부모님은 절 믿어 주셨고 제가 꿈을 포기하지 않도록 해 주셨습니다. 그리고 존 데이비슨 감독님은 굉장히 멋진 분이셨으며 영화에 출연한 다른 동료 스타분들도 그랬습니다. 그 분들이 저 대신 오늘밤 여기에 서야 할 분들입니다.

32 〔모두 듣기〕 **What is this talk about?**

① Why the Americans declared their independence from England

② The history of July 4 from 1776 to the present

③ The foods that most Americans eat on July 4

✓ How many Americans celebrate Independence Day

⑤ Where Americans socialize on Independence Day

이 이야기는 무엇에 관한 것인가?

① 왜 미국인은 영국으로부터 독립을 선언했는가

② 1776년부터 현재까지의 7월 4일의 역사

③ 대부분의 미국인들이 7월 4일에 먹는 요리들

④ 많은 미국인들은 독립기념일을 어떻게 축하하는가

⑤ 미국인들은 독립기념일을 어디서 보내는가

▶ colony 식민지 declare 선포하다 colonial master (식민지의) 종주국 annually 매년 majority of 대다수의 reflect upon …에 대해 숙고하다 countless 무수한, 수많은 make the most out of …을 최대한으로 활용하다 fall (날짜가 어떤 때에) 해당하다 partake in (활동 등에) 참가하다 cookout 야외 파티, 야외 요리 all in all 무엇보다도

M One of the most important holidays in the United States falls on July 4. This holiday is known as Independence Day, for it is the day back in 1776 when the American colonies declared their independence from England, their colonial master. For more than 200 years, Americans have annually celebrated this day in a number of different ways. As it's a national holiday in the U.S., the majority of people get the day off from work. While not so many people take the time to reflect upon their freedoms anymore, countless Americans attempt to make the most out of their day off. Since Independence Day falls in the summer, many Americans partake in outdoor activities. They may have picnics with their families, go camping, watch parades, or even attend baseball games. Additionally, they often have cookouts or barbecues, where hamburgers, hotdogs, and steaks are the main foods. All in all, it's a fun day for many people.

남 미국에서 가장 중요한 휴일 중 하나는 7월 4일이다. 이 휴일은 독립기념일로 알려져 있는데, 1776년에 미국 식민지가 종주국인 영국에서 독립을 선포했던 날이기 때문이다. 200년 이상 미국인들은 매년 이 날을 다른 많은 방식으로 기념해 왔다. 이 날은 미국의 국경일이기 때문에 대다수의 사람들이 직장을 쉰다. 자유에 대해 숙고해 볼 시간을 갖는 사람은 그리 많지 않은 반면에 수많은 미국인들은 휴일을 최대한 활용하려 한다. 독립기념일이 여름에 있기 때문에 많은 미국인들은 야외활동을 즐긴다. 그들은 가족들과 야유회를 가거나 야영을 가기도 하고, 퍼레이드를 구경하거나 야구경기를 참관하기도 한다. 게다가 종종 야외 파티, 즉 바비큐를 하는데, 이때는 햄버거와 핫도그, 스테이크가 주식이다. 무엇보다도 그날은 많은 사람들에게 즐거운 날이다.

---

33 〔모두 듣기〕 **Which of the following sports do the speakers like in common?**

✓ Baseball

② Volleyball

③ Football

④ Basketball

⑤ Soccer

화자들이 공통으로 좋아하는 스포츠는 무엇인가?

① 야구

② 배구

③ 축구

④ 농구

⑤ 축구

▶ imaginable 상상할[생각할] 수 있는, 가능한 scoring 득점, 시합 기록 come to think of it (다시) 생각해보니, 그러고 보니 appreciate 진가를 인정하다[알다] appeal 사람의 마음을 움직이는 힘, 매력

W Are you still watching that football game? I thought you said it was about to end thirty minutes ago.

M There are still two minutes left. Sometimes football games take a long time to end.

W I don't know how you can stand watching those games. You should try another sport like soccer.

M You've got to be kidding. That's the most boring sport imaginable. There's never any scoring like there is in basketball.

W That's yet another sport which takes forever to end.

M I guess you're right about that. At least you don't mind watching baseball games with me sometimes.

W I think the reason is that my brothers both played it when they were young. But, come to think of it, they also played volleyball, and I don't enjoy that sport either.

M I sometimes just think you don't appreciate sports at all. You ought to give them a chance. They're great exercise and really fun to play and watch.

W I don't know. I simply don't get the appeal of most sports.

M Anyway, the game's about to finish. Let me get back to watching it.

여 아직도 그 풋볼 경기 보고 있어? 30분전에 끝날 거라고 말했던 것 같은데.

남 아직 2분 남았어. 풋볼경기는 가끔 끝나는 데 시간이 많이 걸려.

여 그런 경기를 어떻게 참고 보는지 모르겠어. 축구 같은 다른 스포츠를 보려고 해봐.

남 농담하지 마. 그건 상상할 수 있는 한 가장 지루한 운동이라고. 야구에서 같은 득점은 절대 못 올리잖아.

여 하지만 그것도 끝나는 데 시간이 무진장 오래 걸리는 또 하나의 스포츠지.

남 그건 네 말이 맞을 거야. 어쨌든 넌 가끔 나랑 야구 경기를 보잖아.

여 내 생각에 그건 남자형제 둘이 어렸을 때 야구를 했기 때문인 것 같아. 하지만 생각해보니까 그들은 배구도 했는데, 난 그 운동도 싫거든.

남 가끔은 네가 스포츠의 진가를 전혀 모른다는 생각이 들어. 기회를 줘 봐. 스포츠는 훌륭한 운동이고 경기하는 것도 관전하는 것도 정말 재미있어.

여 모르겠어. 난 그냥 대부분의 스포츠는 흥미를 못 느끼겠어.

남 아무튼 이 경기는 막 끝나려고 해. 다시 볼 게.

<table>
<tr><th>문제와 정답</th><th>스크립트</th><th>해석</th></tr>
<tr><td>

34 〔모두 듣기〕 **Which is the relationship between the speakers?**

① A dog owner and a pet shop owner
② A veterinarian and a nurse
③ A nurse and a dog groomer
✓ A veterinarian and a dog owner
⑤ A pet shop owner and a veterinarian

두 화자의 관계를 나타낸 것은?

① 개 주인과 애완동물 가게 주인
② 수의사와 간호사
③ 간호사와 애견 미용사
④ 수의사와 개 주인
⑤ 애완동물 가게 주인과 수의사

▶ scratch 긁다 appetite 식욕 lethargic 졸리는, 무기력한 hearty (식욕이) 왕성한 constant 끊임없이 계속되는 bother 괴롭히다, 귀찮게 하다 formality 형식적인 행위 pick up (감기 등에) 걸리다 flea 벼룩 in no time 곧, 바로

</td><td>

M Good afternoon, Mrs. Baker. What brings you here today?

W I think Choco's got something wrong with her skin. She keeps scratching herself all the time and won't stop.

M Does she have any other problems? For example, has she been suffering from a loss of appetite? Or perhaps she may seem lethargic at times?

W Oh, goodness no. I don't think I've ever seen a more active dog. Choco loves to run around the house and play with her toys. And she still has a hearty appetite.

M That's good to hear. I was worried it might be something serious.

W No, it seems the constant scratching is all that's bothering her. She started scratching right after I took her on a walk four days ago.

M Okay, I think I know what her problem is then. Let me take some skin samples first, but that's really just a formality.

W Why is that? What's wrong?

M She probably picked up some fleas while she was outside. But don't worry. I'll give her some special shampoo and medicine, and she'll be better in no time.

W That's great to hear.

</td><td>

남 안녕하세요, 베이커 부인. 오늘은 어떻게 여기 오셨습니까?

여 초코가 피부에 뭔가 문제가 있는 것 같아요. 항상 끊임없이 몸을 긁는데 멈추질 않아요.

남 다른 문제는 없나요? 이를테면 식욕을 잃고 있나요? 아니면 가끔씩 무기력해 보인다던가요?

여 오, 이런, 아니오. 초코보다 더 활동적인 개는 본 적이 없는 것 같아요. 집을 뛰어다니고 장난감을 가지고 노는 걸 좋아하죠. 또 아직은 식욕도 왕성한 걸요.

남 잘됐네요. 뭔가 심각한 게 아닌가 걱정했는데.

여 아니에요, 계속 긁는 것만 문제인 것 같아요. 4일 전에 산책을 하러 간 직후부터 긁기 시작했어요.

남 알았습니다, 그럼 문제가 뭔지 알 것 같네요. 먼저 피부 샘플을 좀 채취해 볼 건데, 그건 정말 그냥 형식적인 겁니다.

여 왜요? 뭐가 잘못됐죠?

남 아마 야외에 있을 때 벼룩이 좀 붙었나 봐요. 하지만 걱정 마세요. 특별한 샴푸와 약을 좀 줄 테니 곧 괜찮아질 거예요.

여 다행이군요.

</td></tr>
<tr><td>

35 다음을 듣고, 이어지는 영어 질문에 답하시오.

① 4:00
② 6:00
③ 7:00
✓ 8:00
⑤ 10:00

▶ seashell (바다의) 조개, 조가비 while …하는 동안, 반면에 every twelve minutes 12분마다

</td><td>

M At twelve o'clock in the afternoon, Sally and Lisa go to the beach and start looking for pretty seashells. Sally already had eight seashells while Lisa had none. Sally finds a pretty seashell every twelve minutes, but Lisa looks harder, so she finds a pretty seashell every ten minutes.

Q: *What time will Lisa have the same number of seashells as Sally?*

</td><td>

남 오후 12시에 샐리와 리사는 해변에 가서 예쁜 조개를 찾기 시작했다. 샐리는 이미 여덟 개의 조개가 있는 반면 리사는 하나도 없었다. 샐리는 12분마다 예쁜 조개를 발견하고, 리사는 더 열심히 찾기 때문에 10분마다 예쁜 조개를 발견한다.

Q: *리사는 몇 시에 샐리와 똑같은 숫자의 조개껍질을 갖게 될까?*

</td></tr>
</table>

36 주어진 시간 동안 아래 지문을 주의 깊게 읽고, 대화를 들은 후 질문에 답하시오. 〔1분〕

In recent years, there has been something of a revolution in the way that people take care of their banking needs. In the past, people had to go into physical banks to do all sorts of transactions. Once ATMs were invented, then many transactions could be done through these machines. However, thanks to the newest innovation in banking services, many people no longer even need to leave their homes to do their banking. The reason is that Internet banking is becoming popular. Thanks to Internet banking, customers can enter their login and password onto the computer and can then do almost every transaction they want. They can check their account balance, transfer money, and even pay their bills. This keeps them from having to go to the bank for many transactions. However, they still cannot deposit or withdraw money online, but they can apply for loans, including personal loans and mortgages. Best of all is that Internet banking is completely safe. The banks use the most advanced software, which is protected with many safeguards. So long as the customer does not let anyone know his or her login and password, the customer's account information is entirely safe.

Q ___________________________

① Well, you can apply for personal loans online.
② I've just got to transfer some money really quickly.
③ Actually, you still can't deposit money online yet.
④ It keeps me from having to visit an ATM all of the time.
✓ The software is completely protected from hackers.

① 흠, 개인 대출을 온라인으로 신청할 수도 있어.
② 나 정말 급하게 돈을 약간 송금해야 해.
③ 사실, 넌 아직 온라인으로 돈을 예금할 수 없어.
④ 그것 때문에 내가 항상 현금자동인출기를 찾아가지 않아도 돼.
⑤ 소프트웨어가 해커들로부터 완전히 보호돼.

▶ **revolution** 혁명 **banking** 은행 업무, 은행업 **physical** 물리적인 **transaction** 거래 **account balance** 계좌 잔고 **transfer** 옮기다 **bill** 청구서, 청구금액 **deposit** (은행에) 예금하다 **withdraw** 인출하다 **loan** 대출(금) **mortgage** 주택 금융〔융자〕 **best of all** 무엇보다 특히, 첫째로 **safeguard** (기계 등의) 안전장치 **so long as** …하는 한 **unauthorized** 권한이 없는, 허가받지 않은

W Are you ready to go? We're going to be late.

M Hold on a second while I do some banking.

W How are you going to do any banking from your office? Isn't it a little late to be calling your banker?

M No, I'm doing Internet banking. I haven't paid a couple of my most recent bills, so I need to take care of them right now.

W Is that something new? I've never heard of Internet banking.

M It's been around for a while, but not everyone uses it.

W Well, I can understand that. After all, with all of those computer hackers out there, what happens if someone unauthorized gets access to your account? You could lose all of your money.

M I suppose that could happen, but it's actually pretty safe.

W I'm not so confident about that. What makes you believe that it's all right?

M ___________________________

Q: *Which is the best answer to the woman's last words?*

여 갈 준비 됐어? 늦겠어.

남 은행업무 좀 하게 잠깐만 기다려.

여 사무실에서 어떻게 은행업무를 본다는 거야? 은행원에게 전화하기엔 좀 늦지 않았어?

남 아니야, 인터넷뱅킹을 하는 거야. 최근 청구대금 몇 건을 지불하지 않아서 지금 당장 그걸 처리해야 해.

여 그거 새로운 거야? 난 인터넷뱅킹에 대해 전혀 못 들어 봤는데.

남 좀 되긴 했는데 모두가 그걸 사용하진 않아.

여 음, 알겠어. 하지만 컴퓨터 해커들이 있으니까 허가받지 않은 누군가가 네 계좌에 접속하면 어떤 일이 생기겠어? 돈을 모두 잃을 수도 있을 거야.

남 그런 일이 있을 수는 있겠지만 사실은 아주 안전해.

여 난 그렇게 확신 못하겠어. 그게 괜찮다고 넌 어떻게 믿니?

남 ___________________________

Q: *여자의 마지막 말에 대한 남자의 응답으로 알맞은 것은?*

최근 수년 사이에 사람들이 은행 업무를 처리하는 방식에서 혁명적인 일이 있었다. 과거에 사람들은 온갖 종류의 거래를 하기 위해 물리적인 은행에 가야 했다. 일단 현금자동인출기가 발명되자 그 다음엔 많은 거래가 이 기기를 통해 처리될 수 있었다. 하지만 가장 최근에 일어난 은행 업무의 혁명 덕분에 많은 사람들은 더 이상은 은행 업무를 보려고 집을 떠날 필요가 없다. 그 이유는 인터넷뱅킹이 대중화되고 있기 때문이다. 인터넷뱅킹 덕분에 고객들은 로그인과 비밀번호를 컴퓨터에 입력한 뒤 원하는 모든 거래를 거의 다 할 수 있다. 그들은 자신의 계좌 잔고를 확인하고 송금을 하고 심지어 청구대금을 납부할 수도 있다. 이로 인해 사람들은 많은 거래를 위해 은행에 가야 할 필요가 없다. 하지만 사람들은 여전히 돈을 온라인으로 예금하거나 인출할 수 없지만 신용대부와 주택융자를 포함한 개인 대출을 신청할 수는 있다. 무엇보다도 좋은 것은 인터넷뱅킹은 완전히 안전하다는 것이다. 은행들은 최고급 소프트웨어를 사용하는데 이것은 많은 안전장치로 보호된다. 고객이 자신의 로그인과 비밀번호를 아무도 알지 못하게 하는 한 고객의 계좌 정보는 전적으로 안전하다.

<table><tr><th>문제와 정답</th><th>스크립트</th><th>해석</th></tr></table>

37 Which of the following questions does the talk answer?

① Why did Bram Stoker write the novel *Dracula*?
✓ What are the characteristics of a vampire?
③ What is the best way to destroy a vampire?
④ Where do most vampires prefer to live?
⑤ How can a regular person become a vampire?

이 이야기는 어떤 질문에 답하고 있는가?

① 브람 스토커는 왜 소설 〈드라큘라〉를 썼는가?
② 흡혈귀의 특징들은 무엇인가?
③ 흡혈귀를 물리치는 가장 좋은 방법은 무엇인가?
④ 대부분의 흡혈귀들은 어디에 살기를 좋아하는가?
⑤ 보통 사람이 어떻게 흡혈귀가 될 수 있는가?

38 Which of the following is NOT true about vampires?

① They are much stronger than most people.
② They can turn other people into vampires.
✓ They must drink any kind of blood to survive.
④ They can be destroyed by a stake in the heart.
⑤ They can turn themselves into other animals.

다음 중 흡혈귀에 대해 사실이 <u>아닌</u> 것은 무엇인가?

① 그들은 일반 사람들보다 훨씬 더 강하다.
② 그들은 다른 사람들을 흡혈귀로 변하게 만들 수 있다.
③ 그들은 살기 위해 어떤 종류의 피라도 마셔야 한다.
④ 그들의 심장에 말뚝을 박으면 물리칠 수 있다.
⑤ 그들은 다른 동물로 변신할 수 있다.

▶ **stir** 대소동, 대평판 **chronicle** 기록에 올리다, 상술하다 **vicious** 사악한 **that is (to say)** 즉 말하자면 **neither ... nor** …도 …도 아닌 **attribute ... to** …가 …에서 기인한다고 생각하다 **cloud** (먼지, 연기 등의) 자욱한 것, 연기 **in addition** 더구나, 게다가 **stake** 말뚝, 막대기 **holy** 신성한 **expose** 노출시키다, 드러내다 **disintegrate** 산산조각이 나다, 해체되다

(37~38)

M In 1897, Bram Stoker created a stir when he published his novel *Dracula*. In it, he chronicled the story of Count Dracula, a vicious, bloodsucking vampire from Transylvania. While many people believe Stoker created the Dracula legend himself, stories of vampires have actually been around for hundreds, if not thousands, of years. According to legend, vampires are undead creatures. That is, they are neither living nor dead but something in between. Vampires survive by drinking people's blood, which they must do regularly. However, when a vampire bites a person, usually in the neck, that person will soon become a vampire. Legends attribute many special powers to vampires. They have superhuman strength, can typically fly, and can sometimes turn themselves into a bat, a wolf, or even a cloud of gas. In addition, vampires show no reflections in mirrors. Fortunately for humans, vampires can be defeated. A person can kill a vampire by driving a wooden stake into its heart. Also, vampires, being evil creatures, react badly to crosses and holy water. And vampires cannot be exposed to the sun. If any sunlight touches them, they will disintegrate into nothing.

(37~38)

남 1897년 브람 스토커가 소설 〈드라큘라〉를 발표했을 때 큰 반응을 일으켰다. 그 책에서 그는 트란실바니아 출신의 사악하고 피를 빨아먹는 흡혈귀인 드라큘라 백작의 이야기를 기록했다. 많은 사람들이 스토커가 드라큘라 전설 자체를 만들었다고 믿지만 흡혈귀 이야기는 실제로 수천 년은 아니더라도 수백 년 정도 동안 존재해 왔다. 전설에 따르면 흡혈귀들은 죽지 않은 생물이다. 다시 말해 그들은 살아 있지도 죽지도 않은 그 중간적인 존재이다. 흡혈귀들은 사람들의 피를 마셔서 생존하는데, 규칙적으로 그렇게 해야 한다. 하지만 흡혈귀들이 한 사람을 물면, 보통은 목에다 무는데, 그 사람은 곧 흡혈귀가 될 것이다. 전설에 따르면 많은 특별한 힘이 흡혈귀에게 있다고 한다. 그들은 초인적인 힘을 지녔고, 전형적으로 날 수 있으며 가끔은 스스로 박쥐나 늑대, 심지어는 가스 덩어리로 변신할 수 있다. 게다가 흡혈귀들은 거울에 비춰지지 않는다. 인간들에게는 다행히도 흡혈귀들은 퇴치될 수 있다. 사람은 나무로 된 말뚝을 흡혈귀의 가슴에 찔러 흡혈귀를 죽일 수 있다. 또한 악한 생물인 흡혈귀들은 십자가와 성수에 심한 반응을 보인다. 그리고 흡혈귀들은 태양에 노출될 수 없다. 만일 햇빛이 그들에게 조금이라도 닿으면, 흡혈귀들은 흔적도 없이 해체될 것이다.

39 Which of the following is NOT true about the man?

✔ ① He makes a lot of money.
② He is currently employed.
③ He thinks his job is boring.
④ He lacks confidence in his abilities.
⑤ He is considering getting another job.

남자에 대해 사실이 <u>아닌</u> 것은 무엇인가?

① 그는 돈을 많이 번다.
② 그는 현재 직업이 있다.
③ 그는 자기 직업이 따분하다고 생각한다.
④ 그는 자기의 능력에 대한 자신감이 부족하다.
⑤ 그는 다른 직업을 가질 것을 고려 중이다.

40 What is the woman trying to say?

① Making money is the most important aspect of working.
② Experience is the best way to get a new job.
③ Even in a bad economy, people can still get hired.
✔ ④ Enjoying one's job is better than being bored.
⑤ It is more important to be employed than to be happy.

여자가 말하고자 하는 것은 무엇인가?

① 돈을 버는 것은 일하는 것의 가장 중요한 측면이다.
② 경험이 새로운 직업을 얻는 가장 좋은 방법이다.
③ 경기가 나빠도 사람들은 여전히 직업을 얻을 수 있다.
④ 자기의 일을 즐기는 것이 따분해 하는 것보다 낫다.
⑤ 행복해지는 것보다 일자리를 얻는 것이 더 중요하다.

▶ current 현재의 position 직(職), 근무처 in fact 사실은 field 분야, 영역 what if …이면 어떻게 되는가? succeed in 성공하다 care (…인지 아닌지) 궁금해 하다, 개의하다 even if 설령 …하더라도 economy 경제 (활동), 경기 get hired 고용되다 talent 재주, 솜씨 take a risk 위험을 무릅쓰다, 모험하다 I bet 틀림없이 …이다

(39~40)

M I've been doing a lot of thinking about my job lately. I'm not sure if I should stay at my current position or not. In fact, I'm even considering applying for another job.

W Really? What's wrong with the job you're doing now?

M Well, it's just really boring. There's nothing wrong with it. It's just that I had been hoping to do something a little more exciting with my life.

W In that case, why don't you quit your job now and look for a position in another field?

M You know... I'd love to do that, but what happens if things don't go too well? My job is completely boring, but it's still a job. What if I don't succeed in something new?

W Who cares? You should get out and try to do something new. Even if you fail, it'll still be a learning experience for you.

M I don't know. At first, I thought getting a new job would be all right, but the economy isn't very good now. What happens if I don't get hired by someone else?

W You've got a lot of talent and abilities. I'm sure someone will give you a job.

M Do you think so? I'm not so sure about that.

W Of course I do. Anyway, you only live once. Take a risk, and try to find a job you'll actually enjoy. I bet you'll love your life much more once that happens.

(39~40)

남 최근에 직업에 대해 많이 생각해 봤어. 현재의 직장에 남아 있어야 할지 말지 잘 모르겠어. 사실은 다른 직장에 지원하는 것도 생각 중이야.

여 정말이야? 지금 하는 일이 무슨 문제가 있니?

남 음, 그냥 정말 따분해. 일은 아무 문제 없어. 그냥 살면서 뭔가 좀 더 신나는 일을 했으면 좋겠어.

여 그럼 지금 일을 그만두고 다른 분야에서 일자리를 찾아 보면 어때?

남 있잖아… 그러고 싶지만 상황이 잘 돌아가지 않으면 어떡해? 내 일은 완전히 따분하지만 그래도 일이잖아. 새로운 것에 성공 못하면?

여 누가 신경 쓴대? 나가서 새로운 것을 시도해 봐야지. 실패하더라도 여전히 너한텐 배울 만한 경험이 될 거야.

남 모르겠어. 처음엔 새 일을 갖는 게 괜찮을 거라고 생각했지만 지금 경기가 별로 안 좋잖아. 다른 누군가에게 고용이 안 되면 어떡해?

여 넌 재주와 능력이 많아. 분명히 네게 일자리를 줄 사람이 있을 거야.

남 그렇게 생각하니? 난 잘 모르겠어.

여 물론이야. 아무튼 인생은 한 번뿐이잖아. 모험을 해서 정말로 즐기게 될 일을 찾아 봐. 일단 그렇게 되면 네가 인생을 훨씬 더 좋아할 거라고 믿어.

실전모의고사 **04**

01 ③	02 ④	03 ①	04 ②	05 ①	06 ③	07 ④	08 ②	09 ③	10 ④
11 ⑤	12 ②	13 ④	14 ⑤	15 ①	16 ③	17 ②	18 ①	19 ②	20 ③
21 ④	22 ①	23 ②	24 ⑤	25 ④	26 ⑤	27 ④	28 ②	29 ③	30 ④
31 ①	32 ④	33 ③	34 ②	35 ②	36 ③	37 ②	38 ②	39 ②	40 ③

문제와 정답	스크립트	해석

01 다음을 듣고, 이야기와 그림 속의 상황이 일치하지 <u>않는</u> 것을 고르시오.

▶ **depict** 그리다, 묘사하다 **subsequently** 그 후에, 이어서 **rural** 시골의, 농사의 **capture** (영화 등으로) 표현하다, 포착하다 **barn** 헛간, 가축우리 **situated in** …에 위치해 있는 **graze** (가축이) 풀을 뜯다 **give off** (빛 등을) 내다, 풍기다

W My friend is a painter who often depicts real-life subjects. Last week, she visited a local farm and subsequently created a wonderful painting of a rural farming scene. I saw it and realized that she had completely captured the way a farm looks. The focus of the piece was the red barn situated right in the middle of the painting. To the right of the barn is a small pond which has some ducks and other birds swimming in it. There are a few cows which are grazing in the field located on the left-hand side of the painting. And, the sun is setting, so it's low in the sky and also giving off a red light. I was so impressed by this painting. I grew up on a farm, and she accurately managed to depict the essence of a farm. Her painting really reminded me of my earlier life.

여 내 친구는 실물을 대상으로 자주 묘사하는 화가이다. 지난주에 그녀는 지역 농장을 방문한 뒤 시골의 농장 풍경을 멋지게 그렸다. 그걸 봤을 때 난 그녀가 농장의 모습을 완벽하게 표현했다는 것을 깨달았다. 그 작품의 중심은 그림 정중앙에 있는 빨간 헛간이었다. 헛간 오른쪽에는 작은 연못이 있는데, 그곳에선 오리 몇 마리와 다른 새들이 헤엄을 치고 있다. 그림 왼쪽에 있는 들판에는 소 몇 마리가 풀을 뜯고 있다. 그리고 해가 저물고 있어서 하늘에 낮게 내려와 빨간 빛을 비추고 있었다. 이 그림에 나는 매우 감명을 받았다. 난 시골에서 자랐는데 그녀는 농장의 진수를 정확하게 묘사했다. 그녀의 그림은 정말로 내 어린 시절을 생각나게 했다.

02 대화를 듣고, 여자는 다음 중 누구와 친한 친구가 될 수 있을 것인지 고르시오.

① 수미: 난 친구들과 외출하는 걸 좋아하지만 같이 있을 때 말은 별로 안 해. 대신 친구들이 말하는 걸 뭐든 그냥 듣는 걸 더 좋아해.
② 진희: 나는 친구들을 위해 선물을 사는 걸 좋아해. 또 친구들과 집에서 영화를 보며 수다 떠는 것을 좋아하지.
③ 사라: 내가 잘 들어주기 때문에 친구들은 항상 내게 전화해서 문제를 얘기해. 다행히 친구들은 내게 점심이나 저녁 사주기를 좋아하는데, 때로 내가 돈이 부족하기 때문이야.
④ 미미: 난 함께 외출해서 친구들에게 돈을 쓰는 걸 좋아해. 항상 수다를 떨지만 친구들의 말에도 뭐든지 주의를 기울이려고 노력해.
⑤ 정아: 영화를 보러 가는 게 가장 좋아. 또 친구들이 별로 말을 하지 않아도 친구들과 얘기하는 걸 좋아해. 주로 내가 얘기를 가장 많이 하지.

▶ **argument** 말다툼, 언쟁 **ever** 영원히, 언젠가 **ideal** 이상적인 **outgoing** 외향적인 **match** 잘 어울리는 한 쌍 **outdoors activity** 야외 활동 **characteristic** 특징, 특성 **key** 중요한, 중대한 **generous** 인심 좋은, (돈 등에) 인색하지 않은 **hang out with** …와 어울리다, 사귀다 **share** 몫, 분담

M I just had a huge argument with my best friend. I don't think we're ever going to talk to each other again.

W That's too bad. Perhaps you need to choose your friends better in the future.

M I suppose you're right. Well, what's your ideal friend like?

W That's a good question. I'm a pretty outgoing person, so I couldn't be close friends with someone who's very quiet. I don't think that would be a good match.

M Yeah, you're probably correct about that. What else?

W I like to go out a lot, so I need to be friends with a person who enjoys doing outdoors activities. Oh, and my best friend should be a good listener, too.

M Yeah, that's a really important characteristic. That's key for me as well.

W There's one more… A best friend should be generous. I can't stand hanging out with people who never pay for their fair share or who are always begging to borrow money from you.

M It looks like you've thought about this a lot.

W I have, and that's why I have a really good best friend. We get along very well with each other and almost never have any problems.

남 가장 친한 친구와 큰 다툼을 벌였어. 다시는 말을 섞지 않을 거야.

여 안됐다. 앞으로는 친구를 더 잘 골라야겠구나.

남 그런 것 같아. 음, 네가 생각하는 이상적인 친구는 어떤 거야?

여 좋은 질문이네. 난 꽤 사교적이라서 아주 조용한 사람하고는 친한 친구가 될 수 없었어. 잘 어울릴 것 같지 않아.

남 그래, 그건 아마 네가 맞는 것 같다. 다른 건?

여 난 외출을 아주 좋아하니까 야외 활동을 즐기는 친구가 필요해. 아, 그리고 가장 친한 친구는 또 이야기를 잘 들어주는 사람이어야 해.

남 그래, 그건 정말 중요한 특징이야. 그건 나한테도 중요해.

여 하나 더 있어… 가장 친한 친구는 관대해야 해. 나는 자기가 당연히 내야 할 몫을 절대로 안 내거나 항상 돈을 꿔달라고 조르는 사람하고는 어울리지 못해.

남 이 문제에 대해 생각 많이 하는것 같구나.

여 그래, 그래서 내겐 정말로 좋은 가장 친한 친구가 한 명 있지. 우린 서로 아주 잘 어울리고 거의 아무런 문제도 없어.

<table>
<tr><th>문제와 정답</th><th>스크립트</th><th>해석</th></tr>
</table>

03 다음을 듣고, 이 이야기가 무엇을 위한 것인지 고르시오.

✔ ① 상대방의 친절에 감사를 표하기 위해
② 최근의 여행을 되돌아보기 위해
③ 자기를 도와준 두 남자를 칭찬하도록 추천하기 위해
④ 사업 관계를 더욱 돈독히 하고자 하는 마음을 드러내기 위해
⑤ 미래의 여행 계획을 세우기 위해

▶ **hospitality** 환대, 후대 **employee** 직원 **note** 언급하다 **set up** …을 공급하다, 갖추어 주다 **conclude** 끝나다, 종료하다 **polite** 친절한 **efficiency** 능률, 효율 **professionalism** 전문성, 직업의식 **extend** (감사의 뜻 등을) 말하다, 베풀다

M I appreciate the hospitality you and the employees at your company showed during my recent trip to your city. In particular, I wish to note that the hotel you set me up in was excellent; the room was lovely, and the food was fantastic. I would also like you to say thanks to Bob Davies and Fred Thompson for showing me around the city after our meetings concluded. In addition, everyone in your office was polite and showed the efficiency and professionalism I had expected from your company. It was a pleasure doing business with you. Finally, I want to extend a personal invitation to anyone in your company to visit my company and city anytime. I'm not sure if I can provide the same level of hospitality as you and your people did, but I will do my best. Once again, I am really grateful for your helping to make my trip a memorable one.

남 최근 그 도시를 여행하는 동안 귀하와 동료들과 보여주신 환대에 감사를 드립니다. 특히 제게 마련해 주신 호텔은 훌륭했고, 객실도 근사했으며 음식은 환상적이었음을 말씀드리고 싶습니다. 또한 보브 데이비스와 프레드 톰슨에게 회의가 끝난 뒤 도시를 구경시켜 주셔서 감사했다는 말씀을 전해 주시기 바랍니다. 더욱이 귀하의 사무실에 있는 모든 분이 친절했으며 제가 귀사에서 기대한 능률과 전문성을 보여 주셨습니다. 귀하와 함께 일을 해서 즐거웠습니다. 마지막으로 귀사의 모든 분께 저희 회사와 도시에 언제든 오시라는 말씀을 드리고 싶습니다. 귀하와 직원들이 보여 주신 환대에 똑같이 대접할 수 있을지는 모르겠지만 최선을 다하겠습니다. 다시 한 번 추억에 남는 여행이 되도록 도와주셔서 정말 감사드립니다.

04 대화를 듣고, 여자에게 주어진 임무가 <u>아닌</u> 것을 고르시오.

① 항공편을 예약하는 것
✔ ② 회의의 일정을 잡는 것
③ 중요한 파일을 다시 입력하는 것
④ 컴퓨터 문제를 처리하는 것
⑤ 남자를 위해 호텔을 예약하는 것

▶ **account** 예금 계좌, 신용 거래, 고객 **retype** 다시 입력하다 **make a reservation** 예약하다(=book) **get on** (일 등을) 계속하다, (척척) 진척시키다 **get in** 도착하다, 오다 **positive** (의견, 주장에) 확신[자신]이 있는 **reliable** 믿을 만한 **keep an eye on** …을 감시하다, …에 유의하다 **That's it** 그게 다이다, 그것으로 끝이다

M Can I see you for a moment?

W Of course. What can I do for you?

M First, I need the Williams account file retyped with these changes I've made. That has to be done by noon tomorrow. Also, can you make a reservation for me on a flight to Incheon on March 24? I'll be returning on March 27. And book me a hotel room for those dates, too.

W No problem, sir. I'll get on it right away. Is their anything else?

M Yes. The computer specialist is coming to my office this afternoon to check my computer for viruses, but I'm going to be in meetings all afternoon. Please make sure he gets in, but stay in the office while he works. I don't want him copying anything or deleting any important files.

W I'm positive there won't be any problems with that since he's very reliable.

M I know, but we have a lot of sensitive material and need to be careful.

W I understand. I'll be sure to keep an eye on him. Is that everything you need me to do?

M That's it for now. I'm going to lunch and then those meetings. See you tomorrow.

남 잠깐 저 좀 봐주시겠어요?

여 네. 뭘 도와드릴까요?

남 우선 윌리엄스 거래 파일을 내가 수정한 것으로 다시 입력해 줘요. 내일 정오까지 끝내야 해요. 또 3월 24일 인천행 항공편을 예약 좀 해 줄래요? 3월 27일 돌아올 거예요. 그리고 그 날짜로 호텔 예약도 부탁해요.

여 알겠습니다. 당장 진행하겠습니다. 다른 게 또 있으세요?

남 있어요. 컴퓨터 전문가가 오늘 오후에 바이러스 때문에 컴퓨터를 점검하러 사무실에 오는데 난 오후 내내 회의에 참석할 거예요. 그가 왔는지 확인하고 작업하는 동안 사무실에 남아 있어요. 그 사람이 뭔가를 복사하거나 중요한 파일을 삭제하는 건 싫으니까.

여 그는 아주 믿을 만해서 그건 전혀 문제 없을 것 같은데요.

남 알아요, 하지만 민감한 자료가 많이 있어서 주의가 필요해요.

여 알겠습니다. 꼭 주시하겠습니다. 제가 해야 할 건 그게 전부인가요?

남 지금은 그래요. 나는 점심 먹고 회의에 갈 거예요. 내일 봅시다.

05 다음을 듣고, 화자의 심정을 가장 잘 나타낸 것을 고르시오.

✔ ① concerned
② depressed
③ nervous
④ amused
⑤ optimistic

① 걱정하는
② 우울한
③ 긴장된
④ 즐거워하는
⑤ 긍정적인

▶ a streak of 연속적인, 일련의　transfer 전출시키다, 이동시키다　all the way 내내, 줄곧　break up 헤어지다　stimulating 자극적인, 격려가 되는　rent rate 임대료　afford to do …할 여유가 있다　nowadays 요즈음에는　turn around (시장, 경제 등이) 그전과는 반대의 경향을 보이다

W I've had a streak of bad luck lately, and sometimes it seems like it's never going to change. For example, I'd been dating the same guy for two years, but his company just transferred him to another office, so he moved all the way across the country. We had to break up because of that. Additionally, I feel like the job I have now isn't good for me. It isn't stimulating at all, so I don't get any satisfaction out of it. I'd love to find another one, but the economy isn't particularly good, so I doubt I'd be able to get hired anywhere else. Finally, I'm probably going to have to move to a smaller apartment because my neighborhood is getting more expensive. Rent rates are rising, and I simply can't afford to pay that much money. It seems like nothing is going right for me nowadays. I sure wish things would turn around and start looking brighter soon.

여 최근 연속적으로 불운을 겪었는데 가끔은 이런 상황이 절대로 변하지 않을 것 같다. 예를 들면 2년 동안 한 남자와 데이트를 해 왔지만 그의 회사가 얼마 전에 그를 다른 사무실로 전출시켜서 그는 먼 곳으로 이사했다. 그것 때문에 우리는 헤어져야 했다. 게다가 난 지금 하는 일이 맞지 않는 것 같다. 전혀 자극을 주지 않아서 아무런 만족을 얻지 못한다. 다른 일을 찾고 싶지만 경기가 너무나도 좋지 않아서 어디든 다른 곳에 채용될 수 있을지 의문이다. 마지막으로 더 작은 아파트로 이사를 해야 할 것 같은데, 동네가 더 비싸지고 있기 때문이다. 임대료가 올라가고 있는데 내겐 그렇게 많은 돈을 지불할 능력이 없다. 요즈음은 제대로 돌아가는 일이 없는 것 같다. 상황이 바뀌어서 곧 더 나아지길 정말로 바란다.

---

06 대화를 듣고, 영화에 대한 화자들의 의견이 바르게 반영된 것을 고르시오.

	좋았던 점	좋지 않았던 점
① 남자:	음악	특수효과
② 여자:	폭력성	배우들의 연기
✔③ 남자:	배우들의 연기	음악
④ 여자:	재미 있는 대사	폭력성
⑤ 남자:	재미 있는 대사	특수효과

▶ based on …을 바탕으로 한　care for …을 좋아하다　to begin with 무엇보다도 먼저, 첫째로　dialog 대화　for one thing 우선 첫째로, 한 가지는　obviously 명백하게, 아무리 보아도　violence 폭력　be supposed to be …이기로 되어 있다　bother 일부러 …하다, 귀찮게 굴다

W How was your past weekend?

M It was boring except for the movie I watched on Saturday night.

W I saw one on Saturday, too. What did you see?

M I went to that science fiction movie that was based on the television show. It was really crowded there.

W I don't particularly care for science fiction. My husband and I went to a drama about some people in Los Angeles. How was your movie?

M Well, to begin with, the acting was excellent. Additionally, the special effects were fantastic, and the story itself was pretty good with lots of funny dialog. The only problem was the music. It just didn't seem to match the mood of the movie. How did you enjoy your movie?

W Well, I had mixed feelings about it. For one thing, the acting and story were quite good. Those really impressed me a lot.

M But what did you dislike about the movie? There was obviously something.

W You're right. I thought it had too much bad language and violence in it. It was supposed to be a family movie, but it didn't seem like one.

M That's too bad. I guess I won't bother watching it in the future.

여 지난주말 어땠어요?

남 토요일 밤에 영화 본 것 외에는 지루했어요.

여 나도 토요일에 하나 봤는데. 뭐 봤어요?

남 텔레비전 쇼를 바탕으로 한 공상과학 영화를 보러 갔어요. 거기 정말 혼잡하더라고요.

여 난 공상과학은 별로 안 좋아해요. 난 남편과 로스앤젤레스에 있는 어떤 사람들에 관한 드라마를 보러 갔어요. 당신 영화는 어땠어요?

남 음, 먼저, 연기가 훌륭했어요. 거기에다 특수효과가 굉장했고 스토리 자체는 재미있는 대화가 많아 꽤 괜찮았어요. 한 가지 문제는 음악이었죠. 그냥 영화 분위기와 어울리지 않는 것 같더라고요. 당신 영화는 즐거웠어요?

여 음, 복잡한 느낌이었어요. 우선 연기와 스토리는 꽤 괜찮았어요. 그건 정말 엄청 감동적이었죠.

남 하지만 뭐가 영화에서 싫었죠? 분명히 뭔가가 있을 텐데.

여 맞아요. 욕설과 폭력이 너무 많았던 것 같아요. 가족 영화였던 것 같은데 그래 보이지 않았어요.

남 저런. 난 앞으로 그런 걸 일부러 보진 않을 것 같아요.

07

다섯 개의 대화문을 듣고, 자연스럽지 <u>않은</u> 것을 고르시오.

①
②
③
④ ✓
⑤

▶ catch (열차 등을) 잡아타다 had better …하는 것이 낫다, …해야 한다 take a message 메시지를 전하다 contact 연락하다 as soon as …하는대로 곧 in that case 그렇다면, 그 경우에 keep A from B A가 B 하는 것을 막다

① M Excuse me, but do you know the time? I'm trying to catch the seven-thirty train.

W It's twenty-five after seven. You'd better hurry if you don't want to be late.

M Thanks a lot. I appreciate your help.

② W And then I told him I didn't have time to meet until next weekend.

M Oh, so did he get upset about that?

W He wasn't happy, but he understood my situation.

③ M I'm sorry, but Joey isn't home right now. Can I take a message?

W Thanks. It's Sue from school. Can you ask him to call me later?

M Sure, I can do that for you. I'll have him contact you as soon as he gets home.

④ W So, what did the doctor tell you about your problem?

M He told me I need to get some rest because I've been working too hard.

W In that case, why don't we go hiking this weekend? It should be a lot of fun.

⑤ M I'm really sorry, but I'm going to be late for dinner tonight.

W Oh? What's going to keep you from getting here on time?

M Traffic is bad since there was an accident on the road.

① 남 실례지만 몇 시예요? 7시 반 기차를 타려고 하거든요.

여 7시 25분이네요. 늦지 않으려면 서둘러야겠네요.

남 정말 고마워요. 도와주셔서 감사해요.

② 여 그리고 나서 그 사람한테 다음 주말까지 만날 시간이 없다고 말했어요.

남 아, 그래서 그가 그것 때문에 언짢아했어요?

여 좋아하진 않았지만 내 상황은 이해하더군요.

③ 남 미안하지만 조이는 지금 집에 없어. 메세지를 전해 줄까?

여 고맙습니다. 학교 친구 수인데요. 나중에 전화해 달라고 말씀해 주시겠어요?

남 알았어, 그러마. 집에 오는 대로 연락하라고 할게.

④ 여 그래서 의사가 당신 문제가 뭐래요?

남 일을 너무 많이 해서 휴식이 좀 필요하대요.

여 그럼 이번 주말에 하이킹 가는 것 어때요? 정말 재미있을 거예요.

⑤ 남 정말 미안한데 오늘 저녁식사에 늦을 것 같아.

여 어? 뭣 때문에 여기 제시간에 못 오는 거야?

남 도로에서 사고가 나서 교통 상황이 나빠.

08

다음을 듣고, 이야기 속의 This가 무엇인지 고르시오.

① history
② philosophy ✓
③ economics
④ sociology
⑤ physics

① 역사
② 철학
③ 경제학
④ 사회학
⑤ 물리학

▶ branch 부문, 분과 deal with …을 다루다 subject 주제 in particular 특히 existence 존재 ethics 윤리(학) central to …에 있어서 중심적인, 핵심인 discipline 학문 (분야) practitioner 실천가 associated with …와 연관된 field 분야 founder 창시자 primary 근본적인, 주요한 instruction 가르침, 교육 inquiry 질문, 탐구

W This is a branch of the social sciences that deals with the thoughts of men on various subjects. In particular, ideas on where we come from, our existence in the universe, ethics, logic, and the meaning of life are all central to this discipline. Some of the most famous practitioners have come from ancient times, especially from Greece. Plato, Socrates, and Aristotle are among the most famous of the Greek thinkers associated with this field. Plato, who was Socrates's student, is considered one of the founders of this discipline, and his works are often used as primary sources of instruction and study. His student Aristotle didn't agree with many of these methods, so he developed his own methods of inquiry, which have been followed by many up to modern times. In the recent past, the most important practitioners have come from Germany and include such famous thinkers as Immanuel Kant and Friedrich Hegel.

여 이것은 사회과학의 한 분야로 다양한 주제에 관한 인간의 생각을 다룬다. 특히 우리가 어디서 왔는지에 대한 견해와 우주에서의 우리의 존재, 윤리, 이성, 삶의 의미가 모두 이 학문 분야에서 주요하다. 가장 유명한 실천가 중 일부는 고대, 특히 그리스 출신이다. 플라톤과 소크라테스, 아리스토텔레스는 이 분야와 연관된 가장 유명한 그리스 사상가들 중 일부이다. 소크라테스의 학생이었던 플라톤은 이 학문 분야의 창시자 중 한 명으로 여겨지며 그의 저술은 종종 교육과 연구의 근본적인 출처로 쓰인다. 그의 학생인 아리스토텔레스는 이 방법들 중 많은 것에 이견을 보여 자신만의 탐구법을 개발했는데, 그것은 현대까지 많은 사람들이 따르고 있다. 근대에 들어 가장 중요한 실천가들은 독일 출신이며, 이마누엘 칸트와 프리드리히 헤겔 같이 유명한 사상가들이 포함된다.

09 대화를 듣고, 남자의 마지막 말에 대한 여자의 응답으로 알맞은 것을 고르시오.

W: ________________________________

① Okay, then let's meet at two o'clock.
② Oh, I'm sorry, but I won't be here.
③ That's fine with me. I'll see you then. ✓
④ Sorry, but that's too late in the day.
⑤ I look forward to seeing you on Monday.

① 좋아요, 그럼 두 시에 만나요.
② 이런, 미안해요. 난 여기 없을 거예요.
③ 나는 괜찮아요. 그럼 그때 봐요.
④ 미안한데, 시간이 너무 늦네요.
⑤ 월요일에 만나기를 기대하고 있겠습니다.

▶ appointment 약속 business trip 출장 last minute 마지막 순간의, 막바지의 get out of …을 피하다, 도망치다 reschedule (일정을) 재조정하다 Let's see 어디보자, 잠깐만 exception 예외

W Good morning, this is the First Bank of New York. This is Betty White speaking. How can I help you?

M Good day, Mrs. White. This is Scott Andrews. We had an appointment for two o'clock this afternoon, but I'm afraid I can't make it.

W May I ask why you can't make the appointment, Mr. Andrews?

M Of course. My company is sending me out of town today on a business trip. It's a last minute thing, and I can't get out of it.

W I understand. So we'd better reschedule our appointment, hadn't we? Let's see. Today is Tuesday. How does Thursday at the same time sound to you?

M I'm sorry, but that's not good for me. I won't be back in town until Friday evening.

W Then we can meet sometime next week. I'm free all afternoon long on Monday.

M Actually, I was hoping to meet sooner than that. I need to take care of this matter before next Monday.

W We're open on Saturday morning until noon. I wasn't planning to come in, but I suppose that I could make an exception.

M I would appreciate that very much. How does ten Saturday morning sound to you?

W ________________________________

여 안녕하세요, 뉴욕 퍼스트 은행의 베티 화이트입니다. 뭘 도와드릴까요?

남 안녕하세요, 화이트 씨. 나는 스콧 앤드류스입니다. 오늘 오후 2시에 약속이 돼 있는데 지킬 수가 없을 것 같군요.

여 약속을 못 지키는 이유를 여쭤 봐도 될까요, 앤드루 씨?

남 그럼요. 회사에서 오늘 다른 곳으로 출장을 가라네요. 마지막 순간에 그렇게 돼서 어떻게 할 수가 없어요.

여 알겠습니다. 그럼 약속 일정을 재조정해야겠군요, 그렇죠? 잠깐만요. 오늘이 화요일이네요. 목요일 같은 시간으로 괜찮으세요?

남 미안하지만 그땐 안 될 것 같아요. 금요일 저녁까지 못 돌아올 거예요.

여 그럼 다음 주에 만날 수 있겠네요. 저는 월요일에는 오후 내내 괜찮습니다.

남 사실은 그것보다 더 일찍 만나고 싶어요. 다음 월요일 전에 이 문제를 처리해야 하거든요.

여 저희는 토요일 오전 정오까지 영업을 합니다. 출근하지 않을 생각이었지만 예외로 해야겠어요.

남 정말 감사합니다. 토요일 오전 10시 괜찮으세요?

여 ________________________________

---

10 다음을 듣고, 이 이야기가 어떤 질문에 대한 대답인지 고르시오.

① How did Asians introduce tea to the West?
② What is the process by which people make tea?
③ Why do people in the East enjoy tea so much?
④ How do people in various countries consume tea? ✓
⑤ Why do the British and Russians enjoy different kinds of teas?

① 아시아인들은 어떻게 서양에 차를 소개했나?
② 사람들이 차를 만드는 절차는 무엇인가?
③ 동양의 사람들은 왜 차를 그렇게 많이 즐기는가?
④ 다양한 국가의 사람들은 어떻게 차를 마시는가?
⑤ 영국과 러시아인들은 왜 다른 종류의 차를 즐기는가?

▶ explorer 탐험가 reach 도달하다 consumption 소비 depend upon …에 달려 있다, …나름이다 popular 인기있는 serve with …와 같이 내놓다, 대접하다 contain 함유하다, 포함하다 property 고유의 성질, 특성 elaborate 정교한, 복잡한 ritual 의식 regarded as …로 간주되는

M Tea has been drunk in various parts of the world, the Far East in particular, since ancient times. Only after Western explorers reached these lands during the Middle Ages was tea brought to the countries of Europe. The consumption of tea has many different styles, all of which depend upon the culture. In the West, black tea is the preferred drink. Many people take it with sugar and either milk or cream. It's very popular in England, where four in the afternoon is considered "tea time." Additionally, a light meal is often served with tea there. However, Russians enjoy black tea with lemon or honey and drink it after every meal. In the East, green tea is the preferred choice, and many people believe it contains healthy properties. The Japanese are famous for their tea ceremony, an elaborate ritual in which the setting of dishes, the making of the tea, and the pouring and drinking are all regarded as an art form.

남 차는 고대 이후 세계적으로, 특히 극동 지역에서 마셔왔다. 중세에 서구 탐험가들이 이 지역에 도착한 이후에서야 차는 유럽 국가로 전해졌다. 차를 소비하는 데는 여러 가지의 많은 방식이 있으며 그 모든 방식은 문화에 따라 다르다. 서구에서는 홍차를 마시는 것을 더 좋아한다. 많은 사람들이 홍차에 설탕과 우유나 크림을 넣어 마신다. 홍차는 영국에서 아주 인기가 있는데, 그곳에서 오후 4시는 '차 마시는 시간'으로 여겨진다. 게다가 그곳에서는 가벼운 식사에 차가 자주 같이 나온다. 하지만 러시아인들은 홍차를 레몬이나 꿀을 넣어 마시는 것을 좋아하며 매끼 식사 뒤에 마신다. 동양에서는 녹차가 선호되는데, 많은 사람들이 녹차에는 건강에 좋은 성질이 함유되어 있다고 믿는다. 일본인들은 다기와 차 만들기, 따르기, 마시기가 모두 예술적 형태로 간주되는 섬세한 의식인 다도로 유명하다.

<table>
<tr><th>문제와 정답</th><th>스크립트</th><th>해석</th></tr>
</table>

11

대화를 듣고, 여자가 돌려받게 될 금액이 얼마인지 고르시오.

① $4.50
② $5.00
③ $5.50
④ $6.00
✔ $6.50

▶ purchase 구입하다 cost 비용이 들다 on sale 팔려고 내놓은, 특가인 set you back …에게 (얼마의) 비용이 들다 get … a bargain …을 헐값으로 손에 넣다 by the way 그런데 though 하지만, 그래도 discount 할인 receipt 영수증 refund 환불하다

스크립트

M Good evening. Have you found everything you're looking for?

W Yes, I think so. I've got this sweater I'd like to purchase, and I've also got a pair of blue jeans.

M Okay, the sweater costs fifty dollars while the jeans are on sale, so they're only going to set you back forty dollars. That's quite a bargain you're getting.

W I agree. That's why I'm purchasing them. By the way, when is the sale ending?

M Actually, today is the last day of the sale, so you'd better purchase everything you want now unless you like paying higher prices.

W Hmm… That's a good point. I tell you what. I think I'll get a second pair of those jeans. That's probably the smart thing to do. Oh, I've also got this card I'd like to use with my purchase. I'm not exactly sure what it does though.

M Ah, this is a family card which gives you five percent back on everything you purchase here.

W Well, that sounds great. So, do you just give me the discount right here?

M No. You pay the full price here, and then you take your receipt to the counter downstairs where they'll refund your money.

해석

남 안녕하세요. 원하는 것 찾으셨어요?

여 네, 그런 것 같아요. 이 스웨터를 사고 싶고 또 청바지도 있어요.

남 알겠습니다. 스웨터는 50달러이고 청바지는 특가라서 40달러밖에 안 합니다. 아주 싸게 사시는 거예요.

여 그렇죠. 그래서 제가 사려는 거예요. 그런데 염가판매는 언제 끝나죠?

남 실은 오늘이 염가판매 마지막 날이에요. 그러니 더 높은 가격을 지불하지 않으시려면 지금 원하시는 걸 모두 구입하시는 게 낫죠.

여 흠… 좋은 지적이네요. 있잖아요. 저 청바지를 하나 더 사야겠어요. 그렇게 하는 게 현명하겠죠. 아, 또 구매할 때 쓰고 싶은 이 카드가 있어요. 하지만 무슨 소용이 있는지는 정확히 모르겠지만요.

남 아, 이건 패밀리 카드로 여기서 구입하시는 물건 모두에 대해 5퍼센트를 되돌려 드리는 겁니다.

여 잘 됐네요. 그러니까 바로 여기서 그냥 할인해 준다는 거죠?

남 아닙니다. 여기서는 전액을 지불하신 다음 영수증을 가지고 아래층 카운터에 가시면 거기서 돈을 환불해 드릴 겁니다.

12

대화를 듣고, 이 상황에 가장 잘 어울리는 영어 속담을 고르시오.

① A stitch in time saves nine.
✔ Nothing ventured, nothing gained.
③ Every cloud has a silver lining.
④ The early bird catches the worm.
⑤ Don't count your chickens before they are hatched.

① 제때의 한 바늘은 후에 아홉 바늘을 덕본다.
② 모험 없이는 아무것도 얻지 못한다.
③ 괴로움이 있는 반면에 즐거움이 있다.
④ 일찍 일어나는 새가 벌레를 잡는다.
⑤ 김칫국부터 마시지 마라.

▶ handle 처리하다 sales volume 판매량, 매출 tons of 다수의, 엄청난 step (목표로의) 일보, (일련의 행동의) 조치, 방법 invest 투자하다 research 연구, 조사 make sure 확인하다 profit 수익, 이익 at first 처음에는 be ready to do …할 준비가 되다 gamble 도박 risk 위험 reward 보상, 보답

스크립트

W I heard your new Internet business is doing really well. Congratulations.

M Thanks. It's really growing faster than I'd ever expected. I think I'll have to hire three new people just to handle the sales volume.

W I wish I could have my own business. I don't particularly like my job.

M What's stopping you then? There are tons of opportunities to start a new business.

W I know. It's just that it's a huge step. I'm nervous about investing my money and time into something I'm not sure will work.

M Let me give you some advice. Find something you really like because if you're not enjoying yourself, you won't be happy. Then do some research on it. Finally, make sure you have enough money for the first six months since most new businesses don't make a profit at first.

W Now you're making me even more nervous. I don't think I'll ever have that much money.

M If you really want to, you can do it.

W I don't know if I'm ready to do so much work and take such a big gamble.

M There is some risk involved, but the rewards are worth it.

해석

여 새 인터넷 사업이 정말 잘 되고 있다고 들었어. 축하해.

남 고마워. 정말로 예상한 것보다 더 빨리 성장하고 있어. 판매량을 처리하기 위해서만 새롭게 세 명을 뽑아야 할 것 같아.

여 내 사업을 할 수 있다면 좋겠어. 내 일을 그다지 좋아하지 않거든.

남 그럼 뭘 망설여? 새 사업을 시작할 많은 기회가 있잖아.

여 알아. 그냥 그게 엄청난 방법이잖아. 잘 될지 모르는 것에 돈과 시간을 투자하는 게 불안해.

남 충고 좀 할게. 네가 정말 좋아하는 일을 찾아봐. 너 스스로 즐겁지 않다면, 넌 행복하지 못할 거야. 그 다음에 그것에 관해 조사를 좀 해봐. 마지막으로, 처음 6개월 동안 쓸 돈이 충분히 있는지 확인해봐, 대부분의 새 업체들은 처음에는 이익을 못 내거든.

여 지금 넌 날 훨씬 더 불안하게 만들고 있어. 그렇게 많은 돈이 내게 생길 것 같지 않아.

남 네가 정말로 원한다면 할 수 있어.

여 그렇게 많은 일을 하고 그처럼 큰 도박을 할 준비가 됐는지 난 모르겠어.

남 위험이 좀 있긴 하지만 그 보상은 그럴 만한 가치가 있어.

13

다음을 듣고, 이것이 누가 누구에게 하는 이야기인지 고르시오.

① coach → team
② mayor → city residents
③ manager → employees
✓ president → citizens
⑤ professor → students

① 코치 → 팀원들
② 시장 → 시민들
③ 매니저 → 종업원들
④ 대통령 → 국민들
⑤ 교수 → 학생들

▶ election 선거 expert 전문가 tax cut 세금 감면 enact (법률, 조례를) 제정하다, 법규화하다 unemployment 실업 unprecedented 전례없는, 유례없는 boom 벼락 경기, 붐 intrude on …에게 개입하다 least 최소한으로 opponent 상대 pass legislation 법안을 통과시키다 aspect 측면, 요소 hands-off 불간섭의 approach 접근법 office 공직, 직무

M It's a pleasure to be with everyone today. It's an election year, and I'm confident you'll reelect me as your leader for four more years. Thanks to my leadership, the economy is stronger than ever, and experts predict even more future growth thanks to the tax cuts I had enacted. Unemployment is down since thousands of businesses are hiring nowadays. We're in the middle of an unprecedented economic boom, so, if you want it to continue, you'll reelect me next month. In addition to keeping the economy running, I'm going to make sure the federal government intrudes on your lives as little as possible. As I've always said, the government that rules best rules least. My opponent wants to pass legislation that will control too many aspects of your lives. I say that people tend to know what's best for themselves and don't need the government to tell them what to do. And you'll get more of this hands-off approach if you keep me in office this year.

남 오늘 여러분과 함께 하게 되어 반갑습니다. 선거의 해입니다. 저는 여러분이 저를 4년 더 여러분의 지도자로 재선출해 주시리라 믿습니다. 저의 지도력 덕분에 경제가 더 튼튼해지고 제가 제정한 세금 감면 덕분에 앞으로 더 큰 성장을 전문가들은 예상하고 있습니다. 요즘은 수 많은 사업체가 채용을 하고 있어서 실업은 줄어들었습니다. 우리는 전례없는 경제적 붐 한가운데에 있습니다. 그러니 이것이 계속되길 원하신다면 다음달에 저를 재선출해 주십시오. 지속적인 경제 운용과 더불어서 저는 연방정부가 여러분의 삶에 개입하는 것을 가능한 한 줄이겠습니다. 항상 말씀드렸듯이 최상의 정부는 최소한의 통치를 합니다. 상대 후보는 여러분 삶의 너무 많은 측면을 통제할 법안이 통과되길 바라고 있습니다. 저는 사람들은 스스로에게 무엇이 최상인지 알고 있으며 정부가 그들에게 무엇을 하라고 말할 필요가 없다고 주장합니다. 여러분이 올해 저를 계속 재임하게 해 주신다면 이러한 불간섭적 접근 방식을 더 누리게 될 것입니다.

14

대화를 듣고, 두 사람이 이야기하고 있는 동작을 고르시오.

①  ② 

③ 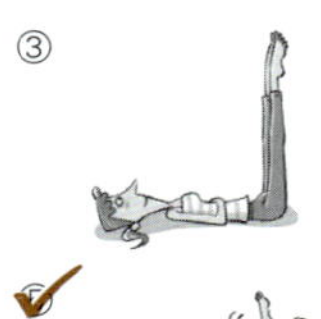 ④ 

✓ 

▶ wonder if …인지 궁금하다 be concerned about …이 걱정되다 thigh 허벅지 tone (건강 등을) 정상으로 하다, 정상 상태로 돌리다 firm 단단하게 하다, 굳건히 하다 raise 올리다 position 자세 somewhat 다소 lift 들어올리다 circular motion 원을 그리는 동작 as if 마치 …처럼 burning 화끈거리는, 얼얼한 after a while 얼마 후에는

W I was wondering if you could give me some advice on making my legs stronger and better-looking. I'm particularly concerned about my thighs.

M Then jogging, riding a bike, and doing aerobics are the best things to do. Here's one for you... Doing an air bicycle exercise for five minutes every day is great for toning and firming the legs.

W What kind of exercise is that? Could you show me how to do it?

M Just lie on your back like I'm doing now. Lift your legs, and then put your hands under your hips for support. But make sure your elbows are on the floor and aren't raised.

W Okay, is this the proper position? It feels somewhat strange.

M But that's exactly what you should be doing. Now, lift your legs higher in the air, and move them in a circular motion as if you were pedaling a bicycle.

W Am I doing it properly?

M Just raise your legs a little more, and then you'll have it. Yes, that's perfect.

W I can already feel my legs burning. This isn't going to hurt later, is it?

M It might hurt at first, but, after a while, your legs will look and feel great.

여 다리를 더 튼튼하고 모양 좋게 만드는 데 관해 상담을 좀 해줄 수 있나 해서요. 특히 허벅지가 걱정이 되거든요.

남 그럼 조깅을 하고, 자전거를 타고 에어로빅을 하는 것이 최상입니다. 여기 환자분을 위한 처방입니다… 매일 5분간 에어 바이시클 운동을 하는 것이 다리를 정상으로 만들고 튼튼하게 하는 데 좋습니다.

여 그게 어떤 운동인가요? 어떻게 하는 건지 가르쳐 주시겠어요?

남 그냥 제가 지금 하는 것처럼 누우세요. 다리를 들어올린 다음 두 손을 엉덩이 아래에 놓아 받쳐 줍니다. 하지만 팔꿈치가 바닥에 닿은 채로 올라가지 않도록 하세요.

여 알겠어요, 이게 적절한 자세인가요? 좀 이상하네요.

남 하지만 바로 그거예요. 이젠 다리를 공중으로 더 높이 들어올리고 자전거 페달을 돌리는 것처럼 다리로 원을 그리며 움직여 보세요.

여 제가 제대로 하고 있나요?

남 다리를 좀 더 올리면 되겠네요. 네, 완벽합니다.

여 벌써 다리가 얼얼하네요. 나중에 아프지는 않겠죠, 네?

남 처음에는 그럴지 모르지만 좀 지나면 다리가 보기 좋게 되고 기분도 좋아질 거예요.

15 대화를 듣고, 대화 후에 남자가 할 행동을 고르시오.

✔① Call his friend and apologize
② Call his parents to ask for money
③ Pay his friend twenty dollars
④ Borrow some money from his friend
⑤ Get his paycheck from his company

① 친구에게 전화해 사과한다.
② 부모님에게 전화해 돈을 달라고 부탁한다.
③ 친구에게 20달러를 지불한다.
④ 친구로부터 돈을 빌린다.
⑤ 회사로부터 돈을 돌려받는다.

▶ long face 시무룩[침통]한 얼굴 as a matter of fact 사실상, 실제로 lend (돈 등을) 빌려주다 cf. borrow (돈 등을) 빌리다 make a mistake 실수를 저지르다 repay (돈을) 돌려주다, 상환하다 payday 봉급일 apologize 사과하다 installment (빚, 월부 등의) 분할분의 1회분, 할부금

W What's with the long face today? You look like you lost your best friend.

M As a matter of fact, I have. We had a big fight yesterday, and he said he never wants to talk to me again.

W I'm so sorry about that. What happened to cause the fight?

M It was about money. He lent me a hundred dollars two months ago, but I still haven't paid him back. I just don't have enough money right now.

W Have you tried borrowing money from your parents or someone else?

M I thought of that, but then I'd be doing the same thing with another person.

W That's a good point. Maybe you could pay him a small amount of money each week. You just need to call him, say you made a mistake, and make a plan to repay the money.

M That's a good idea. Thanks for your help. The only problem is that my next payday isn't for another week, so I can't pay him anything now.

W If he's a true friend, he'll understand. Apologize to him, and say that you'll pay him the first installment on payday.

M I appreciate your help. Thanks for your advice.

여 오늘 왜 침울해? 가장 친한 친구라도 잃은 것 같네.

남 사실은, 그래. 어제 크게 다퉜는데 그가 다신 절대로 나하고 말하고 싶지 않대.

여 참 안됐다. 어쩌다가 싸우게 됐어?

남 돈 때문이야. 그가 두달 전에 나한테 100달러를 빌려줬는데 아직 못 갚았거든. 난 지금 당장 돈이 부족해.

여 부모님이나 다른 사람에게서 빌리려고 해봤어?

남 그 생각은 했지만 그럼 다른 사람에게 똑같은 일을 하는 게 되잖아.

여 좋은 지적이네. 어쩌면 매주 조금씩 돈을 갚을 수도 있을 거야. 그냥 그에게 전화해서 실수했다고 하고 돈을 갚을 계획을 짜봐.

남 좋은 생각이야. 도와줘서 고마워. 한 가지 문제는 다음 봉급일이 1주일을 기다려야 해서 지금은 전혀 갚을 수가 없어.

여 그가 진정한 친구라면 이해할 거야. 사과하고 봉급일에 1차 액수를 갚겠다고 말해.

남 도와줘서 고마워. 충고도 고맙고.

16 다음을 듣고, 이 내용에 대한 예로 알맞은 것을 고르시오.

① 중국의 많은 사람들이 바다 근처에서 산다.
② 유럽 전역에는 많은 농장들이 있다.
✔③ 힌두교도들은 종교적 신념을 이유로 쇠고기를 먹지 않는다.
④ 전세계의 많은 나라들에는 저마다의 독특한 문화가 있다.
⑤ 어떤 나라에는 엄청난 폭우가 내린다.

▶ unique 독특한, 고유의 custom (사회의) 관습, 풍습 terrain 지형 in contrast 반대로 suitable for …에 적합한 condone (죄 등을) 용서하다, 눈감아주다 sacred 신성한 meanwhile 그동안에, 한편 mountainous 산이 많은 arable (토양이) 경작에 알맞은 land 나라, 지방 grain 알곡, 곡식 graze (가축이) 풀을 뜯다 prairie 대초원 raise (가축을) 사육하다

W Every country has its own unique food and customs for food consumption. Much of this is influenced by the country's climate, culture, and terrain. In Asia, many nations eat large amounts of rice because the heavy rainfall and climate are ideal for its production. In contrast, Europeans and North Americans eat lots of bread, which comes from wheat. The climates in these lands are suitable for growing wheat. Additionally, people in some cultures avoid eating certain foods because of their beliefs. For example, some religions do not condone the eating of beef because they believe cows are sacred. Other people don't consume pork because pigs are unclean animals in their belief system. Finally, terrain can also influence food consumption. Countries near the sea have diets heavy in seafood because fishing grounds are so close by. Meanwhile, mountainous countries have little arable land, so their fields are used to grow grains and vegetables, not for grazing cows. In contrast, flat prairie lands are ideal for raising cattle.

여 모든 나라에는 자국만의 독특한 음식과 음식을 소비하는 풍습이 있다. 이 중 다수는 그 나라의 기후와 문화, 지형에 영향을 받는다. 아시아에서는 많은 나라들이 다량의 쌀을 먹는데 호우와 기후가 쌀 생산에 적합하기 때문이다. 반대로 유럽과 북미인들은 밀로 만드는 빵을 많이 먹는다. 이런 나라들의 기후는 밀을 키우기에 적합하다. 게다가 일부 문화권의 사람들은 신념 때문에 특정 음식을 먹는 것을 피한다. 예를 들면 어떤 종교는 소가 신성하다고 믿기 때문에 쇠고기를 먹는 것을 용서하지 않는다. 다른 사람들은 그들의 신앙 체계에서 돼지가 더러운 동물이기 때문에 돼지고기를 먹지 않는다. 마지막으로 지형도 음식 소비에 영향을 줄 수 있다. 바다 근처 국가들은 어장이 아주 가까이 있어서 해산물 음식이 많다. 한편 산악국가는 경작지가 거의 없어서 들판이 소가 풀을 뜯기 위한 것이 아니라 곡식과 채소를 키우는 데 사용된다. 반대로 평평한 대초원 국가는 소를 키우기에 이상적이다.

<table>
<tr><th>문제와 정답</th><th>스크립트</th><th>해석</th></tr>
</table>

17 대화를 듣고, 다음 중 대화 속에서 언급되지 <u>않은</u> 것을 고르시오.

① 남자가 원하는 방의 개수
② ✔ 이용 가능한 대중교통
③ 학교와 관련된 집의 위치
④ 마당의 유무
⑤ 남자가 지불할 수 있는 임대료 액수

▶ require 필요하다　the more..., the more ... …하면 할수록 더욱 더 …하다　available 이용할 수 있는, 수중에 넣을 수 있는　at the moment 지금　attend school 학교에 다니다　school district 학군　budget 예산, 생활비　backyard 마당

W　Why don't you tell me exactly what kind of house you're looking for?

M　I have three children in my family, so we'll require at least four bedrooms and two bathrooms. The bigger the house, the better it is.

W　That's not a problem. We have several of those kinds of homes available at the moment.

M　Great. Also, since my kids are all attending school, I need a house in a good school district and with schools located within walking distance.

W　Of course. I should be able to find you a place close to the local schools. What about your budget? Do you have a certain number in mind you'd like to pay in rent?

M　I'd love to be able to spend less than $1,500 a month if that's possible.

W　Well, that's going to make it somewhat more difficult since you need such a large home, but I'll see what's available.

M　Oh, and there's one more thing. I'd really appreciate it if the places you show me have a backyard of some kind so that my kids can play there. They're pretty active, so they need a place to run around.

W　Sure, most of the homes in this area have yards.

여　정확히 어떤 종류의 집을 찾으시는지 말씀해 주시죠?

남　식구로 아이들 셋이 있어서 최소한 침실 네 개와 욕실 두 개가 필요해요. 집은 클수록 더 좋고요.

여　문제 없습니다. 저희에겐 지금 얻으실 수 있는 그런 종류의 집이 여러 채 있습니다.

남　잘됐군요. 또 아이들이 모두 학교에 다니니까 좋은 학군에 있고 걸어다닐 수 있는 거리에 학교가 있는 집이 필요해요.

여　물론이죠. 지역 학교에 가까운 곳을 찾아 드릴 수 있을 겁니다. 예산은 어떠세요? 임대료로 염두에 두시는 특정 금액이 있나요?

남　가능하다면 월세가 1,500달러 미만이면 좋겠어요.

여　음, 그렇게 큰 집이 필요하신데 그걸로는 좀 어려울 것 같지만 가능한 걸 알아보겠습니다.

남　아, 그리고 한 가지 더 있어요. 보여 주실 곳에 아이들이 놀 수 있게 어떤 종류든 마당이 있으면 정말 고맙겠어요. 아이들이 꽤나 활동적이어서 뛰어다닐 곳이 필요하거든요.

여　알겠습니다. 이곳에 있는 집은 대부분 마당이 있습니다.

---

18 대화를 듣고, 두 사람의 직업이 무엇인지 고르시오.

Man	Woman
✔ lawyer	florist
② fireman	teacher
③ businessman	wedding planner
④ security guard	photographer
⑤ policeman	artist

남자	여자
① 변호사	플로리스트
② 소방관	교사
③ 사업가	웨딩플래너
④ 경호원	사진작가
⑤ 경찰관	예술가

▶ personality 성격　class 학급, 반학생　suit (사람, 물건 등에) 어울리다　creativity 창의성　profession 직업　arrangement 준비, 장치　criminal 범죄자　jail 감옥　courtroom 법원　jury 배심(원단)　look a person in the eye (남을) 똑바로[정면으로] 보다　after all 결국

M　Do you think everyone has a job that matches his or her personality?

W　I'm not sure. My brother is a teacher, and he's one of the shyest people I know. I guess he's a different person when he's in front of his class.

M　You're certainly different than him. Your personality suits your job perfectly.

W　What do you mean?

M　You're so creative even when you aren't working with flowers in your shop. I've seen your drawings and paintings, and they're excellent.

W　Having creativity is necessary in my profession. I have to prepare for so many events, like weddings, funerals, and parades, and everyone wants a different arrangement.

M　I'm certainly glad you took care of all the flowers for my wedding.

W　Well, what about your personality? It certainly doesn't match your job. You're too nice to be putting criminals in jail.

M　That's what my wife says. I actually wanted to be a fireman because I like helping people. But you know, when I'm in a courtroom standing in front of the jury and looking a criminal in the eye, I just feel like it's the right job for me.

W　Maybe your personality goes with your job after all.

남　넌 사람들 모두가 자기 성격에 맞는 일을 갖고 있다고 생각하니?

여　모르겠어. 우리 오빠는 교사인데 내가 아는 가장 부끄러움 타는 사람 중 하나야. 자기 반 학생들 앞에선 다른 사람이 되는 것 같아.

남　넌 오빠와 확실히 다르구나. 성격이 네 일과 완벽하게 맞잖아.

여　무슨 말이야?

남　가게에서 꽃을 다루지 않을 때도 넌 아주 창의적이잖아. 네 스케치와 그림을 봤는데 훌륭하던걸.

여　창의성은 내 직업에선 필수야. 결혼식과 장례식, 퍼레이드 같이 아주 많은 행사를 위해 준비해야 하는데 모든 사람이 다른 걸 원하거든.

남　네가 내 결혼식 꽃을 모두 맡아줘서 정말 기뻐.

여　음, 네 성격은 어때? 확실히 직업이랑 안 맞잖아. 범죄자들을 감옥에 넣기엔 넌 너무 착해.

남　아내도 그 얘기를 해. 사실 난 소방관이 되고 싶었어. 사람들을 돕고 싶었거든. 하지만 말이지, 법원에서 배심원 앞에 서서 범죄자를 똑바로 쳐다보고 있으면 그냥 그 일이 내게 맞는 것 같은 느낌이 들어.

여　어쩌면 결국은 네 성격이 직업과 맞을지도 모르겠다.

19 다음을 듣고, 이 이야기의 내용이 어떤 장르에 속하는지 고르시오.

① a magazine article
✓ a newspaper report
③ a crime novel
④ a movie review
⑤ a textbook excerpt

① 잡지 기사
② 신문 기사
③ 범죄 소설
④ 영화 리뷰
⑤ 교과서 발췌문

▶ crime 범죄 burglary (가택 침입) 강도(죄), 건물 침입죄 rob 강탈하다 lock 자물쇠를 채우다, 잠그다 cautious 주의하는, 신중한 pretend to do …인 체하다 inspector 검사원 leak 새는 곳, 누출 ransack 샅샅이 뒤지다, 샅샅이 찾다 valuables 귀중품 shake up …을 흥분시키다, 동요시키다 regarding …에 관하여 tip 비밀 정보 anonymous 익명의

M The large number of crimes over the weekend has shocked local residents. There were three home burglaries, and a convenience store on Palm Street was robbed at 2 a.m. on Saturday morning. A large amount of cash was stolen, but no one was hurt. Police say that all four crimes may be connected, and they are searching for members of a local gang that may be responsible. Residents are advised to lock all their doors and windows at night and to be extremely cautious when opening the door to strangers. During one of the robberies, the criminals pretended to be gas inspectors checking for leaks. They tied up the elderly couple and then ransacked the house, taking all of the valuables. Although shaken up, the couple was, fortunately, physically unharmed. If anyone has any information regarding these crimes, call Crime Stoppers at 555-6789, or stop by a local police station. All tips are anonymous, and rewards are given for information that leads to an arrest.

남 주말 동안 많은 범죄가 지역 주민들을 경악시켰습니다. 주택 강도가 세 건 있었고 팜스트리트의 편의점이 토요일 오전 2시에 강도를 당했습니다. 많은 현금이 도난당했지만 아무도 다친 사람은 없습니다. 경찰은 네 건의 범죄가 아마도 모두 연관된 것이라고 말하며 관련된 지역 폭력단을 수색중이라고 합니다. 주민들은 야간에는 문과 창문을 모두 닫고 낯선 사람에게 문을 열어 줄 때는 매우 조심하시기 바랍니다. 강도 사건 중 한 건은 범죄자들이 가스 누출을 확인하는 검사인 척 했습니다. 그들은 노부부를 줄로 묶은 다음 집을 샅샅이 뒤져 귀중품을 모두 가져갔습니다. 놀라기는 했지만 부부는 다행히 신체적인 부상은 없습니다. 이 범죄와 관련해 어떤 정보든 갖고 계시면 크라임 스토퍼 555-6789로 전화 주시거나 지역 경찰서에 들러 주십시오. 모든 정보는 익명이며, 범인 체포로 이어지는 정보에 대해서는 보상이 주어집니다.

---

20 대화를 듣고, 앞으로 소년이 잠자리에 들 시각을 고르시오.

① 11 p.m.
② 11:30 p.m.
✓ Midnight
④ 12:30 a.m.
⑤ 1 a.m.

▶ matter 문제, 곤란한 일 academy 학원, 전문학교 fair 공평한, 공정한 What if...? …하면 어떤가? grade 성적 experiment 실험

M Mom, I'd like to talk about my daily schedule. I think it needs to be changed a little.

W What's the matter with it?

M I'd really like to have some more free time, especially so that I can watch television. It would be great to be able to watch some TV before I go to bed every night.

W I don't think that's such a good idea. You're in high school now, and your studies are more important than watching television.

M But I'm so busy all day that I never have any fun. I'm in school until six o'clock, and after that, I study at the art academy until eight PM.

W Yes, and then you come home at eight thirty, do your homework for three hours, and then go to bed.

M It's not fair. All my friends' parents let them watch TV daily.

W There's just no time for you to do that since your schedule is full.

M What if I went to bed half an hour later? Then I could watch something.

W Maybe. Let's try it for one week and see what happens. But if you're too tired and your grades go down, then we're going to end this experiment.

남 엄마, 일일 계획표에 대해 얘기하고 싶어요. 약간 수정해야 할 것 같아요.

여 뭐가 문제인데?

남 특히 텔레비전을 볼 수 있게 자유 시간을 좀 더 갖고 싶어요. 매일 밤 자기 전에 TV를 좀 볼 수 있다면 좋을 거예요.

여 그리 좋은 생각이 아닌 것 같구나. 이제 고등학생인데 공부가 텔레비전 시청보다 더 중요하잖니.

남 하지만 하루 종일 너무 바빠서 전혀 재미가 없어요. 6시까지 학교에 있고 그 후에는 미술 학원에서 8시까지 공부하잖아요.

여 그래, 그리고는 8시 반에 집에 와서 세 시간동안 숙제하고 다음에 자러 가지.

남 불공평해요. 내 친구들 부모님들은 모두 매일 TV를 보게 해 주신단 말이에요.

여 넌 계획이 꽉 차 있으니까 그럴 시간이 전혀 없잖아.

남 30분 더 늦게 자면 어때요? 그럼 좀 볼 수 있을텐데.

여 글쎄다. 한 주 시험 삼아 해 보고 지켜보자꾸나. 하지만 너무 피곤해서 성적이 내려가면 이 실험은 끝내는 거야.

21 다음을 듣고, 그래프에 대해 사실이 <u>아닌</u> 것을 고르시오.

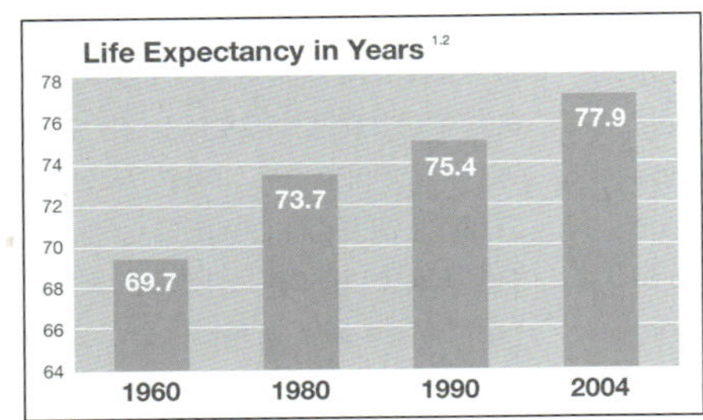

① Koreans lived longer on average in 1990 than in 1980.

② The life expectancy of the average Korean is steadily increasing.

③ The increase in life expectancy from 1960 to 1980 was greater than the increase from 1980 to 1990.

✓ There was an increase in life expectancy of three and a half years from 1990 to 2004.

⑤ The increase in life expectancy of the average Korean from 1960 to 2004 was less than ten years.

① 한국인들은 1980년보다 1990년에 평균적으로 더 오래 살았다.

② 평균적인 한국인의 예상 수명은 꾸준히 늘고 있다.

③ 1960년에서 1980년의 예상 수명 증가는 1980년에서 1990년의 증가보다 더 컸다.

④ 1990부터 2004년까지 3.5년 예상 수명이 늘었다.

⑤ 1960부터 2004년까지 평균적인 한국인의 예상 수명 증가는 10년 미만이었다.

▶ life expectancy (평균) 예상 수명　abundance 풍부함　treatment 치료　tremendously 엄청나게

W　The life expectancy for Koreans nowadays is greater than it has been at any point in the nation's history. There are many reasons for this dramatic improvement in how long people live. For example, the country has an abundance of food, and the medical treatment Koreans receive is tremendously better than what it was merely thirty or forty years ago. The result is that people no longer look at life as something that must be lived day to day but instead can focus on long-term goals and desires. A simple look at a graph will show how, in the past forty-four years, the life expectancy of the average Korean went from just under seventy years of age to 77.9 years of age. This is a number similar to those of the world's developed countries, showing that Korea has reached standards near what people in these countries have. While the life expectancy of most Koreans is expected to stay around eighty years of age, this is a welcome increase from past years.

여　요즘 한국인들의 예상 수명은 한국의 역사상 그 어떤 때보다 더 길다. 사람들이 얼마나 오래 사는가 하는 문제가 이렇게 극적으로 개선된 데는 많은 이유가 있다. 예를 들면 한국에는 음식이 풍부하고 한국인들이 받는 의료 치료는 30, 40년 전 보다도 엄청나게 좋아졌다. 그 결과 사람들은 더 이상 삶을 하루하루 살아가야만 하는 것으로 보지 않고 대신에 장기적 목표와 욕구에 집중할 수 있다. 그래프를 보면 과거 44년 동안 평균적인 한국인의 예상 수명이 70세 미만에서 77.9세로 변했다는 것이 드러난다. 이것은 세계 선진국의 수치와 비슷하며 한국이 이런 국가 사람들이 갖는 수준에 근접했다는 것을 보여준다. 대부분 한국인들의 예상 수명은 80세 정도로 예상되며 이것은 지난 수년부터 증가된 반가운 소식이다.

---

22 대화를 듣고, 남자의 마지막 말을 완성하는 것을 고르시오.

M: If I had done my best, ____.

✓ I'd be successful like you

② I never managed to go to college

③ I have to go back to work soon

④ I haven't gotten married yet

⑤ I'm not really interested in law

① 나도 너처럼 성공했을 거야

② 절대로 대학에 가지 못 했을 거야

③ 나 곧 일하러 돌아가야 해

④ 난 아직 결혼을 안 했을 거야

⑤ 난 법에는 정말 관심이 없어

▶ out of touch 연락을 않는　engineer 기술자 accept 받아들이다　pay attention 주의를 기울이다 lawyer 변호사　firm 회사　a while ago 얼마전에 fantastic 굉장히 좋은

M　It's been a long time since I've seen you.

W　It's been at least ten years. In fact, I don't believe we've seen each other since our high school graduation ceremony.

M　Yeah, I've been out of touch with lots of people from school. Most of you went to university, but I didn't.

W　I thought you'd wanted to become an engineer.

M　I did, but I didn't study very hard at school. So, none of the good universities would accept me. I guess I should have paid more attention in class and tried to plan for my future. What are you doing these days?

W　I'm employed as a lawyer at a firm in Seoul, and I just got married a while ago.

M　That's fantastic. You always studied hard, so I knew you'd be successful. I was too busy having fun and playing games in school.

W　Well, are you working somewhere around here?

M　Yes, I'm employed at my father's store and help him out. It's an okay job I guess, but it's not what I had expected.

W　What do you think would have happened had you studied harder at school?

M　If I had done my best, ________________.

남　우리 만난 지 오래됐지.

여　최소한 10년은 됐지. 사실 고등학교 졸업식 이후 서로 못 본 것 같은데.

남　그래. 학교 사람들과는 연락이 많이 끊겼어. 대부분은 대학에 갔지만 난 안 갔잖아.

여　난 네가 기술자가 되고 싶어하는 줄 알았어.

남　그랬는데 학교 공부를 아주 열심히 하지 않았어. 그래서 좋은 대학은 어느 곳도 날 받아 주지 않았어. 수업 때 좀 더 주의를 기울이고 미래를 계획했어야 했는데. 넌 요즘 뭘 하고 있니?

여　서울에 있는 회사에서 변호사로 고용됐고, 얼마 전에 막 결혼했어.

남　굉장하다. 넌 항상 열심히 공부해서 난 네가 성공할 줄 알았어. 난 학교에서 즐기고 게임하느라 너무 바빴지.

여　음, 너 이 근처 어디서 일하는 거야?

남　응, 아버지 가게를 도와주고 있어. 괜찮은 일이지만 기대했던 건 아냐.

여　학교에서 더 열심히 공부했다면 무슨 일이 생겼을 것 같니?

남　최선을 다했다면, ________________.

<table>
<tr><th>문제와 정답</th><th>스크립트</th><th>해석</th></tr>
</table>

23 다음을 듣고, 여자가 휴가에 대해 가장 만족했던 것을 고르시오.

① chatting with her family
✓ watching the fireworks
③ staying in the cabin
④ having a picnic on the mountain
⑤ going to the barbecue

① 가족들과 이야기하기
② 불꽃놀이 구경하기
③ 오두막집 안에 있기
④ 산으로 소풍 가기
⑤ 바비큐파티에 가기

▶ **absolutely** 완전히, 아주 정말로 **cabin** 작은 집, 오두막집 **scenery** 풍경 **postcard** 엽서 **downpour** 억수, 폭우 **entertain** 즐겁게[재미있게] 하다 **trout** 송어 **sponsor** 주창하다, 후원하다 **barbecue** 야외 파티, 바비큐 **fireworks show** 불꽃놀이 쇼

W I just returned from my summer holiday, which was absolutely fantastic. My family went to a cabin by a lake in the mountains. The scenery by the lake was like something out of a postcard. Unfortunately, there was a downpour the first day, but we still entertained ourselves indoors by playing games and just chatting. On the second day, we went fishing, and my son caught a big trout. He was so proud of it. The day after that, we went hiking up a mountain and had a picnic at the top, where we got a lovely view of the area. But the last day was even better. The local town sponsored this huge barbecue. There was a concert and a fireworks show. That was the best part of the trip. The fireworks simply filled the night sky with all kinds of colors. My children laughed and had a great time watching everything. I'm already planning our vacation for next summer, and I'm sure we'll go back there again.

여 방금 여름휴가에서 돌아왔는데, 휴가가 정말 환상적이었다. 우리 가족은 산에 있는 호수 근처 오두막에 갔다. 호수 옆 경치가 엽서 속에서 나온 풍경 같았다. 안타깝게도 첫날에는 비가 왔지만 우린 그래도 실내에서 게임을 하고 그냥 수다를 떨며 즐겼다. 둘째 날에는 낚시를 갔는데 아들이 큰 송어를 잡았다. 아들은 아주 뿌듯해 했다. 그 다음날에는 산으로 하이킹을 가서 정상에서 소풍놀이를 했는데, 거기서 그 지역의 멋있는 풍경을 봤다. 하지만 마지막 날에는 훨씬 더 좋았다. 지역 마을이 성대한 야외 파티를 후원했다. 콘서트와 불꽃놀이 쇼가 있었다. 그것이 여행에서 최고로 좋은 부분이었다. 불꽃들이 정말 온갖 색상으로 밤하늘을 수놓았다. 아이들은 웃었고 그 모든 걸 지켜보면서 즐거운 시간을 보냈다. 난 벌써 다음 여름 휴가를 계획하고 있는데 그곳에 꼭 다시 갈 것이다.

---

24 대화를 듣고, 여자의 좌석 위치를 고르시오.

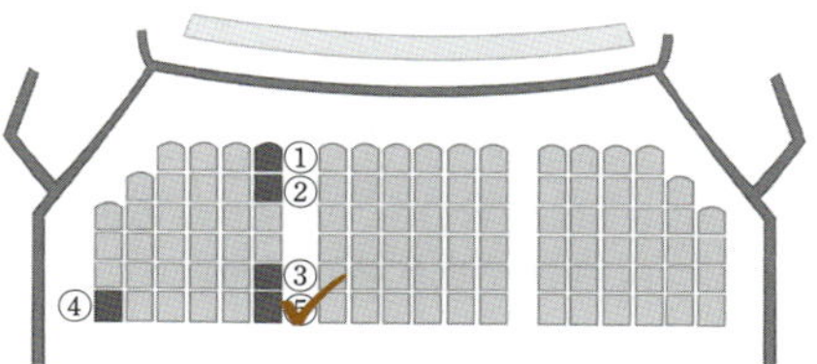

▶ **front** (물건, 장소의) 맨 앞부분 **seating chart** 좌석표 **mark** 표시하다 **screen** (극장 등의) 화면 **angle** 각도 **aisle** (열차, 극장 등의) 좌석간 통로, 길다란 통로 **row** (극장 좌석 등의) 가로줄 **free** (장소, 방 등이) 비어 있는

M Welcome to Cineplex Theater. How may I help you?

W Hi, I'd like to get a seat for the 8 PM showing of that action movie.

M We have tickets, but most of them have already been sold. There are just a few seats left, and they're all on the left-hand side and are close to the front. Take a look at this seating chart, and tell me what you like. The ones available are marked in blue.

W I really can't stand sitting too close to the screen, so I'd prefer something as far away as possible.

M How about seat number twenty-four? It's pretty far away from the screen.

W It is, but it's also on the far left-hand side near the wall, so it's difficult to see the screen from that angle. Is there anything better?

M How about a seat in the aisle? What about this one here? It's still empty.

W That's in the aisle, but it's the fifth row. Isn't there anything in the last row?

M Yes, there is. This seat is free, and it's exactly what you want. Here's your ticket. That will be eight dollars and fifty cents, please.

W Here you are. Thanks for your help.

남 시네플렉스 극장에 잘 오셨습니다. 뭘 도와드릴까요?

여 안녕하세요, 저 액션영화 오후 8시 상영분으로 좌석 한 장 주세요.

남 표가 있긴 하지만 대부분 이미 매진됐어요. 딱 몇 좌석이 남아 있는데 모두 왼쪽면에 있고 맨앞쪽과 가깝습니다. 이 좌석표를 보시고 원하는 걸 말씀해 주세요. 가능한 자리는 파란색으로 표시돼 있습니다.

여 화면에 너무 가까이 앉는 건 정말 못견디니까 가능한 한 멀리 떨어진 걸 원해요.

남 24번 좌석은 어떠세요? 그건 화면에서 꽤 멀리 떨어져 있는데요.

여 그렇긴 하지만 벽 가까이에 있는 왼쪽이라 그 각도에서는 화면을 보기 힘들어요. 더 좋은 자리는 없어요?

남 통로에 있는 좌석은 어떠세요? 여기 있는 이것 말이에요. 아직 비어 있답니다.

여 그건 통로에 있지만 5열이네요. 마지막 줄에 있는 건 없나요?

남 아니오, 있네요. 이 좌석은 비어 있고 손님이 바로 원하시는 겁니다. 여기 표 있습니다. 8달러 50센트 되겠습니다.

여 여기 있습니다. 도와줘서 고마워요.

25 다음을 듣고, 원어민이 절대로 하지 <u>않을</u> 말이 무엇인지 고르시오.

① That's a nice jacket you're wearing.
② You are the same age as me.
③ I will see you in church.
✔ You ought to go on a diet.
⑤ That movie had so many bad words.

① 당신이 입고 있는 재킷 멋지군요.
② 당신은 나와 동갑이네요.
③ 교회에서 봐요.
④ 당신은 다이어트를 해야겠어요.
⑤ 저 영화는 비속어가 너무 많이 쓰였어요.

▶ expression 표현 offensive 모욕적인, 불쾌감을 주는 lest …하지 않게, …하면 안 되므로 comment 의견을 말하다, 비평하다 remark 언급, 의견 appearance 외모 handicap 장애 refrain from …을 삼가다, 자제하다 swear words 욕설 regularly 보통, 통례적으로

M There are many expressions in English that English speakers find offensive. Foreigners who meet English speakers or visit their countries should be aware of what phrases can be insulting to others and then take care not to use them lest there be a bad result. For example, one should never comment on another person's weight. Calling someone "fat" is very insulting. In addition, just about any negative remark on a person's appearance may cause offense. Never ask people their height or why they have a handicap or other physical problem. Age is also a sensitive issue, so refrain from saying that someone is "too old." In fact, you shouldn't even ask how old a person is. The clothes people wear let them express themselves, so never make negative comments about them. In addition, there are many swear words that are regularly used in English-language movies, but most English speakers find them offensive. Finally, be careful about saying something negative about a person's politics or religion.

남 영어 원어민들이 불쾌하게 느끼는 영어 표현이 많이 있다. 원어민을 만나거나 그들의 국가를 방문하는 외국인들은 어떤 구절이 다른 사람들에게 모욕적일 수 있는지 알아야 하며 그런 다음 나쁜 결과가 생기지 않게 그것들을 사용하지 않도록 주의해야 한다. 가령 다른 사람의 체중에 대해 절대로 언급해서는 안 된다. 누군가를 '뚱뚱'하다고 말하는 건 아주 모욕적이다. 게다가 한 사람의 외모에 대해 어떠한 부정적인 언급도 불쾌함을 야기할 수 있다. 절대로 사람들에게 키나 장애나 기타 신체적 문제가 생긴 이유를 묻지 말라. 나이도 민감한 문제이므로 누구를 '너무 늙었다'고 말하는 것을 삼가라. 실제로 심지어는 몇 살이냐고 묻는 것도 안 된다. 사람들이 입는 옷은 자신들을 표현하는 것이므로 결코 그에 관해 부정적인 비평을 하지 마라. 또한 영어 영화에서 보통 사용되는 많은 욕설이 있지만 대부분의 영어 화자들은 그것들을 불쾌하게 느낀다. 마지막으로 어떤 사람의 정치나 종교에 대해 부정적인 말을 하는 데 있어 신중하라.

---

26 대화를 듣고, 남자가 제출해야 하는 것을 모두 고르시오.

ⓐ a copy of his driver's license
ⓑ a copy of his passport
ⓒ a financial statement
ⓓ a copy of his ID card
ⓔ a criminal background report

① ⓐ, ⓑ, ⓒ, ⓓ
② ⓑ, ⓓ, ⓔ, ⓐ
③ ⓐ, ⓑ, ⓓ, ⓔ
④ ⓑ, ⓒ, ⓓ, ⓔ
✔ ⓐ, ⓒ, ⓓ, ⓔ

▶ be of service 도움이 되다 application form 신청서 at one's leisure 한가한 때에, 편리할 때에 submit 제출하다 bank statement 은행예금 내역서 membership fee 회비 should 만약에 …, 가령 … criminal record 전과 기록 absolutely 물론, 그렇다 pride oneself on …을 자부하다, 자랑하다 reject 거부하다 applicant 신청자 document 서류

W Good afternoon, sir. Welcome to the Elite Golf Club. How can I be of service?

M I'm interested in joining your club and would like to know what I need to do to become a member.

W That's not a problem at all. Here's our application form. Please fill this out at your leisure, and then mail it to the club or submit it in person.

M I'm sorry, but according to this, I need to provide you with a bank statement. Why is that?

W Our club has a very expensive annual membership fee, and we must ensure that you can afford it should you join.

M Of course. There's one more thing I'd like to ask about. I'm also required to provide a criminal record check. Is this necessary?

W Absolutely, sir. We pride ourselves on having a top safety record and reject any membership applicant who has a criminal record. We don't want those kinds of people in our club.

M That's good to know. Is there anything else I need to bring?

W Yes, we require copies of your driver's license and national identification card.

M I'll take this home and mail it as soon as possible with all the proper documents.

여 안녕하세요. 엘리트 골프클럽에 잘 오셨습니다. 어떻게 도와드릴까요?

남 클럽에 가입하는 데 관심이 있어서 회원이 되려면 뭘 해야 하는지 알고 싶습니다.

여 문제 없습니다. 여기 신청서가 있습니다. 이걸 편하실 때 작성하신 다음 클럽에 우송하시거나 직접 제출하시면 됩니다.

남 미안한데 여기에는 제가 은행 예금 내역서를 제공해야 한다고 나오는데요. 왜 그렇죠?

여 우리 클럽에는 아주 비싼 연회비가 있어서 가입하실 경우 그 능력이 되는지 확인해야 합니다.

남 그렇군요. 한 가지 더 물어 볼 게 있어요. 범죄 기록 확인서도 제공해야 한다고요. 이게 필요한가요?

여 물론입니다. 우리는 최고의 안전기록을 자부하고 있고 전과가 있는 회원 신청자는 받아들이지 않습니다. 우리 클럽은 그런 류의 사람들은 원하지 않습니다.

남 잘 알았어요. 가져와야 할 다른 게 있나요?

여 네, 운전면허증과 신분증 사본이 필요합니다.

남 이걸 집에 가지고 가서 적절한 모든 서류와 같이 가능한 한 빨리 보낼게요.

<table>
<tr><th>문제와 정답</th><th>스크립트</th><th>해석</th></tr>
</table>

27 **Why did the woman miss her flight?**

① There were too many passengers on the flight.
② She forgot to confirm her reservation.
③ The flight was cancelled because of a problem.
④ She did not get to the airport on time. ✓
⑤ She forgot to pay for her ticket.

여자가 비행편을 놓친 이유는 무엇인가?

① 비행기에 사람들이 너무 많았다.
② 예약을 확인하는 것을 잊었다.
③ 문제가 있어서 비행기가 취소되었다.
④ 제시간에 공항에 도착하지 못했다.
⑤ 티켓값을 지불하는 것을 잊었다.

▶ **back up** (교통 등을) 정체시키다　**by the time** …할 때까지는　**check-in** 탑승수속, 숙박수속　**counter** 카운터　**passenger** 승객　**promise** 약속하다　**solid** 빽빽한, 완전한　**lounge** 휴게실　**hardly** 거의 …않다　**weird** 기묘한, 괴상야릇한

W　I recently had a terrible experience at the airport. I was going to Tokyo from Beijing for an important meeting. Unfortunately, traffic was really backed up outside the airport, so I arrived there late. By the time I got to the check-in counter, they had stopped taking any more passengers. I was so upset that the airline agent promised to get me on the first flight in the morning, which was at 5 a.m. I had to be in Seoul for an 11 a.m. meeting the next day, so I told her to book the flight. Then, I tried to check into the airport hotel, but they were booked solid, so I had to spend the night in the passenger lounge. The chairs were uncomfortable, and I was worried someone would steal my bags, so I hardly slept at all. It was weird since no one else was in the airport at night. It felt so strange being alone in such a big building. I hope I never experience that again.

여　최근 공항에서 끔찍한 경험을 했다. 중요한 회의 때문에 베이징에서 도쿄로 가는 중이었다. 불행히도 공항 밖 교통이 매우 정체되어서 공항에 늦게 도착했다. 탑승수속을 하는 카운터에 도착할 즈음 더 이상 승객을 받지 않았다. 내가 너무 흥분하자 공항 직원은 오전 5시에 있는 첫 비행기를 타게 해주겠다고 약속했다. 다음날 오전 11시에 서울에서 회의가 있어서 난 그녀에게 비행기를 예약해 달라고 했다. 그런 다음 공항 호텔에 체크인을 하려고 했지만 거긴 예약이 다 차 있었다. 그래서 승객 휴게실에서 밤을 보내야 했다. 의자는 불편했고 누가 가방을 훔쳐갈까봐 걱정이 돼서 거의 잠을 자지 못했다. 밤에 공항에는 다른 사람이 아무도 없었기 때문에 기분이 이상했다. 그렇게 큰 건물에서 혼자 있다는 건 아주 이상한 느낌이었다. 다시는 절대로 그런 경험을 하지 않기를 바란다.

---

28 **Which of the following people agrees with the speaker?**

① Jaegyu: I can't wait to retire at 65. It's my dream.
② Hyemi: I'm 65 years old but still healthy. I'm not interested in retiring. ✓
③ Dongsook: Older people can't work as well as younger people.
④ Myungho: The government should make the retirement age lower.
⑤ Chulsoo: I'm happy I retired at 65. I have a lot of free time now.

다음 중 화자의 의견에 동의하는 사람은 누구인가?

① 재규: 난 빨리 65살이 되어서 은퇴하고 싶어. 그건 내 꿈이야.
② 혜미: 난 65세지만 아직 건강해. 은퇴에는 관심이 없어.
③ 동숙: 나이든 사람들은 젊은 사람들만큼 일을 할 수가 없어.
④ 명호: 정부는 퇴직 연령을 더 낮춰야 해.
⑤ 철수: 난 65세에 은퇴할 수 있어서 행복해. 지금 난 여가시간을 누리고 있어.

▶ **be forced to do** …을 강요당하다　**retire** 은퇴하다　*cf.* **retirement** 은퇴　**mandatory** 의무적인, 강제적인　**quality** 양질의, 고급의　**accumulated** 축적된　**a wealth of** 풍부한　**contribute** 기여하다　**pension** 연금　**salary** 봉급　**decent** 온당한, 품위있는　**policy** 정책

M　Some people are forced to retire from work once they reach a certain age. This is known as mandatory retirement. Many countries or companies have laws regarding this situation. In Korea, according to law, the retirement age is sixty-five. However, some companies force their employees to retire when they are even younger. I have a problem with mandatory retirement, especially because many people are being forced to retire while they're still healthy and capable of doing quality work. Additionally, many people in their sixties have accumulated a wealth of experience and wisdom at their jobs and are extremely valuable employees for their firms. If they're physically unable to continue working, then companies should find another way to enable them to contribute. Also, many elderly people are unable to survive just with their company or government pensions. They need their salaries to live decent lives, especially because the cost of living is increasing yearly. The government needs to change the current policy and let people work until they want to retire.

남　어떤 사람들은 일정 연령에 다다르면 직장에서 은퇴를 해야만 한다. 이것은 의무 은퇴로 알려져 있다. 많은 국가나 회사에서 이런 상황에 관한 법이 있다. 한국에서는 법에 따르면 정년이 65세이다. 하지만 어떤 회사는 직원들이 훨씬 더 젊을 때 강제로 은퇴하도록 한다. 난 의무 은퇴에 이의가 있는데, 특히 많은 사람들이 여전히 건강하고 고급 업무를 할 능력이 있을 때 은퇴를 당하기 때문이다. 게다가 60대에 있는 많은 사람들은 자기 일에 대한 풍부한 경험과 지혜를 축적한, 회사에 있어 지극히 귀중한 직원들이다. 그들이 신체적으로 지속해서 일을 할 수 없다면 회사는 그들이 기여할 수 있는 다른 방안을 찾아야 한다. 또한 많은 노인들이 회사나 정부 연금만으로는 연명할 수 없다. 특히나 생활비가 매년 증가하고 있기 때문에 그들에게는 품위있는 삶을 살 봉급이 필요하다. 정부는 현재의 정책을 바꿔 사람들이 은퇴를 원할 때까지 일하도록 할 필요가 있다.

29 **Which of the following is NOT true about the conversation?**

① They will go to her mother's house on Sunday.
② They will see the baseball game on Saturday.
✓ They will see both games this weekend.
④ The man bought tickets for both games.
⑤ The woman likes baseball more than basketball.

대화에 대해 사실이 <u>아닌</u> 것은 무엇인가?

① 화자들은 일요일에 여자의 어머니 집에 갈 것이다.
② 화자들은 토요일에 야구 경기를 볼 것이다.
③ 화자들은 이번 주말에 두 경기를 모두 볼 것이다.
④ 남자는 두 경기의 티켓을 샀다.
⑤ 여자는 농구보다 야구를 좋아한다.

▶ **playoff** 챔피언 결정전 **champ** (경기의) 우승자, 챔피언 **give away** 거저 주다 **instead** 대신에 **there's no point** 소용이 없다, 이득이 없다 **argue about** …에 대해 논쟁하다, 언쟁하다

W What are we going to do this weekend?

M There's a baseball game on Saturday afternoon and a basketball game on Sunday night. I want to attend both of them, and I already have the tickets.

W You're going to both of them? I know you love sports, but I think two games in one weekend are too much for me.

M Come on. It'll be fun. You like baseball, and the home team is trying to win enough games to make the playoffs. You'll have a great time if you go.

W I'll go to the baseball game, but I certainly don't want to see the basketball game. You know I'm not that thrilled about basketball.

M The champs are coming. It's going to be a great game.

W Sorry, but Sunday is our day to do something together with our family. My mother wants us to come for dinner.

M But I bought the tickets for the game yesterday.

W I'm sure one of your friends will buy them from you, or you can just give them away instead.

M I guess there's no point in arguing about it. Call your mother, and tell her that we'll be there.

여 이번 주말에 뭐할 거야?

남 토요일 오후에 야구경기가 있고 일요일 밤엔 농구경기가 있어. 둘다 관람하고 싶어서 표를 이미 샀어.

여 둘다 가려고? 스포츠를 좋아하는 건 알지만 주말에 두 경기는 나한텐 너무 많은 것 같아.

남 제발. 재미있을 거야. 당신도 야구를 좋아하고 홈팀이 플레이오프에 진출할 수 있을 만큼 충분한 경기를 이기기 위해 애쓰고 있잖아. 가면 즐거운 시간이 될 거야.

여 야구 경기엔 가겠지만 농구 경기는 정말 보고 싶지 않아. 농구에는 그다지 흥분하지 않는 거 알잖아.

남 챔피언들이 올 거라고. 멋진 경기가 될 거야.

여 미안하지만 일요일은 가족끼리 뭔가를 하기로 한 날이야. 엄마가 우리가 저녁식사에 왔으면 해서.

남 하지만 어제 경기 표를 샀단 말이야.

여 분명히 당신 친구 중에서 그걸 살 사람이 있을 거야. 아니면 그냥 줘도 되잖아.

남 이 문제에 대해 다퉈도 소용이 없을 것 같다. 장모님한테 전화해서 거기 가겠다고 말씀드려.

---

30 **Which is the best title for this talk?**

① How Our Body Works
② Why People Can Taste Things
③ The Eye and the Brain
✓ The Five Senses
⑤ Understanding the Environment

이 이야기의 제목으로 가장 알맞은 것은 무엇인가?

① 우리의 인체는 어떻게 작용하는가
② 사람들이 왜 맛을 느낄 수 있는가
③ 눈과 뇌
④ 오감
⑤ 환경을 이해하기

▶ **sense** (감각 기관에 의한) 감각, 감각 작용 **auditory organ** 청각 기관 **vibrate** 진동시키다, 떨게 하다 **eardrum** 중이, 고막 **optical nerve** 시신경 **a series of** 일련의 **olfactory** 후각의 **sensor** 센서, 감지장치 **nasal passage** 콧구멍 **distinguish** 구별하다 **pleasant** 기분좋은 **sensation** 지각, 기분

W Our bodies get information from the environment through the various senses. There are five of them, and they are, in no particular order, hearing, sight, smell, touch, and taste. People are able to hear thanks to their ears and the other auditory organs found inside the head. What we hear as noise are actually sound waves vibrating our eardrums. The eyes are connected to the brain by the optical nerves, and the brain records the images the eyes see. The nose picks up smells through a series of olfactory sensors in the nasal passages. The tongue, mouth, and lips have sensors which can distinguish the many different tastes, both pleasant and not so pleasant, that people experience. These allow people to distinguish between a large number of different tastes. The skin covers the entire body. Every skin cell contains sensors that feel sensations such as the touch of another person, heat, cold; and even pain. Without our senses, we would have a very difficult time living in our world's environment.

여 우리 몸은 다양한 감각을 통해 주위 환경에서 정보를 얻는다. 감각에는 다섯 가지가 있는데 무작위로 열거해 보면 청각, 시각, 후각, 촉각, 미각이다. 사람들은 귀와 머리 속에 있는 다른 청각 기관 덕분에 소리를 들을 수 있다. 우리가 소음으로 듣는 것은 실제로는 고막을 진동하는 음파이다. 눈은 시신경에 의해 뇌에 연결되는데 뇌는 눈이 보는 이미지들을 기록한다. 코는 콧구멍 속에 있는 일련의 후각 센서를 통해 냄새를 맡는다. 혀와 입, 입술은 사람들이 체험하는 많은 다른 맛, 기분좋은 것과 그다지 기분좋지 않은 것 두 가지를 구별할 수 있다. 이런 것들로 인해 사람들은 수많은 다른 맛을 구별할 수 있다. 피부는 몸 전체를 덮고 있다. 모든 피부세포에는 또 다른 사람의 접촉과 열, 추위, 심지어 고통 같은 기분을 느끼는 센서가 들어 있다. 우리에게 감각이 없다면 우리는 세상 환경에서 살아가는 데 아주 어려움을 겪을 것이다.

31 〔모두 듣기〕 **Which is NOT a reason the speaker likes his new boss?**

✔ She always has lunch with the staff.
② She is never late for work.
③ She often stays late to help others.
④ She is very nice to the employees.
⑤ She does her job very well.

화자가 새 상사를 좋아하는 이유가 <u>아닌</u> 것은 무엇인가?

① 그녀는 늘 사원들과 함께 점심을 먹는다.
② 그녀는 절대로 지각하지 않는다.
③ 그녀는 다른 이들을 돕느라 종종 늦게까지 회사에 있는다.
④ 그녀는 직원들에게 굉장히 친절하다.
⑤ 그녀는 자신의 일을 잘 처리한다.

▶ supervisor 감독(자), 관리자 promote 승진시키다 head 수석, (집단의) 우두머리 manager 관리인, 경영자 so far 지금까지 replace 대체하다 shout 소리치다 on time 정각에(=sharp), 제시간에 disappear 사라지다 at a time 한 번에 deadline 마감일 previous 이전의 in the first place 애당초 be satisfied with …에게 만족하다

M My department supervisor got promoted to head manager last week, so we have a new supervisor in our department. So far, the new supervisor is excellent. In fact, she's much better than the person she replaced. She's kinder and never shouts at employees if they make a mistake. She knows a lot about her position, which makes our jobs much easier. She also always arrives at work on time and only takes an hour for lunch. The last boss would always come late and would often disappear for hours at a time. Every day this week, she stayed late to help us finish a project in order to complete it by the deadline. Our previous supervisor was out the door at five o'clock sharp every day. Sometimes I wonder why he even got promoted in the first place. Anyway, I'm totally satisfied with my new boss. I just hope she doesn't get promoted, too.

남 우리 부서 상사가 지난주에 관리본부장으로 승진해서 우리 부서에 새 상사가 왔다. 지금까지 새 상사는 훌륭하다. 사실 그녀는 전임자보다 훨씬 더 낫다. 더 친절하고 직원들이 실수했을 경우 절대로 그들에게 소리 지르지 않는다. 그녀가 자기 직책에 대해 아는 것이 많아서 우리 일이 훨씬 더 수월하다. 또 그녀는 항상 정각에 출근하고 점심은 한 시간밖에 안 걸린다. 지난번 상사는 항상 늦게 오고 종종 한 번에 몇 시간씩 사라지곤 했다. 이번주 매일 그녀는 늦게 남아서 우리가 마감일까지 완료하기 위해 프로젝트를 끝내는 걸 도왔다. 이전 상사는 매일 다섯 시에 칼같이 문을 나섰다. 가끔 난 애당초 그가 어떻게 승진되었는지가 의아하다. 아무튼 나는 새 상사에게 완전히 만족한다. 그저 그녀까지 승진되지 않기만을 바랄 뿐이다.

---

32 〔모두 듣기〕 **Which of the following offenses did the woman NOT commit?**

① She was too close to another car.
② She did not signal a lane change.
③ She was driving too fast.
✔ She did not have her seatbelt on.
⑤ She had a broken car part.

다음 중 여자가 위반하지 <u>않은</u> 것은 무엇인가?

① 그녀는 다른 차와 너무 가깝게 있었다.
② 그녀는 차선 변경 신호를 하지 않았다.
③ 그녀는 과속을 하고 있었다.
④ 그녀는 안전벨트를 착용하지 않았다.
⑤ 그녀의 자동차 일부가 부서져 있었다.

▶ vehicle registration 차량 등록증 officer 경관, 순경 violate 위반하다 speed limit (자동차 등의) 제한 속도, 최고 속도 posted 공표된 in a hurry 조급하게 excuse 변명, 핑계 lane 차선 signal 신호를 보내다 taillight (자동차 등의) 미등 cover 덮개 repair 수리하다 distance 거리 ticket 딱지, 교통 위반 카드 from now on 지금부터는

M May I see your driver's license and vehicle registration please, ma'am?

W Yes, officer. Here they are. Could you tell me what I did wrong?

M Actually, you violated a number of laws. First, you were driving ten kilometers over the speed limit. The posted limit is only sixty kilometers per hour, yet you were doing seventy.

W Sorry. I'm late for work, so I was in a hurry.

M That's no excuse, ma'am. Second, you crossed from one lane to another without signaling.

W I guess I forgot, but no one else was signaling, so why did you stop me?

M I stopped you because you also have a broken taillight cover that needs to be repaired as soon as possible. Today would be a good time to do it.

W I'll go to the repair shop at lunchtime. Is that everything, officer?

M No, there's one more thing. You were driving too close to the vehicle in front of you, so try to keep a safe distance in the future. Here's your ticket. Please drive carefully from now on, ma'am.

W I will. Thanks for being so nice.

남 운전면허증과 차량 등록증을 보여주시겠습니까?

여 네. 여기 있어요. 제가 뭘 잘못했나요?

남 사실 많은 법규를 위반했어요. 첫째로 제한속도를 10킬로미터 초과해서 운전중이었죠. 공표된 제한속도는 겨우 시속 60킬로미터인데 70으로 운전하고 계시더군요.

여 미안해요. 직장에 늦어서 조급했거든요.

남 그건 변명이 안 되죠. 둘째로 신호를 보내지 않고 한 차선에서 다른 차선으로 가로질렀어요.

여 깜빡했나봐요. 하지만 다른 사람도 아무도 신호를 안 보냈는데, 왜 저를 세운 거예요?

남 제가 세운 건 가능한 한 빨리 수리가 필요한 미등 덮개도 깨져 있어서입니다. 오늘 그 일을 하시면 좋겠네요.

여 점심 때 수리점에 갈게요. 그게 다인가요, 경관님?

남 아니오, 한 가지 더 있습니다. 앞 차량에 너무 가까이 운전하고 계셨으니 앞으로는 안전 거리를 유지하도록 하십시오. 여기 교통위반 카드입니다. 지금부터는 주의해서 운전하세요.

여 그러죠. 친절하게 대해줘서 고마워요.

33 〔모두 듣기〕 **What is an example of "Don't count your chickens before they're hatched"?**

① A boy gets the birthday present he was hoping for from his parents.

② A student studies hard and receives a very good grade on an exam.

③ A woman buys a lottery ticket and then goes to look at new cars.

④ A man starts a business and becomes very successful after some time.

⑤ A little girl dreams of becoming a ballerina when she grows up.

'알을 까지 전에 닭을 세지 말라'는 이야기의 예는 어느 것인가?

① 소년이 부모에게서 바라는 생일 선물을 받는다.

② 학생이 열심히 공부해서 시험에서 아주 좋은 성적을 받는다.

③ 여자가 복권을 산 다음 새 차를 보러 간다.

④ 남자가 사업을 시작해서 얼마 후 아주 성공하게 된다.

⑤ 어린 소녀가 자라서 발레리나가 되는 꿈을 꾼다.

▶ **convey** (뉴스, 의미 등을) 전달하다, 표현하다 **subtle** 미묘한, 섬세하고 신비적인 **fable** 우화 **folktale** 민화, 전설 **count** 차례로 세다 **hatch** (알을) 부화하다 **dozens of** 수십의, 많은 **lay eggs** 알을 낳다 **daydream** 몽상하다, 공상에 잠기다 **trip** (돌 등에) 걸려 비틀거리다 **moral** (이야기, 경험 등의) 교훈 **depend on** 의존하다 **carelessness** 부주의

W The English language has many expressions which can convey subtle meanings for events or people's personalities. Many expressions come from fables and folktales from the past. An example is "Don't count your chickens before they're hatched." This saying comes from the tale of a man with a basket of eggs. He was walking with a basket full of eggs in his arms while thinking about the dozens of chickens he would have when the eggs hatched. Some chickens he would sell for money, some he would cook for his family, and others he would keep to lay more eggs. Soon, he would have hundreds of chickens. The man was daydreaming about his good fortune when he tripped, fell, and broke every egg in the basket. The moral of this fable is you shouldn't depend on something until it happens. The man was already thinking of chickens while he only had eggs and thus lost everything through his carelessness.

여 영어에는 일이나 사람들의 성격에 대한 미묘한 의미를 전달할 수 있는 많은 표현이 있다. 많은 표현은 과거의 우화와 민담에서 유래한다. 일례는 '알을 까지 전에 닭을 세지 말라'이다. 이 격언은 달걀 바구니를 든 남자의 이야기에서 유래했다. 그는 달걀이 가득 든 바구니를 안고 걸으면서 달걀이 부화했을 때 자신이 갖게 될 수십 마리의 닭에 대해 생각하고 있었다. 몇 마리 닭은 돈을 얻기 위해 팔고 몇 마리는 가족을 위해 요리를 하고 다른 것들은 알을 더 낳기 위해 갖고 있을 것이다. 곧 그에게는 수백 마리의 닭이 생길 것이었다. 그가 행운에 대해 몽상하고 있을 때 그는 발이 걸려 넘어져서 바구니에 든 계란이 모두 깨져버렸다. 이 우화의 교훈은 어떤 일이 발생할 때까지 그것에 기대어서는 안 된다는 것이다. 남자는 달걀만 갖고 있었을 때 벌써 닭을 생각하고 있었고 따라서 부주의로 인해 모든 것을 잃어버렸다.

---

34 〔모두 듣기〕 **Where is this conversation taking place?**

① In a library

② In a police station

③ At 120 Eastern Avenue

④ At the motorcycle repair shop

⑤ At a university

이 대화가 이루어지고 있는 곳은 어디인가?

① 도서관에서

② 경찰서에서

③ 이스턴 애비뉴 120번지에서

④ 오토바이 수리점에서

⑤ 대학교에서

▶ **purse** 지갑, (여성의) 핸드백 **relax** 긴장을 풀다, 진정하다 **describe** 표현하다, 묘사하다 **motorcycle** 오토바이 **grab** 갑자기 꽉 잡다, 잡아채다 **ride** (탈것에) 타다, 타고 가다 **more like** 오히려 …에 가까운[닮은] **scooter** 스쿠터 **stripe** 줄무늬 **visor** (야구 모자 등의) 챙, 햇빛 가리개

M Yes, ma'am. How can I help you?

W I was just robbed. A man just stole my purse from my hands right on the street.

M Just relax, ma'am. I know you're excited and scared, but I need to ask you some questions. Please have a seat at my desk here. Okay, first, what's your name and address?

W I'm sorry, officer, but it was so shocking. My name is Jessica Smith, and I live at 120 Eastern Avenue.

M Now why don't you describe exactly what happened?

W I was leaving the library near the university just down the street from here. I work there. This man drove by on a motorcycle and just grabbed my purse before I knew what was happening.

M What kind of motorcycle was he riding?

W Oh, I don't know much about them. It wasn't a big one. It was more like a scooter. I think it was white with red strips.

M All right. And what did the man look like?

W I didn't get a look at his face because he was wearing a helmet with a dark visor.

남 네, 부인. 뭘 도와드릴까요?

여 방금 강도를 당했어요. 어떤 남자가 길에서 제 손에 있는 지갑을 훔쳤어요.

남 진정하세요. 흥분되고 겁이 난 건 알지만 몇 가지 질문을 해야겠습니다. 여기 제 책상 의자에 앉으세요. 자, 먼저 이름과 주소가 어떻게 되죠?

여 미안하지만 너무 놀랐어요. 이름은 제시카 스미스이고 이스턴 애비뉴 120번지에 살아요.

남 이제 정확히 무슨 일이 일어났는지 말씀해 주시겠어요?

여 저는 여기서 바로 길 아래에 있는 대학 근처의 도서관에서 나오고 있었어요. 거기서 일을 하거든요. 이 남자는 오토바이를 타고 옆을 지나갔는데 그냥 부지불식간에 제 지갑을 낚아챘어요.

남 어떤 종류의 오토바이를 타고 있었죠?

여 아, 그건 잘 모르겠어요. 큰 건 아니었어요. 스쿠터에 더 가까울 거예요. 흰색과 빨간색 줄무늬가 있었던 것 같아요.

남 알겠습니다. 그리고 그 남자가 어떻게 생겼죠?

여 얼굴 생김새는 못 봤어요. 검게 선팅된 헬멧을 쓰고 있었거든요.

35 다음을 듣고, 이어지는 영어 질문에 답하시오.

① Monday
✓ Wednesday
③ Thursday
④ Friday
⑤ Saturday

▶ share 공유하다   on weekends 주말에

M Terry, Jimmy, and Fred share an apartment together. All three of them like watching television at their home at night. Terry usually watches television from Monday to Friday but never on weekends because he goes out with his friends then. Jimmy doesn't watch TV as much as the others because he's a student and needs to study. He enjoys his favorite shows only on Wednesday and the weekend. Fred can be found in front of the television on every day of the week because he really loves it.

Q: *Which day of the week do all three roommates watch television together at home?*

남 테리와 지미, 프레드는 같은 아파트에 산다. 그들 세 명 모두는 밤에 집에서 텔레비전을 보는 것을 좋아한다. 테리는 보통 월요일에서 금요일까지 텔레비전을 보지만 주말에는 절대로 보지 않는데 그때는 친구들과 외출을 하기 때문이다. 지미는 다른 사람들만큼 텔레비전을 보지는 않는데, 학생이라서 공부를 해야 하기 때문이다. 그는 수요일과 주말에만 하는 자신이 좋아하는 쇼를 즐긴다. 프레드가 매일 텔레비전 앞에 있는 걸 볼 수 있는데 그것은 정말로 텔레비전을 좋아하기 때문이다.

Q: *세 룸메이트가 집에서 모두 함께 TV를 보는 날은 언제인가?*

---

36 주어진 시간 동안 아래 지문을 주의 깊게 읽고, 들려주는 질문에 답하시오. (1분)

In eastern Asia, many people visit both Western-trained doctors and Oriental medicine doctors. Oriental medicine differs greatly from Western medicine. To begin with, there is less reliance on surgery and synthetic medicines in Oriental medicine. Instead, it uses methods like acupuncture and herbal remedies to treat patients' aliments. The sick person's body is treated as a whole; the doctor does not just focus upon the particular part that is not functioning properly. For example, if a person had a foot problem, a Western doctor would examine them, take X-rays, and perhaps perform surgery or prescribe medicine for the foot problem. The Oriental doctor, however, would treat the body as one entity by using acupuncture on the feet, by massaging the joints in the back and legs to relieve pressure on the feet, and by giving herbal medicine for high blood pressure, which could be the cause of the foot problem. Western doctors are typically skeptical about Oriental medicine and often believe it has no merits. But this is more a case of professional jealousy than something grounded in fact. Oriental medicine is reliable, it is less expensive than Western methods, and the patient often recovers faster.

Q ___________________

① 환자들에게 수술을 시행한다.
② 환자들에게 마사지를 시행한다.
✓ 환자들에게 약을 처방한다.
④ 환자들에게 침을 놓는다.
⑤ 환자들의 엑스레이를 찍는다.

▶ differ from …와 다르다   reliance on …에 대한 신뢰[의존]   synthetic 인조의, 합성의   acupuncture 침술   remedy 의약품, 치료   ailment (가볍거나 만성적인) 병, 불쾌   prescribe 처방하다   entity 존재, 본질   joint 관절, 마디   skeptical 회의적인

Q: *Which is NOT a difference between Western and Oriental medicine?*

동아시아에서는 많은 사람들이 서양식 교육을 받은 의사와 한의학 의사 모두를 찾아간다. 한의학은 서양 의학과는 매우 다르다. 우선 한방에서는 수술과 인조 약물에 덜 의존한다. 대신 침술과 한약재 같은 치료제를 이용하여 환자들의 병을 치료한다. 아픈 사람의 몸은 전체적으로 치료가 되며 의사는 기능이 제대로 되지 않는 특별한 부분에만 중심을 두는 것이 아니다. 예를 들어 어떤 사람이 발에 문제가 있으면 양의사는 진찰을 하고 엑스레이를 찍고, 어쩌면 수술을 하거나 발 질환에 대한 약물을 처방할 것이다. 하지만 한의사는 발에 침을 놓고 등과 다리 관절에 마사지를 해서 발의 압력을 완화하고 발 질환의 원인이 될 수 있는 고혈압을 위해 약재를 주어, 하나의 존재로서 몸을 치료할 것이다. 양의사들은 일반적으로 한의학에 대해 회의적이며 종종 그것이 아무런 장점이 없다고 생각한다. 하지만 이것은 사실에 근거한 것이라기보다는 직업적인 질시에 따른 경우가 더 많다. 한의학은 믿을 만하며 서양식 방법보다 저렴하며 때로는 환자가 더 빨리 회복한다.

Q: *서양과 동양 의학의 차이가 아닌 것은 무엇인가?*

37 Which of the following is NOT true about the speaker?

① She is married.
✓② She lives in Busan.
③ She is a school teacher.
④ She has children.
⑤ She studied in Australia.

화자에 대해 사실이 <u>아닌</u> 것은 무엇인가?

① 그녀는 기혼자이다.
② 그녀는 부산에 산다.
③ 그녀는 학교 선생님이다.
④ 그녀는 자녀가 있다.
⑤ 그녀는 호주에서 공부를 했다.

38 Choose the title of a book which the speaker most likely wants to read.

① *Journey to the Stars*
✓② *Korea in the Nineteenth Century*
③ *Child Care and You*
④ *New Methods in Education*
⑤ *Adventures in the Jungle*

화자가 가장 읽기 좋아할 것 같은 책의 제목을 고르시오.

① 〈우주로의 여행〉
② 〈19세기의 한국〉
③ 〈육아와 당신〉
④ 〈새로운 교육 방식〉
⑤ 〈정글에서의 모험〉

▶ **degree** 학위 **yoga** 요가 **socialize** 격의없이 교제하다 **passion** 열정, 좋아하는 것 **spy novel** 탐정소설

(37~38)

W Please allow me to introduce myself. My name is Park Heejin, and I'm thirty-nine years old. I was born in Busan and have two older sisters and one younger brother. My parents were both elementary school teachers but have since retired. I finished high school in 1987 and entered Seoul National University to study education. I graduated with my degree in 1992. I was employed as an elementary school teacher for three years before moving to Australia to study English for a year. Following that, I returned to Korea, where I found my current job, which is teaching English at a Seoul middle school. I got married in 1999 and now have two daughters. I like watching baseball and television dramas and also do yoga in my free time. I love hiking, and my husband and I also enjoy socializing with our friends by going out to eat a lot. Reading is my other passion. I love reading history books and spy novels. There's nothing better than staying at home and reading a good book.

(37~38)

여 제 소개를 하겠습니다. 이름은 박희진이며 39세입니다. 부산에서 태어났고 언니 두 명에 남동생이 한 명 있습니다. 부모님은 모두 초등학교 교사였지만 퇴직하셨습니다. 저는 1987년에 고등학교를 마치고 서울대학에 입학해 교육학을 공부했습니다. 1992년에 학위를 받고 졸업했습니다. 초등학교 교사로 3년간 재직하다 호주로 옮겨 1년 동안 영어를 배웠습니다. 그 이후에는 한국으로 돌아와서 현재 서울에 있는 중학교에서 영어를 가르치는 일을 하고 있습니다. 1999년에 결혼하여 지금은 딸이 두 명 있습니다. 야구와 텔레비전 드라마를 보는 걸 좋아하며 자유 시간에는 요가도 합니다. 하이킹을 즐기며 남편과 친구들과 함께 어울려서 자주 외식도 즐깁니다. 독서는 다른 취미입니다. 역사책과 탐정소설을 읽는 걸 좋아합니다. 집에 머물며 좋은 책을 읽는 것보다 더 좋은 것은 없습니다.

<table>
<tr><th>문제와 정답</th><th>스크립트</th><th>해석</th></tr>
</table>

39 Which TV program do the speakers like in common?

① sports programs
② science fiction shows ✓
③ soap operas
④ reality shows
⑤ comedy shows

화자들이 공통적으로 좋아하는 TV 프로그램은 무엇인가?

① 스포츠 프로그램
② 공상과학 쇼
③ 드라마
④ 리얼리티 쇼
⑤ 코미디 쇼

40 What is the reason the woman dislikes reality programs?

① She is easily bored by them.
② She finds them too realistic.
③ She thinks they are staged. ✓
④ They are too violent for her.
⑤ They do not have realistic situations.

여자가 리얼리티 쇼를 싫어하는 이유는 무엇인가?

① 그녀는 리얼리티 쇼에 금새 싫증이 난다.
② 그녀는 그것들이 너무 현실적이라는 걸 알았다.
③ 그녀는 그것들이 일부러 꾸며진 것이라고 생각한다.
④ 그녀에게는 너무 폭력적이다.
⑤ 현실적인 상황이 없다.

▶ **soap opera** (주부 취향의 연속) 멜로드라마 **show** (텔레비전, 라디오의) 프로, 쇼 **unrealistic** 비현실적인 **divorce** 이혼하다 **lost track** …을 놓치다, 잊다 **despise** 경멸하다, 몹시 싫어하다 **so-called** 이른바 **script** 원고를 쓰다, 대본화하다; 대본 **spontaneous** 자발적인, 임의의 **preview** 미리보기 **live** 생방송인, 실황인 **set up** (기계 등을) 조립[설비]하다, 설정하다

(39~40)

M It's too rainy outside to go to the park.

W I guess we can spend the entire day here. My favorite soap opera is about to come on anyway. Turn on the television, please.

M I don't know how you can watch soap operas. They are so unrealistic. My mother watches one show that has a character who has been married and divorced so many times I've lost track.

W Well, I despise those so-called reality programs you like. They must be scripted. I don't believe those programs are spontaneous, and I bet those people are all paid actors.

M There's no script for those shows, and they aren't actors. Everything you see really happens. Hey, the TV guide says that new science fiction show is starting tonight at nine o'clock after the comedy hour.

W I forgot about that. I really want to see that show because the previews I saw were fantastic.

M Yeah, I can't wait to see it. Oh, the soccer game is on another channel right now. It's the Premier league. Can I change the channel?

W Wait until my show is over. You know I'm not a big fan of sports. People are always hitting each other and getting hurt. It's just too much. Why don't you record it?

M But it's my favorite team. It's not the same if it isn't live.

W Okay, just wait until I set up the VCR to record my show.

(39~40)

남 공원에 가기엔 밖에 비가 너무 와.

여 온종일 여기서 보내야겠네. 어쨌거나 곧 좋아하는 드라마가 할 거니까. 텔레비전 좀 켜줘.

남 드라마를 어떻게 보는지 모르겠어. 너무 비현실적이잖아. 우리 엄마가 보는 프로에서는 등장인물이 너무 여러 번 결혼했다 이혼해서 내용을 놓쳤어.

여 음, 난 당신이 좋아하는 이른바 리얼리티 프로그램이 아주 싫어. 그건 분명히 대본에 있는 거야. 그런 프로그램들은 자발적이지 않다고 생각하고, 그 사람들은 모두 보수를 받는 배우들임이 분명해.

남 그런 쇼에는 대본이 없어. 그리고 그들은 배우가 아니야. 네가 보는 모든 게 정말 일어나는 거라고. 있잖아, TV 가이드에서 새 공상과학 프로가 오늘밤 9시에 코미디 시간 뒤에 시작한대.

여 그걸 깜빡 했네. 미리보기를 본 게 아주 좋아서 그 프로는 정말 보고 싶어.

남 그래, 빨리 보고 싶어. 아, 지금 다른 채널에서 축구 경기를 해. 프리미어 리그야. 채널 바꿀까?

여 이 프로 끝날 때까지 기다려 줘. 난 그다지 스포츠팬이 아니라는 거 알잖아. 사람들이 항상 서로 공격하고 다치고. 그건 너무 지나쳐. 녹화하면 안 될까?

남 하지만 내가 좋아하는 팀이야. 생방송으로 보는 거랑은 달라.

여 알았어, 이 프로를 비디오로 녹화 설정할 때까지만 기다려 줘.

실전모의고사 05

01 ⑤	02 ③	03 ①	04 ①	05 ②	06 ④	07 ②	08 ③	09 ④	10 ①
11 ②	12 ⑤	13 ④	14 ②	15 ②	16 ②	17 ⑤	18 ④	19 ④	20 ⑤
21 ④	22 ③	23 ②	24 ④	25 ②	26 ⑤	27 ⑤	28 ②	29 ①	30 ①
31 ②	32 ①	33 ⑤	34 ①	35 ④	36 ⑤	37 ②	38 ④	39 ②	40 ①

문제와 정답	스크립트	해석

01

다음을 듣고, 여자가 찾아갈 가게들이 순서대로 나열된 것을 고르시오.

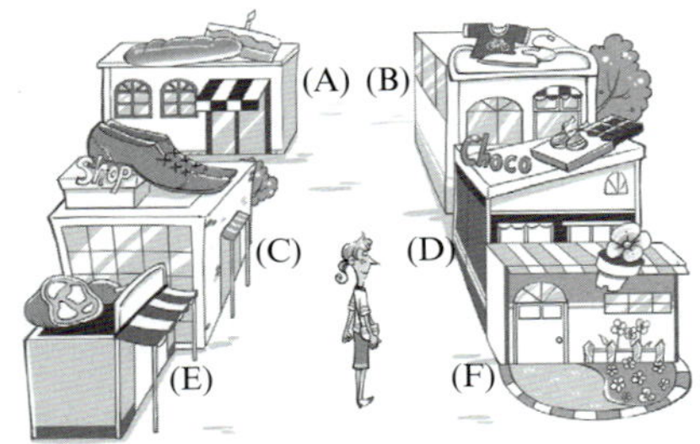

① (A) – (C) – (D) – (F)
② (B) – (D) – (F) – (E)
③ (F) – (C) – (D) – (A)
④ (E) – (F) – (C) – (B)
⑤ (F) – (D) – (C) – (A) ✓

▶ **short of** …이 부족한, 불충분한 **pick up** …을 찾아오다 **risk** 모험하다, 위험에 내맡기다

W I've got some shopping to do today. There are a lot of things to buy, yet I'm pretty short of time. Fortunately, there's one street nearby with some great shops. Now, let me think about the best way to do this. First, I need some flowers for my sister's birthday, so I think I'll visit the florist right away. Oh, I should also buy some chocolates for her as soon as I leave the first place. She loves chocolate, and I heard that the shop is having a sale today. Then, I can cross the street and pick up the shoes I left to get fixed at the store last week after I broke a heel while working. Finally, I need to remember to pick up the cake I ordered for the party at the bakery. I don't want to carry it around everywhere and risk dropping it or anything.

여 오늘 쇼핑할 게 좀 있다. 살 물건은 많은데 시간이 꽤 부족하다. 다행히 괜찮은 가게가 몇 군데 있는 거리가 근처에 있다. 이제, 쇼핑을 가장 잘 할 수 있는 방법에 대해 생각을 해 보자. 첫째로, 여동생의 생일 때문에 꽃이 좀 필요하니까 당장 플로리스트를 찾아가야겠다. 또 첫 번째 장소를 떠나자마자 그녀에게 줄 초콜릿을 좀 사야 한다. 그녀는 초콜릿을 좋아하는데 오늘 그 가게가 특매를 한다고 들었다. 그 다음엔 길을 건너서 지난주에 일을 하다 뒤축을 부러뜨린 뒤에 가게에 수선을 맡긴 구두를 찾으면 되겠다. 마지막으로 파티를 위해 빵집에 주문한 케이크를 찾아오는 걸 기억해야 한다. 그걸 여기저기 들고 다니면서 떨어뜨리거나 어떤 모험을 하고 싶지는 않으니까 말이다.

02

대화를 듣고, 남자의 직업이 무엇인지 고르시오.

① doctor
② businessman
③ librarian ✓
④ lawyer
⑤ teacher

① 의사
② 사업가
③ 사서
④ 변호사
⑤ 교사

▶ **to tell the truth** 사실대로 말하면 **absolutely** 아주, 정말로 **suit** 양복 **previous** 이전의 **nowadays** 요즈음 **surrounded** 둘러싸인 **relax** 편히 쉬다, 긴장을 풀다 **standard** 보통의, 관례적인 **even though** 비록 …하지만 **ideal** 이상적인 **current** 현재의

W How's your new job been going? You must be pretty busy because I haven't seen you around much lately.

M Well, the job's going quite well to tell the truth. I absolutely love it, especially because I don't have to wear a suit like I did at my previous job.

W Yeah, you were always at the office and going on business trips a lot. I remember how busy you used to be.

M But it's much different nowadays. I'm in such a quiet environment now, and there's really not that much stress in my life.

W That's a relief. I never enjoyed hearing stories about all your trips to the doctor's office since you were so stressed.

M You won't hear about those any more. I'm surrounded by books all day long, which really helps to relax me.

W That's good to hear. What about your hours?

M I work a standard nine-to-six day even though we're open until nine. But I get to go home early.

W It sounds like you've found the ideal job for you. Congratulations.

M Yeah, I'm really happy with my current situation.

여 새 일 어때? 최근에 별로 보이지도 않고 꽤 바빴나 봐.

남 음, 사실 일은 꽤 잘 되고 있어. 특히 이전 직장에서처럼 양복을 입지 않아도 돼서 정말 마음에 들어.

여 그래, 넌 항상 사무실에서 있으면서 출장을 많이 다녔잖아. 예전에 네가 얼마나 바빴는지 기억난다.

남 하지만 요즘은 많이 달라. 이젠 아주 조용한 환경에 있고 생활에서 받는 스트레스도 그렇게 많진 않아.

여 그거 안심이 된다. 네가 그렇게 스트레스를 받은 이후로 병원에 다녔다는 이야기를 듣고 마음이 편치 못했는데.

남 더 이상은 그런 얘길 안 듣게 될 거야. 하루 종일 책에 둘러싸여 있는데, 마음을 편히 하는 데 그게 정말로 도움이 되거든.

여 다행이다. 근무 시간은 어때?

남 우리는 9시까지 문을 열지만 난 일반적인 9시에서 6시까지 일해. 하지만 일찍 귀가하지.

여 네게 딱 맞는 일을 찾은 것 같다. 축하해.

남 그래, 현재 상황에 정말 만족해.

03 대화를 듣고, 두 사람의 관계를 가장 잘 나타낸 것을 고르시오.

Man	Woman
✔ interviewer	interviewee
② employer	employee
③ professor	student
④ manager	employee
⑤ company president	manager

남자	여자
① 면접관	피면접인
② 고용주	고용인
③ 교수	학생
④ 관리자	직원
⑤ 회사 사장	관리자

▶ take 견해, 해석 economy 경제 (상태), 경기 nosedive (가격 등의) 폭락 assessment 평가 lay off (일시적으로) …을 해고하다 picky 꽤 까다로운 be up against (곤란 등에) 직면해 있다 stiff 힘든 depend upon …에 달려있다 call … in 부르다, 초대하다 round 한 차례[과정] transcript 성적증명서 I'd say 아마 …이겠지요

M What is your take on the current job market?

W It's not very positive. The economy was great for a couple of years, but it looks like it's about to take a nosedive.

M That's our assessment as well. We're positive a number of companies are going to begin laying off workers relatively soon.

W But that's not the case for your firm.

M Not at all. If it were, you and I wouldn't be talking today. However, that means we can be picky about whom we choose to employ.

W I suppose I'm up against some stiff competition.

M Yes, that's true, but we're impressed with your qualifications. Depending upon how well you do today, we may call you in for a second round.

W That's exactly what I'm hoping for. Like I said earlier, I'm not confident in the economy, so I need to secure some employment really soon.

M Going by your transcript and qualifications, I'd say you'll be sure to do that. Now, why don't I introduce you to some of the other people with whom you'll be speaking today?

W That sounds great to me.

남 현 구직 시장에 대해 어떤 견해를 갖고 있습니까?

여 별로 전망이 좋지 않습니다. 수년간은 경기가 괜찮았지만 곧 폭락할 것 같습니다.

남 우리 평가도 그래요. 많은 회사가 비교적 곧 직원들을 해고하기 시작할 거라고 봅니다.

여 하지만 귀사의 경우는 아니죠.

남 전혀요. 그랬다면 우린 오늘 얘기를 하지 못하고 있을 겁니다. 하지만 그 말은 우리가 채용할 사람을 선택하는 데 까다로울 수도 있다는 뜻이지요.

여 제가 경쟁이 좀 심한 상황에 놓인 것 같군요.

남 네, 맞습니다, 하지만 당신이 갖춘 자격에 감명을 받았어요. 오늘 당신이 얼마나 잘 하는가에 따라서 2차에서 당신을 부를 수도 있지요.

여 그게 바로 제가 희망하는 겁니다. 앞서 말씀드린 것처럼 경기에 대한 확신이 없어서 정말 빨리 일자리를 얻어야 하거든요.

남 당신의 성적증명서와 자격 요건으로 보건대, 꼭 그렇게 될 것 같군요. 이제, 오늘 같이 얘기하게 될 다른 사람을 몇 분 소개시켜 줄게요.

여 좋습니다.

---

04 다음을 듣고, 화자의 심정을 가장 잘 나타낸 것을 고르시오.

① ✔ regretful
② angry
③ jealous
④ ecstatic
⑤ uncaring

① 후회하는
② 화난
③ 질투하는
④ 황홀한
⑤ 부주의한

▶ prestigious 유명한, 신망이 있는 in hindsight 지나고 나서 보니까 job interview (취직) 면접 (시험) fault 잘못, 과실 attend 참석하다 out of breath 숨이 차서, 헐떡이며 sweaty 땀투성이의 shave 면도하다 crooked 비뚤어진, 구부러진 hire 고용하다, 채용하다 top priority 최우선 사항

M I just found out that I failed to get hired by a very prestigious company in Seoul, and, in hindsight, missing out on this opportunity was my own fault. The job interview process was difficult since there were three interviews, but I successfully passed the first two rounds. However, the night before the last interview, I attended a birthday party for one of my high school friends. It was fun, but now I wish I'd never gone. I returned home late and forgot to set my alarm clock. I woke up thirty minutes before the interview and was already upset with myself for being so stupid. I hurried there but was out of breath and sweaty when I arrived. I didn't shave, and my tie was even on crooked. Today, I received an e-mail saying they weren't going to hire me. Getting this job should have been my top priority.

남 나는 방금 서울에 있는 매우 신망 있는 회사에 취직하는 데 실패했는데, 지나고 보니 이번 기회를 잃은 것이 나 자신의 잘못이라는 것을 알았다. 취업 면접 절차는 면접이 세 차례이기 때문에 어려웠지만 난 처음 두 번은 합격했다. 하지만 마지막 면접 전날 밤에 고등학교 친구 중 한 명의 생일 파티에 참석했다. 그것은 재미있었지만 지금은 절대 가지 말았어야 했다는 생각이 든다. 늦게 귀가를 해서 알람시계를 맞춰놓는 것을 잊어버린 것이다. 잠이 깬 것은 면접 30분 전이었고 난 이미 그토록 멍청했던 나 자신에게 화가 나 있었다. 그곳으로 서둘러 갔지만 도착했을 때는 숨이 찼고 땀범벅이었다. 면도도 하지 않았고 심지어 넥타이는 비뚤어져 있었다. 오늘 그들이 나를 채용하지 않을 것이라는 이메일을 받았다. 나는 이 일자리를 얻는 것을 가장 우선시 했어야 했다.

<table>
<tr><th>문제와 정답</th><th>스크립트</th><th>해석</th></tr>
</table>

05

대화를 듣고, 남자가 목적지까지 가는 데 가장 좋은 교통 수단이 무엇인지 고르시오.

① by taxi
✓ by bus
③ by car
④ by commuter train
⑤ by subway

① 택시
② 버스
③ 자동차
④ 통근 열차
⑤ 지하철

▶ downtown (시의 중심을 이루는) 상업 지구, 번화가 parking lot 주차장 be jam-packed (장소에) 빽빽하게 채워넣어지다, 꽉 채워지다 parking spot 주차 공간[지점] be better off 더 좋은 상태이다 subway 지하철 fortune 큰 돈 commuter train 통근 열차 suburb 교외, 근교 silly 어리석은, 바보 같은

M Do you have any plans for the weekend?

W I'm going to stay home with my family. How about you?

M My family and I are going downtown to the new shopping mall this Saturday. We're going to drive there in the afternoon.

W Oh, it's quite nice, but I wouldn't drive there if I were you.

M Why do you say that?

W The parking lots there are simply jam-packed with cars. I drove there last weekend and spent thirty minutes looking around for a parking spot. You'd be better off going there by subway.

M Oh, I didn't know that. I'm not sure about the subway though. There's not a station anywhere near our house.

W Hmm… And it would cost a fortune to take a taxi there. You're nowhere near the commuter train, are you?

M We live in the suburbs, so we could take it, but my youngest is kind of scared of them. It sounds silly, but it's the truth. I guess we'd be better off taking the bus.

W I agree. That sounds like the best way to get to the mall and back.

남 주말에 무슨 계획 있어?

여 가족들이랑 집에 있을 거야. 넌 어때?

남 가족들과 이번 토요일에 시내에 있는 새 쇼핑센터에 갈 거야. 오후에 운전해서 갈 예정이야.

여 아, 근사하다. 하지만 나라면 그곳에 차를 가지고 가진 않을 거야.

남 이유가 뭔데?

여 거기 주차장에는 차들이 아주 꽉 차 있어. 지난 주말에 운전해서 그곳에 갔는데 주차 장소를 찾는 데 30분이 걸렸어. 거기는 지하철로 가는 게 나을 거야.

남 아, 몰랐어. 그래도 지하철은 확신이 안 선다. 우리 집 근처에는 역이 없어.

여 흠… 그곳까지 택시를 타면 돈이 엄청 들 거야. 통근 열차는 좀처럼 없지, 안 그래?

남 교외에 사니까 탈 수는 있겠지만 막내가 그걸 좀 무서워해. 바보 같은 소리지만 사실이야. 버스를 타는 것이 나을 것 같다.

여 그래. 그게 쇼핑센터에 다녀오는 데는 최상의 방법인 것 같아.

06

대화를 듣고, 이 대화가 이루어지고 있는 장소를 고르시오.

① 공항 출국장
② 백화점
③ 슈퍼마켓
✓ 면세점
⑤ 기념품 가게

▶ ought to …해야 한다 purchase 구입하다 waste 낭비하다 tax 세금 item 품목, 물건 less than … 미만의, …을 밑도는 complex 종합 빌딩, 대형 아파트 why not (해도) 좋지 않으냐, 왜 안하느냐 go ahead (망설이지 말고) 진행시키다 section 구역, 부분 flight 정기 항공편, 비행기 여행 notice 알아차리다

W Come here and take a look at this. Do you think I ought to buy it?

M Can't you purchase it somewhere else back at home?

W Well, I might have to look around, but I'm sure I could find it at a store somewhere.

M Then why do you want to waste your money on it here?

W The reason is that it's much cheaper here. Since I don't have to pay any taxes on the item, it costs less than if I were to get it at the complex near our house.

M I never thought about it like that. In that case, why not go ahead and spend the money? We're on vacation after all.

W That's so nice of you to say that. Now, after I get this, let's go to that section over there. We absolutely must buy some presents for everyone back home.

M Okay, but we'd better hurry if we don't want to miss our flight.

W Right. I hadn't noticed how little time we have left.

M Then let's buy what we need to and get out of here.

여 여기 와서 이것 좀 봐. 이걸 사야 할까?

남 귀국해서 어디 다른 데서 구입할 수는 없니?

여 음, 찾아봐야겠지만 어딘가 가게에서 그걸 찾을 수는 있을 거야.

남 그럼 왜 여기서 돈을 쓰려고 해?

여 그건 여기가 값이 훨씬 더 싸기 때문이야. 그 물건에 대해 세금을 전혀 안 내도 되니까 집 근처 빌딩에서 사는 것보다 비용이 덜 들어.

남 난 그런 생각은 전혀 못했어. 그럼 그냥 돈을 써도 되잖아? 어쨌거나 우린 휴가 중이니까 말이야.

여 그렇게 말해 주니 참 고마워. 자, 이걸 산 뒤에 저쪽에 있는 매장으로 가 보자. 고국에 있는 사람들에게 줄 선물을 꼭 사야 하잖아.

남 좋아, 하지만 비행기를 놓치지 않으려면 서둘러야 해.

여 그래. 시간이 얼마 안 남은 걸 몰랐어.

남 그럼 필요한 걸 산 다음에 여길 나가자.

07 다섯 개의 대화문을 듣고, 자연스럽지 **않은** 것을 고르시오.

① 
②
③
④
⑤

▶ **for a while** 잠시, 얼마동안 **performance** 수행, 성취 **stuff** 물건 **happen to** 우연히[어쩌다] …하다 **inadvertently** 부주의하게, 무심코 **throw ... away** …을 팽개치다, 던지다 **wind up** …이라는 처지가 되다, …으로 끝나다 **get rid of** …을 제거하다 **tie the knot** 인연을 맺다, 결혼하다 **opposite** 반대 **break up with** …와 헤어지다 **relative** 친척 **rest** 휴식하다

① M I talked to Jeremy's teacher for a while after school.

W Really? What did she say about his performance?

M She told me he was doing well in school but that he doesn't always do his homework.

W We'll have to make sure he finishes it every night from now on.

② W Did you remember to bring the shopping list with you? I've got to get a lot of stuff today.

M Actually, I don't have it. I thought that you were bringing it.

W Great. Why don't you let me have it so that we can get our shopping done?

③ M Do you have a copy of that memo which Mr. Park sent to everyone?

W Yeah, I think I've got one right here. What happened to the one you got?

M I inadvertently threw it away with some other files.

W You've got to be more careful about that. You might wind up getting rid of something really important one of these days.

④ W Did you hear the news about Sara and Greg?

M Did they finally decide to get married or something? It's about time that they tie the knot.

W Actually, it's the opposite. They broke up with each other last night.

⑤ M How did you enjoy your trip to see your parents?

W It was nice to spend time with them, but the trip was not particularly relaxing.

M Oh? I thought your parents lived out in the country where there's nothing to do.

W That's true, but I had to visit so many of my relatives who lived out there that I never got a chance to rest.

① 남 방과 후에 잠시 제레미의 선생님과 얘기했어.

여 그래? 제레미의 행동에 대해 뭐라고 말씀하셔?

남 학교에서는 잘 하고 있다고 하는데 항상 숙제를 안 한대.

여 지금부터 매일 밤에 숙제를 끝내는지 꼭 확인해야겠어.

② 여 쇼핑 목록 잊지 않고 가져왔지? 오늘 사야 할 물건이 많아.

남 실은 안 가져왔어. 난 당신이 그걸 가져올 거라고 생각했어.

여 잘했군. 그럼 내가 가져와서 쇼핑을 끝내는 거 어때?

③ 남 미스터 박이 모두에게 보낸 메모 사본 갖고 있어?

여 응, 바로 여기에 있을 거야. 네 건 어떻게 했는데?

남 무심코 다른 파일과 함께 버려버렸어.

여 좀 더 주의해야겠다. 언젠가는 정말 중요한 것을 없애버릴지도 모르잖아.

④ 여 사라와 그레그 소식 들었니?

남 드디어 결혼이라도 하기로 했어? 인연을 맺을 때잖아.

여 실은 그 반대야. 어젯밤에 서로 헤어졌어.

⑤ 남 부모님을 뵈러 간 여행 어땠어?

여 같이 시간을 보내는 건 좋은데 여행이 그다지 편하진 않았어.

남 뭐? 난 네 부모님이 할 일이라고는 없는 시골에 살고 계시는 줄 알았는데.

여 맞아, 하지만 거기 살고 있는 아주 많은 친척들을 방문해야 해서 쉴 기회가 전혀 없었어.

---

08 다음을 듣고, 이야기 속의 This가 무엇인지 고르시오.

① a text message
② an e-mail
③ a blog
④ a homepage
⑤ a chat room

① 휴대폰 문자
② 이메일
③ 블로그
④ 홈페이지
⑤ 인터넷 채팅방

▶ **mundane** 평범한, 세속의 **individual** 개인 **daily routine** 일과 **ups and downs** 기복, 고저 **opinionated** 자기 의견을 고집하는, 독단적인 **specific** 구체적인 **grant** 들어주다, 승낙하다

W This is something people write to put on the Internet, and it can only be found there. It often consists of mundane stories about a person's life, giving details of that individual's daily routine and various ups and downs. In many ways, it's often similar to a diary, and it can serve as a personal webpage. It's sometimes very opinionated, giving a person's thoughts on particular issues. Others may cover a specific topic, such as movie reviews, a sports team, or even someone's favorite type of pet. Some become quite popular as thousands of people read through them every day and then leave comments. Others are set up so that only friends and family members can view them, so permission must be granted before new people can obtain access. Some people who write them just for fun get noticed and become famous all from what they've written on the Internet.

여 이것은 사람들이 인터넷에 올리기 위해 쓰는 것으로 인터넷에서만 찾아 볼 수 있다. 종종 어떤 사람의 삶에 대한 평범한 이야기로 구성되며 개인의 일상과 다양한 기복에 대한 자세한 내용을 전달한다. 여러 면에서 그것은 일기와 비슷하며 개인 웹페이지 역할을 할 수 있다. 가끔은 특정 문제에 대한 한 사람의 생각을 전하면서 의견을 아주 강하게 펼치는 곳이 되기도 한다. 다른 것들은 영화 비평이나 스포츠 팀, 심지어는 좋아하는 애완동물 종류와 같은 구체적인 주제를 다룰 수도 있다. 어떤 것은 수천 명의 사람들이 매일 그것을 훑어본 뒤 의견을 남겨서 꽤 인기를 얻게 되기도 한다. 다른 것들은 친구들과 가족만 볼 수 있도록 설정해 놓아서, 새로운 사람들이 접속할 수 있으려면 사전에 허가를 받아야만 한다. 단지 재미를 위해 그것들을 쓰는 어떤 사람들은 인터넷에 자신들이 쓴 것들로 인해 주목을 받고 유명해지기도 한다.

09 대화를 듣고, 여자가 원래 받았어야 할 거스름돈이 얼마인지 고르시오.

① $3.50
② $5.60
③ $5.70
✓ $6.30
⑤ $8.00

▶ be supposed to do ···하기로 되어 있다   cash register 금전 등록기   I don't mind 괜찮다, 신경 쓰지 않는다   appreciate 감사해하다   go over (재)점검하다   purchase 구매(품)   in line 일렬로 늘어선   cold medicine 감기약   on sale 팔려고 내놓은, 특매가의   oops 이런, 아차   honest 정직한, 솔직한

W Excuse me, but I think you just made a mistake. I'm not supposed to get this much money back.

M I don't think so. The cash register says you should get back seven dollars and thirty cents, so that's what I returned to you.

W I don't mind getting back extra money, but I don't think your manager would appreciate it if you did that. Would it be okay to go over my purchases in order to check?

M I guess not. There's no one in line behind you.

W All right, I bought this cold medicine for eight dollars. And this box of candy cost three dollars and fifty cents.

M Right. And the aspirin costs three dollars and twenty cents.

W Okay, and there's one more item I purchased. Let me see what the price is here.

M It's this DVD, which is on sale for nine dollars.

W So, I gave you thirty dollars for my purchase. Did you give me the right amount of change?

M Oops. It looks like I was about to give you a dollar too much. Thanks for being so honest.

여 실례지만 방금 실수를 하신 것 같네요. 제가 이렇게 많은 돈을 받는 것이 아닌 것 같아요.

남 아닌데요. 금전 등록기에 7달러 30센트를 드려야 한다고 나와서 그 금액을 드린 겁니다.

여 돈을 더 받는 건 상관없지만 그럴 경우 관리자가 달가워하지 않을 텐데요. 확인해 보기 위해 제가 구입한 걸 다시 점검해도 괜찮겠죠?

남 괜찮습니다. 손님 뒤에 줄 서 있는 분이 안 계시니까요.

여 좋아요, 제가 산 감기약은 8달러이고요. 또 이 사탕 상자는 3달러 50센트이죠.

남 맞습니다. 그리고 그 아스피린은 3달러 20센트입니다.

여 그래요, 그리고 구입한 물건이 하나 더 있어요. 이건 가격이 얼마인지 보여 주세요.

남 그건 이 DVD인데, 특매가로 9달러입니다.

여 그러니까 제가 구입한 물건에 대해 30달러를 드렸잖아요. 제게 잔돈을 맞게 주셨나요?

남 이런. 제가 1달러를 더 많이 드리려 한 것 같군요. 솔직하게 말씀해 주셔서 감사합니다.

---

10 대화를 듣고, 여자의 마지막 말을 완성하는 가장 알맞은 것을 고르시오.

W: Just hope you don't get fired. After all, ____________.

✓ as you sow, so shall you reap
② it's better to be safe than sorry
③ look before you leap
④ a bird in the hand is worth two in the bush
⑤ a penny saved is a penny earned

여: 네가 해고되지 않기만을 바랄 뿐이야. 어쨌거나, ____________.

① 뿌린 대로 거둘 거야
② 나중에 후회하느니 안전한 편이 나아
③ 돌다리도 두드려 보고 건너라
④ 숲 속의 새 두 마리보다 수중에 든 새 한 마리가 실속 있어
⑤ 티끌 모아 태산이야

▶ chew out 호되게 꾸짖다, 형편없이 깎아내리다   on time 제시간에   ensure 확실하게 하다, 보증하다   give up ···을 포기하다   would rather 오히려 ···하고 싶다   overtime 시간외로   attitude 태도   focus on ···에 집중하다   disagree with ···에 반대하다   yell at ···에게 고함치다   uncalled for 부당한, 공연한   get fired 해고되다

M I just got chewed out by the boss for ten minutes for not finishing my work on time.

W You haven't finished that project? Didn't you start it a month ago?

M Yeah, but I took some vacation time two weeks ago. I never expected the project to take this long.

W You should've known to get your work done on time. Why didn't you work weekends to finish it? I've been here every weekend for the past two months to ensure that I get all my work done on time.

M You don't really think I should give up my weekends, do you? I'd much rather hang out with my friends and do stuff with them.

W Yeah, that would be nice. But you still need to get your work done.

M I'm sorry, but I'm not working overtime. My free time is important to me.

W That's a pretty bad attitude. You need to focus on your work.

M Sorry, but I disagree with you. And I really don't appreciate the boss yelling at me. That was uncalled for.

W Just hope you don't get fired. After all, ____________
____________.

남 금방 상사에게서 일을 제때 마치지 못한다고 10분 동안 엄청 혼났어.

여 그 프로젝트 못 끝냈어? 한 달 전에 시작하지 않았니?

남 그래, 하지만 2주 전에 휴가를 갔었단 말이야. 프로젝트가 이렇게 오래 걸릴 줄은 전혀 예상 못했어.

여 네 일이 제시간에 끝나는지 알고 있었어야지. 왜 그걸 끝내기 위해 주말에 일하지 않았어? 난 내가 맡은 일은 모두 제때 마치려고 지난 두 달 동안 주말마다 여기 왔잖아.

남 너 정말로 내가 주말을 포기해야 한다고 생각하는 건 아니지, 그렇지? 난 친구들과 어울려서 같이 이런저런 걸 하는 게 더 좋단 말이야.

여 그래, 그럼 좋겠지. 하지만 그래도 네 일은 마쳐야지.

남 미안하지만 난 연장근무는 안 할 거야. 여가 시간은 내게 중요해.

여 그건 정말 나쁜 태도야. 네 일에 집중을 해야 해.

남 미안, 하지만 동의할 수 없어. 그리고 상사가 나한테 소리지르는 건 정말 사양이야. 그건 부당하다고.

여 네가 해고되지 않기만을 바랄 뿐이야. 어쨌거나, ____________
____________.

11 다음을 듣고, 우주여행에 대해 사실이 <u>아닌</u> 것을 고르시오.

① 한국 우주인이 우주정거장에서 실험을 했다.
✓ 우주선에 탄 세 명의 우주인 중 한 명은 전에 우주를 방문했다.
③ 이 우주선은 한국이 아닌 다른 국가에서 발사되었다.
④ 우주선에는 2개국의 우주인이 있었다.
⑤ 그 우주선은 이틀 뒤 우주정거장과 도킹했다.

▶ astronaut 우주인 orbit (천체의) 주위를 궤도를 그리며 돌다, 선회하다 exclusive 배타적인, 독점적인 blast off 발사되다, 이륙하다 launch pad (로켓 등의) 발사대 dock (두 우주선이) 대기권 밖에서 도킹하다 on board (배, 비행기 등에) 탄 conduct (실험 등을) 수행하다 zero gravity 무중력 features 용모, 이목구비 originate in …에서 생기다

M Humans have gone into space since 1961 when the first Russian astronaut, Yuri Gagarin, orbited the Earth. Many countries have sent individuals into space since, and now Korea has joined this exclusive club. In April 2008, Korea's first astronaut blasted off from a launch pad in Kazakhstan, and, two days later, her spacecraft docked at the International Space Station. With the Korean astronaut were two Russians. It was the first time in space for all three of them. The Korean astronaut planned to spend ten days on board the station before returning to Earth. During this time, she conducted experiments on the effects of space travel on fruit flies and the effects of zero gravity on her facial features. Other experiments included monitoring dust storms that originate in China and blow into Korea. She returned to Earth with two different astronauts who had just finished their stays on the space station.

남 인간은 1961년 첫 우주인인 러시아인 유리 가가린이 지구궤도를 돈 이후 우주에 진출했다. 그 이후로 많은 국가가 사람들을 우주에 보냈고 이제 한국이 이 독점적인 모임에 가입했다. 2008년 4월 한국의 첫 우주인이 카자흐스탄의 발사대에서 쏘아올려졌고 이틀 뒤 그녀가 탄 우주선은 국제우주정거장에 도킹했다. 한국인 우주인과 함께 두 명의 러시아 우주인이 있었다. 세 명 모두 우주는 처음이었다. 한국 우주인은 우주정거장에 승선해서 10일을 보낸 다음 지구로 귀환할 계획이었다. 이 기간 동안 그녀는 초파리의 우주여행 효과와 자신의 얼굴 모양새의 무중력 효과에 대한 실험을 수행했다. 다른 실험들로는 중국에서 시작되어 한국으로 불어오는 황사를 관찰하는 것이 포함되었다. 그녀는 우주정거장에서의 체류를 끝낸 다른 두 명의 우주인과 함께 지구로 귀환했다.

---

12 대화를 듣고, 여자에게 주어진 조언이 <u>아닌</u> 것을 고르시오.

① Ask her parents for help with her work
② Ask the teacher more questions in class
③ Get a tutor to help with her studies
④ Go over her lessons much more carefully
✓ Talk to the teacher after class finishes

① 공부를 도와달라고 부모님께 부탁하라
② 수업시간에 선생님에게 질문을 더 많이 하라
③ 학업을 도와줄 가정교사를 구하라
④ 수업을 더 주의 깊게 들어라
⑤ 수업이 끝나고 선생님과 상담하라

▶ mathematics 수학 used to do 이전에는 …하곤 했다 material 자료 cover 다루다, 담당하다 in front of …앞에서 confused 어찌할 바 모르는, 혼란한 state 분명히[정확히] 말하다 score 점수, 성적 either …도 또한 (…아니다) see about …에 대해 수단을 강구하다, 고려하다 tutor 가정교사, 개인지도 교수 assist 도와주다, 거들다

M Your mother told me that your last mathematics test wasn't very good. What's been going on with your studies lately? You used to be such a good student, but things seem to have changed.

W I have no idea. It's just that some of the material we cover in class seems too hard. I simply don't understand it much of the time.

M In that case, why don't you ask your teacher to explain it one more time in class?

W Are you serious? Then I'd look stupid in front of all my friends. I can't do that.

M I bet that your friends are all confused too but don't want to ask for the same reason you stated.

W Well, you may be right about that. Their test scores aren't good either.

M Okay, then you should see about getting a tutor to help you.

W Yeah, the school provides them. I can do that. Is there anything else that I should do?

M Sure. You ought to read your lessons more carefully and ask your mother or me for help. Remember that we went to school too, so we can assist you with your schoolwork.

W Oh, right. I never thought of that. Thanks a lot, Dad.

남 네 엄마가 지난번 너의 수학시험 성적이 썩 좋지 않았다고 얘기하더구나. 최근 공부하는 데 뭐 문제가 있니? 예전엔 아주 우수한 학생이었는데, 상황이 변한 것 같구나.

여 모르겠어요. 그냥 수업시간에 다루는 내용이 어떤 건 너무 어려운 것 같아요. 대부분 정말 이해가 안 돼요.

남 그럼 수업시간에 선생님께 한 번 더 설명해 달라고 청해 보지 그러니?

여 진심이세요? 그럼 친구들 앞에서 바보같이 보일 거예요. 그렇게는 못해요.

남 분명히 네 친구들도 모두 헷갈리지만 네가 말한 것과 똑같은 이유로 물어 보고 싶지 않은 걸 거야.

여 음, 그게 맞을지도 모르겠어요. 친구들도 시험 성적이 안 좋거든요.

남 그래, 그럼 너를 도와줄 선생님을 구하는 걸 생각해 봐야겠구나.

여 네, 학교에서 선생님들을 구해 줘요. 그건 할 수 있어요. 제가 해야 할 다른 건 없어요?

남 있어. 수업을 좀 더 주의해서 듣고 엄마나 나한테 도와달라고 요청해야 해. 우리도 학교에 다녔고 그래서 네 학업을 도울 수 있다는 걸 기억해라.

여 아, 맞아요. 그 생각은 전혀 못했네요. 고마워요, 아빠.

13 다음을 듣고, 이 이야기가 어떤 질문에 대한 대답인지 고르시오.

① Where did you go to university?
② Can you tell me about your family?
③ When did you get married?
✔ How did you meet your spouse?
⑤ Have you ever been on a blind date?

① 당신은 어느 대학교를 다녔나요?
② 당신 가족에 대해 얘기해 주시겠어요?
③ 당신은 언제 결혼했나요?
④ 당신은 배우자를 어떻게 만났나요?
⑤ 소개팅을 해 본 적이 있나요?

▶ blind date 소개팅 extremely 대단히, 몹시
settle down (사람, 사태가) 가라앉다, 평온해지다
discover 깨닫다, 알다 in common 공통으로
gladly 기쁘게, 반갑게 soon after 바로 뒤에, 이내

M The first time I saw her was on a blind date that my friend and her friend set up for us. At the time, we were both university students although we attended different colleges. Our first date was in a coffee shop near her university. I was extremely nervous, and I think she was, too. But we got settled down, had some coffee, and then talked for a long time. It was on our very first date that we discovered we had much in common. At the end of the evening, I asked for her phone number, and she gladly provided it for me. We had many more dates after that, and I think we knew we were in love soon after. About one year later, I graduated from university and started working. Then she took me to meet her parents, and we made plans to get married. That was ten years ago. Now we have two children, a boy and a girl, and we're very happy.

남 처음 그녀를 본 것은 내 친구와 그녀의 친구가 우리를 위해 주선한 소개팅에서였다. 그때 우리는 둘 다 다른 대학에 다니긴 했지만 대학생이었다. 첫 데이트는 그녀가 다니는 대학 근처에 있는 커피숍에서였다. 난 너무나 긴장했고 그녀도 그랬던 것 같다. 하지만 우리는 마음을 가라앉히고 커피를 좀 마신 뒤 오랫동안 이야기를 했다. 바로 그 첫 데이트에서 우리는 우리에게 공통점이 많다는 걸 발견했다. 그 저녁이 끝날 무렵 난 그녀의 전화번호를 물었고 그녀는 반갑게 내게 알려 줬다. 그 뒤로 우리는 몇 번을 더 데이트 했고 이내 사랑에 빠진 걸 안 것 같다. 1년 정도 뒤에 나는 대학을 졸업해서 일을 시작했다. 그때 그녀가 날 데리고 자신의 부모님을 만나러 갔고 우리는 결혼을 하기로 계획을 세웠다. 그것이 10년 전이었다. 지금 우리에게는 아들과 딸, 두 명의 아이가 있고 아주 행복하다.

---

14 대화를 듣고, 두 사람에 의해 언급된 교통 표지판이 <u>아닌</u> 것을 고르시오.

①  ② ✔ 

③  ④ 

⑤ 

▶ pass 통과하다, 합격하다 driver's license 운전면허증 go over 복습하다, 되풀이하다 practice 연습하다 arrow 화살표 point 위치[방향]를 가리키다 go straight ahead 곧장 앞으로 가다 curve 휘다, 구부러지다 backwards 뒤쪽으로, 거꾸로 two-way 양방향의 Bingo 해냈어, 맞혔어 recognize 알아보다, 알다 indicate 가리키다, 나타내다

M How am I ever going to pass my driver's license exam? I've got so many things to learn that I'll never remember them all.

W Why don't you let me help you? Here, let's go over some traffic signs and see if you know what they mean.

M I know most of them, but some are pretty hard.

W In that case, let's practice. What's this one with an arrow pointing to the left with a line through it?

M Hmm... I think it means you cannot turn right. And I know what the picture of the arrow going straight ahead and then curving backwards with a line through it means, too. It's saying you can't do a U-turn there.

W Wow, it looks like you know your signs. How about this sign with one arrow going up and the other going down? That's a little confusing.

M I think it means there's two-way traffic on the road.

W Bingo. You're exactly right about that. Here's one I don't recognize. It's got an arrow that curves back and forth and then goes straight ahead.

M Oh, it's indicating that a curve is coming up in the road.

W You know, I don't think you have anything to worry about on your test.

남 운전면허 시험을 어떻게 하면 통과할 수 있을까? 배워야 할 게 아주 많아서 절대로 그걸 다 기억하진 못할 거야.

여 내가 좀 도와줘도 될까? 자, 교통표지판을 좀 복습해 보고 그게 뭘 뜻하는지 알고 있는지 보자.

남 대부분은 다 아는데, 몇 개는 꽤 어려워.

여 그렇다면 연습해 보자. 화살표가 왼쪽을 가리키고 있고 그 위에 선이 그어져 있는 이건 뭐야?

남 흠… 좌회전을 못한다는 뜻 같아. 그리고 화살표가 곧장 앞으로 가다가 뒤로 휘면서 그 위에 선이 그어져 있는 그림이 뜻하는 것도 알아. 그건 거기서 유턴을 못한다는 거야.

여 우와, 표지를 잘 아는 것 같구나. 화살표 하나가 위를 향해 있고 다른 건 아래로 있는 이 표지는 어때? 좀 헷갈리는 건데.

남 내 생각엔 도로에서 교통이 양방향이라는 의미 같은데.

여 맞았어. 정확하게 맞혔어. 여기 내가 모르는 게 있다. 화살표가 앞뒤로 휘었다가 곧장 앞으로 가는 거야.

남 아, 그건 전방에 굽은 도로가 있을 거라는 걸 나타내는 거야.

여 있잖아, 내 생각에 너는 시험에 대해 걱정할 게 전혀 없는 것 같아.

<table>
<tr><th>문제와 정답</th><th>스크립트</th><th>해석</th></tr>
</table>

15 대화를 듣고, 남자가 대화 후에 할 행동을 고르시오.

① 파티에 사람들을 초대한다.
✔ 제과점에 케이크를 주문한다.
③ 슈퍼마켓에서 음식을 구입한다.
④ 집이 깨끗한지 확인한다.
⑤ 파티를 위해 음식을 준비하기 시작한다.

▶ ingredient 재료 What about...? …은 어때?
bakery 빵집 doubt 의심쩍다 either of …중 어느
쪽이든 immediately 당장, 즉시 confirm 확인하다
show up 나타나다, 출석하다 as well …도 또한
mess 엉망인 상태, 지저분한 것 take care of …을
처리하다 right now 지금 당장

M Mom's big birthday party is tomorrow. Why don't we go over everything we're going to do one last time?

W Yeah, we ought to do that since we wouldn't want to forget anything.

M Now, we're going to cook dinner for her at six o'clock. Have you purchased all the ingredients for the dinner yet?

W I haven't gotten all of them, but here's a list of what we have. We'll have to visit the supermarket tomorrow to get the rest.

M Okay, that sounds fine. What about the cake? Are you going to make that?

W Uh, I thought you were going to do that.

M That's not good. We'd better call the bakery and order a cake for Mom since I doubt either of us will have time to make it.

W Then you ought to do that immediately since we'll want it specially ordered. What about inviting everyone to the party?

M Everyone who's been invited knows about it, but we should call them again tomorrow to confirm that they're going to show up. And we need to clean the house as well. This place is a mess.

W All right. I'll take care of that right now, and you do what you have to do.

남 엄마의 생일을 위한 큰 파티가 내일이야. 마지막으로 해야 할 걸 모두 점검해 볼까?

여 그래. 어떤것도 잊어버리면 안 되니까 그렇게 해야겠다.

남 자, 6시에 엄마를 위해 저녁을 요리할 거야. 저녁에 필요한 재료는 이미 다 구입했니?

여 다는 못했지만 뭘 샀는지 목록이 여기 있어. 내일 나머지를 사러 슈퍼마켓에 가야 해.

남 알았어, 그건 된 것 같네. 케이크는 어때? 만들 거니?

여 어, 난 오빠가 할 줄 알았는데.

남 이런. 빵집에 전화해서 엄마를 위해 케이크를 주문하는 게 낫겠어. 우리 둘 다 만들 시간이 있을지 의심스러우니까 말이야.

여 그럼 특별한 걸 주문해야 하니까 당장 해야 해. 파티에 사람들을 초대하는 건 어때?

남 초대받은 사람은 모두 알고 있지만 내일 다시 전화해서 참석하도록 확인해야 해. 그리고 집도 청소해야 하고. 이곳은 엄망이야.

여 좋아. 그건 내가 지금 당장 할테니까 오빠 오빠가 해야 할 일을 해.

---

16 다음을 듣고, 화자의 스케줄 표 중 빠진 부분에 들어갈 알맞은 것을 고르시오.

Schedule

9 a.m.	Arrive at Work
10 a.m.	Sales Meeting
12 p.m.	Lunch with Friend
___	___
3 p.m.	Sales Meeting
5:30 p.m.	Meet the President
6:45 p.m.	Go to Airport

	Time	Activity
①	1 p.m.	Lunch with President
✔②	2 p.m.	Managers' Meeting
③	1:30 p.m.	Sales Meeting
④	2:30 p.m.	Managers' Meeting
⑤	12:30 p.m.	Go Back to Office

	시간	할 일
①	오후 1시	회장님과 점심
②	오후 2시	관리자들 회의
③	오후 1시 반	영업 회의
④	오후 2시 반	관리자들 회의
⑤	오후 12시 반	사무실 복귀

▶ consult 참고하다 anticipate 예상하다, 기대하다
conclude 끝나다, 종료하다 sales figures 판매 수치

W I have many things to do every day, so I always make sure that I write my schedule down and consult it all throughout the day. This Tuesday, I'll arrive at work at nine a.m. as usual. After I check my e-mail and have some coffee to help me wake up, I have my first sales meeting at ten. I anticipate it'll take about two hours. I plan to meet my friend for lunch at twelve o'clock and return to my office by one. At two, I need to attend a managers' meeting, which will hopefully conclude by three o'clock since I have another sales meeting at that time. That one should finish by half past four. Then, I'm scheduled to meet with the president of our company at half past five, during which time he wants to go over the current sales figures. Finally, my husband is returning to town from a business trip that evening, so I promised to meet him at the airport by a quarter to seven.

여 난 매일 해야 할 일이 많아서 항상 꼭 스케줄을 적어놓고 하루 종일 그걸 참고한다. 이번 화요일에는 평소처럼 9시에 직장에 도착할 것이다. 이메일을 확인하고 커피로 잠을 쫓은 뒤에, 10시에 내 첫 판매회의가 있다. 두 시간 정도 걸릴 것이 예상된다. 12시에 친구를 만나 점심을 먹고 1시까지 사무실에 돌아올 계획이다. 2시에는 관리자들 회의에 참석해야 하는데, 3시까지는 끝났으면 좋겠다, 왜냐하면 그 시간에 또 다른 판매회의가 있기 때문이다. 그 회의는 4시 반까지 끝날 것이다. 그런 다음에는 5시 반에 사장을 만나기로 되어 있는데, 그는 현 판매수치를 점검하고 싶어 한다. 마지막으로 남편이 그날 저녁에 출장에서 돌아오기 때문에 7시 15분 전까지 공항에서 만나기로 약속했다.

<table>
<tr><th>문제와 정답</th><th>스크립트</th><th>해석</th></tr>
</table>

17 다음을 듣고, 다음중 이야기 내용과 관련이 <u>없는</u> 것을 고르시오.

① J.R.R. 톨킨의 〈반지의 제왕〉
② 에밀리 브론테의 〈폭풍의 언덕〉
③ J.K. 롤링의 〈해리 포터와 불사조 기사단〉
④ 박경리의 〈토지〉
✓ 윈스턴 처칠의 〈제2차 세계대전〉

▶ **readable** 읽기 재미난 **element** 요소 **imagination** 상상(력), 창의력 **intrigue** 흥미를 끌다, 호기심을 돋우다 **plot** (소설 등의) 줄거리, 구상 **manner** 방법, 방식 **genre** 장르 **outline** 개요, 주요 특징 **progress** 진행, 경과 **give away** 폭로하다 **vital** 긴요한, 매우 중대한 **brilliant** 훌륭한, 멋진 **author** 작가, 저자 **on their way to** … 도중에, 가까워져 **embrace** 기꺼이 받아들이다, 선택하다

W Writing a readable story takes great skill and a lot of time. The key elements to good story writing are having a great imagination, creating an intriguing plot, developing believable characters, and then putting them all together in an enjoyable manner. All good stories start with imagination. It doesn't matter if the genre is science fiction, crime, fantasy, or romance. Without imagination, there would be no story. The plot describes the basic outline of the story, such as the setting, the time, the basic situation, and the progress of the story. A good plot keeps the reader intrigued by not giving away vital information until absolutely necessary. The best novels are those which keep the reader guessing until the very last page. Lastly, a brilliant plot made with a fantastic imagination is wasted if no one believes in or likes the characters. Once authors create the characters that people can see themselves in, they will be on their way to making a great story that will be embraced by many readers.

여 잘 읽히는 이야기를 쓰는 것은 대단한 재주와 많은 시간이 걸린다. 훌륭한 이야기 저술의 주요한 요소들은 뛰어난 상상력을 소유하고 흥미를 끄는 줄거리를 만들고, 신뢰를 주는 인물을 발전시키고, 그 다음으로 그 모든 것들을 유쾌한 방법으로 조합하는 것이다. 모든 훌륭한 이야기는 상상으로 시작한다. 장르가 공상과학인가, 범죄물, 판타지, 로맨스인가는 문제가 되지 않는다. 상상이 없다면 이야기는 존재하지 않을 것이다. 줄거리는 배경과 시간, 기본적인 상황, 그리고 이야기의 진전 같은 이야기의 기본 개요를 묘사한다. 훌륭한 줄거리는 정말로 필요할 때까지 중대한 정보를 주지 않음으로써 독자로 하여금 흥미를 계속 유지하게 만든다. 최고의 소설들은 마지막 페이지까지 독자들이 추리를 하게 만드는 것들이다. 마지막으로, 아무도 등장인물들을 믿지 않거나 좋아하지 않는다면 환상적인 상상력으로 만들어진 뛰어난 줄거리라도 소용이 없다. 일단 작가들이 사람들이 스스로 몰입할 수 있는 등장인물들을 탄생시키면, 그들은 많은 독자들이 호응할 대단한 이야기를 만드는 데 가까이 다가서게 될 것이다.

---

18 대화를 듣고, 현재 시각을 고르시오.

Movie Timetable

Spider-Man 3	4:30
Shrek 3	5:50
Titanic	7:00
The Lord of the Rings	7:30

① 5:30
② 6:00
③ 6:20
✓ 6:40
⑤ 7:10

▶ **It's been a long time since...** …한 지 오래됐다 **film** 영화 **in a while** 한동안, 오랫동안 **in the meantime** 그 사이에 **I suppose** …라 생각하다, …인 것 같다

M I'm so excited to be going to the movies. It's been a long time since I've actually visited the theater and enjoyed a film.

W It's the same for me. Well, let's take a look at what films are playing.

M I haven't seen a good action movie in a while. I hope that *Spider-Man 3* is playing here.

W Well, I've got good news and bad news. The good news is that the movie's playing here, but the bad news is that it's already over. I'm sorry about that.

M That's all right. I can always watch it another time. Say, what do you think about watching *The Lord of the Rings*? I've heard great things about that movie.

W But do you really want to wait around for almost an hour? What are we going to do in the meantime?

M I suppose we could get some dinner. What do you think about that?

W Actually, I had dinner already, so I'm not particularly hungry. Hey, I've got a better idea. *Titanic* is going to be starting in about twenty minutes. Let's just see that.

M Okay, I haven't seen that movie yet.

W I'll get the tickets, and you go to buy the popcorn and cokes.

남 영화를 보러 가게 돼 아주 설렌다. 사실 극장에 가서 영화를 즐긴 지가 오래 됐거든.

여 나도 마찬가지야. 음, 어떤 영화가 상영중인지 한번 보자.

남 한동안 괜찮은 액션영화를 못 봤어. 〈스파이더맨 3〉가 여기서 상영되면 좋겠는데.

여 음, 좋은 소식과 나쁜 소식이 있어. 좋은 소식은 그 영화가 여기서 상영된다는 거지만 나쁜 소식은 이미 끝났다는 거야. 안타깝다.

남 괜찮아. 다른 때 언제든 볼 수 있으니까. 있잖아, 〈반지의 제왕〉을 보는 건 어떻게 생각해? 그 영화에 대해 대단한 얘기들을 들었는데.

여 하지만 정말 한 시간 가까이 기다리고 싶니? 그 사이에 뭘 할까?

남 저녁을 먹을 수도 있을 것 같은데. 넌 어떻게 생각해?

여 사실은 난 이미 저녁을 먹어서 그다지 배가 안 고파. 이봐, 괜찮은 생각이 났어. 〈타이타닉〉이 20분 정도 뒤면 시작할 거야. 그냥 그걸 보자.

남 좋아, 아직 그 영화를 안 봤으니까.

여 내가 표를 살테니 넌 가서 팝콘이랑 콜라를 사.

19

다음을 듣고, 무엇에 대해 이야기하고 있는지 고르시오.

① 모델 선발
② 패션쇼
③ 연기자 오디션
✓ 미인대회
⑤ 탤런트 쇼

▶ **competition** 시합, 대회(=contest) **divid into** …로 나누다 **judge** 심사하다, 심사위원 **not only A but also B** A뿐만 아니라 B도 **intelligence** 총명함 **skill** 능력, 역량 **evening gown** (옷자락이 긴) 여성용 야회복 **rate** 평가하다 **poise** 태도, 착실함 **elegance** 기품 **segment** 부분, 일부(=portion) **contestant** 경쟁자 **at last** 마침내 **finalist** 결승전 출전(자격)자 **crowned** 왕관을 쓴

M This competition is divided into several different activities. The women are judged not only on their looks but also on their intelligence and skills at a particular activity. One of the first things in the competition is the evening gown competition. Each lady wears a lovely dress, and the judges rate her on her poise and elegance. The next step in the contest is the bathing suit judging. In this segment, each lady wears a similar bathing suit and walks before the judges and the audience. Usually the talent portion of the program follows. Here, each contestant must do a performance of some kind. Singing, dancing, and playing music are among the most common of these talents although some will do activities of a different nature. At last, the judges select several finalists, usually five, and ask difficult questions about current events in order to judge their intelligence. Finally, after much discussion, the judges make their selection on who will be crowned the winner.

남 이 대회는 몇 가지의 다른 활동으로 나누어진다. 여자들은 외모뿐만 아니라 지적 능력과 특기에 대해서도 심사를 받는다. 이 대회에서 첫 번째 일 중 하나는 야회복 경쟁이다. 각 숙녀는 멋있는 드레스를 입고 심사위원들은 그녀의 자세와 기품에 대해 평가한다. 이 대회에서 다음 단계는 수영복 심사이다. 이 부문에서 각 숙녀는 비슷한 수영복을 입고 심사위원과 관객 앞에서 걷는다. 보통 이 다음에 오는 프로그램은 재능 부문이다. 여기서 각 참가자는 어떤 종류의 공연을 해야만 한다. 비록 일부는 다른 종류의 활동을 하겠지만 노래와 춤, 음악 연주는 이러한 재능 중 가장 일반적인 것들이다. 드디어 심사위원들은 몇몇 최종단계 진출자들, 보통은 다섯 명을 선출하여 그들의 지능을 심사하기 위해 시사 문제에 관한 어려운 질문을 한다. 마지막으로 많은 논의를 한 뒤에 심사위원들은 누가 왕관을 쓸 승자가 될지 선택을 한다.

20

대화를 듣고, 남자의 요지를 고르시오.

① 정부는 숭례문의 연소에 대해 사과해야 한다.
② 아무도 숭례문의 연소를 상상할 수 없었을 것이다.
③ 일부 국보가 파괴되는 것은 불가피하다.
④ 국보를 보호하는 데 많은 비용을 들일 필요는 없다.
✓ 국보를 보호하는 것은 정부의 책임이다.

▶ **bother** 괴롭히다, 당황하게 하다 **national treasure** 국보 **arson** 방화(죄) **suspect** 의심하다, 수상히 여기다 **burn** 불태우다 **occur** 생기다, 일어나다 **duty** 의무, 책무 **property** 자산, 소유물 **belong to** …에 속하다 **smoke alarm** 화재경보기 **fire extinguisher** 소화기 **security guard** 경비원 **riot police** (폭력 진압) 경찰 기동대 **rebuild** 재건하다

W I can't believe what happened to Sungnyemun. It bothers me that one of our national treasures suffered an arson attack.

M You're right. The government needs to do a better job of protecting them.

W But what can it do? I mean, who'd ever suspect somebody would want to burn something like Sungnyemun down? It never would occur to most people to do that.

M That's true. However, it's the government's duty to protect its citizens and their property, and Sungnyemun belonged to all Korean citizens.

W What do you suggest they do?

M Well, it's too late for Sungnyemun, but the government should provide better security for our national treasures. And, of course, it should put smoke alarms and more fire extinguishers near them.

W But who's going to pay for these security guards?

M I've got an idea. All of those riot police don't have much work to do nowadays. The government is paying them to stand around and do nothing most of the time. They should be employed as guards for all national treasures.

W That idea just might work.

M I hope so. After all, we can rebuild Sungnyemun, but it'll never be the same. We don't want to lose any more of our country's treasures.

여 숭례문에 생긴 일이 믿기지가 않아. 국보 중 하나가 방화를 당했다는 게 당황스러워.

남 그래. 정부가 국보를 더 잘 보호할 필요가 있어.

여 하지만 정부가 뭘 할 수 있니? 내 말은, 누가 어떤 사람이 숭례문 같은 것을 불태워 없앨 거라고 의심이나 하겠어? 대부분의 사람들은 그럴 수 없을 거야.

남 맞아. 하지만 시민과 자산을 보호하는 게 정부의 의무이고 숭례문은 모든 대한민국 국민들의 것이잖아.

여 어떻게 해야 할 것 같니?

남 음, 숭례문은 너무 늦었지만 정부는 국보에 대한 보안을 강화해야 해. 그리고 당연히 근처에 화재 경보기와 더 많은 소화기를 놓아두어야 해.

여 하지만 누가 이런 경비원들에게 보수를 지불할 거야?

남 내게 생각이 있어. 요즘에는 폭동을 진압하는 경찰 기동대원들이 할 일이 많이 없잖아. 정부는 그들이 주변에 서서 대부분의 시간을 아무것도 하지 않는 데 보수를 주고 있어. 그들은 모든 국보를 지키는 경비원들로 고용이 되어야 해.

여 그 생각은 바로 활용할 수도 있겠다.

남 그랬으면 좋겠어. 결국 숭례문을 재건할 수는 있겠지만, 그것은 결코 똑같은 것이 아니야. 더 이상 국보를 잃는 것을 원하지 않아.

21 대화를 듣고, 남자가 말하고자 하는 것이 무엇인지 고르시오.

① Extreme diets help people quickly lose a lot of weight.
② The woman needs to go on a diet as soon as possible.
③ It is ideal to eat a little amount of food for several days.
✔ The woman should be careful about the diet she goes on.
⑤ Eating only one kind of food is an example of an extreme diet.

① 극단적인 다이어트는 사람들이 많은 체중을 빼는 데 도움이 된다.
② 여자는 가능한 한 빨리 다이어트를 할 필요가 있다.
③ 며칠 동안 적은 양의 음식을 먹는 것이 이상적이다.
④ 여자는 자신이 할 다이어트에 대해 신중해야 한다.
⑤ 단 한 가지 종류의 음식만 먹는 것은 극단적 다이어트의 예이다.

▶ **mirror** 거울 **put on weight** 살이 찌다 **go on a diet** 다이어트를 하다 **something of a** 상당한, 얼마간 **fad** 일시적 유행, 취미 **extreme** 극단적인, 과격한 **diet** 제한식, 감식 **cause** 초래하다 **harm** 손상, 위해 **crash** 속성의, 벼락치기식의 **recover** 회복하다

W I'm really concerned about my weight. I've been looking at myself in the mirror, and I seem like I've put on some weight lately. I think I'm going to go on a diet.

M Well, you'd better be careful about which diet you go on.

W Huh? Why do you say that?

M There are a large number of different diets that people are following these days. In fact, it's something of a fad to go on an extreme diet.

W I've never heard of an extreme diet. What exactly is it?

M There are many different kinds, but they typically involve eating very little for several days or eating only one type of food. Those diets often help people lose a lot of weight fast, but there are some problems.

W What's wrong with losing lots of weight fast? That's exactly what I need.

M It's actually quite unhealthy. You can cause serious harm to your body by going on a crash diet.

W Hmm… I never thought of it that way.

M Yeah, so you'd better do some research before you go on a diet. You don't want to do any harm to your body, or you might have a hard time recovering from an extreme diet.

여 정말 몸무게가 걱정이 돼. 거울을 봤는데 최근에 살이 좀 찐 것 같아 보였어. 다이어트를 해야 할 것 같아.

남 음, 어떤 다이어트를 할 건지 신중해야 해.

여 어? 왜 그런 거야?

남 요즘엔 사람들이 따라 하는 다양한 다이어트가 많이 있어. 사실은 극단적인 다이어트를 하는 게 상당히 유행이야.

여 극단적 다이어트에 대해서는 못 들었는데. 정확히 그게 뭐야?

남 여러 종류가 많이 있지만 일반적으로 며칠 동안 아주 적게 먹거나 단 한 가지 유형의 음식만 먹는 거야. 그런 다이어트들은 사람들이 많은 체중을 빨리 빼는 데 도움이 되지만 문제가 좀 있지.

여 많은 체중을 빨리 빼는 게 뭐가 잘못이야? 그거야 말로 내가 필요한 거야.

남 실제로는 건강에 꽤 안 좋아. 벼락치기 다이어트로 몸에 심각한 해를 끼칠 수 있거든.

여 흠… 그렇게는 전혀 생각 못해봤네.

남 그래, 그러니까 다이어트를 하기 전에 연구를 좀 하는 게 나을 거야. 몸이 상하길 원하는 건 아니잖아, 안 그러면 극단적인 다이어트에서 회복하는 데 어려움을 겪을지도 몰라.

---

22 다음을 듣고, 이야기의 내용이 그래프에 잘못 반영된 것을 고르시오.

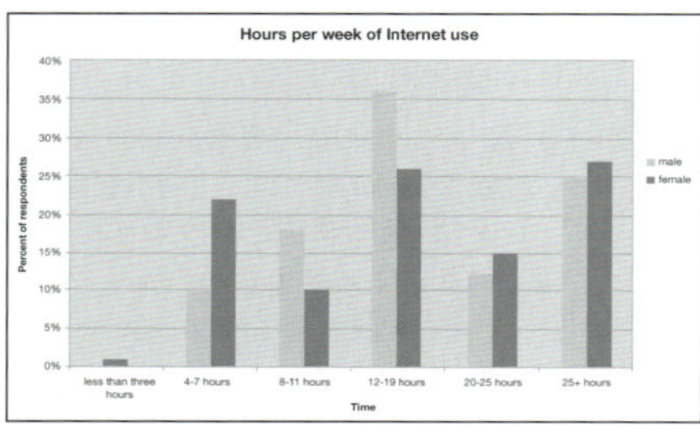

① 최고치를 보인 남성 사용자의 주당 시간
② 주당 25시간이 넘게 인터넷을 사용하는 여성의 퍼센트
✔ 주당 3시간 미만 인터넷을 사용하는 남성의 퍼센트
④ 주당 4시간에서 7시간을 사용하는 남성과 여성 사용자의 비교
⑤ 주당 20시간에서 25시간을 사용하는 남성과 여성 사용자의 비교

▶ **survey** 조사 **result in** …을 낳다 **respondent** 응답자 **claim** 주장하다 **category** 범주, 카테고리 **scale** 규모, 정도 **slightly** 약간 **difference** 차이 **reflect** 초래하다, 반영하다 **lifestyle** 생활방식 **whether ... or not** …인지 아니지

M A recent survey of Internet users resulted in some interesting numbers. The survey asked both women and men about the number of hours they spend using the Internet each week. According to the survey, about thirty-six percent of the male respondents claimed to use the Internet for twelve to nineteen hours each week. This was the largest category for men. Meanwhile, the highest percentage of female respondents—about twenty-seven percent—said they use the Internet over twenty-five hours per week. On the lower end of the scale, about two percent of males and females who responded use the Internet for under three hours per week. More females than males spend four to seven hours a week on the Internet, yet more males than females spend eight to eleven hours a week online. Finally, slightly more females than males use the Internet for twenty to twenty-five hours per week. The difference between time spent on the Internet for males and females may be reflected in their lifestyles and whether they are employed or not.

남 최근 인터넷 사용자들에 대한 조사에서 몇몇 흥미있는 통계가 나타났다. 이 조사에서는 여성과 남성 모두에게 매주 인터넷을 사용하는 데 얼마의 시간을 쓰는지에 대해 물었다. 조사에 따르면 약 36퍼센트의 남성 응답자가 매주 12시간에서 19시간을 인터넷을 사용한다고 주장했다. 이것은 남성들에게 가장 큰 범주였다. 한편 여성 응답자들의 최고 퍼센트는 약 27퍼센트였는데, 주당 25시간이 넘게 인터넷을 사용한다고 말했다. 정도가 낮은 쪽에서는 남녀 응답자의 약 2퍼센트가 주당 3시간 미만의 시간을 인터넷에 사용한다. 남성보다 더 많은 여성들이 주당 4시간에서 7시간을 인터넷에 소비하지만 여성보다 더 많은 남성들이 주당 8시간에서 11시간을 온라인에서 보낸다. 마지막으로, 남성보다 약간 더 많은 여성들이 주당 20시간에서 25시간을 인터넷을 사용한다. 남성과 여성의 인터넷에 소비하는 시간의 차이는 그들의 생활양식과 직업이 있는지의 여부에서 초래될 수도 있다.

23 대화를 듣고, 화자들이 할 행동을 순서대로 나열한 것을 고르시오.

ⓐ Go shopping at the department store
ⓑ Have dinner with the man's parents
ⓒ Take their children to the amusement park
ⓓ Watch a movie with the woman's sister

ⓐ 백화점으로 쇼핑을 간다
ⓑ 남자의 부모님과 저녁식사를 한다
ⓒ 그들의 아이들을 놀이공원에 데리고 간다
ⓓ 여자의 동생과 영화를 본다

① ⓐ - ⓓ - ⓑ - ⓒ
✓② ⓑ - ⓐ - ⓓ - ⓒ
③ ⓑ - ⓐ - ⓒ - ⓓ
④ ⓓ - ⓐ - ⓒ - ⓑ
⑤ ⓒ - ⓐ - ⓓ - ⓑ

▶ relieve 안심시키다 look forward to …을 고대하다 amusement park 놀이공원 likely to do …할 것 같은 would rather 오히려[더욱] …하고 싶다 in mind 생각중인, 계획중인 have got to do …해야 하다 department store 백화점 out of the way 방해가 되지 않도록, 결말이 나서

M I'm so relieved we've got a holiday coming up. I could use a break from work, so I'm looking forward to staying home.

W But don't you remember we promised to take the kids to the amusement park this weekend?

M Oh, that's right. Well, we've got from Friday to Sunday off, so let's go there on Sunday. I guess that'll be the day with the fewest visitors since most people are likely to go on Friday or Saturday.

W That sounds fine, but what do you want to do on the other two days?

M I'd rather spend some time at home, but it sounds like you've got some other plans in mind. Am I right?

W Your parents want us to visit them for dinner, so I thought we'd do that on Friday night. And we've got to go shopping at the department store and see a movie with my sister.

M We're going to be busier than I thought.

W Yeah, I'm sorry about that.

M That's fine. Okay, first thing on Saturday, let's get the shopping out of the way. We can watch the movie with your sister that night as well.

W Great. I'll give her a call and let her know our plans.

남 휴가가 다가오고 있어서 정말 다행이야. 일을 떠나 좀 쉴 수 있어서 집에 있는 것이 기대가 돼.

여 하지만 이번 주말에 애들을 데리고 놀이공원에 가기로 약속한 것 기억 안나?

남 아, 맞아. 음, 금요일에서 일요일까지 쉬니까, 일요일에 거기 가자. 대부분의 사람들이 금요일이나 토요일에 갈 가능성이 있으니까 그 날이 방문객이 제일 적은 날일 거야.

여 좋아, 하지만 나머지 이틀 동안은 뭘 하고 싶은데?

남 난 집에서 시간을 좀 보내고 싶지만 당신한테 다른 계획이 좀 있는 것 같은데. 맞아?

여 당신 부모님이 우리를 저녁식사에 초대하길 원하셔서 금요일 밤에 그렇게 해야겠다고 생각했지. 그리고 백화점에서 쇼핑하고 여동생과 영화를 보고.

남 내 생각보다 더 바빠지겠는걸.

여 그래, 미안해.

남 괜찮아. 알았어, 토요일에 먼저 쇼핑을 끝내자. 그날 밤에 처제랑 영화도 보고.

여 좋아. 동생한테 전화해서 계획을 알려 줄게.

---

24 다음을 듣고, 화자의 현재 취미가 무엇인지 고르시오.

① jazz dancing
② astronomy
③ painting
✓④ photography
⑤ sculpting

① 재즈 댄스
② 천문학
③ 그림
④ 사진
⑤ 조각

▶ stick with (일 등을) 계속하다 moody 변덕스러운 personality 성격 sign up for …을 신청하다, 등록하다 photography 사진 촬영(술) previously 이전에는 be involved in (사람이) …에 몰두하다 sculpture 조각 frustrated 좌절한 astronomy 천문학 all that 모든 그런 종류의 bored 지루한 instructor 강사 strict 엄격한 complicated 복잡한

W I love doing so many things, but I never seem to stick with one hobby for very long. I guess it's because of my moody personality. I get really excited about something, but, the next day, I want to try something else. For example, yesterday I bought a digital camera, and I immediately signed up for photography classes. Previously, I'd been involved in painting but dropped that when I decided to learn how to make sculptures. But I soon got frustrated with that because it takes too much time to finish anything. Besides, I'd just begun studying astronomy with my son's telescope. All that physics and math soon bored me though, so, after a week, I started taking jazz dance lessons. At first it was fun, but the instructor was especially strict, so I had too many problems. But I think I'll continue with what I'm doing now for a while. It doesn't seem to be particularly complicated. However, there's always the possibility I'll get interested in something else soon.

여 나는 아주 많은 일을 하는 것을 좋아하지만 절대로 한 가지 취미를 오랫동안 유지하는 것 같지 않다. 그건 변덕스런 성격 때문인 것 같다. 뭔가에 정말 흥분을 하지만 다음날이면 다른 걸 시도하고 싶다. 예를 들어 어제 디지털 카메라를 사서 당장 사진촬영 강의에 등록을 했다. 이전에는 그림에 몰두해 있었지만 조각을 하는 방법을 배우기로 결정했을 때 그것을 그만둬버렸다. 하지만 어떤 것이든 끝내는 데 시간이 너무 많이 걸려서 곧 조각에 좌절을 느꼈다. 게다가 아들의 망원경으로 막 천문학을 공부하고 있던 중이었다. 하지만 곧 물리학과 수학 같은 것들 때문에 지루해져서 일주일 후에 재즈 댄스 수업을 듣기 시작했다. 처음에 그건 재미있었지만 강사가 엄격해서 문제가 많았다. 하지만 당분간은 지금 하고 있는 것을 계속할 생각이다. 그건 특별히 복잡해 보이지 않는 것 같다. 하지만 곧 다른 것에 흥미를 느끼게 될 가능성은 언제나 있다.

25 다음을 듣고, 남자의 마지막 말에 들어갈 가장 알맞은 것을 고르시오.

> In conclusion, ________________.

① Koreans will likely never accept foreigners in their country
✓ there will be many changes in Korea in the future
③ the government is likely to restrict the number of foreigners it allows in
④ all foreigners should be given equal treatment in Korea
⑤ there will be more foreigners than Koreans in a few years

> 결론적으로, ________________.

① 한국인들은 자신들의 국가에서 외국인들을 결코 받아들일 것 같지 않다.
② 앞으로 한국에서는 많은 변화가 있을 것이다.
③ 정부가 허용하는 외국인들의 수를 제한할 것 같다.
④ 모든 외국인들은 한국에서 동등한 대우를 받아야 한다.
⑤ 몇 년 뒤에는 한국인들보다 외국인이 더 많을 것이다.

▶ multiethnic 다민족의 majority of 대부분의 existence 존속 estimate 추정하다 represent …에 상당[해당]하다 despite …에도 불구하고 reflect 반영하다, 나타내다 ethnicity 민족성, 민족색 adjust 조정하다 definition (단어 등의) 정의

M It's never been clearer than before that Korea is becoming a multiethnic society. For the majority of its existence, Korea has been a closed society with Koreans considering foreigners to be outsiders. Now, there are many signs indicating this will change. There are currently over one million foreigners from all over the world living and working in Korea. In addition, the percentage of Koreans marrying foreign nationals is increasing every year. It is estimated that, by 2030, ten percent of Koreans will be married to foreigners while their children will represent five percent of the population. Despite this, Korean society is having a difficult time accepting non-Koreans. In many nations, the citizens' nationality is not reflected in their ethnicity. Koreans need to adjust their definition of what a Korean is and should learn to accept non-Koreans as full citizens and neighbors. Only then will Korea be able to accept all of its citizens, no matter what their nationality or ethnicity, as Koreans and not as strangers. In conclusion, ________________.

여 한국은 그 어느 때보다도 명백히 다민족 사회가 되어가고 있다. 건국 이래 대부분의 시간동안 한국은 외국인을 이방인으로 생각하는 한국인들로 인해 폐쇄된 사회였다. 이제, 이것이 변할 것이라는 것을 나타내는 많은 신호가 있다. 현재 세계 각국에서 온 1백만 명이 넘는 외국인들이 한국에서 생활하며 일하고 있다. 게다가 외국 국적자와 결혼하는 한국인 비율은 매년 증가하고 있다. 2030년까지 한국인의 10퍼센트가 외국인과 결혼할 것이며 그들의 자녀는 인구의 5퍼센트를 차지할 것으로 추산된다. 이러한 점에도 불구하고 한국 사회는 한국인들이 아닌 사람들을 수용하는 데 어려움을 겪고 있다. 많은 국가에서 시민들의 국적은 그들의 민족성을 나타내지 않는다. 한국인들은 한국인이란 무엇인지에 대한 자신들의 정의를 재조정할 필요가 있으며 한국인들이 아닌 사람들을을 완전한 시민과 이웃으로 받아들이는 걸 배워야 한다. 그러한 경우에만 한국은 모든 시민들을, 국적이나 민족성에 상관없이 한국인으로, 또 이방인이 아닌 존재로 받아들일 수 있을 것이다. 결론적으로 ________________.

---

26 대화를 듣고, 민수의 성격을 가장 잘 나타낸 것을 고르시오.

① Polite
② Tense
③ Selfish
④ Flashy
✓ Considerate

① 정중한
② 예민한
③ 이기적인
④ 충동적인
⑤ 사려 깊은

▶ reimburse 갚다, 상환하다 notebook 공책 photocopy (문서 등을) 복사하다 notes (간단한) 기록 thunderstorm 심한 뇌우: 천둥을 수반하는 일시적인 폭우 awful 무서운, 무시무시한 soaked (비 등으로) 흠뻑 젖은 in the process …의 진행 중에, …의 과정에서

M I didn't expect to see you here tonight. I thought you said that you didn't have any money to spend.

W Well, that's true, but one of my friend's gave me some cash because he knew how much I wanted to see this movie with everyone.

M So when are you going to have to pay him back?

W Oh, I don't have to reimburse him at all. Minsu gave me the money. He's just that kind of a person I guess.

M You're right about that. I remember something that happened at school once. I had lost my notebook, and we were taking a test the next day. Minsu photocopied all of his notes for me and then let me have them. I couldn't believe it.

W That's a good one. I have another story about him as well.

M Go ahead, and tell me what he did.

W He didn't do this for me, so I heard about it from someone else. Do you remember that thunderstorm we had last week?

M Yeah, how can I forget it? It was awful.

W Well, Minsu gave Eunmi his umbrella during it since she didn't have one. He got soaked in the process, but he didn't seem to mind.

남 오늘밤에 여기서 널 볼 줄은 예상 못했어. 돈이 전혀 없다고 했던 것 같은데.

여 어, 맞아. 하지만 내가 모두와 함께 이 영화를 얼마나 보고 싶어 하는지 아는 친구 하나가 돈을 좀 줬어.

남 그래서 그 친구에게 언제 갚아야 하는데?

여 아, 갚을 필요가 전혀 없어. 민수가 돈을 줬거든. 그는 그냥 그런 성격의 사람이야.

남 그건 네 말이 맞아. 언젠가 학교에서 일어난 일이 기억난다. 공책을 잃어버렸는데 다음날이 시험을 치는 날이었어. 민수가 자기가 필기한 것을 복사해서 내게 줬어. 믿을 수가 없었지.

여 다행이야. 그에 관해 다른 이야기도 있어.

남 어서, 그가 뭘 했는지 말해봐.

여 내게 한 일은 아니고, 다른 사람에게서 얘길 들은 거야. 지난주에 천둥치고 비내린 것 기억나니?

남 그래, 어떻게 잊겠어? 끔찍했어.

여 음, 그때 은미가 우산이 없어서 민수가 은미에게 자기 우산을 줬대. 그러다 자기는 흠뻑 젖었는데 개의치 않는 것 같았대.

27 대화를 듣고, 여자의 반지가 있던 위치를 고르시오.

▶ **see if** …인지 보다   **roll** 구르다, 굴러가다
bookshelf 책장   **flashlight** 회중전등, 손전등   **stand** (물건을 올려놓거나 하는) 대, 작은 탁자   **search** 찾다
get down (사람이) 몸을 굽히다, 무릎 꿇다   **horrible** 끔찍한, 지긋지긋하게 싫은   **Hold on a second.** 잠깐만.   **be able to** …할 수 있다   **grab** 움켜쥐다

W Can you come and help me for a minute? I think I've lost my ring. It's somewhere in the living room, but I can't remember where I put it.

M Did you lose your ring again? Okay, let me help you find it. Maybe it's on table next to the sofa like it was the last time you lost it.

W I already checked, but it's not there. Why don't you take a look under the sofa and see if the ring rolled under it?

M Okay, but I don't know how it could have gotten there.

W In the meantime, I'll look on the bookshelves. I sometimes put things there and then forget about them. Are you having any luck?

M Not yet. It's kind of dark here. Let me get a flashlight, and I'll be able to check better. Why don't you look on the TV stand? It might be there.

W No, I already searched there twice. I'll never find it.

M Okay, I've got the flashlight. Let me get down and try again.

W This is horrible. It's not even next to the lamp like it usually is.

M I've got it. Hold on a second, and I'll be able to grab it for you.

여 잠깐 와서 나 좀 도와줄 수 있어? 반지를 잃어버린 것 같아. 거실 어딘가에 있는데 어디다 뒀는지 기억을 못하겠어.

남 또 반지를 잃어버렸어? 알았어, 찾는 거 도와줄게. 어쩌면 지난번에 잃어버렸을 때처럼 소파 옆 테이블 위에 있을지도 몰라.

여 벌써 확인해 봤는데 거기는 없었어. 소파 아래를 보고 반지가 그 밑으로 굴러갔는지 봐줄래?

남 알았어, 하지만 어떻게 거기로 들어갈 수 있었는지 모르겠다.

여 그 사이에 난 책장 위를 볼게. 가끔씩 물건을 거기다 둔 뒤에 잊어버리거든. 잘 되가니?

남 아직. 여긴 좀 어두워. 손전등을 갖고 올게. 그럼 더 잘 살펴볼 수 있을 거야. TV 탁자 위를 보지 그래? 거기 있을지도 모르잖아.

여 아니야, 거긴 이미 두 번이나 찾아봤어. 반지를 절대로 못 찾을 거야.

남 됐다, 손전등을 갖고 왔어. 무릎을 꿇고 다시 볼게.

여 어떡하지. 보통 때처럼 램프 옆에도 없어.

남 찾았어. 잠깐만, 내가 잡을 수 있을 거야.

28 다음을 듣고, 화자의 의견에 동의하는 진술을 고르시오.
① 수진: 부자만이 성형수술을 할 여유가 있으므로 그에 대한 제약이 있어야 한다.
✔ 은주: 얼굴에 손을 좀 대지 않았다면 나는 결코 이 일을 얻을 수 없었을 것이다.
③ 미희: 사무실에 있는 모든 여성들이 성형수술을 받았기 때문에 모두 똑같아 보인다.
④ 현정: 내 친구는 지난해에 성형수술을 받은 뒤에 몇 가지 심각한 문제로 고통을 받았다.
⑤ 정화: 채용은 그 사람의 외모가 아니라 실력에 근거해야 한다.

▶ **plastic surgery** 성형수술   **disagree with** (의견 등에) 이의가 있다   **logic** 논리   **no longer** 더 이상 …않는   **appearance** 외모   **crucial** 결정적인, 매우 중대한   **attached to** …에 붙어있는   **job application** 입사지원서   **discrimination** 차별   **based on** …에 근거한   **illegal** 불법의   **therefore** 그러므로   **enhance** 강화하다   **prospect** (장래에 대한) 전망, 기대   **on one's mind** 신경이 쓰여, 마음이 걸려

W Plastic surgery is incredibly popular in Korea nowadays. Many people spend a lot of money so that they can look their best. Most people who get work done say that they need the surgery in order to compete in society. Getting a good job and finding the perfect husband or wife is not easy, so looking like a model or movie star is a must. I cannot disagree with their logic. Modern society is all about competition, and, if getting plastic surgery is necessary to be successful, then a person should do it. Unfortunately, attending a good university or having the best skills no longer guarantees employment. Appearance is crucial. After all, in Korea, a personal photograph must be attached to all job applications. Discrimination based on appearance is illegal yet impossible to prove. Therefore, many young people are having plastic surgery to enhance their career prospects. Getting married is also on most young people's minds, and being beautiful or handsome is an important step for them to find love and happiness.

여 요즘 성형수술은 한국에서 믿을 수 없을 정도로 대중적이다. 많은 사람들이 최상으로 보일 수 있도록 많은 돈을 쓴다. 성형을 한 대부분의 사람들은 사회에서 경쟁하기 위해 수술이 필요하다고 말한다. 좋은 직업을 얻고 완벽한 남편이나 아내를 찾는 것은 쉽지 않아서 모델이나 영화배우처럼 보이는 것은 필수이다. 나는 이러한 논리에 반대할 수 없다. 현대 사회는 모든 것이 경쟁에 관련돼 있고 성형수술을 받는 것이 성공을 위해 필요하다면 해야 한다. 불행히도 좋은 대학에 다니거나 최고의 기술을 갖는 것이 더 이상 고용을 보장하지 않는다. 외모는 중요하다. 어쨌거나 한국에서는 개인의 사진이 모든 입사지원서에 부착되어야만 한다. 외모에 근거한 차별은 불법이지만 증명하기가 불가능하다. 그러므로 많은 젊은이들은 직업 전망을 높이기 위해 성형수술을 받고 있다. 결혼을 하는 것도 대부분의 젊은이들이 신경을 쓰는 것이며 미남미녀가 되는 것은 그들에게 있어 사랑과 행복을 찾기 위한 중요한 단계이다.

29 **What can be inferred by the woman's last words?**

✓① She thinks the man's grades are not very good.
② She does not consider the man a good friend.
③ She has very few close friends at her school.
④ She does not enjoy socializing with her friends.
⑤ She has not been out with her friends in a while.

여자의 마지막 말로 유추할 수 있는 것은?
① 그녀는 남자의 점수가 그다지 좋지 않다고 생각한다.
② 그녀는 남자를 좋은 친구로 생각하지 않는다.
③ 그녀는 학교에서 친한 친구가 거의 없다.
④ 그녀는 친구들과 어울리기를 좋아하지 않는다.
⑤ 그녀는 한동안 친구들과 나가 놀지 않았다.

▶ care to …하고 싶어하다, 바라다 literature 문학 turn in 제출하다 as ... as possible 가능한 …한 besides 그리고 또, 게다가 assignment 과제 grade (성적) 평점, 평가 disappoint 실망시키다 entire 전체의 workload 작업량 care about 염려하다, 마음 쓰다

M Some of us are going out to eat tonight. Would you care to join us?

W I'd love to, but I've got to finish this paper, so I'm going to spend the rest of the evening in the library.

M Are you talking about that paper for your literature class? I thought it wasn't due until next week.

W You're right, but I like turning in my work as quickly as possible. Besides, I've got several other assignments to work on, so it'll be good to finish this paper tonight.

M Oh, come on. Forget about that report, and have dinner with us. You spend all your time studying and never go anywhere.

W Yeah, but I'm here to get good grades and learn as much as I can. I don't want to disappoint my parents.

M But it's just one time. You don't have to stay the entire evening.

W I'm sorry, but I can't. You all go out and have fun together. Perhaps I can meet everyone in a few weeks when my workload gets lighter.

M I think you care too much about your grades and not enough about your friends.

W Well, perhaps you should try caring more about your grades. It would help you a lot.

남 우리 몇 명은 오늘밤에 나가서 먹을 거야. 같이 갈래?

여 가고 싶지만 이 리포트를 끝내야 해서 남은 저녁시간은 도서관에서 보낼 거야.

남 문학 수업에 필요한 리포트 말하는 거니? 다음 주가 기한인 줄 알았는데.

여 맞아, 하지만 가능한 한 빨리 제출하고 싶어. 게다가 진행해야 할 다른 과제도 몇 개 있어서 오늘밤엔 이 리포트를 끝내는 게 좋을 거야.

남 아, 제발. 그 리포트는 잊고 같이 저녁이나 먹자. 온통 공부만 하고 전혀 아무데도 안 가잖아.

여 그래, 하지만 난 좋은 성적을 받고 가능한 많이 배우려고 여기에 왔어. 부모님을 실망시키고 싶지 않아.

남 하지만 그냥 한 번이잖아. 저녁 내내 있지 않아도 돼.

여 미안하지만 안 되겠어. 너희는 함께 나가서 재미있게 보내. 어쩌면 몇 주 뒤에 할일이 좀 줄면 모두를 만날 수 있을 거야.

남 넌 성적에 대해 너무 신경을 쓰고 친구들에 대해선 별로 신경을 쓰지 않는 것 같아.

여 음, 아마 넌 성적에 대해 좀더 신경을 써야 해. 그럼 도움이 많이 될 거야.

---

30 **What is the purpose of this talk?**

✓① To announce a program time change
② To promote a new doll business
③ To discuss a successful businesswoman
④ To mention a new television program
⑤ To describe an unusual Korean household

이 이야기의 목적은 무엇인가?
① 프로그램의 시간 변경을 알리는 것
② 새로운 인형 사업을 장려하는 것
③ 성공적인 여성 사업가에 대해 논의하는 것
④ 새로운 텔레비전 프로그램을 언급하는 것
⑤ 독특한 한국의 가정을 묘사하는 것

▶ typical 전형적인 suggest 제안하다, 말을 꺼내다 runaway 일방적 승리의, 수월하게 얻은 jealous 시기하는 corporation 기업 provided that …이라는 조건으로, 만약 …이면 give up 포기하다 creation 창작물 tune in 라디오[텔레비전]를 틀다, 주파수[채널]를 (…에) 맞추다 find out 알아보다, 살펴보다 slot (연속한 것, 표 등에서의) 위치, 자리

M Kim Minhee was once a typical housewife who loved making dolls at home. One day, a friend suggested that she start selling dolls over the Internet. Minhee decided to try it, and, overnight, her doll business became a runaway success. Unfortunately, this has created a number of problems for her. Her husband is jealous that she makes more money than he does, and her children want her to spend more time taking care of them. Additionally, a large corporation has recently offered to buy her doll business provided that she gives up the rights to her creation. What should Minhee do? Tune in to Channel 22 every day from Monday to Friday at eleven a.m. to find out. *Life in the Dollhouse* has moved to a new time from its previous ten thirty a.m. slot. Be sure to remember the new time since you won't want to miss Korea's most popular morning TV program, and then you can find out how Minhee will solve her problems in her *Life in the Dollhouse*.

남 김민희는 한때 집에서 인형 만드는 것을 좋아하는 전형적인 주부였습니다. 어느날 친구가 인터넷으로 인형을 팔기 시작하라고 제안했습니다. 그녀는 그것을 시도하기로 결정했고 하루 아침에 그녀의 인형 사업은 크게 성공했습니다. 안타깝게도 이것은 그녀에게 많은 문제를 야기했지요. 남편은 그녀가 자기보다 많은 돈을 버는 것에 질투를 하고 아이들은 그녀가 자신들을 돌보는 데 더 많은 시간을 써 주기를 원합니다. 게다가 대기업은 최근 그녀가 창작물에 대한 권리를 포기한다는 조건하에 그녀의 인형 사업을 매입하려고 제안해 왔습니다. 그녀는 어떻게 해야 할까요? 월요일에서 금요일까지 매일 오전 11시에 22번으로 채널을 돌려 알아보십시오. 〈인형의 집에서의 삶〉은 이전의 오전 10시 반 시간대에서 새로운 시간으로 옮겼습니다. 한국에서 가장 인기있는 아침 TV 프로그램을 놓치지 않으려면 새로운 시간을 꼭 기억하십시오. 그러면 〈인형의 집에서의 삶〉에서 그녀가 어떻게 자신의 문제를 풀 것인지 알 수 있습니다.

31 〔모두 듣기〕 **What is this talk about?**

① A new government law for apartments

✓ Garbage separation at an apartment complex

③ Recycling glass, plastic, and paper

④ Thanking people for following some rules

⑤ The punishment for failing to follow the rules

이 이야기는 무엇에 관한 것인가?

① 아파트에 대한 정부의 새로운 법률

② 아파트 단지에서의 쓰레기 분리수거

③ 유리, 플라스틱, 종이의 재활용

④ 규칙을 지키는 사람들에 대한 감사

⑤ 규칙을 지키지 않는 것에 대한 벌칙

▶ **apartment complex** 아파트 단지 **sort** 분류하다 **container** (물건을 담는) 용기 **collection** 수집, (쓰레기 따위의) 더미 **recyclables** 재활용품 **tin can** 깡통 **dump** 버리다 **regular** 일반적인 **organic** 유기체[생물]의 **dispose of** 처분하다, (쓰레기를) 치우다 **core** (과일, 옥수수 등의) 속, 심 **peel** (채소, 과일 등의) 껍질 **leftover** 나머지, 음식 찌꺼기 **spoiled** 상한 **cooperate** 협조하다

W I've called this meeting once again to stress the importance of doing this. Too many people have not followed the government's and this apartment complex's rules. You must be sure to sort every item into the different bags and containers at the collection point. First, let's talk about the recyclables. Plastic bottles and any other kinds of plastic container go into container number one. Into container number two go newspapers, paper bags, and all other kinds of paper products. Put glass bottles of any type and tin cans into container number three. Finally, too many people are dumping animal, fruit, and vegetable waste matter into the regular garbage bags. Anything organic must be disposed of properly. This includes meat and fish bones, eggshells, apple cores, orange and banana peels, and any leftover or spoiled food. Please cooperate in this matter, and then there shouldn't be any more problems in the future.

여 이 모임을 다시 한 번 소집한 것은 이 행동의 중요성을 강조하기 위해서입니다. 너무 많은 사람들이 정부와 이 아파트 단지의 규칙을 따르지 않았습니다. 여러분은 반드시 모든 물건을 수집장소에 있는 서로 다른 주머니와 용기에 분류해 넣어야 합니다. 첫째, 재활용품에 대해 얘기해보겠습니다. 플라스틱병과 다른 기타 종류의 플라스틱 용기는 1번 용기에 넣어야 합니다. 2번 용기에는 신문과 종이백, 기타 모든 종류의 종이 제품을 넣습니다. 어떤 유형이든 유리병과 깡통은 3번 용기에 넣으세요. 마지막으로 너무 많은 사람들이 축산물과 과일, 야채 폐기물을 일반 쓰레기봉투에 버리고 있습니다. 유기물질은 적절하게 폐기되어야만 합니다. 이것에는 육류와 생선 가시, 달걀껍데기, 사과심, 오렌지와 바나나 껍질, 남은 음식이나 상한 음식이 포함됩니다. 제발 이 문제에 협조해 주십시오. 그러면 앞으로는 더 이상의 문제가 없을 것입니다.

---

32 〔모두 듣기〕 **Which of the following will the student NOT do?**

✓ Learn about Art Deco

② Read a list on her syllabus

③ Study chapters 4 and 5

④ Learn about the Impressionists

⑤ Get some extra books to study

다음 중 학생이 하지 않을 일은 무엇인가?

① 아르 데코에 대해 공부한다

② 강의 계획서에 있는 리스트를 읽는다

③ 4장과 5장을 공부한다

④ 인상주의자들에 대해 공부한다

⑤ 공부하기 위해 추가 서적을 구한다

▶ **mind** 언짢게 여기다, 반대하다 **curious** 궁금한 **midterm** 중간의 **excuse** (행동 등의) 이유[핑계]가 되다 **whatever** 무엇이든 **Impressionist** 인상주의자 **Art Deco** 아르 데코: 1920~30년대의 장식 양식 **set ... aside** …을 제쳐 두다 **in addition to** …에 더하여, …외에 또 **syllabus** (강연, 강의 등의) 개요, 요강 **do well** 잘되다, 성공하다

W Mr. Johnson, do you mind if I ask you a few questions? I'm curious about what's going to be on the midterm exam.

M Weren't you listening in class yesterday? I went over everything then.

W Actually, I wasn't there since I was at the doctor's office. Here's my note excusing me.

M In that case, go ahead and ask whatever you want.

W First, are we going to be tested on the section about the Impressionists?

M Yes, you should know about them, so read chapters 4 and 5 thoroughly since they'll help you understand that time period.

W Okay, thanks. But what about the information on Art Deco? Do we need to know that?

M No, that's going to be on the final exam, so you can set that aside to study another day.

W Great, and are there any books I should study that would help me perform well on the exam?

M In addition to your textbook, there's a list of books on your syllabus that will help you learn the material. Read that list, do some extra reading, and you should do well on the exam.

여 존슨 선생님, 질문을 몇 가지 해도 되나요? 중간고사에 뭐가 나올지 궁금해서요.

남 어제 수업할 때 잘 듣지 않았니? 그때 모두 얘기했는데.

여 실은 병원에 있어서 수업에 없었어요. 여기 사유서가 있어요.

남 그런 경우라면, 뭐든 원하는 걸 물어봐.

여 첫째로 인상주의자 부분에 관해 시험을 치나요?

남 그래, 그들에 대해 알아야 하니까 4장과 5장을 철저하게 읽어라. 그럼 그 시기를 이해하는 데 도움이 될 테니까.

여 알겠어요, 고맙습니다. 그런데 아르 데코에 관한 내용은 어때요? 그걸 알아야 하나요?

남 아니, 그건 기말시험에 나올 거니까 다른 날 공부하도록 제쳐놓아도 괜찮아.

여 잘됐네요. 그리고 시험을 잘 치는 데 도움이 될 공부해야 할 책이 뭐 있나요?

남 교과서와 더불어 강의 계획서에 있는 책들도 그 내용을 배우는 데 도움이 될 거야. 목록을 읽고 추가로 책을 더 읽어봐. 그럼 시험을 잘 칠 거다.

<table>
<tr><th>문제와 정답</th><th>스크립트</th><th>해석</th></tr>
</table>

33 〔모두 듣기〕 **According to the talk, what does the speaker want to be in the future?**

① a flight attendant
② a surgeon
③ a math teacher
④ a tour guide
✔ an airline pilot

이야기에 따르면, 화자는 미래에 무엇이 되고 싶어 하는가?

① 승무원
② 외과의사
③ 수학 선생님
④ 여행 안내인
⑤ 항공기 조종사

▶ navigational 항해(술)의, 항공(술)의 all over the world 전세계에서 correct 교정하다, 조정하다 eyesight 시력(＝vision) perfect 완벽한 be required for …에 필요하다 position 직, 근무처 apply to …에 지원하다, 의뢰하다 private 개인적인, 사적인

M I'm still in high school, but, in the future, I hope to have a successful career, so right now I have to start making plans. I need to get accepted to a good university first, so I must study hard in school. Mathematics is important for my job because it requires a lot of navigational skills, so I'm taking extra math classes now. Also, since my job will take me all over the world and its main language is English, I need to ensure that my English is as good as possible. Next, I need some surgery to correct my eyesight since perfect vision is required for this position. After I finish university, I'll apply to all the big airlines for training. If they don't accept me, then I'll go to a private flying club and get my private license first. After that, I am sure one of them will hire me.

남 나는 아직 고등학교에 다니지만 앞으로 성공적인 직업을 얻기를 바라므로 지금 당장 계획을 짜기 시작해야 한다. 먼저 좋은 대학에 입학할 필요가 있으니 학교에서 열심히 공부를 해야 한다. 수학은 운항기술이 많이 필요한 내 일을 얻는 데 중요하기 때문에 나는 지금 수학 수업을 추가로 듣고 있다. 또한 그 일이 전 세계를 돌아다니는 일이고 주요 언어가 영어이므로 꼭 영어를 가능한 한 잘 할 필요가 있다. 다음으로 이 직업에는 완벽한 시력이 필요하기 때문에 시력을 교정하는 수술이 좀 필요하다. 대학을 마친 뒤에는 훈련을 위해 큰 항공사들에 전부 지원할 것이다. 그들이 날 받아 주지 않는다면 먼저 사설 비행클럽에 가서 개인 면허증을 딸 것이다. 그 뒤에는 그들 항공사 중 한 곳이 나를 채용할 거라고 확신한다.

---

34 〔모두 듣기〕 **How long will the bus take to get to New York?**

✔ 4 hours
② 4 hours and thirty minutes
③ 5 hours
④ 5 hours and thirty minutes
⑤ 6 hours

버스가 뉴욕에 도착하는 데 시간이 얼마나 걸리는가?

① 4시간
② 4시간 반
③ 5시간
④ 5시간 반
⑤ 6시간

▶ preference 선호, 애호 aisle seat (열차, 극장 등의) 통로쪽 좌석(↔ window seat) front 맨 앞부분, 정면 plenty of 다수의…, 다량의… express bus 고속버스 arrive 도착하다 owe ... for …에게 (물건의) 대금을 빚지고 있다 total comes to (금액이) 모두 …이다 cash 현금 assistance 도움, 보조

M Is there something I can help you with today?

W Yes, I'd like a ticket on the next bus for New York, please.

M All right. There are a few seats left on the bus. Do you have any preference as to where you'd like to sit?

W I didn't know we could choose our seats on the bus. If that's the case, how about giving me an aisle seat near the front?

M Sure, I can do that for you. Now, the bus is going to be leaving at 5:30, so that's about fifteen minutes from now. You should have plenty of time to get there before it leaves.

W That's good to hear. I'm in a hurry and need to get to New York as fast as possible.

M Well, you've got a ticket on the express bus, so, once it starts going, it's not going to stop until it arrives there at nine thirty tonight.

W That sounds wonderful. Oh, how much do I owe you for the ticket?

M Your total comes to sixty dollars.

W Here's the cash. Thanks so much for your assistance.

남 오늘 무엇을 도와드릴까요?

여 네, 뉴욕으로 가는 다음 버스 표를 주세요.

남 알겠습니다. 그 버스에 좌석이 몇 석 남아 있네요. 선호하는 좌석이 있으신가요?

여 버스에서 좌석을 선택할 수 있는 줄은 몰랐네요. 그럼 앞 부근의 통로 쪽 좌석은 어때요?

남 괜찮습니다, 그렇게 해드리죠. 자, 버스가 5시 30분에 떠나니까 지금부터 약 15분 후예요. 버스가 떠나기 전에 그곳에 도착할 시간이 충분하시네요.

여 다행이네요. 급해서 가능한 한 빨리 뉴욕에 도착해야 하거든요.

남 음, 갖고 계신 건 고속버스 표니까 일단 출발하게 되면 오늘밤 9시 30분에 도착할 때까지 서지 않고 갈 겁니다.

여 정말 잘됐네요. 표값은 얼마를 드려야 하죠?

남 총액이 60달러입니다.

여 여기 있습니다. 도와줘서 정말 고마워요.

문제와 정답	스크립트	해석

35 다음을 듣고, 이어지는 영어 질문에 답하시오.

① swimming ② baseball ③ golf
✓ table tennis ⑤ volleyball

① 수영 ② 야구 ③ 골프
④ 탁구 ⑤ 배구

▶ out of shape 몸의 상태가 나쁜, 형태가 흐트러진
sport 운동, 스포츠 strategy 전략, 전술 teammate
팀동료

M Eric thinks he's out of shape, so he wants to start playing a new sport. However, he's not particularly good at sports that require a lot of strategy. In addition, he prefers to play sports where he doesn't have any teammates. Finally, he doesn't particularly enjoy being outdoors, and he absolutely can't stand getting wet at all.

Q: Which of the following sports is Eric likely to try?

남 에릭은 몸 상태가 별로인 것 같아서 새로운 운동을 시작하고 싶어 한다. 하지만 그는 많은 전략이 필요한 운동은 그다지 잘하지 못한다. 게다가 팀 동료가 한 명도 없는 운동을 하는 걸 선호한다. 마지막으로 그는 야외에 있는 것을 그다지 즐기지 않고 몸이 젖는 것은 정말로 전혀 못 견딘다.

Q: 다음 중 에릭은 어느 스포츠를 할 가능성이 높은가?

---

36 주어진 시간 동안 아래 지문을 주의 깊게 읽고, 들려주는 질문에 답하시오. 〔1분〕

At the start of the twentieth century, Earth's population was estimated at around 1.6 billion people. In slightly more than one hundred years, however, that number has increased to somewhere around 6.6 billion individuals. This is an astonishing rate of increase in population as the number of people living on Earth has more than tripled in approximately a century. Interestingly enough, some countries around the world are either experiencing negative population growth or are witnessing birthrates lower than necessary for a country to sustain its population. For example, Russia is seeing its population decline while countries like Japan, Italy, and several other European nations all have incredibly low birthrates. For these countries, it is just a matter of time before their populations also begin to decrease. As a general rule, developed countries have lower birthrates while developing countries have much higher ones. The result is that much of the world's population increase is being driven by countries in Asia, the Middle East, and Africa. Unfortunately, many people in these countries cannot economically support such large families, which thereby causes numerous social and health problems because of these countries' quickly increasing populations.

Q _____________________________

① The world's population will triple in the next hundred years.
② Several Asian countries are seeing their populations decrease.
③ Many countries with increasing populations have social problems.
④ There is room for about 1.6 billion more people to live on Earth.
✓ The populations in some developing countries are growing rapidly.

Q: According to the passage, which of the following statements is true?

20세기 초에 지구의 인구는 약 16억 명으로 추산되었다. 하지만 1백 년이 약간 지나는 동안 그 수는 66억 명 가량으로 증가했다. 이것은 엄청난 인구 증가율로, 지구에 살고 있는 사람들의 수가 대략 한 세기 사이에 세 배가 넘었기 때문이다. 아주 흥미로운 것은 전 세계의 일부 국가들은 마이너스 인구 성장을 경험하고 있거나 한 나라가 인구를 지탱하기에 필요한 것보다 더 낮은 출산율을 목격하고 있다. 예를 들면 러시아는 인구 감소를 보이는 반면 일본과 이탈리아, 기타 몇몇 유럽 국가들은 모두 믿기지 않을 정도로 낮은 출산율을 보인다. 이런 국가들에서는 인구가 감소되기 시작하는 것도 단지 시간의 문제일 뿐이다. 일반적으로 선진국은 저출산율을 보이는 반면에 개발도상국들은 훨씬 더 높은 출산율을 보인다. 그 결과 대부분의 세계 인구 증가가 아시아와 중동, 아프리카 국가들에 의해 진행되고 있다. 불행히도 이런 국가들에 있는 많은 사람들은 그런 대가족을 경제적으로 부양할 수 없기 때문에 이들 국가의 급증하는 인구가 수많은 사회 문제와 보건 문제를 낳고 있다.

Q: 지문에 따르면, 다음 진술 중 사실인 것은 어느 것인가?

<table>
<tr><th>문제와 정답</th><th>스크립트</th><th>해석</th></tr>
</table>

① 세계 인구는 다음 백 년 사이에 세 배로 늘 것이다.
② 몇몇 아시아 국가는 인구 감소를 보이고 있다.
③ 인구가 증가하는 많은 국가들은 사회 문제를 안고 있다.
④ 약 16억이 넘는 사람들이 지구에서 살 공간이 있다.
⑤ 일부 개발도상국의 인구가 급증하고 있다.

▶ **billion** 10억의 **astonishing** 깜짝 놀라게 하는, 놀라운 **triple** 3배로 되다 **approximately** 대략, 대체로 **witness** 목격하다 **sustain** 지탱하다, 유지하다

---

37 **Which of the following is NOT an English loanword from another language?**

① sushi
✔ steak
③ pizza
④ cafe
⑤ aloha

다음 중 다른 나라의 언어에서 차용된 영어가 <u>아닌</u> 것은?

① 스시
② 스테이크
③ 피자
④ 카페
⑤ 알로하

38 **Why is the woman reading the book?**

① She has a class assignment on it.
② Someone gave it to her as a present.
③ Her major at school is linguistics.
✔ She is interested in the topic.
⑤ She is taking a class on the topic.

여자가 그 책을 읽는 이유는?

① 그 책에 관련된 수업시간의 숙제가 있다.
② 누군가 그 책을 그녀에게 생일 선물로 주었다.
③ 학교에서 그녀의 전공이 언어학이다.
④ 그녀는 그 주제에 관심이 있다.
⑤ 그녀는 그 주제에 대한 수업을 수강하고 있다.

▶ **borrow** 빌리다, 차용하다 **influence** 영향을 미치다 **straight** 바로, 수정[변경]없이 **linguist** 언어학자 **loanword** 차용어, 외래어 **fascinating** 매혹적인, 흥미진진한 **amazed** 놀란, 경탄한 **check ... out** …을 확인하다, 조회하다

(37~38)

M What book are you looking at there?

W It's a book about the English language I'm reading for fun. It's really quite interesting. Did you know that large numbers of English words come from other languages?

M Sure, but don't most languages borrow from each other? I'm not sure there's anything special about that.

W Well, of course many languages influence one another; however, large numbers of English words have been taken straight from other languages and put into English without any changes at all. For example, the word "sushi" comes from Japanese. In English, it has the same meaning as the Japanese word. Linguists call these loanwords.

M Ah, I see what you're talking about. That's pretty fascinating. What are some other words that come from different languages?

W Hmm… Let me see. The word "café" comes from a French word. And the word "aloha," which we use to mean "hello," comes from the Hawaiian word with the same meaning.

M I never realized there were so many loanwords in English.

W Yeah, I'm totally amazed as well. Here, check this out. The word "gulag," which is a prison, comes from the same Russian word. And, your favorite food, pizza, comes from the Italian word with the same meaning.

M Yum, I'm getting hungry just thinking about that. Let's go get a steak or something to eat.

W Okay, let me read a couple more pages, and then I'll join you for dinner.

(37~38)

남 거기서 무슨 책 보고 있어?

여 재미로 읽고 있는 영어에 관한 책이야. 정말로 흥미로워. 너는 많은 영어 단어가 다른 언어에서 왔다는 것 알았니?

남 그래, 하지만 대부분의 언어가 서로 차용하지 않니? 거기에 특별한 게 있는지는 모르겠는데.

여 음, 물론 많은 언어가 서로 영향을 주긴 하지만 많은 영어 단어는 다른 언어에서 직접 차용되어 아무런 수정도 없이 영어로 받아들여졌어. 예를 들어서 '스시'라는 단어는 일본어에서 왔어. 영어에서 그건 일본어 단어와 똑같은 의미를 지니지. 언어학자들은 이것을 차용어라고 불러.

남 아, 무슨 말하는지 알겠다. 꽤 흥미로운걸. 다른 언어에서 온 다른 단어들로는 어떤 게 있어?

여 흠… 잠깐만. '카페'라는 단어는 프랑스 단어에서 왔어. 그리고 우리가 '안녕'의 의미로 쓰는 '알로하'라는 단어는 똑같은 의미를 지닌 하와이언 단어에서 왔고.

남 영어에 그렇게 많은 차용어들이 있는 줄은 전혀 몰랐어.

여 그래, 나도 정말 놀랐어. 여기, 이걸 한번 살펴 봐. 감옥이라는 뜻의 '굴라그'란 단어는 똑같은 러시아어 단어에서 왔대. 그리고 네가 좋아하는 음식인 피자는 똑같은 뜻을 지닌 이탈리아어 단어에서 왔어.

남 야, 그거 생각만 해도 배고파진다. 스테이크나 뭐 좀 먹으러 가자.

여 알았어, 몇 페이지만 더 읽고 그 다음에 같이 저녁 먹으러 가자.

39 **What is the best title of this article?**

① Coming Summer Fashion Trends
☑ The New Spring Look
③ The Return of Sunglasses
④ The Styles of Earrings
⑤ Fashion from Around the World

이 기사에 가장 적절한 제목은 무엇인가?

① 다가오는 여름 패션 경향
② 새봄의 유행 디자인
③ 돌아온 선글라스
④ 귀고리의 스타일
⑤ 전 세계의 패션

40 **What is NOT mentioned as a hot item for the spring?**

☑ miniskirts
② colored stockings
③ sunglasses
④ plaid skirts
⑤ gold earrings

봄의 유행 아이템으로 언급되지 <u>않은</u> 것은?

① 미니스커트
② 색 있는 스타킹들
③ 선글라스
④ 격자무늬 스커트
⑤ 금 귀고리

▶ **catwalk** (패션 쇼의) 객석으로 뻗은 무대 **latest** 최신의 **go out of style** 유행에 뒤떨어지다 *cf.* **in style** 유행하는 **ladylike** 숙녀다운, 기품 있는 **plaid** 격자 무늬 (천) **definitely** 틀림없이, 확실히 **slight** 약간의 **slit** (스커트 등의) 길게 째진[튼] 데 **along with** …와 함께 **tone** 색조, 색상 **as for** …에 관한 한은, …은 어떠냐 하면 **the more..., the more** …하면 할수록, 더 ~한 **hoop** 링, 고리 **stud** (신체 일부를 뚫은) 보석류, 장신구

(39~40)

M Women's spring fashions are about to hit the catwalk from Milan to New York, and we have the latest news on what and what not to wear this spring. As temperatures start warming, blue jeans will go out of style and more ladylike fashions will come in style. While plaid skirts are definitely in, make sure they're below the knee because miniskirts are no longer fashionable. The best plaid skirts should be gray, red, or brown and have a slight slit at the side. Along with the skirt, most young ladies will wear colored stockings, with dark tones in black, brown, blue, and green being the most popular choices. As for accessories, we have two suggestions: sunglasses and gold earrings. Sunglasses—the bigger the better—are back in style after disappearing for a few years. Now they're being worn by everyone, so grab a pair for yourself. Jewelry accessories are a must, and gold earrings are the hottest items out there. It doesn't matter what kind of earrings you wear. They could be hoops or simple studs. But make sure they're gold, and you'll be in style this spring.

(39~40)

남 여성들의 봄 패션이 곧 밀라노에서 뉴욕까지 패션무대에 등장할 준비를 하고 있는데요, 이번 봄철에 무엇을 입고 무엇을 입지 말아야 할지 최신 뉴스를 전해 드립니다. 기온이 따뜻해지기 시작함에 따라 청바지는 유행에 뒤떨어지게 될 것이며 더 여성스러운 패션이 유행할 것입니다. 격자무늬 스커트는 확실히 유행하겠지만 미니스커트가 더 이상 유행이 아니므로 무릎 아래에 오는지 꼭 확인하십시오. 최상의 격자무늬 스커트는 회색이나 빨간색, 갈색으로, 옆쪽에 약간의 트임이 있는 것이 될 것입니다. 스커트와 더불어 대부분의 젊은 여성들은 색깔 있는 스타킹을 신을 텐데요, 검정색과 갈색, 청색, 녹색의 짙은 색조가 가장 인기를 끌 것으로 보입니다. 액세서리의 경우 두 가지 제안을 할 수 있는데, 선글라스와 금귀고리입니다. 선글라스는 크면 클수록 더 좋은데, 몇 년 동안 사라진 뒤 다시 유행이 되었습니다. 이제는 모든 사람들이 선글라스를 끼고 있으니까 스스로를 위해 하나를 준비해 보십시오. 보석 액세서리는 필수로, 금귀고리는 시중에 나와 있는 가장 인기있는 품목입니다. 어떤 종류의 귀고리를 달 것인가는 상관이 없습니다. 링 귀고리나 심플한 귀고리가 될 수도 있겠지요. 하지만 꼭 금으로 하세요, 그럼 이번 봄에 유행에 동참하시게 될 겁니다.

실전모의고사 06

01 ②	02 ⑤	03 ②	04 ①	05 ⑤	06 ②	07 ⑤	08 ③	09 ①	10 ④
11 ④	12 ③	13 ③	14 ①	15 ④	16 ④	17 ④	18 ②	19 ①	20 ④
21 ③	22 ①	23 ②	24 ①	25 ⑤	26 ①	27 ①	28 ④	29 ③	30 ②
31 ①	32 ②	33 ④	34 ④	35 ②	36 ③	37 ④	38 ③	39 ③	40 ①

문제와 정답	스크립트	해석

01 대화를 듣고, 여자가 구입한 치마를 고르시오.

① 　② 

③ 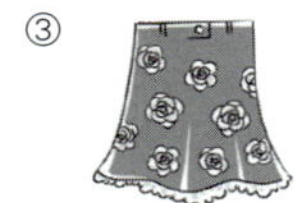　④ 

⑤ 

▶ **out of style** 유행이 지난 *cf.* **in style** 유행하는
way 훨씬, 아주　**knee** 무릎　**either** …도 또한
(…아니다)　**in stock** 비축되어, 재고로　**stripe** 줄무늬
prefer 선호하다　**solid** (색 등이) 고른, 무늬 없는
wrap ... up …을 포장하다

W Excuse me, but do you think you could help me out for a few minutes?

M Sure, what would you like for me to do?

W Well, I'm interested in getting a new skirt, but I'm not exactly sure what is in and out of style these days.

M I think I can help you out with that problem. How about this miniskirt? They're always in style.

W It's nice, but I am not interested in that or in anything that is too long. So I don't want a skirt that goes way past my knees either.

M Okay, then I won't show you any of those in stock. Here's a nice skirt that has stripes. What do you think of it?

W Ugh. That doesn't do anything for me at all. I'd prefer something that's more solid and is medium-length.

M Hmm… I've got two of those. Here's one which has some flower designs on it, and here's one that's a nice solid color.

W Give me the second one. That's exactly what I'm looking for.

M That's an excellent decision. Just let me wrap it up for you.

여 실례지만 잠깐 도와줄 수 있을까요?

남 그럼요, 뭘 도와드릴까요?

여 음, 새 치마를 사고 싶은데 요즘 유행하는 것과 유행이 지난 것을 확실히 모르겠어요.

남 그 문제라면 도와드릴 수 있겠어요. 이 미니스커트는 어떠세요? 항상 유행하는 거죠.

여 좋네요. 하지만 전 미니스커트나 너무 긴 것에는 관심이 없어요. 그래서 무릎 밑으로 너무 내려오는 치마도 안 좋아해요.

남 알겠습니다. 그런 종류의 것들은 보여드리지 않겠습니다. 여기 줄무늬가 있는 괜찮은 치마가 있는데요. 그건 어떠세요?

여 윽, 그건 나한테는 전혀 도움이 안 돼요. 전 단색에 중간 길이인 걸 선호해요.

남 흠… 두 가지가 있네요. 꽃무늬가 디자인된 게 하나 있고 단색이고 근사한 것이 하나 있습니다.

여 두 번째 걸 주세요. 그게 바로 제가 찾는 거예요.

남 탁월한 결정이세요. 바로 포장해 드리겠습니다.

02 대화를 듣고, 두 사람이 만나는 요일과 시간을 고르시오.

① 화요일 오후 2시
② 수요일 오전 10시
③ 목요일 오후 3시
④ 목요일 오후 4시
⑤ 금요일 오후 1시

▶ **I've been meaning to do** …할 작정〔생각〕이었다
contact 연락하다　**get together** 모이다　**definite**
확실한, 명백한　**business trip** 출장　**depend on**
…에 달려 있다　**work** (약 등이 사람에게) 잘 듣다,
효과가 있다　**out of the question** 불가능한, 논외인
in that case 그렇다면

M Anne, I've been meaning to contact you about sitting down for a meeting sometime soon. Do you have any time to get together this week?

W Well, let me think about that for a minute… I can't meet you either today or tomorrow, but I think Wednesday or Thursday is a definite possibility.

M Hmm… I'm going to be out of the office on a business trip both of those days, so do you think we could meet on Friday instead?

W It depends on the time. What time were you hoping to see me?

M I think anytime in the morning works for me. How does ten a.m. sound to you?

W Sorry, but that's completely out of the question. I've got a meeting in Mr. Drummond's office at that time. How about the afternoon? Do you have any time then?

남 앤, 조만간 있을 회의에서 좌석 배치 때문에 연락하려고 했어요. 이번 주에 모일 시간이 돼요?

여 음, 잠깐 생각 좀 해보고요… 오늘이나 내일은 못 만나지만 수요일이나 목요일은 확실히 가능할 것 같아요.

남 흠… 난 그 날 모두 출장 때문에 사무실에 없는데, 그럼 금요일에 만날 수는 있겠어요?

여 시간에 따라 달라요. 몇 시에 만나고 싶어요?

남 난 오전에는 아무 때나 좋아요. 오전 10시는 어때요?

여 미안하지만 그건 전혀 불가능해요. 그 시간에는 드러몬드 씨 사무실에서 회의가 있어요. 오후는 어때요? 그때 시간 있어요?

	M Well, I could meet you at either one or four o'clock, but only for an hour.	남 음, 1시나 4시에 만날 수 있을 것 같지만 한 시간만 될 것 같아요.
	W How much time do you think you'll need?	여 시간이 얼마나 필요할 것 같아요?
	M This should only take about an hour or so.	남 이건 한 시간 정도면 될 거예요.
	W In that case, let's get together right after lunch on that day.	여 그럼 그날 점심 직후에 보는 걸로 하죠.

03 다음을 듣고, 이야기 속의 This가 무엇인지 고르시오.

① a telescope
✓② a microscope
③ eyeglasses
④ a camera
⑤ binoculars

① 망원경
② 현미경
③ 안경
④ 카메라
⑤ 쌍안경

▶ device 장치 tiny 아주 작은 institute 연구소, 학회 sit (물건이) 놓여 있다 specimen (의학, 미생물학상의) 표본, 시험품 rectangular 직사각형의 *cf.* square 정사각형의 subsequently 그 후에, 그 다음에 underneath …바로 밑에 adjust 조절하다 intensity (빛, 열 등의) 세기, 강도 magnification (렌즈 등의) 배율, 확대 enlarge 확대하다 up to …까지 organism 유기체, 생물 atom 원자

W This is a device which is used to observe extremely tiny objects. It is typically found in hospitals, research laboratories, and educational institutes. It can be small enough to sit on a person's desk or large enough to fill an entire room. To use it, the specimen to be observed is placed on a rectangular piece of glass called a slide. The specimen must then be covered by a second smaller square piece of glass. The slide is subsequently set underneath a powerful lens. The user looks through the lens at the specimen and can even adjust the intensity in order to see the item at various magnifications. The most basic ones can enlarge the image up to ten times while huge electronic ones can observe even the tiniest organisms living on Earth. Without this device, much scientific research into diseases and the structure of the atom would be impossible.

여 이것은 엄청나게 작은 대상을 관찰하는 데 사용되는 장치이다. 통상적으로 그것은 병원과 연구 실험실, 교육기관에서 볼 수 있다. 한 사람의 책상에 충분히 놓을 정도로 작거나 방 전체를 충분히 채울 만큼 클 수도 있다. 그것을 사용하려면 관찰되는 표본을 슬라이드라고 부르는 직사각형 유리조각 위에 놓는다. 그때 두 번째의 더 작은 정사각형 유리 조각으로 표본을 덮어야 한다. 그 다음에 슬라이드를 성능 좋은 렌즈 밑에 놓는다. 사용자는 렌즈를 통해 표본을 들여다보고 다양한 배율로 그 물건을 보기 위해 강도를 조절할 수도 있다. 가장 기본적인 것은 이미지를 10배까지 확대할 수 있는 반면 커다란 전자 장치는 지구상에 존재하는 가장 작은 생물체까지도 관찰할 수 있다. 이 장치가 없다면 질병과 원자 구조에 대한 많은 과학 연구가 불가능할 것이다.

04 대화를 듣고, 여자의 감정 변화를 가장 잘 나타낸 것을 고르시오.

✓① concerned → encouraged
② depressed → worried
③ annoyed → amused
④ sad → pessimistic
⑤ angry → pleased

① 걱정되는 → 기운이 난
② 풀이 죽은 → 걱정되는
③ 짜증난 → 즐거운
④ 슬픈 → 비관적인
⑤ 화가 난 → 즐거운

▶ it's just that 그건 단지 …이다 pleased with …에 만족해하는, 마음에 들어 하는 major 전공 goal 목표 calm down 진정하다 No matter what 무슨 일이 있어도, 무엇이 …라 할지라도 no way 절대 …하지 않는 not exactly 전혀 …이 아니다 decent 제대로 된, 온당한 department 학부, 과 totally 전부, 모두 semester 학기 pay for …의 대금을 치르다

M You've been looking a little down lately. I hope you don't have any family problems.

W No, it's just that I've been doing a lot of thinking about my future. I'm simply not pleased with anything right now. I can't stand my major and feel like I don't have any goals in my life.

M Hey, calm down a bit. No matter what you think, nothing's that bad.

W Of course it is. With my major, there's no way I'll ever get a decent job.

M If you're really not happy with your major, then why don't you change it and start studying something else?

W That would be impossible to do. After all, I've been here for two years, so it's too late to change.

M That's not exactly true. My best friend was in the same situation as you last year. He changed departments, and now he's much happier.

W Really? Are you sure about that?

M Totally. He might have to stay here for an extra semester, but that's a small price to pay for his happiness.

W I agree. Thanks. I'm going to check into this right away.

남 최근에 좀 시무룩해 보이더라. 네 가족에게 아무 문제가 없었으면 좋겠다.

여 없어. 그냥 미래에 대해 생각을 많이 해서 그런 것뿐이야. 그냥 지금 당장은 아무것도 만족스럽지 않아. 전공도 견딜 수 없고 인생에서 아무런 목표가 없는 것 같아.

남 이봐, 좀 진정해. 네가 무슨 생각을 하든 어떤것도 그렇게 나쁘진 않아.

여 아니야, 그래. 내 전공으로는 절대로 괜찮은 일자리를 못 구할 거야.

남 전공이 정말 싫으면 전공을 바꿔서 뭔가 다른 공부를 시작해 보지 그래?

여 그건 불가능할 거야. 어쨌거나 2년 동안 여기에 있었고, 바꾸기에는 너무 늦었어.

남 그렇지 않아. 내 가장 친한 친구는 작년에 너와 똑같은 처지였어. 과를 바꿨는데 지금은 훨씬 더 행복해해.

여 정말이야? 확실해?

남 그렇고말고. 한 학기를 더 여기서 보내야 할지도 모르지만 그건 그의 행복을 위해서 치르는 작은 대가야.

여 그래. 고마워. 당장 이 문제를 확인해 봐야겠어.

05

다음을 듣고, 화자가 고등학생일 때 어디에서 살았는지 고르시오.

① Kenya
② The United States
③ India
④ Saudi Arabia
✓ Malaysia

① 케냐
② 미국
③ 인도
④ 사우디아라비아
⑤ 말레이시아

▶ **grow up** 성장하다, 자라다　**civil engineer** 토목 기사　**construction company** 건설회사　**long-term contract** 장기 계약　**accompany** 동행하다, 동반하다　**work on** …에 착수하다　**oil refinery** 정유 공장　**supervisor** 감독자, 관리자　**massive** 대규모의　**seaport** 항구 도시, 해항　**assign** 임무에 앉히다, 선임하다　**head office** 본사, 본점　**frequently** 빈번하게

M When I was growing up, my family moved many times because of my father's job. He was a civil engineer for a construction company, so they sent him to several countries on building projects. Since they were long-term contracts, my family accompanied him. I spent three years in India during elementary school while he helped build a dam there. Soon after that, we moved to Kenya, where his company constructed a highway and an airport. I spent most of middle school in Saudi Arabia when he was working on an oil refinery. From my final year of middle school until I graduated from high school, we lived in Malaysia, where my father was the supervisor of a massive seaport project. Finally, I attended university in the United States when my father was assigned to the head office there in New York. Moving frequently was sometimes difficult, but I've seen some fascinating places.

남 내가 자랄 때 우리 가족은 아버지의 직업 때문에 여러 번 이사를 다녔다. 아버지는 건설회사의 토목 기사여서 회사에서는 아버지를 건설 프로젝트로 여러 나라에 보냈다. 장기 계약이었기 때문에 우리 가족은 아버지와 동행했다. 나는 초등학교 시절 인도에서 3년을 보냈는데, 아버지는 거기서 댐 건설을 도우셨다. 그 후 얼마 뒤에 우리는 케냐로 이사했는데, 거기서 아버지네 회사는 고속도로와 공항을 건설했다. 중학교 대부분은 사우디아라비아에서 보냈는데, 그때 아버지는 정유공장을 추진중이셨다. 중학교 최종 학년에서부터 고등학교를 졸업할 때까지 우리는 말레이시아에서 살았고, 거기서 아버지는 거대한 항구 프로젝트의 감독관이셨다. 마지막으로 나는 미국에서 대학을 다녔는데, 그때는 아버지가 뉴욕 본사에 발령을 받으셨다. 자주 이사를 하는 것은 때론 힘들긴 했지만, 나는 아주 멋진 지역들을 보았다.

06

다섯 개의 대화문을 듣고, 자연스럽지 <u>않은</u> 것을 고르시오.

①
✓ 
③
④
⑤

▶ **pile of** 다수[대량]의　**head down** 향하다　**laundromat** 빨래방, (동전을 넣는) 자동 세탁기　**break down** 고장나다　**repairman** 수리공　**make it to** …에 용케 도달하다　**do the laundry** 세탁하다　**assistance** 도움, 지원　**take up** …에 착수하다, …을 (취미로) 하다　**make up one's mind** 결심하다　**transfer** 전출시키다　**jeopardize** 위태롭게 하다　**ingredient** 재료

① M Where are you going with that big pile of clothes?
   W I'm heading down to the laundromat. My washer broke down the other day, and the repairman hasn't made it to my house yet.
   M In that case, just come over to my house to do your laundry. That's better than heading to the laundromat.

② W I know you're really busy with your work today, but would you mind helping me out for a couple of minutes?
   M Okay, what exactly do you need assistance with?
   W It's the project you're working on now. You're doing it all wrong.

③ M I've decided to take up a new hobby.
   W That sounds nice. Do you know what you're going to do yet?
   M I haven't made up my mind, but I was thinking about learning how to play chess.
   W Good luck. That's not a particularly easy game, so it might take you a while to learn how to play it really well.

④ W You look exhausted. Did you have a long day at the office?
   M Yeah, you wouldn't believe how busy things have gotten. Ever since Mr. Martin got transferred here, he's been working everyone too much.
   W You should have a chat with him and tell him what he's doing.
   M No way. I don't want to say anything that could jeopardize my job.

① 남 옷 뭉치를 잔뜩 갖고 어디로 가는 거야?
   여 빨래방에 가는 중이야. 세탁기가 요전날 고장이 났는데 수리공이 아직 집에 안 왔거든.
   남 그럼 그냥 우리 집에 와서 세탁해. 그게 빨래방에 가는 것보다 낫잖아.

② 여 오늘 일이 정말 바쁜 줄 알지만 잠깐만 좀 도와줄래요?
   남 알았어요, 정확히 어떤 도움이 필요해요?
   여 지금 당신이 추진중인 프로젝트예요. 완전히 잘못하고 있어요.

③ 남 새 취미를 해보기로 결정했어.
   여 잘됐다. 뭘 할지는 정했니?
   남 아직 결정은 못했지만 체스하는 법을 배울까 생각중이야.
   여 행운을 빈다. 그건 그다지 쉬운 게임이 아니니까 정말 잘 하는 법을 배우려면 시간이 좀 걸릴 수도 있겠다.

④ 여 지쳐 보이네. 사무실에서 힘들었어?
   남 응, 일이 얼마나 바빴는지 넌 못 믿을 거야. 마틴 씨가 여기로 전출된 뒤로 모든 사람들에게 너무 많은 일을 시키고 있어.
   여 그와 얘기해서 그가 하고 있는 것에 대해 말해야 해.
   남 절대 안 돼. 내 일을 위태롭게 할 수 있는 건 전혀 말하고 싶지 않아.

⑤ M Have you purchased everything we need to make dinner tonight?

W I'm pretty sure I have. I got all the ingredients for the salad, and I picked up some chicken at the supermarket as well.

M What about the dessert? Did you remember to make that?

W I don't have time to make one, so I bought something from the bakery instead.

⑤ 남 오늘밤에 저녁을 만드는 데 필요한 것들을 모두 구입했어?

여 그런 것 같은데. 샐러드에 필요한 재료를 다 샀고 슈퍼마켓에서 닭고기도 좀 샀어.

남 디저트는 어때? 그거 만드는 걸 잊지는 않았니?

여 만들 시간이 없어서 대신에 빵집에서 뭘 샀어.

---

07 다음을 듣고, 입장료의 총액이 얼마인지 고르시오.

① $10
② $15
③ $20
④ $24
✔ $26

▶ museum 박물관 dinosaur 공룡 exhibition 전시회 entrance fee 입장료 adult 성인 senior citizen 노인 offer …을 제공하다 discount 할인 worth …할 만한, 가치가 있는 collection 수집품 bone 뼈 most of all 그 중에서도, 무엇보다도 bored 지루한 cell phone 휴대폰

W Last Tuesday, my family went to the natural history museum to see the dinosaur exhibition. There were myself, my husband, my ten-year-old son, and my fifteen-year-old daughter. The museum opened at ten a.m. and closed at seven p.m., and we spent most of the day there. We wanted to go on Monday, but it's always closed that day of the week. The entrance fees are ten dollars for adults, five dollars for senior citizens, four dollars for teenagers, and two dollars for children twelve years old or younger. They were offering a ten-percent discount for groups of five or more. It was a bit expensive, but the trip was totally worth it. The exhibition was fantastic, and we saw their wonderful collection of dinosaur bones. My son enjoyed it most of all, but I think my teenage daughter was a little bored. She kept calling her friends on her cell phone.

여 지난 화요일 우리 가족은 공룡 전시회를 구경하러 자연사 박물관에 갔다. 나와 남편, 열 살 난 아들과 열다섯 살 난 딸이 함께였다. 박물관은 오전 10시에 열어서 7시에 문을 닫았는데 우리는 거기서 그날 대부분을 보냈다. 월요일에 가고 싶었지만 주중에 그 날은 언제나 문을 닫는다. 입장료는 성인은 10달러이며 노인은 5달러, 10대는 4달러, 12세 이하 아동은 2달러이다. 다섯 명 이상의 단체에는 10퍼센트 할인을 제공하고 있었다. 다소 비싸긴 하지만 그 나들이는 정말로 가치가 있었다. 전시회는 환상적이었고 우리는 공룡 뼈를 모아놓은 놀라운 수집품을 보았다. 아들은 그걸 가장 좋아했지만 십대인 딸은 좀 지루한 것 같았다. 딸은 계속 휴대폰으로 친구에게 전화를 걸었다.

---

08 대화를 듣고, 남자의 마지막 말에 대한 여자의 응답으로 알맞은 것을 고르시오.

W: _______________

① No, I haven't gotten a job yet.
② Yes, I will talk to him later.
✔ No, I didn't have time to go.
④ Yes, I suppose I should try your method.
⑤ Yes, it's getting really frustrating.

① 아니, 난 아직 직업이 없어.
② 응, 내가 그에게 나중에 얘기할게.
③ 아니, 난 갈 시간이 없었어.
④ 알았어, 네 방법을 시도해 봐야 할 것 같아.
⑤ 응, 정말 실망스러워.

▶ manage to …을 잘 해내다, 애를 써서 …하다 apply for …에 지원하다 submit 제출하다 resume 이력서 application 지원(서), 신청(서) liberal arts 인문과학 search for …을 찾다 picky 까다로운 consulting firm 컨설팅 업체 business 업체 manufacturing 제조(업), 제조의 focus 집중하다, 초점을 맞추다 somehow 어떻게든 하여 sector 부문 counselor 상담자

M Have you managed to apply for any good jobs lately?

W Well, I've submitted my resume to a lot of different companies, but I'm not sure how many of my applications are for good jobs.

M Yeah, I know what you mean. The job market doesn't seem like it's particularly good this year.

W True, but you're an engineer, so you shouldn't have too much of a hard time finding a job. My major is in liberal arts, so it's a little more difficult for me.

M I suppose you're right. What kinds of jobs are you applying for?

W I'm mostly searching for an office job, but I'm not going to be too picky about what I get. I've applied to some consulting firms, big businesses, and even a few manufacturing firms.

M Are you serious? It sounds like you need to focus a little better.

W Maybe, but I need to get a job somehow.

M I agree, but focusing on one sector should help you get a job faster. That's what the job counselor told us. Didn't you attend that meeting on getting a job last week?

W _______________

남 최근에 뭐 괜찮은 일자리에 지원해 봤니?

여 음, 여러 군데 회사에 이력서를 제출하긴 했는데 지원서 중 몇 장이나 좋은 직장에 보낸 건지는 모르겠어.

남 그래, 무슨 말인지 알아. 올해는 취업시장이 특히나 안 좋은 것 같아.

여 맞아, 하지만 넌 기술자니까 취직하는 데 아주 큰 어려움은 없을 거야. 난 전공이 인문과학이라서 더 힘들어.

남 네 말이 맞는 것 같다. 넌 어떤 종류의 일자리에 지원하고 있니?

여 주로 사무직을 찾고 있지만 일자리에 대해 너무 까다롭게 굴지는 않으려고. 컨설팅 회사 몇 군데와 대기업, 그리고 제조업체에도 몇 군데 지원했어.

남 정말이니? 좀 더 집중해야 할 것 같은데.

여 어쩌면 그래, 하지만 어떻게든 취직을 해야 해.

남 그래, 하지만 한 부문에 집중하는 것이 더 빨리 취직하는 데 도움이 될 거야. 취업 상담가가 우리에게 말했어. 지난주 취업 관련 모임에 참석하지 않았니?

여 _______________

<table>
<tr><td>문제와 정답</td><td>스크립트</td><td>해석</td></tr>
</table>

09 다음을 듣고, 이 이야기의 목적이 무엇인지 고르시오.

✔ To instruct
② To complain
③ To warn
④ To criticize
⑤ To praise

① 지도하기 위해
② 불평하기 위해
③ 경고하기 위해
④ 비판하기 위해
⑤ 칭찬하기 위해

▶ pay attention 주의를 기울이다 headquarters 본사, 본부 make sure 확실히 하다, 꼭 …하다 presentable 남 앞에 내놓을 만한, 단정한 under no circumstances 어떤 일이 있더라도 결코 …하지 않는 flashy 야한, 현란한 perfume 향수 cologne 오드 콜로뉴: 독일 쾰른 원산의 향수 manner 태도, 몸가짐

M After finishing university, many people enter the job market. One of the most important skills you need is how to do a job interview. This isn't as easy as it sounds, so pay close attention. First, learn everything you can about the company you're interviewing with. For example, learn about the products it makes or sells, where its headquarters is, and who its president is. Second, make sure you dress your best and look presentable. Under no circumstances should you wear any flashy jewelry or any kind of perfume or cologne. Next, make sure you arrive early for the interview. If you're late, you have already lost the job. During the interview, try to be relaxed, and answer every question in a clear, strong manner. Finally, and most importantly, never ask about the position's salary. If you do, this shows you're there to help yourself, not to help the company.

남 대학을 마친 뒤에 많은 사람들이 취업 시장에 뛰어듭니다. 여러분에게 필요한 가장 중요한 기술 중 하나는 면접을 하는 방법입니다. 이것은 말처럼 쉽지는 않으니까 주의를 잘 기울여 주세요. 첫째로 면접을 할 회사에 관해 여러분이 할 수 있는 모든 것을 습득하십시오. 예를 들면 그 회사가 제조하거나 판매하는 제품들과 본사가 어디에 있는지, 또 사장은 누구인지에 관해 알아두십시오. 둘째로 반드시 가장 좋은 옷을 입고 단정하게 보이도록 하십시오. 절대로 번쩍이는 보석이나 어떤 종류든 향수를 사용해서는 안 됩니다. 다음으로 면접에 일찍 도착하도록 하세요. 늦을 경우 여러분은 이미 그 일자리를 놓친 것입니다. 면접을 하는 동안에는 마음을 편히 하도록 노력하고 모든 질문에 분명하고 씩씩한 태도로 답하십시오. 마지막이자 가장 중요한 것으로, 직책의 급여에 대해 절대로 질문하지 마십시오. 그렇게 할 경우 이것은 여러분이 회사를 돕는 것이 아니라 여러분 자신을 돕기 위해 그곳에 있다는 것을 나타내는 것입니다.

10 대화를 듣고, 남자가 조깅 대신 수영을 시작한 이유를 고르시오.

① 남자는 건강을 증진시키고 싶어 한다.
② 조깅을 하기에는 거리가 너무 혼잡하다.
③ 의사가 수영을 하라고 지시했다.
✔ 남자의 아내가 함께 운동을 하기를 원했다.
⑤ 남자는 아침 일찍 일어나는 것이 싫었다.

▶ jog 조깅: 조깅하다 quit 그만두다 regularly 규칙적으로 instead of …대신 neither …도 또한 …아니다 get sick of …이 싫증나다 crowded 혼잡한 improve 향상시키다 persuade 설득하다 at first 처음에는 can't wait to do 빨리 …하고 싶다, …하고 싶어 기다릴 수 없다 pool 수영장 be sure to do 꼭 …해라 lap (수영 경기에서) 풀장을 한번 왕복하기

W Are you still going on those two-mile jogs every morning?

M Actually, I quit doing those about a month or so ago.

W What? Aren't you the one who was always telling me how I needed to exercise? Why did you suddenly quit jogging?

M I'm not jogging anymore, but I'm still exercising regularly. Instead of jogging, I go swimming four times a week.

W Oh, that's interesting. I never imagined you were the kind of person who'd enjoy that.

M Me neither, but it's actually kind of fun.

W So, what made you take it up? Did you just get sick of jogging and having to run on those crowded city streets?

M Not exactly. My wife's doctor told her she needed to swim to improve her health. She didn't want to do it alone, so she persuaded me to start with her. I wasn't that good at first, but now I can't wait to get to the pool.

W That sounds great. I swim a lot myself. Perhaps I'll see you at the pool sometime.

M I hope so. We'll have to be sure to swim some laps together.

여 아직도 매일 아침에 2마일을 조깅하니?

남 사실은 한 달 정도 전에 그만뒀어.

여 뭐라고? 내게 운동이 얼마나 필요한지 항상 말하던 사람이 너 아니었어? 갑자기 왜 조깅을 그만뒀어?

남 더 이상 조깅은 안하지만 그래도 규칙적으로 운동은 하고 있어. 조깅 대신 일주일에 네 번씩 수영하러 다녀.

여 아, 그거 흥미로운데. 난 네가 그걸 즐길 거라고는 전혀 생각 못했어.

남 나도 그래, 하지만 사실은 재미있더라.

여 어떻게 그걸 시작하게 됐어? 조깅하면서 복잡한 도시 거리를 달리는 것에 싫증났던 거야?

남 꼭 그렇진 않아. 아내의 담당의가 아내의 건강이 좋아지려면 수영이 필요하다고 말했어. 아내가 혼자 하는 걸 싫어해서 날더러 같이 시작하자고 설득하더라고. 난 처음에는 그다지 잘하지 못했지만 지금은 수영장에 가는 게 기다려져.

여 잘됐다. 난 혼자서 자주 수영해. 어쩌면 가끔 수영장에서 볼지도 모르겠구나.

남 그럼 좋지. 꼭 몇 구간을 같이 수영하자.

11 대화를 듣고, 약에 대해 사실이 <u>아닌</u> 것을 고르시오.

① 아무런 부작용이 없다.
② 하루에 네 번 복용한다.
③ 액체 상태의 약이다.
④ 일어난 직후 복용해야 한다. ✓
⑤ 이 약은 복용해도 졸리지 않을 것이다.

▶ **medicine** 약물　**symptom** 증상　**match A for B** B에게 A와 어울리는 것을 찾아 주다　**cough** 기침하다　**sore throat** 인후염　**run** (눈물 등이) 흐르다　**aches and pains** (온몸이) 쑤시고 아픔, 통증　**entire** 전체의　**spoonful** 한 숟가락 가득 (한 분량), 소량　**drowsy** 졸리는　**side effect** (약의) 부작용　**whatsoever** (whatever의 강조형) …하는 것은 무엇이든, 아무리 …일지라도　**see a doctor** 의사의 진찰을 받다　**immediately** 즉시

W I'm trying to find some medicine, but I'm not sure exactly what to buy.

M In that case, why don't you tell me about your symptoms, and I'll try to match the proper medicine for you?

W I've been coughing a lot lately, and I've got a sore throat as well. My nose is running, and I'm experiencing various aches and pains over my entire body.

M All right, I think I know the perfect medicine for you. You want to get this medicine, which should help you feel better quickly.

W That sounds good. How often should I take it?

M You should take one spoonful four times a day. Drink some after every meal and right before you go to bed.

W Is it going to make me drowsy or have any other side effects? I've got to take my kids to school, so I hope it won't do anything bad to me.

M Don't worry about that at all. People who have taken this medicine have reported that it has no side effects whatsoever.

W That's good to hear. Is there anything else I should know?

M Yes, if you don't feel better after a couple of days, you need to see a doctor immediately.

여 약을 좀 구하려고 하는데 뭘 사야 할지 정확히 모르겠어요.

남 그러시다면 증상에 대해 말씀해 주세요. 그럼 적절한 약을 골라드릴게요.

여 최근에 기침을 많이 하고 인후염도 있어요. 콧물이 흐르고 여러 가지로 온몸이 쑤시고 아프네요.

남 알겠습니다. 꼭 맞는 약을 알 것 같네요. 이 약을 드시면 빨리 낫는 데 도움이 될 거예요.

여 잘됐네요. 얼마나 자주 먹어야 하죠?

남 하루에 한 숟가락 정도 네 번을 드셔야 해요. 매끼 식사 후에 또 잠자리에 들기 전에 마시면 됩니다.

여 졸리거나 다른 무슨 부작용은 없나요? 아이들을 학교에 데려다 줘야 해서 안 좋은 일은 없었으면 싶거든요.

남 그건 전혀 걱정하지 마세요. 이 약을 드시는 분들은 어떤 부작용도 전혀 없다고 하셨어요.

여 다행이네요. 제가 알아야 할 다른 게 있나요?

남 네, 며칠 후에도 나아지지 않으면 즉시 진찰을 받아야 합니다.

---

12 다음을 듣고, 이 이야기가 어떤 질문에 대한 대답인지 고르시오.

① What are two happy stories about lottery winners?
② Why do lottery winners lose their money so quickly?
③ What happened to two different lottery winners? ✓
④ Can winning the lottery change my life?
⑤ Do men and women handle success differently?

① 복권 당첨자에 대한 두 개의 행복한 이야기는 무엇인가?
② 왜 복권 당첨자들은 돈을 그렇게 빨리 잃어버리는가?
③ 두 명의 다른 복권 당첨자들에게 무슨 일이 생겼는가?
④ 복권 당첨이 나의 삶을 바꿀 수 있을까?
⑤ 남자들과 여자들은 성공을 다르게 처리하는가?

▶ **poorhouse** 구빈원　**disreputable** 질이 나쁜, 평판이 좋지 않은

M Winning the lottery is a dream come true for many people, but it can also be a nightmare for others. Sudden wealth can bring riches as well as numerous problems when people get all that money. A California woman who recently won the lottery went from the rich house to the poorhouse in less than four years. After winning the lottery, she started buying everything she could. She soon met some disreputable people, who wound up conning her out of her fortune. Very quickly, all of her five million dollars in prize money was gone, and she was left broke and miserable. However, there are many people who manage to handle their sudden wealth much more appropriately than that unfortunate woman. A New York man who won the lottery started by quitting his job and then took his family on a trip around the world. Afterwards, he invested the rest of the money in a business and the stock market. Today, he's successful, wealthy, and much happier than he used to be.

남 복권에 당첨되는 것은 많은 사람들에게 꿈이 실현되는 것이지만 다른 사람들에게는 악몽이 될 수도 있습니다. 갑작스런 부는 사람들이 그 모든 돈을 얻을 때 부유함뿐만 아니라 수많은 문제도 가져올 수 있지요. 최근 복권에 당첨된 캘리포니아에 사는 여성은 4년이 못 지나서 부유한 집에서 구빈원으로 갔습니다. 복권에 당첨된 후 그녀는 할 수 있는 모든 것을 사기 시작했지요. 곧 일부 질 나쁜 사람들을 만났는데, 그들은 결국 그녀에게 사기를 쳐서 재산을 빼앗았습니다. 순식간에 상금으로 받은 5백만 달러가 모두 없어졌고 그녀는 빈털터리가 되어 참담한 상태가 되었습니다. 하지만 불운한 그 여성보다 갑작스런 부를 훨씬 더 적절하게 잘 처리하는 사람들이 많이 있습니다. 복권에 당첨된 뉴욕의 어떤 남자는 먼저 직장을 그만둔 다음 가족을 데리고 전 세계로 여행을 했지요. 이후에는 나머지 돈을 사업과 주식시장에 투자했습니다. 현재 그는 성공했고 부유하며, 예전보다 훨씬 더 행복합니다.

13 다섯 개의 대화문을 듣고, 아래 그림의 상황에 가장 잘 어울리는 것을 고르시오.

① ②  ④ ⑤

▶ break (작업 중의) 휴식, 잠시 동안의 휴식 are for …을 좋아하다 unsweetened 단맛이 없는, 달게 하지 않은 a lot 훨씬, 대단히 employee cafeteria 직원 식당 You can say that again. 맞았어, 바로 그거야 agree with …에게 동의하다 have got to do …해야 하다 deliver 배달하다

---

① W Why don't we stop working and take a quick break for lunch?

M That sounds like a great idea. What do you want to get to eat?

W I'm not exactly sure. Let's walk outside and see which restaurants aren't too busy.

② M What would you like to order for lunch today?

W I think I'll have the chicken salad, please. I'd like that with ranch dressing.

M All right, and would you care for something to drink?

W Yes, I'll have a glass of unsweetened ice tea, please.

③ M I'm so glad I've started bringing my lunch to work these days.

W Yeah, it's a lot healthier than eating at the employee cafeteria.

M You can say that again. It's also cheaper, and I can eat whatever I feel like.

④ W Well, that was a really good lunch.

M I have to agree with you, but it's about time that we head back to the office.

W Yeah, I don't really want to go back, but we've got to get our work done on time.

M Exactly. My wife won't be happy if I come home from work late again tonight.

⑤ W What are you thinking of doing for lunch today?

M Why don't we order something and have it delivered here?

W That sounds like a plan. I don't feel like going out in all this rain.

---

① 여 일하는 거 멈추고 점심시간 동안 잠깐 휴식하는 거 어때?

남 좋은 생각이야. 넌 뭘 먹고 싶어?

여 잘 모르겠어. 밖에 나가서 어느 식당이 분주하지 않은지 보자.

② 남 오늘 점심으로 뭘 주문하시겠습니까?

여 닭고기 샐러드로 갖다 주세요. 렌치 드레싱으로 곁들여 주세요.

남 알겠습니다, 음료를 드시겠습니까?

여 네, 무가당 아이스티 한 잔 주세요.

③ 남 요즘 직장에 점심을 싸오기 시작해서 아주 기뻐.

여 그래, 직원식당에서 먹는 것보다 훨씬 더 건강에 좋아.

남 맞아. 또 더 싸고 뭐든 내가 먹고 싶은 걸 먹을 수 있어.

④ 여 음, 정말 훌륭한 점심이었어.

남 맞아, 하지만 사무실로 돌아가야 할 시간이야.

여 그래, 정말 돌아가기 싫지만 일을 제때 마쳐야 하니까.

남 정말 그래. 오늘밤 또 늦게 퇴근해서 귀가하면 아내가 좋아하지 않을 거야.

⑤ 여 오늘 점심 어떻게 할 생각이야?

남 뭔가 주문해서 여기로 배달시키면 어때?

여 괜찮은 생각이야. 비가 이렇게 오는데 외출하고 싶진 않아.

14 대화를 듣고, 두 사람의 관계를 가장 잘 나타낸 것을 고르시오.

Woman	Man
✓ eyewitness	police officer
② driver	insurance agent
③ pedestrian	tow truck driver
④ shopkeeper	traffic control officer
⑤ passenger	mechanic

여자	남자
① 목격자	경찰관
② 운전자	보험회사 직원
③ 보행자	견인차 운전기사
④ 점원	교통관리 경찰
⑤ 승객	정비사

▶ statement 진술, 한 마디(말) cross 건너다 notice 알아차리다 light 교통신호 slow down 속도를 늦추다 *cf.* speed up 속력을 높이다 hit 충돌하다 intersection (주요 도로와의) 교차점 at fault 죄가 있는 tow truck 견인트럭 on one's way 도중에 if you don't mind 상관 없으시다면, 괜찮으시다면 reach 연락하다(＝contact) insurance 보험 cooperation 협조

W I can't believe what just happened. I saw the entire thing if you want to hear about it.

M Yes, I'd appreciate your giving me a statement. Why don't you tell me exactly what you saw?

W I was waiting to cross the street here. Traffic going north-south was stopped while the cars were moving from east to west.

M Please go on.

W I noticed the light was changing because most of the cars started slowing down. But that red car suddenly started speeding up like the driver wanted to make it through the light. That's when he hit the black car, which was just beginning to move through the intersection.

M Okay, it sounds like you saw exactly what a couple of other people did as well.

W It's very clear who's at fault. I just hope they can get a tow truck here quickly so that traffic won't be stopped for too long.

M We've already called one, so it's on its way. Oh, if you don't mind, I need your name and a telephone number where we can reach you.

W Sure, let me write them down for you.

M You'll probably get contacted by someone in my office as well as both drivers' insurance companies. Thanks for your cooperation.

여 방금 일어난 일을 믿을 수가 없네요. 듣고 싶어 하신다면, 제가 전부 다 봤어요.

남 네, 진술해 주시면 감사하겠습니다. 보신 걸 정확히 말씀해 주실래요?

여 여기서 길을 건너려고 기다리고 있었어요. 차들이 동서로 이동하고 있는 동안 남북으로 가는 교통이 멈췄어요.

남 계속하시죠.

여 대부분의 차가 속력을 늦추기 시작했기 때문에 전 교통신호가 변하고 있다는 걸 알았죠. 하지만 그 빨간색 차가 갑자기 속력을 내기 시작했어요, 운전자가 신호를 통과하고 싶었던 것처럼요. 그때 그가 검정색 차를 들이받았는데, 검정색 차는 막 교차지점을 통과해서 움직이기 시작하고 있었죠.

남 알겠습니다, 다른 몇 사람들이 본 것과도 똑같이 보셨군요.

여 누구 잘못인지는 아주 분명해요. 난 그냥 그들이 빨리 여기에 견인차를 보내서 교통이 너무 오래 멈추지 않았으면 좋겠어요.

남 이미 전화해서 오고 있는 중입니다. 아, 괜찮으시다면 이름과 연락 가능한 전화번호가 필요한데요.

여 그래요, 적어 드릴게요.

남 아마 저희 사무실 직원뿐만 아니라 양 운전자들의 보험사에서도 연락할 거예요. 협조해 주셔서 고맙습니다.

---

15 다음을 듣고, 슬로푸드 운동에 대해 사실이 <u>아닌</u> 것을 고르시오.

① 슬로푸드 운동을 하는 사람들은 어떤 종류의 패스트푸드도 먹지 않는다.
② 슬로푸드 운동은 모든 음식이 유기농으로 재배되어야 한다고 말한다.
③ 슬로푸드 운동을 하는 사람들은 요리가 음식을 먹는 것만큼이나 중요하다고 생각한다.
✓ 슬로푸드 운동의 초창기 회원들은 북미 지역에 살았다.
⑤ 슬로푸드 운동은 전자레인지의 사용을 지양한다.

▶ slow-food movement 슬로푸드 운동: 환경 친화적인 식생활 문화를 지키자는 국제 운동 relatively 비교적 attempt 시도 basic 근본, 기본 원리 productive 생산적인 emphasis 강조(된 것) take one's time 천천히[느긋하게] 하다 dining 식사(하기), 정찬 pleasurable 유쾌한 race 경주 generation 한 세대 organically 유기 재배로 package (포장) 용기 microwave 전자레인지로 요리하다 naturally 자연히, 당연히 spread 퍼지다

W The slow-food movement is a relatively recent attempt to return people to the basics of good eating. Today's lifestyles place too much stress on doing things faster and on being more productive, which leaves little time for eating. The emphasis in the slow-food movement is on taking one's time while dining, whether at home or in a restaurant. According to the members of this group, dining should be pleasurable, not a race to eat as quickly as one can. Members believe that the dining table is a place to relax, enjoy food, and talk to family and friends. Cooking as a group and teaching cooking to the next generation are also very important. Fresh, organically grown food is the choice of slow-food movement members, and they won't touch anything that comes in a package or has to be microwaved. Naturally, they're also against any type of fast-food restaurant or instant food. The movement started in Europe in the 1980s and has since spread both to North America and Asia.

여 슬로푸드 운동은 사람들을 좋은 식사의 근본으로 돌려보내려는 비교적 최근에 일어난 시도이다. 오늘날의 생활 방식은 더 빨리 일 하고 더 생산적이 될 것을 너무 많이 강조하는데, 이것은 식사할 시간을 거의 주지 않는다. 슬로푸드 운동에서 강조하는 것은 집에서든 식당에서든 식사를 하는 동안 여유를 갖는 것이다. 이 집단의 회원들에 따르면 식사는 가능한 한 빨리 먹는 경주가 아니라 유쾌한 것이어야 한다. 회원들은 식탁은 긴장을 풀고 음식을 즐기고 가족 및 친구들과 대화를 하는 곳이라고 생각한다. 단체로 요리하고 요리를 다음 세대에게 가르치는 것도 매우 중요하다. 신선하고 유기농법으로 재배한 음식물이 슬로푸드 운동 회원들의 선택이며 그들은 포장 용기 속에 든 것이나 전자레인지를 이용해야 하는 것은 어떤 것이든 손을 대지 않을 것이다. 당연히 그들은 또 패스트푸드 식당이나 인스턴트 음식은 어떠한 형태든 반대한다. 이 운동은 1980년대에 유럽에서 시작됐으며 이후 북미와 아시아로 확산되었다.

16 대화를 듣고, 카페인 복용의 장단점을 고르시오.

장점	단점
① 경계심 증진	위암 유발
② 지능 증진	손떨림 유발
③ 기억력 증진	신경쇠약 유발
✓ 각성 효과	인체에 해로움
⑤ 집중력 증진	체중 증가

▶ **caffeine** 카페인 **ever since** 그 뒤 줄곧 **concentrate** 집중하다 **ingest** (음식 등을) 섭취하다, 취하다 **cause** 초래하다 **normally** 보통은, 일반적으로 **alert** 기민한, 민첩한 **nowadays** 요즘에 **all that** 모든 그런 종류의 **nervous** 초조한, 불안한 **seriously** 진지하게 말해서 **Do me a favor** 제발 (…해 주시오) **as soon as** …하자마자 **protect** 보호하다, 지키다

W Are you already drinking another cup of coffee? Isn't that the third cup you've had since lunch?

M I really need the caffeine to help me stay awake. I haven't gotten a good night's sleep ever since I started working on this project, so I need something to help me keep awake and let me concentrate better.

W Well, that's true, but all that caffeine can't be good for your body. I read in a magazine that if you ingest too much caffeine, it can cause serious stomach problems.

M That's all right. I don't normally drink caffeine, so, once this project ends, I'll stop. Anyway, I feel so much more alert nowadays. It's a pretty good feeling.

W But look at how much your hands are shaking. They never did that before you drank all that coffee.

M Hmm… I hadn't noticed that before.

W And you're also speaking really quickly and moving around like you're nervous. Seriously, all that caffeine is bad for you. Do me a favor and stop drinking so much of it.

M Okay, I'll do that just as soon as this project comes to an end.

W Great. Your body will thank you for doing that. And you'll be protecting your health in the future.

여 벌써 또 다른 커피를 마시고 있어? 점심 이후에 세 번째 아니냐?

남 깨어 있으려면 정말로 카페인이 필요해. 이 프로젝트를 시작한 이후 잠을 충분히 잔 적이 없어서 계속 깨어 있는 상태로 더 집중하려면 뭔가가 필요해.

여 음, 그건 사실이지만 그렇게 많은 카페인이 몸에 좋을 리가 없어. 잡지에서 읽었는데 카페인을 너무 많이 섭취하면 심각한 위장 장애를 초래할 수 있대.

남 그건 괜찮아. 보통은 카페인을 안 마시니까 일단 이번 프로젝트가 끝나기만 하면 그만둘 거야. 아무튼 요즘은 훨씬 더 말짱한 느낌이야. 꽤 기분이 좋아.

여 하지만 네가 손을 얼마나 떨고 있는지 봐. 이렇게 커피를 마시기 전에는 전혀 안 그랬잖아.

남 흠… 그건 전에 몰랐는데.

여 그리고 또 초조한 것처럼 말을 매우 빨리 하고 여기저기를 돌아다니잖아. 진지하게 말하는 건데, 카페인은 네게 나빠. 제발 그렇게 많이 마시지 마.

남 알았어. 이번 프로젝트가 끝나는 대로 바로 그렇게 할게.

여 좋아. 그럼 몸이 네게 고마워할 거야. 앞으로는 네 건강을 챙겨야 해.

---

17 다음을 듣고, 일기예보와 일치하지 <u>않는</u> 것을 고르시오.

① 토요일의 기온은 30도 가까이 될 것이다.
② 일요일은 덥고 맑은 날이 될 것이다.
③ 토요일은 남부지방이 몹시 흐릴 것이다.
✓ 토요일에 비가 올 가능성이 몹시 높다.
⑤ 월요일에 더 많은 비가 예상된다.

▶ **long-range forecast** 장기 예보 **peninsula** 반도 **high winds** 강풍 **heavy seas** 큰 물결, 거센 파도 **typhoon** 태풍 **head toward** …쪽으로 향하다 **indoors** 옥내에서, 집안에서 **refrain from** …을 자제하다 **temperature** 기온 **climb** 오르다, 상승하다 **at least** 최소한 **coast** 해안 **heat** 더위 **humidity** (상대) 습도 **rainfall** 강우, 강수량

M Now, let's take a look at the long-range forecast for the coming weekend on the Korean peninsula. In the south, there will be continued high winds and heavy seas from the typhoon that is heading toward Japan. People should remain indoors and refrain from driving since, while the typhoon will avoid us, we can still expect some heavy rain. Between fifty and one hundred millimeters are expected. However, the storm should be completely away from Korea by Saturday morning. On Saturday, the skies will still be cloudy in the south, and there will still be a ten-percent chance of light rain. In the north, there will be fewer clouds, and, by Saturday afternoon, the sun should be shining again. Temperatures on Saturday should be in the high twenties. Sunday is expected to be sunny and hot, with the temperature climbing to at least thirty-two degrees on the east coast and twenty-nine degrees in Seoul and the west coast. This heat will bring increased humidity, and, thus, there will be more rainfall on Monday.

남 이제, 다가오는 주말 동안 한반도의 장기 예보를 살펴보겠습니다. 남부에서는 일본 쪽으로 진행되는 태풍으로 인해 강풍과 거센 파도가 계속될 예정입니다. 태풍이 지나가는 동안에도 여전히 호우가 예상되고 있으므로 시민들은 실내에 머무르며 운전을 자제해 주시기 바랍니다. 강수량은 50밀리미터에서 100밀리미터 사이로 예상됩니다. 하지만 폭풍우는 토요일 오전 경 한국에서 완전히 사라질 것으로 보입니다. 토요일 남부지방은 여전히 하늘에 구름이 끼어 있으며 여전히 약한 비가 내릴 확률이 10퍼센트일 것입니다. 북부지방은 구름이 더 적을 것이며 토요일 오후 경에는 해가 다시 비칠 것입니다. 토요일 기온은 30도 가까이 될 것입니다. 일요일은 기온이 동해안은 최소 32도, 서울과 서해안은 29도까지 오르면서 햇살이 비치고 뜨거운 날씨가 예상됩니다. 이 더위로 인해 습도가 증가하여 월요일에는 더 많은 비가 내릴 전망입니다.

<table>
<tr><th>문제와 정답</th><th>스크립트</th><th>해석</th></tr>
</table>

18

다음을 듣고, 이야기의 분위기를 가장 잘 나타낸 것을 고르시오.

① comedic
✓ thrilling
③ silly
④ boring
⑤ nervous

① 우스운
② 스릴 있는
③ 바보 같은
④ 지루한
⑤ 긴장되는

▶ leap 뛰어오르다 dash 돌진하다 alley (좁은) 뒷골목 pour 억수같이 쏟아지다 drench 흠뻑 적시다 thug 악당 on a person's tail 남을 미행하여 dead end 막다른 골목 catch one's breath 한숨 돌리다 lid 뚜껑 closely 차근히 clatter 덜걱 소리를 내다 drawn (칼 등이) 집에서 뽑힌 smash 세게 내려치다, 강타하다 skid 옆으로 미끄러지다 all-out 총력을 기울인, 전면적인 brawl 떠들썩한 싸움 claw 손톱으로 잡으려 하다, 할퀴다 desperate 필사적인 bid 노력, 시도

M Detective Max Gordon leaped from his burning car and dashed into the nearby alley. As he ran, the rain continued to pour and completely drenched him. Not far behind were the two thugs on his tail, and Max had already fired the last bullets from his gun. He turned the corner but saw he was in a dead end. Max stopped to catch his breath and then noticed the lid of a garbage can. He listened closely, and then he heard their footsteps clattering on the asphalt while getting closer and closer. A light overhead cast shadows on the ground, and Max could see two men approaching with guns drawn. When the first one came around the corner Max smashed the garbage lid across the thug's gun hand, and the gun skidded across the ground as the man shouted. And then it was on. There was an all-out brawl as Max smashed, punched, and clawed at the two men in a desperate bid to save his life.

남 맥스 고든 형사는 불타는 차에서 뛰어나와 근처 뒷골목으로 달려 들어갔다. 그가 달릴 때 비가 계속 내려서 그는 완전히 젖었다. 바로 뒤에서는 악당 둘이 그를 바짝 뒤쫓고 있었고 맥스는 이미 총에 들어 있던 마지막 총알들을 발사했다. 그는 모퉁이를 돌았지만 막다른 골목을 보았다. 맥스는 숨을 돌리기 위해 멈췄는데 그때 쓰레기통 뚜껑을 발견했다. 그는 가만히 귀를 기울였고 그때 발자국 소리가 아스팔트 위를 울리면서 점점 더 가까이 다가오고 있는 것을 들었다. 머리 위로 불빛이 바닥에 그림자를 드리우고 있었고 맥스는 남자 두 명이 총을 빼들고 다가오는 것을 볼 수 있었다. 첫 번째 남자가 모퉁이 근처에 왔을 때 맥스가 쓰레기통 뚜껑으로 그 악당의 총을 든 손을 내려쳤고 남자가 소리를 치면서 총이 바닥을 가로질러 미끄러졌다. 그러고 나서 일이 벌어졌다. 전면전이 벌어졌는데, 맥스는 목숨을 구하기 위해 필사적으로 두 명의 남자를 때리고, 주먹질을 하고, 할퀴었다.

19

다음을 듣고, 화자의 직업이 무엇인지 고르시오.

✓ photographer
② artist
③ choreographer
④ film director
⑤ wedding planner

① 사진가
② 예술가
③ 안무가
④ 영화감독
⑤ 웨딩플래너

▶ be ready to do …할 준비가 되다 portrait 초상화, 얼굴 사진 arrange …을 배열하다, …을 정돈하다 in front of …앞에 background 배경 scenery 무대 장치, 배경 hold (어떤 상태로) 두다, 유지하다 pose 자세 adjust (기계 등을) 조절하다 a bit 약간 apart (거리, 위치 등이) 떨어져, 사이를 두고 face …쪽을 향하다 shoot 사진을 찍다, 촬영하다

M Is everyone ready to begin? This is going to be a family portrait with five people, so let me arrange everyone in front of the background scenery. Mr. Kim, can you stand in the back, please? Yes, that's perfect. I want your son to stand next to you on the right. Okay, that's great where he's standing now. I'm going to place the three ladies in front of the men and have them sitting down. Mr. Kim's mother should be in the middle, his daughter should sit right in front of her father, and his wife should be in front of her son. Is everyone fine? Good, everyone please hold that pose. Okay, I need to adjust the lights a bit. Mr. Kim, can you place your hand on your daughter's right shoulder? That yes, that looks better. Now I need the men to move apart just a bit. Both of you turn your shoulders a bit so that you're facing each other more. Thank you. Now we're ready to shoot.

남 모두 시작할 준비 됐어요? 이건 다섯 명의 가족 사진이 될 거니까 제가 배경이 되는 무대 앞에서 모두에게 자리를 잡아 드릴게요. 김 선생님, 뒤에 서 주시겠어요? 네, 완벽합니다. 아드님은 김 선생님 오른쪽에 서시고요. 됐습니다, 지금 서 있는 곳이 좋네요. 숙녀 세 분은 남자분들 앞에서 앉으시죠. 김 선생님 어머님은 중앙에 계셔야 하고, 따님은 아버지 앞쪽 오른쪽에 앉으시고 부인은 아드님 앞에 계시면 됩니다. 모두 괜찮으신가요? 좋습니다, 모두 그 자세를 유지해 주세요. 자, 조명을 좀 조절해야겠네요. 김 선생님, 손을 따님 오른쪽 어깨에 올려 주시겠어요? 네, 그게 더 나아 보이네요. 이제 남자분들은 아주 약간만 이동해 주시면 됩니다. 두 분 모두 어깨를 좀 돌려서 서로 좀 더 마주보도록 하세요. 감사합니다. 이제 촬영 준비가 됐군요.

20

대화를 듣고, 남자에 대해 사실이 <u>아닌</u> 것을 고르시오.

① He wants to stay close to his parents.
② He is not very concerned about money.
③ He does not want to drive his own car.
✔ He is not eager to go to the countryside.
⑤ He would prefer to fly to his destination.

① 남자는 부모님과 가까운 곳에 머무르기를 원한다.
② 그는 돈에 관해서는 그다지 걱정하지 않는다.
③ 그는 차를 직접 운전하는 것을 원하지 않는다.
④ 그는 시골로 가는 것을 아주 바라고 있지는 않다.
⑤ 그는 목적지까지 비행기로 가는 것을 선호한다.

▶ **countryside** 시골, 농촌지방 **waste** 낭비, 허비 **packed** (건물, 방 등이) 사람으로 꽉 찬, 혼잡한 **raise** (임금, 물가 등의) 인상, 상승 **I'd rather be** …인 편이 훨씬 낫다 **no way** 절대 안 돼, 천만에 **dive** (흔히 지하에 있는) 싸구려 숙박소 **bed and breakfast** 조반 제공 숙박(민박) **plenty of** 다수의 **guest** 손님

W We need to talk about our trip to visit your parents in the countryside.
M I was hoping to fly there and then rent a car to drive around.
W That sounds like a waste of money. Why don't we drive there instead?
M I hate driving all those hours to get there. And the roads there are going to be packed since it's a holiday weekend. Besides, money isn't important since I just got that big raise.
W Well, I'd still rather drive there. Anyway, where are we staying? Your parents won't have any room at their place since your brother's family is already there.
M Yeah, I hadn't thought about that. I suppose we could stay at that hotel near their place.
W No way. That place is a dive. You know, I found a nice little bed and breakfast on the Internet that's about thirty minutes from their place. It even has plenty of activities for all the guests.
M Sure, but we're going to be with my family most of the time. We won't have the chance to do any activities. And I'd rather be five minutes away than thirty.
W Well, let me see what I can find. I don't want to stay at that other hotel.

여 시골에 계신 시부모님을 방문하는 여행에 대해 얘기 좀 하자.
남 난 비행기로 간 다음에 차를 빌려서 운전하면서 다녔으면 좋겠어.
여 그건 돈 낭비 같아. 대신 거기까지 차를 몰고 가면 안 될까?
남 도착하기까지 내내 운전하는 건 싫어. 그리고 축제가 있는 주말이어서 그곳 도로가 꽉 막힐 거야. 게다가 봉급 인상이 많이 됐으니까 돈은 중요하지 않아.
여 음, 그래도 난 거기까지 운전해서 가고 싶어. 아무튼 우리 어디서 묵을 거야? 부모님 댁엔 이미 시아주버니 식구들이 있어서 방이 전혀 없잖아.
남 그래, 그 생각은 못했네. 부모님댁 근처 호텔에 묵을 수도 있을 것 같은데.
여 절대 안 돼. 거긴 지하에 있는 싸구려 숙박소야. 있잖아, 부모님댁에서 30분 정도 떨어진 곳에 있는 작고 근사한 곳을 인터넷에서 찾았어. 거긴 손님을 위한 활동도 많이 있어.
여 그래, 하지만 우린 대부분의 시간을 우리 가족과 함께 있을 거잖아. 무슨 활동을 할 기회는 없을 거야. 그리고 난 30분보다 5분 거리가 더 좋아.
남 음, 좀 더 찾아볼게. 난 다른 호텔에 묵는 건 싫어.

21

대화를 듣고, 다음 그래프에 대해 사실이 <u>아닌</u> 것을 고르시오.

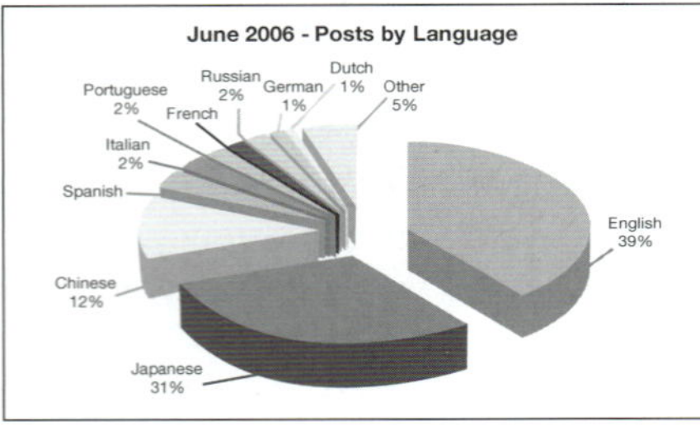

① Japanese people often use cell phones to update their blogs.
② More blogs use English than any other language.
✔ Chinese is about to pass Japanese for the number-two position.
④ Lots of Chinese are getting connected to the Internet.
⑤ Many European languages will not get higher rankings in the future.

① 일본인들은 블로그를 업데이트하기 위해 휴대폰을 자주 이용한다.
② 다른 언어보다 영어를 사용하는 블로그가 더 많다.
③ 중국어가 일본어를 제치고 2위가 되려고 한다.
④ 많은 중국인들이 인터넷에 연결을 하고 있다.
⑤ 미래에는 많은 유럽의 언어들이 상위권에 들지 못할 것이다.

▶ **dominant** 지배적인, 주요한 **by far** 훨씬, 단연 **hooked up** (기기를) 연결하다[접속시키다] **overtake** 따라잡다, 뒤따라 앞지르다

M I have to get home soon. I've got this great idea for a post I want to put on my blog.
W You really love your blog a lot, don't you?
M That's the truth. Nowadays, more and more people all around the world are getting into them. However, the dominant language is still English. Check out this graph that I found.
W Wow, it seems that English and Japanese are by far the main languages people blog in. It's easy to understand why English is the leader since it's an international language. But what's up with Japanese?
M I think many Japanese update their blogs through their cell phones. And you know how important the cell phone culture is in Japan, right?
W Totally. It looks like Chinese is becoming a major blog language.
M That's correct. The reason is that millions of Chinese are getting hooked up to the Internet.
W I'd be willing to bet that Chinese overtakes Japanese in a few years.
M That'll probably happen. But it looks like European languages like Russian, German, and Spanish are going to keep their fairly small numbers.
W I'm sure of that. Not enough people around the world speak those languages for them to get any bigger numbers.

남 빨리 집에 도착해야 해. 블로그에 올릴 게시물을 위한 좋은 생각이 났거든.
여 넌 블로그를 정말 좋아하는구나, 그렇지?
남 맞아. 요즘에는 전 세계에서 더욱 더 많은 사람들이 블로그를 사용하고 있어. 하지만 주요 언어는 여전히 영어야. 내가 발견한 이 그래프 좀 봐.
여 우와, 단연코 영어와 일어가 사람들이 블로그에서 쓰는 주 언어인 것 같구나. 영어는 국제 언어니까 대표인 게 쉽게 이해가 돼. 하지만 일본어는 왜 그런 거야?
남 내 생각엔 많은 일본 사람들이 휴대폰으로 자기 블로그를 업데이트하는 것 같아. 그리고 일본에서 휴대폰 문화가 얼마나 중요한지 너도 알지, 그렇지?
여 그럼. 중국어가 주요한 블로그 언어가 되고 있는 것 같네.
남 맞아. 그 이유는 수백만 명의 중국인들이 인터넷에 접속하고 있기 때문이야.
여 분명히 몇 년 뒤에 중국어가 일본어를 앞지를 것 같은데.
남 어쩌면 그럴지도. 하지만 러시아어와 독일어, 스페인어 같은 유럽어들은 아주 적은 숫자를 유지할 것 같아.
여 그럴 거야. 더 큰 수를 차지할 정도로 그 언어들을 쓰는 사람은 전 세계에 충분히 많지 않으니까.

22 대화를 듣고, 남자의 마지막 말에 들어갈 말로 가장 알맞은 것을 고르시오.

> M: Just remember, _________________.

✓ a little leak will sink a great ship
② all that glitters is not gold
③ empty vessels make the most noise
④ great haste makes great waste
⑤ look before you leap

> 남: 기억해, _________________.

① 조금 새는 물이 큰 배를 가라앉힐 거야
② 반짝이는 모든 것이 금은 아니야
③ 빈수레가 요란한 법이야
④ 너무 서두르면 일을 망치는 거야
⑤ 돌다리도 두드려 보고 건너야 해

▶ in a while 한동안, 오랫동안   cram into …에 억지로 밀어 넣다   legroom (극장, 차 좌석에서) 다리를 뻗을 수 있는 공간   pool (일반적으로 액체가) 괸 곳   liquid 액체   form 형성되다, 생기다   underneath …바로 밑에   sign 표시, 징조   harmless 해가 없는   drop 한 방울, (액체의) 소량   brake fluid (자동차의) 브레이크액   had better …해야 하다, 하는 것이 낫다

W I'm so excited to be going on a trip this weekend. I'm going to love spending time with my friends.

M You're driving to the beach this weekend, right?

W Yeah, I haven't been there in a while, so I'm going to have fun. We're taking my car, but I won't have to drive the entire way. After all, it's a four-hour drive.

M You're taking your car, huh? Are you sure that's a good idea?

W Why not? It has enough room for all six people going on the trip. If we tried to cram into someone else's car, there wouldn't be enough legroom.

M That's not what I'm talking about. Take a look at that little pool of liquid forming underneath your car. That's not a good sign, you know.

W Oh, it's probably harmless. I'm not worried about a couple of drops of some liquid.

M You ought to care. That's brake fluid. It might seem like it's small, but losing some could be the difference between life and death. You might find yourself hitting the brakes but nothing happens.

W Oh, I think I see what you mean. I'd better get that fixed, right?

M Exactly, or you'll have a huge problem. Just remember, _________________.

여 이번 주말에 여행을 가게 돼서 아주 흥분돼. 친구들과 함께 하니까 즐거울 거야.

남 이번 주말에 차 몰고 해변에 갈 거지, 그렇지?

여 응, 한동안 못 갔으니까 재미있을 거야. 차를 갖고 갈 거지만 내가 전부 다 운전하진 않아도 될 거야. 어쨌거나 4시간 운전이니까.

남 네 차를 갖고 가는 거지, 응? 그게 좋은 생각 같니?

여 왜 안돼? 여행 가는 여섯 명 모두를 위한 충분한 공간이 있어. 다른 사람 차에 억지로 타려고 하면 다리 뻗을 공간이 충분치 않을 거야.

남 내가 말하는 건 그게 아니야. 저기 네 차 밑에 액체가 고인 걸 봐. 그건 좋은 징조가 아니야.

여 아, 아마도 문제 안 될 거야. 액체 몇 방울 떨어지는 건 걱정 안 해.

남 신경을 써야 해. 그건 브레이크액이야. 사소한 것처럼 보일지 모르지만 약간만 없어져도 생사를 가를 수 있는 거야. 넌 브레이크를 밟는데 아무 일도 생기지 않는 거지.

여 아, 무슨 말인지 알 것 같아. 그걸 고치는 게 낫겠구나, 그렇지?

남 그렇고말고, 안 그러면 큰 문제가 생길 거야. 기억해, _________________.

---

23 대화를 듣고, 현금지급기의 사용 방법을 순서대로 나열한 것을 고르시오.

ⓐ Select the amount of money
ⓑ Choose the transaction to be made
ⓒ Select the PIN
ⓓ Swipe the bank card

ⓐ 액수를 선택한다
ⓑ 원하는 거래를 선택한다
ⓒ 비밀번호를 선택한다
ⓓ 은행 카드를 긁는다

① ⓓ – ⓑ – ⓐ – ⓒ
✓ ⓑ – ⓓ – ⓐ – ⓒ
③ ⓓ – ⓑ – ⓒ – ⓐ
④ ⓑ – ⓓ – ⓒ – ⓐ
⑤ ⓓ – ⓒ – ⓑ – ⓐ

▶ ATM 현금 자동 입출금기   differently than …와 다른   press the button 버튼을 누르다   transaction 거래   swipe (신용 카드 등)을 해독기에 넣다   withdrawal (예금의) 인출   go ahead 진행하다   PIN 개인 식별번호(personal identification number): (은행 카드의) 비밀번호

W What's wrong with this ATM? I can't get it to work right.

M You're trying one of those new ATMs, aren't you? They work a little differently than the old kind.

W Don't I just put in my card and punch all of the buttons?

M No, not exactly. Actually, the first thing that you need to do is to press the button for whatever transaction you want to make.

W What? You mean I don't swipe my card first?

M No, you don't. You're going to make a withdrawal, right? In that case, go ahead and push the button for that. Then you need to swipe your card next.

W Okay, I can do that. But I really prefer the old style where the card stays in the machine. They're a lot easier to use.

M Yeah, I suppose that you're right about that.

W Okay, now the machine is asking me how much I want to take out. So I just hit the button, and then the money is going to come out. Is that correct?

M You forgot about one thing. You need to punch in your PIN, you know, your personal identification number, before you can get any money. Only then will you be all set.

여 이 현금지급기가 왜 이래요? 제대로 작동이 안 되네요.

남 새로운 현금지급기 중 하나를 쓰고 계시죠, 아닌가요? 그건 예전 종류와는 좀 다르게 작동됩니다.

여 그냥 카드를 넣고 버튼을 누르면 되지 않아요?

남 아니오, 꼭 그렇지는 않습니다. 사실, 가장 먼저 하셔야 할 것은 어떤 것이든 원하는 거래 버튼을 누르는 겁니다.

여 뭐라고요? 그 말씀은 먼저 카드를 긁지 않는다는 건가요?

남 네, 그렇습니다. 인출을 하시려는 거죠? 그렇다면 인출 버튼을 누르세요. 그런 다음 카드를 긁어야 합니다.

여 알았어요, 그건 할 수 있어요. 하지만 난 카드가 기계 안에 남아있는 예전 방식이 더 좋네요. 그게 사용하기가 훨씬 더 쉬워요.

남 네, 그건 맞는 말씀 같습니다.

여 좋아요, 이제 기계가 얼마를 인출하길 원하는지 묻네요. 그러니까 그냥 버튼을 누르고 그 다음에 돈이 나오는 거죠. 맞나요?

남 한 가지를 잊으셨네요. 돈을 받으시기 전에 핀넘버 즉, 개인 식별번호를 누르셔야 합니다. 그래야만 다 된 겁니다.

24 대화를 듣고, 여자의 마지막 말에 담긴 의도가 무엇인지 고르시오.

☑ To be sarcastic
② To be considerate
③ To express her anger
④ To be generous
⑤ To express her sadness

① 비꼬기 위해
② 신중하기 위해
③ 분노를 표현하기 위해
④ 너그러워지기 위해
⑤ 슬픔을 표현하기 위해

▶ absolute 확실한, 명백한 mess 엉망인 상태, 어질러진 것 simultaneously 동시에, 일제히 clean ... up …을 청소[정리]하다 clutter 어질러진 물건, 잡동사니 folder 종이[서류] 끼우개, 폴더 semblance 비슷함, 비슷한 것 order 정돈, 질서 wrapper 포장지 disgrace 창피, 망신거리 tons of 다수의, 엄청난 bug 벌레 partially 부분적으로, 어느 정도 tip 충고, 조언 straighten up …을 정리[정돈]하다

M Take a look at your office. It's an absolute mess.

W Well, I've been busy working on several projects simultaneously, so I haven't been able to clean it up.

M But how can you find anything in all this clutter? I mean, take a look at all of the papers and folders lying around here.

W Strangely enough, I actually seem to know where everything in my office is. It might look messy to you, but I can still find whatever I'm looking for.

M Are you sure about that? It sure doesn't look like there's any semblance of order here.

W Yeah, don't worry about me. At least my office is just messy and not dirty. I don't have any empty pizza boxes or fast-food wrappers lying around here like someone that I know.

M What? Are you talking about me?

W I sure am. You're the one whose office is an absolute disgrace. While mine might have tons of papers lying around, yours is lucky it doesn't have any bugs.

M Hmm… I suppose you may be partially right about that.

W I'm totally right. So, the next time I need some tips on how to straighten up my office, I'll be sure to talk with you. Okay, Mr. Clean?

남 네 사무실을 한 번 봐. 정말 엉망이야.

여 음, 동시에 몇 가지 프로젝트를 하느라 바빠서 청소할 수가 없었어.

남 하지만 어떻게 이런 온갖 잡동사니 속에서 뭔가를 찾을 수가 있어? 내 말은 이 주변에 있는 모든 서류와 폴더를 좀 보라고.

여 참 이상하게도 사실 난 내 사무실의 모든 게 어디 있는지 알 것 같아. 네겐 엉망으로 보일지 몰라도 난 내가 찾는 걸 뭐든 발견할 수 있어.

남 정말 그러니? 여긴 정말 아무런 질서 같은 게 없는 것 같은데.

여 그래, 내 걱정하지 마. 최소한 내 사무실은 그저 엉망일 뿐 더럽지는 않잖아. 내가 아는 누군가처럼 주변에 빈 피자 박스나 패스트푸드 포장지는 없지.

남 뭐라고? 내 얘기하는 거야?

여 물론이야. 너야말로 사무실이 정말 창피스럽잖아. 내 건 수많은 서류가 놓여 있을지 모르지만 네 사무실은 벌레가 전혀 없다는 게 행운이니까.

남 흠… 어느 정도는 네가 맞을 수도 있겠다.

여 정말 그래. 그러면, 다음에 내 사무실을 정리할 방법에 관해 어떤 충고가 필요할 때는 반드시 너와 얘기할게. 됐니, 깔끔씨야?

---

25 대화를 듣고, 두 사람이 이야기하고 있는 도자기를 고르시오.

①  ② 

③  ④ 

▶ oriental 동양의 ceramics 도자기 (공예) I couldn't agree (with you) more. (당신의 의견에) 대찬성이다 fine 훌륭한, 정교한 porcelain 자기, 자기 제품 artwork 예술품 if you ask me 내 생각으로는 thin 가느다란, 두께가 작은 bottleneck 병목 point out 가리키다 practically 사실상, 거의 unusual 독특한 in that …이라는 점에서 as opposed to …와는 대조적으로 crafted (물건, 제품을) 정교하게 만들다, 세공하다

W Ah, we're in my favorite part of the museum. I absolutely love the oriental ceramics exhibition.

M I couldn't agree with you more. Fine porcelain is really like artwork if you ask me. So, what's your favorite type of ceramics? I love ones that have wide bodies but thin bottlenecks.

W I can't say I agree with you. They look rather strange to me. Here, let me point out my favorite one in the museum's collection. There it is.

M What, you mean the one with the flower designs painted all over it?

W No, not that one. I'm talking about the one with flower designs painted only on the neck.

M Ah, yes, that one is pretty nice. I love that it's so thin.

W Yes, it's practically the same size from the bottom to the top. I think that's why I like it so much. It must have been difficult to make it.

M Yes, and it's somewhat unusual in that it has only one handle as opposed to two of them.

W You're absolutely right about that. Having only one handle can sometimes upset the balance of the work, which is why I feel it's so finely crafted.

M Wow, I had never considered that before.

여 아, 우리는 지금 박물관에서 내가 가장 좋아하는 곳에 있네요. 난 정말로 동양의 도자기 전시회가 좋아요.

남 정말 동감이에요. 정교한 자기는 정말이지 예술 작품 같아요. 자, 당신이 좋아하는 도자기는 어떤 유형이죠? 난 몸체는 넓지만 입구가 가는 것을 좋아하죠.

여 저는 당신과는 달라요. 그런 것들은 내겐 좀 이상하게 보여요. 여기, 박물관 수집품에서 내가 좋아하는 것을 가리켜 볼게요. 저기 있네요.

남 뭐라고요, 온통 꽃무늬가 그려져 있는 것 말인가요?

여 아니오, 그것 말고요. 입구에만 꽃무늬가 그려진 걸 말하는 거예요.

남 아, 네, 그건 정말 멋지네요. 아주 가느다란 것이 마음에 드네요.

여 네, 사실상 바닥에서 꼭대기까지 크기가 거의 똑같죠. 그래서 저는 그게 정말 좋은 것 같아요. 그걸 만드는 건 분명히 힘들었을 거예요.

남 네, 또 손잡이가 두 개인 것과는 대조적으로 하나만 있다는 점이 좀 특이하네요.

여 정말 그래요. 손잡이가 하나만 있는 건 가끔은 작품의 균형을 불안하게 하는데, 그게 내가 이 작품이 아주 정교하게 만들어졌다고 느끼는 이유예요.

남 와, 난 전에는 그런 생각을 전혀 못했어요.

26 **What best completes the speaker's last sentence?**

So, you should ______________________ .

✔ ① understand the method of greeting before visiting a different country

② always use the method of greeting people from your own culture

③ know that French women only kiss people whom they like

④ initiate a handshake with another person when in Eastern Asia

⑤ be sure to greet people with "hello" whenever you meet them

마지막 문장을 가장 잘 완성하는 것은?

따라서, 당신은 ______________________ .

① 다른 나라를 방문하기 전에 인사법을 이해해야 한다.
② 항상 여러분 자신의 문화에서 온 인사법을 사용해야 한다.
③ 프랑스 여자는 자신이 좋아하는 사람들에게만 키스한다는 것을 알아야 한다.
④ 동아시아에 있을 때는 다른 사람과 악수를 먼저 시작해야 한다.
⑤ 언제든 사람들을 만날 때는 "hello"라고 인사를 꼭 해야 한다.

▶ greet 맞이하다, 인사하다 shake hands 악수하다 difference 차이 for instance 예를 들면 virtually 사실상, 거의 prohibit 금지하다(= forbid) in public 공개적으로 whereas …임에 반해, …인데도 tend not to … 않는 경향이 있다 unless …이 아니면, …이외에는 bow 허리를 굽히다, 절하다 respect 존경 the more..., the more …할수록 더 ~한 initiate 시작하다, 제안하다 vocal 구두의 component 구성 요소, 성분 vary 가지각색이다, 다르다

M There are many ways to greet people in different cultures. In the West, most people shake hands when they meet, but there are some differences. In Russia, for instance, men shake hands virtually every time they meet while American men usually don't shake hands with people they see everyday. Both traditional Jewish and Muslim cultures prohibit men and women from physical contact in public, so shaking hands is forbidden. In France, when a woman greets a man or woman, she gives a small kiss on the cheek whereas North Americans tend not to kiss unless they haven't met in a long time. In Eastern countries, particularly Japan, China, and Korea, people meet by bowing at the waist. It's considered a sign of respect. Additionally, the deeper you bow, the more respect you show. These cultures also use handshakes, but the older of the two people must initiate it. Most cultures also have a small vocal component of greeting, such as saying "hello" or "hi." This, of course, varies from culture to culture. So, you should ______________________ .

남 다른 문화의 사람들에게 인사하는 데는 많은 방법이 있다. 서양에서는 대부분의 사람들이 만날 때 악수를 하지만 몇 가지 차이가 있다. 가령 러시아에서는 남자들이 거의 만날 때마다 악수를 하는데 반해 미국 남자들은 보통 매일 보는 사람과는 악수를 하지 않는다. 전통적인 유대 문화와 이슬람 문화는 모두 남녀가 공개적으로 신체 접촉을 하는 것을 금하기 때문에 악수가 금지된다. 프랑스에서는 여자가 남자나 여자에게 인사할 때 뺨에 가볍게 키스하는 반면, 북미인들은 오랜만에 만난 것이 아니라면 키스를 하지 않는 경향이 있다. 동양의 국가들, 특히 일본과 중국, 한국에서는 사람들이 만날 때 허리를 굽혀 절을 한다. 그건 존경의 표시로 간주된다. 게다가 더 깊이 절할수록 더 많은 존경을 표하는 것이다. 이 문화권들에서는 악수도 하지만 두 사람 중 연장자가 그것을 시작해야만 한다. 대부분의 문화권에는 말로 하는 짧은 인사도 있는데, "hello"나 "hi"같은 것들이다. 물론 이것은 문화마다 다양하다. 따라서, 당신은 ______________________ .

27 Which of the following is NOT true about Hangeul?

✔ It was created in the fourteenth century.
② It has ten different vowel sounds.
③ A Korean king is credited with inventing it.
④ It can be learned very quickly by some people.
⑤ Several people probably created it together.

다음 중 한글에 대해 사실이 <u>아닌</u> 것은 어느 것인가?

① 그것은 14세기에 창안되었다.
② 그것은 열 개의 다른 모음이 있다.
③ 한국의 왕이 그것을 발명했다고 생각된다.
④ 어떤 사람들은 그것을 아주 빨리 배울 수 있다.
⑤ 아마도 몇몇 사람들이 같이 그것을 만들었다.

▶ refer to …을 언급하다 promote 장려[촉진]하다 create 창조하다 by himself 혼자 힘으로 give a person credit for …을 ~이라고 인정하다, …을 ~의 공로로 삼다 script (손으로 쓴) 문자 literate 학식있는 character 문자 You can say that again. 맞았어, 바로 그거야! consonant 자음 cf. vowel 모음 symbol 부호, 기호 syllabic 음절의 block 큰 덩어리, 블록 combination 조합 illiteracy rate 문맹률 master 숙달하다 sound out 발음하다, 말하다

M Learning Korean is hard, especially because I've got an entire new alphabet to learn.

W You're referring to Hangeul, right? Did you know Hangeul has a pretty interesting history?

M I heard some king invented it a long time ago, but that's about all I know.

W Yes, Hangeul was promoted by King Sejong the Great, who lived from 1397 to 1450. He probably didn't create it by himself, but he's still given credit for it. Hangeul was made because there was no Korean script at the time. Literate Koreans used Chinese characters.

M That makes sense. Hangeul is much easier to read than Chinese characters.

W You can say that again. After all, there are only fourteen consonants and ten vowels. But, since the symbols can be placed into different syllabic blocks, there are thousands of possible combinations.

M Yeah, it seems like you can make so many words. I'm really impressed by that. It makes studying hard though.

W True, but the ease with which people can learn Hangeul has helped Korea decrease its illiteracy rate. After all, many people can learn Hangeul in less than an hour.

M True, but they can't master it that quickly.

W No, but they can still start sounding out words that fast.

남 나로서는 특히나 알파벳 전체를 새로 배워야 하기 때문에 한국어를 배우는 것은 어려워요.

여 한글 말하는 거죠, 그렇죠? 한글에 꽤 흥미로운 역사가 있는 거 알았어요?

남 오래전에 어떤 왕이 발명했다고 들었지만 그게 내가 아는 전부예요.

여 그래요, 한글은 세종대왕이 장려했는데, 그는 1397년에서 1450년까지 살았죠. 아마 혼자서 한글을 창안하지는 않았겠지만 여전히 한글에 대한 공로를 인정받고 있어요. 당시에는 한국의 문자가 전혀 없었기 때문에 한글이 만들어진 것이죠. 학식 있는 한국인은 한자를 사용했어요.

남 이해가 되네요. 한글은 한자보다 훨씬 더 읽기 쉬워요.

여 바로 그거예요. 아무튼 자음 열 네 개와 모음 열 개만 있으니까요. 하지만 그 기호들이 놓여서 다른 음절 블록이 될 수 있기 때문에 수천 건의 조합이 가능하죠.

남 그래요, 아주 많은 단어를 만들 수 있는 것 같아요. 나는 정말 그 점에 감명을 받았어요. 하지만 그래서 공부를 열심히 해야 해요.

여 맞아요, 하지만 사람들이 한글을 쉽게 배울 수 있어서 한국이 문맹률을 줄이는 데 도움이 됐어요. 어쨌거나 많은 사람들이 한 시간 안에 한글을 배울 수 있어요.

남 사실이긴 하지만 그렇게 빨리 숙달할 수는 없어요.

여 그래요, 하지만 매우 빨리 단어를 발음하기 시작할 수는 있어요.

28 Which of the following people agrees with the speaker?

① Jason: My business overseas tripled after the free-trade agreement was ratified.

② Bruce: I need to learn English so that I can have more opportunities at home and abroad.

③ Samantha: My company must expand overseas if it wants to compete at an international level.

✓ Iris: All of my country's citizens should only buy products made in our country.

⑤ Richard: I'll buy a foreign product if it's cheaper and better than what is made here.

다음 중 화자에 동의하는 사람은 누구인가?

① 제이슨: 해외에 있는 내 사업이 자유무역협정이 비준된 후 3배가 늘었다.

② 브루스: 국내외에서 더 많은 기회를 가질 수 있도록 영어를 배울 필요가 있다.

③ 사만사: 우리 회사가 국제적 수준으로 경쟁하기를 원한다면 해외로 확장해야 한다.

④ 아이리스: 우리나라의 시민들 모두는 우리나라에서 만들어진 제품만을 사야 한다.

⑤ 리처드: 나는 여기서 만들어진 것보다 더 싸고 좋다면 외국제품을 살 것이다.

▶ curb 제한[억제]하다 multinational corporation 다국적 기업 free-trade agreement 자유무역협정 couple A with B A와 B를 결부시켜 생각하다

W Anti-globalization is a movement which is primarily concerned with two things: curbing the growing power of multinational corporations and limiting free-trade agreements. Many people fear that some companies are growing too powerful and may one day replace nations as the center of authority in the world. Coupled with this is a sense that national pride and growth are being sacrificed by creating free-trade zones. Anti-globalization believers think that such zones must have limitations or be removed entirely. I couldn't agree more with these people. National industries must be protected from cheap products from other nations. When more foreign products enter a country, that country tends to lose jobs in its domestic industries, which increases unemployment. In addition, the power of corporations must be limited. A nation is run by its duly-elected officials, not by the seemingly unlimited money some of these corporations have. Another aspect of anti-globalization is a feeling that one's culture is being lost. This can especially been seen in the growing use of English as an international language.

여 반세계화는 주로 두 가지 일, 다국적기업의 힘 증가를 막는 것과 자유무역협정을 제한하는 것에 관련된 운동이다. 많은 사람들은 어떤 회사들이 너무 강력해지고 언젠가 세계에서 권력의 중심으로 국가를 대체할지도 모른다는 두려움을 갖고 있다. 이것과 결부하여 자유무역지대를 창출함으로써 국가의 자존심과 성장이 희생되고 있다는 인식이 있다. 반세계화 신자들은 자유무역지대가 한계를 갖고 있다거나 완전히 제거되어야 한다고 생각한다. 나는 이 사람들에게 전적으로 동의한다. 국가의 산업은 다른 국가들의 값싼 제품에서 보호되어야 한다. 더 많은 외국 제품이 어떤 국가에 들어갈 때 그 나라는 국내 산업에서 일자리를 잃는 경향이 있는데, 이것은 실업을 증가시킨다. 더욱이 기업의 힘은 제한되어야 한다. 국가는 이런 기업들의 일부에 있는 무제한적으로 보이는 돈이 아니라 정당하게 선출된 관리들에 의해 운영된다. 반세계화의 또 다른 측면은 국가의 문화가 상실되고 있다는 느낌이다. 이것은 특히 국제언어로서의 영어의 사용이 증가하는 데서 보일 수 있다.

29 What is this food?

① hamburgers

② apple pie

✓ pizza

④ cake

⑤ sandwiches

이 음식은 무엇인가?

① 햄버거

② 애플파이

③ 피자

④ 케이크

⑤ 샌드위치

▶ originate 일어나다, 생기다 flat 납작한 decline 약화, 쇠퇴 version 특정한 형, 변형 green pepper 피망 arrange 배열하다, 정리하다 flag 국기 spread 퍼지다 immigrant 이민자 dish 요리, 음식 establish (학교 등을) 설립하다 popularity 유행, 인기 aboard (배, 항공기 등의) 안에서 slice 얇은 조각, 한 조각

M This food originated long ago with the Greeks and Romans. They would put onions, olives, and other vegetables on flat pieces of bread and then eat them as meals or snacks. The tradition never died but continued, even after the decline of Rome and Greece. In the late nineteenth century in Naples, Italy, one restaurant created a special version of this food for Queen Margarita's visit. It had green peppers, white mozzarella cheese, and red tomatoes on flat bread and was arranged in the shape of the Italian flag. The queen tried it and loved it, and it soon spread all over Italy. When Italian immigrants went to America, they brought this dish with them and even established restaurants in many American cities. During World War II, American soldiers carried this food all over the world, helping increase its popularity. It has even been eaten aboard the space station. Today, almost every country has some version of it, and it's estimated that more than one billion slices are eaten every day.

남 이 음식은 오래전에 그리스와 로마에서 기원했다. 그들은 양파와 올리브, 기타 채소들을 납작한 빵조각 위에 얹은 다음 그것을 식사나 간식으로 먹곤 했다. 그 전통은 전혀 사라지지 않고 심지어 로마와 그리스의 쇠퇴 이후에도 지속되었다. 19세기 말 이탈리아 나폴리의 식당에서 마르가리타 여왕의 방문을 위해 이 음식의 특별한 형태를 만들어냈다. 거기에는 피망과 하얀 모차렐라 치즈, 빨간 토마토를 납작한 빵 위에 얹어서 이탈리아 국기 모양으로 배열했다. 여왕이 맛을 보고 좋아했으며 곧 이탈리아 전역으로 확산되었다. 이탈리아 이민자가 미국으로 갔을 때 그들은 이 음식을 같이 가져왔고 심지어는 많은 미국 도시에서 식당을 차렸다. 2차 세계대전 동안 미국 군인들은 이 음식을 전 세계로 전파했고 그 인기를 더하는 데 도움을 주었다. 그것은 심지어는 우주 정거장에서도 먹어왔다. 오늘날 거의 모든 나라에서 그것의 어떤 형태를 갖고 있으며 매일 10억 개 이상의 조각이 소비되고 있다고 추정된다.

30 What are they mostly talking about?

① The housewarming parties they disliked
✓ Various aspects of past housewarming parties
③ When to have their own housewarming party
④ The housewarming party they liked the most
⑤ What to serve at their upcoming housewarming party

화자들은 주로 무엇에 대해 이야기하고 있는가?

① 그들이 마음에 들지 않았던 집들이 파티
② 과거에 가봤던 다양한 집들이 파티들의 양상
③ 그들의 집들이 파티를 언제 해야 하는지
④ 그들이 가장 좋아했던 집들이 파티
⑤ 다가오는 그들의 집들이에서 어떤 음식을 내놓아야 하는지

▶ settled down (특히 결혼하여) 살림을 차리다, 자리 잡다 host (파티 등을) 개최하다, 열다 housewarming party 집들이 cater (연회, 결혼식 등에) 요리나 서비스를 제공하다 team up 협력[협동]하다 interfere with …을 방해하다 conversation 대화 excellent 탁월한 icebreaker 긴장이나 어색함을 누그러뜨리는 것

W Now that we've finally gotten settled down in our house, we need to start thinking about hosting a housewarming party.

M Yeah, that would let all of our friends see where we live. And we could thank them all for helping us move, too.

W You're right. So I was thinking that we could have the party catered like Dave and Lisa did for theirs.

M No, I don't like that idea. It seems better to make the food ourselves, much like John and Nancy did. It'll be a lot of work, but I think we can do it if we team up.

W Okay, the food at John and Nancy's place was really good, so we'll do that. How did you like the music at Dave and Lisa's party?

M It was great. It wasn't too loud, nor was it too soft, so it didn't interfere with anyone's conversation.

W Yeah, that was the best thing about it. And I really liked that John and Nancy had us all play some different games at their party.

M You're right. They were excellent icebreakers since all their friends didn't know each other.

W We should do the same thing at ours.

M I totally agree with you about that.

여 마침내 우리 집에 살림을 차렸으니까 집들이 하는 걸 생각해 봐야지.

남 그래, 그럼 친구들 모두 우리가 사는 곳을 보게 될 거야. 그리고 친구들한테 우리가 이사하는 걸 도와줘서 고마움을 표시할 수도 있을 테고.

여 맞아. 그래서 내 생각엔 데이브와 리사가 집들이때 했던 것처럼 출장식 파티를 하는 것도 괜찮을 것 같아.

남 아니야, 그건 싫어. 존과 낸시가 그랬던 것처럼 우리 스스로 음식을 만드는 게 더 나은 것 같아. 일은 많겠지만 내 생각엔 우리가 힘을 합친다면 할 수 있을 거라고 생각해.

여 알았어, 존과 낸시네 음식은 정말 훌륭했어, 그러니까 그걸로 하자. 데이브와 리사네 파티에서 있었던 음악은 어땠어?

남 훌륭했어. 너무 시끄럽지도 낮지도 않아서 모두의 대화를 방해하지 않았어.

여 그래, 그 부분이 가장 좋았어. 그리고 난 존과 낸시가 파티때 우리 모두가 놀 수 있게 몇 가지 다른 게임을 한 게 정말 좋았어.

남 그래. 친구들 모두가 서로 알지는 못하니까 그게 어색함을 없애는 데 훌륭한 역할을 했어.

여 우리도 같은 것으로 해야겠어.

남 그건 전적으로 동감이야.

---

31 (모두 듣기) Which sentence is the woman likely to say to her roommate?

✓ Don't poke your nose where it doesn't belong.
② There's more than one way to skin a cat.
③ You are such a yellow-bellied person.
④ You have really come out of your shell.
⑤ That's just the icing on the cake.

여자가 그녀의 룸메이트에게 할 것 같은 말은 무엇인가?

① 남의 일에 신경쓰지 마.
② 방법은 여러가지다.
③ 너 정말 비겁하구나.
④ 너 정말 솔직해졌구나.
⑤ 그거 정말 금상첨화구나.

▶ deceive 속이다, 현혹시키다 must be 틀림없이 …일 것이다 annoying 피롭히는, 짜증나는 decorate 장식하다 considerate 사려깊은, 신중한 rearrange 재배열하다 furniture 가구 redo 장식을 바꾸다, 개장하다 complimentary 칭찬하는, 찬사의 get rid of …을 제거하다 get tough with …에게 엄하게 굴다 ought to …해야 한다 be concerned with …에 관심이 있다, 관여하다

W You won't believe the new roommate I just got. She's an absolute nightmare.

M Really? I thought you told me she seemed nice when you met her the first time.

W Looks can be deceiving. She must be the most annoying person I've ever met.

M What exactly has she done?

W Well, as soon as she got settled in the apartment, she walked into my room and asked me why I'd decorated it like that. Can you believe that?

M That wasn't very considerate of her.

W Oh, that's not all. She even started rearranging all of the furniture in the living room. She told me I have no sense of style and that she wanted to redo the house. And when she saw a picture of my boyfriend, she started making comments about how he looks. She wasn't complimentary at all.

M That's awful. Is there any way for you to get rid of her?

W I need to have a chat with her.

M Get tough with her. You ought to tell her not to be so concerned with other people's business.

여 내가 얼마 전에 구한 새 룸메이트를 넌 이해 못 할 거야. 그녀는 정말로 악몽이야.

남 그래? 난 네가 그녀를 처음 만났을 때 좋아 보인다고 한 것 같은데.

여 외모는 현혹시킬 수 있는 거야. 그녀는 내가 만난 사람들 중에서 가장 짜증나는 사람이야.

남 정확히 무슨 짓을 했는데?

여 음, 아파트에 정착하자마자 내 방으로 와서 내가 왜 그렇게 장식했는지 묻는 거야. 믿기니?

남 그건 별로 사려 깊지는 않구나.

여 아, 그게 다가 아니야. 심지어 거실에 있는 가구 전부를 재배치하기 시작했어. 내가 스타일에 대한 감각이 전혀 없고 자기가 집을 다시 장식하고 싶다고 말하는 거야. 그리고 내 남자친구 사진을 보고 외모에 대해 언급하기 시작했어. 전혀 칭찬하는 말이 아니었어.

남 세상에. 그녀를 내보낼 방법이 뭐 없어?

여 그녀와 얘기를 해야겠어.

남 세게 나가. 다른 사람 일에 그렇게 관여하지 말라고 말해야 해.

32 〔모두 듣기〕 **What is the purpose of the phone call?**

① to complain about a product
✓ to make an order
③ to advertise something
④ to inform someone about an item
⑤ to return a purchase

전화를 건 목적은 무엇인가?

① 상품에 대해 불평하기 위해
② 주문하기 위해
③ 선전하기 위해
④ 어떤 물품에 대해 누군가에게 알리기 위해
⑤ 구입한 것을 반환하기 위해

▶ **satisfied** 만족한 **brewing** (맥주 등의) 양조, (1회의) 양조량 **previous** 이전의 **capacity** 용량 **pot** 냄비, 포트 **timer** 타이머, 타임스위치 **feature** 특징, 특색 **receive** 받다 **by the way** 그런데 **deliver** 배달하다 **gift** 선물

W Hello, I just wanted to say how satisfied I am with the Brew Master 600 that I ordered from your company. It has a faster brewing time than my previous coffee machine, and it keeps the coffee hot all day long. And the twelve-cup-capacity pot is great since everyone in my family enjoys drinking a good cup of coffee. The timer is an excellent feature, and I always set it so that the coffee is ready exactly when we wake up. All my friends asked about it, and I gave them your number. Three of them have received it already, and they say it's the best coffee machine they've ever bought. By the way, the reason I'm calling is that I would really like to get another one delivered to my house. It's my sister's birthday in a week, and I think the Brew Master 600 would make an excellent gift.

여 안녕하세요, 저는 귀사에서 주문한 브루 매스터 600이 얼마나 만족스러운지 말씀드리고 싶었어요. 예전 커피 자판기보다 더 빨리 제조하고 하루 종일 커피를 뜨겁게 유지해 주죠. 또 식구들 모두가 커피를 한 잔 가득 마시는 걸 즐기기 때문에 열두 잔 용량의 포트는 아주 좋아요. 타이머는 탁월한 특징으로 난 항상 정확하게 우리가 깰 때 커피가 준비되도록 설정해 놓는답니다. 친구들 모두 그것에 대해 물어 봐서 귀사의 연락처를 알려 줬어요. 그들 중 세 명은 이미 그것을 받았고 자기들이 산 것 중 최고의 커피자판기라고 말해요. 그런데 전화를 드린 이유는 또 다른 걸 집에 배달해 줬으면 해서요. 일 주일 뒤에 동생 생일인데 브루 매스터 600이 탁월한 선물이 될 것 같거든요.

---

33 〔모두 듣기〕 **Which of the following is NOT true according to the weather forecast?**

① Monday will not experience any snowfall.
② The roads near the ocean will be dangerous on Friday.
③ The coldest day of the week will be Sunday.
✓ Hardly any snow will fall on the east coast.
⑤ There is a good chance of rain on Tuesday.

일기예보에 대해 사실이 <u>아닌</u> 것은?

① 월요일에는 눈이 오지 않을 것이다.
② 바다 가까운 곳의 도로는 금요일에 위험할 것이다.
③ 주중 가장 추운 날은 일요일일 것이다.
④ 동해안에는 거의 눈이 내리지 않을 것이다.
⑤ 화요일에는 비가 올 가능성이 충분히 있다.

▶ **around the corner** (거리, 시간적으로) 임박하여 **balmy** (날씨, 바람 등이) 부드럽고 시원한, 온화한 **temperature** 기온 **cold front** 한랭 전선. *cf.* **warm front** 온난 전선 **freezing** 결빙 (작용), 빙점: 빙점의, 혹한의 **freezing rain** 결빙성의 비, 진눈깨비 **blizzard** 심한 눈보라, 장기간의 폭설 **caution** 주의, 조심 **whiteout** 화이트아웃: 눈의 난반사로 방향이나 거리를 알 수 없게 되는 현상 **condition** 상황 **highway** 주요(간선) 도로 **crisp** (공기, 날씨 등이) 서늘한, 상쾌한

M Winter is just around the corner as the balmy fall days are ending. Expect temperatures to drop this week as a cold front moves down from the north. While no snow is expected at the beginning of the week, temperatures will drop to almost freezing on Monday. A warm front will follow, and there is an eighty-percent chance of rain and freezing rain on Tuesday and Wednesday. On Thursday, a mix of snow and rain is going to turn into a blizzard by Friday. Please use caution when driving as there will be serious whiteout conditions on all highways, especially near the ocean. The snow will continue on Saturday while temperatures will be just below freezing. The east coast mountains are going to get at least ten centimeters of snow by Saturday. A new cold front is expected to move through the area by Sunday, giving us crisp, blue skies and temperatures around ten degrees below freezing.

남 온화한 가을날이 끝나면서 겨울이 곧 다가오고 있습니다. 이번주에는 한랭전선이 북쪽으로부터 내려오면서 기온이 떨어질 것으로 예상됩니다. 주초에는 눈 예보는 없는 반면 기온은 월요일에 거의 0도까지 내려갈 것입니다. 온난전선이 발생하여 화요일과 수요일에는 비와 진눈깨비가 내릴 확률이 80퍼센트입니다. 목요일에는 눈비가 내리다 금요일경 눈보라로 변할 것으로 보입니다. 모든 간선도로, 특히 바다 근처에서는 심각한 화이트아웃 상황이 있을 것이므로 운전중에 조심하시기 바랍니다. 눈은 토요일에 계속되고 기온은 0도를 바로 밑돌겠습니다. 동해안 산악지대는 최소한 10센티미터의 눈이 토요일까지 내리겠습니다. 새로운 한랭전선이 일요일에 그 지역을 거쳐 이동하면서 청명한 하늘과 영하 10도 정도의 기온이 예상됩니다.

34

〔모두 듣기〕 **When are the speakers going to meet?**

① Monday at 10 a.m.
② Monday at 4 p.m.
③ Tuesday at noon
④ Wednesday at 10 a.m.
⑤ Wednesday at 3 p.m.

화자들은 언제 만날 예정인가?

① 월요일 오전 10시
② 월요일 오후 4시
③ 화요일 정오
④ 수요일 오전 10시
⑤ 수요일 오후 3시

▶ make it to …에 용케 도달하다 reschedule 예정을 변경하다 in favor of …에 찬성하여, 편들어 get together 모이다, 합치다 deadline 마감시한 tie up (사람, 교통 등을) 꼼짝 못 하게 하다 factory floor 공장의 작업장, 일반 공원들 luncheon 오찬(회), 점심식사 go for …을 지지하다, 찬성하다 head to …로 향하다

W Jim, I'm sorry I couldn't make it to your office today. Why don't we reschedule our meeting as soon as possible?

M That sounds good. I'm in favor of getting together as soon as possible because we've got a lot to talk about and our deadline is coming up soon.

W All right, well, today is Monday, and I'm all tied up, so how does tomorrow sound?

M It's good, but only in the afternoon. I'm out of the office in the morning.

W Then that's no good for me since I'll be on the factory floor all afternoon.

M In that case, how about the day after tomorrow? What's your schedule like then?

W I've got a lot of free time. What time are you thinking of meeting?

M I was hoping for either nine in the morning or four in the afternoon. I've got a luncheon from twelve to three, so I can't meet any time during the middle of the day.

W Let's go for the morning time. We can chat, and then you can head to your other meeting.

M Great. I'll see you then.

여 짐, 오늘 사무실에 못가서 미안해요. 가능한 빨리 모임 일정을 다시 잡으면 어때요?

남 좋아요. 할 얘기가 많고 마감도 곧 다가오니까 가능한 한 빨리 모이는 것 찬성이에요.

여 그래요. 음, 오늘이 월요일이라 내가 꼼짝을 못하니까 내일은 어때요?

남 좋긴 한데 오후에만 돼요. 오전에는 사무실에 없거든요.

여 오후 내내는 내가 공장에 있어야 하니까 그럼 안 되겠네요.

남 그렇다면 모레는 어때요? 그때 일정은 어때요?

여 여유 시간이 많아요. 몇 시에 만날까요?

남 오전 9시나 오후 4시가 좋겠어요. 12시부터 3시까지는 오찬이 있어서 한낮에는 시간을 전혀 낼 수가 없어요.

여 오전으로 하죠. 얘기를 나눈 뒤에 다른 모임에 가시면 되겠네요.

남 좋습니다. 그때 뵙죠.

35

주어진 시간 동안 아래 지문을 주의 깊게 읽고, 대화를 들은 후 질문에 답하시오. 〔1분〕

One of the greatest advocates for civil rights the United States has ever produced was Martin Luther King, Jr. The son of a preacher, King would go on to become a reverend himself. But that was not what he would become most famous for. It was King's dedication to civil rights that made him a world-renowned figure and, in fact, won him the Nobel Peace Prize in 1964. In the 1950s, many black Americans were upset with the segregation that was going on in the country, particularly in the South. Blacks and whites would often use different facilities, and blacks were not afforded the same treatment that whites were. Many people were ready to resort to violence, but King advocated a nonviolent approach. He led many sit-ins, boycotts, and other events in an attempt to gain equal rights for all Americans, particularly minorities. This culminated in 1963 when he gave his "I Have a Dream" speech in Washington, D.C. Just one year later, the Civil Rights Act became law, thereby giving all Americans equal treatment under the law. Unfortunately, King was assassinated in 1968, but his dream of equal rights still lives today.

M I've got to write a report on Martin Luther King, Jr., but I don't know that much about him.

W Are you serious? He was one of the greatest Americans of all time. He helped change the entire country.

M I know he was big on civil rights, but I'm not exactly sure how.

W Well, he managed to get some legislation passed which gave equal rights to everyone. Remember that several decades ago, not everyone was treated the same in the U.S.

M Right, but I'm a little confused about his tactics. Didn't he ever fight back?

W No, he didn't. Some other groups did, but the people who followed King always tried peaceful measures.

M Like what? What did they do?

W Well, King led the Montgomery Bus Boycott from 1955 to 1956. There was no violence, but he got the city of Montgomery to change its laws.

M Why didn't he ever resort to physically fighting?

W ___________________________________

Q: *Which is the best answer to the man's last words?*

미국이 낳은 가장 위대한 시민권 옹호자 중 하나는 마틴 루터 킹 주니어이다. 전도사의 아들인 킹은 스스로 목사가 되었다. 하지만 그것이 그가 가장 유명하게 된 이유는 아니었다. 그를 세계적으로 유명한 인물로 만든 것은 바로 시민권에 대한 그의 헌신이었으며 실제로 1964년에 노벨평화상을 그에게 안겼다. 1950년대에 많은 미국 흑인들은 미국, 특히 남부에서 계속되고 있는 인종차별주의에 분노했다. 흑인들과 백인들은 종종 다른 시설을 사용하고 흑인들은 백인들과 똑같은 대우를 받지 못했다. 많은 사람들은 폭력에 의존할 준비를 했지만 킹은 비폭력적 방법을 주장했다. 그는 많은 농성과 불매운동, 모든 미국인들, 특히 소수 민족에게 평등권을 획득하기 위한 다른 행사를 지도했다. 이것은 1963년 그가 워싱턴 DC에서 "내겐 꿈이 있다"는 연설을 했을 때 절정에 달했다. 꼭 1년 뒤에 민권법안이 법이 되었고 그에 따라 모든 미국인들은 그 법하에서 동등한 대우를 부여받았다. 불행히도 킹은 1968년에 암살되었지만 평등권에 대한 그의 꿈은 여전히 오늘날에도 살아 있다.

남 마틴 루터 킹 주니어에 관해 리포트를 써야 하는데 그에 관해 아는 게 별로 없어.

여 정말이야? 그는 역사상 가장 위대한 미국인 중 하나잖아. 온 나라를 변화시키는 데 도움을 줬어.

남 그가 시민권에 대해 훌륭했다는 건 알지만 정확히 어떻게 그런지는 몰라.

Q ______________________

① He won the Nobel Peace Prize in 1964.
✓ He believed in using nonviolent methods.
③ He got the Civil Rights Act passed.
④ He became a preacher like his father.
⑤ He wanted blacks to be treated equally.

① 그는 1964년에 노벨평화상을 수상했어.
② 그는 비폭력 방식을 쓰는 것을 믿었어.
③ 그는 민권 법안이 통과되게 만들었어.
④ 그는 아버지처럼 목사가 되었어.
⑤ 그는 흑인들도 평등하게 대우받기를 원했어.

▶ advocates 옹호하다, 주장하다 civil rights 시민권, (특히) 흑인 공민권 preacher 전도사 reverend 목사, 성직자 dedication 헌신 renowned 유명한 figure 인물 segregation 인종 차별 (대우) afford 가져오다, 주다 resort to …에 의지하다 sit-in 연좌(농성) 항의 equal 동등한, 평등한 minority 소수민족 culminate 완결시키다, 클라이맥스에 이르게 하다 thereby 그 때문에 assassinate 암살하다 all time 전대미문의, 사상 legislation (제정된) 법률 tactics 작전, 책략 measures 방책, 수단

여 음, 그는 모든 사람에게 평등권을 준 일부 법안이 통과되도록 애를 썼어. 수십년 전에는 미국에서 모든 사람이 똑같은 대우를 받진 않았다는 걸 생각해봐.

남 그래, 하지만 그의 전략에 대해서는 좀 혼란스러워. 도대체 대항을 하긴 했어?

여 아니, 안 그랬어. 일부 다른 집단은 그랬지만 킹을 따르는 사람들은 항상 평화적인 방법을 시도했어.

남 예를 들면? 그들이 뭘 했는데?

여 음, 킹은 1955년에서 1956년까지 몽고메리 버스 보이콧을 이끌었어. 폭력은 전혀 없었지만 몽고메리 시가 법을 수정하도록 만들었지.

남 왜 그는 전혀 물리적으로 싸우는 데 의존하지 않았니?

여 ______________________

Q: *남자의 마지막 말에 대한 여자의 응답으로 알맞은 것은?*

36

다음을 듣고, 이어지는 영어 질문에 답하시오.

① Sunday
② Monday
✓ Tuesday
④ Wednesday
⑤ Thursday

① 일요일
② 월요일
③ 화요일
④ 수요일
⑤ 목요일

▶ local 지역의, 그 고장의 in a row 잇따라, 연속적으로 playground 운동장 return 돌아오다, 되돌아가다

M Today is Sunday, so Sumi is taking her dog for a walk in the local park like she did yesterday. She always takes her dog to the park for four days in a row. Then she takes her dog for a walk next to the river for three days. Next, she takes her dog to a local school's playground for three days in a row. Finally, she goes to the lake for one day and then returns to the park the next day.

Q: *On which day will Sumi take her dog to the lake?*

여 오늘은 일요일이어서 수미는 어제 그랬던 것처럼 지역 공원에 개를 데리고 산책을 갈 것이다. 그녀는 언제나 4일 연속으로 개를 데리고 공원에 간다. 그 다음에 그녀는 3일 동안 강 옆으로 개를 데리고 산책을 간다. 다음으로 그녀는 3일 동안 연속으로 지역 학교 운동장으로 개를 데리고 간다. 마지막으로 그녀는 하루 동안 호수로 가고, 다음날 공원으로 다시 간다.

Q: *수미는 언제 강아지를 데리고 호수에 갈 것인가?*

37 What is the woman's occupation?

① TV reporter
② newspaper reporter
③ hospital patient
✓ ④ magazine journalist
⑤ TV show host

여자의 직업은 무엇인가?

① 텔레비전 기자
② 신문 기자
③ 병원의 환자
④ 잡지 기자
⑤ TV 쇼 호스트

38 Which of the following are proven false by the doctor? Check all that apply.

ⓐ An all-meat diet can be healthy.
ⓑ It is safe to lose several pounds very quickly.
ⓒ A person needs to eat a balanced diet.
ⓓ It is good to eat a lot of meat.
ⓔ No-vegetable diets are effective.

① ⓐ, ⓑ
② ⓐ, ⓑ, ⓒ
✓ ③ ⓐ, ⓑ, ⓓ
④ ⓑ, ⓓ
⑤ ⓑ, ⓓ, ⓔ

남자의 말에 따르면, 다이어트에 관한 속설 중 잘못된 것으로 판명된 것을 모두 고르시오.

ⓐ 육류 다이어트로 건강해질 수 있다.
ⓑ 매우 빠르게 몇 파운드를 빼는 것은 안전하다.
ⓒ 사람은 균형 잡힌 식단을 먹을 필요가 있다.
ⓓ 고기를 많이 먹는 것은 좋다.
ⓔ 채소를 먹지 않는 다이어트는 효과가 있다.

▶ **fad** 일시적 유행, 취미 **diet** 제한식, 음식물 **harmful** 해로운, 유해한 **side effect** 부작용 **regain** 되찾다, 회복하다 **notion** 인식, 견해 **You must be kidding.** 설마 농담이겠지?, 그럴 리가! **balanced** 균형 잡힌 **recipe** 요리법, 비결 **disaster** 재앙, 불행 **protein** 단백질 **article** (잡지 등의) 기사 **red meat** (쇠고기, 양고기 등의) 붉은 고기 **clog up** (파이프 등을) 막히게 하다, 메우다 **artery** 동맥

(37~38)

W Dr. Weston, because there are so many fad diets out there these days, our readers are very interested in learning the truth about which ones are good and which ones aren't.

M It's true that many people are following some strange diets, which can wind up hurting them more than helping them.

W Now, I've heard it's possible for a person safely to lose several pounds in just a couple of days. What do you think about that?

M I'm sorry, but that's just wrong. A person can lose several pounds very quickly, but it could have some harmful side effects. Plus, most of the weight loss tends to be water, which the person can quickly regain.

W What about the notion of an all-meat diet being very healthy.

M You must be kidding. A person needs to eat a balanced diet, one which includes fruits, grains, and vegetables. Eating only one of the food groups is a recipe for disaster.

W But isn't a lot of meat supposed to be good for you since it is high in protein? I believe our own magazine had an article about that not too long ago.

M Well, meat, of course, does have a lot of protein, but a person should be careful about eating too much of it, especially red meat. It can clog up arteries and lead to heart problems if you overeat it and enjoy it too much.

W Well, that's very interesting to know.

(37~38)

여 웨스턴 박사님, 요즘 시중에는 아주 많은 다이어트가 유행하고 있어서 독자들이 어떤 것이 좋고 나쁜지에 관한 사실을 아는 데 매우 관심이 많습니다.

남 많은 사람들이 일부 이상한 다이어트를 따라 하고 있는 것은 사실인데, 그것은 결국 도움을 주기보다는 해를 끼치게 됩니다.

여 자, 단 며칠만에 안전하게 수 파운드를 빼는 것이 가능하다고 들었는데요. 그에 대해 어떻게 생각하십니까?

남 미안하지만 그건 정말 잘못된 거예요. 아주 급속히 수 파운드를 뺄 수는 있지만 그건 몸에 나쁜 부작용이 다소 있을 수 있어요. 게다가 빠진 살 대부분이 수분이기 쉬운데, 그건 재빨리 다시 얻을 수 있는 거지요.

여 완전 육류 다이어트가 매우 건강에 좋다는 주장에 대해서는 어떠세요?

남 농담이시죠? 사람은 균형 잡힌 식사를 해야 해요, 과일과 곡식, 야채가 들어 있는 것이죠. 식품군 중 하나만을 먹는 것은 재앙을 가져오는 방법이에요.

여 하지만 고기에는 단백질이 많으니까 많은 고기는 몸에 좋아야 하는 것이 아닌가요? 얼마 전에 우리 잡지에서 그에 관한 기사가 실렸어요.

남 음, 물론 고기에는 단백질이 많이 들어있습니다만 그것을 너무 많이 먹는 것은 조심해야 합니다. 특히 붉은 고기인 경우에 그렇죠. 그것은 동맥을 막히게 해서 지나치게 먹고 너무 즐기면 심장 질환으로 이어질 수 있습니다.

여 음, 그건 아주 흥미로운 정보군요.

<table>
<tr><td></td><td></td><td></td></tr>
</table>

39 **What is the best title of this talk?**

① Historic London Places
② The Best Sights in London
✓ A Tour Package to London
④ How to Get to London
⑤ The History of London

이야기의 제목으로 가장 알맞은 것은 무엇인가?

① 런던의 역사적인 장소들
② 런던의 최고 명소들
③ 런던 투어 패키지
④ 런던으로 가는 방법
⑤ 런던의 역사

40 **Which of the following is NOT true about this tour?**

✓ The cost of the hotel is not included.
② There are lower prices for groups.
③ The tours will be done by bus and boat.
④ A palace visit is part of the tour.
⑤ The package is available for three months.

다음 중 이 투어에 대해 사실이 <u>아닌</u> 것은?

① 호텔 값은 포함되어 있지 않다.
② 단체를 위한 할인된 가격이 있다.
③ 투어는 버스와 보트를 이용할 것이다.
④ 왕궁 방문이 투어의 일부이다.
⑤ 이 패키지 상품은 3개월간 유효하다.

▶ **package tour** 〈여행사의〉 패키지 투어 **double-decker** 〈배, 버스 등의〉 이층으로 된 것, 이층 버스 **check out** …을 확인하다 **cruise** 순항, 유람 항해 **Ferris wheel** 〈유원지의〉 페리스 관람차 **available** 이용할 수 있는 **affordable** 〈가격 등이〉 알맞은, 감당할 수 있는 **operator** 관리자, 오퍼레이터 **discount** 할인, 할인율[할인액] **senior** 연장자, 어른

(39~40)

M Are you looking for an exciting place to visit? Why not come to London? It's a fantastic city with a mix of both the old and the new. We have flights three days a week from Seoul to London. Our package tour includes the cost of the flight, four days and three nights at a lovely hotel, and a bus tour of London on a real double-decker bus. On the first day, you will check out Buckingham Palace, Trafalgar Square, the Tower of London, and Westminster Abby in order to get a sense of the history of the city. On the second day, you will go on a Thames River boat cruise to be followed by a visit to the Millennium Dome and the London Eye, one of the world's biggest Ferris wheels. The last full tour day will be yours for shopping or to take in any of the other sights you may wish to enjoy. Our package is available from June to the end of August and is affordable for all. Call one of our operators at our office at 555-2309. And remember to ask about our discounts for group tours and seniors.

(39~40)

여 흥미로운 방문지를 찾고 계십니까? 런던으로 오십시오. 이곳은 옛것과 새것이 혼합되어 있는 환상적인 도시입니다. 서울에서 런던까지 일주일에 3일 항공편이 있습니다. 당사의 패키지 여행에는 항공료와 멋진 호텔에서의 3박4일, 실제 이층버스를 타고 런던을 둘러보는 버스 여행이 포함되어 있습니다. 첫날에는 버킹엄궁전과 트라팔가 광장, 런던탑, 웨스트민스터 성당을 보실 겁니다. 그 도시의 역사를 알아보기 위해 둘째 날에는 템스강을 보트로 유람하고 이어서 밀레니엄돔과 세계에서 가장 큰 페리스 관람차 중 하나인 런던아이를 방문하게 됩니다. 마지막 날은 여러분의 날로 온종일 쇼핑을 즐기시거나 어떤 곳이든 원하시는 다른 관광지를 방문할 수 있습니다. 패키지 여행은 6월부터 8월 말까지 가능하며 여러분 모두를 위한 가격으로 모십니다. 사무실에 있는 저희 관리자에게 555-2309번으로 전화 주십시오. 단체여행과 어르신들을 위한 당사의 할인율에 대해 잊지 말고 물어 보십시오.

실전모의고사 **07**

01 ①	02 ③	03 ⑤	04 ②	05 ②	06 ④	07 ②	08 ③	09 ②	10 ⑤
11 ②	12 ②	13 ④	14 ②	15 ⑤	16 ④	17 ②	18 ③	19 ②	20 ②
21 ③	22 ②	23 ④	24 ①	25 ②	26 ③	27 ④	28 ③	29 ①	30 ③
31 ③	32 ③	33 ④	34 ③	35 ①	36 ③	37 ④	38 ②	39 ④	40 ③

문제와 정답	스크립트	해석

01 대화를 듣고, 두 사람이 이야기하고 있는 장소를 고르시오.

①  ② 

③  ④ 

⑤ 

▶ identification 신분증, 동일함, 동일하다는 증명

스크립트

W May I have your name and address please?

M I live at 12 Baker Street.

W And could you let me know what your telephone number is, please?

M It's 555-6691.

W Okay, I think that should just about do it. Here is your reservation.

M Thanks. I'm glad that we got that taken care of.

W You reserved a small car, right? Are you going to be the only driver?

M Yes, I will be the only one who will be driving.

W Let me make a copy of your license for our records. I'll be right back in a couple of seconds.

M Okay.

W Oh, I see that your license is damaged. Do you have any other form of identification with you?

M I'm afraid that I don't. You know, I've never had anyone else tell me that there's a problem with my license before.

W My manager is very strict, so I need to make sure that I have copies of two forms of identification that belong to you.

M Here's my passport. Will that be sufficient?

W Yes, thank you very much. Have a seat over there. I'll have everything ready for you in a minute.

해석

여 이름과 주소를 알려 주실래요?

남 베이커가 12번지에 살고 있습니다.

여 전화번호를 알려 주시겠습니까?

남 555-6691입니다.

여 좋아요, 그러면 된 것 같군요. 여기 예약사항입니다.

남 고마워요. 처리가 돼서 기쁘군요.

여 소형차를 예약하셨죠, 맞습니까? 고객님만 운전하실 건가요?

남 네, 저만 운전할 겁니다.

여 기록을 위해 운전면허증을 복사할게요. 잠시 후에 돌아오겠습니다.

남 좋아요.

여 이런, 면허증이 손상되었군요. 다른 신분증 있으십니까?

남 죄송하지만 없는데요. 전에는 제 면허증에 문제가 있다고 말하는 사람이 아무도 없었거든요.

여 제 상사가 아주 엄격해서요, 고객님의 신분증 두 개를 복사해야만 합니다.

남 여기 제 여권이 있습니다. 그거면 충분한가요?

여 네, 감사합니다. 저쪽에 앉아 계세요. 잠시 후에 모든 준비를 해드리겠습니다.

---

02 대화를 듣고, 여자가 책장을 파는 이유를 고르시오.

① 책장이 너무 낡아서
② 책장이 부서져서
③ 그녀의 새 아파트에 놓기에는 너무 커서
④ 남자가 책장을 정말로 필요로 하기 때문에
⑤ 그녀의 새 아파트에 놓기에는 너무 작아서

▶ bookcase 책장 advertisement 광고 correct 정확한 condition 상태, 조건 pic up …을 가져 오다 get rid of 제거하다

스크립트

M Hello. May I speak to Mrs. Robinson, please?

W This is Mrs. Robinson speaking.

M Hello, my name is Jack Smith. I'm calling about the bookcase that's for sale. I only saw the advertisement this morning. You haven't sold it yet, have you?

W Actually, you're the first person to call about the ad. So, no, it hasn't been sold.

M The ad mentioned that you're selling it for $50. Is that the correct price?

W Yes, and it's also in perfect condition. I've only had it for two years, but I'm moving to a smaller apartment, so I'm afraid that I won't have enough space for it any more.

해석

남 여보세요, 로빈슨 씨와 통화할 수 있을까요?

여 전데요.

남 안녕하세요, 제 이름은 잭 스미스입니다. 내놓으신 책장에 대해 문의 드리려고 전화했는데요. 오늘 아침에야 광고를 봤습니다. 혹시 벌써 팔린 것은 아니죠?

여 사실, 당신이 처음으로 전화한 겁니다. 책장은 아직 안 팔렸습니다.

남 광고에 보니까 50달러에 팔고 있다고요. 그 가격이 맞습니까?

여 네, 그리고 상태도 아주 좋습니다. 2년밖에 안 갖고 있던 거라서요. 근데 더 작은 아파트로 이사를 갈 예정이라서 책장을 놓을 만한 충분한 공간이 없습니다.

<table>
<tr><th>문제와 정답</th><th>스크립트</th><th>해석</th></tr>
</table>

M I think $50 is a good price. I really want the bookcase, but the problem is that I don't have a car. Do you think that you could hold on to it for a few more days until I can arrange to have one of my friends drive me over to pick it up?

W Let's see… Today's Sunday, and I have to move on Wednesday morning. So I've got to get rid of it by then. Is that going to be possible for you?

M I don't think so. Let me call you back so that I can figure out some way to get that bookshelf out of your place.

남 제 생각에 50달러면 가격도 괜찮고 정말 그 책장을 갖고 싶은데요, 문제는 차가 없다는 것입니다. 친구 한 명이 저를 태워서 책장을 가지러 갈 수 있도록 준비할 때까지 며칠만 더 팔지 않고 계실 수 없을까요?

여 어디 봅시다. 오늘은 일요일이고 저는 수요일 아침에 이사를 가야 합니다. 그래서 그때까지 치워야 하거든요. 그렇게 하는 게 가능할까요?

남 아니요. 책장을 옮길 수 있는 방법을 찾아서 다시 전화를 할 수 있을까요?

---

03 대화를 듣고, 인터뷰를 위해 준비된 것으로 언급되지 <u>않</u>은 것을 고르시오.

① 단정한 복장
② 추천장
③ 자격 요건
④ 경험
✓⑤ 자기 소개서

▶ nervous 긴장되는 qualification 자격, 능력 recommend 추천하다 hard working 부지런한 responsible 책임감이 있는 boring 지루한, 무미건조한 quality 자질

M So, how was your interview?

W I haven't gone to the interview yet. It's tomorrow morning. I'm already nervous.

M Don't worry. You'll be fine. You have the experience and good qualifications. You'll be the best person for the job.

W I hope so. Say, would you write a letter recommending me for the job?

M No problem. I'm sure they'll ask you for one anyway. I'll say that you work well with people and that you're hard working and responsible.

W I sound really boring!

M Nonsense, those are the qualities they look for.

W Thanks for the help.

M Good luck with the interview tomorrow. Dress smartly and speak clearly. You'll be fine.

남 면접은 어땠니?

여 아직 면접 안 봤어요. 내일 아침인데, 벌써부터 긴장되네요.

남 걱정하지 마. 너라면 괜찮을 거야. 넌 경력도 있고 훌륭한 자격요건도 있어. 그 일에 최적인 사람일 거야.

여 저도 그러길 바래요. 그런데, 저를 그 일에 추천하는 편지를 써 주시겠어요?

남 문제 없지. 분명히 그쪽에서도 추천장을 원할 거야. 네가 사람들과 어울리며 일을 잘 하고, 성실하고 책임감 있는 사람이라고 말하마.

여 내가 너무 재미 없는 사람 같이 들리잖아요!

남 말도 안 돼. 바로 그런 게 그들이 원하는 자격 요건이란다.

여 도와주셔서 감사해요.

남 내일 인터뷰에 행운을 빈다. 복장을 단정히 하고 명확하게 말을 하렴. 그럼 괜찮을 거다.

---

04 대화를 듣고, 여자가 외출할 수 <u>없는</u> 이유를 고르시오.

① 그녀는 수업을 위해 해야 할 숙제가 있다.
✓② 그녀는 내일 회사 프레젠테이션이 있다.
③ 그녀는 실직해서 돈이 없다.
④ 그녀는 전날 늦게까지 밖에 있었다.
⑤ 그녀는 대학 시험을 준비중이다.

▶ hectic 몹시 바쁜 presentation 프리젠테이션 get a life 다시 한 번 기회를 얻다 relax 여유를 갖다 complain 불평하다 give a call 전화를 하다

M Jane, how are you doing?

W Oh, hi, Mark. Life is crazy these days, and when I'm not at work, I'm at college.

M I know what you mean. Studying and working at the same time is very hectic. I'm calling because I'm getting together with Lisa and Mike tonight. We're probably going out to eat and then maybe we'll have coffee together. Why don't you come with us?

W I'd really love to, but I have an important work presentation tomorrow.

M That's too bad. But you know we won't be staying out very late. We should be home by 11 p.m. at the latest. Maybe you need a break. When was the last time you were out with all of us? It's time to get a life.

W You don't understand. There's nothing I'd like more. But I haven't finished the presentation yet and the meeting is first thing in the morning.

M All right then. But next time no excuses. You need to relax more. Everyone has been complaining that they never see you these days.

W You're right. There's more to life than working and studying.

M I'll give you a call soon, and hopefully you'll be less busy next time.

W I promise I'll be available.

남 제인, 어떻게 지내고 있니?

여 아, 안녕 마이크. 요즘은 굉장히 바빠서 회사에 있지 않으면 학교에 있어.

남 무슨 말인지 알아. 학업과 일을 병행하는 것은 굉장히 바쁘지. 다른 게 아니라 리사와 마이크랑 오늘밤 만나기로 해서 전화했어. 나가서 저녁 먹은 다음 아마 커피를 마실 거야. 너도 오지 그러니?

여 정말 가고 싶지만 난 내일 중요한 회사 프레젠테이션이 있어.

남 정말 안 됐구나. 하지만 우리가 그렇게 늦게까지 있지는 않을 거라는 걸 너도 알잖아. 최소한 밤 11시까지는 집에 들어갈 거야. 너도 휴식이 필요할지도 몰라. 우리랑 마지막으로 어울린 게 언제였지? 한숨 돌릴 시점이라고.

여 넌 모를 거야. 그것만큼 내가 원하는 것도 없어. 하지만 아직 프레젠테이션을 끝내지 못했고 회의는 내일 아침 일찍 있어.

남 알았어, 그럼. 하지만 다음 번에는 봐주지 않을 거야. 넌 좀 더 쉴 필요가 있어. 모두 요즘 널 못 봤다며 불만이 대단해.

여 맞아. 인생엔 일하고 공부하는 것보다 중요한 게 있지.

남 조만간 다시 전화할 텐데 그때는 좀 덜 바빴으면 좋겠다.

여 그땐 꼭 시간 낸다고 약속할게.

05 대화를 듣고, 남자가 쇼핑몰에 다녀오는 방법을 가장 잘 나타낸 것을 고르시오.

쇼핑몰까지	집까지
① 5번 버스	어머니의 차
✔ 어머니의 차	친구의 어머니의 차
③ 5번 버스	친구의 어머니의 차
④ 어머니의 차	5번 버스
⑤ 5번 버스	어머니의 차

▶ take a show 샤워를 하다 be supposed to …할 예정이다 had better …하는 것이 더 낫다 drop off …을 내려 주다

M Mom, how do I get to the Woods Shopping Mall? I'm planning to go there for a while.

W You can take bus number 5, but if you want to go now, I can drive you there.

M Thanks, Mom. Can you wait while I take a shower?

W Sure, I can wait for you, but don't be too long. I've got to meet some friends of my own after I finish shopping. If you take too long, you'll have to take the bus.

M I won't, Mom. I'm supposed to meet Jim outside the shoe store in thirty minutes. His mother is buying him some new shoes, and he wants me to help him choose a cool pair.

W That's a good idea. How long do you think that you'll be at the mall with him?

M We might see a movie after we find the shoes, or maybe we will get some dinner while we're there.

W I won't wait for you at the mall then since I've got other things to do. You had better take the bus back home.

M Okay, but Jim said that his mom will be able to drop me off, so that's how I plan to get home.

남 엄마, 우즈 쇼핑몰까지 어떻게 가죠? 잠깐 다녀올 계획이에요.

여 5번 버스를 타면 돼. 근데 지금 갈 거면 내가 태워다 줄게.

남 고마워요, 엄마. 샤워할 동안 기다려 줄 수 있으세요?

여 물론, 기다릴 수 있지. 그렇지만 너무 오래 하지는 말아라. 쇼핑 끝내고 친구를 좀 만나야 하거든. 네가 오래 걸리면 버스를 타야 할 거다.

남 안 그럴게요, 엄마. 30분 후에 신발가게 밖에서 짐을 만나기로 되어 있어요. 짐 엄마가 새 신발을 사 줄 건데 짐은 제가 멋진 신발을 고르는 걸 도와주었으면 해요.

여 좋은 생각이다. 짐이랑 쇼핑몰에는 얼마나 있을 생각이니?

남 신발을 산 후에 영화를 볼지도 몰라요. 아니면 아마 거기서 저녁을 먹을 거예요.

여 그럼 엄마도 다른 할 일이 있으니까 쇼핑몰에서 널 기다리진 않을게. 집으로 올 때는 버스를 타는 게 낫겠다.

남 좋아요, 근데 짐이 그러는데 짐 엄마가 저를 중간에 내려 주실 수 있을 거래요. 그게 집에 오는 저의 계획이에요.

---

06 다음을 듣고, 알프레드 노벨이 다섯 가지 상을 제정한 이유를 고르시오.

① 그는 매우 유명한 과학자였다.
② 그는 새로운 발명품들을 선전하고 싶었다.
③ 그는 부정한 방법으로 벌어들인 돈에 대해 양심의 가책을 느꼈다.
✔ 그는 군에 의해 사용되는 자신의 발명품에 대해 괴로워했다.
⑤ 그는 돈이 너무 많았다.

▶ award 상을 주다 physics 물리학 chemistry 화학 literature 문학 medicine 의학 economics 경제학 will 유언, 의지 institute 제정하다 central bank 중앙은행 praise 찬사 anniversary 주기, (해마다 돌아오는) 기념일 inventor 발명가 dynamite 다이너마이트 military 군사적인 asset 자산, 재산 establishment 제정, 설립 promote 촉진하다, 고무하다

W Nobel Prizes have been awarded in Physics, Chemistry, Literature, Peace, Medicine and Economics since 1901. Alfred Nobel, a Swedish scientist, used his will to institute the first five prizes in 1895. The prize for economics was instituted by Sweden's central bank in 1968. All six prizes are widely regarded as very high praise in their subject areas. Except for the peace prize, which is handed out in Oslo, Norway, they are all awarded in Stockholm, Sweden, at an annual ceremony on December 10, the anniversary of Nobel's death. Nobel was himself the inventor of dynamite. Before his death, Nobel became very uncomfortable with the military using the dynamite he invented and therefore decided to leave 94% of his total assets for the establishment of the five prizes to promote study and research.

여 노벨상은 1901년부터 물리학, 화학, 문학, 평화, 의학, 그리고 경제학 부문에서 수여되어 왔다. 스웨덴의 과학자인 알프레드 노벨은 유언장을 통해 1895년 최초로 다섯 가지 상을 제정했다. 경제학 부문의 상은 1968년 스웨덴의 중앙은행에 의해 제정되었다. 여섯 가지의 상 모두 그 영역에 있어서 매우 높은 상으로 폭넓게 인식된다. 노르웨이의 오슬로에서 수여되는 평화상을 제외하면 그것들은 모두 노벨의 기일인 12월 10일 스웨덴 스톡홀름에서 매년 열리는 시상식에서 수여된다. 노벨 자신은 다이너마이트의 발명가였다. 사망하기 전 노벨은 자신이 발명한 다이너마이트가 군사적으로 사용되는 것에 괴로워 했고, 그래서 학문과 연구를 촉진시키기 위한 다섯 가지 상을 제정하기 위해 그의 자산의 94퍼센트를 남기기로 결심했다.

07 대화를 듣고, 남자가 바커 인터내셔널 회사에서 일하는 것에 대해 걱정하는 점이 무엇인지 고르시오.

① 일이 힘들지 않은지
✓ ② 회사의 급여조건과 혜택이 좋은지
③ 연장 근무를 할 필요가 없는지
④ 상사가 좋은 사람인지
⑤ 점심식사가 무료인지

▶ How can I put this? 어떻게 말을 꺼내야 할까요?
rude 무례한 stressful 스트레스가 많은 salary 급여, 보수 offer 제공하다 perk(perquisite) 특혜, 특전 in turn 그 대가로 give a effort 노력하다, 애쓰다 without question 무조건, 이러니저러니 할 것 없이

M Pardon me, but is anyone sitting here?

W No.

M Then do you mind if I join you?

W Please go ahead.

M It's just that… How can I put this? I know that you work for Barker International, and I'm dying to get a job there. Do you mind if I ask you some questions?

W I don't mind at all although I had assumed that you wanted the pleasure of my company for lunch.

M You must think I'm so rude.

W I'd do the same thing if I were you.

M Are you happy working at that company?

W What a difficult question. Yes, I think I am happy although I have a pretty stressful job and a very tough boss.

M But your salary is pretty good, isn't it?

W It's a good salary, yes, and the company offers many perks.

M Such as?

W That's a very personal question.

M But it's important. My present company offers no perks at all.

W I think that you might want to work at Barker International for the wrong reasons. Yes, the company pays us very well. But, in return, you have to give 100% effort without question.

남 죄송하지만, 여기 자리 있습니까?

여 없는데요.

남 같이 앉아도 될까요?

여 앉으세요.

남 그게 저… 어떻게 말을 해야 할지… 현재 바커 인터내셔널에서 일하고 계신 거 알고 있습니다. 전 정말로 거기서 일하고 싶거든요. 제가 몇 가지 질문을 해도 될까요?

여 전 당신이 저랑 같이 점심을 먹고 싶어하는 줄로 생각했지만 괜찮습니다.

남 제가 무례하다고 생각하시는군요.

여 제가 당신이라도 똑같이 했을 거예요.

남 그 회사에서 일하시는 게 행복하십니까?

여 정말 어려운 질문이군요. 네, 일이 스트레스가 많고 상사도 까다롭지만 행복하다고 생각해요.

남 그렇지만 보수는 아주 좋지 않습니까?

여 네, 보수는 좋습니다. 그리고 혜택도 많이 제공되고요.

남 예를 들면?

여 그건 아주 사적인 질문인데요.

남 그렇지만 아주 중요합니다. 현재 제 회사에는 전혀 혜택이 없거든요.

여 제 생각엔 당신이 바커 인터내셔널에서 일하고 싶은 이유가 좀 잘못된 것 같네요. 그래요, 회사가 월급을 많이 주는 것은 사실입니다. 그렇지만 그 대가로 무조건 100%의 노력을 기울여야 합니다.

---

08 대화를 듣고, 여자의 마지막 말에 대한 남자의 응답으로 알맞은 것을 고르시오.

M: ___________________________

① Stop complaining.
② It will be easy. Don't worry.
✓ ③ I look forward to seeing you then.
④ Don't forget to wear shoes.
⑤ If you don't feel like going, call me after lunch.

① 불평은 그만해.
② 쉬울 거야. 걱정 마.
③ 그때 꼭 봤으면 해.
④ 신발 신는 거 잊지 마.
⑤ 가고 싶지 않으면, 점심 이후에 전화해.

▶ get into shape 건강해지다 refreshing 기분전환이 되는 give it a try 시도해 보다 yawn 하품을 하다, 하품

M I'm starting to run before work in the morning since I absolutely have to get into shape.

W Where do you run when you go out?

M I always jog at Center Park. It takes about 35 minutes to go around the park once. I'd love to do more, but I don't have time to do it twice.

W That sounds very tiring, especially if you're jogging before work.

M Not really. I feel so much better after jogging. I even have more energy, and I sleep better at night.

W I used to run in the evenings a long time ago. I remember that it was refreshing.

M Why don't you come with me one morning, and we'll run around the park once? If you don't like it, you don't have to come with me again. But if you do, we can run together every morning. It would be so much more fun to have a partner to go jogging with.

W I don't know if I could do it every day, but I suppose there's no harm in giving it a try.

M Let's meet at the entrance to the park at about 6 a.m.

W That's so early that I'm sure I'll still be yawning, but okay.

M _______________________________

남 건강을 위해 아침에 회사 가기 전에 조깅을 시작했어.

여 조깅하러 나가면 어디를 달리니?

남 센트럴 파크에서 조깅해. 공원을 한 바퀴 도는 데 약 35분 정도 걸려. 더 뛰고 싶은데 두 번 뛸 시간은 없어.

여 많이 피곤할 것 같다. 특히 회사 가기 전에 한다면.

남 실제로는 안 그래. 조깅하고 나면 기분이 훨씬 나아져. 에너지가 더 많이 생기고 밤에 잠도 더 잘자.

여 예전에 저녁에 달리기를 하곤 했었는데 기분전환이 되었던 게 기억나.

남 언제 한번 아침에 나랑 같이 가서 공원을 한 바퀴 돌아보는 건 어때? 마음에 들지 않으면 다시는 안 가면 되잖아. 그렇지만 좋으면 매일 아침 같이 달릴 수도 있어. 같이 조깅할 친구가 있으면 훨씬 더 재미있을 것 같아.

여 매일 할 수 있을지는 모르겠지만 한번 해보는 것도 나쁘지 않을 것 같아.

남 아침 6시쯤에 공원 입구에서 만나자.

여 너무 일러서 분명 하품이 나오겠지만 좋아.

남 _______________________________

09

대화를 듣고, 화자들이 이야기하고 있는 사람을 고르시오.

▶ share 공유하다　interest 관심　skinny 몸이 마른　medium-length 키가 중간인　suit 정장, 양복　have … in common 공동으로 …을 지니다

W How are you enjoying the party? Have you met a lot of people tonight?

M I'm surprised to say this, but I'm having a good time. I don't usually get out, but I've met several pretty interesting people.

W You know, there's someone whom you absolutely have to meet. His name is Kevin. Have you talked to him yet?

M No, I'm afraid I haven't had the pleasure of being introduced to him. Is he one of those guys standing over there in the corner?

W Yes, he is. You and he share a lot of interests, so you'll be sure to like him. He's the guy over there wearing the glasses.

M The one on the right who is kind of short?

W Oh, no. That's Lewis. Kevin is fairly tall and pretty skinny. He's also got medium-length hair.

M We'll there are two guys like that. Is he the one wearing the button-down shirt with the blue jeans, or is he the person with the T-shirt and shorts?

W He's got the button-down shirt on. He actually usually wears suits, so he's going casual tonight.

M Okay, I'll be sure to talk to him if you think that we have so much in common.

여 파티 어떠니? 오늘밤 사람들 많이 만났어?

남 놀랍게도 좋은 시간을 보내고 있어. 평소에 밖에 잘 안 나가는데 아주 재미있는 사람들을 여럿 만났어.

여 있잖아, 네가 꼭 만나봐야 할 사람이 있어. 이름은 케빈이야. 벌써 얘기 나눠 봤니?

남 아니, 아직 소개 못 받았는데. 저기 구석에 서 있는 남자들 중 하나니?

여 그래, 맞아. 나랑 그 사람은 취향에 공통점이 많아서 틀림없이 그를 좋아하게 될 거야. 저기 안경을 쓰고 있는 남자야.

남 오른쪽에 약간 키가 작은 사람?

여 아니. 그 사람은 루이스야. 케빈은 아주 키가 크고 말랐어. 또한 그는 머리 길이가 중간 정도야.

남 그런 사람이 두 명 인데. 청바지에 단추 달린 셔츠를 입고 있는 사람이니? 티셔츠에 반바지를 입고 있는 사람이니?

여 단추 달린 셔츠를 입고 있어. 사실 그는 평소에 정장을 입어서 오늘밤은 캐주얼하게 입고 왔네.

남 좋아, 우리가 공통점이 많다고 네가 생각한다면 꼭 그와 얘기를 나눠 볼게.

10

다음을 듣고, 대기에 대한 설명으로 옳지 <u>않은</u> 것을 고르시오.

① 대기는 지구를 둘러싼 가스층이다.
② 대기는 태양으로부터의 자외선을 흡수한다.
③ 대기는 기온을 낮춰 준다.
④ 카르만 선은 대기와 우주의 경계를 나타낸다.
✓ 대기는 수소와 산소, 아황산가스과 기타 가스들로 구성되어 있다.

▶ atmosphere 대기, 분위기　surround 둘러싸다　gravity 중력　nitrogen 질소　oxygen 산소　argon 아르곤　carbon dioxide 이산화탄소　absorb 흡수하다　radiation 자외선　boundary 경계　fade away 사라지다　outer space (지구 밖의) 우주　astronaut 우주 비행사

M The atmosphere is a layer of gases that surrounds the Earth and which is held in place by gravity. It is made up of nitrogen, oxygen, argon, carbon dioxide, water vapor, and other gases. This mixture of gases is commonly known as air. The atmosphere protects life on Earth by absorbing radiation from the sun. This helps to lower the temperature of the planet, which makes life possible. Three quarters of the atmosphere is within eleven kilometers of the Earth's surface. There is no clear boundary between the atmosphere and outer space. The higher it goes, the thinner the atmosphere becomes until it finally fades away into space. The Karman line, which is 100 kilometers above the Earth, is commonly used as the boundary between atmosphere and outer space. However, it's different in other countries. In the United States, for example, people who travel above a height of 80.5 kilometers above the planet are considered astronauts.

남 대기는 지구를 둘러싸고 있고 중력에 의해 머물러 있는 기체들의 층이다. 대기는 질소, 산소, 아르곤, 탄소, 수증기, 다른 기체들로 이루어져 있다. 이렇게 섞인 기체들은 흔히 공기로 알려져 있다. 대기는 태양으로부터 오는 자외선을 흡수함으로써 지구상의 생명체를 보호한다. 대기 때문에 지구의 기온이 낮아져서 생명이 살아갈 수 있다. 대기의 4분의 3은 지구표면에서 11Km 이내에 있다. 대기와 바깥 우주 사이에는 명확한 경계선이 없다. 높이 올라갈수록 대기는 점점 희박해지다가 마침내 바깥 우주로 사라진다. 지구에서 100Km 떨어진 곳에 있는 카르만 선이 흔히 대기와 바깥 우주의 경계선으로 사용된다. 그러나, 그것은 나라마다 또 다르다. 예를 들면 미국에서는 지구에서 80.5Km 높이 이상으로 올라가는 사람들이 우주 비행사로 간주된다.

11

대화를 듣고, 남자가 여자만큼 배가 고프지 **않은** 이유를 고르시오.

① The man ate an apple and drank some water.
✓ The man ate breakfast, but the woman did not.
③ The man ate some doughnuts earlier.
④ The man ate some cookies earlier.
⑤ The man is trying not to think about food.

① 남자는 사과를 먹고 물을 마셨다.
② 남자는 아침을 먹었지만 여자는 먹지 않았다.
③ 남자는 전에 도넛을 먹었다.
④ 남자는 전에 쿠키를 먹었다.
⑤ 그는 음식에 대해서는 생각하지 않으려고 한다.

▶ starve 몹시 배고프다 survive 견디다 skip 빼먹다, 넘기다 on time 제시간에 sweet 달콤한 it doesn't matter 상관 없다

스크립트

W I'm starving right now. Do you happen to know what time it is?

M It's 11:30 a.m., so we've got another half an hour until lunch.

W I won't survive unless I get something to eat right now.

M Here, why don't you have some water?

W Water? I'd like some food since I skipped breakfast this morning. I was running late and barely got here on time.

M Stop thinking about food, and you should be fine.

W Don't you have a snack that I can eat to help hold me over until lunch?

M Like what? All I have is water and apples.

W You've always got healthy food. However, I'd prefer something sweet like cookies or perhaps a doughnut.

M That sounds terrible. You know that you won't feel like eating lunch if you start eating cookies now, don't you?

W It doesn't matter since I don't have any cookies with me right now. I'm usually fine if I eat breakfast in the morning, but I'm simply starving today.

M It's never a good idea to miss breakfast. I haven't done that in years. That's why I'm feeling fine and you're not.

해석

여 지금 배고파 죽겠다. 혹시 지금 몇 시인지 알아?

남 아침 11시 30분이야. 점심시간까지 30분 더 남았어.

여 지금 뭘 좀 먹지 않으면 죽을 것 같아.

남 여기. 물을 좀 마시는 게 어때?

여 물? 오늘 아침을 걸렀기 때문에 음식을 좀 먹고 싶어. 늦어서 간신히 제시간에 도착했거든.

남 음식에 대해서 생각하지 않으면 괜찮을 거야.

여 점심 때까지 참는 데 도움이 될 만한 간식 같은 거 없니?

남 어떤 거? 나한테 있는 건 물과 사과뿐이야.

여 넌 항상 건강식만 갖고 있구나. 그렇지만 난 과자나 도넛 같은 단 음식이 더 좋아.

남 끔찍하다. 지금 과자를 먹기 시작하면 점심이 먹기 싫어질 거라는 거 알지?

여 지금 나한테 과자가 없으니까 상관없어. 보통 아침을 먹으면 괜찮은데 오늘은 진짜 배고파 죽을 것 같다.

남 아침을 거르는 건 좋은 생각이 아냐. 난 거르지 않은 지 몇 년 됐어. 그게 난 괜찮고 넌 괜찮지 않은 이유야.

12

대화를 듣고, 남자가 구입하려고 하는 것들을 모두 고르시오.

ⓐ computer ⓑ washing machine
ⓒ television ⓓ iron
ⓔ toaster ⓕ microwave oven
ⓖ refrigerator ⓗ bed
ⓘ stove

ⓐ 컴퓨터 ⓑ 식기 세척기
ⓒ 텔레비전 ⓓ 다리미
ⓔ 토스터기 ⓕ 전자레인지
ⓖ 냉장고 ⓗ 침대
ⓘ 스토브

① ⓐ, ⓒ, ⓓ, ⓔ, ⓕ, ⓗ
✓ ⓒ, ⓔ, ⓕ, ⓖ, ⓗ, ⓘ
③ ⓐ, ⓑ, ⓓ, ⓕ, ⓘ
④ ⓑ, ⓒ, ⓓ, ⓔ, ⓖ, ⓗ, ⓘ
⑤ ⓐ, ⓒ, ⓔ, ⓕ, ⓖ, ⓗ

▶ contract 계약 rent 임대하다 furniture 가구 stuff 물건 You're telling me. 내 말이 바로 그거야. figure out 생각하다 refrigerator 냉장고 laundromat 자동 세탁기, 빨래방 stove 스토브, 요리용 화로 microwave 전자레인지 inexpensive 저렴한

스크립트

M I'm so excited. I just signed a contract to rent an apartment, so I'll be moving there in a couple of weeks.

W Congratulations. You must be so excited finally to be getting out of your parents' home so that you can live on your own.

M I am, but now I've got to spend a lot of money on furniture and stuff. There's absolutely nothing in my new place.

W Wow, that's going to be expensive.

M You're telling me. I won't have enough money for everything I need, so I'll have to figure out what the most important things are.

W That's smart. Well, you'll definitely need a bed, refrigerator, television, and washing machine.

M I agree on everything except the washing machine. I'll just have to go to a laundromat for the first couple of months.

W Well, that's not too bad. How about a stove or microwave oven? Surely you'll need one of those.

M I'm going to get both since they're fairly inexpensive. And I'll get a toaster and a sofa but not a computer. I'll just use the one I have at work.

W Great. And I can give you an iron if you want it. I've got an extra one lying around my home.

해석

남 기분 정말 좋아. 방금 아파트 임대계약을 해서 몇 주 후에는 거기로 이사 갈 거야.

여 축하해. 드디어 부모님을 떠나 혼자만의 삶을 살 수 있게 돼서 너무 신나겠다.

남 응, 그렇지만 이제 가구며 물건들을 사는 데 많은 돈을 써야 해. 새로 이사 갈 집에는 아무것도 없거든.

여 와, 정말 돈이 많이 들겠구나.

남 맞아. 필요한 모든 것을 살 돈은 나한테 없어. 그래서 가장 중요한 것이 무엇인지 알아봐야 할 거야.

여 그게 현명하지. 음, 분명 침대, 냉장고, TV, 세탁기가 필요할 거야.

남 세탁기만 빼면 나도 동의해. 처음 몇 달 동안은 그냥 빨래방을 가야 할 것 같아.

여 음, 나쁘지 않네. 스토브나 전자레인지는 어때? 분명 둘 중 하나는 필요할 텐데.

남 별로 안 비싸니까 둘 다 살 거야. 토스터, 소파도 사고 컴퓨터는 안 사고. 그냥 회사에 있는 것을 사용해야지.

여 좋아. 원한다면 다리미 줄게. 집에 여분이 하나 있거든.

13 다음을 듣고, 임주영 박사가 대학에서 가르치기 시작한 해를 고르시오.

① 1970
② 1977
③ 1986
✓ 1987
⑤ 2008

▶ chamber of commerce 상공회의소
appointment 임명   graduate from …을 졸업하다
immigrate 이민 가다, 이주하다   complete (과정을)
마치다, 완성하다

W The Seoul Chamber of Commerce would like to congratulate Dr. Yim Ju Young on his appointment as Executive Vice President of the Seoul Chamber of the Arts and Literature. He will take up his appointment on May 30, 2010. Dr. Yim graduated from the Department of English Literature of Seoul National University in 1970. He immigrated to the United States in 1977, where he went on to complete a two-year master's program in English Literature at the State University of New York. He taught at the University of Wisconsin for seven years before returning to Korea with his family in 1993. He also serves as president of the Korea Foundation for the Arts.

여 서울 상공회의소는 임주영 박사의 서울 예술문화재단의 부회장 취임을 축하드립니다. 그는 2010년 5월 30일까지 재임하실 것입니다. 임 박사님은 1970년에 국립 서울대학교의 영문과를 졸업하셨습니다. 그는 뉴욕 주립대학교에서 2년간의 석사 코스를 마치기 위해 1977년에 미국으로 건너가셨습니다. 그는 1993년에 그의 가족과 함께 한국으로 돌아오기 전 7년 동안 위스콘신대학에서 가르쳤습니다. 그는 또한 한국 예술재단의 회장으로 재임 중이시기도 합니다.

---

14 대화를 듣고, 상황에 가장 잘 어울리는 속담을 고르시오.

① It's like talking to a wall.
✓ Too many cooks spoil the broth.
③ Spare the rod and spoil the child.
④ The grass is always greener on the other side.
⑤ There is no use crying over spilt milk.

① 소귀에 경 읽기이다.
② 사공이 너무 많으면 배가 산으로 간다.
③ 매를 아끼면 자식을 망친다.
④ 남의 떡이 더 커 보인다.
⑤ 엎질러진 물은 도로 담을 수 없다.

▶ presentation 프리젠테이션   complete 완벽한,
완성하다   failure 실패   go wrong 잘못 되다
interrupt …을 방해하다, 끼어들다   agree on …에
대해 합의하다   blame 비난하다   disaster 실패,
엉망진창인 것   avoid …을 피하다

W How did your presentation go this morning?

M It was a complete failure. So many things went wrong that it was really embarrassing.

W But you worked so hard. How could that have happened? What went wrong?

M I prepared the presentation, but, during the meeting, the entire team decided to interrupt me and add things whenever they felt like it.

W But I thought you'd decided that one person would do the presentation and everyone else would answer the questions afterwards.

M Yes, that's what we had decided. But in the meeting, everyone seemed to have forgotten what we had agreed on.

W You must have been really angry. I know that I would have been.

M I was. We looked as if we hadn't prepared properly. My manager said that he wants to see me in his office tomorrow morning. I hope he's not going to blame me for the disaster.

W You should explain exactly what happened. The situation could easily have been avoided, especially since you worked so hard and for so many hours. Maybe he'll give you another chance.

여 오늘 아침 프레젠테이션 어땠어?

남 완전히 실패했어. 너무나 많은 일들이 틀어져서 정말 당황스러웠다니까.

여 그렇지만 넌 열심히 했잖아. 어떻게 그런 일이 있을 수가 있어? 뭐가 잘못됐는데?

남 준비는 내가 했는데 회의하는 동안에 팀 전체가 나를 방해하기로 작정하고 아무때나 토를 다는 거야.

여 그렇지만 원래는 한 사람이 발표를 하고 다른 사람들은 나중에 질문에 답하기로 결정했었던 것 같은데.

남 그래, 그게 원래 결정이었지. 그런데 회의 때는 다들 우리가 동의했던 것도 잊어버린 것 같았어.

여 정말 화났었겠다. 나라도 화가 났을 거야.

남 화났지. 제대로 준비를 안 했던 것처럼 보였어. 과장님이 내일 아침 사무실에서 좀 보자고 하셨는데 이 사태에 대해 날 비난하지 않기를 바랄 뿐이야.

여 정확히 무슨 일이 있었는지 설명해야 해. 특히 네가 정말 열심히 아주 오랜 시간 동안 준비를 했기 때문에 그 상황은 충분히 피할 수 있었어. 어쩌면 다시 한번 기회를 줄지도 몰라.

15 다음을 듣고, 집을 짓는 과정을 순서대로 나열한 것을 고르시오.

ⓐ Negotiate the contract
ⓑ Select the plan for the home
ⓒ Determine a budget
ⓓ Choose the designer and builders
ⓔ Find a plot of land

ⓐ 계약을 협상한다
ⓑ 집을 위한 설계도를 선정한다
ⓒ 예산을 결정한다
ⓓ 설계자와 건축가를 선정한다
ⓔ 부지를 찾는다

① ⓔ - ⓒ - ⓑ - ⓓ - ⓐ
② ⓒ - ⓓ - ⓔ - ⓐ - ⓑ
③ ⓔ - ⓓ - ⓑ - ⓒ - ⓐ
④ ⓒ - ⓒ - ⓓ - ⓐ - ⓑ
✓⑤ ⓒ - ⓔ - ⓓ - ⓑ - ⓐ

▶ purchase 구입하다   process 과정
complicated 복잡한   homeowner 주택 소유자
smoothly 원활하게   make a budget 예산을
세우다   determine 결정하다   lot 부지, 지구
account for …을 고려하다   architect 건축가   plan
설계도   select 선택하다   negotiate 협상하다
construction 건축, 건설

M　These days, many people are choosing not to purchase homes that have already been built. Instead, they're having their own homes made exactly the way they want them. Unfortunately, this process is often complicated, especially for first-time homeowners. But there are a few things they can do to ensure their home gets built as smoothly and as easily as possible. The first thing a future homeowner should do is to make a budget and determine exactly how much money he or she can spend. After that, he or she should choose the lot where the house is going to be built. This, of course, should be accounted for in the budget. Once the lot has been purchased, the individual needs to pick both the architect and the builders. Next, since the architect will undoubtedly present at least two or three different designs for the house, the plan to be followed needs to be selected. Finally, the contract with the builder must be negotiated. Once this is done, construction on the new house can begin.

남　요즘, 많은 사람들이 이미 지어진 집을 사지 않는다. 대신에 정확히 원하는 대로 자신들의 집을 짓는다. 안타깝게도 이 과정은 아주 복잡하다. 특히 처음으로 집을 갖게 되는 사람들에게는 말이다. 그렇지만 집을 가능한 한 원활하게 그리고 쉽게 짓기 위해 할 수 있는 일들이 몇 가지 있다. 미래의 주택 소유주가 해야 할 첫 번째 일은 예산을 짜고 정확히 얼마만큼의 돈을 쓸 수 있는지 결정하는 것이다. 그 후에는 집을 지을 부지를 선택해야 한다. 물론 이것도 예산안에 고려되어야 한다. 일단 부지를 구매했으면 건축가와 인부들을 뽑아야 한다. 다음으로 건축가가 틀림없이 적어도 두세 개의 건물 디자인을 제출할 테니 다음 계획을 선택할 필요가 있다. 마지막으로 건축회사와 협상해서 계약서를 작성해야 한다. 일단 협상이 되면 새집 건축을 시작할 수 있다.

16 대화를 듣고, 내용과 일치하는 것을 고르시오.

① The man wants salt on his popcorn.
② The woman forgot to buy the tickets online.
③ The couple wants to see the new action movie.
✓④ The line moved faster when a new counter opened.
⑤ The couple gave up on seeing the movie they wanted

① 남자는 소금을 넣은 팝콘을 원한다.
② 여자는 인터넷으로 표를 구입하는 것을 잊었다.
③ 두 사람은 신작 액션 영화를 보고 싶어 한다.
④ 새 매표소가 열리자 줄이 더 빠르게 움직였다.
⑤ 두 사람은 보고 싶어 했던 영화 관람을 포기했다.

▶ What a disaster. 끔직한 일이야.   book 예약하다
be sold out 매진되다   in a couple of minutes 잠시
뒤에

W　What a disaster. Look at the line for tickets. It looks like we're going to have to wait for a long time before we get to the front.

M　I'm sorry that I didn't book the tickets online like you asked me to. We could have been sitting down already.

W　I don't think we'll even get in. The tickets will be sold out by the time we get to the ticket counter.

M　Don't worry. I don't think anyone wants to see the movie we're going to watch. Most people are here to see the new action movie that opened today.

W　You may be right about that. Look over there. They've opened a new counter, so now we're moving much more quickly.

M　I've got an idea. I'll stand in line while you go get our drinks. After all, we don't want to walk in after the movie starts.

W　Okay. Would you like me to get you some popcorn?

M　I'd really appreciate it, but make sure there's no salt on the popcorn, please. Oh, and I want a diet soda, too.

W　No problem. I'll meet you in a couple of minutes.

여　끔찍하다. 표 사려고 선 줄을 봐. 한참을 기다려야 앞쪽으로 갈 수 있을 것 같은데.

남　네 말대로 인터넷으로 표를 예약하지 않아서 미안해. 벌써 자리에 앉아 있을 수도 있었는데.

여　심지어 들어갈 수 있을지도 의심스러워. 우리가 매표소까지 갈 때 쯤엔 표가 매진될 거야.

남　걱정 마. 우리가 보려는 영화를 보고 싶어하는 사람들은 없을 것 같아. 대부분의 사람들은 오늘 개봉한 액션영화를 보러 온 거야.

여　네 말이 맞을지도 몰라. 저기 봐봐. 매표소를 새로 열었네. 훨씬 더 빨리 줄이 움직이겠다.

남　좋은 생각이 떠올랐어. 네가 가서 음료수를 살 동안 내가 줄 서 있을게. 어차피 영화가 시작한 후에 걸어 들어가고 싶지는 않아.

여　좋아. 팝콘도 사다 줄까?

남　그럼 고맙지. 근데 소금 안 넣은 걸로 부탁해. 아, 그리고 다이어트 콜라도.

여　문제없어. 이따가 보자.

17 다음을 듣고, 다음 문장의 빈칸에 어울리지 <u>않는</u> 것을 고르시오.

When people are outside in the summer, they need to ________________________.

① drink water every couple of hours
✓ keep their bodies dehydrated
③ try to keep from sweating too much
④ wear long-sleeved clothes and hats
⑤ protect themselves from the sun

사람들이 여름에 야외에 있을 때는 ________________ 필요가 있다.

① 몇 시간마다 물을 마실
② 탈수 상태를 유지할
③ 땀을 지나치게 흘리는 것을 피해야 할
④ 긴팔 옷과 모자를 착용할
⑤ 태양으로부터 자신들을 보호할

▶ outdoors 야외에서 precaution 주의사항 suffer from …로 고생하다 heatstroke 일사병 heat-related 더위와 관련된 hydrate 수분을 유지하다 sweat 땀을 흘리다 dehydrate 탈수되다 blaze 타오르다 sunscreen 자외선 차단제 exposure 노출

W Now that summer is beginning, people are going to be spending lots of time outdoors. Unfortunately, most people don't take all the precautions they should so wind up suffering from heatstroke or developing other heat-related problems. In order to remain in perfect health, people should remember to do a few important things. First, and most importantly, people need to keep their bodies hydrated. So long as they are outside in the sun, they should drink lots of water. Even when they're not thirsty, they still need water, especially if they're sweating a lot. Without water, the body will dehydrate quickly and suffer numerous problems. Additionally, people shouldn't stay in the sun for too long. Remaining under the blazing sun can cause people to suffer from heatstroke. Finally, if people have to be in the sun for any length of time, they should wear sunscreen and protect themselves with the proper clothes. They should wear light clothes, not dark ones, and protect their heads from too much exposure to the sun.

여 이제 여름이 시작되면 사람들은 많은 시간을 야외에서 보낼 것이다. 안타깝게도 대부분의 사람들은 주의사항을 지키지 않아서 일사병에 걸리거나 다른 더위와 관련된 질병에 걸린다. 완벽한 건강을 유지하기 위해 사람들은 몇 가지 중요한 사항을 기억해야 한다. 먼저, 가장 중요한 것으로, 몸에 수분을 유지할 필요가 있다. 햇빛을 받으며 밖에 오래 있을 때는 물을 많이 마셔야 한다. 목이 마르지 않을 때에도 물이 필요한데, 특히 땀을 많이 흘릴 때는 그러하다. 물을 안 마시면 금방 탈수가 되어 여러 가지 문제가 생길 것이다. 또한 너무 오랫동안 햇빛을 받으면 안 된다. 불타는 태양 아래 있으면 일사병에 걸릴 수가 있다. 마지막으로 얼마 동안이든 햇빛을 받아야 될 때에는 자외선 차단제를 바르고 적절한 옷으로 보호해 주어야 한다. 어두운 색이 아닌 밝은 색의 옷을 입어야 하며 머리도 햇빛에 너무 많이 노출되지 않도록 보호해야 한다.

---

18 대화를 듣고, 여자의 마지막 말에 대한 남자의 응답으로 알맞은 것을 고르시오.

M: ________________________

① No, I already have a copy of the book.
② I think that I'll pass on the offer.
✓ Yes, I'd love to talk to that person.
④ Yes, it is a really interesting book.
⑤ I'm pretty sure he wants too much for it.

① 아니, 난 이미 그 책이 한 권 있어.
② 그 제안은 그냥 무시할까봐.
③ 응, 그 사람과 꼭 이야기하고 싶어.
④ 응, 그건 정말로 재미있는 책이야.
⑤ 분명 그 사람은 높은 가격을 원할 거야.

▶ used bookstore 헌책방 browse …을 훑어보다 overhear 엿듣다 be willing to 기꺼이 …하다 price 가격

W Eric, you'll never guess what I found today.

M I give up. Go ahead and tell me.

W Well, I know you've been looking all over for that book on early American history. You know what I'm talking about, right? It's the one which was printed about a hundred years ago.

M Sure, that's the book by Roger Jackson. I know what you're talking about… Wait a second. Don't tell me you actually found a copy of it. You didn't, did you?

W Well… I didn't exactly find a copy, but I got the next best thing.

M Okay, hurry up and tell me about it. You know I've been dying to get my hands on a copy of that book.

W All right, let me see. I was at the local used bookstore just browsing around for anything interesting. Well, for some reason, I decided to ask the clerk if they had the Jackson book.

M Did they?

W No, they didn't. But someone overheard me talking to the clerk, and he mentioned that he had two copies of that book in his collection and would be willing to part with one if the price was right. So, are you interested in his number?

M ________________________.

여 에릭, 오늘 내가 뭘 발견했는지 모르지?

남 몰라. 어서 말해.

여 네가 초기 미국역사에 관한 책을 찾느라고 다 뒤져본 거 알거든. 내가 무슨 얘기하는지 알지? 한 백년 전에 인쇄된 책 말이야.

남 물론이지, 로저 잭슨이 지은 책이잖아. 무슨 말 하는지 알아… 잠깐만. 설마 그 책을 찾았다고 얘기하는 건 아니지, 찾았어?

여 음… 정확히 말하면 그 책을 찾은 건 아니고 그 다음으로 좋은 걸 찾았어.

남 좋아, 어서 말해 봐. 그 책을 손에 넣고 싶어서 죽을 것 같았던 거 알지?

여 좋아, 가만 있자. 뭐 좀 재미있는 게 있나 보려고 우리 동네 헌책방에 갔었거든. 근데 웬일인지 점원한테 그 책이 있는지 물어보기로 했어.

남 있다고 하든?

여 아니, 없대. 근데 어떤 사람이 내가 점원이랑 하는 얘기를 듣고는 자기가 수집한 것 중에 그 책이 두 권 있다는 거야. 그래서 가격만 맞으면 기꺼이 한 개를 주겠다는 거야. 자, 전화번호 알려 줄까?

남 ________________________

<table>
<tr><th>문제와 정답</th><th>스크립트</th><th>해석</th></tr>
</table>

19 다음을 듣고, 화자의 의견에 동의하는 진술을 고르시오.

① Sungmin: I haven't had much time to prepare for my interview.

✓ Yujin: I had someone look over my application for errors.

③ Hyowon: I told my interviewer about the problems his company has.

④ Jaegyu: I didn't bother dressing up for my interview.

⑤ Soohee: I brought an old copy of my resume to give to the interviewer.

① 성민: 난 면접을 준비할 시간이 별로 없었어.
② 유진: 난 다른 사람이 내 지원서에 실수가 있는지 검토해 보게 했어.
③ 효원: 나는 면접관에게 그의 회사가 가진 문제점들에 대해 얘기했어.
④ 재규: 난 면접을 위해 귀찮게 옷을 잘 차려 입지 않았어.
⑤ 수희: 난 면접관에게 주기 위해 나의 옛날 이력서 한 부를 가져 왔어.

▶ first impression 첫인상 employer 고용인 qualification 자격, 능력 sufficiently 충분히 get hired 고용되다 common sense 상식 interviewee 면접 받는 사람 formally 격식을 갖춰 resume 이력서 cover letter 자기소개서 proofread 교정을 보다 potential 잠재적인, 미래의 courteous 정중한 accomplishment 성과물 arrogant 거만한

M When going to a job interview, you must be careful to make a good first impression with the people who may eventually become your employers. Too many people, even those with excellent qualifications, fail to prepare sufficiently for their interviews and therefore don't get hired. All it takes is a little bit of common sense to avoid making these foolish mistakes. Interviewees should make sure they are dressed both formally and neatly. Wearing blue jeans and a T-shirt to an interview is a sure way not to get hired. Additionally, resumes and cover letters should be proofread so that they have zero mistakes. Many potential employers will throw out any job applications that are poorly written or which have mistakes in them. Interviewees should also be kind, courteous, and well-spoken. They should take every opportunity to talk about their accomplishments during the interview, yet they should also be careful not to come across as arrogant. By acting in this manner, the chances of a person getting hired will increase dramatically.

남 면접을 보러 갈 때는 나중에 상사가 될지도 모르는 사람들에게 좋은 첫인상을 주기 위해 주의해야 한다. 너무나 많은 사람들이, 심지어 훌륭한 자격조건을 갖추고 있는 사람들도 면접을 충분히 준비하지 않아서 떨어지곤 한다. 필요한 것은 어리석은 실수를 피하기 위한 다음과 같은 약간의 상식뿐이다. 면접 받는 사람은 깔끔하게 정장을 입어야 한다. 청바지와 티셔츠를 입는 것은 면접에 떨어지는 확실한 방법이다. 또한 이력서와 자기소개서는 실수가 없도록 다시 한번 교정을 봐야 한다. 많은 미래의 고용인들은 대충 작성되었거나 실수가 있는 지원서는 던져 버린다. 면접 받는 사람은 또한 친절하고 정중하게 말을 잘해야 한다. 면접 중 자신들의 성과에 대해 기회가 있을 때마다 말해야 하지만 거만하다는 인상을 주지 않도록 조심해야 한다. 이렇게 행동함으로써 뽑힐 가능성은 급격히 높아질 것이다.

---

20 대화를 듣고, 내용과 일치하는 것을 고르시오.

① It is very difficult to be a vegetarian.

✓ The man has found healthy alternatives to meat.

③ The man avoided meat to improve his health.

④ The people are going to an Italian vegetarian restaurant.

⑤ The woman will become a vegetarian.

① 채식주의자가 되는 것은 무척 어렵다.
② 남자는 고기를 대체할 건강식을 찾았다.
③ 남자는 건강을 증진시키기 위해 고기를 피했다.
④ 두 사람은 이탈리안 채식주의 레스토랑에 갈 예정이다.
⑤ 여자는 채식주의자가 될 것이다.

▶ as a way of …의 방법으로 vegetarian 채식주의자 meat 육류 soy food 콩으로 만든 음식 in better shape 더 건강한 as a matter of fact 사실

W Thanks for your help on that project. I couldn't have done it without you.

M It was my pleasure, so don't worry about it.

W I'd like to buy you lunch at that new Italian place that just opened as a way of thanking you.

M That sounds nice, but you know that I'm a vegetarian, right?

W I didn't know that. What made you decide to give up meat?

M I just stopped enjoying it and then decided that I should stop eating it altogether.

W So what do you eat instead?

M I eat eggs and drink milk, or I have nuts and soy foods. Being a vegetarian is not as difficult as people think it must be. As a matter of fact, we actually have many choices.

W It sounds as if your diet is very healthy as well.

M It is. And my doctor says that I'm in much better shape ever since I stopped eating meat.

W Well, I'll find a restaurant that serves the kind of food you'd like to eat, and then we'll go there.

여 프로젝트 도와줘서 고마워. 네가 없었다면 할 수 없었을 거야.

남 고맙긴, 너무 신경 쓰지 마.

여 감사의 마음으로 얼마 전에 문을 연 이탈리아 레스토랑에서 점심을 사고 싶어.

남 그거 좋은데, 근데 나 채식주의자인 거 알지?

여 몰랐어. 왜 고기를 안 먹겠다고 결심한 거니?

남 그냥 고기를 즐겨먹는 걸 그만두었다가 그 다음에 완전히 안 먹기로 결심했어.

여 그럼 대신에 뭘 먹는데?

남 계란과 우유를 먹어. 아니면 땅콩이나 콩으로 만든 음식. 채식을 하는 것은 사람들이 생각하는 것처럼 어렵지는 않아. 사실은 먹을 게 많아.

여 네가 먹는 것도 건강식인 것 같다.

남 맞아. 의사가 고기를 안 먹고 나서 몸이 훨씬 더 건강해졌다고 하더라.

여 음, 네가 먹고 싶어하는 종류의 음식을 파는 식당을 찾아볼게. 찾으면 거기 가자.

<table>
<tr><th>문제와 정답</th><th>스크립트</th><th>해석</th></tr>
<tr>
<td>

21 대화를 듣고, 두 사람이 주로 무엇에 대해 이야기하고 있는지 고르시오.

① How hard it is to make business contacts
② How difficult learning to play golf is
☑ How important golf is in business
④ How they should meet to play golf
⑤ How to find a nice club to play golf at

① 사업적 만남을 갖는 것이 얼마나 어려운 일인가
② 골프를 배우는 것이 얼마나 어려운가
③ 사업에서 골프가 얼마나 중요한가
④ 골프를 치기 위해 두 사람이 어떻게 만날 것인가
⑤ 골프를 칠 멋진 클럽을 어떻게 찾을 것인가

▶ beginner 초보자 get tired of …에 싫증나다 contact (사업적으로) 교섭하는 사람 businesspeople 사업가들

</td>
<td>

W Do you still play golf these days?

M Of course I do. I love to play that game. Why do you ask?

W My husband is learning to play and is looking for a golf partner for this weekend.

M Tell him to give me a call. I'd love to play a game or two with him. How good is he?

W I don't think he's very good yet since he's only been playing for about two months.

M If he's just a beginner, then it's possible that I could teach him a few things.

W He'd love that and really appreciate it. It's so important to him to play well because most of his business contacts play golf. He thinks it's a good way to get closer to some of the people he does business with.

M He's absolutely right. That's one of the reasons why I started playing. I got tired of having to buy people dinner all the time. Now I just invite my contacts to play golf instead. Most businesspeople enjoy playing the game after all.

W My husband will probably give you a call this evening. I hope you both have a great time together.

</td>
<td>

여 요즘에도 계속 골프 하시나요?

남 물론 하지요. 골프를 너무 좋아하거든요. 왜 물으시죠?

여 남편이 배우고 있는데 이번 주말에 같이 칠 사람을 찾고 있어요.

남 저한테 전화하라고 말해 주세요. 기꺼이 한 게임 하죠. 남편은 얼마나 잘하시죠?

여 골프를 한 지 두 달밖에 안 됐기 때문에 잘하는 것 같지는 않아요.

남 남편이 초보자라면 몇 가지 가르쳐 드릴 수도 있습니다.

여 아주 좋아하고 정말 감사드릴 거예요. 골프를 잘 치는 게 너무나 중요해요. 왜냐면 대부분의 사업상 만나는 지인들이 골프를 치거든요. 남편은 골프가 같이 사업을 하는 사람들과 더 가까워질 수 있는 좋은 방법이라고 생각해요.

남 남편 분 말이 맞습니다. 그래서 저도 골프를 시작했거든요. 사람들에게 항상 저녁을 사야 하는 것에 싫증이 났지요. 대신에 지금은 사업상 만나는 사람들에게 골프를 치자고 초대합니다. 대부분은 결국엔 골프를 치는 것을 즐기게 되죠.

여 아마도 오늘 저녁에 남편이 전화를 할 거예요. 같이 즐거운 시간 보내시길 바랍니다.

</td>
</tr>
<tr>
<td>

22 대화를 듣고, 총 몇 명이 식사를 할 것인지 고르시오.

① 6
☑ 5
③ 4
④ 3
⑤ 2

▶ have a reservation 예약을 하다 extra 추가의, 여분의 non-smoking area 금연석

</td>
<td>

W Good evening, sir. Do you have a reservation?

M Yes, I do.

W What is your name?

M My name is Brad Pitt.

W Let's see. Oh yes, you made a reservation for four people. Is that correct?

M Yes, that's correct. Will it be a problem if one extra person joins us?

W It shouldn't be too much of a problem. I'll tell your waiter to set an extra place at the table.

M Thank you.

W Your reservation is for the non-smoking area, isn't it?

M Yes, non-smoking please.

W Come this way, please. We have a table for you right next to the window.

M That's great. We can look out over the river while we eat.

W I hope you enjoy your evening.

</td>
<td>

여 안녕하세요, 손님. 예약을 하셨습니까?

남 네, 그렇습니다.

여 성함이 어떻게 되시죠?

남 브래드 피트입니다.

여 한번 볼까요. 오, 여기 있네요. 4인석을 예약하셨네요. 맞나요?

남 네, 맞아요. 그런데 한 사람이 더 와도 문제가 안 될까요?

여 큰 문제는 없을 겁니다. 웨이터에게 테이블에 한 자리를 더 만들라고 얘기하겠습니다.

남 고마워요.

여 금연석으로 예약하셨죠?

남 네, 금연석으로 부탁해요.

여 이쪽으로 오세요. 창가 바로 옆에 테이블을 준비했습니다.

남 멋지네요. 식사를 하면서 강을 볼 수 있겠어요.

여 좋은 저녁 되시기 바랍니다.

</td>
</tr>
</table>

문제와 정답	스크립트	해석

23 대화를 듣고, 남자가 무엇을 팩스로 받을지 고르시오.

① An invitation to a party
② An invitation to the party for his partner
③ A recipe for garlic bread
✓ Directions to the woman's new house
⑤ A list of things to bring to the party

① 파티 초대장
② 파트너를 위한 파티 초대장
③ 마늘빵 조리법
④ 여자의 새로운 집으로 가는 길 안내
⑤ 파티에 가져갈 것들의 목록

▶ invitation 초대장 throw a party 파티를 열다
end up 마침내는 …하게 되다 hopelessly 가망 없이,
절망적으로 add 추가하다 garlic 마늘

스크립트

M Hi, how are you doing today?

W I'm doing well today. Thank you for asking.

M I just received an invitation to your party next weekend. I was so surprised.

W I really hope that you can come. I haven't thrown a birthday party in about three years.

M So it's next Saturday at your house, right?

W That's right. Don't forget that I'm not living at the same address as before.

M Oh, yes. Do you think I can call you to learn the way to your house on the day before the party? I always end up driving around in places I don't know and then get hopelessly lost.

W I'll draw a map and fax it over to you, so you shouldn't have any problems.

M That's even better.

W So you're definitely going to come, right? Shall I add you to my list?

M Please do that. But what can I bring to the party?

W You could bring some of that delicious garlic bread that you make.

M Great.

해석

남 안녕, 오늘 어때?

여 잘 지내고 있어. 물어봐 줘서 고마워.

남 방금 다음 주말에 있을 네 파티의 초대장을 받았어. 깜짝 놀랐어.

여 네가 올 수 있으면 정말 좋겠다. 거의 3년 동안 제대로 된 생일파티를 열지 않았거든.

남 다음 주 토요일 너의 집에서지, 맞니?

여 맞아. 전과 같은 주소에 살고 있지 않다는 거 잊지 마.

남 아, 그래. 파티 전에 네 집으로 가는 도중에 길을 물어보려 전화해도 될까? 난 항상 모르는 곳을 운전하다가 완전히 길을 잃어버리곤 해서 말이야.

여 지도를 그려서 팩스로 보낼게. 아무 문제 없도록 말이야.

남 그게 훨씬 낫겠다.

여 그럼 넌 확실히 오는 거지? 내 목록에 널 넣어도 될까?

남 그렇게 해줘. 근데 파티에 뭘 가져 가지?

여 네가 만든 그 맛있는 마늘빵 좀 가져 오면 되겠다.

남 좋아.

---

24 대화를 듣고, 남자의 직업을 고르시오.

✓ He is a salesperson.
② He works at an advertising company.
③ He works at a marketing company.
④ He is an office worker.
⑤ He is the manager of a clothing store.

① 그는 판매원이다.
② 그는 광고 회사에서 일한다.
③ 그는 마케팅 회사에서 일한다.
④ 그는 사무직이다.
⑤ 그는 옷가게의 매니저이다.

▶ have a sale 세일을 하다 drop (가격의) 하락
show up 나타나다 garment 의상 stop by 들르다
convince 납득시키다, 확신시키다

스크립트

M We're having a big sale tomorrow. All dresses and shoes will be on sale for 25% off.

W Wow! That's a very big drop in prices.

M Our doors open at 7:30 a.m., and I imagine that we'll be very busy all day long.

W I hate the crowds that show up at these sales.

M We hate them, too. Most of us will come to work at about 7 a.m. and wind up leaving at about 10 p.m. tomorrow.

W That's too bad. How long will the sale continue?

M It's only going to last one day.

W What a pity. I don't know if I'll have a chance to come and look at everything. I'm going to be busy at the office.

M All the best garments will probably sell out early in the morning. Why don't you stop by the store before going to work?

W I don't know if I'll have enough time. I'll see.

M The next time we'll have another big sale will be next year. Don't miss this one.

W Now I see why you do such good work at your job. You've convinced me to show up.

M Excellent.

해석

남 내일 엄청나게 세일을 할 거예요. 드레스와 신발 모두 25% 할인해서 판매합니다.

여 와! 엄청난 가격인하네요.

남 아침 7시 반에 개점합니다. 그리고 하루 종일 굉장히 바쁠 거예요.

여 이런 할인판매를 할 때 오는 엄청난 사람들이 난 싫어요.

남 저희들도 싫어요. 내일 저희들 대부분은 아침 7시쯤에 출근해서 저녁 10시쯤에 퇴근할 거예요.

여 안 됐군요. 할인판매가 얼마 동안 계속되나요?

남 하루 동안만이요.

여 그것 참 유감이네요. 와서 둘러볼 기회가 있을지 모르겠어요. 회사에서 바쁠 것 같아서요.

남 좋은 옷들은 틀림없이 아침 일찍 매진될 거예요. 회사 가기 전에 잠깐 가게에 들리는 건 어때요?

여 시간이 충분할지 모르겠어요. 두고 보죠.

남 다음에 우리가 또다시 세일을 할 때는 내년이 될 거예요. 이번 기회 놓치지 마세요.

여 왜 일을 그렇게 잘하시는지 이제 알 것 같아요. 제가 오도록 설득시키셨네요.

남 아주 좋네요.

25 다음을 듣고, 화자의 요지를 가장 잘 나타낸 것을 고르시오.

① Homeschooling should not be allowed according to the law.
✓ Homeschooled students perform better than public school students.
③ While homeschooling is effective, not every student should try it.
④ Virtually every homeschooled student gets accepted to prestigious universities.
⑤ Public schools are too restrictive, so homeschooling is a better option.

① 홈스쿨링은 법으로 금지되어야 한다.
② 홈스쿨링을 한 학생들은 공립학교 학생들보다 우수하다.
③ 홈스쿨링이 효과적이기는 하지만, 모든 학생들이 해서는 안 된다.
④ 명백하게 모든 홈스쿨링을 한 학생들이 일류 대학에 입학한다.
⑤ 공립학교는 너무 제약이 많으므로 홈스쿨링이 더 좋은 선택이다.

▶ homeschooling 홈스쿨링 be referred to …로 불리다 in comparison to …와 비교해서 on average 평균적으로 spelling bee 철자 맞추기 대회 educate 교육 시키다 prefer to …하는 것을 선호하다 religion 종교 influence 영향 bullying 약자 피롭히기, 따돌림 undoubtedly 의심의 여지 없이

W A popular trend among American parents is for them not to send their children to regular schools but to have them study at home. This is referred to as homeschooling. While it may appear unusual, homeschoolers often do very well in comparison to students at regular schools. For example, on average, they score better on standardized tests, win more contests like spelling bees, and get into higher ranking schools more often than students attending public schools. Parents homeschool their children for several reasons. Some feel that public schools don't educate their children well enough, so they prefer to do it themselves. Others like teaching their children subjects, like religion, for example, that aren't covered in public schools. And others feel that public schools are bad influences on their children with regards to bullying and other problems. Whatever the case, many homeschooled students are highly motivated and, as it turns out, extremely well-educated upon finishing their high school curriculum. Undoubtedly, more students will be choosing the homeschooling option in the future.

여 미국의 학부모들에게 요즘 유행하고 있는 경향은 아이들을 학교에 보내지 않고 집에서 공부하게 하는 것이다. 이것을 홈스쿨링이라고 부른다. 이것은 색다르게 보일 수도 있지만 집에서 공부하는 아이들이 학교에서 공부하는 학생들에 비해 공부를 잘하는 경우가 많다. 예를 들면, 평균적으로 공립학교를 다닌 학생들보다 표준화된 시험에서 더 높은 점수를 얻고, 철자맞추기 대회 같은 많은 대회에서 우승을 하며 더 좋은 대학교에 입학한다. 학부모들은 여러 가지 이유로 자녀들을 집에서 교육시키는 것이다. 어떤 학부모들은 공립학교가 자녀들을 충분히 잘 가르치지 못한다고 생각해서 직접 교육을 하는 것을 선호한다. 또 어떤 학부모들은 자녀들에게, 예를 들면, 종교와 같은 공립학교에서 다루지 않는 과목들을 가르치는 것을 좋아한다. 또 어떤 학부모들은 공립학교가 집단 따돌림과 다른 문제들과 관련해서 자녀들에게 나쁜 영향을 미친다고 생각한다. 어떤 경우든 간에 많은 집에서 교육을 받은 학생들이 동기부여가 잘 되어 있고 결과적으로 고등학교 교과과정을 끝내는 데 있어서도 매우 교육을 잘 받게 된다. 의심할 여지 없이, 앞으로는 더 많은 학생들이 홈스쿨링을 선택할 것이다.

---

26 대화를 듣고, 다음 공지사항 중 잘못된 부분을 고르시오.

Restaurant

Qualifications: ⓐ energetic and outgoing person
ⓑ Previous experience is essential.
When: ⓒ on Wednesday, 7 August from 8:00 a.m. to 6:00 p.m.
Where: ⓓ at Seoul City Restaurant, Gangnam
Open positions: ⓔ 16

레스토랑

자격요건: ⓐ 활기차고 사교적인 사람
ⓑ 경력이 필수적임
일시: ⓒ 8월 7일 수요일 오전 8시부터 오후 6시까지
장소: ⓓ 강남의 서울 씨티 레스토랑
채용 인원: ⓔ 16인

① ⓐ ② ⓑ  ✓ ⓒ ④ ⓓ ⑤ ⓔ 

▶ dedicated 헌신적인 professional 전문가 turnover 회전율 mature 성숙한 application 지원서 qualification 자격 요건

M The biggest and busiest restaurant in Seoul is seeking rising stars to join its team of dedicated professionals. If you have experience in restaurants with a high turnover of customers and are looking for a challenge, we would like to meet you. We are looking for mature, neatly groomed, and energetic people. An outgoing personality is a must, and you should get along well with people. Previous experience in the restaurant business is essential. If these characteristics describe you, then submit an application as soon as you can. If you do not meet these qualifications, then your enquiry or application will not be considered. We will be holding interviews on Tuesday, August 7, from 8:00 a.m. to 6:00 p.m. at Seoul City Restaurant. The location of our restaurant is Gangnam. Please call us for an appointment. We only have sixteen positions to fill.

남 서울에서 가장 크고 가장 손님이 많은 식당에서 헌신적인 전문가들로 구성된 팀에 합류할 차세대 주자를 찾고 있습니다. 손님 회전율이 높은 식당에서 일한 경험이 있거나 도전이 될 만한 일을 찾고 있다면 당신을 만나고 싶습니다. 저희는 성숙하고 용모단정하며 활력이 넘치는 사람들을 찾고 있습니다. 외향적인 성격은 필수이고 다른 사람들과 잘 어울릴 줄 알아야 합니다. 기존 요식업 분야에서의 경험이 아주 중요합니다. 이러한 특징들을 갖고 계시다면 가능한 한 빨리 지원서를 제출해 주세요. 이러한 자격조건들을 갖추고 있지 않다면 여러분의 문의사항이나 지원서는 검토되지 않을 것입니다. 면접은 8월 7일 화요일, 아침 8시부터 저녁 6시까지 서울 씨티 레스토랑에서 있을 예정입니다. 저희 식당의 위치는 강남에 있습니다. 전화해서 약속시간을 잡아 주세요. 채용중인 자리는 16개뿐입니다.

27 대화를 듣고, 대화의 내용과 물건 위치가 일치하지 않는 것을 고르시오.

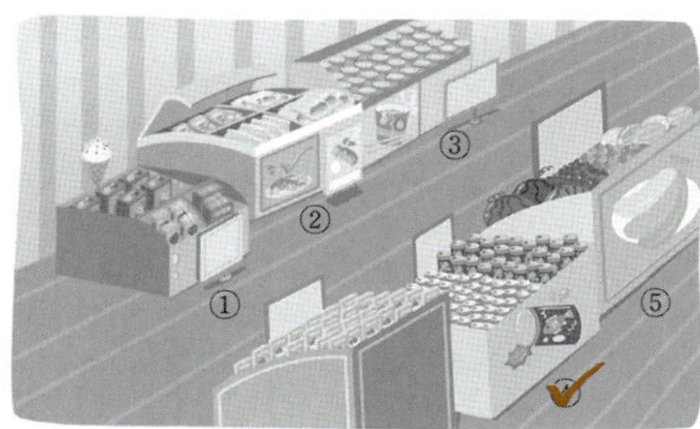

▶ frozen foods 냉동 식품 purchase 구입하다
canned goods 통조림 류 spice 양념 mushroom
버섯 produce 농산물, 천연 산물 assist 돕다,
지원하다 vermicelli 베르미첼리(스파게티보다 가는
굵기의 파스타)

M Excuse me, but could you let me know where your pasta section is?

W It's right over there by the frozen goods.

M Okay, and where are the sauces? I need to purchase some tomato sauce, too.

W You can find that in the canned goods section, which is next to the pasta section.

M Well, thanks. Oh, by the way, do you sell spices?

W Sure, they're all over here.

M I need to get some oregano and basil.

W Here they are. Will you be needing anything else?

M Well, I guess I could use some vegetables. Let's see… I need mushrooms, peppers, and onions. And that should be everything I need.

W Sir, you can find the vegetables in our produce section. Someone there will be able to assist you.

M Oh, there is one last thing. Do you happen to sell fedelini?

W I've never heard of it. It sounds like it's a type of pasta.

M Yes, it is. It's a lot like vermicelli only thicker.

W You could check in the pasta section, sir, but I can't guarantee you'll find it.

M Thanks so much.

남 실례합니다만, 파스타 섹션이 어디 있는지 알려 주시겠습니까?

여 바로 저기 냉동식품 옆에 있어요.

남 그렇군요, 소스류는 어디 있죠? 토마토소스를 좀 사야 하는데요.

여 통조림류 파는 데에 있을 거예요. 파스타 섹션 옆에요.

남 음, 고마워요. 아, 그런데 양념도 파나요?

여 물론이죠, 이쪽에 다 있어요.

남 오레가노 오일과 바질이 필요해요.

여 여기 있습니다. 다른 것 뭐 필요한 것 없으신가요?

남 음, 야채를 좀 샀으면 하네요. 어디 보자… 버섯, 고추, 양파가 필요해요. 그럼 다 산 거예요.

여 손님, 야채는 농산물 파는 곳에 있습니다. 가면 점원이 도와드릴 겁니다.

남 아, 마지막으로 한 가지 더요. 혹시 페델리니도 파나요?

여 처음 듣는 건데요. 파스타 같은 건가요?

남 네, 맞아요. 베르미첼리 정도 굵기에요.

여 파스타 파는 곳에 가보세요, 손님, 꼭 찾으신다는 보장은 없지만요.

남 정말 고맙습니다.

---

28 Why must the woman remind the man about the meeting after work?

① He does not have an assistant.
② He does not know that the flight has been delayed.
✔③ He forgot about the last meeting.
④ He has too few staff members.
⑤ He did not receive an email about it.

왜 여자는 남자에게 퇴근 후의 회의에 대해 알려 주어야 했는가?

① 그는 조수가 없다.
② 그는 비행기가 연착되었다는 것을 모른다.
③ 그는 지난번 회의를 잊었다.
④ 그에게는 직원이 너무 적다.
⑤ 그는 그것에 관한 이메일을 받지 못했다.

▶ interrupt 방해하다 reminder 상기시키는 것
employee 직원, 피고용인 client 고객 flight 항공편
be delayed 연착되다

W I'm sorry to interrupt you right now, but I have a message for you.

M What's wrong? Is there something I need to fix right now?

W It's not bad news. I'm just supposed to give you this reminder about the meeting after work tonight.

M Oh, yes. I'd completely forgotten about tonight's meeting.

W I knew you were going to do that since you didn't remember to go to the last meeting as well.

M With all the extra work I have right now, it's not surprising that I can't remember to do everything.

W You've still got too few staff members in your office, don't you?

M Yes, but I have just hired two new employees who will start working for me next week.

W That's a relief. Maybe we'll be able to get more work done after they get here.

M Yes, and then you won't have to remind me about all of the important things any more.

W So the meeting tonight is at 7 p.m.

M Why are we having it so late after work?

W We are meeting the Japanese clients, but their flight has been delayed by a couple of hours.

여 방해해서 죄송합니다만 전달할 내용이 있어요.

남 뭐가 문제죠? 지금 당장 고쳐야 할 것이라도 있습니까?

여 나쁜 소식 아니에요. 단지 오늘밤 일 끝나고 있을 회의에 대해 상기시켜 드리려고요.

남 아, 네. 오늘밤 회의에 대해서는 완전히 잊고 있었네요.

여 그럴 줄 알았어요. 지난번 회의에 가는 것도 깜빡 했었잖아요.

남 지금 하고 있는 이 늘어난 일거리들을 보면 할 일을 다 기억 못하는 것도 놀라운 일은 아니죠.

여 사무실에 아직도 직원이 너무 적죠?

남 네, 그런데 방금 다음 주에 저를 위해 일을 시작할 새 직원을 두 명 고용했어요.

여 다행이네요. 아마 새 직원이 오면 일을 더 많이 끝낼 수 있을 거예요.

남 네, 그러면 당신이 나에게 더 이상 온갖 중요한 일들을 상기시켜줄 필요도 없죠.

여 오늘밤 회의는 저녁 7시에 있습니다.

남 회의를 왜 그렇게 일 끝나고 늦게 하죠?

여 일본인 고객을 만날 건데 비행기가 두세 시간 연착되었어요.

29 Why is blushing similar to stuttering in a social situation?

① They are both due to shyness. ✓

② They are both due to a lack of confidence.

③ It is possible to hide these two things.

④ People need to control them.

⑤ It will not stop once it starts.

얼굴이 붉어지는 것은 사람들 앞에서 말을 더듬는 것과 왜 비슷한가?

① 둘 다 수줍음 때문이다.

② 둘 다 자신감 부족 때문이다.

③ 이 두 가지를 숨기기가 가능하다.

④ 사람들은 그것을 조절해야 한다.

⑤ 한 번 시작하면 멈출 수 없다.

▶ invitation 초대 What a relief. 다행이다, 안심이다 stutter 말을 더듬다 get rid of 없애다, 제거하다 confident 확신에 찬, 자신만만한 shyness 수줍음, 숫기 없음 blush 얼굴이 붉어지다

M Hello, it's so good to see you today.

W Hi, I'm so glad that you made it here tonight.

M Thanks for the invitation.

W Why don't you come in to the dining room? A few other people have already arrived.

M It looks as if I know almost everyone here. What a relief. You know I'm really shy, so when I meet new people, I often start stuttering. It's a habit I had as a child, and I haven't managed to get rid of it.

W I had no idea that you stuttered. You're always so confident when we're in the office.

M It's not caused by a lack of confidence. It's because of my shyness. I worry that I'll start stuttering and that people will think I'm strange.

W When I was a teenager, I was always very shy. I used to blush whenever a stranger said something to me. It's like stuttering in a way. It's something you can't hide. But I've since learned to control my blushing, so now I'm fine.

M That's lucky for you. Unfortunately, I still haven't managed to control my stuttering.

남 안녕, 오늘 보니까 너무 좋다.

여 안녕, 오늘밤 여기 와 주어서 너무 반가워.

남 초대해 줘서 고마워.

여 어서 식당으로 와. 다른 사람 몇 명은 벌써 도착했어.

남 여기 있는 사람들 거의 다 알 것 같아. 다행이다. 알다시피 난 정말 수줍음이 많아서 처음 보는 사람을 만나면 말을 더듬기 시작하지. 어릴 때 갖고 있던 버릇인데 아직도 없애지를 못했어.

여 네가 말을 더듬었다니 전혀 몰랐어. 회사에 있을 때 넌 항상 자신감에 차 있었잖니.

남 자신감 부족 때문이 아니야. 내 수줍음 때문이지. 말을 더듬기 시작해서 사람들이 날 이상하다고 생각할까봐 걱정이야.

여 10대 때는 나도 항상 수줍어했어. 낯선 사람이 나에게 무슨 말을 할 때마다 얼굴이 붉어지곤 했지. 어떤 면에서는 말을 더듬는 거랑 비슷해. 숨길 수가 없는 거야. 그렇지만 그 후로 얼굴이 붉어지는 것을 조절하는 법을 알게 돼서 지금은 안 그래.

남 운이 좋구나. 불행히도 난 여전히 말 더듬는 것을 조절할 수가 없어.

30 What will probably happen next?

① The man will receive a new order of fried rice.

② The man will start shouting at the waiter.

③ The man will speak to the manager and then leave. ✓

④ The man will sit down at a different table.

⑤ The man will rush back to work.

어떤 일이 벌어질 것인가?

① 남자는 새로 주문한 볶음밥을 받을 것이다.

② 남자는 웨이터에게 소리치기 시작할 것이다.

③ 남자는 매니저와 얘기한 후 떠날 것이다.

④ 남자는 다른 테이블에 앉을 것이다.

⑤ 남자는 급히 일로 복귀할 것이다.

▶ customer 손님, 고객 fried rice 볶음밥 order 주문 allergic 알레르기가 있는 calm down 마음을 가라 앉히다 chef 주방장 on the house (비용을) 식당에서 부담하는

M I'd like to see the manager, please.

W Could you hold on for a moment, please? He's busy with another customer at the moment.

M Tell him that there's an angry customer waiting to speak to him.

W Is there anything I can do to help you, sir?

M I'm so angry. I just found some seafood in my fried rice. And I don't eat seafood.

W I'm sorry. They must have mixed up your order.

M I usually don't mind getting the wrong order, and I don't get angry very easily. But I told the waiter that I'm allergic to seafood. I get really sick if I eat it, but he still managed to get my order wrong. I don't think he was listening to a word that I said.

W I can understand why you're angry. Why don't you take a seat and calm down? I'll make sure that the chef prepares a new order for you. And your meal will be on the house.

M I'm not staying here another minute. I want to see the manager, and then I'm leaving.

남 매니저를 만나고 싶습니다.

여 잠시만 기다려 주시겠어요? 매니저가 현재 다른 손님 때문에 바쁘셔서요.

남 화가 난 손님 하나가 매니저와 얘기하기를 기다리고 있다고 전해 주세요.

여 도와드릴 일이 있습니까, 손님?

남 너무 화가 나요. 방금 볶음밥에서 해산물을 발견했어요. 전 해산물을 안 먹거든요.

여 죄송합니다. 분명 다른 주문과 혼동했나 봅니다.

남 전 보통 주문한 게 잘못 나와도 신경 안 씁니다. 그리고 그렇게 쉽게 화를 내지도 않고요. 그렇지만 저는 해산물에 알레르기가 있다고 웨이터한테 말했거든요. 먹으면 정말 병이 납니다. 그런데도 그 웨이터는 제 주문을 잘못 받았어요. 그가 제가 한 말을 한 마디라도 제대로 듣고 있었던 것 같지 않군요.

여 왜 화가 나셨는지 이해합니다. 좀 앉아서 진정하시는 게 어떨까요? 요리사가 다시 요리를 준비하도록 하겠습니다. 그리고 비용은 저희 가게에서 부담하겠습니다.

남 더 이상 1분도 여기 있지 않을 거예요. 매니저를 만나고 싶고, 그런 다음 떠날 겁니다.

<table>
<tr><th>문제와 정답</th><th>스크립트</th><th>해석</th></tr>
</table>

31 〔모두 듣기〕 **How does the man probably respond to the woman?**

① Don't worry. I'll go to the restaurant alone.

② I'll bring you a sandwich from the restaurant.

✓ Okay, I'll call them and ask if they deliver.

④ I'm not hungry anymore.

⑤ I think their food is terrible anyway.

남자는 여자의 말에 어떻게 대답했을까?

① 걱정 마요. 내가 레스토랑에 혼자 갈게요.

② 레스토랑에서 샌드위치를 가져다 줄게요.

③ 알았어요. 내가 전화해서 배달해 주는지 물어 볼게요.

④ 난 더 이상 배가 안 고파요.

⑤ 그 집 음식은 어쨌든 끔찍하다고 생각해요.

▶ **take a break** 휴식을 취하다   **feel like -ing**
…하고 싶은 기분이 들다   **deliver** 배달하다   **at least**
적어도, 최소한   **statistics** 통계, 통계학

W Why don't we take a break for lunch right now? We've been working nonstop since we arrived here this morning.

M I agree. What do you feel like eating?

W I feel like having a toasted sandwich and a cup of strong coffee.

M That's not real food. It's just a snack. Let's go to the restaurant around the corner and get some proper food.

W I'd like that, but we don't have enough time to go out for a long lunch.

M The service at that restaurant is fast, so we'll be back in an hour.

W Maybe I'll try their spaghetti and tomato sauce with basil. Didn't you have that last time we went there together?

M I did. It was so delicious. In fact, I think that I might order the same thing again.

W Why don't we call and ask them to deliver our lunch to the office?

M I'd like that, but I don't think they deliver food.

W Let's try at least. We really need to finish these statistics before the end of the day.

M ___________

여 점심시간이니 잠깐 쉬는 게 어떻겠습니까? 오늘 아침에 출근한 이후로 한 번도 안 쉬고 일만 했잖아요.

남 동의해요. 뭐 드시고 싶으세요?

여 토스트에 구운 샌드위치랑 진한 커피 한잔을 마시고 싶네요.

남 그건 식사가 아니라 간식이잖아요. 길 모퉁이에 있는 식당에서 가서 제대로 된 음식을 먹죠.

여 그러고 싶지만 밖에 나가서 오랫동안 점심식사를 할 만한 시간이 없어요.

남 그 레스토랑은 음식이 빨리 나와서 한 시간 안에 돌아올 수 있을 거에요.

여 그럼 바질이 들어간 토마토소스를 곁들인 스파게티를 먹어야겠어요. 지난번에 같이 갔을 때 그걸 먹지 않았어요?

남 그랬죠. 너무 맛있었어요. 사실 이번에도 똑같은 것을 주문해서 먹을까요.

여 전화해서 배달이 되는지 물어 보는 것은 어떨까요?

남 그러고 싶지만 배달은 안 될 것 같아요.

여 최소한 시도는 해 봐요. 오늘 내로 이 통계 내는 것을 끝내야 되잖아요.

남 ___________

---

32 〔모두 듣기〕 **What is the reason the Great Mall is offering some special promotions?**

① to promote the mall

② to celebrate the tenth annual fundraiser for shopaholics

✓ to celebrate its tenth anniversary

④ to hold its year-end clearance sale

⑤ to offer free makeovers for mall patrons

그레이트몰이 특별 판촉행사를 제공하는 이유는 무엇인가?

① 매장을 홍보하기 위해

② 쇼핑광들을 위한 열 번째 연 모금행사를 축하하기 위해서

③ 10주년을 축하하기 위해

④ 연말 창고정리 세일을 열기 위해

⑤ 쇼핑몰 후원자들을 위해 무료 외모 변신 서비스를 제공하기 위해

▶ **celebrate** 기념하다   **anniversary** 기념일, 주기
promotion 판촉 행사   **shop up a storm** 한바탕
쇼핑을 하다   **pamper** 만족시키다   **makeover**
(외모의) 변신   **therapist** 치료사, 테라피스트
treatment 미안술

W The Great Mall is celebrating its tenth anniversary during the month of July. A series of special events are being organized to mark this special event. Most of the stores in the mall will run special promotions during July. Designer stores will be offering up to 70% off selected goods on July 12 starting at nine in the morning. And once you've shopped up a storm, the Face Store will pamper you with a free makeover. Sorry, guys, but this is an offer for ladies only. The best hairdressers, stylists, and beauty therapists will be on hand to provide facial treatments and hair care. The first fifty customers that day receive a 50% discount on a treatment and beauty package.

여 그레이트몰은 7월 한 달 동안 10주년 기념행사를 할 예정입니다. 일련의 특별 행사들이 이 특별한 날을 기념하기 위해 만들어지고 있습니다. 쇼핑몰 안에 있는 대부분의 가게들은 7월 중 특별 판촉행사를 할 계획입니다. 디자이너 가게들은 7월 12일 아침 9시부터 일부 품목에 대해 70%까지 할인행사를 할 것입니다. 그리고 일단 잔뜩 쇼핑을 하셨다면 페이스 스토어에서 무료 변신으로 여러분을 만족시켜 드릴 겁니다. 남자분들에게는 죄송하지만 이건 여성들에게만 해당되는 서비스입니다. 최고의 헤어디자이너, 스타일리스트, 그리고 치료사들이 미안술과 머리손질을 제공 해드리기 위해 대기하고 있습니다. 그날 제일 먼저 오시는 50분의 고객에게 미안술과 미용 패키지 상품을 50% 할인해 드리겠습니다.

33

[모두 듣기] **Why is it so easy for the women to trick people?**

① They dress the same.
② They have the same friends.
③ They have the same hairstyles.
✓ They are identical twins.
⑤ They like to have fun.

여자들이 사람들을 속이는 것이 그렇게 쉬운 이유는 무엇인가?

① 그들은 옷을 똑같이 입는다.
② 그들은 공통의 친구가 있다.
③ 그들은 헤어스타일이 같다.
④ 그들은 일란성 쌍둥이이다.
⑤ 그들은 장난치는 것을 좋아한다.

▶ twin 쌍둥이 identical 일란성의 tell apart …을 구분하다 confuse 혼동하다 difference 차이 fool …을 속이다, 놀리다 play tricks on …을 놀리다

M I saw you at the coffee shop last night, but you didn't even greet me. Why didn't you say hi to me?

W I wasn't at the coffee shop last night. I was here at home studying all night long.

M No, you weren't. I definitely saw you there.

W You must have seen my sister and thought she was me. We're twins, so people often get confused.

M I didn't know you had a twin. And you two are identical, aren't you?

W Yes, we are.

M And you even have the same hairstyles.

W But we don't dress the same, so that's one way to tell us apart.

M Do your parents ever confuse the two of you?

W They haven't done that in a long time. They can always tell the difference between us.

M What about your friends? It must be easy to fool some of them.

W Well, sometimes we play tricks on them. Last week, I went to the movies with her friends, and they didn't realize I had tricked them. It was a lot of fun.

남 어젯밤 커피숍에서 널 봤는데 나한테 인사도 안 하더라. 왜 인사 안 했니?

여 어젯밤에 커피숍 안 갔는데. 밤새 집에서 공부했어.

남 아냐. 분명히 너 봤거든.

여 내 여동생을 보고 나라고 생각한 것이 틀림없어. 우리는 쌍둥이야. 그래서 사람들이 많이 헷갈려 해.

남 쌍둥이 자매가 있는 건 몰랐네. 일란성 쌍둥이지?

여 그래, 맞아.

남 심지어 헤어스타일도 똑같아.

여 그렇지만 옷은 다르게 입어. 옷이 우리를 구별하는 하나의 방법이야.

남 부모님들은 헷갈려 하시지 않니?

여 옛날부터 그러지 않으셨어. 항상 우리 둘 사이의 차이점을 구별하시지.

남 친구들은 어때? 친구들을 속이기 쉬울 것 같은데.

여 음, 가끔은 장난을 치기도 해. 지난주에는 동생 친구들이랑 영화를 보러 갔어. 근데 내가 속이는 줄도 모르더라. 정말 재미있었어.

34

[모두 듣기] **What advice do you think the woman offers the man?**

① Don't put all your eggs in one basket.
② Don't believe everything you're told.
✓ Don't count your chickens before they're hatched.
④ Don't daydream too much.
⑤ Don't dream too big.

여자는 남자에게 어떤 충고를 줄 거라고 생각하는가?

① 모든 달걀을 바구니 하나에 담지 마.
② 들은 얘기를 모두 믿지 마.
③ 달걀이 부화하기 전에 닭을 세지 마.
④ 헛된 꿈을 꾸지 마.
⑤ 너무 큰 꿈을 갖지 마.

▶ promote 승진시키다 deserve …할 만 하다 lazy 게으른 get the promotion 승진하다 catch up on (잠, 공부 등을) 만회하다

M My boss says that he's so happy with my work that he might promote me very soon. I've been waiting for this day for a really long time.

W That's good news. Did he say when he's going to promote you?

M No, he didn't, but it will probably happen soon. I sure know that I deserve it.

W Just make sure you don't get lazy and give him a reason not to promote you.

M I won't. I'm going to focus on the vacation we'll go on when I get the promotion. I think we should go to Hawaii. The weather there is great, and we can swim in the ocean every day. You can read your books there, and I'll catch up on my sleep.

W I'd love to go to Hawaii. I've wanted to go there for years.

M And when we come back, I'll buy one of those new cars you love so much. Perhaps we can even find one that's red. You can drive it wherever you want when I'm not using it.

W You haven't gotten the job yet. ___________

남 우리 상사가 그러는데 내가 한 일이 아주 마음에 들어서 곧 나를 승진시킬지도 모르겠대. 난 정말 오랫동안 이런 날을 기다려왔어.

여 좋은 소식이구나. 언제 승진시킬 예정인지 말했니?

남 아니, 얘기하지 않았어. 그렇지만 곧 승진될 거야. 난 그럴 자격이 있어.

여 게을러져서 널 승진시키지 않을 만한 이유를 만들지 않도록 해.

남 안 그럴 거야. 일단 승진이 되면 우리가 가기로 한 휴가에 집중하려고 해. 내 생각엔 하와이에 가고 싶어. 거긴 날씨도 좋고 매일 바다에서 수영도 할 수 있어. 넌 거기서 책도 읽을 수 있고 그동안 못 잔 잠도 실컷 잘 수 있고.

여 정말 하와이에 꼭 가고 싶네. 몇 년 동안이나 가고 싶었어.

남 그리고 휴가 다녀 오면 네가 좋아하는 걸로 새 차를 살 거야. 빨간색 차를 살 수도 있겠지. 내가 안 쓸 때는 네가 운전해서 가고 싶은 곳은 어디든지 가.

여 너 아직 승진한 거 아니야. ___________
___________ .

<table><tr><th>문제와 정답</th><th>스크립트</th><th>해석</th></tr></table>

35 다음을 듣고, 이어지는 영어 질문에 답하시오.

✓① Monday
② Wednesday
③ Thursday
④ Saturday
⑤ Sunday

① 월요일
② 수요일
③ 목요일
④ 토요일
⑤ 일요일

▶ movie theater 영화관 agree to …에 동의하다
watch a film 영화를 보다

M Minsu met his friend and saw a movie together with him three days ago. Two days before that, they had agreed to have dinner together on Friday night, but, when they met, they changed their minds so that they could watch a film instead.

Q: *What day is it today?*

남 민수는 3일 전에 친구를 만나서 같이 영화를 보러 갔다. 영화 보기 이틀 전에는 금요일 밤에 같이 저녁을 먹기로 했지만 막상 만났을 때는 마음을 바꿔서 대신에 영화를 보기로 했다.

Q: *오늘은 무슨 요일인가?*

---

36 주어진 시간 동안 아래 지문을 주의 깊게 읽고, 대화를 들은 후 질문에 답하시오. 〔1분〕

Anyone who has seen the movie *Armageddon* knows that asteroids present a constant threat to our planet. An asteroid impact wiped out the dinosaurs, and a disaster of equal or greater proportion could happen again. Unlike the characters in the movie though, we probably will not see the big rock coming; it would be invisible to the naked eye until it hit Earth's atmosphere. If a telescope happened to spot the deadly asteroid in time to give a warning, which is highly unlikely, we could still do nothing but wait. At the moment, there are no missiles in existence powerful enough to escape Earth's gravity, and there are no rockets capable of going even as far as the moon.

① And it could be worse than the one that killed the dinosaurs.
② But there are better ways to stop an asteroid.
✓③ But there is nothing we can do about it.
④ And it is possible a telescope would find it first.
⑤ But I just do not like the ending of the movie.

① 그리고 그건 공룡을 멸망시킨 것보다 더 나쁠 수도 있어.
② 하지만 소행성을 멈추게 할 더 좋은 방법들이 있어.
③ 하지만 우리가 할 수 있는 일은 없어.
④ 그리고 망원경으로 먼저 그것을 발견해낼 수 있어.
⑤ 하지만 난 그냥 그 영화의 결말이 마음에 들지 않아.

▶ give away scary 무서운 asteroid 소행성
smash into 공격하다 destroy 파괴하다 humanity
인류 extinction 멸종, 멸망 realistically 현실적으로
completely 완전히 orbit 궤도 unpredictable
예측불허의

M I picked up some DVDs. Want to watch *Armageddon* with me?

W Okay. I've already seen it, but I promise I won't give away the ending.

M Oh, I already know the ending. A big, scary asteroid is about to smash into the Earth, so a group of heroes flies off into space and destroys it, saving humanity from extinction.

W Right. It's a great story, but I wish movies would treat scientific topics more realistically. The plot of that movie is completely different from reality.

M It's not completely different. Asteroids are real, and there are huge numbers of them that cross Earth's orbit in unpredictable ways. One of them could head for us at any time.

W That's true. ________________________
________________________ .

Q: *Which best completes the woman's last words?*

영화 〈아마겟돈〉을 본 사람들은 소행성이 지구에 지속적인 위협을 준다는 것을 알 것이다. 소행성의 충격은 공룡을 멸종시켰고, 그에 상응하거나 더 큰 비중의 사건이 다시 일어날 수 있다. 영화 속 캐릭터들과는 달리, 우리는 큰 암석이 날아오는 것을 보지 못할 것이다. 그것은 지구의 대기와 충돌할 때까지는 육안에 보이지 않을 것이다. 만약 망원경이 경고해 줄 수 있는 시간에 우연히 그 치명적인 소행성을 잡아내더라도 우리는 기다리는 것 말고는 아무것도 할 수 없다. 지금 당장은 지구의 중력에서 벗어날 수 있을 정도로 강력한 미사일은 존재하지 않으며 달까지 갈 수 있는 로케트도 없기 때문이다.

남 DVD 몇 개 사왔어. 〈아마겟돈〉 같이 볼래?

여 좋아, 난 벌써 봤지만 결말은 말 안 할게.

남 아, 나 이미 결말 알아. 큰 무시무시한 소행성이 지구와 충돌할 위기에 있었는데 지구를 구할 영웅들이 우주로 날아가 그 소행성을 파괴해서 인류의 멸종을 막는 거지.

여 맞아. 대단한 이야기야. 그렇지만 난 영화들이 과학적인 주제를 좀더 현실감 있게 다루었으면 해. 이 영화의 플롯은 완전히 현실과 동떨어져 있어.

남 완전히 다르지는 않아. 소행성은 실제로 있고, 예측불허의 방식으로 지구 궤도에 진입하는 소행성들은 엄청나게 많아. 그것들 중 하나는 아무 때나 지구 쪽으로 향할 수 있어.

여 그건 사실이야. ________________________
________________________ .

Q: *여자의 마지막 말에 들어갈 가장 알맞은 것은?*

37

Which of the following is true of the conversation?

① The boy is eager to attend the summer camp.
② The boy is going to visit his grandparents this summer.
③ The girl still wants to receive an allowance every week.
✓ Both their parents don't usually change their minds easily.
⑤ The girl thinks going to the camp is a good idea.

대화에 대해 사실인 것은 무엇인가?

① 남자는 여름 캠프에 무척 가고 싶어 한다.
② 남자는 올 여름에 할아버지 댁을 방문할 것이다.
③ 여자는 여전히 매주 용돈을 받기를 원한다.
④ 보통은 두 사람의 부모님 모두 쉽게 마음을 바꾸지 않는다.
⑤ 여자는 캠프에 가는 것이 좋은 아이디어라고 생각한다.

38

What does the girl imply she is going to do during summer vacation?

① She will stay at her grandparents' home.
✓ She is going to find a part-time job.
③ She will work as a waitress at a restaurant.
④ She is going to hang out with the boy.
⑤ She will go to the same summer camp as the boy.

여자는 여름방학 동안 무엇을 하게 될 것이라고 말하고 있는가?

① 그녀는 할아버지 댁에 머무를 것이다.
② 그녀는 아르바이트를 찾을 것이다.
③ 그녀는 식당에서 웨이트리스로 일할 것이다.
④ 그녀는 남자와 함께 놀러 갈 것이다.
⑤ 그녀는 남자와 같은 여름 캠프에 갈 것이다.

▶ **bother** …을 귀찮게 하다, 괴롭히다 **be all ears** 귀 기울여 듣다 **hang out with** …와 어울리다 **prepare for** …을 준비하다 **convince** 납득시키다, 확신시키다 **stubborn** 완고한 **allowance** 용돈 **jump at** 흔쾌히 응하다

(37~38)

M Do you mind if I talk to you? There's something that's been bothering me.

W I'm all ears. Go ahead and let me know what's going on.

M I'm trying to decide what to do during summer vacation. My parents really want me to go to summer camp, but I'm not too eager about it. Instead, I'd rather get a part-time job at a restaurant and spend the rest of the time hanging out with my friends.

W What kind of summer camp is it?

M It's actually more of a study camp. It's a five-week program where they teach you extra classes to help you prepare for college. I really have no desire to do that. Plus, I don't need to go since my grades are already really good.

W Have you tried explaining this to your parents to make them see your side? If you did that, you might convince them you'd be better off working this summer.

M I tried earlier, but both my parents are set on sending me to camp.

W That's too bad. But you ought to try talking to them again. After all, my parents wanted to send me to my grandparents' for the summer, but I convinced them to let me get a job.

M How'd you manage that? Your parents are almost as stubborn as mine are.

W Actually, it was pretty easy. I told them that if I got a part-time job, they wouldn't have to pay me an allowance anymore. They jumped at that opportunity.

(37~38)

남 얘기 좀 나눌 수 있을까? 날 성가시게 하는 문제가 있어서 말이야.

여 어서 얘기해봐. 잘 듣고 있으니까. 무슨 일인지 말해 봐.

남 여름방학 때 뭘 할 건지 결정하는 중인데 부모님은 여름 캠프에 가길 바라셔. 근데 난 별로 그러고 싶지 않거든. 대신에, 식당에서 아르바이트하면서 남는 시간에는 친구들과 어울려 놀고 싶어.

여 어떤 여름 캠프인데?

남 사실 공부하는 캠프에 더 가까워. 대입을 준비하는 데 도움이 되는 수업을 추가로 가르쳐주는 5주간의 프로그램이야. 정말 하고 싶지 않아. 게다가, 내 성적은 이미 꽤 좋기 때문에 굳이 할 필요도 없어.

여 부모님한테 이걸 잘 설명 드려서 네 입장을 알리려는 시도해 봤어? 그런다면 이번 여름에 일을 하는 게 더 낫다는 것을 설득시킬 수도 있을 거야.

남 벌써 해 봤지. 근데 부모님 두분 다 날 캠프에 보내기로 마음을 굳히셨어.

여 안 됐다. 그렇지만 다시 얘기를 해야 돼. 어쨌거나 우리 부모님도 여름에 할아버님 댁에 날 보내고 싶어 하셨는데 내가 일자리를 구할 수 있게 설득시켰거든.

남 어떻게 그랬니? 너희 부모님도 우리 부모님만큼이나 완고하시잖아.

여 사실, 아주 쉬웠어. 내가 아르바이트를 하면 부모님이 더 이상 용돈을 안 주셔도 된다고 말했거든. 흔쾌히 응하셨어.

39 남자의 취직에 대한 생각을 가장 잘 요약한 것은 무엇인가?

① 면접이 취직하는 데 가장 중요한 것이다.
② 월급이 근무 환경보다 더 중요하다.
③ 일의 종류와 근무 시간은 중요하지 않다.
④ 취직이 힘들기 때문에 면접관들에게 좋은 인상을 주는 것이 중요하다.
⑤ 일요일에 일하는 건 문제가 된다.

40 여자가 "It's only a job."이라고 말한 이유는 무엇인가?

① 남자가 인터뷰에 너무 많은 시간을 투자해서
② 남자가 일자리 찾느라 공부를 소홀히 해서
③ 남자가 인터뷰 복장에 너무 신경을 써서
④ 남자가 구직에 실패한 것을 위로하려고
⑤ 여자가 구직에 실패한 것을 변명하려고

▶ **well-dressed** 잘 차려 입은 **application letter** 지원서 **impress** …에게 깊은 인상을 주다, 감동을 주다 **well-paying** 보수가 좋은 **resume** 이력서 **cover letter** 자기소개서 **make a good impression** 좋은 인상을 주다 **depend on** …에 달려 있는, …에 따라 다른

(39~40)

W You are very well-dressed. Where are you going?

M I'm going to a job interview. I sent an application letter to a bank, and they wrote an e-mail saying that they wanted to interview me. Do you think I look all right for an interview?

W You look good. They might think you're trying to impress them. It's only a job.

M But I do want to impress them. Don't you understand how difficult it is to find a well-paying part-time job? Most of the students in my class have jobs with the best companies. I've been trying to find a job for two months now.

W You're right. All I think about are my studies.

M You should think about finding a job when you graduate next year. It's more difficult than you think. You have to write a really good resume and a good cover letter. And if they decide to interview you, you'll have to make a good impression.

W You sound as if you know what you're talking about. How much money do you think they'll offer you?

M I don't know. It depends on the kind of work and the working hours. I can only work in the afternoon and perhaps on weekends.

W But banks aren't open on weekends.

M I'll be working in the office. Sometimes the office staff works on Saturdays.

W But do you want to work on weekends, too?

M I really want this job experience. I don't even mind working Sundays, too.

(39~40)

여 옷을 잘 차려 입었구나. 어디 가니?

남 면접 보러 가. 은행에 지원서를 냈는데 면접을 보고 싶다는 이메일이 왔어. 면접에 적당한 것처럼 보이니?

여 좋아 보여. 네가 좋은 인상을 주고 싶어 한다고 생각할 거야. 그냥 일자리일 뿐인데 말이야!

남 하지만 정말 좋은 인상을 주고 싶어. 보수가 좋은 아르바이트를 구하는 게 얼마나 어려운지 모르겠니? 우리반 학생 대부분은 다들 좋은 회사에서 일하고 있어. 난 두 달 동안이나 일자리를 구하려는 중이고.

여 네 말이 맞아. 난 맨날 공부만 생각해.

남 내년에 졸업하면 너도 일자리에 대해 생각해야 해. 생각보다 어려워. 이력서와 자기 소개서를 정말 잘 써야 하거든. 그리고 면접이 결정되면 좋은 인상을 주어야 할 거야.

여 전문가처럼 들리는데. 임금은 얼마나 준대?

남 몰라. 일의 종류와 근무시간에 따라 달라지겠지. 난 오후랑 주말에만 일할 수 있어.

여 은행은 주말에 문 안 열잖아.

남 난 사무실에서 일할 거야. 사무실 직원들은 가끔 토요일에 일해.

여 근데 주말에도 일하고 싶니?

남 꼭 이 회사에서 직장 경험을 하고 싶어. 일요일에 일하는 것도 상관없어.